THE STORY OF

World War II

Donald L. Miller

REVISED, EXPANDED AND UPDATED
FROM THE ORIGINAL TEXT BY
HENRY STEELE COMMAGER

A Lou Reda Book

SIMON & SCHUSTER

New York   London   Toronto   Sydney   Singapore

SIMON & SCHUSTER
Rockefeller Center
1230 Avenue of the Americas
New York, NY 10020

For information about special discounts for bulk purchases,
please contact Simon & Schuster Special Sales:
1-800-456-6798 or business@simonandschuster.com

Designed by Richard Oriolo
Maps by Guenter Vollath

Manufactured in the United States of America

1   2   3   4   5   6   7   8   9   10

Library of Congress Cataloging-in-Publication Data
Miller, Donald L., date.
The story of World War II / Donald L. Miller ;
original text by Henry Steele Commager.
p.   cm.
Rev., updated, and reworked version of: The story of the Second World War /
edited with historical narrative by Henry Steele Commager. 1945.
Includes bibliographical references (p.   ) and index.
1. World War, 1939–1945. I. Title: Story of World War Two. II. Title: Story
of World War 2. III. Commager, Henry Steele, 1902– IV. Story of
the Second World War. V. Title.
D743.M546 2001
940.53—dc21   2001049638
ISBN 0-7432-1198-7

PHOTO CREDIT KEY

LRP—Lou Reda Productions   USAAF—U.S. Army Air Force
M25—M25 Studio   USCG—U.S. Coast Guard
NA—National Archive   USMC—U.S. Marine Corps
SC—U.S. Army Signal Corps   USN—U.S. Navy

ACKNOWLEDGMENTS

MY DEBTS ARE SUBSTANTIAL. TO LOU REDA, who assisted in every way with his terrific energy. To his wonderfully cooperative staff and collaborators, who went out of their way to help me: Mort Zimmerman, Joan York, Norman Stahl, Sharon Stahl, John McCullough, Joseph H. Alexander, Samuel Jackson, Tracy Conor, Lydia Bruneo, Douglas Joiner, Lou's beautiful wife, Timi, and Rod Paschall, editor of the *Military History Quarterly*, who read this book in manuscript. Mort Zimmerman, Mark Natola, and John McCullough were especially helpful with the photographs and Mark Natola loaned me transcripts of interviews he conducted with B-29 crewmen. At Lou Reda's studios I was fortunate to be working with three World War II veterans, Lou, Mort Zimmerman, and John McCullough, all of whom I interviewed for this book. Lou helped steer me to many other veterans and opened doors for me all over the country.

Special thanks to Douglas Brinkley, director of the Eisenhower Center at the University of New Orleans, and to Stephen E. Ambrose, its founder and presiding spirit, who made available to me their vast collection of oral histories, written memoirs, and letters; and to others at the Center, especially Kevin Willey and Michael Edwards, who made the Eisenhower Center a welcoming home away from home during work on this book. Thanks also to the immensely helpful librarians at Lafayette College, especially Douglas Moore and Therry Schwartz, who ran a nonstop interlibrary loan operation for me. To Margaret Drain at WGBH-TV Boston, who provided me with transcripts of interviews from World War II film documentaries presented on *The American Experience*. To Benis M. Frank, former director of the U.S. Marine Corps Oral History Project, who gave me voluminous source material on the Marines in the Pacific and shared with me his experiences as a young warrior in the assaults on Peleliu and Okinawa.

I wish to thank Mary Commager, Henry Steele Commager's widow, for providing me with biographical material on Commager from the Henry Steele Commager Papers at Amherst College and for encouraging me to write this book. I owe a special debt to Lafayette College's Excel Program and its former director, Jeff Bader, for providing me with two superb student assistants, Rebecca Waxman and Janine Stavrovsky. They were with me every step of the way, and I am grateful to them. Two other Lafayette students helped with the photographs, Carter Figueroa and Pete Gannon. And Lauren Sheldon, another Excel scholar, was an indispensable fact-checker. Lafayette students Rose Pilato and John Krystofik also helped with some of the research.

Donald Myerson read parts of the manuscript and was my most valuable sounding board and source of inspiration. A combat veteran, he knew what it was like. Also offering help and encouragement were my agent, Gina Maccoby, my secretary, Kathy Anckaitis, and my good friend, Jim Tiernan. My conversations with Jim helped give the book shape. My thanks to the late Eugene B. Sledge for giving me permission to quote from his unpublished book, to Judy Crichton for allowing me to use a segment of her late husband Robert's unpublished war memoir, to Christine Herbes Sommers for encouraging me to make this a "personal book," to my brother Larry and my cousin John Steber for providing me information on the service records of my father, my uncle, and others close to us who served in the war, to Pat Caruso for making available to me the prisoner of war diary of her father, and to Ray "Hap" Halloran for sending me pictures and records of his service in the Pacific. "Hap" and the two hundred or so other veterans of World War II I interviewed or corresponded with made the writing of this book an enlivening experience.

Bob Bender and Johanna Li at Simon & Schuster assisted me at every juncture of this project. Simon & Schuster is a vast enterprise, but Bob and Johanna turn it, for me, into a small and friendly shop. My copyeditor, Fred Chase, saved me from some embarrassing errors, and his probing mind made this a better book. Gypsy da Silva, Associate Director of Copyediting, was as always, gracious and brilliant. John Morgenstern and Peter Vabulas assisted her.

Lastly, I thank my wife, Rose, who was there with help whenever it was needed—and always with loving encouragement. And to the new ones in our lives, "the Miller girls," Alyssa, Alexis, Ashlee, and the "Medina Boys," Devin, Mason, and Austin. This lively gang has given me a second life. And special thanks to Alyssa. Our evening "conversations" on the bench at the World War II memorial in front of her house on Washington Boulevard helped me appreciate how important it was to write this book at this moment in my life.

Donald L. Miller
Easton, Pennsylvania

This book is for my mother, Frances,
and in memory of my father, Donald L. Miller.
With love and gratitude.

CONTENTS

IN 1995, THE DEATH OF MY FATHER, a World War II veteran, reawakened my interest in the war that transformed his life and the lives of his friends and family in the close-knit working-class neighborhood where he grew up, graduated from high school, and met my mother. They were married not long after my father entered the Army Air Forces in 1942 at the age of nineteen. And when he left Reading, Pennsylvania, for basic training, she took a job at a local plant that produced parts for the planes of the air arm he served in for the next three years. Her father, a Slovak immigrant, worked in a steel mill that forged weapons of war for General Dwight D. Eisenhower's great army of liberation. In 1944, that army swept across France and into Hitler's Germany, where my uncle, John Steber, a mud-slogging infantryman, was captured and spent the remainder of the war in a Nazi prison camp. Before that, he had served in North Africa and fought and nearly died on Omaha Beach on D-Day.

Except for those like him who saw combat, Americans did not directly experience the plague of war. We were not invaded, nor were our great cities turned to rubble and ash. Yet Americans at home did suffer. Born in late 1944, I was too young to experience the war, but engraved in my mind is the living room of our neighbors, the

Adamses, turned for many years after the war into a shrine for the boy who never came back. After the war, my father was President of the Catholic War Veterans post that was named after Francis Adams, and it was there, over a number of years, that I coaxed and pulled stories of the war out of tight-lipped veterans, many of them tough steel workers, like my uncle, who wanted to forget.

When my father died, these stories took a stronger hold on me. At the time, I had just finished one book and was well into the research for another, a history of the Vicksburg Campaign, the turning point of the American Civil War. But as I was about to begin writing, I discovered a book that moved me in the direction I really wanted to go. This was Henry Steele Commager's *The Story of the Second World War*.

I found the book on a pile of papers in the office of my friend Lou Reda, a documentary film producer who has made over a hundred films on World War II for national television, all of them in his small shop in Easton, Pennsylvania, where I live with my family and teach at Lafayette College. Commager had played a part in my life. In college, the first serious book I read on American history was the magisterial work he co-authored with Samuel Eliot Morison, *The Growth of the American Republic*, one of the most influential, entertaining, and widely read general histories of the United States. That book and a number of others I read over the course of a lazy summer, playing basketball and chasing the girl I would marry, convinced me to switch my major from business administration to history, and years later, Commager himself gave my career a push by encouraging an editor to publish one of my first books. By 1995, I had read almost all of Commager's work, yet I had no idea he had written a book about World War II. I was embarrassed to admit this to Lou Reda, who had been a close friend of Commager's and made a film for television, *The Blue and the Gray*, with Commager and Bruce Catton serving as historical consultants.

Reda handed me one of his spare copies of *The Story of the Second World War*, and I took it home and got lost in it for the next two days. Written during the war, while Commager, a forty-three-year-old professor at Columbia University, was working as a propagandist and historian for the War Department in London, Paris, and Washington, it brought together some of the best stories of the war, many of them by correspondents whose work drew them into the thick of the fight. There are also official reports, public speeches, newspaper and magazine pieces, radio broadcasts, and selections from popular histories written while the war was being fought. Commager stitched together these various accounts with a vigorously written history of the war. He wrote with passion and patriotic fervor, picturing World War II as a clearly drawn conflict between good and evil. It is a work of history as well as moral partisanship, from the pen of an aroused humanist who believed that fascist tyranny threatened to plunge civilization into a new dark age. As his Columbia colleague Allan Nevins said: "When [Commager] takes up a cause . . . it is with fervor almost volcanic." [1]

Commager did not set out to write a comprehensive history of the war. In late 1945 it was too soon for that; the official records were not yet available. "But war is not only a matter of information and statistics," he wrote in the book's preface. "It is felt experience, and no later generation can quite recapture that experience. Here is the story of the war as it came to the American and British people—as it looked and felt while the fighting was going on." [2]

For me, the book's pulling power was these qualities of immediacy and emotional empathy, the feeling it gave of living inside a tremendous moment in historical time. Reading of those grim days in the middle of the war, when it looked to knowing observers in the West that the Axis powers might prevail, one is quickly disabused of the idea of historical inevitability. It was a war the Allies could easily have lost.

This was a book, I thought, that deserved to be back in print, but in a greatly revised and updated form, to reflect not only the latest scholarship on the war but also the eyewitness accounts of those who lived through that world-transforming event.

Commager was, understandably, too emotionally involved in the war to write an unsparing account of it. He also had to contend with wartime censorship. There was tight government censorship of the letters of American servicemen and of the dispatches of war correspondents. This was done for reasons of military security, but the military also did not want folks back home to know how ferocious the fighting was on land, at sea, and in the air. Until the middle of the war, no pictures were published in the American press showing dead American boys, not even photographs of fallen fighting men with blankets covering their battered bodies.

Some of this censorship was self-imposed. "We edited ourselves," John Steinbeck remarked, "much more than we were edited." [3] Steinbeck and his fellow war correspondents wanted to contribute to victory by bolstering home-front morale—not by twisting the truth but by not telling everything. Or as playwright Arthur Miller writes of the legendary war reporter Ernie Pyle: by telling "as much of what he saw as people could read without vomiting." [4] There was a shared feeling "that unless the home front was carefully protected from the whole account of what war was like," Steinbeck writes, "it might panic." It was only after the war, when those who had seen it up close began telling their stories in novels and memoirs, that the protected American public learned what a "crazy hysterical mess" much of the war had been. [5]

Commager had access only to the filtered reports of combat, and he never got close to the dirty and dangerous front lines. Here was an opportunity to enrich and broaden his book, drawing on material he might have used had it been available to him. Starting in my own community, I began interviewing World War II veterans, and I pulled out the notes I had made, years ago, on conversations with my father, my uncle, and their wartime buddies. At this point, Lou Reda became an enthusiastic partner in the enterprise. He gave me unrestricted access to the written transcripts and videotapes of over 700 interviews his production teams have conducted over the past thirty years with participants in the war—generals and GIs, corpsmen and nurses, combat correspondents and innocent victims of a total war that killed almost sixty million people, most of them civilians. None of this material had ever been used by historians.

When I described my project to Douglas Brinkley and Stephen Ambrose, the present and the former director, respectively, of the Eisenhower Center in New Orleans, they generously made available to me their capacious collection of oral testimonies, including 200 or so eyewitnesses' accounts that they had recently acquired but had not yet catalogued. Margaret Drain, executive producer of *The American Experience,* also gave me access to transcripts of interviews in the archives of WGBH-TV Boston. This fresh material was especially valuable for reconstructing the Pacific War, which Commager, an ardent Anglophile—a native of Pittsburgh who spoke, dressed, and acted like an Oxbridge man—does not give the coverage it demands.

What began as a modest effort to update an unjustly forgotten work became, in this way, a new book but a book faithful, I hope, to Commager's belief that the war was an event deeply based in human emotions that could not be understood by a cold recounting of the facts.

Readers who compare the original with the revised version of this book will notice that the narratives are structured differently. Commager used short historical accounts of his own to introduce longer published pieces by others, most of them correspondents and popular historians. I weave shorter—and many more—eyewitness accounts, most of them by men and women on the front lines, into a fuller, more personal, and more critical narrative than Commager had the resources—or, in fact, the intention—to write. And while people and their stories predominate, this is a history not only about what happened but also about why it happened.

In Commager's original version of this book, the words and works of great men form the spine of the narrative. My revision is written from the ordinary fighting man's point of view, the American fighting man primarily, because it is the on-the-spot accounts of these men that were available to me and because I am an American interested in the character and conduct of my countrymen.

"A battle exists on many different levels," wrote the novelist and World War II veteran Irwin Shaw, author of *The Young Lions*, one of the truest works of fiction to come out of the war. "Generals sit in different pressed uniforms, looking at very similar maps, reading very similar reports, matching their moral strength and intellectual ingenuity with their colleagues and antagonists a hundred miles away. . . .

"The men on the scene see the affair on a different level. . . . They see helmets, vomit, green water, shell-bursts, smoke, crashing planes, blood plasma. . . .

"To the General sitting before the maps eighty miles away . . . the reports on casualties are encouraging. To the man on the scene the casualties are never encouraging. When he is hit or when the man next to him is hit . . . it is inconceivable at that moment to believe that there is a man eighty miles away who . . . can report, after it has happened . . . that everything is going according to plan."[6]

After the war, General Sir Archibald Wavell, one of Britain's most respected commanders, said that if he were to write a history of the past conflict he would focus on "the 'actualities of war'—the effects of tiredness, hunger, fear, lack of sleep, weather. . . . The principles of strategy and tactics, and the logistics of war are really absurdly simple: it is the actualities that make war so complicated and so difficult, and are usually so neglected by historians."[7] This book is written in the spirit of General Wavell's remark and from the down-close-in-the-dirt perspective of Irwin Shaw's "man on the scene."

It is a book about what the historian John Keegan calls "the face of battle." But the principal characters are civilians who were shot at and bombed as well as fighting men who did the shooting and bombing. Included, also, are medical personnel and correspondents, women and men who put their lives on the line at the front and suffered high casualty rates. "If you stayed a correspondent long enough and went to the things that were happening, the chances were that you would get it," recalled John Steinbeck.[8]

I share Commager's conviction that this was a war against modern barbarism. Writing in the midst of the emotional letdown that followed this tumultuous event—not only the greatest war, but perhaps the greatest human catastrophe, in recorded history—he wanted to assure his readers that the cause had been worth all the bloodshed and suffering. His assertive and dramatic style turns parts of the book into a prose hymn to the Allied war effort. But the war was more than a heroic crusade; it was a tragic and complex human experience. In battling evil, the armies of the democracies committed cruelties that sometimes rivaled those of the enemy, and in the maelstrom of combat, many men broke down or ran.

Just as every American fighting man wasn't a hero, every general wasn't a genius. Allied commanders made stupid blunders that resulted in the unnecessary deaths of thousands of young men, blunders that were covered up by military censors or by reporters who feared public criticism would jeopardize the war effort—or their own jobs. The American armed forces also practiced a policy of racial prejudice that was in obscene defiance of the ideals America claimed to be fighting for; and for long after the war, the military refused to recognize the enormous contribution to victory made by African-American and Japanese-American fighting men. I have tried to set the record right without losing sight of the democratic principles Commager rightly believes the war preserved.

I am not sure that the American men and women who saw combat duty in this war were the Greatest Generation, but they were certainly a great generation, one to whom the nation owes an unpayable debt. They took part in what Walter Lippmann called at the time "the greatest human experience that men have passed through for many centuries."[9] But only when we know, through their own words, the full horror of what they experienced, and the depth and complexity of their feelings when under fire, can we appreciate how they held together and saved the world from despotism. The American fighting man "was often bored; he wasn't always brave; most times he was scared," wrote Sergeant Debs Myers at the end of the war. "Maybe he didn't know what fascism was—maybe he did. [He] did not destroy fascism. But he helped defeat the fascists, and he took away their guns. . . .

"With his allies he saved the world and hoped to God he'd never have to do it again."[10]

There is no need to embellish the deeds of these men; there is heroism enough in what they did.

The war left scars that never healed. This was a war that was so savage it turned some soldiers into savages, human beings who had to kill in order to keep on living. On the tiny Pacific island of Peleliu, one of the most murderously fought battles of the war was waged in tropical heat that reached 115 degrees. There was never a break in the action, and the enemy, sworn to fight the American "barbarians" to the last man, would not surrender. So neither side took prisoners. The fighting was continuous, day and night, and men broke down under these conditions. Some of them mutilated enemy corpses in retaliation for unspeakable atrocities committed on living and dead American prisoners. A group of Marines even killed one of their fellow Marines, whose mind had cracked in combat, so that his wild screams of anguish would not give away their position to the enemy.[11]

This is one of the reasons combat veterans were reluctant to talk about the war after it was over. Only those who had been there could truly understand what they had been through.

Telling the story of the war as it was—refusing to sanitize it or glorify it for our own current purposes—does not diminish good men who in bad situations did things they would later regret. Rather, it underscores the tragedy of total war, warfare without mercy or let-up.

This kind of fighting brought out the best as well as the worst in men. Boys who had barely begun to shave carried out stirring acts of heroism and selflessness, throwing themselves on grenades to save their comrades and carrying their wounded buddies in stretchers to aid stations—in the open, under withering enemy fire. And Army and Navy nurses went into the fire zones, right onto the sands of Iwo Jima and Omaha Beach, risking everything to care for and evacuate the wounded. The war tested these young people as they would never be tested again and brought many of them to their highest pitch as human beings, forcing combat veterans especially to draw on emotional and spiritual resources that were as important to them, said General Eisenhower, as their training and weapons. As one veteran recalled: "In combat the biggest battle is not with the enemy but with yourself. Facing death every second, you find out who you are. Will you fight or run? Will you risk your life to save a friend, or will you only try to save yourself? And if you live and win, and knowing how scared and angry you are, will you treat your prisoners decently or will you, if you have the chance—and can get away with it—shoot them?"[12]

"Don't get the notion that your job is going to be glorious or glamorous," an American colonel told an Eighth Air Force bomber crew. "You've got dirty work to do and might as well face the facts: You're going to be baby killers." That didn't sit well with bombardier Frank Clark, the son of a Wisconsin factory worker. "What I don't like, and didn't talk about to anyone," he admitted after the war, "was the fact that we were bombing industrial towns that were largely populated with working people— much like the towns a lot of us came from. . . .

"To me the war had a human face."[13]

The Good War that was seemingly bereft of moral ambiguity was suffused with it. We can only know this by getting as close to it as we possibly can. And that is only possible through the ancient art of story telling, the kind of tales I first heard at my father's Catholic War Veterans Post, just down the street from where I was born.

So we begin as John Steinbeck began his collection of war correspondence. "There was a war, long ago—once upon a time . . ."[14]

The Nazi Juggernaut

THE FAILURE OF APPEASEMENT

Before dawn of September 1, 1939, clouds of bombers and fighters flew eastward into the skies over Poland, raining death and destruction on helpless towns and villages, on airfields, railroads, bridges, and factories. From East Prussia, Pomerania, Silesia, and Slovakia gray-clad armies poured across the frontiers into the doomed country. The greatest of wars was on, a war which was, in the end, to involve the whole world in one vast conflagration.

How did it happen that a generation still healing the deep wounds of the War of 1914–18 permitted this second and more terrible war to come?

The explanation was to be found in the breakdown of the system of collective security and the growth of international anarchy, moral and political, in the post–World War I years.

Across the seas, unappreciated by the average American, there had arisen a new threat to peace, to law, and, ultimately, to American security. This was totalitarianism, as expressed in the political organization of Italy, Germany, and Japan. The essence of totalitarianism was the subordination of all individual or social interests to the interests of the "master race" as represented in the State; its object, the division of the world into spheres of influence, each sphere to be controlled by a master nation; its method, the ruthless use of force. Italy, under Benito Mussolini, had inaugurated the first totalitarian state in 1922; Adolf Hitler, who became Chancellor of Germany in 1933, improved greatly on the Italian model; Japan, long inured to despotism, fell increasingly under the control of reactionary military leaders who, with Emperor Hirohito's active compliance, ruthlessly suppressed all political opposition and preached the doctrine of Japanese racial superiority and the nation's sacred mission to free Asia of "contaminating" Western influences.[1]

Early in the 1930s the first of these totalitarian nations felt strong enough to strike. Determined to establish its hegemony in the Far East, Japan invaded Manchuria in September 1931, crushed Chinese resistance, and, a year later, set up the puppet state of Manchukuo. The United States protested and the League of Nations condemned the aggression, but Japan ignored the American protest, withdrew from the League, and prepared to extend its Asian conquests in order to end its economic dependence on white Western powers.

The moral was not lost on other discontented nations. Throughout the 1920s Germany had wrestled with the economic disorganization and social demoralization that followed its defeat in World War I, and the crisis was, by 1930, acute. German democracy seemed unable to cope with this crisis, but Adolf Hitler and his National Socialist (Nazi) Party promised relief from economic ills, escape from the "bondage" of the Versailles Treaty, and the union of the entire German race under one strong government. In 1933 the aged President Paul von Hindenburg was persuaded to appoint Hitler, a transplanted Austrian and failed artist, to the chancellorship, and within a few months all opposition leaders were in jail and the National Socialist Party had an iron grip on the political and military machinery of the country. Hitler moved swiftly to consolidate his position and implement his promises. Determined to make Germany the greatest military power in the world, he contemptuously withdrew from both the Geneva Disarmament Conference and the League of Nations and embarked upon a full-scale program of rearmament. And, as if to dramatize his dissociation from the moral standards of the Western world, he invoked the discredited doctrine of Aryan superiority to justify a reign of terror against the Jews.

Meanwhile, Mussolini, the founder of Fascism, thought the time was now ripe to reestablish the Roman Empire of ancient days. Ethiopia, which blocked the way from Italian Libya to Italian Somaliland, seemed an easy victim to start on. Early in 1935

Mussolini persuaded the slippery French Premier, Pierre Laval, to consent to an Italian conquest of Ethiopia, and during the winter of 1935–36 that conquest was consummated. Haile Selassie, the Ethiopian Emperor, appealed to the League of Nations, but he was powerless to stop Italy. On March 7, 1936, when the conquest of Ethiopia was all but complete, Hitler ordered his army into the demilitarized Rhineland, an audacious move to retake Germany's "traditional" Aryan territories and a flagrant violation of the Versailles Treaty. The French, with the strongest army in the world, offered no resistance.

The identity of interest of these two totalitarian states was shortly dramatized in one of the great crises in the history of modern democracy—the Spanish Civil War. In 1931, the Spanish people had overthrown their decrepit monarchy and established a republic. The following years were troubled by escalating conflict between conservative and radical groups. The election of February 1936 placed a left-wing Popular Front coalition government in uneasy control of the nation, but reactionary groups still commanded the support of the Church, the great landowners, and the army, led by General Francisco Franco. The Nationalists, as these reactionary groups came to be known, revolted, and in midsummer 1936 Spain was plunged into a ferociously fought civil war that had much the same relation to World War II that the Kansas struggle of the 1850s had to the American Civil War.

The governments of Great Britain and France failed to appreciate the implications of this war, or feared that intervention might lead to a widening of the conflict, which would involve all Europe. Communist Russia alone actively supported the beleaguered Spanish Republic, but its support further discouraged the timid governments of the democracies. So while Germany and Italy, fearing the triumph of Bolshevism in Spain, hurried hundreds of planes and tens of thousands of "volunteers" into the Nationalist camp, Britain and France adopted a policy of nonintervention, and the United States Congress clamped an embargo on the shipment of munitions to either side. These divergent policies ultimately decided the outcome of the war, and a Nationalist dictatorship was set up under General Franco in 1939.

Once more, it was Japan's turn. In July 1937, the Kwantung Army invaded China. Immensely superior in armaments, the Japanese swept from victory to victory, overrunning most of northern China and all the important seaports. After taking the walled city of Nanking in December 1938, Japanese soldiers slaughtered over 200,000 military prisoners of war and unarmed civilians, raping, castrating, and beheading tens of thousands of them, in what has been called a Hidden Holocaust.[2] To the entire world, the Japanese served notice that this was the new meaning of Bushido, the medieval code of the Japanese warrior that originally called for compassion toward one's enemies.

The pattern and the menace of totalitarian conquest were becoming clear enough, yet the democracies, unprepared to risk war, continued to follow a policy of appeasement. Taking advantage of this, Nazi Germany moved swiftly to achieve three major objectives: the reincorporation into a greater Germany of all German peoples, the control by Germany of Middle Europe and the road to the Middle East, and the erection of a totalitarian barrier against Communism. Already in 1936 Hitler had called into existence the Rome–Berlin Axis, an anti-Communist alliance which shortly embraced Japan, Italy, Spain, and Hungary. He then began a policy of territorial aggrandizement.

Austria was the logical place to begin; it was small and defenseless, and its population was almost entirely German-speaking. In March 1938, the blow fell. While Britain and France held futile conferences, a Nazi fifth column in Austria took control of the Army and the police. The Austrian Chancellor, Kurt von Schuschnigg, who had resisted Nazi aggression to the last, abdicated, and on the night of March 11 the German mechanized Army sped across the border and the union of Austria and Germany was formally announced. A triumphant Hitler rode like a king through the neighborhoods where he had once lived as a struggling artist in miserable flophouses. And SS officials and Viennese Nazis launched a wild urban pogrom against the Jews.

G. E. R. Gedye, the veteran British correspondent in Vienna, described a city taken over by Hitler thugs wearing brown shirts and marching menacingly behind enormous swastika flags:

NAZI TROOPS WELCOMED BY ETHNIC GERMANS IN THE SUDETENLAND, OCTOBER 1, 1938 (M25).

IT WAS AN INDESCRIBABLE WITCHES' SABBATH—stormtroopers, lots of them barely out of the schoolroom, with cartridge belts and carbines, the only other evidence of authority being swastika brassards, were marching side by side with police turncoats, men and women shrieking or crying hysterically the name of their leader, embracing the police and dragging them along in the swirling stream of humanity, motor lorries filled with stormtroopers clutching their long-concealed weapons, hooting furiously, trying to make themselves heard above the din, men and women leaping, shouting, and dancing in the light of the smoking torches which soon began to make their appearance, the air filled with a pandemonium of sound in which intermingled screams of: "Down with the Jews! Heil Hitler! Heil Hitler! Sieg Heil! Perish the Jews!"[3]

Hitler's power in Germany was now absolute; his popularity with the German people overwhelming. He had restored the confidence of a shaken and badly divided nation, wiped out the humiliation of the Treaty of Versailles, pulled Germany out of a paralyzing economic depression, and won a succession of territorial conquests without shedding a drop of German blood. That this was accomplished by the complete suppression of civil liberties, the crushing of Leftist political parties, and a vicious policy of ethnic cleansing against the Jews, "was seen by most as at least a price worth paying—" writes historian Ian Kershaw, "by many as positively welcome."[4]

Before the democracies had recovered from the shock of the *Anschluss,* or incorporation of Austria, Hitler moved against Czechoslovakia, demanding the cession of the Sudetenland, along the German border, home to more than three million ethnic Germans. Throughout the spring and summer of 1938 Hitler stormed at the hapless Czechs while he alternately threatened and cajoled their allies, Britain and France. Finally at the Munich Conference of September 29–30, Britain and France abandoned the little democracy to her fate. "[I bring you] peace with honor," said Prime Minister Neville Chamberlain on his return to London. "I believe it is peace for our time."[5]

Writing to his sister, Chamberlain declared that "in spite of the harshness and ruthlessness I thought I saw in [Hitler's] face, I got the impression that he was a man who could be relied upon when he had given his word."[6]

War

In March 1939, Hitler proved Chamberlain both a poor prophet and a poor judge of character, sending his army into Czechoslovakia, and, while Britain and France looked helplessly on, dismembering that country. Back in the United States, Senator Albert Borah, a strident isolationist, explained to Congress that this was not a violation of the Treaty of Versailles, and as if to confound him, Mussolini three days later seized Albania. In May, the two totalitarian leaders concluded a formal military alliance, directed against France and Britain. Then the German Fuehrer turned on Poland, demanding the return of territory it had been forced to cede to Poland by the terms of the Treaty of Versailles, the "Polish Corridor," a wide stretch of land, inhabited mostly by Germans, that cut off East Prussia from the rest of Germany.

Convinced now that Hitler wanted war, England and France attempted to repair the damage of prolonged appeasement. But the diplomatic humpty-dumpty had had so great a fall that it was impossible to put it together again. France distrusted Britain, and Britain, France—and both with reason; Russia had lost confidence in both of them; the smaller nations could not fail to read the moral of Munich and of Prague. Yet Britain and France pushed ahead. They offered to guarantee Poland against aggression—though they failed conspicuously to indicate how they proposed to do this. As if to test the realism of the British, Russia proposed an alliance on the understanding that she be permitted to march troops into Poland and to take the Baltic states of Latvia, Lithuania, and Estonia into "protective custody." Acquiescence in this proposal might have exposed the British government to the charge of insincerity in its zeal for the welfare of the nonaggressor nations, and the proposal was rejected. Russia then turned to Germany, and on August 23 the two great antagonists concluded a nonaggression pact, which freed Germany to seize Poland without risking war with Russia.

Though there was a strong faction in both Britain and France that advocated further appeasement, this time the two governments did not back down. Hitler renewed his demands on Poland, but when he offered to "guarantee" the British Empire in return for a free hand in Poland, the British refused, informing him that they had obligations to Poland that they intended to honor.

Hitler was unimpressed. "Our enemies are small worms," he told his generals. "I saw them in Munich."[7] On the morning of September 1, 250,000 German soldiers stormed across the Polish border, and 1,600 Luftwaffe aircraft smashed Polish towns and cities. Hitler issued no declaration of war, claiming Germany had been attacked by Poland.

THE BELLIGERENTS

On September 3, millions of people in the Western world, their radios alert to every step in the unfolding tragedy in Europe, heard the grave but firm voice of Neville Chamberlain announcing that Britain, in fulfillment of her commitments, was at war with Germany. That same day, reluctantly, France too went to war. And, with the single exception of Ireland, the British Commonwealth of Nations rallied to the support of the mother country. The war Hitler had hoped to confine to a series of episodes was underway; and the great combination against him was already beginning to be formed.

"Hitler's 'counterattack' on Poland has on this Sabbath day become a world war!" William L. Shirer, the CBS newscaster, wrote in his diary. "To record that date: September 3, 1939."

Shirer was in Berlin's Wilhelmplatz when the announcement was made over the loudspeakers that England had declared war on Germany. A small crowd of people was standing there. When the announcement was finished, "there was not a murmur," he wrote. "They just stood there as they were before. Stunned. The people cannot realize yet that Hitler has led them into a world war." There was, he said, "not even any hate for the French and the British—despite Hitler's various proclamations to the people . . . accusing the 'English war-mongers and capitalistic Jews' of starting this war."[8]

POLAND

The Allies had a larger combined Army than Germany and a far stronger Navy, but Hitler's Army was more highly mechanized, with five crack panzer divisions, and Germany's industrial prowess was only second to that of the United States, a nonbelligerent. Germany also had a heavy advantage in airpower and had developed its air arm as a lethal offensive weapon. And while France and England had largely maintained their peacetime economies right into 1939, the entire Nazi war machine had been preparing for a lightning offensive strike for fully six years.

Poland had no time to organize its defense, nor did France or England have time to come to its aid. So Poland fought alone.

The conquest of Poland was swift, violent, and overwhelming, a stunning revelation of the potentialities of mechanized, blitzkrieg warfare and a dress rehearsal for action in the West. Within a week the Nazis had broken through to the defenses of Warsaw; within a month the Poles had capitulated, and the fighting was over. The Nazis had massed 1.5 million men, nearly 2,000 tanks, and over 4,000 planes for the invasion. Against this tremendous array the Poles were able to mobilize only some twenty-two infantry divisions, eight cavalry brigades, a single motorized brigade, and perhaps 1,000 planes, most of them antiquated.

The German campaign was planned with masterly skill, drawing on the audacious ideas of General Heinz Guderian, who envisioned a new kind of warfare using tanks, motorized infantry, mobile artillery, and fast-striking air power. Three great armies converged on Warsaw—one from East Prussia, one from Pomerania, and one, under Field Marshal Gerd von Rundstedt, from the south. Western Poland offered no natural barriers to an advancing enemy, no convenient defense line. Hopelessly outnumbered, the Poles fought heroically, sending in horsemen armed with swords and lances against massive German tanks until their defenses cracked. The *New York Times* Berlin correspondent, Otto D. Tolischus, who was expelled by the Nazis the following year—the year he won the Pulitzer Prize—describes what happened in the first week of the German campaign:

WITH THE GERMAN ARMIES IN POLAND, September 11—Having hurled against Poland their mighty military machine, the Germans are today crushing Poland like a soft-boiled egg. . . .

The Germans have proceeded not only with might and speed, but with method, and this bids fair to be the first war to be decided not by infantry, "the queen of all arms," but by fast motorized divisions and, especially, by the air force. . . .

Today the German rule of the air is so complete that, although individual Polish planes may still be seen flying at a high altitude, the German army has actually abandoned the blackout in Poland. It is a strange sensation to come from a Germany thrown into Stygian darkness at night to a battlefront town like Lodz, as this correspondent did the night after the Germans announced its occupation, and find it illuminated although the enemy is only a few miles from the city.

With control of the air, the Germans moved forward not infantry but their tanks, armored cars and motorized artillery, which smashed any Polish resistance in the back. . . . As a purely military matter, the German army is the height of efficiency.[9]

The fall of Warsaw would not necessarily have spelled the end of Poland. But in the midst of the fight against the Nazi invader, a new situation arose. On September 17 the Russians, anxious now for their own defense, marched in from the east. Confronted with the Wehrmacht on the west, the Red Army on the east, Polish resistance collapsed. On September 28, as the battered remnants of Warsaw surrendered, Germany and Russia arranged the partition of Poland, which, as it had so many times before, disappeared from the map. To Russia went the larger territory, but only one third the population and few of the industrial resources in which western Poland was so rich. But what Russia wanted was space in which to erect a barrier against a possible German attack. For this even eastern Poland was not enough. The following June, when the collapse of France had freed the Germans for further ventures, Russia took over the Baltic republics of Estonia, Latvia, and Lithuania.

One other frontier gave the Russians concern, and to that, having secured themselves along the Baltic Sea, they now turned their attention.

FINLAND

The Nazi conquest of Poland had made Joseph Stalin nervous. He was successful in building up a defense barrier from the Baltic to Romania. But he wanted to protect himself similarly in the north. When negotiations to gain territorial concessions from Finland failed, the Red Army invaded on November 30. The world, which had expected an easy conquest, was shortly astonished at the ferocity of the Finnish defense. The Russians, unprepared for winter fighting, unfamiliar with the terrain, and underestimating the fighting ability of perhaps the most warlike people in Europe, suffered costly defeats. North of Lake Ladoga the Finns cut three Russian divisions to pieces; at Suomussalmi two more divisions were wiped out. The American correspondent and author Virginia Cowles describes this battlefield of ice and snow, white forests and glassy lakes, shortly after the Russian defeat:

DURING THE PREVIOUS SEVEN WEEKS, over a hundred thousand Russian troops had crossed the frontier, in repeated attempts to cut Finland in two. But the Finns had repulsed the onslaughts with some of the most spectacular fighting in history; they had annihilated entire divisions and hurled back others thirty and forty miles to the border from where they started.

To understand how they did it, you must picture a country of thick snow-covered forests and ice-bound roads. You must visualize heavily-armed ski patrols sliding like ghosts through the woods; creeping behind the enemy lines and cutting their communications until entire battalions were isolated, then falling on them in furious surprise attacks. In this part of Finland skis out-maneuvered tanks, sleds competed with lorries, and knives even challenged rifles.

We approached the village of Suomussalmi just as dawn was breaking, and here I witnessed the most ghastly spectacle I have ever seen. It was in this sector that the Finns, a few weeks previously, had annihilated two Russian divisions of approximately 30,000 men. The road along which we drove was still littered with frozen Russian corpses, and the forests on either side had become known as "Dead Man's Land." Perhaps it was the beauty of the morning that made the terrible Russian *débâcle* all the more ghastly when we came upon it. The rising sun had drenched the snow-covered forests, with trees like lace valentines, with a strange pink light that seemed to glow for miles. The landscape was marred only by the charred framework of a house; then an overturned truck and two battered tanks. Then we turned a bend in the road and came upon the full horror of the scene. For four miles the road and forests were strewn with the bodies of men and horses; with wrecked tanks, field kitchens, trucks, gun-carriages, maps, books, and articles of clothing. The corpses were frozen as hard as petrified wood and the color of the skin was mahogany. Some of the bodies were piled on top of each other like a heap of rubbish, covered only by a merciful blanket of snow; others were sprawled against the trees in grotesque attitudes.

All were frozen in the positions in which they had died. . . . They were everywhere, hundreds and hundreds of grotesque wooden corpses; in the ditches, under the trees, and even in dugouts beneath the snow where they had tried to escape from the fury of the attack.[10]

After these costly defeats the Russians abandoned the effort to drive through snowbound wilderness and began a direct attack upon the Mannerheim Line, along the Karelian Isthmus. Here Russian superiority in manpower, artillery, and planes could make itself felt, and here after two months of the hardest kind of fighting, a breakthrough was achieved. On March 12, Finland ceded to Russia all the lands demanded before the invasion. The cost to the Soviets was high: over 200,000 dead soldiers, compared to some 20,000 Finnish fatalities.

The following month, Stalin ordered the massacre of almost all Polish officers captured by the Red Army in 1939. This was done secretly. The bodies of many of the victims were finally discovered in the spring of 1943 in the Katyn forest, near Smolensk. Why had Stalin done this? Probably to make sure neighboring Poland remained weak in the postwar years by eliminating 15,000 anti-Communist leaders.

Meanwhile, Hitler began the systematic slaughter of Polish Jews, Gypsies, and political "undesirables." By the end of the war, 5.5 million Poles would be killed, most of them civilians, almost 16 percent of the population. (Poland suffered the greatest human losses in the war; Yugoslavia and the Soviet Union followed, with 10 percent and 5 percent dead respectively.) By early 1940, the world had begun to see that this war would be more barbaric than any civilized person might have imagined.

DENMARK AND NORWAY

In March, William Shirer confided to his journal*:

I HOPE I DIDN'T put myself out on a limb, but from what I've heard this week I wrote tonight in my broadcast: "Some people here believe the war may spread to Scandinavia yet. It was reported in Berlin today that last week a squadron of at least nine British destroyers was concentrated off the Norwegian coast and that in several instances German freighters carrying iron received warning shots. . . . From here it looks as if the neutrals, especially the Scandinavians, may be drawn into the conflict after all." [11]

Shirer was not out on a limb. At four o'clock in the morning of April 9, German armies poured across the unfortified frontier of Denmark, with whom the Germans had recently concluded a nonaggression pact. Denmark, however, was not to be "conquered." It was to be a model protectorate, a laboratory of the New Nazi Order. But even when on their good behavior, the Nazis were unable to conciliate the people of an occupied country. Soon the usual process of exploitation and looting began, and soon, too, the Danish resistance movement was organized and began its long and heroic campaign of sabotage.

As German troops were marching across the Danish frontier, powerful elements of the German Navy were steaming into every important Norwegian port: Oslo, Kristiansand, Stavanger, Bergen, Trondheim, and Narvik. The Norwegians were caught unprepared. Yet everywhere but at Narvik they put up a stout resistance, inflicting heavy losses.

The Norwegian government had fled to Elverum, near the Swedish frontier, and the Nazis had established a new government under the leadership of Vidkun Quisling, whose name was soon to be a synonym throughout the world for traitor. German armies pushing rapidly northward from Oslo brushed aside fierce but unorganized

*His *Berlin Diary* was published in 1941 and became a bestseller.

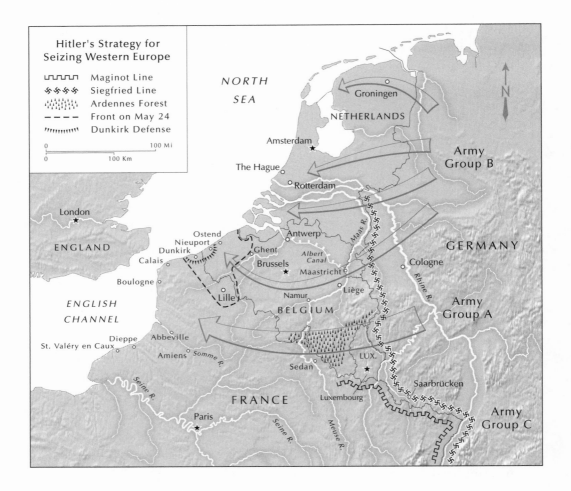

NORTH
SEA

Groningen

NETHERLANDS

Amsterdam

The Hague

Rotterdam

Army
Group B

London

ENGLAND

Ostend
Nieuport
Dunkirk
Calais

Boulogne

ENGLISH
CHANNEL

Ghent
Brussels

Antwerp

Albert
Canal

Maastricht

Maas R.

GERMANY

Cologne

Rhine R.

Army
Group A

Dieppe
St. Valéry en Caux
Abbeville
Amiens

Lille

Namur

Liège

BELGIUM

Somme R.

Seine R.

Sedan

FRANCE

Luxembourg

LUX.

Saarbrücken

Meuse R.

Army
Group C

Paris

Seine R.

resistance. Within a week the British had landed reinforcements—British, French, and Polish—but they were too little too late. The enemy controlled the sea-lanes and air, and by the end of April the Allied forces, outnumbered and outpowered, were forced to withdraw.

In just two months Hitler had conquered Denmark and Norway and had isolated Sweden. His policy of appeasement thoroughly discredited by Hitler's treachery, Chamberlain was forced to retire, and on May 10 a new government was formed under the leadership of Winston Churchill. He inspired the British people, and free peoples everywhere, with an implacable resolution to endure the worst that the Nazis could hurl against them and fight through to ultimate victory. It was entirely fitting that on the very day that Hitler launched his attack on the Low Countries, France, and ultimately Britain, he should be confronted by that indomitable man who, more than any other, was to be responsible for frustrating his wicked designs.

THE LOW COUNTRIES

"The hour has come," Hitler told his army, "for the decisive battle for the future of the German nation. For 300 years the rulers of England and France have made it their aim to prevent any real consolidation of Europe and above all to keep Germany weak and helpless. With this your hour has come. The fight which begins today will decide the destiny of the German people for 1,000 years. Now do your duty."

The army's imperative was to conquer Holland, Belgium, and Luxembourg, overrun France, and bring Britain to her knees. It was one of the great campaigns in military history.

Holland and Belgium, mortally afraid of giving Germany any excuse to attack, had failed to mobilize their armies or coordinate their defenses with those of France. The French had dispersed their forces in the north, in the Maginot Line, and along the Italian frontier. The British were still frantically building up their Army and Air Force.

At early dawn, May 10, the Germans struck all along the Western Front, from the North Sea to Luxembourg. The major attack rolled through the rugged Ardennes toward the Meuse River. Planes bombed helpless cities, parachutists seized airfields and bridges, fifth columnists spread confusion and terror behind the lines.

The Dutch put up a stout resistance, but within four days most of Holland was in German hands. Then, while negotiations for the surrender were underway, the Luftwaffe bombed the center of Rotterdam, killing 814 civilians and leaving 80,000 homeless, the beginning of the war's "terror bombing" campaigns. Under the threat to subject every Dutch city to similar treatment, resistance ceased. The conquest of Belgium was equally swift.

Meantime, Gerd von Rundstedt had broken through the Ardennes. This rugged forest-covered country, crisscrossed by winding roads and swift rivers, was thought to be unsuitable to mechanized warfare and was therefore lightly defended. It was assumed that it would take weeks for the Nazis to fight their way through here, and in that time the French could bring up the whole of their Ninth Army. But with Heinz Guderian's panzer columns in the lead, the Wehrmacht smashed through in two days, crossed the Meuse River, and sped toward the English Channel.

It was a catastrophe of the first order. On May 21, the Germans reached the English Channel at Abbeville, and the encirclement of the Belgians and the British Expeditionary Force was complete. On May 26, Lord Gort, commanding the BEF, was authorized to reembark his army to Britain, and began to concentrate his forces on the only remaining port, Dunkirk. At this juncture, the whole situation was altered, the entire BEF threatened, by the unexpected surrender of the Belgian Army.

DUNKIRK

The BEF, as well as remnants of the French and Polish armies along the Channel—some 400,000 men—seemed doomed as the Germans closed the ring around them. But the sea was still open, and Britain still ruled the waves. With a valor that aroused the admiration even of the enemy, the French fought rearguard actions at Lille, Cassel, and in Dunkirk itself. A small British force held out with fanatical courage at Calais.

Then came Operation Dynamo or, as John Masefield has called it, the Nine Days' Wonder. The Germans pressed on Dunkirk from all sides. Their artillery subjected it to ceaseless pounding, their planes smashed at piers and docks and at the embarkation fleet. The town was aflame, the water supply gone, the docks a shambles.

The Admiralty had already anticipated the task of reembarking the army from France. When it became clear that the withdrawal could no longer be delayed, the word went out for the gathering of the ships. The most fantastic armada in history— numbering 665 civilian craft and 222 naval units—assembled in the British ports nearest Dunkirk.

For nine days the evacuation went on, from May 26 to June 3, and even on the 4th and 5th a few stragglers and last-ditch fighters were brought out. Arthur D. Divine, who took part in the whole operation, has described it:

WHEN I HEARD THAT SMALL BOATS of all sorts were to be used at Dunkirk I volunteered at once. . . . The evacuation went on for something over a week, but to me the most exciting time was the night before the last.

I was given a motorboat about as long as my drawing room at home, 30 feet. She had one cabin forward and the rest was open, but she had twin engines and was fairly fast. For crew we had one sub-lieutenant, one stoker and one gunner. For armament we had two Bren guns—one my own particular pet which I had stolen—and rifles. In command of our boat we had a real live Admiral—Taylor, Admiral in charge of small boats.

We first went out to French fishing boats gathered off Ramsgate, boats from Caen and Le Havre, bright little vessels with lovely names—*Ciel de France, Ave Maria, Gratia Plena, Jeanne Antoine.* . . .

They went as the leaders of the procession, for they were slow. With them went . . . dockyard tugs and towing barges. There were sloops, mine sweepers, trawlers, destroyers. There were Thames fire floats, Belgian drifters, lifeboats from all around the coast, lifeboats from sunken ships. . . .

There was never such a fleet went to war before, I think. As I went round the western arm of the harbor near sunset, passing out orders, it brought my heart into my throat to watch them leave. They were so small! Little boats like those you see in the bight of Sandy Hook fishing on a fine afternoon. . . .

When this armada of oddments was under way, we followed with the faster boats—Royal Air Force rescue launches, picket boats and the like. . . .

It was the queerest, most nondescript flotilla that ever was, and it was manned by every kind of Englishman, never more than two men, often only one, to each small boat. There were bankers and dentists, taxi drivers and yachtsmen, long-shoremen, boys, engineers, fishermen and civil servants. . . .

It was dark before we were well clear of the English coast. . . . [But] even before it was fully dark we had picked up the glow of the Dunkirk flames. From a glow they rose up to enormous plumes of fire that roared high into the ever-lasting pall of smoke. . . .

The picture will always remain sharp-etched in my memory—the lines of men wearily and sleepily staggering across the beach from the dunes to the shad-ows, falling into little boats, great columns of men thrust out into the water among bomb and shell splashes. . . .

Some of the big boats pushed in until they were almost aground, taking appalling risks with the falling tide. The men scrambled up the sides on rope nets, or climbed hundreds of ladders. . . .

The din was infernal. The 5.9 batteries shelled ceaselessly and brilliantly. To the whistle of shells overhead was added the scream of falling bombs. Even the sky was full of noise—anti-aircraft shells, machine-gun fire, the snarl of falling planes, the angry hornet noise of dive bombers. One could not speak normally at any time against the roar of it and the noise of our own engines. We all developed "Dunkirk throat," a sore hoarseness that was the hallmark of those who had been there.

COLONEL GENERAL HEINZ GUDERIAN, THE
GREAT THEORIST OF BLITZKRIEG WARFARE,
DIRECTS THE PANZER ASSAULT ON FRANCE
FROM HIS COMMAND VEHICLE (M25).

Yet through all the noise I will always remember the . . . astonishing discipline of the men. They had fought through three weeks of retreat, always falling back without orders, often without support. Transport had failed. They had gone sleepless. They had been without food and water. Yet they kept ranks as they came down the beaches, and they obeyed commands.

Veterans of Gallipoli and of Mons agreed this was the hottest spot they had ever been in, yet morale held.[12]

All the equipment mobilized for the Battle of France was left behind on the beaches. But 335,000 British and Allied fighting men had been rescued to fight another day.

"To me Dunkirk was one of the great turning-points," Field Marshal von Rundstedt said later. "If I had my way the English would not have gotten off so lightly at Dunkirk. But my hands were tied by direct orders from Hitler himself," orders that historians claim von Rundstedt agreed with at the time, only to change his story after the war.

While the English were climbing into their ships on the beaches Rundstedt was sitting uselessly outside the port with his infantry and five panzer divisions. Hitler had ordered him not to attack, insisting that, because of earlier losses, he did not have enough tanks in good repair to destroy the retreating British forces. "He did not realize," Rundstedt explained in a later effort to clear himself of blame, "that many of the tanks reported out of action one day could, with a little extra effort on the part of the repair squads, be able to fight in a very short time."[13] Hitler also feared that the canal-crossed ground around the port was flooded and unsuitable for tank warfare. Two days later Hitler reversed his order but that delay had given the British time to organize their spectacular retreat, a retreat that may have saved Churchill's government and prevented England from negotiating with Germany to withdraw from the war.

The Fall of France

Even while the remnants of the BEF were being evacuated, the Germans began the final campaign of the Battle of France. In a few days they had crossed the Somme and by the 10th of June were hammering the Marne, scene of some of the bloodiest battles of the last war. Other armies were driving into Brittany, across the Loire toward Nantes, down along the Maginot Line toward Lyon. At this juncture, with France reeling from thunderous blows, Mussolini decided that it was safe to declare war on the Allies.

By this time France was in a state of panic. The government had fled to Tours, and from there moved on to Bordeaux. The armies, still large, and potentially powerful, but demoralized, were in headlong retreat, their progress impeded by hundreds of thousands of refugees, most of them in automobiles, jamming all the roads to the south.

"It was," said Virginia Cowles, "the first *mechanized* evacuation in history."

IN THAT WORLD OF TERROR, panic and confusion, it was difficult to believe that these were the citizens of Paris, citizens whose forefathers had fought for their freedom like tigers and stormed the Bastille with their bare hands. For the first time, I began to understand what had happened to France. Morale was a question of faith; faith in your cause, faith in your goal, but above all else, faith in your leaders. How could these people have faith in leaders who abandoned them? Leaders who had given them no directions, no information, no reassurances; who neither had arranged for their evacuation nor called on them to stay at their places and fight for Paris until the last? If this was an example of French leadership, no wonder France was doomed.[14]

On the 14th the Germans entered Paris, one of the few Open Cities they had seen fit to spare. The French cabinet voted to ask for an armistice. Prime Minister Paul Reynaud resigned and the aged Marshal Henri Philippe Pétain, hero of Verdun, was asked to form a government. Pétain promptly threw in the sponge, calling an end to the fighting, and later forming a puppet government at the resort town of Vichy. Five years later a French jury would find him guilty of treason to the republic. His death sentence commuted to life imprisonment, he died on a remote Atlantic island in 1951, at the age of 95.

On June 21 came the formal surrender in a railroad carriage in the forest at Compiègne, the same carriage, preserved as a museum piece, that Marshal Foch had used when he dictated terms to the Germans in November 1918. Hitler, who had ordered the carriage brought to the forest clearing, had his revenge. France was dismembered. The North and the Western coast were put under Nazi occupation, and the rest of the country was ruled as a vassal state from Vichy. "The humiliation of France, of the French, was complete," wrote William Shirer.[15]

Not all Frenchmen accepted Pétain's surrender. General Charles de Gaulle, who had fought courageously against Guderian's panzer columns, fled by plane to London, where he went on the radio and declared the existence of "Free France." The Frenchmen who joined him fought on in exile under the red cross of Lorraine, which Joan of Arc carried when she freed France at Orléans.

Britain Stands Alone

THE BLITZ

Dunkirk was a catastrophic defeat which the British turned, miraculously, into a moral victory. When, on June 4, 1940, the Nine Days' Wonder was complete and the last troops evacuated from Dunkirk, Churchill hurled defiance at the enemy hosts crowding the French channel ports:

> EVEN THOUGH LARGE TRACTS OF EUROPE and many old and famous States have fallen or may fall into the grip of the Gestapo and all the odious apparatus of Nazi rule, we shall not flag or fail. We shall go on to the end, we shall fight in France, we shall fight on the seas and oceans, we shall defend our Island, whatever the cost may be, we shall fight on the beaches, we shall fight on the landing grounds, we shall fight in the fields and in the streets, we shall fight in the hills; we shall never surrender.[1]

Had Hitler invaded at once, he might have driven the British from their "ancient and famous island." Yet invasion would have been a risky business. The Royal Air

Force, as the summer was to show, still commanded the skies over Britain; the Royal Navy still swept the seas; the British Army and the home guard were fired by determination to resist any assault. British scientists had prepared a warm welcome for invasion barges: vast walls of flame from gasoline piped far out into the sea, other walls of flame on land. All that summer the Nazi soldiers sang *"Wir fahren gegen England,"* but they never did more than sing about it. And from Norway, Belgium, Holland, France, Poland, Czechoslovakia, exile governments fled to London, while remnants of their armies, navies, and air forces trained in Britain for the counteroffensive that would some day come.

But first Britain would have to defend itself from an expected invasion. "The Battle of France is over," Churchill told a hushed House of Commons. "I expect that the Battle of Britain is about to begin."[2] Hitler hoped that a land invasion would not be necessary. The Luftwaffe would reduce Britain to rubble, while the U-boats, launched from new bases in Norway and France, would cut the precious lifeline of the Atlantic, starving Britain to submission. Still, he mobilized an immense invasion armada in the Channel and North Sea ports just in case.

All through May, June, and July the British and the Germans had bombed each other, somewhat ineffectually. Now, Field Marshal Hermann Goering prepared to launch the Luftwaffe in a full-scale attack on what he thought a helpless island. First came an effort to destroy the ports and the airfields; then a blow at London; then attacks on all the major industrial cities. This was the Battle of Britain—the first great air battle of history and Hitler's first major defeat in the war. Beginning in August, it reached its crescendo in October and November, exacting a terrible toll of life and destruction. But the RAF fought back with skill and courage; antiaircraft gunners put a roof of flak over the island; firefighters, wardens, ambulance drivers, home guard, and all the other agencies of defense performed miracles of bravery and endurance.

The RAF, outnumbered four to one, proved itself plane for plane and man for man better than the Luftwaffe. Here is the story of twenty-one-year-old Pilot Officer John Maurice Bentley Beard, as he himself told it. He and other heroic RAF pilots were fighting for the very survival of their country.

I WAS SUPPOSED TO BE AWAY on a day's leave but dropped back to the airdrome to see if there was a letter from my wife. When I found out that *all* the squadrons had gone off into action, I decided to stand by, because obviously something big was happening. While I was climbing into my flying kit, our

Hurricanes came slipping back out of the sky to refuel, reload ammunition, and take off again. The returning pilots were full of talk about flocks of enemy bombers and fighters which were trying to break through along the Thames Estuary. . . . I was crazy to be off. . . .

On we went, wingtips to left and right slowly rising and falling, the roar of our twelve Merlins drowning all other sound. We crossed over London, which, at 20,000 feet, seemed just a haze of smoke from its countless chimneys, with nothing visible except the faint glint of the barrage balloons and the wriggly silver line of the Thames.

I had too much to do watching the instruments and keeping formation to do much thinking. But once I caught a reflected glimpse of myself in the windscreen—a goggled, bloated, fat thing with the tube of my oxygen supply protruding gruesomely sideways from the mask which hid my mouth. Suddenly I was back at school again, on a hot afternoon when the Headmaster was . . . droning on and on about the later Roman Emperors. . . .

It was an amazingly vivid memory, as if school was only yesterday. And half my mind was thinking what wouldn't I then have given to be sitting in a Hurricane belting along at 350 miles an hour and out for a kill. *Me* defending London! I grinned at my old self at the thought.

Minutes went by. . . . I scanned the sky and there *they* were!

It was really a terrific sight and quite beautiful. . . . I could see the bright yellow noses of Messerschmitt fighters sandwiching the bombers, and could even pick out some of the types. The sky seemed full of them, packed in layers thousands of feet deep. They came on steadily, wavering up and down along the horizon. "Oh, golly," I thought, "golly, golly . . ."

And then any tension I had felt on the way suddenly left me. I was elated but very calm. . . .

The squadron leader's voice came through the earphones, giving tactical orders. We swung round in a great circle to attack on their beam—into the thick of them. Then, on the order, down we went. I took my hand from the throttle lever so as to get both hands on the stick, and my thumb played neatly across the gun button. You have to steady a fighter just as you have to steady a rifle before you fire it.

My Merlin screamed as I went down in a steeply banked dive on to the tail of a forward line of Heinkels. I knew the air was full of aircraft flinging themselves about in all directions, but hunched and snuggled down behind my sight, I was conscious only of the Heinkel I had picked out. As the angle of my dive increased, the enemy machine loomed larger in the sight field, heaved toward the red dot, and then he was there! . . .

When he was square across the sight I pressed the button. There was a smooth trembling of my Hurricane as the eight-gun squirt shot out. I gave him a two-second burst and then another. Cordite fumes blew back into the cockpit, making an acrid mixture with the smell of hot oil and the air-compressors.

I saw my first burst go in and, just as I was on top of him and turning away, I noticed a red glow inside the bomber. I turned tightly into position again and now saw several short tongues of flame lick out along the fuselage. Then he went down in a spin, blanketed with smoke and with pieces flying off.

I left him plummeting down and, horsing back on my stick, climbed up again for more. The sky was clearing, but ahead toward London I saw a small tight formation of bombers completely encircled by a ring of Messerschmitts. They were still heading north. As I raced forward, three flights of Spitfires came zooming up from beneath them. . . . They burst through upward and outward, their guns going all the time. They must have each got one, for an instant later I saw the most extraordinary sight of eight German bombers and fighters diving earthward together in flames.

I turned away again and streaked after some distant specks ahead. Diving down, I noticed that the running progress of the battle had brought me over London again. I could see the network of streets with the green space of Kensington Gardens, and I had an instant's glimpse of the Round Pond, where I sailed boats when I was a child. In that moment, and as I was rapidly overhauling the Germans ahead, a Dornier 17 sped right across my line of flight, closely pursued by a Hurricane. And behind the Hurricane came two Messerschmitts. He was too intent to have seen them and they had not seen me! They were coming slightly toward me. It was perfect. A kick at rudder and I swung in toward them, thumbed the gun button, and let them have it. The first burst was placed just the right distance ahead of the leading Messerschmitt. He ran slap into it and he simply came to pieces in the air. His companion . . . [made] one of the speediest and most brilliant "getouts" I have ever seen. . . .

As I turned I had a quick look round the "office" (cockpit). My fuel reserve was running out and I had only about a second's supply of ammunition left. . . . I put my nose down and [headed for home].[3]

By September 1, after a month of heavy fighting, the Germans had failed to destroy the fighters and pilots of the Royal Air Force. Then they switched tactics and began terror bombing London. The first great blow came on September 7, when 375 bombers—a small number by 1945 standards but stupendous for that day—unloaded their bombs on the capital in full daylight. The next day they were over London again, and the next, and the next, day after day, trying to knock out the world's largest city, break British morale, and create massive panic and hysteria, a breakdown in public morale that would bring Britain to the bargaining table, making an invasion unnecessary.

London was stunned—but defiant. With astonishing rapidity and efficiency the whole complex organization of antiaircraft warfare and fire fighting was brought into play. The RAF rose to challenge the invaders, and on one day, September 15, shot down 185 Nazi aircraft. Firefighters worked day and night to cope with the flames which raged through the capital. Ambulance drivers—many of them mere girls—rescued the trapped and the wounded; wardens and other relief workers provided temporary food and shelter. And the antiaircraft gunners threw a "roof" over the city, forcing the enemy higher and higher into the skies. Failing to gain air superiority over southern England, on September 17, Hitler postponed the invasion, code-named Operation Sealion, indefinitely.

Germany had lost the Battle of Britain, but the Blitz went on. By the end of October the Nazis were forced, by mounting losses, to give up the daylight bombing and shift to night attacks—less accurate but no less murderous. The American correspondent Ernie Pyle described a night attack on London:

THEY CAME JUST AFTER DARK, and somehow you could sense from the quick, bitter firing of guns that there was to be no monkey business this night.

Shortly after the sirens wailed you could hear the Germans grinding overhead. In my room, with its black curtains drawn across the windows, you could feel the shake from the guns. You could hear the boom, crump, crump, crump, of heavy bombs at their work of tearing buildings apart. They were not too far away.

Half an hour after the firing started I gathered a couple of friends and went to a high, darkened balcony that gave us a view of a third of the entire circle of London. As we stepped out onto the balcony a vast inner excitement came over all of us—an excitement that had neither fear nor horror in it, because it was too full of awe.

You have all seen big fires, but I doubt if you have ever seen the whole horizon of a city lined with great fires—scores of them, perhaps hundreds.

There was something inspiring just in the awful savagery of it. . . .

Into the dark shadowed spaces below us, while we watched, whole batches of incendiary bombs fell. We saw dozens go off in two seconds. They flashed terrifically, then quickly simmered down to pin points of dazzling white, burning ferociously. These white pin points would go out one by one, as the unseen heroes of the moment smothered them with sand. But also, while we watched, other pin points would burn on, and soon a yellow flame would leap up from the white center. They had done their work—another building was on fire.

GERMAN BOMBER OVER THE LONDON DOCKS, SEPTEMBER 1940 (M25).

The greatest of all the fires was directly in front of us. Flames seemed to whip hundreds of feet into the air. Pinkish-white smoke ballooned upward in a great cloud, and out of this cloud there gradually took shape—so faintly at first that we weren't sure we saw correctly—the gigantic dome of St. Paul's Cathedral. . . .

Later on I borrowed a tin hat and went out among the fires. That was exciting too; but the thing I shall always remember above all the other things in my life is the monstrous loveliness of that one single view of London on a holiday night—London stabbed with great fires, shaken by explosions, its dark regions along the Thames sparkling with the pin points of white-hot bombs, all of it roofed over with a ceiling of pink that held bursting shells, balloons, flares and the grind of vicious engines. And in yourself the excitement and anticipation and wonder in your soul that this could be happening at all.

These things all went together to make the most hateful, most beautiful single scene I have ever known.[4]

An Englishwoman, Mollie Panter-Downes, describes how it was for the people on whom the rain of fire fell:

FOR LONDONERS, there are no longer such things as good nights; there are only bad nights, worse nights, and better nights. Hardly anyone has slept at all in the past week. The sirens go off at approximately the same time every evening, and in the poorer districts, the queues of people carrying blankets, thermos flasks, and babies begin to form quite early outside the air-raid shelters. The air *Blitzkrieg* continues to be directed against such military objectives as the tired shop-girl, the red-eyed clerk, and the thousands of dazed and weary families patiently trundling their few belongings in perambulators away from the wreckage of their homes. After a few of these nights, sleep of a kind comes from complete exhaustion. The amazing part of it is the cheerfulness and fortitude with which ordinary individuals are doing their job under nerve-racking conditions. Girls who have taken twice the usual time to go to work look worn when they arrive, but their faces are nicely made up and they bring you a cup of tea or sell you a hat

A LONDON TUBE PLATFORM SERVES AS A BOMB SHELTER DURING THE BLITZ (M25).

chirpily as ever. Little shopkeepers whose windows have been blown out paste up "Business as usual" stickers and exchange cracks with their customers.

On all sides, one hears the grim phrase: "We shall get used to it."[5]

"This night bombing is serious and sensational," Edward R. Murrow reported from London that September. "It makes headlines, kills people, and smashes property; but it doesn't win wars . . . [and] will not cause this country to collapse."[6] Frustrated, the Luftwaffe turned to the industrial Midlands in November and December. The most murderous of the attacks on England's manufacturing was the night-long bombing of Coventry on November 14, but other Midland cities suffered devastating raids: Birmingham, Manchester, Liverpool, and Sheffield. The toll of civilian dead mounted to over 40,000; hundreds of thousands of houses were wrecked or damaged; essential services—gas and electricity and water and transport—were paralyzed; factories were laid in ruins.

Millions of Americans listened with horror to Edward R. Murrow's radio broadcasts of the London Blitz, some of them made from the roofs of the city. But when the war correspondent A. J. Liebling returned briefly to America, he was shocked by the reaction of his friends to the situation in Europe. "Getting off the plane and meeting people who had stayed in America was a strange experience, because they hardly seemed to know that anything was wrong. When you started to tell them they said soothingly that probably you had a lot of painful experiences, and if you just took a few grains of Nembutal so you would get one good night's sleep, and then go out to the horse races twice, you would be your own sweet self again. It was like the dream in which you yell at people and they don't hear you."[7]

The Atlantic Lifeline

The fight against the Luftwaffe was only part of the titanic contest which Britain waged throughout the world. Cut off from its former continental Allies, Britain depended more and more upon its dominions and empire—and, increasingly, upon the United States. Above all it was essential to her survival to guard the Atlantic and Mediterranean lifelines: if either of them were cut the consequences might be fatal. Upon the British Navy and its air arm was placed the almost intolerable burden of patrolling the water lanes of the world, hunting down marauding cruisers, destroyers, and pocket battleships, protecting convoys against packs of U-boats, sweeping mines from its harbors, getting supplies through not only to Britain but from the mother country to Gibraltar, Malta, Egypt, Russia, India, and the Far East.

In the beginning the combined British and French navies had unchallenged superiority over the German. But with the fall of France the balance shifted. Not only was the French Navy immobilized—soon the British went in to destroy it—but Italy brought to the Axis a powerful modern surface fleet and perhaps a hundred submarines. Germany, too, though weak in surface ships, could boast two giant battleships, *Bismarck* and *Tirpitz*, and three fast pocket battleships, in addition to several older battleships like *Scharnhorst* and *Gneisenau.* From nearby airfields German planes could bomb convoys approaching the British Isles and sow mines in British harbors. And Germany had close to 100 submarines which could operate from pens all along the Atlantic from Norway to the Spanish border.

The seriousness of the U-boat menace was speedily dramatized when, within two weeks of the outbreak of war, a submarine sank the aircraft carrier *Courageous.* The following month another U-boat penetrated the supposedly impregnable British fleet at Scapa Flow in the Orkney Islands and sank the battleship *Royal Oak,* in what was the most sensational U-boat attack of the war. British submarines retaliated, the *Salmon* torpedoing the cruisers *Leipzig* and *Bluecher*. Then, in the distant waters off Uruguay, three British cruisers ran down the German pocket-battleship *Graf Spee,* damaged it, and drove it into Montevideo harbor, where its commander scuttled it.

Other German warships roamed the Atlantic preying upon convoys from the United States and Canada. But the German surface raiders and battleships did not have things their own way. In May 1941, the *Bismarck* and the heavy cruiser *Prinz Eugen* slipped out of their hiding places in a Norwegian fjord to harry British convoys. Reconnaissance planes of the Coastal Command spotted the ships almost at once, and the hunt was on. The raiders were intercepted on the morning of May 24, off the coast of Greenland. The British battle-cruiser *Hood* was fatally hit soon after the engagement opened, but the rest of the attack force chased the *Bismarck* through the ice floes, caught her, and sank her with torpedoes from planes and destroyers and salvos from 14- and 16-inch guns. Almost 2,300 sailors went down with the *Bismarck*, with her flag still flying.

Prinz Eugen got away, to join her sister ships, the battlewagons *Gneisenau* and *Scharnhorst.* Bombed again and again, these ships somehow managed to escape and, under cover of fog, make a spectacular dash around Brittany and up the English Channel to their home ports. Fully repaired, *Scharnhorst,* lurking in the fjords of northern Norway, preyed upon the huge convoys carrying tanks, trucks, and planes to Russia. Finally on December 26, 1943, the incessant efforts of the Royal Navy to lure her into a fight were rewarded and *Scharnhorst* was sunk.

By the early summer of 1941 the Royal Navy had won command of the surface seas, but the menace from mines and submarines remained. Mines were cheap to make, easy to lay, hard to detect or avoid but the minesweepers of the Royal Navy cleared a path for the convoys. Most dangerous of all was the minesweeping in the English Channel, for here the sailors were exposed not only to the mines but to attack from the air and bombardment from coastal batteries.

The U-boats remained the deadliest menace, however. Despite continuous bombing raids on German submarine pens along the coast of occupied France and on the plants inside Germany manufacturing parts, submarine production increased tremendously during the war. Destroyers afforded some protection to the convoys but there were still enormous losses. On October 31, 1941, a U-boat struck the USS *Reuben James* on convoy duty out of Iceland. The German commander, Erich Topp, who would ultimately sink thirty-four Allied ships, describes the incident:

GERMAN U-BOAT PENS (M25).

AT THE END OF 1941, we learned that President Roosevelt had declared that half of the Atlantic Ocean would be under American control and we knew that he had already given 50 destroyers to the British, even though America was still technically a noncombatant.

This was the situation when I was operating in the western part of the Atlantic. On the early morning of the 31st of October, I made contact with a convoy and hit one of the destroyers. I was sure it was a British destroyer escort, but I had only seen the silhouette through my periscope. But soon by radio I heard that I had hit the *Reuben James*. When I hit it, there was a tremendous explosion, and a volcanic foundation of water came out of the ship, and after a time, an additional fountain of water. This was an explosion of the depth charges they used against our U-boats. Then a big fire started on the ship, and this was all I saw.

Later I heard of the tragedy of the *Reuben James:* that more than 100 men had been victims of my attack, and that men were caught in the ship and in freezing water filled with fire and oil.[8]

Commander Griffith B. Coale witnessed this tragedy and recorded it in his journal.

OCTOBER 31, 1941. . . . a sudden loud explosion brings me upright. Know instantly that it is a torpedo and not a depth charge. Spring from my bunk, jump for the bulkhead door . . . and land on the deck in a split second, with General Quarters still rasping. It is not us. A mile ahead a rising cloud of dark smoke hangs over the black loom of a ship. With a terrific roar, a column of orange flame towers high into the night as her magazines go up. . . . All the ship forward of No. 4 stack has disappeared. We move rapidly down upon her, as her stern rises perpendicularly into the air and slides slowly into the sea. A moment, and two grunting jolts of her depth charges toss debris and men into the air. Suddenly my nostrils are filled with the sickly stench of fuel oil, and the sea is flat and silvery under its thick coating. Before we know it, we hear the cursing, praying, and hoarse shouts for help, and we are all among her men, like black shiny seals in the oily water. . . .

"We are the *Reuben James'* men!" comes a chorus from one raft, and then we know. The spirit of these huddled greasy forms, packing the overloaded life rafts, is magnificent. . . . But the bobbing blobs of isolated men are more pitiful. Thrice blown up and choking with oil and water, they are like small animals caught in molasses. We are now in a black circle of water, surrounded by a vast silver ring of oil slick. The men to port are drifting toward us and the hove lines are slipping through their greasy, oily hands. Soon many eager hands are grasping our cargo net, but our ship's upward roll breaks their weak and slippery hold. Instantly officers and men are begging permission to go over the side, and in no time three of our officers are ten feet from the ship on a reeling raft, and several chief petty officers are clinging to the net, trying to make lines fast around the slimy bodies of the survivors so that dozens of strong arms above on the deck can heave them aboard. The first man is hauled over the amidship rail vomiting oil. Forward from the lofty bridge I see an isolated man below me and hear his choking curses. Half blind, he sees the bridge above him. His cursing ceases—"A *line,* please, Sir!" I cup my hands and shout. A line is hove and he is towed amidships to the nets. Crossing to the starboard side, I see the obscure mass of another loaded raft. One man ignites a cigarette lighter and waves it in the darkness. They shout in chorus, but our lines fall short. They are drifting away to leeward. We shout through megaphones: "Hang on! We'll get you!" One man alone is trying to swim toward us. "Come on, buddy!" I bellow, "you can make it!" But the line hove with great skill falls short—and we chart the course of their drift. It is a lengthy and desperately hard job to get these men aboard. Our men are working feverishly, but less than half have come over the rail and thirty-eight minutes have passed. The horizon is dull red with the coming of the dawn, and the increasing light makes the mass of our inert ship an easy target for the submarine which must be lurking near. One of our destroyers is continually circling us, as the Captain bellows from the bridge: "Get those men aboard!" After sixty-five minutes a few exhausted men still bob along our side. The Captain says to me: "We are in great danger. I cannot risk the ship and her company much longer." Now there are two or three left. . . . A contact directly astern with a submarine! The telephone buzzes in the wheelhouse—the other destroyer gets it too! . . . We order the ensigns on the raft aboard with all haste . . . and we leap away, leaving two survivors to swirl astern. We roar away and the other destroyer lets go a pattern of depth charges. . . . We search, lose contact, and return, and the other ship picks up eleven men while we circle her. We hope she got the two we had to leave! A third destroyer comes back to relieve us with orders to search the spot until noon, and we with thirty-six survivors, and the other rescue ship, catch up with the fleeing convoy at twenty-five knots.

"Secure from General Quarters!" Ten-thirty and we can go to breakfast! Hot coffee—Lord, it's nectar! We have been on the bridge since five twenty-three! The ship is a mess—her decks, rails, and ladders are covered with oil and the smell of it. . . . Ropes, life jackets, and the men's clothes are piled along the decks in black and soggy masses. Four men with hemorrhages are put into officers' bunks. We learn that all the officers died with the blowing up of the forward part of the ship, and we had many friends among them.[9]

LEND-LEASE

During the dismal days of Dunkirk, the fall of France, and the Blitz, many Americans all but despaired for Britain. The overwhelming majority hoped for a British victory and gradually, as Britain gathered her resources to strike back, the conviction grew that the Nazis might be stopped, and ultimately defeated. More important was the growing realization that Britain's fight was, in the end, America's fight; that Britain defeated would mean America isolated in a hostile world. From the beginning President Roosevelt was frankly anti-Nazi, and in this he faithfully reflected the attitude of the American people. Bolder than most of his followers, however, he was prepared to translate attitude into conduct. In September came the first important contribution from the United States: a transfer to Britain of fifty overage destroyers in return for ninety-nine-year leases on a series of bases from Newfoundland to British Guiana. But it was not enough. When Churchill pleaded with Roosevelt to give Britain "the tools . . . to finish the job," FDR submitted to Congress his proposal for a lend-lease arrangement, and after two months' heated discussion the plan became law in March 1941, committing America to become the "great arsenal of democracy." [10]

The most urgent demand on America's productive capacity was for ships—for without ships, the planes, the tanks, the food so badly needed by Britain and its Allies could not reach their destination. And in no field—not even in that of airplane production—did America reveal her industrial might and technological genius more clearly than in shipbuilding. Organized as vast assembly lines, American shipyards turned out eight million tons of merchant ships in 1942, almost 20 million in 1943. With the help of American war production and convoys, the Atlantic lifeline was held and Britain transformed, eventually, from a last outpost of defense to a forward base of attack.

WAR IN THE MEDITERRANEAN

After the Battle of Britain, the principal theater of war for the British was the Mediterranean. Italy's entry into the war, together with the collapse of France, enormously increased the difficulties that confronted Britain. Not until Hitler had conquered the Balkans and immobilized the threat from Russia could he cut Britain's lifeline to the Far East or obtain Persian oil. But Mussolini was now in a position to achieve these objectives. Could Britain, fighting for her life, spare sufficient forces to resist Mussolini? At first glance the task seemed insuperable. Mussolini dominated the Mediterranean. He had built up the Italian Navy to a first-class battle fleet; he boasted over 100 submarines. His planes, taking off from fields in southern Italy and Sicily, could cut far-flung British communications to Egypt. In Africa, his flank was secured by the surrender of France and he had a friendly government in Spain. His control of Libya also threatened Egypt from the west.

The most immediate threat was naval, for if Mussolini could make the Mediterranean his sea, the British were in terrible trouble. By itself the Italian fleet was no match for the British. But now the British fleet was engaged in defending the home island and the Atlantic lifeline, while there was grave danger that Italy and Germany might get control of French warships that had found refuge in a port near Oran, in French Algeria, and turn its guns upon the British. British commander Vice Admiral Sir James Somerville gave the commander of the French Squadron an ultimatum. When the French commander refused to surrender his ships, the British opened fire, sinking the battleship *Bretagne,* several destroyers, and the new battle cruiser *Dunkerque,* killing 1,300 French sailors. There were still powerful elements of the French navy at Toulon, but with the action at Oran, the threat of Axis control of the French fleet passed, and Britain was left to deal with Italy alone in the Mediterranean. The outraged Vichy government broke off diplomatic relations with England, and moved closer to active collaboration with Germany.

The British promptly took—and kept—the offensive. In one of the first torpedo plane attacks of the war, British fliers surprised and crippled half the Italian battle fleet at its base at Taranto. Then, in late March 1941, the Royal Navy inflicted a crushing defeat on the Italian fleet at Cape Matapan, southwest of Crete.

Taranto and Matapan effectively disposed of the Italian fleet, but the menace of the submarine and the plane continued. At all costs, the supply lines through Gibraltar and across the Mediterranean to the British Army in Egypt had to be kept open. Astonishingly enough Hitler failed to move through Spain to seize Gibraltar. Perhaps one reason for this failure—a failure which in retrospect seems as fatal as any which he made in the course of the war—was his belief that Italian planes and submarines, operating out of southern Italy and Sicily, could take care of any convoys that attempted to run the gauntlet. This assumption seemed sound enough, but its realization required the early reduction or neutralization of Britain's island fortress of Malta. Malta did not fall, however, nor did it ever cease to serve as a base for punishing offensive action against German supply lines to North Africa.

DESERT AND MOUNTAIN VICTORIES

The Italians had already begun the offensive in North Africa that was designed to win them a vast empire. The prospects were splendid. They had almost half a million soldiers in Africa: against them the British could muster barely 100,000. The British were also badly outnumbered in tanks and planes, and while the Italian lines of communication were short, those of the British were almost 2,000 miles, all of them perilous. The Italian plan envisioned an invasion of Egypt from the south and east by its army in Ethiopia and, simultaneously, an attack from the west by a large and well-equipped army under Marshal Rodolfo Graziani. In September, Graziani began his advance through Libya and into Egypt. But the attack bogged down at Sidi el Barrani. There, in December, General Sir Archibald Wavell, the British commander in the Middle East, struck the Italians sixty miles inside Egypt and sent them hurtling back across the frontier. In a brilliant eight-week campaign, Wavell pursued and destroyed Graziani's Army, capturing over 130,000 prisoners and great quantities of matériel.

Italy's plans for the conquest of Egypt from Ethiopia were going badly too. Here the Italians had some 200,000 troops, outnumbering the British seven to one. Early in 1941 the British launched their offensive and within less than three months all Italian resistance in Ethiopia was wiped out, and Haile Selassie was once more on his ancient throne.

TERROR IN THE BALKANS

Wavell's rapid advance along the Libyan coast came to an abrupt end as he was called upon to send half of his meager forces to the defense of Greece.

In October of the previous year, Mussolini, hoping to secure new outposts for his attack on Egypt, had launched an unprovoked attack upon Greece. The first Italian advance had pushed into the Pindus Mountains along the Albanian border, but by the end of winter, the Greeks had thrown the invaders back across the border and overrun almost half of Albania. Then the situation changed radically. Hitler, who had already determined to attack Russia, prepared to launch an invasion of the Balkans designed at once to secure his southern flank, rescue his Axis partner, and tie up with Vichy forces in Syria the pro-Axis elements in Iraq and Iran. All through 1940 he waged a war of nerves against the Balkan countries, and one by one Romania, Bulgaria, and Yugoslavia fell, although in Yugoslavia guerrilla bands, under General Draja Mihailovitch and the iron-willed Communist insurgent Josip Broz, known as Tito, harried the invaders, immobilizing entire divisions of Nazi troops, and killing Italians and Germans in great numbers.

In March 1941, Wavell shifted approximately half of his forces from North Africa to Greece—a total of some 60,000 men—but was unable to stem the furious

Nazi advance. On April 27, as the Nazis raised the swastika over the Acropolis, which Hitler ordered his airmen not to bomb, the British, hammered relentlessly by the Luftwaffe, were pulling out of Greece in what was another Dunkirk.

Miraculously, the British managed to evacuate to the nearby island of Crete some 50,000 of their 60,000 troops, along with remnants of the Greek army and King George II of Greece. If the Germans were to realize their plan for the conquest of North Africa and the control of the Middle East, possession of Crete was essential. In ten days the Nazis overran Crete, forcing Britain to engage in yet another humiliating evacuation.

DEFEAT

Things were going badly in North Africa as well. The Italian Army of some seven divisions had now been reinforced by the powerful Afrika Korps, under the command of General Erwin Rommel, the "Desert Fox." Late in March Rommel attacked, and rapidly pushed the British back into Egypt. The retreat, however, was not complete, for the British left one Australian division in the Libyan port of Tobruk. These "rats of Tobruk," as they came to be known, withstood an eight-month siege and were a constant threat to Rommel's flank.

In this black chapter of defeat there was but one encouraging page. In the vast and strategically important Middle East, which stretches from the eastern shores of the Mediterranean to India, the British had outguessed, outnumbered, and outfought the Axis and its agents. The importance of this area can scarcely be exaggerated. If the Axis came to dominate Syria, Iraq, and Iran, they could secure for themselves the oil that supplied the Mediterranean fleet, immobilize Turkey, interpose an insurmountable barrier to lend-lease supply to Russia via the Persian Gulf, and threaten India from the west. But Britain moved with audacity to gain control of Iraq, Syria, and along with Russia, Iran.

After Wavell failed to break Rommel's siege of Tobruk, Churchill replaced him with General Sir Claude Auchinleck, whose British forces were now consolidated into the Eighth Army. In November 1941, reinforced with new armored divisions and equipped with American lend-lease supplies, he took the offensive against Rommel in another effort to relieve the garrison at Tobruk. The offensive got off to a bad start when British tanks were outfought at Sidi Rezegh and Rommel cut across Auchinleck's rear to invade Egypt. But Rommel too overplayed his hand, and soon he was forced by British armored and air superiority to retreat all the way back to El Agheila, in north-central Libya, where he had begun his offensive. There he received reinforcements, and the British, who were by this time overextended, were in turn forced to retreat toward Tobruk, near the Egyptian border with Libya.

In the ensuing months, the opposing armies raced to build up their armor—a race the Germans initially won by virtue of their short line of communications. On May 26, Rommel, heavily reinforced, mounted his most dangerous offensive. In this campaign the British were both outclassed and outfought. On "Black Saturday," June 13, the Desert Fox lured the British Army into a trap at Knightsbridge and destroyed all but seventy of 300 tanks. It was one of the most stunning defeats of the war in Africa, but worse was still to come. On June 21, 1942, Tobruk, which had held out for so long against Axis attacks, surrendered, with 28,000 men. Winston Churchill, then in Washington, privately confessed that he was the most miserable Englishman in America since Burgoyne had surrendered at Saratoga. "The fall of Tobruk made an enormous impression in Berlin and throughout Germany," wrote the Swedish journalist Arvid Fredborg. "Public spirits rose at once to a peak not experienced since the conclusion of the Battle of France in 1940. Rommel [promoted to Field Marshal] was the man of the day to whom nothing seemed impossible. Perhaps we can win the war after all, everybody said." [11]

EL ALAMEIN AND BEYOND

But the British were not finished. General Auchinleck set up a defense line in the narrow neck between El Alamein and the impassable Qattara Depression and here, barely sixty miles from Alexandria, the Eighth Army hung on, preventing Rommel from advancing all the way to the Suez Canal.

President Roosevelt ordered every spare Sherman tank sent to the imperiled Egyptian front. Churchill himself came out to encourage the troops with his presence. And in August, Auchinleck was removed and command of the Middle East was entrusted to General Sir Harold Alexander. His close friend General Bernard Law Montgomery took over the Eighth Army. The American reporter John Gunther gives a glimpse of Montgomery in Egypt:

HE WAS HEARTILY DISLIKED when he first arrived in Cairo. He was cavalier about his predecessors, which was considered bad form in the extreme, and many officers thought him insolent. Monty paid no attention. He went up forward and wandered around for a day or two, inspecting every position, talking to every man he met, making intimate personal contact with the troops. What he had to pray for was time. "Give me a fortnight," he said, "and I can resist the German attack. Give me three weeks, and I can defeat the Boche. Give me a month, and I can chase him out of Africa." Meantime, he *took hold*. Within forty-eight hours the difference in spirit at the Alamein front was prodigious. The previous commander had scarcely ever visited or even talked to his own men. But within forty-eight hours of Monty's arrival, every man in Egypt knew that a fresh new wind was blowing, that their new commander was something quite different, something unique. He instilled into them, magically, his own magnificent superconfidence.[12]

The Allies—and the United States was, by this time, an ally—won the final lap of the battle for supply. During the summer months hundreds of Sherman tanks, thousands of jeeps and trucks, almost a hundred 105mm self-propelled guns, and hundreds of planes arrived from the United States. The British too strained every nerve to rush in supplies, and by October Montgomery had clear superiority in armor and in the air.

On the night of October 23, Montgomery hurled all his might at the enemy. The battle of El Alamein was, as Churchill said, "the end of the beginning," one of the turning points of the war. Lieutenant Colonel J. O. Ewert, one of Montgomery's intelligence officers, describes it:

THE TWENTY-THIRD OF OCTOBER, 1942, was a still and moonlit night in the desert. At 9:40 the roar of 800 guns broke the silence and marked the start of the battle of Alamein. Twenty minutes of flashing, deafening chaos . . . For these twenty minutes the sky was lit by the winking flashes along the horizon, then a quiet broken by the sound of tank tracks and the rattle of small arms. The Eighth Army was unleashed. . . .

Rommel had fenced himself in behind barriers of mines and wire, sandwiching Italian battalions between German battalions. It was the deepest defense that either side had constructed in Africa, and there was no possibility of outflanking it. In front of the main position, a strong line with great keeps, there was a forward line. It was not so strong, but was joined to the main ladder. The front parts of the line between the "rungs" were weaker, so that our attacks would be canalized into a series of hollows and would lose direction. Into the "Devil's Gardens," as Rommel named them, a murderous defensive fire was to be laid down. In some areas there were as many as nine successive minefields to overcome.

General Montgomery had decided to make a break-in in the north, using the 30th Corps, which now included the 9th Australian Division (the Rats of Tobruk). . . . He chose the north because a breakthrough in the north threatened the coastal road, the enemy's life, and imperiled the security of all his forces on the southern part of the line. . . .

By first light on the 24th . . . we had bitten deep into the enemy's main defenses. Gaps had been made in the minefields and the armor of the 10th Corps had started to move up. We had broken in, but not through. . . .

The first phase of the battle continued until the 26th. While our infantry ground down the enemy defenses slowly and steadily and beat off the counterattacks of the 15th Panzer Division, the sappers were making the corridors for the armour behind. The second phase began on the 27th. A purposefulness appeared in the enemy's movements. We guessed that Rommel was back. [He had briefly returned to Germany on sick leave.] Subsequent evidence proved that we were right. He took an immediate grip on the situation, and concentrated all his reserves in the north. Meantime Montgomery was building up a hitting reserve behind the "bulge" as it was now called [and] . . . was making his plan for the breakthrough. . . .

The plan had the simplicity of genius. It was to persuade the Germans that we were going one way, and then to go the other. It worked perfectly. On the 29th the 9th Australian Division after bitter fighting, advanced due north across the coast road almost cutting off an enemy force of about two regiments in a strong point known as Thomson's post. The Australians were exposed in this precarious salient, but they were told to stay there. Rommel was drawn. [Soon] the whole of the enemy reserve . . . was concentrated astride the road, right in the north. It was tired and battle worn. The Australians had not yielded an inch.

It was the moment Montgomery was waiting for. . . . On November 2nd the whole weight of the Eighth Army's armour poured west straight out of the bulge. The Germans were caught off balance. Their attention was toward the north. . . . Before [Rommel] could reconcentrate to meet the threat from a new direction, the 1st and 10th Armoured Divisions were among him. A fierce battle was fought at El Aqqaqir, and it was here in this flat out, hammer and tongs fighting on murderously open and featureless ground that the final pressure was applied. By nightfall the enemy had cracked, and was starting to disengage. . . .

Rommel's main stocks and dumps and workshops were at Daba, some twenty miles up the coast road. To cover their evacuation he tried to stand, but . . . the retreat for the moment became a rout. Tanks, guns, vehicles, stores were abandoned, burnt out and scattered along the roadside, while Rommel tried to break right away. Past Daba, where the tank workshops were left almost intact, and a train was still steaming in the station, past Fuka, the Axis remnants streamed, pounded ruthlessly by the R.A.F. Tanks were abandoned in panic when they ran out of fuel, aircraft abandoned intact on the Daba landing grounds.

Nose to tail, two deep, the Eighth Army poured west, back past the old familiar places, tanks, guns without number, without an enemy aircraft disturbing them. In the other direction marched long columns of tattered, tired, dejected Germans and Italians, to join the four divisions Rommel had abandoned in the southern part of the line, and to continue their dreary march into captivity in Egypt, the land they had so nearly conquered. The Axis had suffered its first great defeat and the tide had turned.[13]

Hastily Rommel pulled back his shattered Afrika Korps, hoping to make a stand, as so often before at Tobruk or Derna or Benghazi. But the pursuit was relentless, for 1,400 miles, all the way to Tunisia. By January 1943, Egypt was saved and the Eighth Army was at the gates of Tripoli.

The British reporter John Pudney describes the desert carnage the victorious Army marched through:

BELOW THEM STRETCHED NOTHING BUT DEATH and destruction to the very horizon. Shattered trucks, burnt and contorted tanks, blackened and tangled heaps of wreckage not to be recognized; they scattered the landscape as thickly as stars in the sky. Like dead stalks in the sand, rifles were thrust upright—a denuded forest. And each one meant a man who had been maimed or killed. . . . In dug-outs, pits and trenches the dead lay tangled and piled. Here and there from a heap of dead a hand reached forth as if in supplication, or a pair of eyes stared up accusingly—and would stare so until they rotted into the skull. Here was a body with limbs torn from it or without a head; and somewhere else a head lay on its own. Ripped-apart bellies with the viscera swelling outwards like some great sea-anemone; a throat impaled by the long shard of a shell. These are details of the scene repeated again and again in every corner of the desert landscape: a great rubbish-heap of metal and human flesh. So the victors sat, gazing across the gigantic desolation.[14]

From the Vistula
to the Volga

THE ATTACK ON RUSSIA

On June 22, 1941, Hitler took his greatest gamble.

"I decided today again," he announced, "to lay the fate and future of the German Reich and our people in the hands of our soldiers." As he spoke, his armies were rolling across the plains of eastern Poland into Russia. Hitler called it Operation Barbarossa, after the medieval German emperor who had won spectacular victories against the Infidel in the East.

Why did he do it? Germany had a nonaggression pact with Russia and, presumably, her eastern frontiers were safe. Yet neither Germany nor Russia put much confidence in that pact. Already Russia had moved in to create a defensive barrier in eastern Poland, Finland, and the Baltic states. Already Germany had extended its influence to Hungary, Bulgaria, and Romania and smashed its way into Yugoslavia and Greece. The nonaggression pact was a mere marriage of convenience, to be broken when it suited the parties to break it.

Hitler had wanted temporary security in the East while Germany fought in the West. Stalin had wanted time to prepare to repulse an attack if it came, although when it came, he was surprised, probably because it made no sense to him.

Even he underestimated the depth of Hitler's hatred of Bolshevism and the Slavic people. Nor did he understand that, in Hitler's mind, smashing Russia, the last hope on the continent of Europe against Germany, was a way to bring England to the bargaining table. "The thrust . . . of the entire campaign is clear," wrote Joseph Goebbels, Hitler's minister of propaganda. "Bolshevism must fall and England will have its last conceivable continental weapon knocked out of its hand." [1]

SS TROOPS CELEBRATE GERMANY'S EARLY VICTORIES IN OPERATION BARBAROSSA (M25).

It was a reckless move. The Soviet Union was a nation of 190 million, with vast resources of territory and wealth. "This war with Russia is a nonsensical idea," Field Marshal von Rundstedt wrote privately that May, "to which I can see no happy ending." [2]

Yet if ever there was to be a test of strength, now was the moment when that test might be made most advantageously by Germany, Hitler calculated. With his allied, vassal, and conquered states he could muster formidable power. With immunity in the West, he could hurl against the Soviet Union a larger initial force—and a far better equipped one—than Stalin could mobilize.

It was a decision that would transform the shape of the modern world. It brought into the war one of the two officially neutral countries—the other was the United States—that, together, would make it impossible for Germany to win the war. And it set in motion the most terrible slaughter in the entire history of warfare. More people died on the Eastern front than on all the other fronts of the war combined.

THE BLOODIEST FRONT IN HISTORY

The Germans launched a three-pronged offensive with three enormous army groups, comprising over 3 million troops, slightly more than the number of Soviet sol-

PANZER GRENADIERS PREPARE FOR AN ATTACK ON
STALINGRAD (M25).

diers opposing them. One offensive, under Field Marshal Wilhelm von Leeb, drove through the Baltic states toward Leningrad and a juncture with the Finns—who had joined in the war—coming down from the north. The second and major offensive, under Field Marshal Fedor von Bock, headed straight west toward Moscow. The third and, as it turned out, most successful, under Rundstedt, smashed through southern Poland toward the Ukraine, the Crimea, and the Black Sea.

At first, all three offensives met with spectacular success, the beneficiary of Stalin's pathetic unpreparedness. The northern army plunged into Lithuania and by August was striking at the outskirts of Leningrad. The central army penetrated the Stalin Line and attacked Smolensk. The southern forces overran Kiev, while eager Romanian divisions swept down on Odessa.

But the Germans badly underestimated their enemy. When Russian soldiers were surrounded they kept on fighting and killing Germans until they were overwhelmed. And Stalin, once he recovered his confidence, employed a "defense in depth" system against the Wehrmacht's vaunted blitzkrieg tactics. Every time the Germans smashed through Russian defenses they found new Soviet armies in the rear. Soon Hitler was forced to change his strategy. "Instead of trying for a quick knockout by driving straight through Moscow, Leningrad and the Caucasus," the American reporter Frederick Oechsner explained, "the Nazis had now to attempt to win by destroying the Soviet armies one after the other in a series of bloody *Vernichtungsschlachten* or 'annihilation battles.'"[5] The result was the most terrible slaughter of the entire war. It was, as Oechsner pointed out, the bloodiest front in history:

WHEN HITLER, CULMINATING SIX MONTHS of secret preparation, hurled the German army across the Russian frontier, it attacked with an unparalleled mixture of hatred and fanatic zeal. This spirit had been implanted by twenty years of Nazi vituperation against Communism—except for a cynical two years of Nazi-Soviet "friendship" on paper—and the conviction that German *Kultur* must be brought to the benighted east. Also by a very great yearning for Russian food and raw materials. Millions of young fighters were impelled by this fanaticism, which had been lacking in the western campaigns.

The utterly ruthless character of the Nazi attack was best illustrated for me by an incident told me by a Nazi soldier. On the morning of the attack, that twenty-second of June, 1941, the Russian and German guards at a bridge straddling the frontier were due to be changed as usual. The German sentries approached their Russian colleagues for the customary meeting and salute in the middle of the bridge, but, instead of the usual civilities, whipped out their guns and shot the Russians dead.

That was the style of the onslaught along the whole huge front. It enabled the Germans to chalk up the victories of Bialystok, Minsk, Smolensk, Bryansk, Uman, Nikolaev, and finally Kiev and Odessa. But the Russians held eventually at Leningrad and Moscow, constantly inflicting huge losses on the attackers.

No, this campaign in the east was not like the march through Holland, Belgium and France, as I was able to see on a 2500-mile tour of the southern sector last autumn. I had been on the western front a number of times, too, and even for me, a non-participant, it had been different. In Belgium and France there had been numerous towns and cities with beds to sleep in. The food had not been bad. In Russia I slept on straw and ate raw bacon; I didn't have my clothes off my body for ten days running. There were miles upon miles of empty country with only here and there a small, dirty village.

I could see why the German soldiers didn't like the Russian show. It was a tougher war, resistance was more bitter, losses were greater, there was incredible punishment of equipment on the Russian roads. In the east there were not things to buy in the conquered territory: no silks or wine or chocolate to take home when you went on leave. Nor were the girls the same. I could see distaste written in the grim, weathered faces of thousands after thousands of German youngsters moving forward to the battle lines; I had seen these same youths in France, and their faces were different there.[4]

By mid-July the Germans were at Smolensk and there occurred the first great battle of the Russian campaign, a battle which ended with the Russians in headlong retreat and the Germans in possession of a shattered city. Meantime Rundstedt's armies had moved on to drive the Red Army out of Kiev.

The Germans announced fabulous captures—324,000 prisoners on July 10, another 310,000 at Smolensk in August, 103,000 at Uman that same month, 675,000 in the Ukraine in September. The expectation was that all these prisoners, along with most of the urban population of East Russia, were to be starved to death, opening that vast area for German resettlement.[5] By the end of September, the Red Army had lost some 2.5 million men and SS troops, assisted by special murder squads, indiscriminately slaughtered Jews, along with "subhuman" Slavic peasants, in horrific numbers. Hitler's racial crusade against the Slavic people would backfire, however, driving potential Nazi collaborators, alienated by Stalin's brutality, back into the arms of the tyrannical dictator.

THE BATTLE OF MOSCOW

As German armies to the north opened the siege of Leningrad and to the south the siege of Odessa, Bock prepared for the knockout blow against Moscow. By October

A DETERMINED SS SOLDIER PREPARES TO THROW A "POTATO MASHER" GRENADE IN THE BATTLE OF MOSCOW (NA).

the stage was set for one of the titanic battles of the war. The government moved to Kuibyshev, on the Volga, and Moscow prepared to fight for its life. The Red Army fell slowly back, meeting blitzkrieg war with fanatical resistance. The *New York Times* correspondent C. L. Sulzberger captures the barbaric nature of the fighting on the approaches to Moscow:

IN THE VASTNESS OF THIS STRUGGLE, there have been few pitched battles on static lines. But day after day, night after night, thousands of men are dying, while others crawl to the rear wounded. The terrain over a 2,000-mile front varies only in foliage and climate. It is a monotonous flatland from the southern Ukraine to the wooded shores of Lake Ladoga, rarely broken by geological highlights. There is only this fundamental difference: from the Arctic to the central front the fields are enveloped by great forests . . . while to the south there is the open steppe.

There is no real front. When the battle is joined, the opposing troops come out of their slit trenches and dugouts and fight it out until the tide swings backward or forward. . . .

My diary, describing a typical region northeast of Yelnya on the Moscow front, reads:

". . . Most of this area has been reconquered, and the slightly sour smell of death hovers over it. Enormous bomb craters scar the roadsides, some of them 18 feet deep and more than 30 feet across. Fields have been chewed by tractor and tank treads, and pitted by shell bursts.

"Soldiers drive herds of cattle forward to fill the stewpots at soup kitchens. Privates labor in some of the fields. Crows and magpies peck at the blood-soaked earth.

"This is gray, gloomy, desolate territory. Villages have been smashed and leveled, and trees ripped apart. Fragments of wrecked machinery are seen everywhere. Here is a piece of a Messerschmitt hurled into the ocher-colored earth. There is a Skoda reconnaissance car or a Mercedes gun hauler; cases of mortar shells, tattered uniforms, rifle butts. . . ."

These words describe a quiet day in a quiet area. In general the Russians remain on the defensive, making the Germans pay heavily for every attack, chipping down the size of the *Wehrmacht* day by day. They realize that Hitler's greatest weakness, manpower, is their own chief strength—that no matter how much matériel the Führer can squeeze out of the slave factories of Europe he must have soldiers to use it. General Vassily Sokolovsky, [Marshal Semen K.] Timoshenko's husky chief of western staff, described the Russian tactic to me as one of "blitz grinding." The object is to chew the enemy slowly to pieces.[6]

The major battle was launched on October 2. The Germans planned a series of grand encirclements designed to destroy the Red Army on the central front, capture Moscow, and end the Russian war. The Moscow correspondent for the Associated Press, Henry C. Cassidy, describes the Battle of Moscow after the first unsuccessful German offensive:

THEIR PLAN WAS TO TAKE MOSCOW by encirclement, rather than by frontal assault. Snow was falling, the thermometer was dropping, the winter campaign, on which the Germans had not counted, was starting. There was need to hurry, for the Germans, but this time, there must be no mistake, for a mistake would mean disaster.

But Stalin, in his Kremlin, had another plan. The Red army command, either from direct information or from deduction, seemed to have known or to have figured out the second German offensive in advance. Stalin's plan to meet it provided for concentration in depth of reserves both before Moscow and outside the ring of encirclement, strong defense along fortified lines to drain enemy strength, and finally a powerful, perfectly timed counteroffensive to defeat the enemy.

Moscow, meanwhile, had been declared in a state of siege October 19, the capital had been emptied of industries, commissariats, and civilians not essential for its defense, and General [Georgi] Zhukov was announced to be in command of the western front—a post he had already been holding throughout the battle—while Marshal Timoshenko went to bolster the sagging southwestern front.

The people of Moscow were called upon to play a major part in the drama of life or death of their city. . . . Thousands of women, mobilized by their house committees and still wearing their city clothes, went by train, bus, and truck into the mud, slush, and cold west of Moscow, there to dig tremendous trenches and anti-tank ditches, running like scars across the countryside. The fortifications extended back into the city itself, where steel, sandbag, and earthwork barricades were raised. The Palace of Soviets, a naked skeleton of steel girders, which was to have risen as the world's highest building, started to come down as raw material for defense. The Moscow Métro, most modern subway system in the world, was given over to movements of troops and supplies. . . .

The Russians, being intensely human, did not undergo this strain without a tremor, any more than they had faced their first bombing without a qualm. When the mass evacuation began October 15, there were three days of stampede. People swarmed the railroad stations, seeking transportation, and when there was none, started on foot into the vast spaces of the east. Queues formed at food stores for the extra rations of bread, sausage, and cheese allotted to evacuées. There was a boom on the matrimonial market, as people married to go along with others whose offices or factories were being evacuated. . . .

The Germans started their second general offensive against Moscow November 16. The great armies collided, the plan and counter-plan started working. . . . [At first] the German plan [of encirclement] seemed to be succeeding. But the Russian plan also was in full operation. It called, in the first phase, for a stubborn defense. What this meant was exemplified on November 16, the first day of the German offensive, in the Volokolamsk sector, by one of the grandest acts of heroism of the war.

Major-General I. V. Panfilov, a dapper little fellow who had been military commissar of the middle-Asiatic Khirgiz Republic, defended the Volokolamsk–Moscow highway with the 316th Red army infantry division. . . . General Panfilov died in the field. Twenty-eight of his troops, isolated at one point, died in their trenches. But they exacted, as the price of their lives, eighteen enemy tanks. And they checked the Germans.

Those twenty-eight became Soviet immortals. . . .

The four Moscow Communist divisions went into action in the first lines. They had had little training, there were not enough automatic guns to go around, but they sacrificed their bodies to the defense. Their losses were horrible, but their resistance was strong. In sheer desperation, they delayed the Germans, while in the rear and on the flanks, other forces were gathering. . . .

Those were bright days for the Germans. They had estimated the maximum strength of the Red army at three hundred and thirty divisions. . . . Now, before them appeared a few ragged new divisions of hastily mobilized workers, fighting with the spirit of demons but without the arms, training, or experience of regular troops. The Germans thought the end was in sight. Berlin editors were advised, December 2, to leave space on their front pages to announce the fall of Moscow.

During the first week of December, the Germans reached their farthest points of advance . . . the outskirts of the little Moscow-Volga canal port Khimki, five miles north of Moscow, connected with the capital by a commuters' bus line.

In the meantime, regularly, as often as every quarter of an hour, trains were passing along railway lines to the front, carrying fresh young troops, dressed in warm winter uniforms and armed to the teeth. . . .

The Russians' hour to strike, with their full force, had come.

The Red army launched its counteroffensive on December 7. . . .

In the battle of Moscow, from November 16 to December 10, the Soviet high command estimated the Red army killed more than 85,000 Germans.[7]

On December 7, with snow blanketing the land (what Stalin called "General Winter," his greatest commander), Zhukov went over to the offensive. After wiping out Nazi salients to the north and south, he pushed the whole front back for varying distances from fifty to 200 miles, saving Moscow and proving that the Wehrmacht was not invincible.

During the Battle for Moscow the Germans had suffered defeats in the far north and at Rostov in the far south. They were unable to take Leningrad. And they had lost over one million men. "Never again," one observer wrote, "would this German army be strong enough to attack in more than one large sector at a time. The following summer it was not all Russia they were attacking, but only southern Russia."[8]

GUERRILLAS AND SCORCHED EARTH

The Germans had advanced hundreds of miles, smashed one army after another. But their "scorched-earth" policy brought them only barren space, and in the area they conquered, guerrilla armies sprang up like weeds in wheat fields. As one reporter wrote:

THIS WAS A FORM OF WARFARE with which the Nazis had never reckoned when they built their beautiful dream castles in the Ukraine and Moscow. Moreover, it was one which they could not understand and which they passionately resented. The Nazi newspapers and radio railed ceaselessly at the "bestial" Russians who continued this "senseless" resistance and had not the human intelligence to know when they were beaten. Only "sub-humans" could fight like this and keep on killing Germans, they wailed.[9]

The Germans had met resistance movements in Poland, Norway, and France, and they were to find a formidable one in Tito's Yugoslavia. But this was their first experience with large-scale, relentless guerrilla resistance, and they were unprepared for it.

Here is an account from "Batya," commander of the Smolensk guerrillas:

WHEN THE GERMANS INVADED the Smolensk region we headed for the forests and marshlands, took up arms and struck out at the scoundrels wherever we could. Every day saw new detachments coming into being. Today we number thousands.

We are steadily extending the so-called "small front" which stretches behind the battle line of the main Red armies. We have fought 300 engagements and liberated more than 300 villages. Six thousand Germans have met death at our hands. We burned or destroyed 17 tanks which were sent against us, and derailed five trains carrying reserves, tanks and other military equipment for the front.

We show no mercy to traitors who sell out to the foe. Wherever we set foot, Soviet power is restored and the people once again take up their peaceful labors. Today we possess not only submachine guns, trench mortars, and machine guns, but also artillery and tanks, all of which we have captured from the Germans. . . .

We fight in the localities where we were born and bred. This enables us to attack the foe suddenly. Moving through forests and marshland, we converge imperceptibly on German units and swoop down on them. Every day our men mine the ways by which the enemy passes.[10]

No less upsetting to Nazi grand strategy was the transfer of factories and machinery to the region east of the Urals. With its industrial area overrun and without adequate supplies from Britain or the United States, Russian armament production should have been paralyzed. That is what the Germans counted on. Instead, production increased.

LENINGRAD

While the vast armies of Bock and Timoshenko were locked in combat before Moscow, Leeb's armies were sweeping north of Leningrad and within two months these armies, together with a Finnish force under Marshal Carl Mannerheim, the Finnish commander-in-chief, all but completed the encirclement of the city. The siege of Leningrad was on, one of the most heroic in all history. For the people of Leningrad it was hold on or die, for Hitler had ordered his commanders not

RUSSIAN SOLDIERS DEFENDING THE APPROACHES TO LENINGRAD (M25).

to accept the surrender of the city. It was to be destroyed, and with it, its three million people.

William Mandel, an American reporter in Russia, gives a picture of the siege:

SIX THOUSAND CANNON, 4,500 trench mortars, 19,000 machine guns, 1,000 planes and 1,000 tanks, armoring forty divisions of troops, or approximately 600,000 men were hurled against Leningrad by the Germans in August, 1941. Salvos from the Germans' huge railway guns reached every corner of the city. With all that huge power they expected to smash into the city in a short time. . . .

The Red Army dug in against the assault. As many as 160,000 workmen dropped their tools and took up rifles, women and children replacing them at the factories.

Twelve railroads, a modern canal system, a huge deepwater port, and three excellent highways had been built to supply the three million people of Leningrad and its industries. By the middle of September, the Germans had cut all of these except the water route across Lake Ladoga. Supplies of food, fuel and raw materials rapidly dwindled. When the lake froze and the Germans took Tikhvin on the railroad running to its shore, it seemed that all was lost.

Tikhvin, however, was recaptured, and a truck highway was laid across the ice of Lake Ladoga. The single road kept the city alive during the winter. Even here, munitions and industrial raw materials got priority. Rations were cut again and again, until, for a short period, they reached a low, for the non-working population, of four ounces (five thin slices) of bread and a little watery soup per day. . . .

Though freezing and weak from hunger, the population worked eleven hours a day, took military training in its spare (!) time and walked to and from work through the uncleared snow-drifts and the rubble left by the bombs. Had there been food other than bread and fish, there would have been no way to cook it, for there was no kitchen fuel. Neither could the water supply be maintained in the face of continual German bombardment and lack of power for their pumps. Water had to be brought from wells, the river and the numerous canals. . . .

Not only industry but science, arts and education continued to function. Leningrad's colleges graduated 2,500 students during the siege. Its entertainers put on 20,000 performances for the men at the front lines outside the city. Its publishing houses issued, among other books, a 100,000 copy edition of Tolstoy's *War and Peace*, which people somehow found the time to read. And its artists put together mosaics for the new subway line just opened in Moscow.[11]

When the Germans cut the railroads to Moscow and the east, and the Finns and their German supporters the railroad to Murmansk, it seemed that Leningrad was doomed. People began to eat their domestic animals, along with hair tonic and Vaseline. Artillery pounded the stricken city day and night, while the Luftwaffe bombed it with a thoroughness reminiscent of the Blitz on London. But Russian planes and anti-aircraft guns brought down more planes than the enemy could afford to lose, and Russian artillery proved superior to German. All through the winter, and the next year, fighting raged around the outskirts of the city and guerrilla bands plagued the invader.

It was estimated that almost a million Russians lost their lives during the siege, mostly by starvation. But life and work went on. The Russian writer and Moscow correspondent for the London *Sunday Times*, Alexander Werth, interviewed the people of besieged Leningrad:

An Architect

THE FAMINE HAD PECULIAR PHYSICAL effects on people. Women were so run-down that they stopped menstruating. . . . So many people died that we had to bury most of them without coffins. People had their feelings blunted, and never seemed to weep at the burials. It was all done in complete silence without any display of emotion. When things began to improve the first signs were when women began to put rouge and lipstick on their pale skinny faces. Yes, we lived through hell right enough; but you should have been here the day the blockade was broken—people in the streets wept for joy and strangers fell round each other's necks. And now, as you see, life is almost normal. There is this shelling, of course, and people get killed, but life has become valuable again. . . ."

Peter S. Popkov, President of the Leningrad Soviet

IT WAS OUR PEOPLE and not the soldiers who built the fortifications of Leningrad. . . . During the three black months of 1941, 400,000 people were working in three shifts, morning, noon, and night, digging and digging. I remember going down to Luga during the worst days, when the Germans were rapidly advancing on Luga. I remember there a young girl who was carrying away earth inside her apron. It made no sense. I asked her what she was doing that for. She burst into tears, and said she was trying to do at least that—it wasn't much, but her hands simply couldn't hold a shovel any longer. And, as I looked at her hands, I saw that they were a mass of black and bloody bruises. Somebody else had shoveled the earth onto her apron while she knelt down, holding the corners of the apron with the fingers of her bruised, bloodstained hands. For three months our civilians worked on these fortifications. They were allowed one day off in six weeks. They never took their days off. There was an eight-hour working day, but nobody took any notice of it. They were determined to stop the Germans. And they went on working under shellfire, under machine-gun fire and the bombs of Stukas.[12]

STALINGRAD

The most successful of the German offenses, in terms of distance traveled, territory taken, prisoners captured, and production destroyed, was Rundstedt's drive to the south—a drive in which the Germans had the aid of powerful Hungarian and Romanian divisions. After the destruction of the Russian army east of Kiev, the whole Ukraine fell into German hands. The Russians fell back to the south on the Crimea, to the east on the Donets River. Kharkov, a city of almost a million, was defended heroically, but fell late in October. Meantime Romanian troops had laid siege to the vital Black Sea port of Odessa, which finally fell after two months of desperate fighting— but not until the Russians had evacuated everything that was movable and destroyed the rest.

With Odessa in their hands, and the main Russian forces retreating, the Germans under Field Marshal Fritz Erich von Manstein turned south to take the strategically important Crimea with its mighty naval base of Sevastopol. By December they had broken through to Sevastopol and laid siege to it. The first assault on the city cost an estimated 35,000 German and Romanian casualties. The final attack, which raged all through June before it finally succeeded, took a far larger toll. Sevastopol was in German hands by July 1. Ten days earlier, Rommel had taken Tobruk, the double victories giving the German people an enormous injection of confidence.

With Sevastopol and the whole of the Crimea secured, the Germans prepared for a giant movement that was intended to outflank Moscow from the south, cut communications with the Urals, secure the Volga River and its valley, and capture the rich oil fields of the Caucasus, bringing the Soviet war machine to a halt. No campaign on a more prodigious scale, involving larger armies, and bringing richer rewards, had been seen.

At first all went according to plan. German armies swept north past Kharkov toward Voronezh on the Don. Other armies crossed the Donbas region toward Stalingrad on the Volga. And to the south still other armies moved down from Rostov and into the Caucasus. By August the path to the Caspian oil fields seemed open. Then Russian resistance stiffened, and the Germans were pushed slowly back.

The crucial battle, however, was at Stalingrad—one of the decisive battles of history. As Hitler's 16th Panzer Division approached the Volga River in September 1942, the sprawling industrial city of Stalingrad was already burning from the first Luftwaffe raids, relentless air attacks that would eventually kill thousands of civilians. But Stalingrad held, in what was perhaps the most savage struggle of the war and the battle, more than any other, that convinced the Allies that Hitler could be beaten.

The ferocity of the fighting is suggested by Major Velichko's on-the-spot account of the 62nd Army, led by General Vasily Chuikov, who had been summoned by Commissar General Nikita Khrushchev to defend the city:

A LIGHT YU. 2 PLANE soared slowly over the wide Don steppe. Down below foreign hordes crept eastwards along all the roads over the plain. Like metal worms the Germans crawled over the Russian soil, making their way to Stalingrad and the Volga.

The Yu. 2's passenger was making notes on a map. He was Lieutenant-General Chuikov, commander of the Soviet 62nd Army. He knew that it was not particularly safe to go cruising over the battlefield on his old coffeegrinder, as the Germans call the Yu. 2. He could easily have taken a faster plane. But during this leisurely amble across the sky he could see everything in perfect detail.

The enemy was forging ahead, pressing towards the city. Stalingrad was already ablaze. The headquarters of the 62nd army was installed on a height which gave a view over the whole city and the expanse of the Volga.

Chuikov returned. He tramped Stalingrad's streets, looked over the houses and basements, broke open the stone to make a fortress, dug a grave for the enemy in the hard soil. Every window must shoot at the enemy, every paving stone must crush him, every city square must strangle him.

The 62nd Army set about making Stalingrad into a shield that would bar the way to the Germans.

The Germans, incomparably superior in numbers, bit bloodily into the defenses. At one time it seemed that the 62nd Army must crumble, that human flesh and blood could never withstand this trial. The Military Council discussed the situation. Chuikov, worn out yet unwearying, pointed to a line on the map and said: "The Guards must take up positions here."

At dawn the Germans struck. [They] . . . had forced [their] way ahead some distance when the Guards launched a thunderbolt of a flank attack. The enemy had not even considered the possibility of such a blow. [They were] . . . mutilated, [their] thrust diverted from its course. Only a narrow German tongue reached the Volga crossing. . . . And that was as far as the Germans ever managed to get.

The scale of the Stalingrad battle grew day by day. Thirteen thousand machine guns were at work on both sides sixteen hours a day. The Luftwaffe made 2,000 flights a day over the city. But the 62nd Army fought back.

It created a university of street fighting. Its Red Army men students sat in trenches. Blockhouses were their lecture halls. Hatred of the enemy was their textbook.

The Red Army and the enemy tested each other's mettle. It was in those days that Vasily Zaitsev, one of Stalingrad's most famous snipers, coined the phrase: "There is no land for us on the other bank."

It was a war of grenades. They were stored everywhere: at headquarters, in passageways, in messes and kitchens, near sentry posts, in special dumps. Every niche in every trench was packed with grenades.

The turrets and treads of German tanks could be seen buried under piles of brick and rubble. And under this layer was another and another of buried Germans and their armor. The counterattacks of the 62nd Army grew more and more daring. The Germans went mad. On October 14 the battle grew to monstrous proportions and all scale for comparison was lost.

Command posts and dugouts caved in. The bombardment was so terrific that men staggered in passageways as though on a ship in heavy seas. In the air bombers howled maliciously. Tens of thousands of bombs came down on the 62nd Army. It seemed that the Volga and her banks had moved from their places.

The terrible vibration shattered empty glasses. All the wireless stations went out of commission. Then the oil-covered Volga caught fire.

The Army and the city grew into one. Every soldier became a stone of the city, and a city cannot retreat.

Chuikov decided on a subterranean offensive. The first underground attack was launched by two sections under Vladimir Dubovoy and Ivan Makarov. Their blow was directed against a big centre of resistance from which the Germans kept the Volga under fire. They went down a well 16 feet deep and from the base of the well began to make a tunnel 32 inches wide and a yard high. They probed for 45 yards. For 14 days oil wicks shimmered in the tunnel. The sappers forgot what daylight was, what it felt like to stand on one's feet. The air was foul. Their eyes grew sunken and their faces green.

At last they heard the German voices overhead. Three tons of explosives were placed in a chamber under the Germans. An explosion of terrific force shook the Volga bank.

Strong winds blew at night. They brought the ruins of many-storied buildings crashing to earth. A Red Army man from Kirghizia looked at the debris of a house and said: "The city is tired, the house is tired, the stones are tired. We are not tired." [13]

No battle in history was more ferociously waged. Hitler had issued orders that the entire male population of Stalingrad, a city of a million people, be killed and that all females be deported. And in desperately defending the city the Russians executed 13,500 of their own soldiers for crimes ranging from desertion to failure to kill a comrade retreating without orders. Early in the battle, before the full fury of the Russian winter set in, a German officer described the desperate nature of the fighting, street to street, and in cellars and sewers and blasted-out buildings. "Ask any soldier what hand-to-hand struggle means. . . . And imagine Stalingrad; eighty days and eighty nights of hand-to-hand struggle. . . . Stalingrad is no longer a town. By day it is an enormous cloud of burning, blinding smoke; it is a vast furnace lit by the reflection of the flames. And when night arrives, the dogs plunge into the Volga and swim desperately to gain the other bank. The nights of Stalingrad are a terror for them." [14]

German soldiers could not understand the grim tenacity of the Russian people. A corporal wrote home: "Father, it's impossible to describe what is happening here. Everyone in Stalingrad who still possesses a head and hands, women as well as men, carries on fighting." [15]

Later, the American journalist Edgar Snow asked General Chuikov what important tactical errors the Germans had made. Chuikov said that he had observed none.

"The only great error they made was strategic."

"Why was that?"

"They gave Hitler supreme command." [16]

By November the Red Army was ready to go over to the offensive. Albert Parry, an American reporter born in Russia, describes the great Russian advance:

WHEN THE RUSSIANS OUTSIDE STALINGRAD finally struck, it was mid-November, the beginning of the dreaded winter of the steppe. . . . The timing was perfect. Winter weather was grounding whatever Nazi planes had not been taken from this front to the new menacing lines then being established by the Americans and British in North Africa and at Italy's doorstep. And air power was practically the sole weapon in which the Nazis had superiority in the Russian steppes. . . .

In mid-November 1942 the German–Russian front stretched some 2,000 miles all the way from the Baltic Sea to the Black Sea. . . . And now the Nazi generals began to worry about the Stalingrad winter in earnest. . . .

But besides the winter there were two other factors the Nazis feared in Russia: night fighting and bayonet charges. . . . The Nazis defeated themselves psychologically when they babbled excitedly and self-pityingly about the hardships of winter and night battles in the steppes. It was only in the matter of bayonet charges that they truly lacked the stamina and training of the Russian foot soldier. . . .

As the Russians attacked in November, they proceeded to do precisely what the Nazi generals had nervously expected they would do. The Red Army began to drive from two directions at once in a gigantic pincer movement designed to cut off the German Sixth Army at Stalingrad from the Nazi bases in the Don Cossack land. The drive succeeded.

A partial encirclement of the Sixth Army was accomplished on November 19. Four days later the ring was closed. . . .

From the chief, Colonel General Friedrich von Paulus, down to the lowest subaltern, the Nazi officers told their soldiers not to worry: "We have to hold firm, soldiers," they said, "large forces of reserves are coming to our aid. They will cut through the Russian encirclement and relieve us." In December, a panzer division, sent by Field Marshal Fritz Erich von Manstein, indeed tried to break the ring southwest of Stalingrad . . . but was knocked out by the troops of General Rodion Malinovsky and retreated ignominiously.

The Nazi high command then put its hope in the air transport as a means of supply. Perhaps, reinforced by air with food and weapons, the Sixth Army and other trapped units would be able to counterattack and smash through to freedom on its own. But the hope went for naught. . . .

Food shortly became a thorny problem. The diet of horseflesh was not improved by a terrible-smelling soup, made of pressed cabbage. A Nazi machine gunner, surrendering to the Red Army outposts, revealed that, from one liter per man daily, the ration of the horrid soup was cut to one-quarter liter. Other captives related that dogs and cats were being eaten by the beleaguered Germans.

Munitions, too, gave out. . . .

On January 8 von Paulus was presented with the Soviet ultimatum to lay down his arms by the tenth. The Nazi general refused, blindly obeying his insane Fuehrer. . . .

On January 25 the southern group of the Nazis gave up. The next day the Russians cut their way through the remainder, cleaving it into two smaller pockets. Hitler still urged von Paulus to keep on fighting [but] . . . he had only a few thousand soldiers left, and most of them were lying in cellars nearby—hungry, in rags, suffering from frostbite.

On the last day of January [1943] von Paulus directed one of his generals to tell the Russians to come and take him and whoever else of the Nazis was yet alive and in the vicinity. A young Russian lieutenant—aged only twenty-one!— marched in with a group of his infantrymen and accepted the surrender. . . .

In twenty days alone, from January 10 to 30, an incomplete count established that the Red Army had annihilated more than 100,000 German officers and men in and near Stalingrad. . . .

Thus perished the infamous Sixth Army of the Nazis which in the summer of 1940 had rolled treacherously into Holland and Belgium, crushing those peaceful countries quickly and completely. Retribution had to wait more than two years, but it came.[17]

Toward the end of the pitiless slaughter, the German high command had begged Hitler, for whom Stalingrad had become an insane obsession because of its name, to allow the Sixth Army to attempt a breakout before the Russian encirclement was complete. He refused, ordering General von Paulus to fight to the last man. When Paulus finally gave up, in defiance of Hitler's orders, he surrendered 91,000 battered, freezing, emaciated, lice-ridden troops. This was all that remained of the great army of 300,000 he had led to the River Volga. And almost half of them died by the coming of spring.

The Soviets lost more than half a million people in the Stalingrad campaign, among them 40,000 citizens of the wasted city. But the surrender of Stalingrad was an irreparable blow to the Nazi cause. For three days after the catastrophe on the Eastern Front, German official radio suspended normal broadcasting and played Anton Bruckner's solemn Seventh Symphony. Hitler wanted Paulus to commit suicide; instead he went over to the enemy, broadcasting radio messages to the German armies to surrender. When a reporter in Russia suggested to a German general captured at Stalingrad that "the Red Army was a better army and a better led army" than the Wehrmacht, he "snorted and went almost purple with rage."[18]

Else Wendel, German housewife:

WE ALL HAD FRIENDS on the Russian Front and we tried not to talk too much about them to each other. But one day an old friend of mine—Edith Wieland—wrote, begging me to visit her, as she had just lost her husband in the battle. I found, as she opened the door, a thin, old woman in black, not the proud confident Edith I had known. She began to cry as she asked me inside.

In the lounge she showed me her husband's last letter from Stalingrad. He asked her to forgive him for anything he might have ever done to hurt her. . . . It was for her alone that he was now living and he loved her more than his life. This was no empty phrase he wrote, because they were now facing death, and it would only be a matter of days or weeks. But as long as he felt his death served a purpose he would be willing to give his life for the Fatherland. . . .

I was utterly shaken. I could see him standing before me in his officer's uniform. . . . He had been a strong and virile man, honest as the day.

"Was he wounded when he wrote this letter?" I asked Edith.

"No," she said quickly. . . . "They have written that death came instantaneously. He got a bullet through the head as he came round the corner of a house."

While I was searching desperately for the right words, Edith spoke again. "There is one thing that haunts me. I have heard a rumor that they could have escaped, but that Hitler forbade it!"

I was frightened. I had not heard that rumor myself at the time. "No! Impossible!" I said. "It would be plain murder. Hitler would never do such a thing. You know that, surely?"

Very slowly Edith lifted her head. "I am not so sure," she said in a low voice. "I keep re-reading that sentence in Albert's letter ('as long as I feel my death serves a purpose'), that doesn't sound a bit like Albert. It sounds as though his confidence was waning, and he was beginning to doubt."[19]

The Rising Sun

PEARL HARBOR

As the Germans were preparing to attack Moscow in November 1941, and the British were battling Rommel in the North African desert, relations between Japan and the United States were reaching a crisis point.

On November 17 the Japanese ambassador, Admiral Kichisaburo Nomura, brought his colleague Saburo Kurusu to the office of Secretary of State Cordell Hull. Kurusu had just arrived. Alarmed by the unfavorable American reaction to its expansion into Thailand and the Southern part of French Indochina, the Japanese government had rushed this special peace envoy over to Washington to restore harmony to Japanese-American relations. But the Japanese demands were extreme—Japan refused to give up its now economic colonies. And the American attitude was inflexible—Roosevelt froze Japanese assets in the United States and imposed a total embargo on oil and gasoline exports to Japan. Late in November Hull presented America's demand that Japan withdraw immediately all military forces from China and Indochina. The Japanese government, now headed by General Hidecki Tojo, a hard-line proponent of

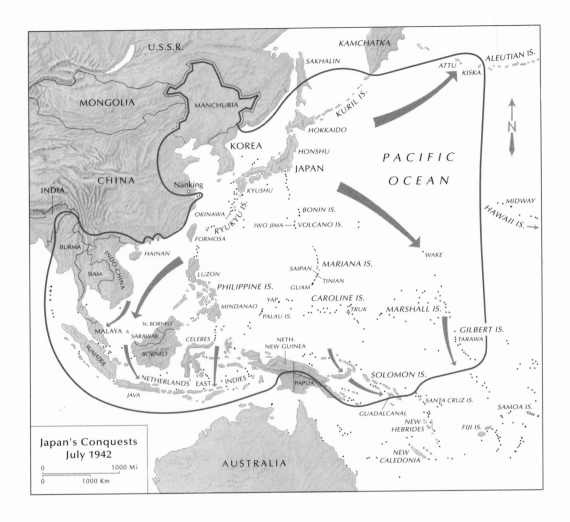

Japan's Conquests
July 1942

0   1000 Mi

0   1000 Km

Imperial expansion, saw this "ultimatum" as tantamount to a declaration of war, a war Tojo wanted.

At 2:20 the next day, Sunday afternoon, December 7, the two emissaries appeared once more at Hull's office with their final reply, just after Roosevelt had telephoned Hull with the news that the Japanese were at that very moment bombing Pearl Harbor. The secretary was told to receive the diplomats' reply and quickly dismiss them. After pretending to examine the document, Hull glared at the two men with cold disdain and said: "In all my fifty years of public service I have never seen a document that was more crowded with infamous falsehoods and distortions—infamous falsehoods and distortions on a scale so huge that I never imagined until today that any

Government on this planet was capable of uttering them." He then waved the two diplomats to the door.

Later that day, Nomura wrote in his diary: "The report of our surprise attack against Hawaii reached my ears when I returned home from the state department; *this might have reached Hull's ears during our conversation"* (Nomura's emphasis).[1]

The objective of the surprise strike on the home base of the American Pacific Fleet was to destroy the only naval force in the Pacific that could interfere with simultaneous Japanese attacks on the Philippines and Malaya, giving Japan, an over-

JAPANESE DIVE BOMBERS OVER PEARL HARBOR (NA).

populated island nation with insufficient natural resources, time to seize a vast area in Southeast Asia it needed to guarantee it economic self-sufficiency. The war in Europe had created an irresistible opportunity for Japan to take over these colonies of France, Britain, and the Netherlands, particularly of the Dutch East Indies and British Malaya, with their invaluable supplies of oil rubber, and tin. The attack was brilliantly planned by Admiral Isoroku Yamamoto, commander of the Combined Fleet, and carried out almost flawlessly by Air Admiral Chuichi Nagumo. It was a daring move. A major naval base had never been attacked in broad daylight by a carrier force, and a number of high American military officials considered Pearl Harbor, the greatest concentration of American military might in the world, impregnable. Success depended on the strictest secrecy.

On November 27, the Japanese put to sea a massive task force composed of the Imperial Navy's six newest and largest carriers and accompanied by battleships, light cruisers, destroyers, fleet submarines, supply ships, and tankers. At sunrise, December 7, 230 miles north of the Hawaiian island of Oahu, the air was alive with the roar of enemy planes. At 7:02 two Army privates manning an experimental radar system reported a large flight of incoming planes, but their superior officer irresponsibly assumed that these were B-17 bombers due in from California on their way to the Philippines. Just minutes earlier, the destroyer *Ward* attacked a tiny two-man Japanese submarine trying to slip into Pearl Harbor. These were the opening shots of World War II for the United States. The *Ward*'s skipper, Lieutenant William W. Outerbridge, reported the attack but senior commanders were skeptical. There had been false submarine sightings in that same area—even whales had been depth-charged—so they would wait for verification. While they waited, 183 Japanese attack planes homed in on the radio beam of station KGMB in Honolulu, which guided them straight to their target.

The attack was a complete surprise. American cryptanalysts had broken Japan's diplomatic code and had warned Roosevelt and his advisors of an imminent attack, but all indications were that the strike would occur in Southeast Asia, not at Pearl Harbor. The Japanese carrier force had moved from the remote Kurile Islands, north of Japan, across the empty North Pacific, under absolute radio silence, confounding American naval intercept units. As historian David Kahn, an authority on World War II intelligence, has written, "code-breaking intelligence did not prevent and could not have prevented Pearl Harbor, because Japan never sent any message to anybody saying anything like 'We shall attack Pearl Harbor.'" Japan's ambassadors in Washington had not even been told of the plan. "The real reason for the success of the Pearl Harbor attack lies in the island empire's hermetic security. Despite the American code-breakers, Japan kept her secret."[2]

Captain Mitsuo Fuchida led the attack from the flagship carrier *Akagi*. He was thirty-nine years old and a devoted admirer of Adolf Hitler, even to the point, with his trim black mustache, of trying to look like him. When he received orders to launch the strike at dawn, he thought to himself, "Who could be luckier than I?" Here is the story of the attack in his words:

AT 5:30 A.M., 7 DECEMBER, the cruisers *Chikuma* and *Tone* each catapulted a "Zero" floatplane for a pre-attack reconnaissance of Pearl Harbor. On carrier flight decks, readied fighter and attack planes were lined up. The flying crews, also primed for the operation, were gathered in the briefing room. The ships pitched and rolled in the rough sea, kicking up white surf from the predawn blackness of the water. At times waves came over the flight deck, and crews clung desperately to their planes to keep them from going into the sea. . . .

On the flight deck a green lamp was waved in a circle to signal "Take off!" The engine of the foremost fighter plane began to roar. With the ship still pitching and rolling, the plane started its run, slowly at first but with steadily increasing speed. Men lining the flight deck held their breath as the first plane took off successfully just before the ship took a downward pitch. The next plane was already moving forward. There were loud cheers as each plane rose into the air.

Thus did the first wave of 183 fighters, bombers, and torpedo planes take off from the six carriers. . . .

Under my direct command were forty-nine level bombers. About 500 meters to my right and slightly below me were forty torpedo planes. The same distance to my left, but about 200 meters above me, were fifty-one dive-bombers, and flying cover for the formation there were forty-three fighters ["Zeros"]. . . .

A speedometer indicated 125 knots and we were favored by a tail wind. . . . But flying over the clouds we could not see the surface of the water, and, consequently, had no check on our drift. I switched on the radio direction finder to tune in the Honolulu radio station and soon picked up some light music. By turning the antenna, I found the exact direction from which the broadcast was coming and corrected our course, which had been five degrees off. . . .

At 7:30 we had been in the air for about an hour and a half. It was time that we were seeing land, but there was only a solid layer of clouds below. All of a sudden, the clouds broke, and a long white line of coast appeared. We were over Kahuku Point, the northern tip of the island, and now it was time for our deployment. . . .

Meanwhile a reconnaissance report came in from the *Chikuma*'s plane giving the location of [the battleships and cruisers] . . . in the harbor. . . . Now I knew for sure that there were no carriers in the harbor. The sky cleared as we moved in on the target, and Pearl Harbor was plainly visible from the northwest valley of the island. I studied our objective through binoculars. They were there all right, all eight [battleships]. "Notify all planes to launch attacks," I ordered my radioman, who immediately began tapping the key. The order went in plain code: "To, to, to, to. . . ." The time was 7:49. . . .

Lieutenant Commander Takahashi and his dive-bombing group . . . lost no time in dashing forward. His command was divided into two groups: one led by himself which headed for Ford Island and Hickam Field, the other, led by Lieutenant Akira Sakamoto, headed for Wheeler Field.

The dive-bombers over Hickam Field saw heavy bombers lined up on the apron. Takahashi rolled his plane sharply and went into a dive, followed immediately by the rest of his planes, and the first bombs fell at Hickam. The next places hit were Ford Island and Wheeler Field. In a very short time, high billows of black smoke were rising from these bases. [Then the torpedo planes and bombers swooped down on the battleships.] . . .

Knowing the Admirals Nagumo and Yamamoto and the General Staff were anxious about the attack, I decided that they should be informed. I ordered that the following message be sent to the fleet: "We have succeeded in making a surprise attack. Request you relay this report to Tokyo. . . ."

The code for a successful surprise attack was *"Tora, tora, tora."* . . . There is a Japanese saying, "A tiger (tora) goes out 1,000 ri (2,000 miles) and returns without fail."

I saw clouds of black smoke rising from Hickam and soon thereafter from Ford Island. . . . It was not long before I saw waterspouts rising alongside the battleships, followed by more and more waterspouts. It was time to launch our level bombing attacks, so I ordered my pilot to bank sharply, which was the attack signal for the planes following us. . . .

As my group made its bomb run, enemy antiaircraft suddenly came to life. Dark gray bursts blossomed here and there until the sky was clouded with shattering near-misses which made our plane tremble. Shipboard guns seemed to open fire before the shore batteries. I was startled by the rapidity of the counterattack which came less than five minutes after the first bomb had fallen. . . .

Ignoring the barrage of shells bursting around us, I concentrated on the bomb loaded under the lead plane, pulled the safety bolt from the bomb-release lever and grasped the handle. It seemed as if time was standing still. . . .

While my group was circling over Honolulu for another bombing attempt, other groups made their runs, some making three tries before succeeding. Suddenly a colossal explosion occurred in Battleship Row. A huge column of dark red smoke rose to 1,000 feet and a stiff shock wave reached our plane. I called the pilot's attention to the spectacle, and he observed, "Yes, Commander, the powder magazine must have exploded. Terrible indeed!" The attack was in full swing, and smoke from fires and explosions filled most of the sky over Pearl Harbor.

My group now entered on a bombing course again. Studying Battleship Row through binoculars, I saw that the big explosion had been on the *Arizona*. She was still flaming fiercely and her smoke was covering the *Nevada*, the target of my group. Since the heavy smoke would hinder our bomber accuracy, I looked for some other ship to attack. The *Tennessee*, third in the left row, was already on fire; but next in the row was the *Maryland*, which had not yet been attacked. I gave an order changing our target to this ship, and once again we headed into the antiaircraft fire. Then came the "ready" signal and I took a firm grip on the bomb release handle, holding my breath and staring at the bomb of the lead plane.

Pilots, observers, and radiomen all shouted, "Release!" on seeing the bomb drop from the lead plane, and all the others let go their bombs. I immediately lay flat on the floor to watch the fall of bombs through a peephole. Four bombs in perfect pattern plummeted like devils of doom. The target was so far away that I wondered for a moment if they would reach it. The bombs grew smaller and smaller until I was holding my breath for fear of losing them. I forgot everything in the thrill of watching the fall toward the target. They became small as poppy seeds and finally disappeared just as tiny white flashes of smoke appeared on and near the ship.

From a great altitude, near-misses are much more obvious than direct hits because they create wave rings in the water which are plain to see. Observing only two such rings plus two tiny flashes, I shouted, "Two hits!" and rose from the floor of the plane. These minute flashes were the only evidence we had of hits at that time, but I felt sure that they had done considerable damage. I ordered the bombers which had completed their runs to return to the carriers, but my own plane remained over Pearl Harbor to observe our successes and conduct operations still in progress.

After our bomb run, I ordered my pilot to fly over each of the air bases, where our fighters were strafing, before returning over Pearl Harbor to observe the result of our attacks on the warships. Pearl Harbor and vicinity had been turned into complete chaos in a very short time.

The target ship *Utah*, on the western side of Ford Island, had already capsized. On the other side of the island, the *West Virginia* and *Oklahoma* had received concentrated torpedo attacks as a result of their exposed positions in the outer row. Their sides were almost blasted off, and they listed steeply in a flood of heavy oil. The *Arizona* was in miserable shape; her magazine apparently having blown up, she was listing badly and burning furiously.

Two other battleships, the *Maryland* and *Tennessee*, were on fire; especially the latter whose smoke emerged in a heavy black column which towered into the sky. The *Pennsylvania*, unscathed in the dry dock, seemed to be the only battleship that had not been attacked. . . .

As I observed the damage done by the first attack wave, the effectiveness of the torpedoes seemed remarkable, and I was struck with the shortsightedness of the United States in being so generally unprepared and in not using torpedo nets. . . .

It took the planes of the first attack wave about one hour to complete their mission. By the time they were headed back to our carriers, having lost three fighters, one dive-bomber, and five torpedo planes, the second wave of 171 planes commanded by Lieutenant Commander Shigekazu Shimazaki was over the target area. Arriving off Kahuku Point at 8:40 A.M., the attack run was ordered fourteen minutes later and they swept in, making every effort to avoid the billowing clouds of smoke as well as the now-intensified antiaircraft fire.

In this second wave there were thirty-six fighters to control the air over Pearl Harbor, fifty-four high-level bombers led by Shimazaki to attack Hickam Field and the naval air station at Kaneohe, while eighty-one dive-bombers led by Lieutenant Commander Takashige Egusa flew over the mountains to the east and dashed in to hit the warships.

By the time these last arrived, the sky was so covered with clouds and smoke that planes had difficulty in locating their targets. To further complicate the problems of this attack, the ship and ground antiaircraft fire was now very heavy. But Egusa was undaunted in leading his dive-bombers through the fierce barrage. The planes chose as their targets the ships which were putting up the stiffest repelling fire. This choice proved effective, since these ships had suffered least from the first attack. Thus, the second attack achieved a nice spread, hitting the least-damaged battleships as well as previously undamaged cruisers and destroyers. This attack also lasted about one hour, but due to the increased return fire, it suffered higher casualties, six fighters and fourteen dive-bombers being lost.

After the second wave was headed back to the carriers, I circled Pearl Harbor once more to observe and photograph the results. I counted four battleships definitely sunk and three severely damaged. Still another battleship appeared to be slightly damaged and extensive damage had also been inflicted upon other types of ships. The seaplane base at Ford Island was all in flames, as were the airfields, especially Wheeler Field.

A detailed survey of damage was impossible because of the dense pall of black smoke. Damage to the airfields was not determinable, but it was readily apparent that no planes on the fields were operational. In the three hours that my plane was in the area, we did not encounter a single enemy plane. It seemed that at least half the island's air strength must have been destroyed. . . .

My plane was just about the last one to get back to the *Akagi*, where refueled and rearmed planes were being lined up on the busy flight deck in preparation for yet another attack. I was called to the bridge as soon as the plane stopped, and could tell on arriving there that Admiral Nagumo's staff had been engaged in heated discussions about the advisability of launching the next attack. They were waiting for my account of the battle.

"Four battleships definitely sunk," I reported. "One sank instantly, another capsized, the other two settled to the bottom of the bay and may have capsized." This seemed to please Admiral Nagumo, who observed, "We may then conclude that anticipated results have been achieved."

Discussion next centered upon the extent of damage inflicted at airfields and airbases; and I expressed my views saying, "All things considered, we have achieved a great amount of destruction, but it would be unwise to assume that we have destroyed everything. There are still many targets remaining which should be hit. Therefore, I recommend that another attack be launched."

The factors which influenced Admiral Nagumo's decision—the target of much criticism by naval experts, and an interesting subject for naval historians—have long been unknown, since the man who made it died in the summer of 1944 when U.S. forces invaded the Marianas. I know of only one document in which Admiral Nagumo's reasons are set forth, and there they are given as follows:

1. The first attack had inflicted all the damage we had hoped for, and another attack could not be expected to greatly increase the extent of that damage.
2. Enemy return fire had been surprisingly prompt, even though we took them by surprise; another attack would meet stronger opposition and our losses would certainly be disproportionate to the additional destruction which might be inflicted.
3. Intercepted enemy messages indicated at least fifty large planes still operational; and we did not know the whereabouts of the enemy's carriers, cruisers, and submarines.
4. To remain within range of enemy land-based planes was distinctly to our disadvantage, especially since the effectiveness of our air reconnaissance was extremely limited.

I had done all I could to urge another attack, but the decision rested entirely with Admiral Nagumo, and he chose to retire without launching the next attack. Immediately flag signals were hoisted ordering the course change, and our ships headed northward at high speed.[5]

In 1941, the Japanese made up about 40 percent of the Hawaiian population, and almost all of them were strongly pro-American. On December 7, seventeen-year-old Daniel K. Inouye, a second-generation Japanese-American (and later a seven-term senator from Hawaii), was dressing for church when he heard over the radio that Oahu was being bombed by Japanese warplanes:

"PAPA!" I CALLED, THEN FROZE into immobility, my fingers clutching that [radio] button. I could feel blood hammering against my temple, and behind it the unspoken protest, like a prayer—*It's not true! It is a test, or a mistake! It can't be true!*—but somewhere in the core of my being I knew that all my world was crumbling as I stood motionless in that little bedroom and listened to the disembodied voice of doom.

Now my father was standing in the doorway listening, caught by that special horror instantly sensed by Americans of Japanese descent as the nightmare began to unfold. . . .

"Come outside!" my father said to me, and I plunged through the door after him. . . .

We stood in the warm sunshine on the south side of the house and stared out toward Pearl Harbor. Black puffs of anti-aircraft smoke littered the pale sky. . . . And then we saw the planes. They came zooming where we stood and climbing into the bluest part of the sky. . . .

I fell back against the building as they droned near, but my father stood rigid in the center of the sidewalk and stared up into that malignant sky, and out of the depths of his shock and torment came a tortured cry: "You fools!"

We went back into the house and the telephone was ringing. It was the secretary of the Red Cross aid station where I taught. "How soon can you be here, Dan?" he said tensely.

"I'm on my way," I told him. I felt a momentary surge of elation—he wanted me! I could do something!—and I grabbed a sweater and started for the door.

"Where are you going?" my mother cried. She was pointing vaguely out the window, toward the sky, and said, "They'll kill you."

"Let him go," my father said firmly. "He must go." . . .

It would be five days, a lifetime, before I came back. The kid who set out on his bicycle for the aid station at Lunalilo School that morning of December 7 was lost forever in the debris of the war's first day, lost among the dead and the dying, and when I finally did come home I was a seventeen-year-old man.

The planes were gone as I pumped furiously toward the aid station, more than a mile away. The acrid smell of smoke had drifted up from Pearl and people, wide-eyed with terror, fumbling for some explanation, something to do, had spilled into the streets. What would become of them, I agonized, these thousands, suddenly rendered so vulnerable and helpless by this monstrous betrayal at the hands of their ancestral land? In those first chaotic moments, I was absolutely incapable of understanding that I was one of them, that I, too, had been betrayed, and all of my family.

An old Japanese grabbed the handlebars of my bike as I tried to maneuver around a cluster of people in the street. "Who did it?" he yelled at me. "Was it the Germans? It must have been the Germans!"

I shook my head, unable to speak, and tore free of him. My eyes blurred with tears, tears of pity for that old man, because he could not accept the bitter truth, tears for all these frightened people in [our] teeming, poverty-ridden [neighborhood]. They had worked so hard. They had wanted so desperately to be accepted, to be good Americans. And now, in a few cataclysmic minutes, it was all undone, for in the marrow of my bones I knew that there was only deep trouble ahead. And then, pedaling along, it came to me at last that I would face that trouble, too, for my eyes were shaped just like those of that poor old man in the street, and my people were only a generation removed from the land that had . . . sent those bombers . . . sent them to rain destruction on America. . . . And choking with emotion, I looked up into the sky and called out, "You dirty Japs!"[4]

The USS *Solace* was the only hospital ship at anchor at Pearl Harbor that morning. On board was corpsman James F. Anderson of Fort Worth, Texas:

ON THAT PARTICULAR MORNING we were off the end of Ford Island with a clear view of Battleship Row. . . . I had cleaned up and was standing in line waiting for eight o'clock to roll around, when our liberty boats would come. We were standing at a large cargo hatch looking out across the bay and could clearly see the old battleship *Utah*, which was used as a target ship. I could see the men milling around on her deck as they waited to catch their liberty boats. About this time some planes came down through the mist of the early morning. I said to a friend beside me, "Well, it looks like we're going to have another one of those damn sham battles this morning."

A RESCUE BOAT SAVES A SURVIVOR FROM THE *WEST VIRGINIA* (NA).

But as these planes came in—there were five of them, I remember—they dropped torpedoes, and I said, "That's too much. They don't drop torpedoes." As the torpedoes were going through the water and before they hit the *Utah*, the planes flew up over the top of our ship. I could see the red balls on their wings. "My God, those are Japanese. Let's get this damn hatch shut."

At that moment the torpedoes hit the *Utah* and the ship appeared to jump—oh, ten, maybe twenty feet in the air. This giant ship. . . .

Our old chief pharmacist's mate came running out. He was pulling his suspenders up over his shoulders and was in his sock feet. The officer of the deck, a young ensign, was in absolute panic. He didn't know what to do. The chief sent him to the bridge and told him to make the ship ready for getting under way, then picked up the phone and told the engine room to fire up the boilers and make ready for getting under way.

All the men from my ward, following what we had learned from our drills in the past, began to put metal covers over the windows. While we were doing this, I kept turning around to see what was going on, and I saw more planes coming in, passing over Battleship Row dropping bombs. I remember very clearly what looked like a dive-bomber coming in over the *Arizona* and dropping a bomb. I saw that bomb go down through what looked like a stack, and almost instantly it cracked the bottom of the *Arizona*, blowing the whole bow loose. It rose out of the water and settled. I could see flames, fire, and smoke coming out of that ship, and I saw two men flying through the air and the fire, screaming as they went. Where they ended up I'll never know. . . .

Almost immediately we started getting casualties, and from that point on I was very busy in our surgical ward. I remember only one of the men we got was able to tell us his name. The others were all in such critical condition they couldn't talk at all. They were all very badly burned from the oil and flash burns. The one who gave us his name did not have a single stitch of clothing on. The only thing left was a web belt with his chief's buckle, his chief-master-at-arms' badge, and the letters USS *Nevada*. He survived but he had a very long cut down the top of his head and every time he breathed his scalp would open up and I could see his skull.

We were using tannic acid for the burns. Every sheet we had in the ward was immediately brown. Many of the men who came in had their ears burned completely off, their noses badly burned, and their fingers bent like candles from the intense heat they had been in. Their bodies were just like hot dogs that had fallen in the fire and burned. All we could do for those poor fellows was give them morphine and pour the tannic acid over them. . . .

I think we must have gone through forty-eight hours without any sleep—all spent tending to our patients. There was so much adrenaline pumped into the body a person couldn't sleep. But after forty-eight hours I got to the point where I was staggering around. One of the bunks became empty—a man died and we put him on a stretcher to take him down to our morgue. A nurse came along and said, "You get on that bunk and grab some sleep." I don't know how long I slept, but after a while somebody woke me up because another patient had to go in the bunk. I got up and went back to work again. Nobody ever thought of asking for relief.

In the days after the attack, boats from our hospital ship had the awful job of going out alongside the battleships and picking up the remains of the bodies that had floated to the surface. Our corpsmen tried very hard to salvage any part of a human body that could be identified. We brought these parts back and tried to identify fingerprints or teeth or anything of this kind. It was a gruesome job but we had to do it—the detail was assigned to us. The parts were brought to the morgue, where we would clean them of oil and try to identify them.[5]

On December 7 and 8, rescue crews worked frantically to reach sailors trapped in the battleship *Oklahoma*, which was hit by five aerial torpedoes and overturned.

One of the thirty-two seamen caught in the doomed ship, which rested upside down at the bottom of the shallow harbor, a part of its massive hull exposed above the water, was nineteen-year-old Stephen Bower Young, a native of Massachusetts. The ship had been his "home," and now he expected it would be his tomb.

ON THE MORNING OF DECEMBER 7, 1941, I was in the living compartment of the gun crew of the battleship *Oklahoma*'s no. 4 gun turret, one deck below the main deck. There were thirty or so of us there and I was preparing to go on liberty as soon as I finished my duties as mess cook. It was a beautiful Sunday, a perfect day for going to the beach and doing some surfing.

Our ship, along with most of the Pacific Fleet, had been at sea on maneuvers and had only yesterday returned to Pearl Harbor. There were eight battleships in port, and we thought this was strange, for tensions were running high with Japan. As a precautionary move, it had been the practice to keep some of the battlewagons at sea. Like all the other ships, we had our antiaircraft ammunition stored away under lock and key in preparation for a fleet admiral's inspection the following day, Monday the 8th. For the inspection, we also opened up all watertight compartments below the waterline. When in port, we usually closed these compartments, as a safeguard against flooding in the event of an attack or an accident. But for the admiral's inspection we even opened the spaces in the watertight protective blisters that ran along the length of the ship. The blisters were designed to absorb the explosions of torpedoes before they could penetrate the skin of the ship and do heavy damage. So our ship, like the other battleships in port, was in a state of complete nonreadiness that Sunday.

Around eight o'clock that morning an announcement came over the ship's speaker system. "Man the antiaircraft batteries! Man the antiaircraft batteries!" This stunned us. Why were we having drills on Sunday—and in port? What the hell was going on?

The sailors who manned the antiaircraft guns flew to their battle stations, but our stations were in the No. 4 gun turret and our three big 14-inch guns couldn't be used against aircraft. So we stalled momentarily and looked at each other. Then, almost immediately, there was another announcement. "All hands, man your battle stations! This is no shit, Goddamn it! Jap planes are bombing us!"

Ensign Herbert Rommel, our chief turret officer, had just seen a torpedo from one of the Japanese planes slam into a cruiser and had instinctively raced to the ship's general announcing system and given this warning. This was not Navy protocol, Navy language, but it sure got everybody's attention, and we raced toward our battle stations in the turret.

To understand what happened next you have to understand how the gun turret was set up. The enormous 1,400-pound projectiles were hoisted up into the gun chamber from the shell deck, where more than 150 of them were stored, standing on end, in cradles, and lashed against the bulkhead with light rope to prevent them from flipping over. After they were loaded into the breeches, powder bags from the powder-handling room, four decks below, were sent up on hoists into the hoist room, where I worked. We then sent the powder into the gun chamber, where it was loaded with the projectiles.

It was possible to enter the turret from topside, through a small hatch, and from there, scramble down through the turret to your station. But I preferred to enter from below, through a heavy steel door into the powder-handling room, and climb a ladder to my station.

That morning, as I raced down to the lower entrance of the turret with other men in my crew I felt the ship jump and then shake. We had been hit by a torpedo from a Japanese plane, but we all thought we had been bombed. "It's the Japs, the frigging Japs!" a sailor up top yelled down the hatch to us. "The shit's hit the fan!"

By the time I got to the next deck, we were hit by another torpedo and our lights went out. Complete darkness. But someone had a flashlight, and we knew our way so well that there was no problem going down a ladder to the level of the entrance to the gun turret. There was a ladder there and I scrambled up through the powder-handling room to the shell deck. The auxiliary lights came back on and we all thought we were safe there for the moment, four decks down and protected by the heavy armor of the gun turret. And nobody thought an airplane could sink a battleship!

But then the ship started to list badly as water poured into the gaping holes in her side, surging through the blisters and all the open hatches that were ordinarily closed in port. Then we started to hear terrible noises. The tremendous stress of the water began to twist and break up the ship. It sounded as if the old battleship was groaning in pain. We also heard crashing noises as bunks, mess tables, lockers, dishes, everything, began to be thrown around. And we could hear the screams of sailors caught in the path of the rushing water, or in the direct force of the torpedo blasts. We didn't know it, but the *Oklahoma*, our home, was mortally wounded.

As the water began to reach us, the sailors slammed down the watertight door to the powder-handling room. The entire turret was now watertight. It was less than three minutes since we had been called to our battle stations.

I was moving up through the turret with some other men to our battle station when we ran into Ensign Rommel. He was very excited. He told us to go below

to the powder-handling room. We couldn't fire our big guns anyway, and we
would be safer there. So I climbed back down and joined twenty or so other
sailors there.

The ship was then hit by another torpedo, number three. We were now listing 25 or 30 degrees and water started coming in the lower side of the compartment. At the same time, we were being drenched by oil that came pouring down
from the damaged machines in the shell deck above, and this made the floor dangerously slippery. We knew we had to get up to the next deck, the shell deck, as
soon as possible, for the ship was sinking. From the shell deck it was possible to
climb to the top of the ship and jump overboard.

As the ship listed hard, everything that was not tied down went rolling and
smashing along the slippery steel deck of the powder-handling room. Sailors
were slipping and sliding and falling down. As I clung to a bulkhead for support,
I looked at the faces of my shipmates. Men looked scared and unbelieving. Then
there was another tremendous hit, the fourth torpedo. The ship rocked and shud-

dered. Water poured from up above, down through the openings in the deck and spaces overhead—ventilator shafts, portholes, hatches—as the ship heeled well over on her port side. We tried to hold on to anything that would keep us above the water. Several sailors lost their grip and fell into the oily water and lay there, still. I could do nothing but hold on desperately.

Sailors started up the ladder, one at a time. I was right behind them but the ladder was so jammed it was impossible for me to move. I could hear noises from the crew manning the shell deck. As the ship listed, the cradles holding the big shells started to swing. When I saw all those shells rocking back and forth in their cradles on the shell deck, and heard the men yelling, I jumped off the ladder and onto a bulkhead, grabbed a piece of iron, and held on for dear life.

Then the 1,400-pound projectiles broke loose from their rope lashings. The last thing the men on the shell deck saw was dozens of huge steel shells rolling down the deck at them. They screamed as they were crushed into the deck. Then it got real quiet. We looked up but couldn't see. The hatch had been knocked shut. Our shipmates were crushed to death, we knew. Later I learned that three of my best friends were killed on the shell deck.

At that moment, several sailors realized that there was only one other way out—through the same hatch door by which we had entered the powder-handling room. "Get the goddamn door open!" someone yelled. "We've got to get out of here!"

But the ship was rolling over and the door was quickly getting out of reach as it rose above our heads with the listing of the ship. It was also tightly secured and we didn't have the proper tools to open it. But somehow the men forced it open and a couple of them managed to make it topside before the ship went completely over. The water poured down on them but they made it, struggling, choking, gasping for air, not able to see in the pitch dark. "God help me," one guy said as he went through the hatch.

On the other side of the handling room, a dozen or so of us were making our own fight for survival, for we couldn't get to the hatch in time. We thought maybe we could get up the ladder to the shell deck and force the hatch open. Just then, the emergency lights went out. The darkness was absolute. Several of us struggled to open the hatch, but the shells must have jammed it shut. We were trapped! We were going to die!

At that moment the ship took her fifth torpedo and rolled over and her great masts dug into the mud bottom of Pearl Harbor, forty feet down. Her lower starboard side and bottom remained a few feet above water, we learned later.

But at that moment I was so disoriented by the darkness and the wild confusion about me that I didn't even realize the ship had capsized. I had felt the ship lurch. The deck slipped out from under me and my hands snatched at empty air. I was tossed and spun around, pitched into a great nothingness, suspended in air as the ship turned about me. The water roared in and took me under. I surfaced, gulped for air, and began to tread water. I was amazed to find myself still alive. There were two or three dead bodies floating in the water. Just then, I heard my friend Bill "Popeye" Schauf cry out, "I can't swim. So long, boys." I swam over to him, grabbed what little hair he had, and held his head above the water as we thrashed around.

He said, "We are over." The ship had rolled to about 135 degrees. For all intents and purposes, it was upside down. Suddenly, everything got quiet, as many of us realized that our fight for survival had just begun.

When men started to talk there was a lot of anger directed at Ensign Rommel. After telling us to go below, he had climbed to the top of the turret and escaped, swimming from the listing ship to a rescue vessel. At the time, we didn't know what had happened to him but clearly he had abandoned ship, without telling his men to do the same. This would haunt him for the rest of his life.

Yet one man had yelled down to us, through the turret, to abandon ship before we capsized. It was turret captain Harald Oleson. He then risked his life to get everybody out of the upper turret, but he couldn't get to the men below. Thanks to a number of unsung heroes like him we lost only one third of our crew, 448 men.

Meanwhile, at the bottom of Pearl Harbor, fifteen or sixteen men remained trapped in the bowels of the *Oklahoma*. We had a large flashlight but we rarely turned it on for fear of using up the batteries. After our brief exchange about Rommel, there was little talk. We didn't want to use up our limited supply of air.

About this time, we realized that there was a narrow emergency escape hatch which led directly all the way to the main deck. One of the seamen, Clarence Mullaley, decided that he would try to make it down the escape hatch, four decks, all underwater, across some thirty feet of main deck, and then up to the surface, another thirty feet at least. He took a deep breath, filling his lungs with air, ducked underwater and pulled himself into the escape hatch. It was an act of desperate courage. After he left somebody said he would never make it out, but unbelievably he did and he was picked up by a motor launch and taken to the hospital ship *Solace,* although none of us knew that then. It was about eleven o'clock and we had been trapped almost three hours. It was Mullaley, by the way, who told his rescuers we were trapped in the ship and were still alive.

Down below, as water continued to ooze in and the air got thinner, I said to my buddy, "Wimpy" Hinsperger, "Wimpy, I'll bet you a dollar we'll suffocate before we drown."

"I'll take that bet," he said. "I think we'll drown first."

All avenues of escape seemed closed to us except the escape hatch and I wasn't ready to make that desperate, final effort. Not yet. Every now and then one of us rapped out the distress call SOS in Morse code with a wrench on the steel bulkhead. Maybe the Navy would rescue us. But for all we knew, the Japanese had taken over control of Pearl Harbor and they would never try to get us out. "We'll never get laid again," one sailor said.

Just about then, a body of a shipmate floated by, and someone pushed it away. Sooner or later we might join him, I thought. I took out a handful of change from my pocket and tossed the coins in the oily water. But I must have retained a shred of hope, because I kept my folding money—a ten and a one—in my wallet.

While we were sitting there, wondering what to do, a big awkward guy named Daniel Weissman spoke up, "Frig it. I'm going down the escape hatch and I can't swim!" I was sure he couldn't make it, but it was his life he was risking. We had no right to stop him. He ducked underwater and didn't come back. But he made it, we later found out, and several hours later a third man went down the hatch and, unknown to us, made it out. There were no more attempts to escape. It was too late. The air was getting bad and none of the eleven of us who remained had the strength to try to escape.

As the water continued to rise in the turret, we broke into the locked Lucky Bag, the ship's clothing storage room. It was dry there and we could stretch out on a bed of clothing and mattresses.

I was lying against the bulkhead in the Lucky Bag when I was startled to hear voices on the other side of the steel wall. I said, "Who's in there?" "We're radiomen," a voice came back. They said they were trapped and that there were also some guys trapped in a compartment right next to them. They knew of no rescue efforts. "It looks bad," they said. So we stopped talking. There was no whining or complaining. There was nothing that we could do. And we were worn down mentally and physically. Yet though we had nothing to eat or drink for almost a day, I was, amazingly, not hungry or thirsty.

Our watches had been broken and we had lost all track of time. Yet it didn't seem to matter. We were in a kind of limbo zone, a state of semiconsciousness between waking and sleeping. Then, all of a sudden, we heard a hammering sound, in short bursts, somewhere in the ship. I sat straight up and I could hear my heart pounding in my chest. Was somebody trying to get us? Then the rapping noises stopped. But a few minutes later they started again. My whole body tensed up. This went on for a couple of hours, first the noises, closer and closer, then silence. Someone said it was a pneumatic air hammer. They were trying to get to us to cut us out.

We frantically banged the SOS with the hammer, louder and louder, to let them know where we were. All of a sudden, we heard the rescuers break through to the men in the radio compartment. "There's some guys trapped in there, in the Lucky Bag," I heard one of the radiomen say. "We'll get 'em," a confident voice replied. We were going to live! As it turned out, the Lucky Bag was appropriately named.

The rescuers, led by a Portuguese civilian Navy yard worker named Julio De Castro, drilled a small hole through the bulkhead, only inches from where I was. Now at least we could see. But just then we heard a violent hissing sound. Trapped air had begun rushing out the tiny hole in the bulkhead and water started coming into the Lucky Bag in a torrent. It was jetting in through the watertight door we hadn't thought necessary to close. The sudden reduction in air pressure in the air pocket caused by the hole the rescuers had drilled was allowing the water to pour in and flood the area; there was no longer opposing pressure to hold back the waters of Pearl Harbor. And what little air we had left was escaping through that hole.

As the workers used a chipping hammer powered by an air compressor to cut a larger hole in the steel bulkhead, three or four of our guys struggled to get the heavy hatch door closed. They could barely see and the force of the water was unbelievable. "Hurry up! Get that fucking door closed," someone shouted. We all thought we were going to drown in that tiny compartment, just when we were a quarter of an inch of steel from being rescued. But Castro kept assuring us: "Keep calm, young men, we'll get you out."

We were at last able to get the door shut, although we couldn't seal it tight, so water kept gushing in the sides of the door and air kept escaping with an ominous hissing sound. The water was now up to our waists and we yelled for the rescuers to hurry up. Men on both sides of that quarter-inch steel bulkhead knew it would be close, a race against time.

Finally the big chipping hammer cut part of an opening in the bulkhead, and the rescuers slammed the steel back with tremendous blasts from a sledgehammer. The hole was barely big enough for us to squeeze through. And it appeared just in time, for the water was up to our shoulders. I was the first or second to climb out, and a big Hawaiian yard worker said to me, "Up on my back, boy." I said, "Thanks, but I'm okay." And he boosted me up to the next level. When I got to the bottom—what was now the top—of the ship, the air was fresh and the sun was shining.

As we crawled out of the overturned ship the sailors on the battleship *Maryland*, which had been tied up alongside the *Oklahoma*, cheered. We waved back at them and smiled. We stood on the *Oklahoma*'s bottom, oil-covered and almost naked.

Along with the radio guys, we were among the first to be pulled out of the ship. More than 400 men had gone down with the *Oklahoma*. But there would only be a few more survivors. All together, De Castro and his Navy yard team saved thirty-two *Oklahoma* sailors trapped below.

It was 0900, Monday, December 8. We'd been trapped for twenty-five hours. A motor launch from the hospital ship *Solace* came alongside the overturned *Oklahoma* and took us away. One of our guys looked around at the smoke and devastation in the harbor, and said, "Looks like we lost the war."

As our launch moved across the harbor, past the sunken *West Virginia* and the still smoking wreckage of the *Arizona*, we were too shocked to speak. It would take time to realize the enormity of that attack on Pearl Harbor. But we all knew that nothing would ever be the same for us. The world had changed. We knew that at the time, we really did.

By the way, when De Castro got back to his shop in the Navy yard, after twenty-seven hours of backbreaking, dangerous work, he was called to task for putting in too much overtime. It was late and he couldn't find a ride home, so he walked the five miles. Later, he received a Navy Commendation for his heroism. He didn't make a big deal of this. He claimed he was just doing his job. We were just survivors. He was a hero.[6]

The *Oklahoma* lost 448 men at Pearl Harbor, more men than any other ship except the *Arizona*. Together the crews of these two ships accounted for nearly one third of the dead at Pearl Harbor. These were the only battleships that were not repaired and returned to duty. The *Arizona* remains where it sank, with 1,103 men entombed in the wreckage, men who died before they knew who or why they were fighting. The explosion that finally sank the *Arizona* killed more human beings than any single explosion in recorded history, a record broken less than four years later by the atomic bombing of Hiroshima, which some considered revenge for Pearl Harbor.

Using heavy electric winches, Navy workers righted *Oklahoma* and divers removed the remains of over 400 men who had gone down with her. The old battlewagon, however, was too badly damaged to be repaired and sent back to sea. After the war, she was sold for scrap. While being towed to the West Coast she took on a list—the same heavy port list she'd taken on December 7, 1941—and sank. Better an honorable ocean grave, her former crew rejoiced, than to be cut up, as sailors say, to make razor blades.

Stephen Bower Young returned to service on the light cruiser *Honolulu*. He received a Navy Unit Commendation and five Battle Stars while serving in the Aleutian, Guadalcanal, and New Georgia campaigns. After the war, he graduated from Harvard.

During his thirty-five-year naval career, Captain Herbert F. Rommel commanded five ships. He received the Bronze Star for combat while commanding a destroyer during the Korean War. When he was still an ensign, he told Stephen Bower Young that he deeply regretted not having told the sailors he left behind in turret No. 4 to abandon ship.

Turret Captain First Class Harald R. A. Oleson, who had risked his life to go back inside turret No. 4 to warn his shipmates to abandon ship and then helped rescue four men in the boiling waters of Pearl Harbor, even though he couldn't swim, was killed later in the war. His ship came alongside the aircraft carrier *Princeton*, which had been turned into an inferno by Japanese planes during the Battle of Leyte Gulf. Oleson could have stayed in his gun mount, but he helped fight the fire and was killed by an explosion, which blew off both his legs. He was never awarded a medal or commendation for what he did then or on December 7, 1941, "a day," as Stephen Bower Young observes, "when many acts of bravery went unnoticed."

One of the heroes on that terrible Sunday was a twenty-two-year-old mess attendant from Waco, Texas, Doris Miller. When a piece of shrapnel struck the captain of the *West Virginia*, Mervyn S. Bennion, mortally wounding him, Miller, the ship's heavyweight boxing champion, carried him through flames and smoke to a safer place. After Bennion died, Miller manned an abandoned machine gun, which an ensign showed him how to operate, and began blazing away at enemy planes. He was the first African-American to receive the Navy Cross and was later featured in a recruiting poster after he was killed in action off Makin Island on November 24, 1943.

Eight battleships, three light cruisers, three destroyers, and four auxiliary craft were either sunk or damaged in the lightning attack that lasted less than two hours. *Arizona* and *Oklahoma* were wrecked beyond repair, and three battleships, *West Virginia, California,* and *Nevada,* were put out of action temporarily. The Army and Navy lost 165 aircraft, most of them on the ground. The Navy lost 2,008 men killed and 710 wounded, over twice as many as in the Spanish-American War and World War I combined. The Army and Marine Corps together lost 327 killed and 433 wounded. Sixty-eight civilians were killed. By comparison, Japan lost five midget submarines and only twenty-nine of the 354 planes launched from its carrier task force, although many others were badly shot up. It was one of warfare's most one-sided victories.

It was America's greatest military disaster, but not as the Japanese had hoped, an irretrievable one. The three carriers in the Pacific Fleet, *Enterprise, Saratoga,* and *Lexington*—the fleet's main striking force in the new age of aerial warfare that Pearl Harbor helped to inaugurate—were not in port that morning. And the Japanese did not attack the enormous fuel dump at Pearl Harbor, the submarine base, or the naval repair shops. Without fueling or repair facilities the entire fleet would have had to return to the West Coast. Except *Arizona* and *Oklahoma,* all of the war ships that were sunk or damaged were back in active service within a year. The waters of Pearl Harbor were so shallow that ships were salvaged that would have been lost forever had they been sunk in open seas.

It was the first attack by a foreign power on American territory since the War of 1812 and the nation reacted with utter incredulity, then with indignation and a deep desire for revenge. The attack on Pearl Harbor "shook the United States as nothing had since the firing on Fort Sumter," wrote Admiral Samuel Eliot Morison, the navy's chief historian.[7] Republicans and Democrats, interventionists and isolationists, labor and capital, closed ranks in a solid phalanx, and the nation moved from peace to war with a unity which it had never known before in time of crisis. Shortly after noon on December 8, President Roosevelt appeared before a joint session of the Congress to ask for a declaration of war against Japan. Congress responded with only a single dissenting vote.

The previous morning, back in Tokyo, Emperor Hirohito had been told that the surprise attack on Pearl Harbor was successful. "Throughout the day," one of his aides wrote in his diary, "the emperor wore his naval uniform and seemed to be in a splendid mood."[8]

On December 11, Germany declared war on the United States, a decision perhaps even more calamitous for its cause than its invasion of Russia. "Now it is impossible for us to lose the war!" Hitler excitedly told his skeptical generals. "We now have an ally who has never been vanquished in three thousand years."[9]

Mussolini declared war on the United States hours after Hitler's announcement. Now it was truly a world war.

The French correspondent Robert Guillain was under internment in Tokyo when the newspapers hit the streets announcing the attack on Pearl Harbor. He watched people's reactions as they read the papers they hurriedly bought from bell-ringing vendors:

THEY TOOK A FEW STEPS, then suddenly stopped to read more carefully; the heads lowered, then recoiled. When they looked up their faces were again inscrutable, transformed into masks of seeming indifference. Not a word to the vendor, nor to each other. This was a Monday, and the war had stricken these people as they were returning peacefully to work after a fine, sunny Sunday. Not one of them dared voice his feelings, open himself candidly to his neighbors or to his unknown countrymen pressing around the old man selling papers.

"Sensô! Sensô!"

I knew them well enough to understand their reaction. The astonishment and consternation they felt was visible under their impassive expression. They had instigated the war and yet they did not want it. Out of bravado, and to imitate their leaders, they had talked constantly about it, but they had not believed it would happen. What? A new war? For it was now added, superimposed, on the China war that had dragged on for three and a half years. And this time what an enemy: America! . . . The America which the Japanese for a quarter of a century had thought of as the champion of modern civilization, the ever-admired, ever-imitated model. . . .

Japan was at war with terrifying America. The Japanese people's feelings had always been divided; they were torn between the official slogan exhorting them to intransigence and a secret intuition that told them this was madness. Their strongest feeling on that morning of December 8 was one of consternation. Collectively, the nation had let itself be carried away by war hysteria, but individually, each Japanese, always so different when he is on his own, isolated from the group, feared the war. He could already see himself giving up all his little comforts, uprooted by mobilization from the narrow compass of his daily life, and he knew perfectly well that on that day he would appear brave in public. Alone, or at home, he would be green with worry, would have sudden crying jags.

"*Sensô!* War! A Japanese-American war!"

Tokyo was afraid. The Japanese were frightened by what they had dared to do.[10] The war news that came back to Japan after December 8 changed the public mood from anxiety to exuberance.

On the afternoon of December 7, Private James Jones was being transported with his unit from Schofield Barracks to Pearl City. As the line of trucks passed Pearl Harbor, with smoke columns rising "as far as the eye could see," he recalls thinking "that none of our lives would ever be the same, that a social, even a cultural watershed had been crossed which we could never go back over, and I wondered how many of us would survive to see the end results. I wondered if I would. I had just turned twenty, the month before."[11]

BATAAN

On the morning that Pearl Harbor was attacked the Japanese bombed Singapore and sent troops from Siam (now Thailand) toward Malaya in preparation for a full-scale assault on the fortress city. Admiral Sir Tom Phillips, commander of the British Far Eastern Fleet, put to sea with the cruiser *Repulse* and the battleship *Prince of Wales* to prevent an amphibious landing in northern Malaya. As the two ships steamed northward, Japanese warplanes sank them on December 10.

Even as the *Repulse* and the *Prince of Wales* went down, Japanese forces were approaching the Philippines. Senior commander General Douglas C. MacArthur anticipated an attack. Work on new airfields was going forward and troop and plane reinforcements were on the way from the United States, but all this was too late. After reading a report on the slaughter at Pearl Harbor, Lieutenant Edwin Ramsey went to the officers club for a drink with the Army chief of intelligence for the island. " 'Lieutenant, are you religious,' he asked me. 'No sir, not particularly,' I answered.

Then he said, 'I think you better give your soul to God because your ass belongs to the Japanese.' " [12]

Nine hours after the attack on Pearl Harbor an air armada descended on Clark and Iba fields and destroyed most of the American planes on the ground. "At 12:35 in the afternoon . . . we heard the airplanes," recalled Lester I. Tenney, a Jewish kid from Chicago whose tank battalion was in position around Clark Airfield, expecting the landing of Japanese paratroopers. "As we looked up into the sky, we saw . . . bombers flying very high over Clark Field. Just as I was about to say, 'They're not ours,' the ground beneath us shook. . . . The war we feared was upon us." [13]

MacArthur's "failure in this emergency is bewildering," writes biographer William Manchester. We will probably never know why he allowed his air force to be slaughtered on the ground because, as Manchester notes, "we know little about his actions and nothing of his thoughts that terrible morning." [14] MacArthur, who rarely admitted doing anything wrong, was never forthright about this humiliating disaster. Nor was there ever an official inquiry, although Pearl Harbor was the subject of eight investigations.

After Pearl Harbor, the Japanese had been expecting MacArthur's air force to set out immediately for their air base in Formosa. "We put on our gas masks," a Japanese officer recalled, "and prepared for an attack." [15] But orders for the mission were inexplicably stalled, and when the Japanese struck Clark Field the B-17 Flying Fortresses, along with the rest of the air fleet, were sitting wingtip to wingtip, with no fighter cover, while their pilots and crews were having lunch.

With the American Air Force all but destroyed and the Navy's small force of warships retreating southward, the Japanese landed in full force just north of Manila on December 22. MacArthur declared Manila an Open City in a futile attempt to save it and fled to the rock fortress of Corregidor, an island at the entrance of Manila Bay. From there, he directed a fighting retreat to the wilderness peninsula of Bataan.

The mountain jungles of Bataan are almost ideal for defensive fighting. But MacArthur's Filipino-American army of 80,000 men was poorly armed and desperately low on food. Before long, the troops were eating horses, mules, and monkeys; 20,000 were down with malaria; and thousands more were stricken with dysentery, scurvy, hookworm, and beriberi.

General Masaharu Homma had expected to make quick work of Bataan. But in weeks of miserable jungle fighting, American and Filipino troops held him off. After pushing back the initial Japanese offense, General Jonathan Wainwright, the skinny, hard-drinking leader of the jungle defense, reported to MacArthur that barely one quarter of his army was still fit to fight. Men were so sick and hungry they could barely crawl out of their foxholes. The cautious Homma, with a supply line extending back to Japan, settled in for a siege.

A gaunt and weary MacArthur, his wife and three-year-old son by his side, directed the Battle of Bataan from the 1,400-foot-long Malinta Tunnel, his underground command post on Corregidor. Those around him never questioned his bravery. To the alarm of his family and aides, he would stand out in the open without a helmet, coolly puffing on a Lucky Strike cigarette, as Japanese bombers pounded Corregidor. Yet the brave commander paid only one visit—for a day, in a Ford staff car—to his trapped and demoralized army on the Bataan peninsula, only three miles away by water. Perhaps he was ashamed to face his men, for the relief force that Roosevelt had promised to send never arrived.

Some troops called him "Dugout Doug," and composed poems that cruelly but accurately described their own desperate plight—abandoned by Washington because, by agreement with Churchill, the chief target in the war was to be Germany. Frank Hewlett, an American correspondent at the front, wrote what was to become the war's most famous piece of doggerel:

> *We're the battling bastards of Bataan;*
> *No mamma, no papa, no Uncle Sam;*
> *No aunts, no uncles, no nephews, no nieces;*
> *No rifles, no planes, or artillery pieces;*
> *And nobody gives a damn.*

After Roosevelt and Secretary of War Henry L. Stimson privately informed Churchill that they considered MacArthur's army doomed, Stimson wrote in his diary: "There are times when men have to die." [16]

But not MacArthur. He had become an American hero, commander of the only Allied army still holding out against Japan's Pacific blitzkrieg. A master of public relations, MacArthur's official dispatches gave all the credit to the general for the defense of the Philippines.

Roosevelt abhorred MacArthur—both the man and his conservative politics—but he was counting on him to lead the upcoming counteroffensive in the Pacific. Others, including MacArthur's former aide, General Dwight D. Eisenhower, thought he should have been stripped of his command for being caught unprepared by the enemy. Roosevelt obviously needed MacArthur more than he did the men blamed for the Pearl Harbor attack, Admiral Husband E. Kimmel, commander of the Pacific Fleet, and Lieutenant General Walter Short, the army commander at Hawaii, both of whom were relieved and subsequently retired from the service.

General George C. Marshall, the Army chief of staff, begged MacArthur to leave the Philippines. But MacArthur wired back that he and his family would share the fate of his men. Finally, on February 22 MacArthur received direct orders from Roosevelt to escape to Australia. He stalled until March 11 and then left with his family and staff in a PT boat captained by Lieutenant John D. Bulkeley. After a harrowing 600-mile run through the Japanese blockade, MacArthur and his party arrived on the Philippine island of Mindanao and were flown to Australia. On his arrival in Melbourne he made one of the most famous statements of the war, "The President of the United States ordered me to break through the Japanese lines and proceed from Corregidor to Australia for the purpose, as I understand it, of organizing the American offensive against Japan. A primary purpose of this is the relief of the Philippines. I came through and I shall return."

The American government asked him to change this to "We shall return." MacArthur refused. Was it megalomania? Perhaps. But the original author of the phrase, the Filipino journalist Carlos Romulo, informed a MacArthur aide that this pledge was intended for Filipinos, not Americans. "America has let us down and won't be trusted. But the people still have confidence in MacArthur. If *he* says *he* is coming back it will be believed." The aide told this to MacArthur and he naturally agreed.[17]

Back on Bataan, one of his staff, General William E. Brougher, spoke for many of those MacArthur had left behind. "A foul trick of deception has been played on a large group of Americans by a commander in chief and small staff who are now eating steak and eggs in Australia. God damn them!"[18]

Hunger and disease wore down the "Battling Bastards of Bataan" to the point where further resistance was suicidal. "Our stamina was gone," recalls Lester Tenney, "our food was gone, our health was deteriorating, and our ammunition and gas had just about run out. We were helpless. We troops felt let down, even betrayed. If we had been supplied with enough ammunition and guns, troops, and equipment, and food and medical supplies, we believed that we would have been able to repel the Japanese."[19]

On April 8, the Japanese launched a massive attack on the American lines. General Wainwright, who succeeded MacArthur at Corregidor, ordered a counterattack. It was the last flicker of the flame of defiance. The next day 78,000 American and Filipino troops under General Edward P. King, who had replaced Wainwright as commander on Bataan, surrendered. It was the largest surrender by the United States Army in its history.

A handful of the troops and nurses on Bataan managed to make their way to Corregidor to join the 13,000 defenders of that tunneled island rock. For almost a month the Japanese blasted it from air, sea, and land; and on May 6, they crossed the narrow channel and fought their way to the mouth of the tunnel. Concerned that the enemy would sweep through the tunnel guns blazing, killing his soldiers as well as the courageous American nurses who were caring for them, Wainwright ordered his men to lay down their arms. "In Western civilization, capture has always been viewed as being better than death," Lester Tenney wrote later of his capture on Bataan. "Our bad luck was that we were being captured by a people from a civilization that believed death was preferable to surrender." [20]

The ancient Japanese code of Bushido admonished warriors: "Do not survive the dishonor of capture." It did not, however, call for the mistreatment of enemy prisoners. The warlords who took over the Japanese government in the 1930s added that to it, even though the Japanese military had treated prisoners humanely in the Russo-Japanese War of 1904–05 and in World War I.

Soldiers of the new regime were indoctrinated with the idea that they were members of a super race that all other races would eventually have to serve, and that prisoners of war, especially whites, were a species of craven cowards, nonhumans who deserved to be treated like animals for the dishonorable act of surrender.

The prisoners at Bataan and Corregidor were not completely aware of this, but they had heard frightening reports of the atrocities committed by the Japanese in Nanking—of Chinese women raped and burned alive, and of tortured men left for dead with their penises sewed to their lips. "I was scared spitless," said Inez McDonald, one of the fifty-four Army nurses captured on Corregidor.[21] When his Japanese captors approached him, Lester Tenney's "knees began shaking, my hands felt cold and clammy, and sweat broke out on my neck and forehead. We were all scared beyond anything imaginable." [22]

After caring for their patients in the Malinta Tunnel for two months, the nurses were sent to Santo Tomás Internment Camp in Manila, where they suffered hardships and hunger but were not physically molested. The American and Filipino troops on Corregidor were loaded onto freighters, taken to Manila, where they were marched through the streets, and then packed into ovenlike boxcars and shipped to a desolate POW camp. There 2,000 Americans died in the first two months of captivity.

AMERICAN POWs CAPTURED ON BATAAN (NA).

The men captured on Bataan went through an unimaginable nightmare: the Bataan Death March.

When the defenders of Bataan surrendered, the Japanese expected to receive about 25,000 prisoners, who were to be marched nineteen miles to a dispatch station and then taken by truck and train sixty-five miles north to Camp O'Donnell, a former training facility for the Phillipine Army, in central Luzon. But General Homma found himself saddled with three times that number of prisoners and almost all of them were sick and starving. Some of the prisoners were taken by truck to Camp O'Donnell, but most were forced to walk much of the way under the blazing April sun (April is the hottest month in the Philippines) and over sand-covered roads lined with filthy drainage ditches. "The men were in such terrible condition from malnutrition and disease, and pure physical weaknesses from long days of incessant combat, that they didn't have a chance," said nurse Hattie Brantley, who had served with them in Bataan.[25]

Before they were ordered into line, the men were stripped of canteens, food, and personal items. Japanese guards cut off the fingers of officers to get their West Point rings, and prisoners found with Japanese money were shot, on the assumption that it had been taken from a fallen soldier of the empire. Five prisoners who were too sick to make the march were bayoneted in their beds.

General Homma had instructed his officers to treat the prisoners well. But the Japanese guards were in an ugly mood. They were exhausted, sick, and hungry, and they had lost comrades on Bataan. They also came from a culture of cruelty. Japanese military training was "filled . . . with beatings," recalls Sakata Tsuyoshi, a retired World War II soldier. Senior officers would regularly inflict physical punishment on the men under them, slapping them, punching them, kicking them, and beating them with the leather straps of their swords, often while other officers stood by laughing. "This method of inflicting brutal punishment without any cause and destroying our power to think was a way of transforming us into men who would carry out our superiors' orders as a reflex action."[24]

With such training, Japanese soldiers on Bataan did not need orders to inflict violence on prisoners they already regarded with cold disdain.

The American and Filipino prisoners marched four abreast, in long columns, and were given only enough food and water to survive the march. They felt like "walking corpses." Lester Tenney was one of them:

ONE DAY OUR TONGUES WERE THICK with the dust kicked up from the constantly passing trucks, and our throats were parched. We saw water flowing from an artesian well, and . . . a marching buddy, Frank, and I ran toward the well . . . and started to swallow water as fast as we could. . . .

Within a few minutes, another ten to fifteen prisoners ran to the well. . . . At just that time a Japanese guard came over to the well and started to laugh at us. The first five of us drank our fill, and when the sixth man began drinking, the guard suddenly pushed his bayonet down into the man's neck and back. The American prisoner fell to his knees, gasped for breath, and then fell over on his face. . . .

About two hours later, we passed a carabao wallow about fifty feet off the road. After one look at the water, I could see it was not fit to drink; green scum floated on top and two carabao were in the water cooling themselves off. The men were dying of thirst, however, and ready to do anything for a drop of water. . . . One of the men mentioned to a nearby guard and in sign language asked if he could get some of the water. The guard started to laugh and made a hand movement that indicated it was OK.

In a matter of minutes dozens of half-crazed men ran toward the carabao-occupied water. The men pushed the green scum away and started splashing the infested water all over themselves and drinking it. . . .

Only a few minutes went by before a Japanese officer ran to the wallow and began hollering at the Americans in the water. . . . He did not use any sign language to indicate there was trouble, but the fellows in the water ran back into line to continue the march. Then the unbelievable happened. The officer, with a big broad smile on his face, began prancing around the area where the Americans were lined up and ordered the guards to search our ranks for any men who had water-soaked clothes. The guards picked them out of our group of marching men and lined them up on the side of the road. Then the officer ordered the guards to shoot all of them. . . .

Many of the men on the march were just too weak and had too many illnesses to continue. If they stopped on the side of the road to defecate, they would be beaten within an inch of their lives or killed. . . .

On the fourth day of the march, I was lucky enough to be walking with two of my tank buddies, Walter Cigoi and Bob Bronge . . . when a Japanese officer came riding by on horseback. He was waving his samurai sword from side to side, apparently trying to cut off the head of anyone he could. I was on the outside of the column when he rode past, and although I ducked the main thrust of the sword, the end of the blade hit my left shoulder, missing my head and neck by inches. It left a large gash that had to have stitches if I were to continue on this march and continue living.

As the Japanese officer rode off, Bronge and Cigoi called for a medic to fall back to our position. The medic sewed up the cut with thread, which was all he had with him, and for the next two miles or so, my two friends carried me so that I would not have to fall out of line. We all knew that falling out of line meant certain death.

On the fourth day, as the prisoners entered the town of Balanga, Filipino civilians began throwing them food—rice cakes, small pieces of fried chicken, and chunks of sugarcane. When the guards spotted this they opened fire, killing randomly. The Japanese seemed to take malicious delight in killing Filipinos who had fought with or supported the "white devils." Lieutenant Kermit Lay saw a Japanese soldier beat to death a Filipino man with a baseball bat; and at one point in the march, Japanese guards rounded up 300 or 400 Filipino soldiers, tied them together with telephone wire, and bayoneted or beheaded them from behind. The slaughter went on for two hours.[25]

Tenney picks up the story:

WE CONTINUED MARCHING into the center of town, and when nighttime finally came we were herded into a large warehouse. . . . When the warehouse was filled to capacity, the guards pushed and shoved another couple hundred men inside. We were so tightly packed together that we sprawled on each other. When one of us had to urinate, he just did it in his pants, knowing that the following day the heat from the sun would dry them out. Those who had to defecate found their way back to one of the corners of the building and did it there. That night, the human waste covering the floor from those who had dysentery caused many others to contract this killing disease.

The stench, the sounds of dying men, and the whines and groans of those too sick to move to the back of the building had become so unbearable that I put small pieces of cloth into my ears in a feeble attempt to drown out some of the noise. Nothing could be done about the smell. . . . The Japanese guards, also unable to bear the horrible smell, closed the doors to the warehouse, put a padlock on them, and kept watch from outside.

About twenty-five men died in the warehouse that night. In the morning their bodies were tossed like garbage into a field behind the building.

Tenney:

ON THAT FIFTH DAY OF THE MARCH, I witnessed one of the most sadistic and inhumane incidents on the entire march. . . . We had just stopped for a brief rest while waiting for another group to catch up with us. When the other group finally arrived, the guard ordered us to stand up and start walking. One of the men had a very bad case of malaria and had barely made it to the rest area. He was burning up with fever and severely disoriented. When ordered to stand up, he could not do it. Without a minute's hesitation, the guard hit him over the head with the butt of his gun, knocked him down to the ground, and then called for two nearby prisoners to start digging a hole to bury the fallen prisoner. The two men started digging, and when the hole was about a foot deep, the guard ordered the two men to place the sick man in the hole and bury him alive. The two men shook their heads; they could not do that. . . .

Without warning . . . the guard shot the bigger of the two prisoners. He then pulled two more men from the line and ordered them to dig another hole to bury the murdered man. The Japanese guard got his point across. They dug the second hole, placed the two bodies in the holes, and threw dirt over them. The first man, still alive, started screaming as the dirt was thrown on him. . . .

Immediately after witnessing the execution-style burial, my mind turned to the positive side for survival. What, I wondered, can I do to overcome the total despair I felt when I was forced to witness these brutalities? . . . I had to keep a positive attitude. . . . I vowed to walk with determination, my head high, shoulders back, and chest out. This posture would make me feel righteous, and the guards did not harass or belittle the men who looked healthy and in control of themselves.

As the men trudged on like zombies, twelve hours a day for several more days, they began to spot headless corpses in the roadside ditches. One American started counting heads. At twenty-seven, one head per mile, he stopped counting because what he was doing was making him crazy.

Lester Tenney witnessed one of these beheadings:

AT ONE POINT ON . . . THE MARCH, we were ordered to double time, or run, and try to keep up with a fresh group of guards. As we passed a group of Japanese soldiers, our guards ordered us to stop. When we looked over to where the group of soldiers were, we saw an American soldier kneeling in front of a Japanese officer. The officer had his samurai sword out of the scabbard. . . . Up went the blade, then with a great artistry and a loud "Banzai," the officer brought the blade down. We heard a dull thud, and the American was decapitated. The Japanese officer then kicked his body . . . over into the field, and all of the Japanese soldiers laughed and walked away. As I witnessed this tragedy and as the sword came down, my body twitched, and I clasped my hands in front of me, as if in prayer. I could hardly breathe.

Later, Tenney said: "What made the beheading especially sickening was that the man's body shook and twitched well after he was dead."[26]

Tenney and his fellow prisoners struggled on for several more days until, barely able to stand, they were ordered to make a double-time march to the little city of San Fernando. There they were crammed into small railway boxcars used for hauling animals and taken on a five-hour ride to Capas, near their final destination, the barbed wire compound called Camp O'Donnell. In the steaming boxcars, some men couldn't breathe and died standing up. There was no room to fall down.

The exact numbers are lost to history, but about 750 Americans and as many as 5,000 Filipinos died on the march. Those that made it, said an American doctor who survived, did it "on the marrow of their bones."[27]

"If I had to do it all over again, I would commit suicide," said Kermit Lay, fifty years later.[28]

The dying did not stop at Camp O'Donnell. Over sixteen thousand prisoners, 1,600 of them Americans, would die in this loathsome compound in the next two months. As Tenney relates:

THE MEN WERE DYING at a rate of a hundred and two hundred a day. Malaria was a big killer and dysentery was horrible. It was so bad that men would go to sleep next to a slit trench so that if they had to defecate they would just roll over.

And when they died, we had to bury these men, which meant we had to go in a field and dig a hole in marshy soil. If you dug a hole too deep, water would come up and make the dead man float. So you had to take pieces of bamboo and hold the man down with them while you threw dirt on the body.

Let me tell you this. When a man said there's no use in going on any longer, he died. When he said there's no sense in waiting because the Americans are not coming, he died. The men who had positive attitudes, the men who said, "I know I'm going home," are the ones who came home.[29]

After the war, Lester Tenney began to have nightmares that have never gone away. They occurred with particular intensity when, as a college professor, he started writing his memoirs. He had thought he had put it behind him, but his deep hatred of the Japanese returned. In time, however, he came to consider hating "as a sickness." Today, he says he cannot blame an entire people for what happened to him during the war. The only hatred he still harbors "is for those who beat me." [30]

Kermit Lay feels differently. "I hate the Japanese. I won't talk to them, and I won't buy their products. It's just the way it is." [31]

WAKE ISLAND

Between Hawaii and the Philippines lay the three small but strategically important islands of Midway, Wake, and Guam. To control the Pacific west of Hawaii, Japan had to capture these island outposts.

At 8:45 on December 8 (the calendar is one day later west of the International Date Line), eighteen Japanese bombers smashed the military installations on Guam. The small garrison of Navy personnel and Marines had neither antiaircraft batteries nor coastal defense guns. Their few planes were quickly put out of action. The first landing came before dawn on the 10th, and within a few hours all resistance had been overcome.

The defense of Wake is one of the heroic chapters of American history. A naval station north of the Marshall Islands only 600 miles from Japanese bases, Wake was lightly defended by a dozen obsolete Navy fighter planes and a Marine battalion of about 450 men under Major James P. S. Devereux. But when the Japanese tried to land an invasion force on December 11, they were repulsed by devastating, close-range artillery fire and by the four Wildcat fighters that had not been knocked out of action in the initial bombing. Wake's defenders sank or severely damaged six Japanese ships, causing the humiliated Japanese commander to call off the landing.

Back in the United States, headlines blared MARINES HOLD WAKE, and the *Washington Post* compared the desperate defense of the island to the last stand at the Alamo.

The Japanese returned on December 23, this time with six heavy cruisers and two carriers from Nagumo's Pearl Harbor strike force. Carrier-based bombers knocked out the coastal gun emplacements that had chewed up the first invasion fleet, and land-based bombers from Kwajalein, in the Marshalls, pulverized the island. A naval relief force was assembled at Pearl Harbor and sent to sea, but it was recalled when word came in that the Japanese had already landed troops on Wake. One of the last radio messages from the island defenders was a grim piece of understatement: "Urgent! Enemy on island. The issue is in doubt."

Without Navy support, the Marines were helpless to stop a landing force of over 1,000 Japanese. After holding on for thirty hours in furious fighting, the garrison surrendered to avoid a senseless slaughter. Major Devereux walked out to meet the enemy with a white flag tied to a mop pole. Prisoners were taken to Shanghai. A hundred or so civilian construction workers were kept on Wake to rebuild it. All were later executed in reprisal for an American naval strike on the island.

Midway, too, was attacked the day Pearl Harbor was hit, but its shore installations were so effective that the small task force assigned to the job turned and ran. The big fight for Midway would occur later.

SINGAPORE

The attack on the American islands in the Pacific was part of a coordinated assault that targeted British and Dutch outposts in Southeast Asia.

Hong Kong was the first to fall. This great naval base formed, with Singapore and Manila, a triangle of Anglo-American power in the Pacific. As early as 1940, however, Japanese occupation of nearby Canton had made it all but indefensible. The Japanese attacked on December 8, 1941, and for two weeks the great city was subjected to continuous bombardment from land and air. The British garrison might have stood up to this, but the Japanese had cut off the water supply. Confronted with the responsibility for misery or death of hundreds of thousands of civilian inhabitants, the British commander, Sir Mark Young, surrendered on Christmas Day.

Next came Penang, then Singapore. Wearing sneakers and moving by foot and bicycle, with small bags of rice wrapped around their necks, 70,000 Japanese troops under General Tomoyuki Yamashita swept through 580 miles of rice fields, swamps, and rubber forests, crossed the Straits of Johore, and laid siege to the island city, which was packed with fleeing refugees. Running dangerously low on supplies and water, and with panic spreading through the city, British commander Sir Arthur Percival surrendered over 130,000 soldiers and internees to an army about half the size of his force.

Legend has it that Singapore's defenses "faced the wrong way," toward the sea. But that is wrong. The guns faced the mainland, but were armed with the wrong ammunition, shells unsuited for battle against ground troops.

The capture of Singapore opened the way to the resource-rich Dutch East Indies (now Indonesia) and was as important a victory for the Japanese Army as Pearl Harbor was for the Imperial Navy.

THE DUTCH EAST INDIES

Japanese ambitions embraced far more than merely the Philippines and the eastern Asiatic mainland. They looked westward to the conquest of China, Burma, and India, and south to the Dutch East Indies, a vast archipelago which stretched 4,000 miles from Malaya to the Solomons and included Sumatra, Java, Borneo, the Celebes, New Guinea, New Britain, and thousands of smaller islands. This island empire was a storehouse of oil, rubber, timber, rice, and metal production, and from here Japan could threaten Australia, only 300 miles to the south. Within Japan's grasp lay an empire stretching from the Arctic to the Antarctic, from Hawaii to India—an empire with a population of a billion potential slave workers, and an immeasurable supply of raw materials. Never before in history had so splendid a prospect unfolded before the eyes of conquerors.

With terrifying speed, the Japanese swept down into the Dutch East Indies in December 1941. The Allies could put up almost no resistance to this inexorable land and sea blitz, speedier and on a vaster scale than anything Hitler had imagined. The Battle of the Java Sea was the last desperate effort to save the sprawling archipelago. Admiral K. W. F. Doorman of the Dutch Navy was in command of an Allied force of five cruisers and about a dozen destroyers when, on February 27, it ran into two enemy flotillas, far superior both in numbers and firepower to his fleet. In this, the biggest surface naval battle since the Battle of Jutland in 1916, the Japanese annihilated their opponent and solidified their supremacy in the South Pacific.

Now there was nothing to stop the Japanese conquest of Java. From Sumatra and Borneo, 100,000 troops invaded the all but defenseless island. On March 9, the Dutch East Indies surrendered. These easy conquests confirmed Japan's view of the capitalist West as decadent and hopelessly weakened by materialism.

Australia looked like the next target, and it was vulnerable, for its best combat forces were fighting with the British in North Africa. Unknown to the Allies, however, the Japanese had no intention of invading Australia. Their aim was to establish bases off Australia's northern coast in order to cut the American supply line to the island continent. The Japanese correctly saw Australia for what it became, the jumping-off point for an American counteroffensive in the South Pacific.

As early as February 19 the Japanese had bombed Port Darwin, Australia's only major military and naval base in the north. All through that winter and into the spring, the isolation of Australia went on, as the Japanese landed in northern New Guinea and seized the Australian naval and air base at Rabaul, a magnificent harbor on the island of New Britain. Rabaul would be a bulwark against the expected American counterattack and a base from which to launch invasions to capture other strategic positions in the South Pacific, chief among them the Solomon Islands, southern New Guinea, and—the Allies suspected—Australia.

On March 17, 1942, Douglas MacArthur arrived to take charge of the pathetically weak Allied force in Australia. The general decided to defend Australia by going on the offensive. He would begin at the little town of Port Moresby, which faced Australia on the south coast of New Guinea. His forces were a corporal's guard compared to the Japanese arrayed against him. But by late July his engineers had built airfields and bomber strips. Then they moved 150 miles down the coast to Milne Bay at the extreme southwestern tip of New Guinea, and in this "green hell" they built a base, a launching point for a drive on the Japanese concentrations at Buna and Gona on the island's northeast coast. This was to be the starting point for MacArthur's march of revenge to retake the Philippines.

MacArthur hoped to move troops to northern New Guinea by air and water. He did not believe it possible to mount an offensive over the towering, jungle-clothed Owen Stanley Mountains that divide New Guinea as the breastbone divides a chicken, for only a single narrow trail leading through the village of Kokoda crossed this forbidding range. The Japanese thought otherwise. In July they advanced up the Kokoda Trail and, on reaching the reverse slope, began to drive MacArthur's Australian outposts before them. The fighting was prolonged and bitter. On August 25 Australians and Americans repulsed an attempted Japanese landing at Milne Bay. But it was not until mid-September that starvation, bombing, and stiff resistance on the ground halted the Japanese advance against Port Moresby and the Australians took the long trail back to Kokoda.

By then, Vice Admiral William "Bull" Halsey, one of the first American heroes of the war, had already seized the offensive. In January 1942 he sent his carriers against

TOKYO BOUND. A B-25 CLIMBING OFF THE DECK OF THE USS *HORNET*, APRIL 18, 1942 (NA).

Japanese positions in the Marshall Islands, sinking seventeen ships and destroying forty or fifty planes. Three weeks later the carrier *Enterprise* led a force that bombarded Wake Island, and Halsey's carrier planes hit enemy bases on the north coast of New Guinea.

THE DOOLITTLE RAID

Then, on April 18, 1942, Halsey's task force of *Enterprise* and *Hornet* stunned the Japanese by launching a bombing strike on Tokyo.

The attack had been planned by President Roosevelt and his top naval advisors and was intended to revive sinking home front morale. It was one of the great gambles of the war.

Since American aircraft carriers were unable to get close enough to Japan to launch their short-range bombers, Navy planners decided to load the deck of a carrier with mid-range army bombers, even though planes this large had never flown from a carrier in warfare. In total secrecy, volunteer pilots were trained at a Florida base to take off at precariously short distances. The flight decks of carriers were too short for retrieval; the bombers would have to fly, eleven hundred additional miles beyond Japan, to friendly bases in China. Command of the mission was given to Lieutenant Colonel James H. Doolittle, "King of the Sky," a racing pilot known for his daredevil aerial stunts, but also for his deep knowledge of aviation (he had earned a doctorate from MIT in aeronautical engineering).

In April, the carrier *Hornet* steamed toward Japan with sixteen twin-engine B-25s on its deck, each carrying three 500-pound bombs and one incendiary bomb. None of the pilots had ever taken off from the deck of a carrier, and the men did not learn their target was Tokyo until they were far out to sea. When it was announced over the ship's bullhorn—"Now hear this. Now hear this. This force is bound for Tokyo"—sailors and airmen cheered wildly. This would be payback for Pearl Harbor.

Halsey hoped to get within 500 miles of the target before launching Doolittle's bombers. But when *Hornet* and its powerful escort force reached a point 650 miles from the Japanese coast they ran into enemy picket boats. The task force destroyed them, but there was the possibility that the Japanese had already radioed the presence of the Americans. Doolittle doubted that his planes could fly from this point, hit Tokyo, and still make the Chinese mainland. It was abort or go. Halsey said to go. "The wind and sea were so strong that morning that green water was breaking over the carrier's ramps," Halsey wrote later. "Jimmy led his squadron. When his plane buzzed down . . . the *Hornet*'s deck . . . there wasn't a man topside who didn't sweat him into the air." [32]

Doolittle's raiders achieved total surprise. Swooping in at rooftop level, they hit Tokyo and five other Japanese cities, killing about 50 civilians, without the loss of a single plane. Captain Ted W. Lawson tells what happened over Tokyo:

TOKYO WAS BRILLIANT IN THE MID-DAY SUN and looked as limitless as an ocean. . . .

It took about five minutes to get across our arm of the bay, and, while still over the water, I could see the barrage balloons strung between Tokyo and Yokohama, across the river from Tokyo. . . .

In days and nights of dreaming about Tokyo and thinking of the eight millions who live there, I got the impression that it would be crammed together, concentrated, like San Francisco. Instead it spreads all over creation, like Los Angeles. There is an aggressively modern sameness to much of it and now, as we came in very low over it, I had a bad feeling that we wouldn't find our targets. I had to stay low and thus could see only a short distance ahead and to the sides. I couldn't go up to take a good look without drawing anti-aircraft fire, which I figured would be very accurate by now because the planes that had come in ahead of me all had bombed from 1,500 feet. . . .

I was almost on the first of our objectives before I saw it. I gave the engines full throttle. . . . We climbed as quickly as possible to 1,500 feet. . . .

There was just time to get up there, level off, attend to the routine of opening the bomb bay, make a short run and let fly with the first bomb. The red light blinked on my instrument board, and I knew the first 500-pounder had gone. [33]

Robert Guillain was still interned in Tokyo when Doolittle's squadron was first spotted:

ON APRIL 18TH, AT 12:30 P.M., I was at home when, from not very far away, I heard a ragged, powerful series of explosions. Bombs? Suddenly, there was the sound of feeble antiaircraft fire. Still, if it were a raid, we'd have heard the sirens.

Four minutes later, the staccato moans of the sirens filled the air with a dismal call that soared into the blue, sunlit sky over Tokyo. A raid at high noon! Our first raid! So *they've* come! I rushed outside. I lived in the center of the city and it took me only minutes to reach Toranomon, a large intersection near the principal ministries. This was the time of the day when clerks and typists in their blue smocks ate, usually at their desks. . . . Instead of sending everyone to shelter, the sound of the bombs and the warning brought people to their windows or out into the streets and then to the square. Noses in the air, they waited. Suddenly, there was the sound of a plane. At the windows, fingers pointed toward the Ginza. It was at that instant that, looking in that direction, I spotted a dark airplane traveling very fast, practically at rooftop level. Far behind it exploded a line of small, thin, ridiculous-looking clouds, the air defense's shells. A much smaller plane, well behind the bomber and all alone, came into sight: a Japanese fighter. A second series of explosions was heard—more bombs.

And that was all there was to Colonel James Doolittle's famous air raid.[34]

Although the raid did little damage, it lifted American morale. Asked from what base the planes had flown, President Roosevelt whimsically replied, "Shangri-la."

Aided by a strong tailwind, fifteen of the sixteen planes made it to China but ran out of fuel and crashed before they could reach their bases; one made it safely to Siberia. Sixty-four of the fliers, including Doolittle, escaped, spirited to safety by the Chinese underground. The Japanese forces in China captured eight airmen. Three were later executed, in violation of international law and with the Emperor's approval, and one died in prison after being tortured.

But it was the Chinese who suffered the most grievous consequences. In a four-month reign of terror, 250,000 Chinese were slaughtered by the Japanese in reprisal for a few brave peasants lending assistance to the downed Doolittle crews, "a scale of murder," a historian has written, "equal to that of the Rape of Nanking."[35]

The raid caused the Japanese to keep hundreds of planes in the home islands that otherwise would have gone to the South Pacific. More importantly, it was a deep psychological blow to the Japanese, one that led, in retaliation, to the grandiose expansion of Japanese military ambitions that brought on the Battle of Midway.

CORAL SEA

As its naval strength grew, America was prepared to stop Japanese expansion southward as well as eastward. The first major battle came in the Coral Sea, which washes the shores of New Guinea, the Solomons, and New Caledonia. In early May, a Japanese invasion fleet steamed into the Coral Sea from Rabaul, headed for Port Moresby. American intelligence had decrypted the Japanese naval code and the Pacific command sent a task force of two carriers, *Lexington* and *Yorktown*, under Rear Admiral Frank Jack Fletcher, to surprise the enemy.

This was the first major engagement in naval history in which surface ships did not exchange a single shot. Separated by 175 miles of water, the two fleets never got close enough to see one another. Carrier-based planes did all the fighting; and there was so much confusion in this swirling aerial battle that several Japanese planes, in darkness and bad weather, tried to land on the deck of *Yorktown*. American planes sank one Japanese carrier and heavily damaged another, but *Lexington* was lost and *Yorktown* was badly mauled and had to limp back to Pearl Harbor.

This historic battle, which took place in the days following General Wainwright's surrender of Corregidor, was not a clear-cut American victory, but it prevented the enemy from landing at Port Moresby and taking all of New Guinea. The fate of Port Moresby would be decided in a bitter land engagement in some of the most difficult terrain in the world. To support the coming fight for Port Moresby, the Japanese began secretly building an airbase on a tiny island called Guadalcanal.

The Battle of the Coral Sea convinced the crews and commanders of the Pacific Fleet that they could fight on at least equal terms with the powerful and more experienced Japanese Navy. At the end of May, *Yorktown*, repaired in a record seven days, joined *Enterprise* and *Hornet* to fight another carrier-to-carrier battle in the waters off Midway Island.

MIDWAY

On the morning of June 3, 1942, a Catalina patrol plane sighted a Japanese flotilla some 700 miles west of Midway Island. It was part of Admiral Yamamoto's vast armada of 165 ships heading toward Hawaii to deal a knockout blow to the U.S. Pacific Fleet.

Yamamoto was in personal command of the Midway operation on his flagship *Yamato,* the world's largest battleship. Infuriated by the Doolittle Raid, he had convinced Imperial Headquarters to bring on the decisive naval battle of the war.

Yamamoto's carrier commander was Vice Admiral Nagumo. Sailing under strict radio silence, he expected to surprise and slaughter the American fleet, as he had at

Pearl Harbor. A diversionary force was sent toward the American base at Dutch Harbor in the Aleutians. It was to draw the American fleet northward, opening the way for Yamamoto to take Midway, a strategically important atoll that guarded the western approaches to the Hawaiian Islands. When the Pacific Fleet learned it had been fooled and raced back to Midway, it would be, Yamamoto vowed, "annihilated." "Every man was convinced that he was about to participate in yet another brilliant victory," said Captain Mitsuo Fuchida, who had led the Pearl Harbor air attack.[36]

This time the Americans were not caught napping. An intelligence team headed by Lieutenant Commander Joseph Rochefort, the unsung hero of the upcoming battle, had broken the Japanese code, and as reports of a concentration of enemy forces came into headquarters at Pearl Harbor, cool-headed Admiral Chester Nimitz, the new commander of the Pacific Fleet, took immediate countermeasures. Calling the strategic signals from Pearl Harbor, Nimitz ordered Admirals Fletcher and Raymond A. Spruance (Halsey would have been in charge but was hospitalized with a skin infection) to ignore the Japanese feint and concentrate all available warships in the waters around Midway. *Yorktown* sailed from Pearl Harbor with repairmen still on board; B-17 Flying Fortresses were flown in from as far as Ireland; and the defenses of Midway were greatly reinforced.

Nimitz's plan was elegantly simple: he would hide his three carriers until Nagumo's planes hit Midway. Then he would launch his planes and destroy the unprotected Japanese flattops. It was the Japanese, not the Americans, who would sail into an ambush.

As Nimitz expected, the great battle was fought entirely by planes and submarines, in what was to become a new and deadly form of naval warfare. As in the battle of the Coral Sea, the opposing carrier fleets never saw one another. The Americans struck first. On the afternoon of June 3, Flying Fortresses from Midway attacked, but missed, a squadron of enemy landing ships. The Japanese now knew that surprise was lost and Nagumo reacted sharply with a heavy bombing of Midway the following day—an attack that severely damaged shore installations but failed to knock out the island's airfields.

When the flight leader of the raiding force urged a second strike, Nagumo rearmed the torpedo planes he had intended to use against the American fleet, if it showed up, with fragmentation bombs for another attack on Midway. But by this time, the carriers *Enterprise, Hornet,* and *Yorktown* had come within striking distance—150 miles—of his own carriers, and swarms of planes, led by the soon to be famous

Torpedo Squadron 8 from *Hornet,* set out to find their prey. Gilbert Cant, the *New York Post*'s Pacific correspondent, describes the opening phase of this attack:

FORTY-ONE TORPEDO PLANES were among the many groups sent out from the American carriers: fifteen from Torpedo Squadron Eight, attached to the *Hornet;* fourteen from Torpedo Squadron Six *(Enterprise)* and twelve from Torpedo Squadron Five *(Yorktown).* From the *Enterprise* there were, in addition to the fourteen torpedo planes, thirty-six dive-bombers . . . ten fighters, and an extra scout plane for the group commander, Lieutenant Commander Clarence [Wade] McClusky. . . .

Torpedo Eight, flying obsolete Douglas Devastators—not the new Grumman Avengers used by its reserve—was led by Lieutenant Commander John C. Waldron. It became separated from the other formations in the long search for the Japanese ships. A group of bombers and fighters which failed to find the enemy at the assigned position . . . had to be ordered to land on Midway as they were running out of gasoline. . . . But Waldron reasoned that if the Jap ships were not where they were supposed to be, it was probably because they had found the welcome too warm for their comfort and had decided to retire some distance, if not entirely. He therefore backtracked along their previously known course. McClusky arrived at the same conclusion, but not until after he had overshot the enemy's reported position by seventy-five miles or more. Then he too set out to intercept them to the northwest. The effect of these identical decisions made at different times was to bring Waldron's squadron within sight of the enemy. . . .

Waldron found the main enemy force with few fighter planes in the air, but his squadron had been out a long time and was running short of gas. It had accomplished part of its mission merely by locating the retiring Japanese and reporting their position. Waldron radioed his information and added: "Request permission to withdraw from actions to refuel." The admiral to whom the request was passed had an awful decision to make. To permit these planes to withdraw might make all the difference between sinking or crippling three carriers (Waldron had not sighted the fourth) and giving them a chance once more to slip out of sight under a squall. Three carriers could determine the balance of power in this 1942 sea war, in which the carrier was a capital ship at least in importance to the battleship, and actually of greater importance judged by performance in these first six months. Hypothetical scores of ships and hypothetical thousands of lives were on one side of the scale; on the other side were fifteen planes and the lives of their three-man crews. The admiral ordered: "Attack at once."[37]

Before taking off, Waldron had met with his pilots: "I want each of us to do his utmost to destroy our enemies. If there is only one plane left to make a final run in, I want that man to go in and get a hit. May God be with us all."[38]

All of Torpedo 8's planes was blown out of the sky by whirling Zeros and a murderous sheet of antiaircraft fire, "and for about one hundred seconds the Japanese were certain they had won the Battle of Midway, and the war," writes Samuel Eliot Morison.[39]

Ensign George Gay, the only man to survive this American-style kamikaze attack, was shot down and wounded, and watched the rest of the air battle from his floating seat cushion. Two other torpedo squadrons attacked the four carriers. The Zeros, flying at deck level, cut them up, too. Not a single Japanese ship was hit in this massacre.

The torpedo planes, however, had been unintended sacrificial lambs. As the Zeros did their work on them at low altitude, Ensign Gay saw McClusky's dive-bombers come boring down from above, unopposed. They caught Nagumo's carriers in their most vulnerable position, with their decks crowded with planes refueling and rearming, this time with torpedoes, for an expected wipe-up attack on the American carriers.

"At 10:20 Admiral Nagumo gave the order to launch when ready," Matsuo Fuchida recalled. "The big ship began turning in the wind. Within five minutes all her planes would be launched.

"Five minutes! Who would have dreamed that the tide of battle would shift completely in that brief interval of time."[40]

At 10:25 A.M. McClusky's dive-bomber group was about to deliver what historian John Keegan has called "the most stunning and decisive blow in the history of naval warfare."[41]

Lieutenant Clarence E. Dickinson was in McClusky's *Enterprise* group:

AS I PUT MY NOSE DOWN I picked up our carrier target in front of me. I was making the best dive I have ever made. . . . We were coming down in all directions on the port side of the carrier, beautifully spaced. . . . I recognized her as the *Kaga*; and she was enormous. . . .

The target was utterly satisfying. . . . I saw a bomb hit just behind where I was aiming. . . . I saw the deck rippling and curling back in all directions exposing a great section of the hangar below. . . . I dropped a few seconds after the previous bomb explosion. . . . I saw the 500-pound bomb hit right abreast of the [carrier's] island. The two 100-pound bombs struck in the forward area of the parked planes. . . .

Then I began thinking it was time to get myself away from there and try to get back alive.[42]

When McClusky's dive-bombers came screaming down on the Japanese carriers, Matsuo Fuchida learned what it was like to be on the other end of a surprise air strike. He was on the *Akagi* but was not flying that day, having come down with a case of appendicitis:

AT 10:34 THE ORDER TO START LAUNCHING came from the bridge by voice-tube. The Air Officer flapped a white flag, and the first Zero fighter gathered speed and whizzed off the deck. At that instant a lookout screamed: "Hell-Divers!" I looked up to see three black enemy planes plummeting towards our ship. Some of our machine guns managed to fire a few frantic bursts at them, but it was too late.[43]

Within less than a minute the enormous ship was turned into an inferno. Nagumo, with tears in his eyes, reluctantly abandoned the doomed *Akagi*. Fuchida stayed behind to try to hold off the inevitable, but broke both his ankles jumping from

USS *YORKTOWN*, HIT AT MIDWAY (NA).

one deck to another to avoid the explosions and raging fires. He was strapped to a bamboo stretcher and lowered to a boat, which carried him to a rescue ship.

That night *Akagi* and *Kaga* both sank. A third carrier, *Soryu*, was hit by 3,000 bombs and horribly damaged. When its commanding officer, Captain Ryusaku Yanagimoto, refused to abandon ship, a Japanese wrestling champion was sent aboard to bring him to safety, by force if necessary. But Chief Petty Officer Abe respected the will of the greatly loved commander and left him on the bridge, his samurai sword in hand, calmly singing *Kimigayo*, the Japanese national anthem. An American submarine sent *Soryu* to the bottom.

The initial attack that did most of the damage to the Japanese carriers had taken exactly five minutes. After it was over, Ensign George Gay was pulled from the sea. He had participated in and witnessed one of history's greatest naval engagements.

The Japanese were battered, but still capable of fight. Planes from the carrier *Hiryu* struck back. Fletcher Pratt, a war correspondent for the *New York Post*, tells what happened:

THERE WAS LIFE in those Japanese yet; there was one punch left in the *Hiryu.* Our carriers had turned and were steaming southwestward, keeping their distance from those fast Japanese battleships. . . .

It was the *Yorktown*, the northernmost ship, that was struck just after 1 o'clock by 36 dive bombers from the *Hiryu.* . . . "Stand by to repel air attack," said her loudspeakers, and the fighter patrols of the other carrier joined the *Yorktown*'s. "It was damned spectacular," said an officer of one carrier. "On the horizon there would be a flash of flame and a mass of thick black smoke plunging downward to the sea. There would be another flash and another downward pencil; finally it looked like the sky over there was covered by a curtain of smoke streamers."

Only seven Jap planes came through that hornet's nest of American fighters, but they came in a mood of Oriental desperation, and despite losing three more at the ship, they planted bombs. One hit the *Yorktown* . . . and started a fire; another hit in the forward elevator well and started more fire from the tanks of the planes on the hangar deck; and still another bomb went through the side of the funnel, blowing out the fires in the ship's engine room. The *Yorktown* stopped; watching her from the *Hornet*'s deck they could see a tall column of smoke shoot straight up. . . .

All the planes in the fleet still fit for work were refueled and remunitioned, while the pilots grabbed sandwiches and coffee, and then took off again to get that last Jap carrier, the *Hiryu,* and break up her flight deck. . . .

It must have been after 4:00 before [the planes] reached the *Hiryu* group. Now the day-long losing battle that the Japanese airmen had fought began to have its effect. Their fighter opposition was weak. Their antiaircraft fired furiously enough, but the men who fired must have reached the point of black despair over the endless procession of star-marked planes that came out of the clouds to pound their dying ships. Hardly a blow from all that group of American planes missed its target; the *Hiryu* was hit and hit again with bombs timed to pierce her deck till she burned from end to end. Both battleships were hit, the cruiser and the destroyer were hit, while our loss was next to nothing.[44]

Hornet and *Enterprise* raced westward after the decimated Japanese forces, which split up to make detection more difficult. But neither this strategy nor the bad weather that set in saved them from further punishment. The major damage, however, had been done. The Japanese lost four carriers and the Americans only one, *Yorktown.* Abandoned by her crew, she was sunk two days later by a Japanese submarine as the Navy tried to tow her home. Midway was the Imperial Japanese Navy's first major defeat since 1592. As Yamamoto ordered a withdrawal, he turned to his worried officers on the *Yamato:* "I'll apologize to the Emperor myself." [45]

The Japanese people were not told of the shattering defeat at Midway. When Mitsuo Fuchida returned to Japan on a hospital ship, he was not taken ashore until dark "when the streets were deserted. I was taken to the hospital on a covered stretcher and carried through the rear entrance. My room was in complete isolation. No nurses or corpsmen were allowed in and I could not communicate with the outside. It was like being a prisoner of war among your own people." [46]

Military intelligence as well as military might won the Battle of Midway. "Had we lacked early information of the Japanese movements, and had we been caught with carrier forces dispersed . . . the Battle of Midway would have ended differently," said Admiral Nimitz.[47] Working a twenty-hour day in a windowless basement at Pearl Harbor, dressed in a red smoking jacket and slippers, Commander Joseph Rochefort had given Nimitz the key to victory. It was the most important intelligence finding of the Pacific war.

The Battle of Midway decisively changed the course of the war in the Pacific.

The powerful Japanese First Air Fleet was smashed, and from this point on in the war, just six months after Pearl Harbor, the damaged but still formidable Japanese Navy was thrown back on the defensive by America's newest weapon, the carrier task force.

Later that summer, back at Honolulu, James Jones, now a corporal, watched "the victorious carrier pilots of Midway drunk and having fist fights on the lawns of the Royal Hawaiian. . . . None of them expected to come back, and they wanted everything they could get of living on the way out, and that included fist fighting."[48]

RETREAT IN BURMA

If the outlook in the South Pacific was brighter, it was black elsewhere in Asia. While the Japanese were besieging Singapore they were attacking Burma.

Burma, a British province, was one of the vital points in the Far East. From Lashio in the northeast ran the Burma Road, connecting at one end with Mandalay and Rangoon, at the other with Chungking in China. After the Japanese occupied the main Chinese seaports in 1937–38, this road was China's lifeline to the outside world. Burma was also the key to India.

By December 1941, Japan had massed some 200,000 troops in Siam and Indochina and had powerful air forces operating from bases in Siam. The invasion was launched in December but the main attack was made late in January by Siamese puppet troops. The British fell back on Rangoon, Burma's largest port. Pounded by air, they called upon the Flying Tigers, a group of volunteer American pilots commanded by General Claire Chennault.

The Flying Tigers had been hired by Chinese Nationalist Generalissimo Chiang Kai-shek in the summer of 1941 to defend the Burma Road. Flying obsolete P-40s, they had destroyed over 300 Japanese planes. In the battle for Rangoon they shot down another forty-six planes, but there was no stopping the enemy onslaught. Late in February, the Japanese drove British Indian troops back toward Rangoon, which was evacuated in March, severing all supply routes for Allied troops in the interior. Chinese forces under the brilliant American General "Vinegar Joe" Stilwell came down from the north to help hold the line, but the Japanese brought another army in from Siam, cut the Burma Road north of Lashio, and forced Stilwell to retreat. The American reporter Jack Belden describes that epic retreat through an almost impenetrable jungle filled with king cobras and other vipers:

OUR CHIEF PROBLEM before we started seemed to be food. When our party had originally set out from Shwebo, we had been equipped with thirty days' dry rations for sixty-five people. But during the journey, stray groups fastening on us here and there had increased our numbers to almost double their original total. . . .

I looked at the general.

"I'm also radioing the British to get police, guides, food, and water on this road. If they don't, there's going to be a catastrophe. Everyone trying to get out and everyone out of hand. Thousands will die."

Stilwell was right. Thousands did die.

The retreat from Burma was one of the bitterest retreats in modern times, ranking only below the Long March of the Chinese Communists in point of physical hardship and duration of march. Even as late as October 1942, as I wrote these lines, it was still going on. Remnants of the Allied armies, six months after the finish of the Burma campaign, were still lost in the jungles, wandering at the base of the Tibet fastnesses, fed by airplane drops, but slowly dying of malaria, exhaustion, and starvation, still unable to escape. . . .

At half past three on the morning of the 7th of May, while sleep still gripped our tired camp like a disease, I rose from a blanket on the ground, turned my jeep headlights across the yard where weary men lay, and shouted: "Rise and shine!" . . .

Slowly everyone rose. Indian cooks started breakfast bonfires, revealing cans of discarded butter in the yard. Over the fires of Pinky Dorn, the general's aide, burned codes—our radio had been destroyed during the night. The girls marched into the camp from the village, singing, already wide awake before the drowsiness had left the eyes of the men. Carriers came into camp by ones and twos, their shirts hanging loose over their skirts. . . . Rags were wrapped around their heads. They sat quietly smoking white cheroots. . . .

General Stilwell shoved a carrier guide out in front of him on the path and called to General [Franklin] Sibert: "Okay, Si! Let her go."

Sibert held a police whistle to his lips and blew a sharp blast. "Fall in," he shouted. . . .

Stilwell slung a tommy gun over his shoulder, called: "Forward march," and started down the path at a slow pace.

We were off to India. . . .

The jungle along the banks grew thinner, the sun beat down harder, and the water became deeper. It washed sand and gravel into our shoes, crept up around our knees, and pressed like a wall against our legs, which grew heavier. We splashed, stumbled, and went slower. Men began to waver, complain, and curse. . . .

The sun beating down with naked flames on that open beach drove us to seek refuge among the trees, brambles, and bushes on an embankment hanging over the other side of the stream. . . .

Looking at . . . the tired bodies around him, the general audibly wondered "if this gang can march three hours tonight." Half to himself, he said: "If we don't go on, that mob in back will come down on us and that's going to be bad in this narrow stream."

A meal of rice, bully beef, and tea was served on the sands about four o'clock. . . . Then we started marching once again. . . .

The general sloshed with the same steady pace through the water, the tommy gun still on his back, but the main group could not keep up with him. Stragglers began to fall behind so that we had to form a straggler's detachment to pick them up. . . .

At the start of the trip it had been generally feared that our rate of march would be dictated by the comparative slowness of the girls, but there on the first day, at any rate, they not only were marching as fast as anyone else, but were doing so in high spirits, bouncing, splashing and playing in the water, kicking up their legs, holding their skirts high, and singing like chorus girls. . . .

Their high-pitched, girlish voices, raised in song and echoing through the cliffs enclosing the streams, provided in moments of drooping morale and excessive fatigue marching rhythms, varying in mood and effect from the soothing to the stirring, that no military band could have equaled. Their own native Karen songs, war songs, they had learned from Chinese soldiers, Christian hymns, and ancient American jazz were, save for General Stilwell's dogged, cool perseverance, the one invigorating influence we had on the march. With a feeling of nostalgia I can still hear them sloshing through the river, stumbling through the jungles, and streaming down steep mountain sides, singing in their childish, abandoned way.[49]

By the end of May the Japanese conquest of Burma was complete, and so, too, the isolation of China. With the Burma Road gone, the only supply route to China was by air "over the Hump," the Himalayas—one of the most hazardous air routes in the world.

CHAPTER 5

The Hard Way Back

GUADALCANAL

The first phase of the battle for the Pacific ended at Midway. The second began with Guadalcanal, a remote island in the Solomons chain, 10 degrees below the Equator. An epic land, air, and naval struggle, the Guadalcanal campaign stopped Japan's triumphant expansion and put America on the offensive for the first time in the war. Guadalcanal was also the only Pacific campaign that American forces came perilously close to losing.

From the sunny deck of his incoming troopship, Corporal James Jones looked out at what he thought was a piece of paradise: "the delicious sparkling tropical sea, the long beautiful beach, the minute palms of the copra plantation waving in the sea breeze, the dark band of jungle, and the dun mass and power of the mountains rising behind it to rocky peaks."

But when he landed, Jones found himself in "a pestilential hellhole."[1] It was oppressively hot and humid, with torrential downpours that soaked the men's clothing and bedding and led to appalling outbreaks of skin infection and fungal diseases. The

Guadalcanal 1942

vine-choked rain forest was filled with slimy mud and rotting vegetation. This damp undergrowth gave off a vile, unforgettable smell and was a breeding farm for voracious insects and dozens of debilitating jungle diseases. And everywhere there were snakes and scorpions, and spiders as big as a man's fist. "If God ever created a hell-on-earth contest the island . . . would have made it to the finals," said one Marine.[2]

Guadalcanal was thinly populated and had no economic value. But recently and unexpectedly it had become the most vital strategic spot in the Pacific. The Japanese had occupied the Solomons in the spring of 1942, and during that summer their Army had begun constructing an airfield on Guadalcanal. Thanks to the intelligence of Commander Rochefort, the Americans learned of the airstrip even before the Japanese Navy did. If the Japanese completed the airfield by August, as expected, their land-based bombers would control the skies over American shipping lanes to Australia, over which huge amounts of men and supplies were arriving weekly to reinforce Australian units that were being called back from North Africa.

In the gray morning light of August 7, the 1st Marine Division, commanded by Major General Alexander A. ("Archie") Vandegrift, a veteran of jungle warfare in Central America, landed 19,000 troops on Guadalcanal and the tiny neighboring islands of Tulagi, Gavutu, and Tanambogo. Opposition was fierce on Tulagi, but the Guadalcanal landing was unopposed and the Marines moved inland to seize the airfield that was abandoned that morning by the badly outnumbered Japanese. The Marines named it Henderson Field in honor of a Marine pilot killed at Midway, and from this day it became the focus of the campaign.

When the Marines landed, the Japanese had only about 2,500 men on the island, most of them construction workers at the crushed coral airfield. But in the coming months, both sides poured in reinforcements—the Americans to hold the airfield, the Japanese to retake it.

At first, things went badly for the Marines. Covering the initial landing was a carrier force commanded by Vice Admiral Frank Jack Fletcher, veteran of Coral Sea and Midway. Fletcher feared his three carriers were sitting targets for Japanese aircraft in the area and abruptly left a day earlier than planned, a move that necessitated the withdrawal, as well, of the transports that were bringing in supplies and almost 2,000 additional men. It was a cowardly decision, and it left the abandoned Marines short of artillery, ammunition, and food—and without air cover and those extra 2,000 fighting men. After the Navy left, "there was a lot of talk about Bataan," said one Marine.[5] It was a siege now, and not even Washington was confident the Marines could be saved.

Japanese reaction to the American landing was swift and devastating. The next evening a naval strike force came racing through the Slot, the deep channel through the central Solomons, and pounced on the unsuspecting fleet that was in Savo Sound screening the American beachhead. Marine combat photographer Thayer Soule was

MARINE CAMP, GUADALCANAL (USMC).

HENDERSON FIELD. THIS "PAGODA" WAS HEADQUARTERS
FOR U.S. MARINE AND NAVY FLYERS (USMC).

nearby in a troopship waiting orders to head in to the beach. Most of the men had gone to bed. "At 0200 we were awakened by general quarters. The Japanese had arrived early. The sky near Savo [Island] was ablaze with orange and white flashes. Tremendous explosions shook our ship. After only a few minutes, the firing stopped. We could hear only the rain falling on the canvas overhead. . . . Except for the glow of a burning ship, the night was black once more."

Without losing a single ship, Admiral Gunichi Mikawa's expert night-fighting force sank four cruisers and inflicted nearly 2,000 casualties. Predatory sharks tore into the men as they hit the water. Sailors pulled out of the sea were so badly burned that corpsmen could find no place to stick hypodermic needles. It was the worst defeat suffered on the high seas by the U.S. Navy. Yet it could have been worse. "They could have crushed our landing, marooned our troops, destroyed our supplies, and crippled our navy for months to come. But they sailed away," Soule wrote later.[4] Mikawa had not dealt the "mortal blow" because he feared American carrier planes would hit him at first light. It was one of the great mistakes of the war, for Fletcher was fleeing south, out of range of Mikawa.

But that was thin consolation for the Marines who watched the last of the transports leave the next evening. "Bastogne was considered an epic in the ETO [European Theater of Operations]," writes historian William Manchester, a Marine veteran of the Pacific Theater. "The 101st Airborne was surrounded there for eight days. But the marines on Guadalcanal were to be isolated for over four months. There have been few such stands in history."[5]

Thereafter the battle for Guadalcanal was a seesaw affair, a series of ferociously fought sea and air engagements and a long and punishing land campaign. Except in the mountains and jungles of New Guinea, Americans had never waged war under harder conditions than those which the Marines—and later Army infantry reinforcements—encountered on Guadalcanal.

The Marines had to hold the airstrip until they had enough men to drive the Japanese off the island. The Navy had to resupply and reinforce Guadalcanal and stop the "Tokyo Express," the swift-running destroyer convoys that brought troops and supplies down the Slot from the Japanese bastion at Rabaul. The Marines helped out with their own small air force commanded by Major General Roy Geiger. The pilots at Henderson Field lived on meager rations, battled malaria and dysentery, and were pounded day and night from both sea and air. Led by their ace, Captain Joseph J. Foss, who won the Medal of Honor for downing twenty-six enemy aircraft, they covered the naval supply effort and did excellent work against Japanese bombers and Zeros. They were helpless, however, to prevent the Tokyo Express from massively building up Japanese troop strength on the island. The Tokyo Express brought in reinforcements at night; the Marines could fly only in daylight.

It became a brutal war of attrition. In a succession of tremendous naval struggles, the tide swung back and forth, with both sides suffering devastating losses, including, for the United States, the carrier *Hornet*, which had ferried Doolittle's planes to Japan. The Americans won some victories. But until October, when Admiral Bull Halsey took over command in the South Pacific from the super-cautious Admiral Robert Ghormley and began pressing his commanders to challenge the enemy in night fighting, the Japanese controlled the waters around Guadalcanal. The turning point, the Naval Battle of Guadalcanal, took place in mid-November 1942.

On the night of November 13, two Japanese battlewagons, with a screen of destroyers, came barreling through the Slot, headed for Guadalcanal. Yamamoto had sent them to bomb Henderson Field into submission and provide cover for a landing force of 10,000 fresh troops arriving on fast transports and destroyers. American intelligence had once again broken the Japanese code and Halsey had time to prepare. First to meet the Japanese fleet was a badly outnumbered destroyer-cruiser force under Rear Admiral Daniel J. Callaghan, a close personal friend of President Roosevelt. Defying the odds, Callaghan attacked, fighting at perilously close range, in what was the seagoing equivalent of hand-to-hand combat.

It was a moonlit night and the American correspondent Ira Wolfert was on shore with the Marines to witness what Admiral Ernest King, commander-in-chief of the U.S. Fleet, called "one of the most furious sea battles ever fought."[6]

THE LAND FORCES HAD GIRDED THEMSELVES for a repetition of the October 13 bombardment. Men huddled in foxholes, and asked each other silently with their embittered faces, "Where's our Navy?" and wondered what would be left to stop the Jap transports.

Those seven hours of darkness, with each moment as silent as held breath, were the blackest our troops have faced since Bataan, but at the end of them our Navy was there, incredibly, like a Tom Mix of old, like the hero of some antique melodrama. It turned the tide of the whole battle by throwing its steel and flesh into the breach against what may be the heaviest Jap force yet engaged by surface ships in this war.

Again the beach had a front-row seat for the devastating action. Admiral Callaghan's force steaming in line drove headlong into a vastly more powerful Jap fleet which was swinging around tiny Savo Island with guns set for point-blank blasting of Guadalcanal, and loaded with high-explosive shells instead of armor-piercing shells. Matching cruisers and destroyers against battleships is like putting a good bantamweight against a good heavyweight, but the Japs unquestionably were caught with their kimonos down around their ankles. They could have stayed out of range and knocked out our ships with impunity, and then finished us on the ground at their leisure.

We opened fire first. The Jap ships, steaming full speed, were on us, over us, and all around us in the first minute. . . . The range was so close that the Japs could not depress their guns enough to fire at the waterline, which is why so many hits landed on the bridge and two of our admirals were killed.

The action was illuminated in brief, blinding flashes by Jap searchlights which were shot out as soon as they were turned on, by muzzle flashes from big guns, by fantastic streams of tracers, and by huge orange-colored explosions as two Jap destroyers and one of our destroyers blew up within seconds of one another. . . . The sands of the beach were shuddering so much from gunfire that they made the men standing there quiver and tingle from head to foot.

From the beach it resembled a door to hell opening and closing, opening and closing, over and over. The unholy show took place in the area immediately this side of Savo Island. Our ships, in a line of about three thousand yards, steamed into a circle of Jap ships which opened at the eastern end like a mouth gaping with surprise. They ran, dodged, and reversed their field, twisted, lurched, and lunged, but progressed generally along the inside of the lip of the Japs.

Since the Jap circle was much bigger than our line, the Jap ships, first at one end and then the other, fired across the empty space into one another. It took about thirty minutes for our ships to complete the tour of the circle and by the end of the tour the Jap ships had ceased to exist as an effective force.[7]

It was over in twenty-four minutes, "a barroom brawl after the lights had been shot out," an American officer described it.[8] The Japanese lost a battleship and were prevented from bombing Henderson Field and landing troops. But Wolfert was wrong about one thing. It was the American ships that "had ceased to exist as an effective force."

Callaghan and another admiral, Norman Scott, were killed on the bridges of their ships and a cruiser and four destroyers were lost. The next day, the cruiser *Juneau* was blown to pieces by a torpedo from a Japanese submarine. Seven hundred men perished, among them the five Sullivan brothers from Waterloo, Iowa. They had enlisted in the Navy to avenge a friend's death, and through sheer persistence had overcome government reluctance to have members of the same family serve together. The Navy claimed they had gone down with the ship and launched a propaganda campaign, featuring their parents, to boost war production. But the Sullivan boys, along with 135 other men on *Juneau*, had survived the spectacular blast that took the ship under. The survivors lived hour to hour, without food or water, under a boiling sun, and were attacked by sharks as they hung to the netting of their life rafts. They were not found for a week because of a botched search and rescue mission. When they were finally picked up, only ten of them were still alive. The public was never told.

The damaged but still formidable Japanese fleet steamed on toward Guadalcanal. Vice Admiral Willis Lee, with a force of four destroyers and two battleships—*Washington* and *South Dakota*—met the enemy head-on in Savo Sound. It was another night fight and one of the only battleship engagements of the entire war. Almost the instant the two fleets collided the Japanese sank two destroyers and damaged the other two. At this critical moment, *South Dakota,* nicknamed the Big Bastard by its crew, experienced a power failure that put out its radar. Without its "night eyes," it became an easy target for skilled Japanese night fighters. They put forty-two hits into it, smashing the ship's superstructure, knocking out its communications, and killing and mangling its crew.

Robert L. Schwartz, a reporter for *Yank,* the GI paper, interviewed men on the *South Dakota* and pieced together what went on inside the ship after it was hit:

HODGEN OTHELLO PATRICK . . . talker on the Big Bastard's sky patrol, highest lookout post where the ship took its first hit during the Battle of Savo Island, came as reasonably close to being killed as can be expected of any man.

Patrick remembers squaring for battle and from his high perch seeing the Jap ships come up. He saw the first salvo leave the flagship up ahead. His next recollection is of being thrown against a bulkhead and finding somebody's arm, without a body, across his face. A dead weight lay across his chest, pinning him.

"I'm dead," he thought, and the remembrance of it is still clear in his mind. "Here I am dead. This is what it's like to be dead." But the earthly touch of shrapnel in his knee and his hip convinced him that he was still alive. He looked around. The two officers lay dead. Seven enlisted men were still. Four wounded looked at Patrick, not knowing what to do next.

Patrick pressed the button on his headset. "Sick bay," he called, "send help." . . . But no help came.

Patrick ordered two wounded to go below and then put tourniquets on the other two, using their own belts. He applied the same treatment to his own leg above the bleeding knee, then remembered to loosen all three every 15 minutes throughout the night. He hunted a long time for morphine before he found it and divided it with the others. As he was about to take his share of the sedative he noticed that several of the men he had thought dead were stirring. Without a moment's hesitation he divided his share among them. He didn't feel heroic about it. He didn't even think about it.

Despite his injuries, Patrick found that he could get to his feet. He saw that he could report better while standing and remained that way until the end of the battle. Afterward, he fell again to the deck but never stopped his regular reports until he was relieved the next morning.

Patrick was the only enlisted man of the crew who was recommended for the Navy Cross.

When general quarters sounded on the *Big Bastard*, Rufus Mathewson . . . took his post as a talker in the conning tower.

"It'll be a push-over," he heard someone say. "Just a bunch of armed transports. We'll knock 'em off like sitting ducks."

Mathewson said to himself, "I wish I was home." . . .

Hours ticked by. Shortly after midnight the loudspeaker carried a cold steady voice from the plot room. "Target 20,000 yards, bearing 240° . . . target 19,800 yards, bearing 241° . . ." Slowly the target drew closer.

There was a terrific explosion up ahead. Mathewson dashed to one of the slits and felt his stomach drop as he saw a battleship ahead silhouetted by flame. "Lord, let me out and I'll change my ways," he said aloud. A direct hit had dissolved one of the destroyers. . . .

Over the lookout's phone came a voice, "Destroyer sinking on our starboard bow." The captain ordered left rudder, and the helmsman swung the wheel. They skirted the destroyer, then came back on their course. From over the phone came the Admiral's voice: "Fire when ready." . . .

Thirty seconds later shells screamed out. The captain and the navigator were jarred away from their positions at the 'scopes, but voices came in over the phone.

"Right on!"

"The damned thing has dissolved!"

"Looked like a cruiser."

"That was a battleship!"

In rapid succession Mathewson heard a loud crash, a rolling explosion, and then the searing rattle of metal fragments as they crashed into cables, guns, and superstructure. The ship shrugged, leaned back into a volley of 6- and 8-inch shells that raked through the sky control tower, topmost position on the ship.

Quickly Mathewson called sky control on the battle phone. "Patrick, you there?"

"Here, but our officers are dead, and all of us are wounded."

Mathewson asked for permission to go relieve Patrick but his request was denied. Mathewson and Patrick were close friends, and now the thought of Patrick lying wounded on sky control beyond the help of anyone because of fires burning below him almost brought tears to his eyes.

Methodically *Big B* went on firing. . . .

Six- and 8-inch shell fire peppered the bridge with steel fragments. It was almost impossible for shrapnel to penetrate the armor of the bridge but the men inside heard one shell smack through the gun director just aft the bridge and then explode against the chart house. Directions for course and bearing stopped coming in.

Over the amplifier from the chart house came a voice. "My God, this man's bleeding to death. Send help. Hurry. Please hurry."

Melvin McSpadden, the engine control talker, was first to answer. "Sick bay is on this circuit and they'll send a doctor. Give us some bearings."

"This poor guy's bleeding to death. Have you got any bandages? I can't leave him like this."

McSpadden tore down a blackout curtain hanging over one of the slots, stuffed it through the aperture and shouted to a seaman on the catwalk outside, "Take this to the chart house quick." . . .

Batt II, which is the auxiliary control room situated inside the superstructure below the sky control tower, was the hardest hit portion of the ship. One of the talkers in Batt II was Tom Page . . . of Greensburg, Pa.

Page remembers it was a beautiful night. There was a big moon and it was very warm and quiet. The smell of gardenias was strong from off Florida Island. The association of the gardenias with the action that followed caused Page to lose all desire to smell a gardenia again.

Over the amplifier came a voice, "Guadalcanal on our starboard hand." Big vivid flashes lit the sky—some of it gunfire in the distance, some of it lightning. Everybody in Batt II was tense. Not until the *Big Bastard*'s guns went off did everyone's confidence return. . . .

Page sat in a corner on an overturned bucket, feeling comfortable now that the big guns were booming. He noticed that the commander, usually a very nervous man, was very calm. Then he was knocked off his bucket by a shell hit. The molten metal from the shell ran across the floor like lava and he stepped out of the way. Steam pipes were broken, electrical fires sputtered. Noise and heat from the steam were unbearable. He screamed over the phone to engine control to shut off the auxiliary steam line. . . . Somebody on the bridge answered, "They heard you, Page," and in a moment added, "Secure and get out if there's nothing else you can do." . . .

During the entire action one of the lookouts standing by a slot kept repeating in a low voice: "Lord, I'm scared. Nobody has any idea how scared I am. How could anyone be this scared? My God, I'm scared." He said that over and over for about 10 minutes. Nobody thought it was strange.

Men began crawling to their feet. Above the noise of the steam and the fire there rose excited voices. Men asked each other who was hurt, where was the ship damaged, how high were the flames. They speculated on their own chances of getting out. Occasionally they shot glances at the executive officer looking for help. He noticed but didn't know what to say. Finally he blurted out, "Shut up! I'll do all the talking in here!"

The talking stopped. Only the noise of the steam escaping could be heard above the gunfire below. Then the gunfire ceased and within a minute the steam went off. A new noise could be heard now—the moans of the injured and the dying. Pharmacist's mates went among them, injecting shots of morphine. From below came the noise of damage control parties, fighting their way through with hoses and extinguishers. . . .

When John P. Buck left Athens, Ohio, and enlisted in the Navy he went in as an apprentice seaman. Several months later, while cruising the Pacific, the chaplain found that Buck could type. He got him a rating and had him placed on the muster roll as chaplain's yeoman.

Buck's duty at general quarters was after-battery lookout. . . .

Buck leaned against the open door to the compartment and felt the warmth and silence of the night. . . . About 65 feet aft from where he stood, Buck could see the big 16-inch barrels poked out over the starboard rail. He was lazily watching them when they suddenly fired a salvo with a deafening roar. Buck was picked up bodily and thrown inside the compartment. He heard his helmet fly off and strike a bulkhead 30 feet away, then roll around the floor. The explosion blinded him for about 15 minutes, during which time he groped on the floor and found his helmet. When he took it off the next morning he found it wasn't his. Whose it was and where it came from, he never learned.

Regaining his sight and finding that there was a lull in the battle, Buck offered to aid the pharmacist's mates in caring for the wounded. Before he could leave, however, the after battery once again opened fire, so Buck stayed where he was.

Over five miles away a 14-inch shell came screaming out of the muzzle of a gun on a Jap battleship. Buck first saw it when it was about two miles away from him, looming larger and larger as a red dot in the sky. He knew it was going to hit and knelt down in the compartment.

The shell came through at exactly deck level. . . . There was a blinding flash and roar, and shrapnel rained down like cinders. Buck mentally marked turret No. 3 off his list. But when he went out to look he found that the turret was still there but beside it was a yawning hole in the deck.

Looking over the starboard rail he saw a Jap ship racing up. He reported it but worriedly wondered how they were ever going to hit it with the after turret almost certainly out of action. Then he heard the secondaries open fire with a staccato bang-bang-bang, finally reaching the ear-splitting regularity of machine-gun firing . . .

The after turret, meanwhile, turned slowly toward the approaching ship, now so close that the elevation on the barrels was almost nil.

Nobody was more amazed than Buck when the after turret fired. He had no idea it was still in action. Then he saw that the Jap ship had been hit almost point-blank by all three shells. There was a big flash where the ship had been and then smoking, bubbling water. In the few seconds before the Jap went under, Buck had seen one of its turrets fly high into the air and the ship start to split in the middle. But it sank before it had a chance to fall apart.

The firing stopped and Buck left to help in the care of the wounded. At sick bay he found men stretched out on every available table with doctors and pharmacist's mates working over them while standing in 4 inches of blood and water on the deck.

He was sent with a doctor to the top of the superstructure to help the wounded men who had been cut off there. Only Patrick was still there. The doctor stayed with Patrick, giving Buck Syrettes of morphine to administer inside the superstructure on the way down.

Descending on the inside of the tower, Buck found a man lying on one of the upper levels with one leg shot off. He took out his knife and walked over to a dangling electrical wire, cut it loose and wrapped it around the injured man's leg. He wrenched loose the shattered rung of a ladder and used it to twist through the wire, making a tourniquet.

On the next level down he felt his feet get tangled in something in the water on the deck. An officer came along with a flashlight and they discovered that his legs were entwined by someone's insides floating on the water.

He kicked himself loose and went down to the main deck where he saw a man sitting wearily against a bulkhead.

"Hey, Mac, are you okay?" asked Buck.

No answer came so Buck asked him again. When he got no answer this time, Buck reached down to feel his pulse. The man was already cold. Buck left and went back to his post.

Up above the deck the wounded Patrick was giving out morphine. Page was trying hard to keep breathing above the escaping steam, and Buck was trying to recover his sight after being dazed by shell fire. Below decks, in the engine control room, was Chief Yeoman Cheek reading an old issue of the *Reader's Digest*.

The huge panel of gauges in front of him was functioning perfectly. The engine was at top speed, the boilers were maintaining a magnificent head of steam, and the blowers were keeping the room quite cool and comfortable. When a command came through, Cheek carried it out, then returned to his reading.

There was nothing else to do.

The noise of the battle was distant and removed. . . . So Cheek kept on reading the *Reader's Digest*. . . .

It was morning when Cheek walked up onto the deck and saw the destruction. Then he realized, for the first time, how many shells had ripped into the ship during the night.

After he saw the damage, he couldn't sleep for three days.[9]

The Japanese couldn't put the Big Bastard out of action and its powerful batteries helped *Washington* sink the battleship *Kirishima*. When that happened the superior Japanese force withdrew. On the morning of November 15, American planes, ships, and artillery pounced on the abandoned troop carriers. In this bloodbath, the Japanese were able to land only about 2,000 men. Running in transports under Japanese guns, the Navy, meanwhile, had built up the fighting force on Guadalcanal to over 35,000 men, and many of the outnumbered Japanese were beginning to starve.

After the Naval Battle of Guadalcanal, victory in the Solomons was no longer in doubt. There was plenty of fighting ahead—not until February were the last Japanese cleared out of Guadalcanal, and the fight for New Georgia, Choiseul, and Bougainville in the northern Solomons continued through most of the next year. But the naval losses the enemy suffered in this prolonged campaign constituted a disaster second only to that of Midway: two battleships, twenty-three other warships, 600 aircraft, and almost 2,300 irreplaceable aviators.

The United States lost two carriers, and about as many other combat ships as the Japanese, many of them in the waters between Guadalcanal and Savo Island, called Ironbottom Sound for the number of ships sunk there. What went unreported to the

American public was the loss of almost 5,000 sailors in some of the most savage naval fighting in history. With the war beginning to go well, not only in the South Pacific but also in North Africa and at Stalingrad, the Navy thought it prudent to suppress these horrific figures. While mourning the death of his friend Daniel Callaghan, Roosevelt announced that the "turning-point in this war has at last been reached." [10]

But before American seamen and airmen gained the upper hand in November, Marines and infantry on Guadalcanal fought a series of desperate survival battles in the malarial jungle and around the grassy perimeter of Henderson Field. Most of General Vandegrift's Marines were fresh-faced, poorly trained recruits who had enlisted right after Pearl Harbor. One of them was Paul Moore, Jr., just out of Yale College. Years later, in an interview, Moore described the making of a Marine on Guadalcanal:

> SOMEBODY TOLD ME about the Marine Corps. I knew so little about the Marine Corps that I thought it was just like the Navy except you had a prettier uniform. There was a young Marine Corps officer at Yale who drove around the campus with his blues on, in a convertible car with whitewall tires, and I thought he was the best thing I'd seen in a long time. I wanted to be just like him, so I enlisted in the Marine Corps.

Moore was sent to Quantico for basic training, and there, in his words, he made "a damned fool" of himself.

> I REMEMBER WRESTLING with a machine gun, trying to take it apart. It suddenly came apart and I hit myself in the forehead and blood streamed out of my head all over the classroom. The lieutenant turned around and said, "There's an example of a man who cannot follow orders." No sympathy. In any case, the first marking period I was tenth from the bottom of the class of four hundred and way below qualification level for an officer.
>
> I went in to the lieutenant and asked him what I could do about it. He just put his head in his hands, and then shook his head and said, "Moore, you just don't look like a Marine and you never will." . . . Luckily, we went out on the rifle range shortly after, and I did very well at rifle shooting. I'd had a little bit of experience. We used to do it in the Adirondacks. . . . So I did pass and qualify to get my commission.

After qualifying as a rifle platoon leader, Moore was sent to the Pacific with 5,000 other Marines in July 1942. They embarked on a converted ocean liner that Moore had recently sailed on, first class, on a European vacation. When they arrived in Wellington, New Zealand, the locals were happy to see them, but they had some concerns.

ALL OF THEIR YOUNG MEN were away fighting in the [North African] desert, and to have twenty thousand Marines piling into a rather old-fashioned Victorian English city, with all the young women there, I think made them a little nervous. Understandably! So we were given this very elaborate cultural lecture to deliver to our platoons about how conservative English society was. They said, "You never speak to a young woman in New Zealand, whoever she is, without being properly introduced. You don't go out without a chaperone." Well, we landed in New Zealand. I had duty so I didn't get off for about an hour. By the time I walked up the main street of Wellington, every Marine had a girl on his arm.

After a short training stint in New Zealand, Moore's company went to the Fiji Islands for maneuvers.

ALL WE HAD WAS ONE OR TWO DAYS in the Fiji Islands. Then we got back on board, and as we were steaming toward our next destination, they told us . . . our battalion was to join a Raider battalion [a battalion of Marines trained for difficult landings in the Pacific] and attack Tulagi, which was a small island across the gulf from Guadalcanal. The rest of the division disembarked on Guadalcanal.

As we went on our way we were protected by a few destroyers and a couple of cruisers, but each morning as we got up and looked across the sea, we'd see more and more naval vessels. It was the most incredible experience, to look out at these battleships, aircraft carriers, destroyers, cruisers—this enormous fleet of I suppose a hundred ships. It seemed like a thousand. It felt like the Greeks going to Troy. . . . You felt totally invincible.

There had been no attack by United States troops before this time. This was the first.

The night before the landing . . . we were anxious and excited and tense. Dawn broke. We got up in the darkness and got ready to go over the side. In those days you went down a sort of landing net, a webbing made out of stout rope which they would otherwise use to load cargo. They'd put these nets over the side and we'd use them as a rope ladder to go down into the Higgins boats . . . [small] wooden powerboats. Even with a fairly medium-sized sea the Higgins boat would go up and down and the ship would go up and down, and to try to get down that swaying cargo net with about eighty pounds of equipment on your back without killing yourself or getting jammed between the Higgins boat and the ship was quite a stunt. . . .

When the signal was given the Navy ensign in command of the Higgins boat would take off and the boats would go in a preordained pattern toward the beach. All during this time, from dawn on, the cruisers and destroyers had been shelling the shore. We'd never seen a shot fired in anger before, and we didn't see how any animal, much less any human being, could live under this enormous barrage.

Although resistance was strong on Tulagi, Moore did not see any combat. After two weeks, his company was sent across Ironbottom Sound to Guadalcanal. On landing, he was told his best friend from college was one of the first Marines killed on the island.

OUR OUTFIT WAS ON THE MOVE all the time—first we were moved over to Henderson Field, and then within a few days there was a counterattack by those Japanese who were still there, on so-called Bloody Ridge, where a Raider battalion [led by Lieutenant Colonel Merritt "Red Mike" Edson] was dug in. It was the first big battle of Guadalcanal itself, and our troops resisted it, but the Japs almost broke through to Henderson Field and so our battalion was rushed up the second night to support this unit.

One thing I noticed was the relationship between being in one place and emotional stability. . . . We were always on the move. We never had a chance to really make our foxhole our home. If a Marine can dig his foxhole, and dig out a little shelf for his canteen and another little shelf to put a photograph of his girl-friend on, have a little shelter of palm trees to keep the sun off, and make a little home for himself, it makes a tremendous difference to his emotional stability. . . .

The second night the Japanese . . . attack[ed] again and we were thrown into combat, which merely amounted to holding the line against some fairly light Japanese fire. . . . The strange thing was that after the battle was over, one of my men flipped and went into total hysterics, screaming and yelling in the middle of the night. . . . I didn't know whether a Japanese had snuck through the wire and knifed him to death or what. It turned out this guy went absolutely out of his mind. . . .

This kind of thing happened all the time. . . . I had three or four men who went crazy in my platoon, which was 15 percent . . . and this was true of the other platoons in my company. . . . And though it was not a scientific experiment, it seemed to me there was a direct relationship between this and the fact that we were moving all the time.

After Bloody Ridge we were put into another emplacement at the other end of the line. . . .

I was in one of the battles at the Matanikau River. It was a jungle river about two hundred yards wide where it emptied into the bay. The Matanikau was outside of our lines, and for a long time there was sort of a seesaw between the Japanese troops and our own—sometimes the Matanikau was ours, sometimes it was theirs. So from time to time troops would be sent out to try to secure the river. I went out there on patrol, coming at it from inland with our company. I was responsible for leading seven hundred men single file through this impenetrable jungle, with machetes and a compass. . . . When we got within maybe a tenth of a mile of the coast, we heard this battle going on. . . . Another unit had gone up the beach, tried to cross the Matanikau, and was being thrown back by the Japanese.

Lieutenant Colonel Lewis "Chesty" Puller [perhaps the most renowned Marine combat leader of the war] was in charge of this operation, and his tactics were to send one platoon after another across a totally exposed sandspit which closed off one end of the river. . . . The order given to each of these platoons was to run across the sandspit until they were opposite the bank, wade across the river, and attack the Japanese battalion, which was dug in with automatic weapons and hand grenades and mortars in the bank. . . . Well, one platoon went over and got annihilated. Another platoon went over and got annihilated. Then another. We were lined up just behind the shore, ready to go. Ours was the fifth platoon to go over, and you know, we all realized it was insane. We heard what had happened to the other platoons. But if you're a Marine, you're ordered across the goddamn beach and you go. So we went . . . zigzagging and running as best we could so that we wouldn't be exposed, and finally we lined up along the ocean side of the sandspit, just peeking over the top, with our weapons trained on the embankment across this little river. . . . The intelligence was that we could wade across. Well, our two scouts went out and found the water over their heads. . . .

Art Beres, one of my corporals, got to the opposite bank. I remember him holding on to a root, with the bank about a foot over him, and when he turned around I saw his whole face had been shot away. Two other guys had been killed at that particular moment, and I went across to get Art. . . . He was swimming. But by that time I'd called for us to attack (even though we were swimming we were told to attack, so we attacked). First of all I retrieved Art . . . and got him back so that he could get behind the sandspit and be protected until he could be taken to the aid station. Then I turned around to continue swimming across the

CROSSING THE MATANIKAU RIVER (USMC).

river with the rest of my platoon, and I remember—this sounds absolutely impossible but it actually happened—looking up and seeing mortars and hand grenades going over my head and the water as if it were raining, with bullets striking all around us.

I guess we got almost to the opposite bank and at that point realized two or three people had been killed, two or three others wounded, and there was just no way we could do it, so I called for retreat. We . . . swam back, and when we got to the bank I found two men who were unconscious on the beach. I and another fellow looked to see how they were and found out both of them were dead. So we just left them there and ran back to the protection of the sandspit.

I remember when I was leaning over trying to bring one of my men to safety seeing bullet marks in the sand around my feet and thinking, you know, if I get out of this, maybe it means I should do something special. . . . I don't know . . . whether it's superstition or what, but certainly I felt that I had been extremely fortunate, and that I was, in a sense, living on borrowed time, and that this was another good reason to give my life to the Lord, and it seemed that being a priest was that way.

Four years after the war Moore was ordained a priest in the Episcopal Church. In 1972 he was installed as thirteenth bishop of New York.

WHEN I GOT BACK, I asked if I could see Colonel Puller, to report to him what had happened. I wasn't particularly proud of the fact that we had retreated, but it seemed to be the necessary thing to do. Otherwise we would all have been killed and the emplacement still would not have been taken. I can still see him. He had a fat belly. He was sitting under a coconut tree. . . . I saluted and told him . . . what had happened, what I saw of the Japanese emplacement. He not only didn't answer me, he didn't even turn his head to speak to me. It's as if I hadn't been there. After a while I just left.

We did not get across the Matanikau River at that point. We fell back to our lines on the perimeter of the airfield. . . .

We took off the next morning and went up again to the Matanikau River, but this time we went across way up in the headwaters where there wasn't any resistance. . . .

Morale was very bad. But there was something about Marines—once we were ordered to attack we decided we damn well were going to do it . . . You're very nervous before you go in, of course, like before a football game . . . But once you get in it . . . your psyche gets sort of numbed, and therefore you can do acts of bravery, so-called, without necessarily having to be very brave. You just do them because in the excitement of combat you see this is the thing you're supposed to do, and you do it. It isn't making a decision that requires an enormous amount of courage. . . . Also, once you get into the excitement of the action you tend to forget about being vulnerable. When the machine-gun nest needed to have a hand grenade, I got up and threw the hand grenade, without timidity, though obviously it made me very vulnerable. I'm fairly tall even on my knees, and I got up and threw it, and as I threw it, got shot.

I received the Navy Cross for that, my part in that operation. But it really wasn't any great act of bravery. Some of the more extraordinary heroic actions that take place in combat, I think, are understandable. You read about them and say, "Oh my God, I would never do that!" But when you get in combat you do it without thinking too much about it. You do it automatically. And the flip side of the coin is brutality, the imperviousness to killing other people, even brutally; some of the people, I think, become sort of sadistic. Also the act of being fairly impervious to the death of your colleagues—not that you don't regret it, and not that you aren't trying to prevent it and care for them, but you don't burst into tears when you see this guy you've worked with for a few months lying there dead. "So he's dead. I wonder who I'll get to replace him, to take his place on the line?"

To get back to the Matanikau. . . . Although I was shot I was not unconscious. The bullet . . . came through my chest between two ribs, slightly shattering them, went past my heart, as the doctors later told me, when it must have been on an inbeat instead of an outbeat, and then missed my backbone as it went through the other side of my body about an inch. So it was a very close shave. . . . The air was going in and out of a hole in my lungs. That didn't mean I was finished, but I thought I was dead, going to die right then. . . . I wasn't breathing through my mouth but through this hole. I felt like a balloon going in and out, going *pshhhh*.

I was thinking to myself: now I'm going to die. And first of all it's rather absurd for me, considering where I came from, my early expectations of a comfortable life and all the rest, for me to be dying on a jungle island in combat as a Marine. That's not me. . . .

Shortly, a wonderful corpsman crawled up and gave me a shot of morphine, and then a couple of other people got a stretcher and started evacuating me.

... At Henderson Field they had deep dugouts for the wounded. I spent the night in a dugout, then the next day I was flown out. That night I'll never forget, because in this dugout, which I remember was about ten feet deep and about twenty feet square, the wounded were packed just like sardines, and it was terribly hot, there was bad ventilation, terrible smells, and these poor guys were yelling and screaming all night. That was a real horror story. The next morning a plane was able to get in, and they put us aboard and flew us back to Espíritu Santo, a Navy medical hospital.[11]

From there, Moore was taken on the hospital ship USS *Solace* to Auckland, New Zealand.

One problem that historians have in re-creating the past is that their readers know how it will turn out, so events often seem inevitable. But they are not. An Allied victory in World War II was not preordained; nor was an American victory at Guadalcanal. "If our ships and planes had been routed in . . . [the Naval Battle of Guadalcanal], if we had lost it, our troops on Guadalcanal would have been trapped as were our troops on Bataan," Admiral Bull Halsey wrote later. "We could not have reinforced them or relieved them. Archie Vandegrift would have been our 'Skinny' Wainwright and the infamous Death March would have been repeated. (We later captured a document which designated the spot where the Japanese commander had planned to accept Archie's surrender.) Unobstructed, the enemy would have driven south, cut our supply lines to New Zealand and Australia and enveloped them."[12]

Halsey and the Navy deserve much of the credit for driving the Japanese from Guadalcanal. But, in the end, it came down to the men on the ground. They fought two enemies: the jungle and the Japanese. In that dense and unfathomable jungle, a friend of Paul Moore's was shot by one of his own men when his part of the line got lost and doubled back without realizing it. In total darkness, the men would hear "strange jungle noises for the first time," Moore recalls. "Whether these were birds squawking in the middle of the night or some strange reptiles or frogs, I don't know, but we were terrified by any noise whatsoever because we'd been told that the Japanese signaled each other in the jungle by imitating bird calls. So we knew we were being surrounded by them, and once in a while our men would fire. We lost two or three men in the company by that kind of tragic mistake."[15] Other companies suffered losses under similar circumstances. "We were not fully prepared for the mysteries of those jungles," says Guadalcanal veteran Carl Hoffman.

The enemy was the other surprise. Before the war, "our instructors . . . used to joke about the fact that the [near-sighted] Japanese couldn't hit anything on the rifle range," Hoffman remembers. "When we got [to Guadalcanal] we realized that we'd been too quick to write off these little men." They were "courageous, bright, and tenacious . . . and [they] could fire [their] weapons pretty well." [14]

Then there was the way they fought: with fanatical courage, tearing out of jungle hideaways in the black of night on screaming banzai charges. Their suicidal bravery was incomprehensible to American troops, and their adeptness at jungle warfare was positively frightening even though they had not been trained to fight in the jungles of the South Pacific. "They take to the jungle as if they have been bred there," wrote reporter John Hersey. [15] This led some American troops to believe that "the enemy isn't truly human but a furtive jungle animal," a Marine remembered. [16] "I wish we were fighting against Germans," said another Marine. "They are human beings, like us. . . . But the Japanese are like animals." [17]

The Japanese were also treacherous, unfair fighters, in the eyes of the American soldiers. Their wounded would feign death and then pull out grenades and try to kill men who were taking them prisoner.

Most frightening of all was the way the Japanese treated their prisoners. Early in the fighting, a report swept through the American camp of the beheading of several Marine captives. In his novel *The Thin Red Line*, James Jones probes the reaction of raw recruits to such enemy atrocities.

"A cold knifing terror in the belly was followed immediately by a rage of anger. . . . There was a storm of promises never to take a . . . prisoner. Many swore they would henceforth coolly and in cold blood shoot down every Japanese who came their way, and preferably in the guts." [18]

Beginning at Guadalcanal, the war in the Pacific would be a war without quarter. Prisoners were rarely taken and atrocities were answered in kind. Marine Donald Fall tells of the moral reversal that began to occur: "On the second day on Guadalcanal we captured a big Jap bivouac [and] found a lot of pictures of Marines that had been cut up and mutilated on Wake Island. The next thing you know there are Marines walking around with Jap ears stuck on their belts with safety pins. . . . We began to get down to their level." [19]

Or as Guadalcanal veteran Ore Marion put it:

WE LEARNED ABOUT SAVAGERY from the Japanese. Those bastards had years of on-the-job training. But those sixteen-to-nineteen-year-old kids we had on the Canal were fast learners. Example: on the Matanikau River bank after a day and night of vicious hand-to-hand attacks, a number of Japs and our guys were killed and wounded. At daybreak, a couple of our kids, bearded, dirty, skinny from hunger, slightly wounded by bayonets, clothes worn and torn, whack off three Jap heads and jam them on poles facing the "Jap side" of the river. . . . Shortly after, the regimental commander comes on the scene. . . . The colonel sees the Jap heads on the poles and says, 'Jesus, men, what are you doing? You're acting like animals.' A dirty, stinking young kid says, 'That's right, Colonel, we are animals. We live like animals, we eat and are treated like animals, what the fuck do you expect.'[20]

Marines were told that mutilation was a court-martial offense, but it was hard to take that order seriously when Admiral Halsey was constructing billboards all over the Solomons with this simple message: "Kill Japs, kill Japs, kill more Japs."

In his history of World War II, novelist James Jones claims that the great question of 1942 was: "Did we have the kind of men who could stand up eyeball to eyeball and whip the Japs." America was "a peace-loving nation, had been anti soldiering and soldiers since the end of World War I. And we were taking on not only the Japs in the Far East, but the Germans in Europe as well. The Japanese with their warrior code of the bushi, had been in active combat warfare for ten years; the Germans almost as long. Could we evolve a soldier, a *civilian* soldier, who could meet them man to man in the field? . . . Not everyone was sure."[21]

This was the significance of Guadalcanal. In its green vastness, American boys evolved into the gritty island fighters who were needed to turn back the equally tough Japanese. In two furious night attacks on the Henderson Field, one in September, the other in October, the Japanese were thrown back in hellish fighting at bayonet range. In the first attack, Red Mike Edson and 700 Marines, including Paul Moore, held off 3,000 attacking Japanese troops for two nights on a small ridge in front of the airport. When dawn broke on the 14th of September, over a thousand Japanese dead and wounded lay in heaps on the blasted slopes that ran up what the Marines would call Edson's Ridge, or Bloody Ridge.

Bloody Ridge caused both sides to bolster reinforcements and on October 25, Chesty Puller and a force of Marines and Army infantry made an equally epic stand on the ridge, in darkness and driving rain. In this all-out attack, the Japanese lost over 3,500 elite troops and any chance of taking Henderson Field and Guadalcanal.

After the September raid, reporter Richard Tregaskis, author of the now classic

Guadalcanal Diary, hurried to Red Mike Edson's headquarters to get his story of the battle. "He told us about the individual exploits of his men and their collective bravery, but did not mention the fact that he himself had spent the night on the very front line of the knoll, under the heaviest fire.

"He did not mention it, but the fact was that two bullets had actually ripped through his blouse, without touching him."

Edson and his officers "told us some good stories of valor," Tregaskis wrote. "The outstanding one was Lewis E. Johnson's." He was hit three times in the leg, and "at daybreak placed in the rear of a truck with about a dozen other wounded, for evacuation. But as the truck moved down the ridge road, a Jap machine gunner opened up and wounded the driver severely. The truck stopped." Johnson dragged himself into the cab and tried to start the engine. When it wouldn't start, he "pulled the truck a distance of about 300 yards over the crest of the ridge. Then he got the engine going and drove to the hospital."

Feeling revived, he drove back to the ridge and picked up another load of wounded Marines.

Days later, over breakfast, Major Kenneth Bailey, one of the heroes of the ridge, said something to Tregaskis about taking chances in combat. "You get to know these kids so well when you're working with 'em . . . and they're such swell kids that when it comes to a job that's pretty rugged, you'd rather go yourself than send them." [22]

Bailey was killed three days later.

At Guadalcanal, Bailey's boys "fought bravely and better than the enemy," wrote John Hersey. "They had shown themselves to be men, with the strength and weaknesses of men. That had given me, an unprofessional onlooker, a new faith in our chances of winning the war in the visible future." [23]

What turned "kids" like Paul Moore and James Jones into fighting machines? For Jones, it was the acceptance that you were going to die, that you were "written down in the rolls of the already dead." Only when a soldier makes "a compact with himself or with Fate that he is lost" can he fully function under fire. Then he has "nothing further to worry about."

Yet strangely the "giving up of hope" creates a compensatory kind of hope, Jones adds. "Little things become significant. The next meal, the next bottle of booze, the next kiss, the next sunrise, the next full moon. The next bath."

When you know you're going to die, "every day has a special, bright, delicious, poignant taste to it that normal days in normal times do not have. Another perversity of the human mechanism?" [24]

In December, the 1st Marine Division left Guadalcanal. Although they had been reinforced earlier by Army units, they had done most of the fighting up to then and the men were tired, sick, and emotionally drained. Many of them had malaria and most of them had dysentery but they had been told that no one would be pulled off the line unless he was a litter case.

By the time General Vandegrift turned over command at Guadalcanal to Army General Alexander M. Patch, the Japanese high command had decided that Guadalcanal was a lost cause. Many of its soldiers on the island were so undernourished and racked by jungle diseases that their hair and nails had ceased to grow. In the next two months, infantry soldiers and remaining Marines began a great push westward from Henderson Field that ended when over 11,000 Japanese troops were evacuated by destroyer convoys at Cape Esperance, a Pacific Dunkirk. On February 9, General Patch sent a radio message to Admiral Halsey: "Tokyo Express no longer has terminus on Guadalcanal."

Approximately 60,000 Army and Marine Corps ground forces fought on Guadalcanal. Almost 1,600 were killed in combat. Over 4,700 were wounded and twice that number were evacuated after being struck down by jungle diseases or battle psychosis. The Japanese lost close to 25,000 men.

Samuel Stavisky, a reporter for the *Washington Post*, was there for the "mop-up," when worn-down American troops went into jungle hellholes to hunt down the diehard Japanese who had not been able to get off the island and refused to surrender. "Killed all the yellow slant-eyed bastards," a Marine announced to no one in particular as he emerged with his death squad from a growth-covered gorge. He said it matter-of-factly, almost wearily, for he and his fellow Marines were too tired and sick to feel any elation in victory. Just then, Stavisky saw "four skinny, starved, wounded, and unconscious Japs . . . dragged out. The rest were dead: shot, bayoneted, blasted by grenades. Rooted out. Grubbed out. Rubbed out."

"It's over guys," the lieutenant told his men.[25]

It was for them, that day, in that place, on that island. But in stopping the Japanese juggernaut at Guadalcanal, these never-to-be-the-same boys had committed themselves and their country to the greatest reoccupation effort in history.

Great battles, said Winston Churchill, are those that "won or lost, change the entire course of events, create new standards of values, new moods, new atmospheres in armies and in nations."[26] That was Guadalcanal.

ANONYMITY

Two weeks after an infantry fight on Guadalcanal, James Jones was assigned to Grave Registration detail. His unit was ordered to go up into the hills and dig up the bodies of dead comrades:

"The dead were from another regiment, so men from my outfit were picked to dig them up. That was how awful the detail was. And they did not want to make it worse by having men dig up the dead of their own. Unfortunately, a man in my outfit on the detail had a brother in the other outfit, and we dug up the man's brother that day."

As they dug up the bodies, the officer in charge told them to take one dog tag off each man before putting him into a body bag. It was awful work anyway, but these men had been dead for two weeks.

WHEN WE BEGAN TO DIG, each time we opened a hole a little explosion of smell would burst up out of it, until finally the whole saddle where we were working was covered with it up to about knee deep. Above the knees it wasn't so bad, but when you had to bend down to search for the dogtag (we took turns doing this) it was like diving down into another element, like water, or glue. We found about four bodies without dogtags that day.

"What will happen to those, sir?" I asked the lieutenant. . . .

"They will remain anonymous," he said.

"What about the ones with dogtags?" I asked.

"Well," he said, "they will be recorded."

As Jones wrote later, "To accept anonymity, along with all the rest he has to accept, is perhaps the toughest step of all for the combat soldier. . . . It is one of the hardest things about a soldier's life." [27]

NEW GUINEA

While the battle of Guadalcanal still raged, General MacArthur was fighting an equally ugly war of attrition in New Guinea. In September, after the Japanese failed to take Port Moresby in a forced march over the Owen Stanley Range, MacArthur's troops chased them back over these forbidding mountain jungles toward their bases at

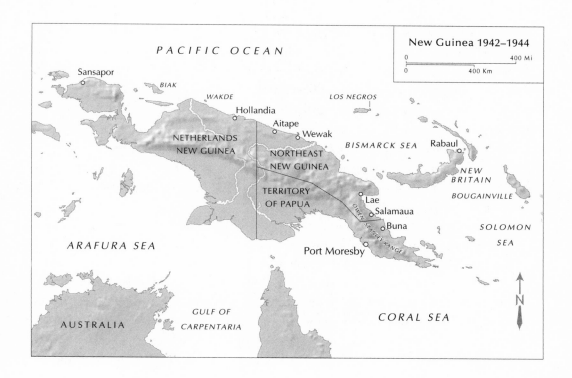

Buna and Gona on the north coast of New Guinea. The Australian correspondent George H. Johnston describes the road back over the rugged Kokoda Trail at the height of the rainy season. The Australians, with American support, led the advance.

I MAY BE WRONG, for I am no soothsayer, but I have an idea that the name of the "Kokoda Trail" is going to live in the minds of Australians for generations, just as another name, Gallipoli, lives on as freshly today, twenty-seven years after it first gained significance in Australian minds. For thousands of Australians who have walked the weary, sodden miles of this dreadful footpath—and these Australians are the fathers of the next generation—it will be the one memory more unforgettable than any other that life will give them. . . .

The weather is bad, the terrain unbelievably terrible, and the enemy is resisting with stubborn fury that is costing us many men and much time. Against the machine gun nests and mortar pits established on the ragged spurs and steep limestone ridges our advance each day now is measured in years. Our troops are fighting in the cold mists of an altitude of 6,700 feet, fighting viciously because they have only a mile or two to go before they reach the peak of the pass and will be able to attack downhill—down the *north* flank of the Owen Stanleys. That means a lot to troops who have climbed every inch of that agonizing track, who have buried so many of their cobbers and who have seen so many more going back, weak with sickness or mauled by the mortar bombs and the bullets and grenades of the enemy, men gone from their ranks simply to win back a few hundred yards of this wild, unfriendly, and utterly untamed mountain. . . .

Fresh troops are going up the track. . . . The men are bearded to the eyes. Their uniforms are hotch-potches of anything that fits or is warm or affords some protection from the insects. . . .

In the green half-light, amid the stink of rotten mud and rotting corpses, with the long line of green-clad Australians climbing wearily along the tunnel of the track, you have a noisome, unforgettable picture of the awful horror of this jungle war. . . .

The Japs have made their stand in the toughest area of the pass through the Owen Stanleys—a terrible terrain of thick mountain timber, great rocks drenched in rain, terrifying precipices and chasms. Often the troops have to make painfully slow progress by clawing with hands and feet at slippery rock faces overlooking sheer drops into the jungle. The almost constant rain or mist adds to the perils of sharp limestone ridges, narrow ledges flanked by chasms, slimy rocks, and masses of slow moving mud.

In this territory the Japanese are fighting, with a stubborn tenacity that is almost unbelievable, from an elaborate system of prepared positions along every ridge and spur. Churned up by the troops of both armies, the track itself is now knee deep in thick, black mud. For the last ten days no man's clothing has been dry and they have slept—when sleep was possible—in pouring rain under sodden blankets. Each man carries all his personal equipment, firearms, ammunition supply and five days' rations. Every hour is a nightmare. . . .

The Australians have reconquered the Owen Stanley Range. Today, on November 2 [1942], they marched into Kokoda unopposed, through lines of excited natives who brought them great baskets of fruit and decked them with flowers. . . .

Kokoda, "key to the Owen Stanleys," has been abandoned by the Japanese without a fight.[28]

The Allies trapped the Japanese at the coastal villages of Buna and Gona. The Americans under General Edwin F. Harding concentrated on Buna, while the

Australians moved against Gona. At Buna, the Japanese dug in behind massive cam-ouflaged bunkers, fronted by nearly impassable swamps. Under orders from MacArthur at Port Moresby, Harding's green, poorly trained infantry attacked repeat-edly and recklessly and were massacred. With the remaining troops near collapse from hunger, fever, and energy-sapping heat, a frustrated MacArthur replaced Harding with Lieutenant General Robert L. Eichelberger. "Bob, I want you to take Buna, or not come back alive," MacArthur told him.

When Eichelberger landed near Buna on December 1 the horrible stink of the coastal swamp told him that he and his army were "prisoners of geography. . . . We would never get out unless we fought our way out." The troops were "riddled with malaria, dengue fever, tropical dysentery, and were covered with jungle ulcers." But Eichelberger quickly found out that "sick men can fight." [29]

Eichelberger was an inspirational leader, but his men could never have held on without supplies flown in over the Owen Stanley Range by MacArthur's new Air Force chief, Major General George Kenney, one of the greatest air commanders of the war. On December 9, the Australians broke through and took Gona; then Eichelberger reopened the assault on Buna.

"It was a sly and sneaky kind of combat," Eichelberger wrote in his memoirs, "which never resembled the massive and thunderous operations in Europe, where tank battalions were pitted against tank battalions and armies the size of city populations ponderously moved and maneuvered. The Pacific was a different war. In New Guinea, when the rains came, wounded men might drown before the litter bearers found them. Many did. No war is a good war, and death ignores geography. But out here I was convinced, as were my soldiers, that death was pleasanter in the Temperate Zone."[30]

In jungle fighting, troops didn't bother to build elaborate trenches; the daily rains would have filled them up. And the fighting was "informal," reported *Yank* correspondent Sergeant Dave Richardson:

> WHEN AMERICANS, AUSTRALIANS, AND JAPS clash, no more than a few dozen men on either side are involved. There's none of that dramatic "over the top" stuff here. Patrols go out every day to feel out the Jap pillboxes and strong points. Then stronger forces come in to knock them out, supported by mortar and light artillery.
>
> When the pillboxes and machine-gun nests are gone, more Yanks and Aussies come in to mop up the snipers and occupy the area.
>
> The Yanks, most of them from Wisconsin's thickly wooded country, are beating the Japs with tactics borrowed from America's original fighting men—the Indians. These tactics involve swift, silent movement, sudden thrusts out of jungles. The rifle is the basic weapon.[31]

The last fighting around Buna took place in torrential rains that prevented the Japanese from burying their dead. The stench of decomposing bodies stacked in heaps just outside the Japanese lines was overwhelming. "We wondered," said a combat reporter, "how the live Japs had borne it until we discovered they were wearing gas masks as protection against their own dead."[32]

On January 2, 1943, Buna fell. The cost of the campaign was high for both sides. The Americans suffered 3,000 casualties and almost three times as many men were treated for serious diseases. Japanese and Australian losses were horrifying: 21,000 Australians troops killed, wounded, or treated for disease; 13,000 Japanese killed.

Eichelberger attributed the victory to sheer stubbornness. "The Japanese morale cracked before ours did."[33] But it cracked only because the besieged enemy ran out of food.

The diaries of Japanese soldiers found in the enemy's bunkers and dugouts record the grinding attrition of the battle and slowly changing Japanese perceptions of the American combat soldier. These excerpts, taken from several diaries, follow chronologically the progress of the siege:

THE ENEMY HAS RECEIVED almost no training. Even though we fire a shot they present a large portion of their body and look around. Their movements are very slow.

The enemy has been repulsed by our keen-eyed snipers. In the jungle it seems they fire at any sound, due to illusion. From sundown until about 10 P.M. they fire light machine guns and throw hand grenades recklessly.

The enemy has become considerably more accurate in firing.

The nature of the enemy is superior and they excel in firing techniques.

Artillery raking the area. We cannot hold out much longer. Our nerves are strained; there is a lack of sleep due to the continuous shelling.

Mess gear is gone because of the terrific mortar fire. Everyone is depressed. Nothing we can do. It is only fate that I am alive today. This may be the place where I shall find my death. I will fight to the last.

Now we are waiting only for death. . . . Can't anything be done? Please God."[34]

In the final stages of the siege, the hemmed-in Japanese ate the flesh of dead enemy soldiers. When hope ran out, they attacked and died rather than surrender. As an Australian reporter wrote: The battle had to be fought until there was "not one Japanese left who was capable of lifting a rifle."[35]

Eichelberger had done the impossible, but MacArthur took credit for the victory, even though he had never left his headquarters in Port Moresby, forty minutes away by air. After Buna was taken, Eichelberger wrote with unconcealed wrath: "The great hero went home [to Australia] without seeing Buna before, during, or after the fight while permitting press articles from his GHQ to say he was leading his troops in battle." After the war, MacArthur approached Eichelberger and said, "Bob, those were great days when you and I were fighting at Buna, weren't they?" Eichelberger took this as "a warning not to disclose that he never went to Buna."[36]

Coming just a month before the Japanese evacuation of Guadalcanal, Buna was the first great victory by American ground forces in the Pacific, and it gave Kenney air bases from which to attack Japanese strongholds in the region. Guadalcanal would be a defensive victory; this was an offensive strike, the beginning of what the troops called "The Hard Way Back."

For MacArthur, the victory had personal meaning. "The dead of Bataan will rest easier tonight," he told reporters after Buna fell. [37]

INVASION!

In the summer of 1942, while MacArthur was just beginning to plan his New Guinea campaign, Roosevelt and Churchill had decided to invade French North Africa. This was a controversial and hotly contested move. It meant postponing a cross-Channel attack against Hitler's Fortress Europe, the "second front" that both Stalin and top American military planners favored. Churchill thought an invasion of northern France was premature and, using all his persuasive powers, convinced a vacillating Roosevelt. Churchill was right. An adequate invasion fleet had not yet been built, German U-boats were inflicting heavy damage on Atlantic convoys headed for England, and the Luftwaffe still patrolled the skies over Northern France. But Stalin was incensed and so was Roosevelt's chief military advisor, General George C. Marshall, who feared the war might be lost unless a second front was established to take pressure off the beleaguered Russians, who were then—before their great victory at Stalingrad—being pushed back by the Germans to their inner defenses. But with congressional elections coming up in November, Roosevelt was under tremendous political pressure to get American ground forces in action against the Germans as soon as possible. And North Africa, with British assistance, was the only place the still-mobilizing Americans were strong enough to take on the German war machine.

Command of Operation Torch was given to Lieutenant General Dwight D. Eisenhower, a Marshall protégé who had originally sided with his chief against the plan. It was the first battle command of his long Army career, and it involved a complete revision of America's planning priorities. A great part of the Atlantic convoy system had to be diverted from England and Russia to the Mediterranean; three American divisions that had been shipped to England had to re-shipped south; hundreds of thousands of troops trained for combat in Western Europe had to be retrained for mountain and desert warfare; and the most delicate diplomatic and secret services negotiations had to be conducted, for the landings would take place on French soil, and

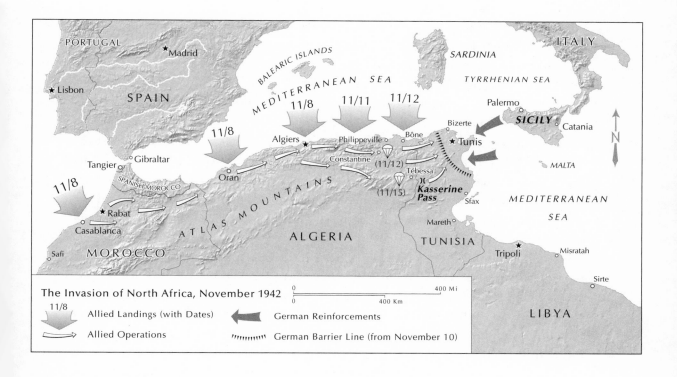

The Invasion of North Africa, November 1942

11/8 Allied Landings (with Dates)

Allied Operations

German Reinforcements

German Barrier Line (from November 10)

no one knew if the French would contest them. Hitler had not occupied a great part of France on the understanding that the Vichy government would defend its colonial empire against the Allies.

On October 24, 1942, as Montgomery broke through the Afrika Korps at El Alamein, a vast troop convoy set sail from American ports to North Africa. The next day two other convoys sailed from Britain. At 3:00 A.M. on November 8, 1942, 85 cargo and war ships converged, with machinelike precision, on their main objectives. An American force landed at Casablanca, on the Atlantic coast of Morocco, and two other task forces made up of British and American troops landed at Oran and Algiers on the Mediterranean coast of Algeria. Altogether, 65,000 troops were put ashore. In a gigantic pincer movement, they would pressure Axis troops from the west while General Montgomery's British Eighth Army came at them from the east. Strenuous efforts had been made to win over the Vichy government, for ultimate success depended in large part upon the speed with which the Allies would get from Morocco and Algeria to Tunisia, to secure it before the Germans did.

But diplomatic negotiations with the French broke down, and the Allies encountered stiff resistance from French colonial troops, especially near Casablanca, where General George S. Patton's Western Task Force went ashore. Resistance might have been prolonged to the point where it imperiled the success of the expedition, but on November 11, Admiral Jean Darlan, a notorious Nazi collaborator and commander-in-chief of Vichy's armed forces, ordered a cease fire, in a sordid deal that gave him Allied recognition as high commissioner for French North Africa. With Darlan's capitulation went not only undisputed control of Morocco and Algeria, but the whole of French West Africa.

The Allies then raced forward through Algiers toward the Tunisian border, hoping to capture the ports of Bizerte and Tunis before the Germans could smash them from the air or rush over enough reinforcements to hold them. The Nazi reaction was swift. Strong forces seized the Tunisian ports, and transport planes brought over thousands of reinforcements from Sicily and Italy, while other thousands were ferried over from southern France. These reinforcements allowed the Axis to consolidate their hold on Tunisia and stop the Allied offensive out of Algeria. While the Axis armies prepared their defenses in the rugged mountains of Tunisia, Hitler ordered the immediate military occupation of the rest of France, and Churchill and Roosevelt, together with high-ranking officers of the Allied armies, met for ten days at Casablanca to plan future military operations.

At Casablanca Marshall continued to push for a 1943 invasion of Northwest Europe, but Britain was still the stronger of the two partners, and Churchill called the shots. The next offensive, it was decided over Marshall's objections, would be in the Mediterranean the following summer, probably against Sicily, and as a concession to the Americans, a larger percentage of the war effort was to be allocated to the Pacific theater. At a press conference at the conclusion of the meetings, Roosevelt sprung a surprise, announcing that the Allies would demand nothing less from the Axis powers than "unconditional surrender." It was apparently a spontaneous statement, but Churchill immediately endorsed it, for the two leaders had recently discussed the idea. This meant nothing at the time, as it was made from a position of military weakness, but it was to have huge consequences later in the war when a fully mobilized America had the unrivaled power to back up its bellicose language.

As Roosevelt flew home from Casablanca, his major concern was how the untested, hastily trained American troops would perform in their first test against the Desert Fox, the most feared field commander of the war. Rommel had recently arrived in Tunisia from El Alamein with his retreating but still formidable Afrika Korps to reinforce General Jurgen von Arnim, commander of the divisions that Hitler had rushed to Tunisia after the Anglo-American landing. The two opponents were now

U.S. ARMORED CAR PASSES DESTROYED AFRIKA
KORPS TANK IN TUNISIA (SC).

more nearly equalized. Yet the Germans realized that time fought on the side of the Allies, whose air campaign against their convoys and air transports moving from Sicily to North Africa was devastatingly effective. Rommel decided to strike, choosing as his target the weak American II Corps, commanded by the irresolute Major General Lloyd Fredendall. The blow came on February 14, with a powerful armored thrust, supported by mobile artillery and screaming Stuka dive-bombers. After throwing back two American counterattacks, the Nazis poured through the Kasserine Pass, their massive tanks tearing through the lighter American Shermans. Then Rommel turned north, toward the town of Tebessa, threatening to cut the Allied armies in two. For four days, fighting raged back and forth. Two American infantry divisions raced eastward from Oran in one of the most spectacular forced marches of the war; Allied planes flew thousands of sorties; powerful new Churchill tanks joined the American Shermans to hold off the enemy. By February 25 Rommel acknowledged defeat and fell back through Kasserine Pass to defensive positions. He had lost a thousand men but left 6,000 American dead or wounded.

Death of an Army

George Patton was then given command of II Corps, with General Omar Bradley as his deputy. Patton performed a minor miracle, turning it, with his élan and driving discipline into a crack desert fighting force. Now Montgomery from the south, and Patton from the north, closed in for the kill. Realizing the desperateness of his position, Rommel, always an offensive fighter, hurled himself at the Eighth Army in a series of uncoordinated attacks that were bloodily repulsed. Two weeks later, on March 21, Montgomery took the offensive. In a brilliant operation, reminiscent of Robert E. Lee's at Second Manassas, he sent his Northumbrian Division on a frontal attack against the Mareth Line and his New Zealand division on a wide sweep around its southern flank to strike from the rear. Threatened by encirclement, the Axis forces abandoned the Mareth Line and retreated toward Cape Bon. By this time, Rommel had returned to Germany, too ill to continue in the field.

Then began the great push that ended in the annihilation of the Axis forces. Patton's II Corps and the British First Army fought their way from one mountain range to another, while from the south the Eighth Army and the Free French LXI Corps pushed toward Cape Bon. The hardest fighting came at Hill 609, dominating Mateur, which the Americans captured on May 1. On May 7, the British First Army broke through to Tunis. That same day, at almost the same hour, the Americans entered the port of Bizerte. On May 3, the Axis armies surrendered.

At a cost of some 70,000 casualties the Allies had captured 266,000 and killed or wounded another 60,000 enemy soldiers. All Africa was now cleansed of the Axis stain and restored to Allied control. The danger of Spanish intervention was past. The Suez was safe. The Near East was secure. And Italy, the southern flank of the Axis, was in mortal danger.

North Africa had been a testing ground for American troops and although they did not do well at first, at Hill 609 in Tunisia they performed with valor. "The capture of the formidable 609," wrote General Eisenhower, "was final proof that the American ground forces had come fully of age."[38]

Ernie Pyle was with the American Army in Tunisia. He wrote this before the Axis surrender.

WE'RE NOW WITH AN INFANTRY OUTFIT that has battled ceaselessly for four days and nights.

This northern warfare has been in the mountains. You don't ride much any more. It is walking and climbing and crawling country. The mountains aren't big, but they are constant. They are largely treeless. They are easy to defend and bitter to take. But we are taking them.

The Germans lie on the back slope of every ridge, deeply dug into foxholes. In front of them the fields and pastures are hideous with thousands of hidden mines. The forward slopes are left open, untenanted, and if the Americans tried to scale these slopes they would be murdered wholesale in an inferno of machine-gun crossfire plus mortars and grenades.

Consequently we don't do it that way. We have fallen back to the old warfare of first pulverizing the enemy with artillery, then sweeping around the ends of the hill with infantry and taking them from the sides and behind. . . .

Our artillery has really been sensational. . . .

All the guns in any one sector can be centered to shoot at one spot. And when we lay the whole business on a German hill the whole slope seems to erupt. It becomes an unbelievable cauldron of fire and smoke and dirt. Veteran German soldiers say they have never been through anything like it.

Now to the infantry—the God-damned infantry, as they like to call themselves. I love the infantry because they are the underdogs. They are the mud-rain-frost-and-wind boys. They have no comforts, and they even learn to live without the necessities. And in the end they are the guys that wars can't be won without.

I wish you could see just one of the ineradicable pictures I have in my mind today. In this particular picture I am sitting among clumps of sword-grass on a steep and rocky hillside that we have just taken. We are looking out over a vast rolling country to the rear.

A narrow path comes like a ribbon over a hill miles away, down a long slope, across a creek, up a slope and over another hill.

All along the length of this ribbon there is now a thin line of men. For four days and nights they have fought hard, eaten little, washed none, and slept hardly at all. Their nights have been violent with attack, fright, butchery, and their days sleepless and miserable with the crash of artillery.

The men are walking. They are fifty feet apart, for dispersal. Their walk is slow, for they are dead weary, as you can tell even when looking at them from behind. Every line and sag of their bodies speaks their inhuman exhaustion.

On their shoulders and backs they carry heavy steel tripods, machine-gun barrels, leaden boxes of ammunition. Their feet seem to sink into the ground from the overload they are bearing.

They don't slouch. It is the terrible deliberation of each step that spells out their appalling tiredness. Their faces are black and unshaven. They are young men, but the grime and whiskers and exhaustion make them look middle-aged.

In their eyes as they pass is not hatred, not excitement, not despair, not the tonic of their victory—there is just the simple expression of being here as though they had been here doing this forever, and nothing else.

The line moves on, but it never ends. All afternoon men keep coming round the hill and vanishing eventually over the horizon. It is one long tired line of antlike men.

There is an agony in your heart and you almost feel ashamed to look at them. They are just guys from Broadway and Main Street, but you wouldn't remember them. They are too far away now. They are too tired. Their world can never be known to you, but if you could see them once, just for an instant, you would know that no matter how hard people work back home they are not keeping pace with these infantrymen in Tunisia.[39]

In a dispatch he filed just after Tunisia was won, Pyle wrote that there were days when he sat alone in his tent "and gloomed with the desperate belief that it was actually possible for us to lose this war." The home front didn't seem to be contributing with full energy and the raw GIs seemed no match for the battle-hardened Germans. But then American production went into high gear. The world's greatest automobile society stopped making cars and transformed its auto plants into production machines for the making of every imaginable instrument of mobile warfare—tanks and planes and mobile artillery that Eisenhower and Patton began using in the North African desert with devastating effect. And after going through "hill-by-hill butchery" the GIs became calloused, hard-cursing warriors whom their folks back home would hardly have recognized. "Apparently it takes a country like America about two years to become wholly at war," Pyle wrote. "We had to go through that transition period of letting loose of life as it was, and then live the new war life so long that it finally became the normal life to us." America had finally become "a war nation." While Pyle was not sure how it would happen or how long it would take, "no longer do I have any doubts at all that we shall win."

On Guadalcanal, John Hersey had come to the same conclusion. Neither reporter, however, could give his readers the "Big Picture." Living in the field with the men, theirs was the "worm's eye" view of war. "Our segment of the picture," Pyle observed, "consists only of tired and dirty soldiers who are alive and don't want to die; of long darkened convoys in the middle of the night; of shocked silent men wandering back down the hill from battle; of chow lines and atabrine tablets and foxholes and burning tanks . . . of jeeps and petrol dumps and smelly bedding rolls and C rations and cactus patches and blown bridges and dead mules and hospital tents and shirt collars greasy-black from months of wearing; and of laughter too, and anger and wine and lovely flowers and constant cussing. All these it is composed of; and of graves and graves and graves." [40]

Along with Guadalcanal and Buna, El Alamein and Stalingrad, Tunisia "clearly signified to friend and foe alike," Eisenhower wrote later, "that the Allied nations were at last upon the march." [41]

THE BATTLE OF THE ATLANTIC

Behind these ringing victories—making them possible—was victory in the greatest naval confrontation of the war, what Churchill called the Battle of the Atlantic. This was the mortal struggle to prevent German U-boats from severing the oceanic lifeline between Britain and her allies, as well her fighting forces around the world. "The Battle of the Atlantic," said Churchill, "was the dominating factor all through the war. Never for one moment could we forget that everything happening elsewhere, on land, at sea, or in the air, depended ultimately on its outcome." [42]

It was a fight for survival. A vulnerable island economy despite its prodigious industrial machine, Britain imported much of its nonferrous metal, one half of its food, and all of its oil. If blockaded successfully by the undersea fleet of Admiral Karl Doenitz, commander of the German submarine service, it would be starved into submission. Short of achieving economic strangulation, the blockage still threatened to cut off the shipment from Britain to Russia of vitally needed planes and tanks to stop the German invasion, of men and supplies to North Africa, and of wheat, oil, and engines of warfare from America to England. "The only thing that really frightened me during the war," Churchill said later, "was the U-boat peril." [43]

One month after Pearl Harbor, Germany extended the U-boat war to the shores of North America. Doenitz called it Operation Drumbeat, and the audacious plan worked to perfection, exposing America's vulnerability at a time when it was trying to stem the furious Japanese advance in the Pacific. Taking advantage of a pitifully unprepared United States Navy, five long-distance U-boats, captained by an equal number of Hitler's "aces," roamed almost at will from Canada to the Caribbean, slaughtering Allied shipping. They struck at night, on the surface, using both guns and torpedoes, and commanders like Reinhard Hardegen of U-123, the most skilled undersea fighters in the world, sank freighters and oil tankers with shocking ease. Many of these ships were put to the bottom within sight of shore because coastal cites like New York, Atlantic City, and Miami refused to impose a blackout, fearing a loss of their tourist trade. Their bright lights gave U-boat captains a perfect background to site and sink unescorted cargo carriers headed out of port. Ships were sunk and men died because Americans at home wanted to live life as usual.

The U-boat crews had not been told their destination until they were halfway across the Atlantic. Diving his boat to twenty meters and assembling most of the crew in the control room, Lieutenant Commander Hardegen addressed them. "Men, I have opened our Operation Order and reviewed it with the officers. We are going against America. Our first destination is New York. . . .

"The five boats will start attacking suddenly, all at once. . . . The element of surprise favors us. The state of readiness of the American defenses is a question mark. Our patrol area is from New York to Cape Hatteras, which is a much-trafficked area some four hundred miles south of New York. The harbor at New York where we will begin is one of the busiest, if not the busiest, in the world. We should not lack for targets."[44]

The maritime massacre began on January 12, 1942, when Hardegan jumped the gun and sank the British freighter *Cyclops* near Nantucket, the first of seven ships he would destroy in a week. As he moved down toward New York Harbor, he could see the lights atop the ferris wheel at Coney Island. Hardegan's submariners sank merchant

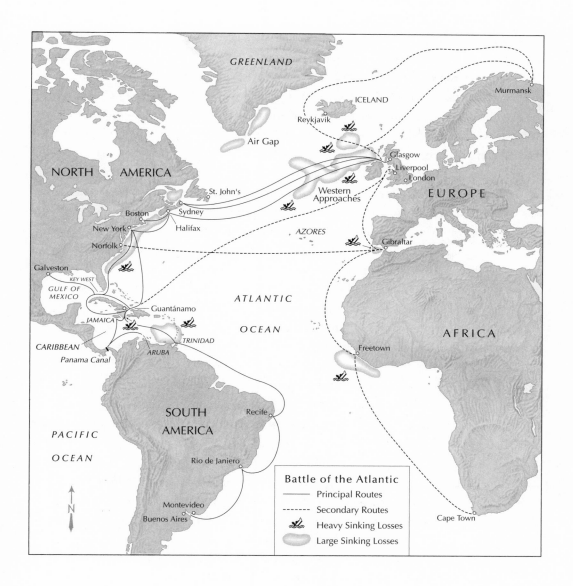

ships thirty miles offshore, here and all the way down to the Virginia Capes, three or more on some days. Passengers landing at airports in New York could see flaming wrecks from their windows, and in a rare daylight attack, bathers at Virginia Beach witnessed two U-boat kills right in front of them. "Our U-boats," Doenitz proudly told a German war correspondent, "are operating close inshore along the coast of the United States of America, so that bathers and sometimes entire coastal cities are witnesses to the drama of war, whose visual climaxes are constituted by the red glorioles of blazing tankers."[45]

When American patrols started to pick them up, the five U-boats—with seven additional boats, all of them armed with thirteen torpedoes—moved down the coast to Miami and then into the Caribbean, feasting on oil tankers sailing out of Venezuela. "The losses by submarines off our Atlantic seaboard and in the Caribbean now threaten our entire war effort," George Marshall wrote Admiral Ernest King, the American naval chief.[46] With a shortage of small ships and destroyers, King refused to form convoys, insisting—against the sound advice of the British—that a weak convoy was worse than no convoy. But under pressure from Marshall he finally established a convoy system in May and improved antisubmarine aviation. The number of sinkings dropped dramatically and Doenitz ordered his assault boats back into the Central Atlantic, where the Battle of the Atlantic had begun two years earlier.

In a mere six months, the German raiders sank nearly 400 ships in U.S. Navy–protected waters, a calamitous setback for the Allied cause. Officials in Washington calculated that the sinking of one freighter with a full cargo was the equivalent of the loss of goods carried on four railroad trains of seventy-five cars each.

Then there was the human cost of what one historian has called "The Atlantic Pearl Harbor."[47] As many as 5,000 Allied lives were lost in Operation Drumbeat, most of them merchant sailors. In the spring of 1942, merchant seamen had a higher likelihood of being killed than American troops trapped in the jungles of Bataan. And they died hideously—blown to pieces, frozen solid in icy Atlantic waters, or boiled at sea by oil fires that burned with raging force for miles around sunken tankers.

On February 2, 1942, the tanker *W. L. Steed*, hauling 65,000 barrels of oil, was eighty miles off the Delaware Capes, plowing through high seas and a driving snowstorm. On watch was Sydney Wayland, second mate. This is part of his report:

WITHOUT WARNING OF ANY KIND the ship was suddenly struck by a torpedo on her starboard side . . . setting the oil afire. . . .

The next thing I heard was the engine being stopped by the captain in the pilot house and the general alarm sounded. The master ordered me to get the two amidships boats ready for lowering.

Wayland carried out his orders and took fourteen other men with him in boat No. 2. He reported that all lifeboats cleared, but said he never saw any of the other men again.

HASTILY DUG GRAVE OF A U.S. MARINE (USMC).

WEATHER CONDITIONS WERE FIERCE, with the snowstorm and dangerous northwest seas running. Everyone in the boat was suffering from cold, due
mostly to lack of clothes.

The men in lifeboat No. 2 died one after another until February 5, when Chief
Mate Einar A. Nilsson and myself were the only ones alive.

On the morning of February 6, Nilsson showed signs of weakening and
extreme fatigue. At about 9:30 A.M. I sighted a steamer coming close to us and
made every effort, waving and hailing, to get her attention, as she seemed to go
past, but finally she hove around, headed for us, and picked us up.

Mr. Nilsson died the following morning.[48]

In the six months after Pearl Harbor, the casualty rate for merchant seamen was
three times greater than for any branch of the armed forces; and for the entire war,

only the Marines matched their casualty rate. In waterfront bars, mangled and badly burned men gathered for drinks with fellow sailors. The American journalist Helen Lawrenson, who was married to Jack Lawrenson, a leader in the National Maritime Union, wrote this account at the height of the "battle off the beaches."

A GROUP OF SAILORS are drinking beer at a bar called George's in Greenwich Village. The jukebox is playing "Deep in the Heart of Texas," and every time it stops someone puts another nickel in and it starts up again. A little man with curly hair and bushy eyebrows turns and glares fiercely at it.

"Can't that machine play nothing else?" he roars. He looks tough enough and mad enough to eat it, record, needle, and all.

"Stop beating your gums, brother," drawls the tall sailor with the black jersey. "I like it. It's catchy."

"I just come back from Texas," adds a third whose face is a complete pink circle, illumined by twinkling blue eyes and a cherubic grin.

"How was it?"

"Oh, dandy!" says Cherub, sarcastically. "Just dandy. Fine trip for your health. A Nazi tin fish chased us for three days. We never seen a patrol boat nor a plane the whole time. Saw one destroyer going hell-bent for election into Charleston one afternoon about dusk, but we all figured she was trying to get safe home before dark when the subs come out.

"We was carrying fifty thousand barrels of Oklahoma crude and fifty thousand of high-test gasoline. It sure gives you a funny feeling. I thought we'd get it any minute. Man, those nights are killers! You sleep with your clothes on. Well, I don't exactly mean sleep. You lie in bed with your clothes on. All of a sudden the old engines slow down and your heart speeds up. Someone knocks on the door, and you rise right up in your bed and seem to lie there in the air. So it turns out it's only the watch. You settle down again and try to light a cigarette if your hand don't shake too much. Not that you're scared of course. Oh, noooh!"

The others laugh. "Who ain't scared?" growls the little man with the bushy brows. "A torpedo connects with one of them tankers and it's just like lighting a match to cellophane. You ain't got a chance. Boom! And you're in the hero department. Just like that. And the next thing all the guys you used to know are going around saying, 'Well, he wasn't such a bad guy after all. Poor old Joe Bananas! . . . ' "

"Well, let's have a beer anyway," says Slim, in the black jersey. "Here, Cherub, it's on you. You just got paid off. How about springing for another round?"

"Okay," says Cherub. "Might as well spend it now. It don't do you no good when you're floating around in a lifeboat. No kidding, a guy's a sucker to go through nights like that. You can't believe it. The next morning you come out on deck, and the sea's blue and beautiful and the sun's shining. The night before—with the zigzagging and the sub alarms and the lying there in your bunk, scared stiff and waiting—it can't be true. That night can't have happened to *me*. Impossible. . . ."

What worried him most, he adds, was a remark made during lifeboat drill just before sailing. "We was practicing and everything goes off pretty good. Then the Inspector, he says, 'Now just in case any of you fellows have to *jump*—remember when you go over the side to pull down on your lifebelt as hard as you can. Cause if you don't when you hit the water it's liable to break your neck.' . . . My God, I thought. Now I got to worry about holding on to my papers and my chocolate bar and my cigarettes and at the same time I got to hold on to my lifebelt so my neck don't get broke!"

"So you have your choice," says Slim, "burn to death, drown, be blown to bits when the torpedo hits the engine room, starve to death in a lifeboat, or get your neck broke when you first jump over the side. Any way you look at it, you're a gone sucker. Only a lame-brained sailor would go for that. You gotta be muscle-bound between the ears to do that for a living. And what for?"

"I'll tell you what for," says Bushy-Brows. "If the rising sun and the swastika and that bundle of wheat ain't gonna be flying over the White House we gotta keep 'em sailing. They gotta have oil and ore and stuff to fight this war, ain't they? And how we gonna get it to 'em if guys like us don't keep on sailing the ships? So that's what for!"

This scene is typical of those being enacted every night in the waterfront bars of ports all over the land. . . .

"I was asleep when the torpedos hit us—" said John Walsh, wiper, survivor of the Cities Service tanker, *Empire,* torpedoed off Fort Pierce, Florida "—three of them. I rushed up on deck and helped get one of the lifeboats over the side. I saw our captain on a life raft. He and some of the other men were on it. The current was sucking them into the burning oil around the tanker. I last saw the captain going into a sheet of orange flame. Some of the fellows said he screamed. . . . Monroe Reynolds was with me for a while. His eyes were burned. He was screaming that he was going blind. The last time I saw him he jumped into the fiery water. That was his finish, I guess. . . ."

In the first four months of this year over a hundred American merchant ships were attacked by enemy U-boats off our own coasts. About 950 seamen were killed. Despite improvements in the patrol system, the ships are still being sunk. The average during April was five or six a week. . . .

Hundreds of American seamen have had to stand by and watch enemy subs sink their ships from under them without guns to fight back. . . .

The law to arm the merchant marine was signed by President Roosevelt on November 18, 1941, but most of the ships which have been sunk have been unarmed. A few which *were* armed have fought off submarines and either damaged them or frightened them away.

Guns are being put on the ships now as fast as possible, but some of the ships are so old and broken down that a gun is almost more of a liability than an asset. As one sailor says, "That rust-pot I just come off, they must of got her out of the Smithsonian Institute! Sure, we had a gun on her. But Holy Mackerel! if we'd ever of had to fire it the whole ship would have fallen apart." . . .

When the *Lahaina* was sunk, 34 survivors spent ten days in a lifeboat with a capacity of 17. Two of them became half-crazed with hunger and thirst, jumped overboard, and were drowned. A third lost his mind completely, had to be lashed to the bottom of the boat, and died the next day. A fourth died from exposure. . . .

All the seamen know what they are facing when they ship out. Yet they keep on sailing. Remember, they don't have to. They are in the private merchant marine, and they can quit any time they want to. Most of them could get good shore jobs, working in shipyards as riggers and welders and mechanics and whatnot, where the chief worry would be the danger of someone dropping a wrench on their feet. It isn't the money that keeps them sailing. On the coastwise run, from New York to Texas, they get a war bonus which works out to around $2.33 a day, hardly worth risking your life for. Also the bonus doesn't apply to the Gulf.

As a matter of fact, former seamen who have been working in shoreside jobs are going back to sea. A few months ago the National Maritime Union issued a call to former seamen. Since then over 2,000 ex-sailors have turned up to ship out again, hundreds of them at the union hall in the port of New York alone, among them men who have been working as furriers, truck drivers, electricians, office workers, actors, construction workers, miners, painters, and bakers.

Those who have been torpedoed and rescued ship right out again as soon as they can get out of the hospital. That takes plenty of nerve, but the merchant seamen have it. They don't get much publicity, and you seldom hear anyone making speeches about them. They don't get free passes to the theater or the movies, and no one gives dances for them, with pretty young actresses and debutantes to entertain them. No one ever thinks much about their "morale" or how to keep it up. It was only recently that a bill was passed to give them medals. And because they wear no uniforms they don't even have the satisfaction of having people in the streets and subways look at them with respect when they go by.

It is not that the seamen, themselves, are asking for any special credit or honors. When you mention words like heroism or patriotism to them they look embarrassed. "Listen, brother, there's a war on!" they say. Ashore, they frequently pretend that they are not brave at all. Not long ago I was talking to a man called Windy, who had just come off the Texas run and had been chased by a submarine for three days. "No more of that for me!" he said. "I tell you, any guy who keeps on shipping these days has got bubbles in his think-tank. The only safe run is from St. Louis to Cincinnati. I'm going to get me a shore job. Why commit suicide at my age?" We believed him; and not one of us could blame him. . . . The next day we heard he had shipped out again. He is now on the high seas, en route to India.[49]

In 1942, it looked like the Allies might lose the Battle of the Atlantic, as U-boat production soared and Doenitz's boats began attacking convoys in "wolf packs." Submarines, operating on the surface, would spread out across a wide band of ocean and search for convoys. When one was spotted, land-based radio operators would vector the other boats to the prey and they would close in for the kill, attacking in numbers that would overwhelm the escort ships. They would attack on the surface, where they had greater visibility and speed. A submarine—Allied or Axis—would usually only dive when attacked or when alone and badly outnumbered.

In 1942 the U-boats sank over a thousand Allied ships in the Atlantic, at a cost of only eighty-six submarines. England was imperiled and Churchill fell into a deep gloom. That summer was high tide for the Axis powers, on land and sea.

Later that year, however, a brilliant intelligence coup helped change the course of the Battle of the Atlantic. U-boat captains used sophisticated little Enigma machines, each with a complex system of three rotors and a typewriterlike keyboard, to encode and decode messages. The Germans were confident this message system could not be compromised. But beginning in 1940, British cryptographers, operating out of Bletchley Park, a top secret facility near Oxford, began using computerlike machines called "bombes" and Enigma machines and codebooks seized from captured U-boats to break the supposedly unbreakable German naval codes, allowing the British naval office to deflect convoys from prowling wolf packs. The Germans never learned their code was broken but kept changing it to insure its security, making necessary continuous raids on U-boats to capture Enigma machines and codebooks.

In February 1942 the German navy switched to a new, ultra-secret "Triton" code and altered its Enigma cipher machines, adding a fourth rotor. This left Bletchley Park "blind" for more than ten months, unable to read German messages. But the following December, in one of the stunning intelligence breakthroughs of the war, Bletchley Park cryptographers, led by Alan Turing, an eccentric Cambridge University mathematician, broke into the new four-rotor system. Once again, the Atlantic convoys could be guided around U-boat patrol lines. At the same time, the Allies used hugely improved antisubmarine technology to sink greater numbers of U-boats. Still, the carnage continued on the convoy runs, as Doenitz now had the 300 U-boats he had boasted he needed to bring England to her knees. "The Germans never came so near to disrupting communication between the New World and the Old as in the first twenty days of March 1943," declared an Admiralty staff review.[50] In this three-week period, after the biggest convoy battle ever, ninety-seven Allied ships were sunk, the vast majority of them in the "Black Pit," a 600-mile air coverage gap to the south of Greenland that Allied land-based planes could not reach. The U-boats simply waited in the Pit for their kills.

Then came the most sudden and dramatic turnaround of World War II. By May, the Allies had gained supremacy in the Atlantic, sinking forty-one U-boats, more than they had sunk in the first three years of the war. Tremendous advances in industry, technology, and tactics prepared the way.

On one level, it was victory by industrial attrition. America, the new shipmaking capital of the world—with ninety-five new shipyards—began building more merchant carriers than the U-boats could sink. Construction impresario Henry J. Kaiser, builder of the Boulder, Bonneville, and Grand Coulee dams, used women welders, prefabricated parts, and Henry Ford's assembly line techniques to mass-produce almost 600 Liberty Ships by the end of 1942. In a blaze of showmanship, he completed one ship, from keel laying to launching, in less than four days. These were the Model Ts of the seas, slow, ungainly-looking things that carried prodigious amounts of military cargo. By 1943 Kaiser was launching 140 Liberty Ships each month. And it was Kaiser who convinced Roosevelt to use small escort carriers against the U-boat menace. Kaiser built these baby flattops, each capable of carrying two dozen aircraft. They, along with sixty long-range B-24 bombers that Roosevelt prodded Admiral King to transfer from the Pacific Theater, closed the mid-ocean air gap, while planes equipped with improved radar and new homing torpedoes made the airplane the U-boat's deadliest foe. Unless it was submerged, a U-boat would be found and destroyed—even at night, with the use of high frequency direction finders and the Leigh light, a high-powered sea light mounted on the belly of a plane. "All these things came to a head at once and when they did we slaughtered the U-boats for three months, April, May, and June of 1943, when we sank a hundred U-boats and just rocked the U-boat fleet right back on their heels," recalls Captain—later Admiral—Daniel V. Gallery.[51]

The Nazis would call it Black May, and at the end of the month Admiral Doenitz pulled his boats from the North Atlantic and put them in safer waters. "We had lost the Battle of the Atlantic," he privately admitted.[52]

In the next several months, sixty-two convoys of merchant ships crossed the Atlantic without losing a single ship. A former Olympic wrestler, Daniel Gallery headed one of the Allies' new hunter-killer groups—comprised of fast destroyers and escort carriers deploying torpedo planes and fighters. They made a sortie into the Atlantic a virtual death sentence for Doenitz's submariners. Now the Allies began using the convoys to lure in and slaughter U-boats with their search-and-destroy teams, just as Eighth Air Force would later use bomber formations escorted by P-51 Mustangs to bait and kill Luftwaffe fighters.

The toll on the brave German submariners was appalling. Of a force of 39,000 men, 27,491 would die in iron coffins, including two of Doenitz's sons. An additional 5,000 would be taken as prisoners. The Allies would sink 754 of the 863 U-boats that sailed out into the war. It was a military massacre almost without precedent. Yet these undersea warriors had done their work with alarming effectiveness, sinking almost 2,775 Allied merchant ships and 175 warships. "Beaten Nazis may take comfort in reflecting that no army, fleet or other unit in World War II, with the exception of their own people who murdered defenseless civilians, wrought such destruction and misery as the U-boats," wrote Samuel Eliot Morison.[53] Had Hitler poured more resources into U-boat construction from the beginning of the war he could have prolonged the conflict by at least a year, although it is doubtful he could have altered the outcome. "The U-boat attack was our worst evil," Churchill wrote in his history of the war. "It would have been wise for the Germans to stake all upon it." [54]

By May of 1943, the U-boat was obsolete, having been overwhelmed by the Allies' technology and productive power. From this point on, the Allies would apply American industrial might with crushing impact, on land, on sea, and in the air. That May, after initial successes unlike any in modern warfare, both Germany and Japan had been stopped. Now the Allies, building up for the kill, would begin the great drives toward Tokyo and Berlin. "The age of managerial, organizational war was in full flex," James Jones recalls of that May 1943, "almost without having realized it had been born." [55]

THE CAPTURE OF U-505

Nothing better illustrates the new Anglo-American hegemony in the Atlantic than the capture in June 1944 of U-505, the only U-boat boarded and captured at sea in the entire war. It was, as well, a major intelligence windfall. Captain Daniel V. Gallery was commander of the USS *Guadalcanal,* the small escort carrier that was the nucleus of a five-ship hunter-killer force that pulled off the daring capture.

His newly built carrier had a complement of 1,200 men, almost all of them green. After several successful Atlantic missions, he shoved off from Norfolk, Virginia, with the intention of capturing and towing home a submarine, a wild idea that would sound sane only to "a bunch of completely inexperienced kids," he said in an interview after the war.

I WAS PRETTY FAMILIAR with the habits of submarines by this time. . . . I knew that when you got one cornered and hammered him with depth charges and punished him so much that he figured he was . . . going to sink, it was standard operational procedure for submarines to blow their tanks and come up and abandon ship, giving the crew a chance to get overboard so they could be rescued and then open the scuttling valves and sink the ship. I figured if we could get aboard in time and close the scuttling valves we might be able to keep it afloat and tow it home. It was a long gamble, but of course the prize would be well

U-BOAT SINKING AFTER BEING TORPEDOED BY A U.S. NAVY GRUMMAN
AVENGER. THE SURVIVORS ARE HUDDLED ON DECK (M25).

worth the gamble. Among other things we'd get the submarine codes, the main thing we would be after.

At the departure conference for this cruise . . . I outlined this plan to the boys and told them that I wanted everybody to organize boarding parties and to keep a whale boat ready to lower. And that if we brought a sub up this next cruise, instead of immediately throwing the works at him and trying to blast him out of the water and sink him, we would just shoot a lot of small stuff at him to keep him away from his guns, discouraging him from shooting torpedoes, and to expedite his abandon ship rule so the skipper could get his people off of there and we could get our people aboard and try to close the scuttling valves.

Off the Gold Coast of Africa, fighter planes from the Task Force spotted a submarine they had been tracking for a week, U-505.

WE CAUGHT HIM COMPLETELY BY SURPRISE. He was running submerged and a destroyer [USS *Chatelain*] picked him up on sonar. We depth charged him. The first attack shook him up a bit but didn't do much damage. . . .

We dropped another depth charge which shook him up pretty badly, rolled him over on end under water and dumped everything into the bilges. [As we learned later] the crew were just sitting down to their Sunday dinner and everything was dumped on top of them. The captain jammed his rudder hard over and it created panic among the crew. They came swarming out of the after torpedo room yelling that the pressure hull had been ruptured and that the after torpedo room was flooding. The skipper took their word for it.

So he blew his tanks and surfaced and abandoned ship. He came up and the crew went overboard and left the sub running at about seven knots on the surface . . . The sub popped up almost in the middle of the task group. The destroyers immediately opened up on it with their small stuff—20 millimeter and machine guns and some 3-inch. . . . When the sub surfaced . . . small crouching figures popped out of the conning tower and plunged overboard. When these men were running for their lives amid a hail of bullets, I broadcast to the Task Force, "I want to capture that bastard if possible." We dropped our boarding boats in the water. The motor whale boat from the [destroyer] *Pillsbury* was the first one to get there. Lieutenant [Albert] David was in charge of the boarding party of ten men. They chased the sub around in a circle and finally caught up with it and threw a line aboard. A boy jumped out of the whale boat and tied it to the back of the submarine.

Incidentally, I was about half a mile away and watching this thing through the binoculars. I broadcast over the loudspeaker, "Heigh-ho Silver, ride 'em, Cowboy," when they got the line aboard. Then David and two other lads [Arthur Knispel and Stanley Wdowiak] were the first aboard. They beat it up to the conning tower, which was open. . . . no one in that boarding party had ever set foot in a submarine . . . before.

We'd seen a number of people go overboard but we were by no means sure that everybody had gone overboard. It was a good chance that there were still people on board waiting for intruders down there to greet them with a machine gun. But David, [Knispel], and Wdowiak plunged down the conning tower and found to their amazement that the sub was all theirs. That is, she was all theirs if she didn't sink or blow up. She was completely abandoned, the skipper and everybody gone. [They were in lifeboats] watching the death struggle of their stricken boat.

[U-505] was in almost neutral buoyancy by this time, just about ready to up end and go down. Water was pouring into her and as far as I knew there were booby traps all over her. They soon found the place where the water was coming in, which was the bilge strainer that had the cover knocked off. Then one of the men [Zenon Lukosius] found the cover lying right there on the floor plates. That was lucky for us. If the thing had gone down into the bilges where he couldn't find it, we wouldn't have been able to save the sub. But he was able to jam the cover back in place. . . . He screwed on the nuts and stopped the water just in the nick of time. . . . [Luke] said he was too busy to be scared. But when he tore his Mae West life jacket on a sharp projection . . . that really shook him—because he didn't know how to swim.

Then the *Pillsbury* came up alongside her to try to take her in tow. Instead of taking her in tow astern she tried to take her in tow alongside, but the big bow flippers on the sub stick out in the water and they cut into the side of the *Pillsbury* and ripped a long underwater gash in her and flooded the two main compartments, and she had to back clear. I thought we were going to lose her because she had flooded the two compartments. The *Pillsbury* radioed to me that she didn't think a destroyer could do this towing job. So I said, "All right, destroyers stand clear, I'll take her in tow myself." I took the *Guadalcanal* over and backed down and put the stern up close to her bow and got a towline over. By that time we had maybe twenty of our people on board the sub . . . including Commander Earl Trosino [who kept] the sub afloat. He too had never been aboard a submarine before. But he had spent time as a chief engineer in Sun Oil tankers. . . . He spent the next couple of hours fighting to keep the sub's head above water. . . .

While I was lying there with the bow of the sub not more than twenty feet from my stern I said sort of a short prayer: "Dear Lord, I've got some young lads on board that submarine. Please don't let any of them monkey with the firing switch or torpedoes." Well, they didn't, and we finally got her in tow and started to haul her away.

After personally boarding U-505 and checking for booby traps—the first time he had ever been on a submarine—Gallery received orders to tow his capture to

Bermuda, 2,500 miles away. The Navy sent out a tanker to meet him on the way and refuel his ships. A fleet tug took over the towing job.

Lieutenant Albert David's boarding party had made an important intelligence find. Among the valuable Enigma codebooks they hauled off U-505 was an "address book" containing the code used to convert references on a grid chart into the names and exact locations of U-boats. For the first time since the Enigma code was broken, American and British intelligence experts tracking U-boats would be able to recognize immediately references to the location of boats mentioned in decoded Enigma messages.[56]

WE PUT THEM [THE CODE BOOKS] in a sack and put them on this other destroyer and sent her on ahead of us. She rushed this thing to Bermuda where it was picked up and flown to Washington.

There they immediately put a watch on U-boat frequencies and for the rest of the war we read the [operational] traffic of the U-boats. Of course the Germans had periodic changes that they made about every two weeks in the code, but the key to all the changes was in the codebooks that we captured so we could follow the changes right along.

The Germans did not learn of the capture of their sub until the end of the war. And that leads me to what I think was probably the most remarkable part of this whole remarkable episode—the fact that we were able to keep it secret. This was very important on account of the codebooks. If they had known they were captured they would have thrown away the old codebooks and put in completely new codes and we wouldn't have been able to read their stuff. So it was very important to keep the capture a secret.

But . . . I had 2,400 young lads in my task group, all of them just bursting with the best story of their lives. I had to get them together and explain to them the vital necessity of keeping their mouths shut. They couldn't say a word to anybody when they got home, not even their wives, mothers, sweethearts—nobody. That's one hell of a big order. So I'm proud of the fact that the boys did keep their mouths shut and the Germans didn't find out about this capture. I think that speaks very highly indeed of devotion to duty and sense of . . . responsibility in the average young American in bell-bottom trousers.

She was kept in Bermuda for the rest of the war and her crewmen were all interned in Bermuda in a special camp all by themselves. They left the sub in Bermuda because it is an island and the British had very tight control over everything going out by mail, telephone, radio, and press. . . . Also the fact that the crew was kept separate from any other German prisoners meant that there wasn't any word getting back to the homeland . . . through the mails.

Incidentally, in the original skirmish the [U-boat] skipper [Harald Lange] had been hit in the leg with a 50-caliber gun and he eventually lost that leg. When we got him aboard my ship he was down at sick bay and he hadn't actually seen us take his ship in tow. . . . He thought his order to scuttle her had been carried out.

I went down to see him . . . the next day and told him we had his ship in tow and he didn't believe it. So I sent over to his cabin and got a picture of his wife and kids off the desk and gave it to him. Then he believed it and . . . kept shaking his head and saying, "I will be punished for this, I will be punished for this." Eventually I got to be good friends with Lange. . . . That's a funny way to make friends with a guy—you shoot his leg off and take his ship away from him . . .

To further ensure that the sub's capture was kept secret, Gallery ordered his men to hand in all the souvenirs they had taken from U-505. The next day, he was swamped with pistols, cameras, caps, and whatnot. He told the men their booty would be returned after the war. He shipped off the souvenirs to Washington and that was the last he or any of his men saw of them.* "The chairborne commandos in the Pentagon glommed onto them for keeps. Now, whenever I meet one of the lads who was in that boarding party, I know exactly what his first words will be—'Captain, where the hell are those binoculars you made me turn in?' "

For extreme heroism, Lieutenant Albert David received the Congressional Medal of Honor and other members of the original boarding party received Navy Crosses or silver stars. Gallery's reckless courage went unrewarded. Admiral King was furious with him for not sinking U-505, and considered having him court-martialed for endangering the Enigma secret. But the captured codes were, as Gallery

---

*After the war, the Navy planned to sink U-505 in the Atlantic, but Gallery protested. Today, it is on display in the Museum of Science and Industry in Chicago, Gallery's hometown. The city of Chicago raised the money to have it towed to the lakeshore, just blocks from the museum, where it was hauled on special tracks to its present site, adjacent to the museum building.

says, "one of the main reasons for our high rate of sinkings during the last year of the war." [57]

When the crewmembers of U-505 were shipped to the United States, they were isolated there, as well. Even the Red Cross was denied access to them. Their families and friends did not know they were alive until 1947, when they were released and sent home.

The Dead of Tarawa

PRELUDE: THE ALEUTIANS

With Guadalcanal secured, the United States sent an invasion force in May 1943 to retake two barren islands far to the north, in the Bering Sea sealing grounds off Alaska. During the Battle of Midway, a Japanese diversionary fleet had attacked and occupied Attu and Kiska in the Aleutians, the long string of islands between Asia and the American continent. This occupation caused a surge of concern in the United States. Alaska and the Pacific Northwest now seemed vulnerable to enemy aggression. These fears were unfounded, but America wanted to finish the business the Japanese had started, expelling them from U.S. territory.

On May 11, the U.S. 7th Division began landing on the forbidding Arctic landscape of Attu. Seventeen days later the cornered and starving Japanese staged a desperate banzai charge, screaming that they would drink American blood. The few who survived the slaughter pressed hand grenades to their chests and pulled the pins. The Americans buried some 2,400 Japanese and took only twenty-nine prisoners, but they suffered an appalling 1,700 casualties. Attu turned out to be one the bloodiest island battles of the Pacific war in proportion to the number of men engaged. *Time-Life* correspondent Robert Sherrod was there and saw this "primitive, man-against-man fighting" as an ominous harbinger of the approaching island warfare in the Central Pacific.[1]

Three months later, American and Canadian forces invaded Kiska, but discovered that the entire Japanese garrison had evacuated under the cover of night and heavy fog. A report said they had left only a few dogs and some hot coffee. "What does this mean?" Navy Secretary Frank Knox asked Admiral King, who was with him when this report reached Washington. "The Japanese are very clever," replied King. "Their dogs can brew coffee."[2]

RABAUL

While this campaign of fog and ice was being fought, General Douglas MacArthur was advancing across the long north coast of New Guinea, an island twice the size of France. At the same time, Bull Halsey's South Pacific Fleet, with Marine and Army amphibious troops, was moving up the long ladder of the Solomons toward the northernmost island, Bougainville. The objective of this coordinated offensive was the Japanese air and naval bastion at Rabaul, at the eastern tip of New Britian, just northwest of Bougainville.

In early March 1943, the Japanese had tried to stop MacArthur by landing 7,000 troops from Rabaul on New Guinea's northeastern coast. Land-based bombers from George Kenney's Fifth Air Force swooped in at mast-high level, and in the three-day Battle of the Bismarck Sea sank four destroyers and all the transports. Three thousand troops drowned or were machine-gunned in the water by PT boats and fighter planes, a reprisal, the men said, for similar atrocities by the enemy.

With the Allies having complete air superiority in the region, Japanese hopes of holding northern New Guinea ended. The following month Admiral Yamamoto launched a last-ditch air attack on American shipping and air bases in the area, but his planes did little damage. In an effort to rally his pilots, the admiral flew to inspect air bases in the Solomons. The Americans broke the Japanese code, and under orders straight from Nimitz ambushed the plane from the sky, sending it spinning and burning into the jungle. Admiral Mineichi Koga replaced the audacious Yamamoto as commander-in-chief of the Combined Fleet.

By September, MacArthur had occupied the small ports of Lae and Salamaua in

northern New Guinea, battling sweltering heat, jungle leeches, tropical ulcers, and starving enemy troops. He then swung north and west, landing the 1st Marine Division, veterans of Guadalcanal, in the rain-soaked jungles of Cape Gloucester, at the western tip of New Britain, on the day after Christmas. One month later, in ferocious fighting, the Marines seized the airfield there. With that and Halsey's establishment of airfields on Bougainville the previous November, Rabaul was caught in the deadly American pincer. Bombers from Bougainville and Gloucester pounded Rabaul relentlessly. With 100,000 of the Emperor's infantrymen, Rabaul prepared for an invasion, the troops vowing to die in a final fight. They waited for the Americans, but the Americans never came; and this proud and embittered Imperial Guard was forced to live out the entire war in humiliation on the bypassed island fortress.

The American high command decided there was no need to try to take Rabaul in a costly offensive; it had been outflanked and neutralized. As Samuel Eliot Morison noted: "Tarawa, Iwo Jima, and Okinawa would have faded to pale pink in comparison with the blood which would have flowed if the Allies had attempted an assault on Fortress Rabaul."[3]

At first, MacArthur angrily protested the decision to avoid Rabaul, but this tactic, first employed by Halsey in the Solomons, would become his signature strategy in the South Pacific. Instead of hitting Japanese strongholds, he flew over them, letting them "die on the vine," saving lives and time. Beginning in the spring of 1944, his forces started that series of leaps along the New Guinea coast—Wewak, Hollandia, Biak—that eventually brought them within striking distance of the Philippines. This "leapfrogging" movement was one of the most brilliantly conceived offensives of the war, conducted without a major carrier force, with a small air arm, and only a minimal number of divisions.

After the war, a high Japanese military official declared that MacArthur's island hopping "was the type of strategy we hated most." MacArthur, he said, "with minimum losses, attacked and seized a relatively weak area, constructed airfields and then proceeded to cut the supply lines to [our] troops in that area. . . . Our strongholds were gradually starved out. The Japanese Army preferred direct [frontal] assault, after the German fashion, but the Americans flowed into our weaker points and submerged us, just as water seeks the weakest entry to sink a ship. We respected this type of strategy . . . because it gained the most while losing the least."[4] For every one of his men that was killed, MacArthur killed ten Japanese.

New Guinea opened one road to Japan. Another was through the vast Central Pacific—the Gilbert, Marshall, Caroline, and Mariana islands. Clearing this road would be the job of the United States Navy, with Marine and Army ground forces. MacArthur pleaded for supreme command of the Pacific Theater and a single offensive along the line he had been pursuing. But the Navy was unwilling to risk big carriers in the treacherous shoals of New Guinea, and Admirals King and Nimitz wanted the war in the Central Pacific to be an entirely Navy affair. Roosevelt, prodded by Admiral King, made the decision: the offensive against Japan would be twin-pronged and simultaneous, with two separate commanders. MacArthur would continue his drive toward the Philippines while Nimitz cut across the Central Pacific, capturing strategically important islands all the way to the innermost reaches of the enemy's defensive system, where bases would be built to bomb Japan. This strategy would also cut off Japan from its resource-rich colonies in the South Pacific. It was a cumbersome command structure and strategy, a compromise between two insistent commanders—King and MacArthur—but it turned out to be surprisingly effective.

Both offensives would employ amphibious warfare, but with a difference. Distances between neighboring islands were not nearly as great in the Southwest Pacific as they were in the Central Pacific. Employing excellent intelligence, MacArthur preferred surprise landings, usually at night, using newly developed amphibious craft to ferry his troops and heavy armor from shore to shore, with Kenney's ground-based aircraft covering the operations. It was a march of the airfields. Once MacArthur captured a position, his engineers would cut an airstrip out of tangled jungle and the troops would move, under an umbrella of air cover, to the next objective. This was triphibious warfare—ground, air, and sea—and it revolutionized the way wars were fought.

Nimitz and the Marines were also committed to triphibious warfare but they would conduct it in their own way in the wide-open spaces of the Central Pacific, where distances between enemy strongholds were daunting. Great carrier fleets would make these giant leaps, landing troops at daybreak on small, hotly defended islands, where they expected to be met, head-on, at the water's edge. These would be high-risk Storm Landings, usually by Marines, who would apply maximum killing power on a concentrated objective, getting in and out as fast as possible. There would be none of the deliberateness of MacArthur's big-unit jungle campaigns.

The ground forces would be supported by ship-to-shore fire and raids from carrier-based planes. After the Marines took an island, they would turn it over to the Seabees, naval construction battalions recruited from the civilian building trades. The Seabees would build airfields, submarine bases, port facilities, roads, hospitals—an entire island infrastructure that would be garrisoned by support troops, including small numbers of African-American Marines. After rest and recuperation, the reinforced strike force would assemble and train for the next island assault.

These were operations of vast distances, great speed, and awesome striking power. The Navy would spearhead seven of them, beginning with Tarawa, and the battles would be short, violent, and decisive, battles of "a magnitude and ferocity that may never again be seen in this world," writes historian Joseph H. Alexander.[5]

The prodigious expansion of the Pacific Fleet made these lightning landings possible. By late 1943, the United States Navy had grown to the point where it was not only the largest and most powerful in the world, but larger than the combined navies of all other warring powers. Seven new battleships had joined the fleet, mostly to provide ship-to-shore fire. Even more significant was the astonishing growth of the Navy's air arm. The Pacific Fleet added seven enormous *Essex*-class carriers and eleven lighter carriers, augmented by numerous escort carriers. The new *Essex*-class carriers were fast, heavily armed, and capable of carrying over a hundred aircraft— the most formidable of them the new F6F Hellcat, which could outfight the feared Japanese Zero. The ships formed carrier task forces made up of troop transports and amphibious vessels protected by battleships, cruisers, destroyers, submarines, and minesweepers, along with a "sea train" of fuel, cargo, repair, and hospital vessels that allowed the task forces to operate out of port for as long as seventy days. Each carrier group was refueled every four days by oilers, which also brought the mail and the latest movies.

Vice Admiral Marc "Pete" Mitscher's Task Force 58, controlling a large part of the fast carriers, was alone more powerful than the entire Japanese Navy. In the words of two reporters:

> TASK FORCE 58 is really something new under the sun. It is so big that one captured Jap pilot said he knew they'd lost the war when he got his first bird's-eye view of its hundreds of ships, from destroyers to huge carriers and 45,000-ton battlewagons, spread over 40 square miles of ocean. It is so fast that no pre–Pearl Harbor battleship could keep pace with it. And it is relentless, because it never has to go home. "When you go to sea with Mitscher, by God, you stay at sea!"[6]

TARAWA

As James Jones would write: "For the first time American corporation war and its managerial technology showed up in the Pacific."[7] Now this relentlessly modern Navy was ready to strike a series of hard blows. The first was aimed at Tarawa in the Gilbert Islands, 2,400 miles west of Hawaii and at the far end of the defensive perimeter Japan had established to protect its island empire. The landing here was significant both strategically and tactically, strategically because it inaugurated the great ocean-borne offensive and put American forces within striking distance of the next and greater objective, the Marshall Islands to the north, tactically because it taught valuable and painful lessons in island-landing.

Tarawa is an atoll, a ring of tiny coral islands that nearly encloses a picture-pretty lagoon. The target on Tarawa was Betio, its largest island, but only a tiny speck in the vast Pacific, about the size of New York's Central Park. It is less than two miles long and little more than 700 yards wide at its center, and it is pancake flat, with no point rising more than a few feet above the surf line. While Marines reduced it and seized its nearly completed airfield, Army troops would storm lightly fortified Makin atoll, 100 miles to the north.

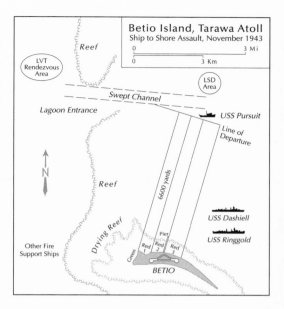

Vice Admiral Raymond Spruance, a hero at Midway, was in charge of Operation Galvanic, the invasion of the Gilbert Islands. Thirty-five thousand troops and 6,000 vehicles were carried by fast transports protected by the Fifth Fleet's nineteen carriers, twelve battleships, and a supporting flotilla of cruisers, destroyers, and minesweepers. The entire armada covered fifty square miles of ocean. It was "the most powerful naval force [then] ever assembled under one flag."[8] And a good part of it was committed to Betio.

Betio was garrisoned by 4,600 men, over half of them Japanese Imperial Marines, volunteers known for their fighting spirit and stoic discipline. These elite troops would be fighting behind the most formidable system of defenses Americans had yet encountered in the Pacific. The assault force was General Julian C. Smith's 2nd Marine Division, half of them veterans of Guadalcanal who had been recuperating from malaria in New Zealand.

U.S. Marine Corps correspondents described the island garrison their comrades were sent against:

THE JAPANESE OVER A PERIOD of fifteen months did a very sound job in perfecting their defenses for . . . Betio. They transformed its flat insignificance into one solid islet fortress which they felt, with considerable justification, would prove impregnable.

For its beaches and the reef were lined with obstacles—concrete pyramid-shaped obstructions designed to stop landing boats, tactical wire in long fences, coconut-log barricades, mines, and large piles of coral rocks.

And for its beach defense there were numerous weapons—grenades, mortars, rifles, light and heavy machine guns, . . . antiboat guns, [and] . . . coast-defense guns . . .

The emplacements for these weapons were often seven feet thick, of solid concrete, reinforced by steel, coral sand, and coconut logs.

The pillboxes for the automatic weapons, and even the riflemen's pits, were scientifically constructed to withstand heavy bombardment. Around a concrete floor in a three- to five-foot excavation was built a twelve-inch reinforced concrete wall. Over this were alternate layers of coral sand, coconut logs, and sandbags. The roof was made in the same way with coral sand covering the entire outside, then tapering off gradually to prevent the casting of shadows which would show in aerial photographs.

In places the blockhouses were of concrete with a roof thickness of five feet, on top of which were palm-tree trunks with a diameter of eighteen inches, and a final layer of angle irons made of railroad steel.

Guarded by these defenses was a landing field: the long, dusty airstrip that gave the Japanese a position of strategic importance in the Central Pacific because it was their nearest point to our travel routes from San Francisco to Hawaii to Australia, because it was our first major obstruction on the road to Tokyo.

In addition to these Japanese-made defenses there were the barriers and hazards of nature. There was the reef. There were the tides.

The Japanese who manned this islet fortress of Betio were not of the ordinary run. They were all volunteers. They possessed a finer physique and training than any other group in the Emperor's forces. . . . Their rear admiral in command at the atoll [Keijo Shibasaki] is known to have stated that the invading Americans faced certain annihilation, for "a million men could not take Tarawa."

The Admiral's confidence was based on realism. . . .

We were not underequipped for Tarawa. Offshore stood the mightiest fleet ever assembled up to that time in the Pacific. In the two years since Guadalcanal, an amazing variety of special landing craft had been developed to meet the needs of transporting men and material for massive seaborne invasions.

Yet Tarawa, too, was a gamble. For the first time in martial history a sea-borne assault upon a heavily defended coral atoll was to be launched. As General Julian Smith told his troops on the eve of D-Day:

"We are the first American troops to attack a defended atoll. What we do here will set a standard for all future operations in the Central Pacific area." [9]

On the morning of November 20, three hours before the Marines climbed down the cargo nets and boarded their landing craft, the Navy unleashed a spectacular bombardment, the largest yet of the war. "We will not neutralize; we will not destroy; we will obliterate the defenses of Betio," declared the admiral in charge of cracking the island's coastal defenses.[10] "We thought that most of the Japanese would be dead by the time we got on the island," reporter Robert Sherrod recalled. "There was even a debate on the troop transport I was on as to whether or not the Japanese had evacuated the island, as they did at Kiska. B-17 pilots who bombed the island the day before reported seeing no signs of life—no return fire, nothing. What we hadn't figured out, of course, was that this was the most heavily defended beach in the world, yard by yard, and that there were an awful lot of Japanese waiting for us." [11]

Unknown to the Marines, the bombardment failed to destroy the enemy's craftily disguised blockhouses and pillboxes, almost 500 of them. The fleet assaulted the island from its lagoon side, where the defenders least expected it, but the Navy stopped the bombardment twenty minutes before the troops landed because of visibility problems. This gave the Japanese time to switch their mobile defenses from the south, or sea beach, to the north side of narrow Betio, turning the dreamy lagoon into a murderous fire zone for their machine guns and mortars.

But the most forbidding defense the enemy possessed was the jutting coral reef that extends 300 to 900 yards into the placid blue-green lagoon formed by the atoll. On the morning of the invasion the tide was unusually low, and the defenders did not believe the invaders could get over it with the wooden landing boats—Higgins boats—they had used at Guadalcanal. But unknown to the Japanese, the Americans had a new weapon that could climb over reefs and operate as a tank on land. The Americans did not, however, have enough of them, only 125.

The first wave of Marines went in on the newly-developed amphibious tractors—LVTs (landing vehicle tracked), which had propellers to move them through water and caterpillar tracks to carry them over land. The amphtracs crawled over the reef and churned onto the beach, machine guns blazing. The sight of these strange metal monsters that could move across water and land struck fear into some defenders, but the Japanese quickly recovered and hit the invaders with a crushing crossfire, forcing them to take protection behind a low seawall of coconut logs that ran along the beach. Still, the LVTs delivered 1,500 men to the beaches in the first fifteen minutes, with only minor casualties. America's first Storm Landing was off to a good start. The problem would be maintaining momentum.

Almost everyone else coming ashore on D-Day rode in Higgins boats, which were larger and had a deeper draft than the amphtracs. They needed four feet of water to get over the reef, but the tide that day was not accommodating. It was an exceptionally unusual "dodging tide" that stayed low for the next thirty hours, confounding the predictions of Marine intelligence experts that there would be at least five feet of water covering the reef. The diesel-powered Higgins boats slammed into the reef and grounded, forcing the Marines to wade in to the shore in chest-deep water, under searing fire. "I couldn't even see the beach because of the tremendous smoke," said Major Michael Ryan.[12] His battalion, like others landing after the first wave, was cut to shreds.

It was now 0920. "Back home the football crowds [were] gathering; chickens and turkeys, dressed and ready for Thanksgiving, crowd[ed] the markets; on Broadway 'Life With Father' [was] in its fifth year, and 'Oklahoma!' [took] the mind off war." [13]

But in the bullet-swept lagoon at Betio, young Americans were dying.

Marines in slow-moving amphtracs returned to the reef to try to ferry in stranded comrades and were blown out of the water, men leaping from them with their clothes aflame. "In the distance I could see the beach," recalled Marine Karl Albrecht. "It was lined with amphracs, all of which appeared to be burning and smoking. . . . The attack appeared to have dissolved in confusion. I was terror stricken and amazed at the same time. We were Americans and invincible. We had a huge armada of warships and a division of Marines. How could this be happening? . . . I discovered the rows of Marines along the beach weren't lying there waiting for orders to move. They were dead. There were dead all over. They appeared to outnumber the living." [14]

The pilot of a Navy patrol plane described the scene: "The water never seemed clear of tiny men, their rifles over their heads, slowly wading beachward. I wanted to cry." [15] Only at the northwestern tip of Betio did the Marines have any success. There Major Michael Ryan led ashore survivors of the 3rd Battalion, 2nd Marines after spotting a lone Marine landing through a gap in the Japanese defenses. Ryan took charge of these scattered Marine units and created the only organized fighting force on Betio for a day and a half. He had just 200 men and two tanks.

It was almost nine o'clock when it came time for Robert Sherrod to start in with the fifth wave. He was part of a small band of civilian and Marine corps correspondents and cameramen, ranging in age from seventeen to fifty-four, who would cover the battle. World War I veteran Kerr Eby, one of America's greatest combat artists, was the oldest man to land on Betio; Harry Jackson, an aspiring sculptor, was the youngest. Sherrod would write a superb book on Tarawa; Kerr Eby would capture the battle's ferocity with his brooding charcoals of anonymous Marines, their helmets hiding their faces; and Staff Sergeant Norman Hatch and a team of Marine Corps photographers, headed by Hollywood star Captain Louis Hayward, would produce a film documentary of the fighting that would win an Academy Award. On this morning, all the correspondents and cameramen put themselves in as much danger as any Marine in the assault force. Two of them would die and three would be wounded or injured.

The pilot of Sherrod's landing boat dropped him off near the reef, in neck-deep water. "No sooner had we hit the water than the Jap machine guns really opened up on us. . . . It was painfully slow, wading in such deep water. And we had seven hundred yards to walk slowly into that machine-gun fire, looming into larger targets as we rose onto higher ground. I was scared, as I had never been scared before."[16]

"The water was red," recalls Harry Jackson. "It takes a lot of blood to make water red." Jackson waded through the lagoon with his buddy Whitey Cronin, a still photographer. "A mortar hit and I looked around and said, 'Whitey, Whitey where are you?' There was a gyrene behind me and he said, 'Is this Whitey?' And I looked and there is Whitey for sure. The whole front of his skull had been blown off, and I looked right into the cave, this incredibly red-black cave of his being. There is no way to describe what one feels in that instant. I was standing shoulder to shoulder with a Marine, and he said to me, 'You've been hit.' And I looked at him and said, 'You are too.' "[17] When enemy fire took down the Marine next to him, Associated Press photographer Frank Filan dropped his cameras in the water to help him. Later, he would borrow a camera to take a famous shot of battered Betio.

One coxswain went out of his mind. "This is as far as I go!" he screamed after running into a hail of bullets. He then dropped the ramp of his Higgins boat and twenty Marines, loaded down with gear, jumped out and drowned in fifteen feet of water.[18]

Robert Sherrod's aiming point was a long pier that stretched from the beach to the reef. Its coconut log stanchions offered him some cover. From there he crawled 400 yards to the beach and jumped into a foxhole in the sand. "I took my first close look at . . . Betio. . . . From the water's edge to the seawall there was twenty feet of sand and brown green coral. These twenty feet were our beachhead. The Japs controlled the rest of the island." [19]

He was in a sector of the beach commanded by a big, red-mustached major named Henry "Jim" Crowe. After catching his breath, Sherrod walked over to Crowe and asked if he had seen any other war correspondents or photographers. Crowe said he hadn't but unknown to him, sitting in a foxhole not thirty yards away, was Norman Hatch, the only motion picture cameraman on the beach. Hatch had gone in to Betio with Crowe and become separated from him on the reef. His film footage, along with Sherrod's reporting, would make Crowe an American hero.

Years later, Staff Sergeant Norman Hatch gave his story of the first day on Tarawa:

BACK IN NEW ZEALAND, when I was put in charge of a group of motion picture photographers for the Tarawa engagement, I selected the one man that I wanted to go into the beach with. His name was Jim Crowe and he had been a hero on Guadalcanal. I wanted to go in with him because he was aggressive. Wherever he went there was bound to be plenty of action to film.

I went to see him and said, "Major, I'm a motion picture cameraman and I'm assigned to go with you in the upcoming engagement." And he barked, "I don't want any goddamn Hollywood Marines with me." I said, "I'm not a Hollywood Marine, I'm a regular, I shot expert with the rifle." I also told him that the film that I would shoot would be as useful to the Marine Corps as the physical combat would be. He looked at me for a minute and said, "You can go, but stay the hell out of my way." When it came time to go in on the Higgins boat I sat on the engine hatch with him and he took one look at me and muttered, "Jesus, you're here."

He was battalion commander and was not due in until the fifth or sixth wave; his executive officer had gone in with first wave. As we approached the reef all the boats were hung up, and Crowe looked in toward the beach and saw that his men were packed together against the seawall, with enemy fire and shattered assault craft pinning them into a tiny square of sand and coral. And all of a sudden Crowe yells, "I've got no beachhead." So he shouts to the coxswain, "Put this goddamn boat in right now. I've got to get in there and straighten out that beach." He was afraid he was losing his beachhead and wouldn't have room for the next companies that were scheduled to come in.

MAJOR "JIM" CROWE DIRECTS ACTION FROM HIS IMPROVISED
COMMAND POST ON THE CROWDED BEACH (USMC).

There was no water on the reef and we ran up on it fast and hit it hard, sending everyone flying. Then the coxswain tried to drop the metal ramp of the plywood boat and it wouldn't go down. It was panic time, for all hell was breaking loose around us, and we were a sitting duck. Crowe told everyone to go over the side, and that's not easy to do on an LCVP, especially under fire with all your battle gear, weighing about sixty to seventy pounds. The gunwales are almost shoulder high and we had to climb over them and drop into water that was about chest level. My assistant, Bill Kelliher, and I had to be very careful. We couldn't get our cameras and film wet. So Kelliher went over the side first, and I loaded him with his cameras and gear, which he carried on his shoulders. Then I went over the side and one of the boat handlers loaded me with my camera equipment.

It was about 400 yards to the beach and we followed the men who had gotten out of the boat ahead of us. But they were all low in the water; all that was sticking out was their helmets. They looked like a herd of turtles. Nobody was standing up and walking, except Kelliher and me. This was my first time in combat and I could see the bullets hitting in the water all around me, and there was a sniper firing at us from under the pier. And I kept saying to Kelliher, "We got to stay upright, don't get down, don't get under the water."

If you ever walked through water you know what an effort it is, and we were weighted down and were wearing heavy boots. We were carrying something else, by the way, a big load of fear and anxiety. I don't know how we made it to the beach, with guys going down all around us, some of them getting hit while they were submerged in water.

When we got to the beach I fell into a shell hole and started shooting film. But before I did I got a sense of what a mess we were in when I looked up and saw a Marine lying right in front of me with his left buttock shot off. All the flesh was exposed and bleeding. My face was about two feet away from his wound, and I thought, Jesus! That could be me!

While I was lying in that hole I got a graphic shot of Jim Crowe standing up and leaning on an LVT, while everyone around him was sucking sand. He was an inspiration to some mighty scared boys who were hugging that seawall. He was walking around cradling a shotgun in his arm and clenching a cigar in his teeth and barking, "Look, the sons of bitches can't hit me. Why do you think they can hit you? Get moving. Go over that wall and kill some goddamned Japs." This got people up and moving to establish a perimeter in front of us, some kind of toehold on that beach. But these guys soon got pushed back. There were too many of them and not enough of us. And we couldn't see the bastards. They were dug in like rodents. But Crowe had the right idea. Unless we went over that wall we were going to die.

This is the crazy thing about being a combat photographer. Here we were in this big mess, and all I could think about was getting it on film. It's like your camera is your gun. You have no sense of danger; you block it out. When you're looking through the viewfinder you're divorced from what's going on around you. What you're doing is looking at a movie out there—that's right, the battle seems like a movie—and your entire intention is to get that movie. Subconsciously, you know guys are shooting at you, but you dismember yourself by looking through that viewfinder. Capturing the story of the battle becomes the most important thing in your life.

And I had a big responsibility, after all. This was the first time the Marines had made an assault on a fortified beachhead, and I was the only Marine cameraman to get onto the beach that day. The rest couldn't get in until the next day. If I didn't capture this on film, no one would.

There is one still shot of me that you see in histories of the battle. Everybody else in it is crouching down and running around in a crouch, and I'm standing up. It's because I wanted to get the shot. Guys would say to me, "You don't have to be here, why the hell are you here?" And I always said, "I have to be here, just like you. We both have jobs to do. I'm doing mine—just like you're doing yours." [20]

A Marine killed on D-Day wrote in the last letter to his wife: "Marines have a way of making you afraid—not of dying, but of not doing your job." [21]

As the battle deteriorated, General Julian Smith, on the bridge of the flagship *Maryland*, radioed Marine General Holland "Howlin' Mad" Smith, supreme commander of both the Tarawa and Makin operations, on the battleship *Pennsylvania*, near Makin. He wanted reinforcements, the 6th Marines, which were being held in reserve, and he ended with the ominous words, "ISSUE IN DOUBT."

This message had been sent after getting word of the situation on Betio from the commander of the assault forces, Colonel David M. Shoup. Robert Sherrod got to know Shoup both at Tarawa and later:

HE WAS A STOCKY, BULLNECKED PROFANE TYPE from Battleground, Indiana, of all places, and he had been an honors graduate of DePaul University. But he talked as though he never got beyond the third grade. And he was a very hard-boiled type. . . . But I found out afterward that he had a soft inner core. He wrote poetry, and sent me some after the battle.

Shoup became very nervous on Tarawa. He had a hard time landing like everybody else, and was wounded in a number of places, although he didn't want anybody to know it. He was awfully nervous about whether we were going to lose the battle or not, but his troops would never have known it. He's one of the reasons the battle was not lost. Directing the fight from an improvised command post right behind a Japanese blockhouse, with the enemy still in it, he was a rock. I can see why he got the Medal of Honor. [22]

Five thousand Marines assaulted the beach on D-Day. By midnight, 1,500 of them were dead or badly wounded, making this the bloodiest day up to then in Marine Corps history. This was the crisis moment of the battle, when it could easily have been lost. That night, the terrified Marines were packed so tight on the narrow beach that no one could move without stepping on somebody else, and hanging in the tropical air was the stench of their own dead, piled up behind them on the water's edge. Lots of guys thought they were trapped and doomed. It was "like being in the middle of a pool table without any pockets," said one Marine.[23] Norman Hatch recalled:

WE FULLY EXPECTED A BANZAI ATTACK. But Jim Crowe told us, "I don't want a single shot fired on the beach tonight unless the Japs hit us with everything they got." He said if any Japs come crawling in over the seawall, "get 'em with your knives." And the reason was simple. We had so many troops on the beach that if we started firing at Japanese infiltrators we'd be killing our own people.

I remember drifting off to sleep, and in the middle of the night I heard somebody yelling, "There's a Jap in here and he's killing people." Then I heard another guy yell and I reached for my knife and couldn't find the goddamned thing. I finally got it out and we were looking around for this Jap. Then all of a sudden the guy yells, "I've got him."

He had crawled in among us and stabbed and killed some of the wounded that were piled up near the water. But one of our guys found him and put a knife in him.

You know, we probably would have pulled out that night if we could have because I'm convinced that if the Japanese had been able to mount a force, they would have pushed us right off the beach. I don't think there's anything we could have done about it because we didn't have enough people ashore. They really missed a big chance.[24]

Lying on another sector of the beach, Robert Sherrod, like Hatch, was sure that this was his "last night on earth."[25]

For fifty years after the battle, historians surmised that the Japanese did not attack because Admiral Shibasaki's wire communications had been knocked out by the naval bombardment, making it impossible for him to orchestrate a coordinated counterstrike. But recently translated Japanese war records reveal that Shibasaki was killed by the initial naval bombardment, slaughtered out in the open with most of his staff while they were moving from one bunker to another. This is why his Imperial Marines were in no position to mount a countercharge.

The following morning Norman Hatch and Robert Sherrod sat at separate spots against the seawall looking out into the lagoon, one taking notes, the other scanning the action with a camera, recording a slaughter even worse than the one they had just survived.

After spending the night in their boats—seasick, wet, and scared—a group of Marine reinforcements started coming in. As Hatch tells it,

> THEY CAME IN ON HIGGINS BOATS. And when they smashed into the reef and grounded, the batteries opened up on them. The Japanese were zeroed in on that reef edge. It was almost uncanny to watch a ramp go down and a bunch of guys make a surge to come out and a shell explode right in their faces. It was like the guy had dead aim and was looking right down into that boat. It didn't happen once. It happened a dozen times. Boats were blown completely out of the water and bodies were all over the place. If Hollywood tried to duplicate that it would not be believed.
>
> Crowe was the only commander with a working radio, and he called in air strikes, but they didn't do much good, because the enemy was so well hidden. Hundreds of guys died in the water. It was far worse than the first day.[26]

Seasick Marines caught on the reef began to be rescued by a Navy salvage boat officer named Edward Heimberger, whom some of them recognized as the movie star Eddie Albert. He was sent out to salvage broken boats, but all he did was salvage Marines. "As I looked around I saw a lot of men in the water, wounded, so I tried to pick them up," Albert recalled years later. His boat was carrying drums of high-octane gasoline and was taking fire from at least five machine gun nests. "The bullets were incendiary and armor piercing and they came right through the boat and skittered around on the floor. Fortunately somebody was watching over us and the bullets didn't hit any of those tanks."

Asked if he thought he was a hero, Albert replied: "They were wounded. You had to get them out of there, for God's sake. There was nothing heroic [about it]."

A group of Marines who were not wounded, but had lost their rifles, refused Albert's offer to evacuate them. "They said 'take the wounded in.' " Then they asked

Albert if he was coming back. "And I said, 'Yeah.' And they said, 'Bring some rifles.' So I dropped off the wounded [on the hospital ship] and came back. By that time they had all been killed." [27]

"We were losing, until we won," General Julian Smith would say years later. [28] The Marines started winning on the afternoon of the second day. But even on that dismal morning some things began to go right. It all started when Major Michael Ryan took a ragtag unit of "orphans" from other battalions and, with the help of two tanks and naval gunfire, fought his way down the west coast of the island and captured a large beach, called Green Beach. Now General Julian Smith could land reinforcements securely, along with heavy weapons. While Smith was assembling a landing force of the 6th Marines, the men on the main invasion beaches started to move out, over the seawall, and take enemy bunkers. As Hatch recalled, the inspiration was Major William Chamberlin:

> HE WAS AN OLD MAID, in training and aboard ship, a college professor who was always telling the guys to put on their tee-shirts so they wouldn't get sunburned. But on the beach that second day he was a goddamned wild man, a guy that anybody would follow in combat.
>
> Early in the morning he came over to me and said, "We're going to take that command post," pointing to a monstrous bunker about forty feet high and on a slope. "Are you interested in coming along and getting some good pictures?" Staff sergeants don't argue with majors, so I told him that sounded like a good idea.
>
> He got his junior officers around him in a foxhole and said, "All right. We're going to jump off at 0900 and we're going to go right over the top of that thing and blow them the hell out." Then he told everybody to synchronize their watches, just like they do in the movies. "When I give the signal, we're off and running."
>
> We were in a foxhole together and at 0900 sharp the major gets up and looks at me and says, "Are you ready?" Then he charges out yelling, "Follow me." We ran right up to the top of that blockhouse. When we got there I looked around and it was only the major and me. And there were about a dozen Japanese looking up and wondering what the hell we're doing on top of their command post. I said, "Major, where's your weapon?" And he said, "I gave my carbine to somebody else and I lost my pistol." All I had in my hands were my cameras, so I said,

"We'd better get the hell out of here." So we turned and ran down back off the other side and jumped into a foxhole.

Then there was a little ass-chewing and he got everybody together again and they took that blockhouse by dropping charges down the air vents, shooting in fire from flamethrowers, and firing their weapons through the gun slits. After they did that, we waited, and several squads of troops came rushing out to engage us, figuring we were surrounding them. We annihilated them, and I was able to capture this on film. This is where my forty-five seconds of fame started which lasted me sixty years. In the Pacific war one hardly ever saw the Japanese, and this was the only time we caught a shot of the enemy in some strength fighting us at point-blank range.

After this, the battle became an island-wide search-and-destroy mission.[29]

A PARTIALLY CAMOUFLAGED JAPANESE BLOCKHOUSE
ON HEAVILY FORTIFIED TARAWA (USMC).

It was called "blind 'em, blast 'em, and burn 'em." That's how Tarawa would be taken, just the way Chamberlin took that big blockhouse. Withering rifle fire drove the Japanese defenders away from their firing slits so that demolition men could heave TNT satchel charges into the bunkers. Then Marines carrying napalm tanks on their backs poured fire and flame through the openings, burning up the oxygen inside and suffocating the defenders. The work was done in teams, but one Marine, Scout Sniper William Deane Hawkins, went on a one-man rampage, attacking pillbox after pillbox—crawling up to them in the sand, firing into the gun ports, and tossing grenades inside—until he was ripped apart by mortar fire. He was awarded the Medal of Honor posthumously, and the airfield at Betio was named Hawkins Field.

Some bulldozers and additional light tanks were landed on the afternoon of the second day, when the tide finally rose, and they were used to break the bunkers. The tanks went in close and blasted away. Bulldozers, manned by Seabees, were brought up to seal the entrances to blockhouses. Gasoline was poured into the vents and ignited with explosives. The charred corpses were not removed. The bulldozers finished the job, entombing the victims under tons of coral and sand.

"The improved situation is reflected in everyone's face around headquarters," Sherrod wrote in his notebook late that afternoon. "The Japs' only chance is our getting soft, as they predicated their whole war on our being too luxury-loving to fight. Of this much I am certain: the Marines are not too soft to fight. More than three thousand of them are by this time assaulting pillboxes full of the loathsome bugs, digging them out." [30] It is about this time that Shoup sent the fleet his now famous situation report: "Casualties: Many. Percentage Dead: Unknown. Combat Efficiency: *We Are Winning.*" [31]

On the evening of the second day, the 6th Marines began landing on Green Beach, with Mike Ryan's "orphans" providing cover. They came in across the heavily mined lagoon on rubber rafts, led by Ryan's good friend Major William Jones, the "Admiral of the Condom Fleet," his men called him. Beginning at dawn the next day, Jones's men moved slowly, but with violent effect, across the south coast of Betio, in the wilting heat, reducing one enemy stronghold after another. They took heavy hits from infantry in log and sand forts and from snipers who had tied themselves to the trunks of coconut trees, but they fought "like men who were anxious to get it over with." [32] Another battalion landed on Green Beach, and these fresh troops marched through Jones's depleted forces, "walking beside medium tanks which bored into the fading Japs."

With enemy resistance collapsing, Merritt "Red Mike" Edson came in to relieve an exhausted David Shoup as beach commander. With him came more tanks and other heavy armor. The tanks "had a field day with the Japs," Sherrod wrote later. "[And] . . . armored half-tracks, mounting 75-mm. guns, paraded up and down Betio all day, . . . pouring high explosives into pillboxes," Observing the progress his Marines were making, Edson smiled and said, "It won't last as long as Guadalcanal." [33]

In every part of the island, Marines found Japanese who chose suicide over surrender. The accepted way was to lie down, remove the split-toed jungle shoe from the right foot, put the barrel of an Arisaka rifle in the mouth, or up against the forehead, and squeeze the trigger with the big toe.

With most of the island under American control, the reporters went out to a transport ship and began writing their stories on typewriters borrowed from the Navy. Less than an hour after they left, the Japanese staged the first of a series of all-night assaults on William Jones's thin front lines, culminating in an early morning banzai charge, with the troops screaming "Marine you die!" and officers swinging samurai swords. "We're killing them as fast as they come at us, but we can't hold out much longer. We need reinforcements," the company commander pleaded with Jones on the field phone. "We haven't got them," Jones replied. "You've got to hold." Supported by naval guns that fired within 500 yards of the American lines, the Marines locked up in hand-to-hand combat with knives and bayonets. "Everyone got into the fight," said Jones. "It was a madhouse."[54] The next morning, a stunned Marine with bloodshot eyes crawled out of his foxhole, looked at the 300 or so massacred Japanese lying around him, and said, "They told us we had to hold . . . and, by God, we held."[55]

Marine veteran William Manchester would write later: "At the time it was impolitic to pay the slightest tribute to the enemy, and [Japanese] determination, their refusal to say die, was commonly attributed to 'fanaticism.' In retrospect it is indistinguishable from heroism. To call it anything less cheapens the victory, for American valor was necessary to defeat it."[56]

These desperate attacks hastened the end of what could have been a prolonged battle had the Japanese decided to hold out in their bombproof bunkers. "I had a chance to walk the lines in front of my front lines," Major Jones recalls. "And tears came to my eyes because of all the dead Marines mingled with dead Japanese." Marine photographers came up and took moving pictures of the bodies. Then Jones called for the big gallon cans of "torpedo juice" (straight alcohol used by the Navy as torpedo fuel) that a sailor had given him back in New Zealand. "And we opened it up and had a cocktail party in one of the tank traps."[57]

The next day, November 23, 1943, the fighting ended. Betio was declared secured at 1312 hours on the fourth day. It had been seventy-five hours and forty-two minutes since the Marines hit the beach. Makin was taken, with light casualties, the same day, giving the Americans control of the Gilbert Islands. What they had did not seem like much. "I'm on Tarawa in the midst of the worst destruction I've ever seen," a Marine officer wrote his wife.[58] But as Admiral Nimitz said, they had kicked open the door to the Japanese heartland. Already, Hellcats were landing on Betio's airstrip; and from

there, reconnaissance planes would soon be flying over the Marshall Islands, gathering intelligence for the next Storm Landing.

THE DEAD OF TARAWA

At Tarawa, the Marines and Navy suffered 3,407 casualties. Losses were similar at Guadalcanal, but "this was . . . worse than Guadalcanal," said the old Marine Raider Evans Carlson as the fighting wound down. "It was the damnedest fight I've seen in thirty years of this business."[39] Tarawa was a horror because the killing was so com-

MARINE DEAD ON THE BEACHES OF TARAWA (USMC).

pressed in time and space. Marines were in Guadalcanal, a much larger island, for six months. They were at Tarawa four days, and the total acreage of Betio is only one-half square mile. In this compacted space there were almost 6,000 dead soldiers, enemy and American.

In an awful indication of the ferocity of the fighting, burial details were able to identify only half of the 997 dead Marines. The fighting was so brutal and continuous that the men had almost no time to eat or sleep. "There was just no way to rest; there was virtually no way to eat. Mostly it was close, hand-to-hand fighting and survival for three and a half days. It seemed like the longest period of my life," Major Carl W. Hoffman recalled.[40]

At Guadalcanal, the Japanese evacuated their forces when the cause became hopeless. On Betio, they left crack troops to fight and die. Only seventeen Japanese soldiers were captured. It wasn't an American victory; it was a small holocaust. Even the killing ground was massacred. There was nothing standing on Betio but the blackened stumps of palm trees and the defiant walls of empty, blown-out blockhouses. The air was still, and the stink of death was in it.

When the correspondents came back to Betio at the end of the fighting their senses were assaulted. "As I walked up the pier, from the comparatively clean-smelling sea, the overwhelming smell of the dead hit me full in the face," Sherrod recalls, "and I vomited a little. By dark I was used to it again." No picture, he said, could capture the devastation of Betio. "You can't smell pictures."[41]

On the final day, Eddie Albert was back in the lagoon picking up marble white corpses that had been in the water for two days. "In the heat, they float very quickly in the warm water. And so I picked them up and took them back for a proper burial."[42] When the tide came in, it carried the mangled and swollen bodies of men who had died off the reef. Corpsmen waded in and fished them out of the water and placed them on the sand. Some of the men had been in the water so long their hair had washed off. "I always expected them to lift their heads for air but they never did," said one Marine.[43]

The bodies were placed in a long line on the sand. Nearby, a man in a bulldozer prepared a large trench. The uncovered bodies were placed in it, and a chaplain performed the last rites. "The bulldozer pushes some more dirt in the Marines' faces and that is all there is to it. Then the bulldozer starts digging a second trench."[44]

It was high tide. Watching the water splash against the seawall to a depth of three feet, carrying the dead who were on the beach to the seawall itself, where they floated grotesquely, it struck Sherrod that the death tide of Tarawa might have saved more Marines than it killed. If the tide had come in earlier the invaders would not have had a beachhead on D-Day. They would have had to go over the seawall and into killing fire, or else back into the lagoon.

When the battle was over, Sherrod walked the island's perimeter, recording what he saw in his notebook. "Betio would be more habitable," he wrote, "if the Marines could leave for a few days and send a million buzzards in."[45] Meeting up with a group of generals who had come on the island to assess the damage, he spotted something that ennobled all this human savagery. It was a dead Marine, leaning forward against the seawall, with one upraised arm on it, supporting his body. Just beyond his hand, on the top of the wall, was a blue and white flag, a beach marker to designate the spot where his assault wave was to land. Looking at it, General Holland Smith said: "How can men like that ever be defeated?"[46]

Sherrod would say later: "If we ever fought a battle in which courage was the dominant factor, it was at Tarawa."[47]

When the Marines left the island, William Jones and his men had to stay behind to bury the Japanese who had killed so many of their friends. They buried them as their fellow Marines had been originally buried, in big trenches, the bodies stacked like the coconut logs of the Betio fortifications. "Then we unburied our dead," Jones recalls, "and put them on a ship to take them back to Honolulu. After the war, the Japanese came back and removed their dead for proper burial."[48]

Robert Sherrod left Tarawa convinced of something that people back home did not want to hear. "It . . . seemed that there was no way to defeat the Japanese except by extermination." In late 1943, when American production began to reach its fabulous potential, a lot of Americans expected the war to end soon, brought to a climactic conclusion by fire from the sky. We would bomb Germany and Japan back to the stone age; close combat would be unnecessary. Tarawa put the lie to this. The road from Tarawa to Tokyo would be one of the bloodiest campaigns in all of history, and every fight would be to the death. There would be no more enemy evacuations as at Kiska and Guadalcanal, a chilling thing to contemplate. "When I told my mother what the war was really like, and how long it was going to take, she sat down and cried," said a bomber pilot who returned home from the Pacific in 1943. "She didn't know we were just beginning to fight the Japs." [49] But how was this to be made known to the American public?

Sherrod and a number of others who covered the war believed the American people were being lied to. There were combat correspondents who filed unvarnished reports, but government censors and cooperating news agencies rewrote them, playing up the positive and shielding the public from the bloody harvest of the war. After Tarawa, Sherrod returned to an America that was "not prepared psychologically," he wrote, "to accept the cruel facts of war." [50]

Sherrod's stories in *Time* and *Life* gave the double-barreled bad news of Tarawa's butcher's bill and the certainty of higher costs to come. But it was the visual evidence that really struck home. Since World War I, the government had prohibited the media from showing pictures of dead American soldiers, even of bodies covered with blankets. This changed two months before Tarawa, when the head of the newly created Office of War Information, Elmer Davis, the "Mt. Everest" of radio news commentators, asked President Roosevelt to lift the ban on the publication of photographs of dead American soldiers. The public, Davis insisted, "had a right to be truthfully informed" about the war, subject to restraints dictated by military security. Roosevelt relented, and *Life* magazine led the way, publishing a photograph by George Strock of three dead American soldiers lying on a desolate beach at Buna. This provoked tremendous controversy, and readers and other news writers assailed *Life* for giving people more of the war than they could take, or for engaging "in morbid sensationalism." [51]

This was the situation when Norman Hatch returned from Tarawa with 3,700 feet of film. The Marines had imposed no censorship restrictions on photographers and correspondents at Betio; they had been free to document the battle as they witnessed it. Still, Hatch expected to run into trouble with the military censors. He was shocked when the Navy released all of his film to the newsreels. Theaters across the country began showing the first unrestricted combat shots that the American public had ever seen, and Hatch's name was put on the marquees. Hatch's footage was also used in a color-tinted documentary film the Marine Corps produced for general distribution. But the film, *With the Marines at Tarawa*, could not be released without Roosevelt's approval.

The President was in a quandary. Photographs of the carnage at Tarawa had already appeared in the press, along with a statement from Holland Smith that Tarawa was taken only because of the willingness of the assault forces to die.[52] This caused a storm of outrage, as did the release of the casualty lists. Why, people wondered, had American boys paid such a frightful price to take an obscure stand of coral that should

THIS PHOTO OF A SHATTERED JAPANESE PILLBOX
REVEALS THE FEROCITY OF THE FIGHTING (USMC).

have been blasted into oblivion. Was this some horrible intelligence blunder by the Navy? Some congressmen called for a special investigation, and Nimitz's office was flooded by mail from mothers who accused him of killing their sons.

Roosevelt had heard that the Tarawa film was graphic and wondered if the public was ready for it. On the other hand, the war bond drive was flagging, and a film like this, showing what America was up against in the Pacific, might give it a boost. Robert Sherrod helped the President make up his mind, as he recounted years later:

> I WAS TOLD ABOUT THIS TARAWA FILM and allowed to see the rough cuts before it was edited. And they were pretty raw, pretty bloody. People didn't know the war was that bad.
>
> I went to one of Roosevelt's press conferences and stayed afterward and had a chat with him, as I had done before many times during the war. He had been in Teheran meeting with Stalin and Churchill at the time of the Tarawa battle and they hadn't told him a great deal about it apparently, because he said to me, "Why didn't they use the battleship shells to blow up the island?" And [I told him] they had used the battleship shells. They used everything they had. Then the President said, "What about that movie they shot? I hear it's pretty raw, pretty rugged."
>
> "Yes sir," I said. "That's the way it is out there." And I recommended that he release it.
>
> The movie was shown. Not the rawest part, but enough to indicate that this is going to be a hard war to finish fighting in the next two years.
>
> [After] it was released, I saw the chief of public relations at Marine Corps headquarters, and he said, "What were the consequences of releasing that film? Enlistments fell off 35 percent." [55]

But war bond sales increased dramatically, the film won an Oscar in 1944 for best documentary, and the wide-angle photograph that Frank Filan shot on the first day from the beach, "Tarawa Island," won a Pulitzer Prize. Like Mathew Brady's Civil War exhibition, "The Dead of Antietam," the film and photographs of Tarawa showed Americans on the home front a war they had not yet seen. In doing this, they helped strengthen public resolve for even grimmer struggles ahead. "We must steel ourselves now," the *New York Times* warned, "to pay [the] price." [54]

Tarawa rewrote the book on Storm Landings, pointing up the need for greater and more accurate preliminary fire, for frogmen and underwater demolition teams to clear obstacles and scout beaches and tides, for more and better amphibious assault vehicles. But the principal weapon on Tarawa needed no improving. When interrogators asked a prisoner at Betio when he thought the battle was lost, he replied, "When the dying Americans kept coming, one after the other." [55]

Up the Bloody Boot

W HILE AMERICAN MARINES WERE STORMING the beaches of Betio in late November 1943, Ernie Pyle's foot-slogging infantry was fighting the mud, the snow, and the Germans in the forbidding mountains of central Italy, in a campaign that was as abysmally planned and ferociously fought as Tarawa. It was a campaign that had begun with great promise the previous summer.

With North Africa cleared and control of the waters of the Mediterranean assured, the Allies prepared the first blow against Europe. The objective, however, was not northern France, as the Americans hoped, but what Churchill erroneously called Europe's "soft underbelly."

Sicily was the first target, and the decision to invade mainland Italy would not be made until the Sicilian campaign was underway. George Marshall, America's chief war planner, opposed putting U.S. troops in Italy, arguing that an Italian campaign would suction off resources from the main objective of the European war, a cross-Channel invasion of German-occupied France. Churchill insisted, however, that an Italian campaign would have multiple advantages. It would bring down the weakened Mussolini regime, taking one of the three main Axis partners out of the war. The airfields at Foggia, in southwest Italy, would enable Allied air forces to reach southern Germany and the abundant oil fields of Romania. And an Allied offensive in Italy would force Hitler to divert combat divisions from the Russian Front.

Churchill also wanted to delay the invasion of "Fortress Europe." His naval leaders had informed him that there would not be enough landing craft to conduct the cross-Channel offensive until the summer of 1944. But with Stalin bearing the brunt of the land war, a major offensive had to be made somewhere in Europe. That was the deciding factor for the Americans. On July 17, 1942, Eisenhower, the area commander, ordered that the conquest of Sicily be followed up immediately by the invasion of Italy.

It was a costly and controversial decision. The Allied high command was convinced that the Germans would not commit to an all-out fight in Italy because of long supply lines and British-American mastery of the air. But Hitler poured in massive reinforcements, fearing the Allies would use Italy as a base to attack the Balkans, a major source of his raw materials. And the Germans held on with fanatical zeal for over 500 days, not surrendering until May 2, 1945, the day the Berlin garrison capitulated, effectively ending the war in Europe. That surrender produced a hollow victory that hardly anyone paid attention to, even though the fighting in Italy had been horrible and heroic beyond belief. Lieutenant General Mark W. Clark's Fifth Army, which fought from invasion to surrender, received 20 percent of the Medals of Honor awarded to all the services in World War II.

The Italian campaign was a nightmare of "mud, misery, and death."[1] It was the longest campaign fought by the Western allies and a horrid throwback to the useless bloodletting of World War I. The Allies would suffer 312,000 casualties, 188,000 of them Americans. The Germans would lose 435,000 men. But the largest loser was Italy itself. Museums, archives, cathedrals, archaeological treasures, and ancient monasteries were blasted and burned, and hundreds of towns were pulverized beyond recognition, their half-starved survivors turned into war-shocked refugees.

British General Sir Harold Alexander, the last man off the beach at Dunkirk, was named ground commander for the invasion of Sicily. But the actual conquest of the island and its garrison of 300,000 Axis troops under Field Marshal Albert Kesselring was assigned to Bernard Montgomery's Eighth Army and the American Seventh Army under George Patton.

It was the largest amphibious operation ever launched to that date. After a thunderous naval bombardment, 160,000 troops landed on the southern coast of Sicily on

July 10, 1943. British troops fought up the east coast, over cruel mountain terrain and miserable roads and against the heaviest German concentrations, toward the port of Messina, where they hoped to prevent the enemy's escape across the narrow Strait of Messina to mainland Italy. Patton went up the west coast and was initially to do little more than secure Montgomery's flanks. General Alexander had not been impressed by the performance of the Americans in Tunisia and assigned them a subordinate role in this invasion plan.

After a sharp tank battle at Gela, where Navy guns helped break up a determined German attack, Patton's forces swept around the western corner of the island to capture Palermo, the first major city on the continent to be liberated. Then, with Montgomery delayed by terrain and the enemy, Eisenhower unleashed Patton, sending him toward Messina against the greatly outnumbered German Army. Meeting tough resistance along the way, Patton got there too late. More than a hundred thousand troops escaped in a spectacular emergency boatlift. The German command was incredulous that the Allies had not seized the Strait of Messina at the opening of the campaign, forcing them into what would have been a death struggle in the mountains of Sicily.

It took just thirty-eight days to capture Sicily, but it nearly cost the Americans one of history's legendary commanders. During his "go like hell" drive to Messina, George Patton stopped at several field hospitals, where he physically abused two soldiers who were suffering from battle fatigue. "You yellow son of a bitch," he shouted at one of them. "I won't have these brave men who have been shot seeing a yellow bastard sitting here crying. . . . You ought to be lined up against a wall and shot." Patton then slapped him across the face.[2] Eisenhower kept the incident secret, with the complicity of print journalists, but when radio commentator Drew Pearson broke the story, Ike had to withstand heavy public and official pressure to remove a general he considered indispensable to the war effort. Eisenhower ordered Patton to apologize to his troops. When the general assembled his men they chanted and cheered to prevent him from speaking. Patton began to cry and walked off.

As the Axis forces prepared to cross the Strait of Messina, the Fascist regime was tottering. On July 25 Benito Mussolini was ousted from the dictatorship he had held for twenty-one years. Confessing the futility of further resistance south of the Po Valley, he had presented a plan to the Fascist Grand Council to defend only the prosperous industrial north. The plan was voted down, Mussolini dismissed. King Victor Emmanuel appointed Marshal Pietro Badoglio, the conqueror of Ethiopia, to head the new government. Badoglio met in secret with Anglo-American officials and on September 3 signed an armistice with the Allies.

When word reached Hitler that Italy had defected, he disarmed the Italian Army, shipped off 600,000 Italian troops to slave labor camps in Germany, and rescued Mussolini from his Italian captors in a daring raid on a mountain top hotel by parachutes and SS troops in gliders. Then he occupied the country and sent in the SS. Anti-Fascist partisans were hunted down and executed, and Mussolini's largely verbal campaign against the Jews was turned into an organized manhunt. Hitler ordered Rome's 12,000 Jews rounded up and sent to extermination camps. Pope Pius XII, who would not protest the slaughter of German Jews, stood by silently while twelve hundred Jews were arrested in Rome and held in a building a block from the Vatican before they were sent to Auschwitz, where most of them were gassed. But many priests, nuns, and Catholic laity opened the doors of convents, monasteries, and homes to Italian Jews, saving thousands. Almost 80 percent of Italy's 32,000 Jews survived the war.

On to Naples

Italy was a surprise to American GIs. "[It] wasn't what the travel posters had cracked it up to be," one of them wrote, "all blue skies and crowds of pretty girls coming down the streets singing opera. It rained and kept on raining until the weather got too cold for rain, and then it snowed. There was mud and slush everywhere, and men went around in the mud up to the top of their leggings and sometimes up to their belly-buttons."[3]

The Germans had more than weather—some of the worst winters of the century—on their side. Hitler moved in front-line forces from Russia and France, including some of the best combat engineers in the Wehrmacht. These seasoned troops—twenty divisions strong—had the advantage of geography, a chain of precipitous mountains, wall after wall, running up the spine of the peninsula, rising in places to 10,000 feet and traversed by rivers cutting through deep valleys to the sea. It was terrain perfect for defense, and Albert Kesselring, the German commander, was a master of delay and attrition.

Allied strategy also worked in Hitler's favor. Napoleon, who had overrun Italy in a tremendous offensive in 1800, had said that Italy is a boot that you enter from the top. That way the country would be cut off from help from the north. But the Allies went up the boot from toe to top in a murderous campaign from one treacherous hill and river valley to the next, with a lot of the fighting done at night. And the campaign had no clear strategic objective. The only place to be taken was Rome, but Rome had no military value.

On September 3, 1943, General Montgomery's Eighth Army crossed from Messina and advanced up the Italian toe, hoping to draw German troops away from the main invasion force, which was to land six days later at Salerno, south of Naples, near the ancient ruins of Paestum. General Mark Clark's Fifth Army, a multinational force made up of troops from nearly every Allied nation, with Americans predominating, would make the assault. Montgomery was to push up from the south and link up with him.

Clark seemed born to command. Tall, lean, and handsome, he had compiled a distinguished record in World War I and had been a superb staff officer. But he was vain, arrogant, and doctrinaire. When Patton was briefed on Clark's risky plan for Salerno, he pointed to a critical weak point, a seven-mile gap between the two corps that were to land on the beach, one British, the other American. Patton said the Germans would find that seam and exploit it. Clark refused to change his plan.

The Italian Campaign

— Gothic Line

▭ Gustav Line

0   100 Mi

0   100 Km

Convoys bearing the Fifth Army put out from ports in Africa and Sicily on September 8, 1943. John Steinbeck was with them, covering the Salerno invasion, one of the riskiest amphibious operations of the war, for the *New York Herald Tribune*.

It was a cloudless night and the sea was calm. "On the iron floors of the L.C.I., which stands for Landing Craft Infantry, the men sit about and for a time they talk and laugh and make jokes to cover the great occasion. They try to reduce this great occasion to something normal, something ordinary, something they are used to. They rag one another, accuse one another of being scared, they repeat experiences of recent days, and then gradually silence creeps over them and they sit silently because the hugeness of the experience has taken them over."

As the ship moved closer to the black shore and the radios went dead, the men began searching "the faces of their friends for the dead. Who will be alive tomorrow night? I will, for one. . . . Each man, in this last night in the moonlight, looks strangely at the others and sees death there."

These were green troops; they had not yet faced enemy fire. "No man . . . knows whether he will run away or stick, or lose his nerve and go to pieces, or will be a good soldier," Steinbeck wrote. "There is no way of knowing and probably that one thing bothers you more than anything else."[4]

The next night Steinbeck filed this dispatch from the invasion beach:

THERE ARE LITTLE BUSHES on the sand dunes at Red Beach south of the Sele River, and in a hole in the sand buttressed by sandbags a soldier sat with a leather covered steel telephone beside him. His shirt was off and his back was dark with sunburn. . . .

"When'd you come ashore?" he asked. And then without waiting for an answer he went on. "I came in just before dawn yesterday. I wasn't with the very first, but right in the second." He seemed to be very glad about it. "It was hell," he said, "it was bloody hell." He seemed to be gratified at the hell it was, and that was right. The great question had been solved for him. He had been under fire. He knew now what he would do under fire. He would never have to go through that uncertainty again. . . .

"It was dark as hell," he said, "and we were just waiting out there." He pointed to the sea where the mass of the invasion fleet rested. "If we thought we were going to sneak ashore we were nuts," he said. "They were waiting for us all fixed up. . . . They had machine guns in the sand dunes and 88's on the hills.

"We were out there all packed in an L.C.I. and then the hell broke loose. The sky was full of it and the star shells lighted it up and the tracers crisscrossed and the noise—we saw the assault go in, and then one of them hit a surf mine and went up, and in the light you could see them go flying about. I could see the boats land and the guys go wiggling and running, and then maybe there'd be a lot of white lines and some of them would waddle about and collapse and some would hit the beach.

"It didn't seem like men getting killed, more like a picture, like a moving picture. . . . Then all of a sudden it came on me that this wasn't a moving picture. Those were guys getting the hell shot out of them. . . .

"They had lots of 88's and they shot at everything. I was just getting real scared when we got the order to move in, and I swear that is the longest trip I ever took, that mile to the beach. I thought we'd never get there. . . . Then we bumped the beach and the ramps went down and I hit the water up to my waist.

"The minute I was on the beach I felt better. It didn't seem like everybody was shooting at me, and I got up to that line of brush and flopped down and some other guys flopped down beside me and then we got feeling a little foolish. We stood up and moved on. Didn't say anything to each other, we just moved on.[5]

Kesselring had guessed exactly where the Allies would land and was waiting for them in the hills overlooking the beachhead with the best German soldiers in Italy, with the Luftwaffe controlling the skies over the beaches. And Montgomery wasn't there to help. He was being held up by German engineers, who were blowing up mountain roads and bridges along his torturous line of advance.

On September 12 Kesselring made the slashing counteroffensive Patton had foreseen. A panzer force smashed through American lines, and Clark, shaken by the ferocity of the attack, considered calling in the Navy and evacuating the entire invasion force. But the Germans ran into overwhelming American artillery fire, causing them to pull back temporarily. Clark then got support from the Northwest African Air Force, which flew 1,888 sorties over the beachhead in one day, from the Navy ships, which pulled within rifle range and blasted the enemy, and from the 82nd Airborne Division, which made a perilous night drop on the beach. By September 15 the counterattack had lost its force and the Germans began an orderly withdrawal to the north. Clark's Fifth Army joined up with Montgomery's Eighth, coming up from the south, and closely pursued them.

It had been a close call. Of all the American amphibious landings of the war, this one and Tarawa came nearest to failing.

The Allies entered Naples on October 7. The Germans had withdrawn from the great port but had destroyed the harbor facilities and the water supply, mined buildings and streets, and seized everything on wheels. The *New York Times* correspondent Herbert Matthews describes one of their most heinous crimes:

ON SUNDAY THE GERMANS BROKE into the university after having carefully organized their procedure—squads of men, trucks with dozens and dozens of five-gallon gasoline tins and supplies of hand grenades. Their objective was deliberate and their work was as methodical and thorough as German work always is. The university was founded in 1224 by Emperor Frederick II.

The soldiers went from room to room, thoroughly soaking floors, walls, and furniture, including archives that went back for centuries. . . .

When everything was ready, the second stage began. The soldiers went from room to room, throwing in hand grenades. At the same time, in an adjoining building a few hundred yards up the street, an even greater act of vandalism was being perpetrated. There was something apt about it, something symbolic of the whole German attitude. It did not matter to the Germans that they were destroying the accumulated wealth of centuries of scientific and philosophical thinking.

The rooms of the Royal Society contained some 200,000 books and manuscripts, from not only Italy but every country in the world. These books were stacked neatly and soberly on shelves along the walls; in the middle of the rooms were plain wooden tables with chairs. In several rooms there were paintings—some of them by Francesco Solimene of Nocera, the great Baroque architect of the seventeenth century. These had been lent by the National Museum, but they will never be returned.

Like everything else they are now heaps of ashes that I plowed through today like so much sand on a beach. Here too the Germans used the same efficient techniques—gallons and gallons of gasoline and then hand grenades. . . .

Everyone knows how difficult it is to burn one solid unopened book thoroughly until nothing remains but a heap of fine ashes. The Germans burned some 200,000 books in that way. Of course, the fire had to rage a long time and—also of course—the German thoroughness was going to see to it that nothing interfered with the fire.

Under fire from Germans holding the high ground at Anzio (SC).

They set it at 6 P.M. on Sunday. At 9 P.M. the Italian firefighting squads came up to extinguish the flames. German guards prevented them from entering the Via Mezzocannone. For three days those fires continued burning and for three days the German guards kept Italians away.[6]

SLOGGING FORWARD

Withdrawing from Naples, the Germans retired to strong defenses on the steep northern bank of the Volturno River. Ordinarily the Volturno is a mild stream, but that October it was swollen with rains. Muddy ground turned southern Italy's primitive road network into rivers of mud, badly hampering ground operations. "We privates got to know Italian dirt and the Germans rather well," recalls Carter Roland. "When it rained, it got slick, then soupy. It was difficult just to stand, much less walk or run, because nothing was level. Italy was one hill after another and when it was wet, you were either going up, too slow, or down, too fast, but always the mud. And every hill had a German gun on it. They were choosing the ground and they were always looking down on us. Even today, I subconsciously look for something to hide behind when I'm in clear view of a hill."[7]

On October 16 the enemy flanks were pushed back, and as the Germans retired they left behind them broken bridges, mines, booby traps, and small knots of snipers to hold up the Allied advance. And mud. "Mud," Carter Roland says, "prevented you from getting your mail on time. It slowed food and ammunition getting up to the front. Mud kept fuel, blankets, tents, or anything to make life bearable from arriving on time. I can tell you, every GI, because of that mud, was convinced Italy would be better left to the Nazis."[8]

"Between Naples and Rome Mr. Winston Churchill's 'soft underbelly of Europe' was pregnant with hard mountains and well-placed German machine guns," writes the photojournalist Robert Capa. "The valleys between the mountains were soon filled with hospitals and cemeteries."[9] By this time, Generals Montgomery, Patton, and Eisenhower had gone to England to prepare for the cross-Channel invasion, and Harold Alexander was left behind as the supreme commander in Italy. The stream of supplies from the United States was also diverted to England. Relegated to a secondary role in the big strategic picture, Clark's men slogged ahead, wet, tired, and miserable. Herbert Matthews was with them:

A BATTLE IS A LONG, SLOW PROCESS. . . . The picture you want to get into the mind is that of a plugging, filthy, hungry, utterly weary young man straggling half dazed and punch drunk, and still somehow getting up and over and beating the Germans, and hanging on against the enemy counterattacks.

That is what wins battles and wars, and only that. . . .

In every evacuation or base hospital you will find cases which are due simply to fatigue, although they would take the form of insomnia, shell shock, broken arms and legs. So it is a great problem, and one that all armies fight as they do any illness. Wherever possible the troops are withdrawn to rest areas and replaced as soon as they get too fatigued.

Under normal conditions, for instance, the same soldiers would not be kept more than three days on the actual summits of front-line mountains. However, the conditions during a campaign like this are rarely normal. The Forty-fifth Division, for instance, fought from day to day on the Salerno beachhead for forty consecutive days without rest. The Third Division, which came in later, did fifty-seven consecutive days.[10]

Most troops developed the ability to sleep while they marched. "It's not a very healthy sleep; you might call it a sort of coma," wrote Bill Mauldin, who covered the Italian campaign for *Stars and Stripes*. "You don't feel very good when you wake up, because there is a thick fuzz in your head and a horrible taste in your mouth and you wish you had taken your toothbrush out before you threw your pack away. It's a little better when you lie down, even in the mud. Rocks are better than mud because you can curl yourself around the big rocks, even if you wake up with sore bruises where the little rocks dug into you. When you wake up in the mud your cigarettes are all wet and you have an ache in your joints and a rattle in your chest."[11]

Even reporters began to break down from fatigue and lack of sleep. John Steinbeck describes the approach of mental and physical meltdown:

YOUR SKIN FEELS THICK AND INSENSITIVE. There is a salty taste in your mouth. A hard, painful knot is in your stomach where the food is undigested. Your eyes do not pick up much detail and the sharp outlines of objects are slightly blurred. . . . The whole world becomes unreal. . . . Gradually your whole body seems to be packed with cotton. All the main nerve trunks are deadened and out of the battered cortex curious dreamlike thoughts emerge. It is at this time that many men see visions. . . . And out of the hammered brain strange memories are jolted loose, scenes and words and people forgotten, but stored in the back of the brain. These may not be important things, but they come back with startling clarity into the awareness that is turning away from reality. And these memories are almost visions." [12]

Dodging shells from unseen German positions in the hills above them gave the men a feeling of helplessness and made some of them anxious to meet the enemy on more personal terms. There was a lot of talk about that, but it was the rare soldier who looked forward to hand-to-hand combat. Bayonet fighting was an especially frightening prospect. "The one thing that scared me the most," said one GI later in the war, "was the thought of being run through with a German bayonet. The thought of that long steel blade going through my body was bad enough, but the worst part would be when he would violently withdraw the bayonet, taking my guts out. I would be left to die an agonizing slow death." [13]

In November, Clark's troops made their first assault on the Winter Line—a series of interlocking defensive positions, ten miles deep, in the highest peaks of the granite and marble Apennines. Ernie Pyle describes mountain fighting in terrain where mules were as valuable as riflemen:

THE COUNTRY WAS SHOCKINGLY BEAUTIFUL, and just as shockingly hard to capture from the enemy. The hills rose to high ridges of almost solid rock. We couldn't go around them through the flat peaceful valleys, because the Germans were up there looking down upon us, and they would have let us have it. So we had to go up and over. A mere platoon of Germans, well dug in on a high, rock-spined hill, could hold out for a long time against tremendous onslaughts. . . .

Our troops were living in almost inconceivable misery. The fertile black valleys were knee-deep in mud. Thousands of the men had not been dry for weeks. Other thousands lay at night in the high mountains with the temperature below freezing and the thin snow sifting over them. They dug into the stones and slept in little chasms and behind rocks and in half-caves. They lived like men of prehistoric times, and a club would have become them more than a machine gun. . . .

If there had been no German fighting troops in Italy . . . our northward march would still have been slow. The country was so difficult that we formed a great deal of cavalry for use in the mountains. Each division had hundreds of horses and mules to carry supplies beyond the point where vehicles could go no farther. On beyond the mules' ability, mere men—American men—took it on their backs. . . .

The mountain fighting went on week after dreary week. For a while I hung around with one of the mule-pack outfits. There was an average of one mule-packing outfit for every infantry battalion in the mountains. Some were run by Americans, some by Italian soldiers.

The pack outfit I was with supplied a battalion that was fighting on a bald, rocky ridge nearly four thousand feet high. That battalion fought constantly for ten days and nights, and when the men finally came down less than a third of them were left.

All through those terrible days every ounce of their supplies had to go up to them on the backs of mules and men. Mules took it the first third of the way. Men took it the last bitter two-thirds, because the trail was too steep for even mules. . . .

On an average night the supplies would run something like this—85 cans of water, 100 cases of K ration, 10 cases of D ration, 10 miles of telephone wire, 25 cases of grenades and rifle and machine-gun ammunition, about 100 rounds of heavy mortar shells, 1 radio, 2 telephones, and 4 cases of first-aid packets and sulfa drugs. In addition, the packers would cram their pockets with cigarettes for the boys on top; also cans of Sterno, so they could heat some coffee once in a while. . . .

Mail was their most tragic cargo. Every night they would take up sacks of mail, and every night they'd bring a large portion of it back down—the recipients would have been killed or wounded the day their letters came.[14]

Ernie Pyle was the GIs' favorite reporter. The troops loved him, thought he captured their feelings exactly. But it was Bill Mauldin, the combat artist, who wrote the best description of the rifleman's day-to-day battle for survival. Mauldin wrote it for those folks back at home who might have been wondering what it was like to be in a foxhole on the front lines.

DIG A HOLE IN YOUR BACKYARD while it is raining. Sit in the hole while the water climbs up around your ankles. Pour cold mud down your shirt collar. Sit there for forty-eight hours, and, so there is no danger of your dozing off, imagine that a guy is sneaking around waiting for a chance to club you on the head or set your house on fire. Get out of the hole, fill a suitcase full of rocks, pick it up, put a shotgun in your other hand, and walk on the muddiest road you can find. Fall flat on your face every few minutes, as you imagine big meteors streaking down to sock you. . . . Snoop around until you find a bull. Try to figure out a way to sneak around him without letting him see you. When he does see you, run like hell all the way back to your hole in the backyard, drop the suitcase and shotgun, and get in. If you repeat this performance every three days for several months you may begin to understand why an infantryman gets out of breath. But you still won't understand how he feels when things get tough." [15]

Progress was slow all along the front. In early December, newly formed units of liberated Italy came up to fight in the front lines against their former Axis partner, and Mussolini, with Hitler's help, formed a fascist government in northern Italy and began sending troops to Kesselring. In Italy, world war merged with civil war.

In mid-January, Clark's men consolidated their positions for another drive on the Winter Line. They broke through, only to run into a new and even stronger defense system high in the rugged mountains south of Rome—the Gustav Line.

Robert Capa was with the 34th Infantry Division when it first tried to break through the Gustav Line. As he climbed the steep slopes of Mount Pantano the dead had not yet been buried.

EVERY FIVE YARDS A FOXHOLE, in each at least one dead soldier. Around them, torn covers of pocket books soaked through and through, empty cans of C-rations, and faded bits of letters from home. The bodies of those who had dared to leave their holes were blocking my path. Their blood was dry and rusty, blending with the color of the late autumn leaves fallen about them.

The higher I climbed, the shorter the distance between the dead. I could not look anymore. I stumbled on toward the hilltop, repeating to myself like an idiot, "I want to walk in the California sunshine and wear white shoes and white trousers." The correspondent's war neurosis was setting in.

Two days before Christmas, Capa decided that "the Fifth Army and I—we had had it. I knew the war would not be decided in Italy." He asked for a jeep to take him to Naples, packed his bags, and followed Eisenhower and the war to London. [16]

ANZIO AND CASSINO

Capa left a campaign that had become a horrible stalemate. That December, Churchill proposed a daring offensive to break it. The English and Americans would land an amphibious force behind the Gustav Line, on the beaches of Anzio, about thirty-five miles south of Rome. It would move out from the beachhead to seize the Alban Hills, cutting the only roads from the Gustav Line to Rome, preventing a German escape from the south. Clark's army would then smash though the middle of the Gustav Line near Monte Cassino, link up with the Anzio force, trap the retreating Germans between the two armies, and capture Rome.

On January 22, 1944, almost 50,000 men—far too few to do the job—landed at Anzio. The enemy was caught off-guard. The only Germans on the beach were four drunken officers who drove their military car into the open door of an Allied landing ship. Under advice from Clark to proceed cautiously, Major General John Lucas failed to take advantage of the enemy's absence and move inland quickly to the Alban Hills, twenty-eight miles from Rome. Expecting a heavy German counterattack, he dug in and consolidated his position, with the approval of both Clark and the chief commander, General Alexander. Only when he secured the beachhead would he move out.

While Lucas delayed, Kesselring brought in 100,000 troops and secured the high ground around the beach's perimeter, turning Anzio into a deadly trap. Here, as elsewhere in Italy, the war came down to a battle of long-distance projectiles against all but defenseless troops—steel against flesh. Under Lucas, a brilliant artillery commander, the Allies gave as good as they got, but they were on vulnerable ground. "On the beachhead every inch of our territory was under German artillery fire," Ernie Pyle wrote from Anzio. "There was no rear area that was immune, as in most battle zones. . . . The land of Anzio beachhead is flat, and our soldiers felt strange and naked with no rocks to take cover behind, no mountains to provide slopes for protection. . . .

"Never had I seen a war zone so crowded. Of course, men weren't standing shoulder to shoulder, but I suppose the most indiscriminate shell dropped at any point on the beachhead would have landed not more than two hundred yards from somebody." [17]

The battlefield was so saturated by firepower that many of the dead could not be removed and rotted for months. "You know what a direct hit by a shell does to a guy?"

a member of a Graves Registration detail said to a reporter. "Sometimes all we have is a leg or a hunk of arm."

When there was an intact body on the Anzio beachhead, and it had not been found for a while, it bloated and changed color. "They don't all get blue," said the Graves Registration man, "some of them get black. But they all stink. There's only one stink and that's it. You never get used to it, either. And after a while, the stink gets in your clothes and you can taste it in your mouth.

"You know what I think? I think maybe if every civilian in the world could smell that stink, then maybe we wouldn't have any more wars." [18]

At one point, on February 16, the shelling strangely stopped for a moment. Seconds later, the Germans threw everything into a furious counterattack that nearly drove the invaders back into the sea. Hospitals were bombed, nurses and patients were killed, and cooks and truck drivers were put on the line to stem the enemy advance. In desperate fighting, the Allies held, just barely, saved by tremendous point-blank artillery fire, along with Navy and air support.

They could not break through, however. All they could do was build a perimeter defense and wait for help while the Germans poured down fire on them day and night. The Germans were so close in places that they were able to roll down grenades on the Allies' positions, but they too were not strong enough to smash the enemy.

It was a World War I–style standoff, with fighting reminiscent of that war. There were long lines of opposing trenches, with a shell-shattered no-man's-land of tangled barbed wire and minefields between them. And the Germans had a World War I–sized railroad gun—"Anzio Annie"—firing 564-pound shells from its 154-foot-long barrel. To move anywhere on the beachhead in daylight was potentially lethal. Said a GI trapped in a chest-deep foxhole:

AND THE NIGHTS WERE WORSE. The hole got about six inches of water, and you couldn't do anything but try to bail it out with your helmet. We wrapped shelter halves and blankets around us, but they didn't do much good. They got soaked with rain and then you sat on a piece of wood or something and shivered and cussed. . . .

Jerry threw in a lot of artillery and mortars. The best thing to do was to pull in your head and pray. Some of that big stuff would cave in the side of a wet foxhole . . . and a couple of the boys got buried right in their hole fifty yards away from me. We had two or three casualties every day, mostly from artillery and mortars. If you got it at night you were lucky, because they could get you out right away. God help you if you got hit in the daytime.[19]

As Anzio veteran Bill Mauldin would say: you were trapped in two dimensions. Trapped by the sea at your back and the mountains in front of you; and by shells above you and cold mud below you. One of the only consolations the troops had was the wine they found buried all over the area. The wine barrels had supporting iron bands and thirsty men found them by using mine detectors.[20]

In the four months the invasion force was trapped on the Anzio beachhead, the Americans alone suffered 59,000 casualties. Before the siege was over, General Lucian Truscott, who had fought under Patton in Sicily and was as aggressive as his former commander, replaced General Lucas. John Lucas was fired by his superiors for doing what they had told him to do when he landed at Anzio.

Both parts of the Anzio plan failed, for Clark's forces were unable to break through the Gustav Line, one of the strongest defensive positions in the history of warfare. In front of the Army were two swollen, fast-flowing rivers, the Garigliano and the Rapido, and behind these loomed Monte Cassino, the keystone of the Gustav Line. It rose 1,700 feet above the Liri River Valley and commanded the main road from Naples to Rome. At the top of Monastery Hill stood the abbey founded by St. Benedict in the sixth century. Looted and destroyed by a succession of invaders, it stood formidable and forbidding in its reconstructed Baroque form, looking more like a fortress than a religious shrine. The German panzer corps commander, General Fridolin von Senger und Etterlin, had not occupied the abbey, partly because he was a lay Benedictine and partly because he had a better observation post on a high hill behind the monastery. Expecting the worst, he brought in trucks to remove to Rome all the artworks and one of the great libraries of the world, containing original manuscripts of Cicero, Virgil, Ovid, Seneca, and other luminaries. Only the abbot, who was in his eighties, five monks, and a party of caretakers were permitted to remain in the monastery.

Clark had made a head-on attack on Cassino two days after the Anzio landing, using the U.S. 34th Division, supported by General Alphonse Juin's North African troops. The 34th was savaged after a nearly three-week battle in violent rain and snow. Then Clark, who had desperately wanted this to be an American victory, reluctantly turned over the battle to General Alexander's reserves. These were international units made up primarily of New Zealanders and Indians and commanded by New Zealand's Bernard Freyberg, a hard campaigner who had twenty-seven separate wounds on his body from previous fighting. Like many of the men in the valley beneath Cassino that had become a Nazi shooting gallery, Freyberg was convinced that the Germans were using the monastery as an artillery observation post. And he must also have seen the enormous and intact monastery as a hated symbol of enemy defiance and personal failure. Before he began his assault, he requested that the abbey be obliterated. Clark and Alexander were not convinced the Germans were using the monastery, but they yielded to the field commander on the firing line. On February 15, 135 B-17s dropped 500-pound bombs and incendiaries on one of the sacred treasures of Christendom. They were followed by waves of medium bombers, which did most of the damage.

Holding a wooden cross in front of him, the abbot of Monte Cassino led a group of survivors out of the devastation and toward the German lines. At the bottom of the valley, troops cheered wildly as they saw great columns of smoke and flame rising from the holy place.

It was a monstrous act and it was all for naught. The Germans had not been using the monastery, but they did use the mountain of rubble created by the bombing to build an almost impregnable defensive position—and from it, repulsed the New Zealanders.

On March 15, a shattering aerial and artillery bombardment leveled the town of Cassino, but when Freyberg's New Zealanders tried to inch forward over rain-washed mountain passes they found it impossible to use tanks on roads pockmarked with shell craters and choked with debris. A hundred or so members of the German 1st Parachute Division, under orders from Hitler to hold or die, crawled out from under the blasted remains of the town and stopped the drive.

Even when the fighting ceased momentarily, conditions were appalling. At night the mud froze like cement and the winds blew with terrific force, shaking the towering, snow-shrouded trees. In their foxholes, men's wet feet froze and trench foot became epidemic. If men "couldn't stand the pain, they crawled out of their holes and stumbled and crawled (they couldn't walk) down the mountains until they reached the aid station," wrote Bill Mauldin. "Their shoes were cut off, and their feet swelled like balloons. Sometimes the feet had to be amputated. But most often the men had to make their agonized way back up the mountain and crawl into their holes again because there were no replacements and the line had to be held." [21]

In a place the GIs called Purple Heart Valley, dead American soldiers were frozen to the ground and packs of wild dogs chewed on their throats.

By April, the Allies had advanced only seventy miles in eight months and there was

THE RUINS OF MONTE CASSINO ABBEY AT THE END OF THE SIEGE (SC).

no relief for the men on the front lines. This was the infantryman's catch-22: the better a soldier you were the less likely they were going to let you go home. The only ticket home was a wound that didn't kill. "That's all [the men] talk about," said one GI.[22]

On to Rome

In May the Allies finally cracked the Gustav Line. They did it not, as in the past, with piecemeal attacks, but with a full fourteen-division offensive organized by Alexander, one that gave them overwhelming numerical superiority. The French force, made up largely of Moroccan mountain fighters who preferred to kill silently with knives, scaled the steep peaks behind the Germans and broke through to the Liri Valley. The Americans and British hammered at the flanks.

Then it was up to the Polish Corps. It went straight for Cassino and the elite Nazi parachute group that was holding it. Paul Green, a reporter for *Stars and Stripes,* joined the Poles after they took the monastery in a sacrificial charge:

> AS WE STOOD ON ABBEY HILL, we had a perfect view of the surrounding countryside. A scene of utter desolation unfolded before us. The pine forest below the hill was stripped so bare of branches and bark that it resembled a matchstick replica. The huge abbey itself was a mass of ruins. All we could see was rubble. . . .
>
> Polish troops, their victory achieved at great price, basked outside in the bright afternoon sun. . . . Through an interpreter, the Poles told us of their savage battle to evict the Germans. A battle of annihilation, one officer called it. Neither side gave any quarter and even the wounded fought to the death. But as soon as a key hill, Colle San Angelo, fell, the Germans knew they had been outflanked. With that hill in Polish hands, and Highway 7 cut by the British, there was no way for reinforcements or supplies to reach them. Though these vaunted parachutists boasted of fighting to the death, from that moment they decided to surrender, but to the British rather than the Poles whose retribution they feared with good reason." [25]

That same day the greatly reinforced VI Corps at Anzio, under Lucian Truscott, burst from its defensive perimeter and in wild fighting took the Alban Hills, the last German position defending Rome.

As Clark's army began moving north, Eric Sevareid noticed a dead German soldier lying inside a doorway, his boots sticking into the street. "Two American soldiers were resting and smoking cigarettes a few feet away, paying the body no attention. 'Oh, him?' one of them said in response to a question. 'Son of a bitch kept lagging behind the others when we brought them in. We got tired of hurrying him up all the time.' Thus casually was deliberate murder announced by boys who a year before had taken no lives but those of squirrel or pheasant." [24]

Two days later, on June 4, Clark's armored columns entered Rome. There were no wild cheering crowds. Romans hid behind locked doors, fearing a final German reprisal. "When we got to Rome, it was eerie," recalls retired Army officer Edward H.

Thomas. "It was like no one was there. It appeared to be a city from which everyone had moved." But as they advanced toward the center of Rome, people came streaming out of buildings to greet their liberators, throwing roses, offering wine, and climbing on the tanks to kiss the hands of the exhausted, unshaven Americans.[25]

In taking Rome, Mark Clark might have prolonged the Italian campaign. The main objective was the German Army, but Clark had ignored Alexander's orders to strike northeast from the Alban Hills and cut off Kesselring's line of retreat. Instead, he had sent a token force after the Germans and ordered his main columns to head north for Rome, a decision that allowed the Germans to slip away and fight again. Clark wanted his Fifth Army, not the British, to have the honor of liberating Rome, the first Axis capital to fall.

Alexander covered up for Clark, calling Rome—a city of symbolic rather than strategic value—a great and important victory. This failed to convince correspondents who were covering the Fifth Army. "[Clark] had a reputation as a shameless publicity seeker," Paul Green wrote. Nothing was going to deter him from capturing "Capitoline Hill where he was determined to have his picture taken to be published, he hoped, on the world's front pages."[26] The photographers snapped their pictures, but the liberation of Rome was pushed off the front pages by a greater Allied breakthrough, the Normandy invasion, launched two days after Clark rode triumphantly into Rome.

It had taken five months to move the short distance from Cassino to Rome, via Anzio, and had cost over 100,000 broken or buried men. What had been gained? Valuable airfields at Foggia from which to strike at Romania and the Reich; this and the tying down of German divisions that would have been used elsewhere. Some asked: was it worth it?

That December, Ann O'Hare McCormick of the *New York Times* wrote a story about a delegation of American congressmen who visited the Italian front at the conclusion of a tour of European battlefields. The congressmen were shocked by what they found. Nothing they had seen could compare, they said, with the "inhumane conditions" under which American troops were fighting and dying in Italy. Folks at home were not being told how bad it was here, and they wanted to know who was responsible for the cover-up.

McCormick claimed the press was not to blame. "Stories have been written and have been printed, [but] the thing is indescribable." Civilians lived in one world, fighting men another, "an abnormal world" that was nearly impossible to picture to people back in the States.[27]

Eric Sevareid saw things differently. He and other correspondents had been unable to get the full story to their readers because of Allied censorship, which in Italy was controlled by the British. General Harold Alexander had his staff tell reporters "not only what they should not write" Sevareid claimed, "but what they should." Sevareid admitted, as well, that he and other reporters felt constrained to publicly criticize the high command in Italy "while men were dying." Had the American people got the full truth about Italy there might have been a public outcry to stop what Sevareid called a senseless slaughter.[28]

The Germans fell back from Rome to the Gothic Line, a new and even stronger defense chain in front of the Po Valley, north of Florence. After Rome, this became the Allies' objective. All through June and July Allied forces pursued the Germans, delayed by mines, mud, lengthening supply lines, and long processions of refugees. With almost all the village men fighting, crops had not been put in the ground and families were starving. They stayed alive by stealing rations from the Allied armies or by buying them on the black market. Prostitution was rampant. Mothers sold their bodies to GIs for K rations to feed their hollow-eyed children.

As the Germans retreated north, the Allied armies occasionally ran into anti-Fascist Partisans who had been fighting a guerrilla war against both German units and Mussolini's diehard supporters. That summer a strangely dressed character approached an Anglo-American encampment. Sergeant Harry Sions, writing in *Yank*, tells the story of "The Partisan from Brooklyn."

THE STRANGER WORE BRITISH ARMY SHOES, mustard-colored cotton pants, a torn GI paratroooper's jacket and an Italian straw hat with an orange band. Cpl. Milo Peck of Barre, Mass., who was standing guard at the gate, was not impressed.

"And what do you want inside?" asked Peck.

"I want to report to my outfit," the stranger said. "I'm Manuel Serrano. Don't you remember me?"

"Serrano!" said Peck. "I thought you were dead a long time ago, back in Tunisia. Where the hell have you been all this time?"

"Well," said Serrano, "I've been to a lot of places, but for the last 10 months I've been fighting with the Eyetie Partisans up in the hills."

"Well, I'll be damned," said Peck. "Come on in."

And that was how Sgt. Manuel Serrano, the first American soldier known to have fought with the Italian Partisans, returned to his outfit after an absence of 20 months.

Serrano is a six-footer, deeply sunburned and husky. He has a small black moustache and thick black hair streaked with gray. Born in Puerto Rico 24 years ago, he had lived in Brooklyn, N.Y., since he was 5, and before the war played the maracas and drums in a rumba band in a Greenwich Village hot spot. In February 1942 he volunteered for the Paratroops, trained at Fort Benning, Ga., and found himself in rapid succession . . . in England and on the North Africa invasion.

A month after the November 1942 landing in Tunisia, Serrano . . . was on a mission to blow up a bridge near El Djem. His patrol was surprised by the Jerries, a few of the 38 GIs were killed and several, including Serrano, were captured.

Four days later Serrano was put on an Italian destroyer with a batch of other Allied prisoners and shipped to an Italian prison camp at Palmero, Sicily. . . .

His first stop in Italy was a concentration camp called No. 59, at Servigliano on the Adriatic coast. He stayed there for nine months. No. 59 had an assortment of American and British prisoners, Yugoslav Partisans, Albanians, and Jews of various nationalities. When they heard via the grapevine of the Italian surrender in September 1943, they made a general break.

The day after the break, Serrano met three of the Yugoslavs in the hills. They were on their way to an Italian Partisan camp in the mountains near Sarnano, about 60 miles to the south. Serrano asked the Yugoslavs what the Italians did and was told they killed Germans and Fascists. That was good enough for him, so he went along.

It took Serrano and the Yugoslavs three days to make the Partisan camp. The hide-out was buried so deeply in the mountain underbrush that they would never have found it except for the help of a friendly farmer. At the hide-out they met 50 Italians and a few more Yugoslavs. . . .

Two weeks later Serrano was picked to go on his first raid. Like all Partisan raids, it would be made at night. The objective was Penna, about 15 miles to the east, where the raiders were to pick up several of the town's leading Fascists and bring them back to camp for trial.

Early in the afternoon a couple of Partisans dressed in civvies circulated through the town to check on the number of Jerries there. If the place was heavy with Jerries, the raid would have to be postponed. There were only a few Jerries around. The raid was on.

Serrano and 19 other Partisans made their way down the mountain paths to the outskirts of the town where they waited for complete darkness. They sneaked in, one by one.

"I was pretty nervous," says Serrano. "They taught me a lot of tricks at Benning and in England, but Fascist-hunting wasn't one of them. . . .

Serrano headed for the house of a Partisan sympathizer, first making sure that a red light was showing in the window; this meant that the coast was clear. Inside he found the other Partisans. The sympathizer led them to the houses of the five Fascists on the night's calling list. Four or five Partisans worked each house, quietly and smoothly. They bound and gagged the Fascists and carried them swiftly out of town and up to the Partisan camp in the hills.

"They hanged those five Fascists," says Serrano. "They gave them a trial and then they hanged them. . . .

"Some of the Fascists we let go—if they weren't active in the party but just paid their dues or tuned on the radio to listen to Il Duce when they were ordered to. We scared the sugar out of them first before we let them go. Some of them even wanted to join up with us, but the Partisans wouldn't have them.

"And then there were some in-between Fascists we let go, but we gave them the castor-oil treatment first—just so they'd have a taste of what they used to hand out. We'd raid the Fascist headquarters and grab their stocks of bottled castor oil. Then we'd dose it out. If a Fascist was in the party for 10 years, then we'd give him 10 doses, a dose a year. . . ."

When the going was tough, the Partisans hid out for weeks in the mountain recesses, in caves or in forest groves on the hillsides. They wore nondescript uniforms—part British, part German, part American, part civilian clothes. Their only weapons were a few old Italian Army rifles and *ballila* (hand grenades) and some captured German pistols. They carried sharpened Italian bayonets and used them as knives. Six months after Serrano joined the Partisans, British planes dropped machine guns and rifles to them.

The band of Partisans to which Serrano belonged was evidently only one of many bands operating all over Italy, wherever the Germans were. The units were organized and controlled through a radio station known as *Italia Combatte* (Italy Fights).

"Every night," Serrano says, "we'd turn on the radio to listen to our code signal, 'Sole tra monte (the sun is between the mountains).' When we heard that, we'd take down the instructions for our next raid. . . ."

Serrano recalls one order about catching a big-shot Fascist in the town of Ascoli. "The radio listed the homes the Fascist lived in at different times, his favorite coffee shops and the hours he visited them, his latest mistress, and the color of her hair, and the address of their love nest. We located that Fascist late at night in the love nest, where he was waiting for his girlfriend to show up. We didn't bother taking him back to the mountains. We let him have it right there." . . .

The Partisans in Serrano's band came from all classes. There were workers and a couple of businessmen. There were Italian sailors, and officers and men of the Italian Army. And for a few months there were a couple of GIs from the 1st Division who had been captured and then escaped.

One of the most important Partisan jobs was to help escaped American and British prisoners. Serrano estimates that his band helped more than 100 prisoners back to Allied lines. . . .

But not all the escaped prisoners were able to make the Allied lines. Many of them were caught. If the Germans got them, the prisoners were usually taken back to the prison camps. But they weren't always that lucky if the Fascists caught them first.

One morning in March, while the Partisans were camping in the hills near Comunanza in the La Marche region, a farmer reported that the Fascists had captured and killed six escaped Allied prisoners. They had stripped the prisoners of their identifications and clothes, he said, and had taken them to a field nearby. Then they had forced the prisoners to dig a long shallow ditch. When the ditch was dug, the Fascists machine-gunned the prisoners, threw their bodies into the ditch and covered them with a few shovelfuls of dirt.

"That night," Serrano says, "three of us made for the field. We saw the ditch but the bodies had disappeared. We checked around and learned that nuns had taken the bodies to the convent in Comunanza after the Fascists left. We went to the convent and there were the six bodies, wrapped in white sheets and laying on slabs of wood. The nuns had cleaned the bodies and wrapped them in the sheets. I lifted up the covers from the faces and recognized them all. Four were GIs from the 1st Division, the other two were British. The nuns said they would give them a decent burial. Then we left.

"I walked out of that convent and back up the hills to camp. When I got to the top of the first hill I turned around toward the convent and those six dead soldiers, and I swore that for each one of those soldiers I would kill a Fascist with my bare hands. I think for the first time I really knew what it meant to be a Partisan." . . .

From April to June the Germans started going after the Partisans in earnest. Jerry planes tried to bomb them out of the hills and mortars tried to blast them out. In the last week of April a mixed unit of Fascists and Jerries had the band surrounded for three days.

"Most of us got away," says Serrano, "but five were caught. The Fascists hanged them. Not a quick hanging like we gave them, but the slow Fascist hanging. They pulled the bodies up above the ground, then let them down slowly till the toes touched the ground, then up again after a while. That way the hangings could last a couple of days. I tell you, those Fascists were no good. The Yugoslavs were right. When we had that first trial, they said: 'What are you wasting time with trials for? Hang the swine.' "

The Partisans did not let the enemy hold the offensive against them but struck back. . . . As the Germans retreated by night over the back roads before the advancing British, the Partisans struck and ran and struck again. For three straight nights they raided all the neighboring towns, seizing and shooting all the Fascists they could find. . . .

"I told the Partisans," Serrano says. "I told them: 'Get all the Fascists now, before the Allies get here. They might be too easy on them.' "

On the fourth day the captain called the Partisan band together and told them their work in La Marche was done. Those who wished could go up north to continue the fight behind the enemy lines.

Serrano made his way back up to Servigliano and rested for a few days in the home of an Italian friend. Those were happy, confused days for the people of Servigliano. The Germans had gone and so had most of the town Fascists, but the British had not yet arrived. The people dug up all the *vino* they had hid from the Nazis and they danced in the streets. At night they gathered in their homes and drank and sang the half-forgotten songs of a free Italy, songs they had not dared to sing in the open for 22 years. Partisans who hadn't seen their families for months came back, hailed as heroes.

On the day Serrano left, he made a speech in the town *piazza.* "I told them

I'd be back some day," he says, "and that I would tell the American soldiers what I had learned from the Partisans. They begged me to stay. They even wanted to make me mayor of the town. In fact, they wanted to give me the town's prettiest girl for a wife. But I guess I'll wait till I get back to Brooklyn and find a nice Italian girl there. I like these Eyeties. Maybe it's because I'm Latin, too, and understand them a little better than some other American soldiers."

Forty miles from Servigliano, Serrano met an American Paratroop major, who told him where Serrano's old outfit was stationed. It wasn't very far away. A truck gave Serrano a lift and dropped him about eight miles from his unit camp.

"I walked those last eight miles," says Serrano. "But it felt like floating on air."

Back in camp Serrano met his old buddies. There were 75 left out of the original outfit as it was activated at Benning more than two years ago. After Tunisia, where Serrano was captured, the battalion had gone on to fight in Sicily and in Italy.

"I don't know what the outfit's going to have me do," says Serrano . . . "but I know what I'd like to do. I'd like to drop back behind the Jerry lines again with an M1 and take 20 of these fellows with me." [29]

In their march northward, the Allied armies liberated Siena, Perugia, and other ancient towns. Seventy-five thousand German troops were unable to stop the British advance up central Italy toward Florence. Patrols reached Florence on August 4. In the city itself every bridge spanning the Arno was destroyed except for Ponte Vecchio. The Germans spared it because it could not handle the heavy trucks and armor of the advancing enemy. But house-to-house fighting did immense damage to other city treasures.

THE GOTHIC LINE

City by city—Pisa, Lucca, Prato, Remini—the Allied armies marched northward. Gains were not dramatic and were won only by punishing attrition, for Allied troops, including the hard-fighting Japanese-American units, were sent that summer to take part in an invasion of southern France. Offered high command in this operation, Clark turned it down to stay with Fifth Army and finish the job.

That September, the British Eighth Army, using Britons, Canadians, Poles, and Indians, punched through the Gothic Line. Martha Gellhorn, the veteran correspondent for *Collier's,* described this advance:

THE GREAT GOTHIC LINE . . . would, under normal circumstances, be a lovely range of the Apennines. In this clear and dreaming weather that is the end of summer, the hills curve up into a water-blue sky: in the hot windless night you see the very hills only as a soft, rounded darkness under the moon. Along the Via Emilia, the road that borders the base of these hills, the Germans dynamited every village into shapeless brick rubble so that they could have a clear line of fire. In front of the flattened villages they dug their long canal to trap tanks. In front of the tank traps they cut all the trees. Among the felled trees and in the gravel bed and the low water of the Foglia River, they laid down barbed wire and they sowed their never-ending mines, the crude little wooden boxes, the small rusty tin cans, the flat metal pancakes which are the simplest and deadliest weapons in Italy.

On a range of hills that is the actual Gothic Line, the Germans built concrete machine-gun pillboxes which encircle the hills and dominate all approaches. They sank the turrets of tanks, with their long, thin snout-ended 88-mm. guns, in camouflaged pits so that nothing on wheels or tracks could pass their way. They mined some more. They turned the beautiful hills into a mountain trap four miles deep where every foot of our advance could be met with concentrated fire. . . .

It was the Canadians who broke into this line on the Adriatic side by finding a soft place and going through. . . . They got across the mined river and past the dynamited villages and over the asphalt road and up into the hills and from then on they poured men and tanks into the gap and they gouged the German positions with artillery fire and they called in the Desert Air Force to bomb it and in two days they had come out on the other side of the Gothic Line at the coast of the Adriatic. But before that . . . the main body of the Eighth Army moved from the center of Italy to the Adriatic coast in three days' time, and the Germans did not know it. . . . This enormous army ground its way across Italy and took up positions on a front thirteen miles long. The Eighth Army, which was now ready to attack the last German fortified line outside the Siegfried Line, had fought its way to these mountains from the Egyptian border. In two years since El Alamein, the Eighth Army had advanced across Africa through Sicily and up the peninsula of Italy. And all these men of how many races and nationalities felt that this was the last push and after this they would go home. . . .

Historians will think about this campaign far better than we can who have seen it. The historians will note that in the first year of the Italian campaign, in 365 days of steady fighting, the Allied armies advanced 315 miles. They will note this with admiration because it is the first time in history that any armies have invaded Italy from the south and fought up the endless mountain ranges toward the Alps. Historians will be able to explain with authority what it meant to break three fortified lines attacking up mountains, and the historians will also describe how Italy became a giant mine field and that no weapon is uglier, for it waits in silence, and it can kill any day, not only on the day of battle.

But all we know who are here is that the Gothic Line is cracked and that it is the last line. Soon our armored divisions will break into the Lombardy plain and then at last the end of this long Italian campaign will become a fact, not a dream. The weather is lovely and no one wants to think of what men must still die and what men must still be wounded in the fighting before peace comes.[30]

One of the GIs in this fight was nineteen-year-old Geddes Mumford, son of the noted New York writer Lewis Mumford. As early as 1938, Lewis and his wife, Sophia, had been ardent advocates of American military intervention against Hitler. Geddes shared their passion and dropped out of school to enlist in the Army. He was ruggedly handsome, an outdoorsman, an avid hunter and fisherman with a wild streak that sometimes got him in trouble with his parents and teachers. But the Army had given him a dose of discipline and he had a steady girlfriend now, who had a taming influence on him. They planned to marry.

Just before Geddes went overseas his mother wrote to him:

I FIND MYSELF WAKING UP in the middle of the night and thinking about you and about the other boys at war and hating civilians, and hating being a civilian. . . . We can't all go off to war, I know. But we could all be *in* the war to the same extent. . . . I find it intolerable that with eight million men under arms the rest of the country's population can go ahead living as they please, with no compulsion toward the common goal. . . .

Seeing what you have become, Geddes my darling, has given me a great thrill of pride. God bless you and keep you well.

With deep love, Your Mother.

Geddes reached Italy in June and got his first taste of combat the following month. After a long silence, his worried parents finally heard from him that July:

YOUR DEAR LITTLE BOY has finally seen the more gruesome side of this man's war. I celebrated my birthday by coming as close to getting killed as I ever want to. I felt the machine gun bullets passing my shoulder. Two of my buddies were hit by the same burst. It's a great life if you like excitement.

It's not all that rough, don't you worry.

That August, Geddes was appointed a scout, one of the most dangerous combat assignments. The next month his division was ordered to make an assault on the mountain passes of the Gothic Line.

All that summer his father wrote him, asking him to describe what combat was like so he could share Geddes's experiences with him in his imagination and feel closer to him. On August 14, his son finally answered him:

DEAR DAD:

While I have written you several letters since I have been in combat I, as you know, have refrained from describing the nature of fighting because of the difference of experience between you and I. It is impossible to make a person who has not been in combat understand it fully. I'll do what I can though and just hope you get something from it.

Fighting behind enemy lines, alone in the night, Geddes had killed his first German. That had been scary, he told his father, and so were the firefights against machine gunners, but nothing compared to being shelled:

YOU HEAR A SHELL COMING two or three seconds before it hits. . . . It's the ones that come fast and at you that really scare. You just hit the ground and wait. Wonder if it's got your dog tag number on it. If it's a really close one you don't hear it [until] the moment before it hits. That fraction of a second between the time it stops hissing and before it explodes gets pretty long. When those moments start coming every few seconds it gets pretty hard. I've seen men cry like babies after they have been under it too long. I've seen men almost unable to walk just from nervous exhaustion. . . .

The small arms part of war is all right. It's a deadly but exciting game; an overdone version of hunting. The artillery, bombs, rockets, and mortars are the hard part. You have no personal comeback against them. You can shoot a man, but you can only hope and wait with a shell. Killing a man in war leaves almost no mark on a man's soul. It's the wine and crunch of shells and the mutilated bodies of your buddies and friends that tears a man to pieces.

You have asked me for a description of combat I've done what I can. Maybe your writer's imagination will help you a bit. There's only one way to really find out and you can thank your damn lucky stars you're not in the infantry overseas to do it.

There it is Dad.

Love

Geddes

On September 6, Geddes's division moved across the Arno. His unit's objective was Monticelli, a broken ridge 3,000 feet high. The Germans had all the approaches covered.

Before he went into combat, Geddes wrote his parents, trying to explain why he and his fellow GIs found it so difficult to tell people back home what they were experiencing:

IT'S HARD FOR MEN, who live only because they co-operate, to explain things to people who live only as semi-isolated individuals. A front line soldier will almost always *give* you half of his last dollar or one of his last two cigarettes. An American civilian finds it hard to lend you half of his surplus.

A man who has gone but a few hundred yards with death in his footsteps and the fear of God in his heart appreciates his fellow man just a bit more than before. The returning front line soldier will find himself, first shocked and then embittered by this difference in outlook. This will be one of the problems of a post-war world.[31]

In his next letter Geddes told his worried parents he had no great urge to be a hero, and "a Purple Heart is something I don't intend to get. With luck I'll be home for my next birthday." There was one more letter, from behind the lines. Then the first telegram from the War Department: Geddes was reported missing in action. On the 17th of September, the second telegram arrived, the only kind that was delivered by hand, not over the phone.

Geddes Mumford was cut down by German gunfire just before his division broke through the Gothic Line. His company was spearheading the attack, and he was out in front of them, an advanced scout.

"When you lose a friend," wrote Bill Mauldin, "you have an overpowering desire to go back home and yell in everybody's ear, 'This guy was killed fighting for you. Don't forget him—ever. Keep him in your mind when you wake up in the morning and when you go to bed at night. Don't think of him as a statistic which changes 38,788 casualties to 38,789. Think of him as a guy who wanted to live every bit as much as you do." [32]

When Lewis and Sophia Mumford learned of the death of their son they wrote to his regiment to find out how he had died and if anyone—perhaps a friend—was with him at the end. But no one saw him get it and no one knew where he was buried. "He was a very young boy and was well liked by the members of his Company," one of his former officers replied. "However, so many replacements have been made in the Company we were unable to find a real 'Buddy' of his." [33]

Before the Allied armies progressed far beyond the Gothic Line, in their drive for Bologna and the Po Valley, bad weather set in and the Germans put up strong resistance. When the cold rains came in October, the German Army was still entrenched in a line of fortifications that had been built along the slopes of a fifty-mile-deep mountain range with the labor of 17,000 Italian and Slovak prisoners. One of the most closely watched American combat units in front of the Gothic Line that fall was the 92nd Division, the only African-American division to see combat in Europe. They called themselves the Buffalo Soldiers after the black cavalry regiments that had served in the American West after the Civil War, and they were a fiercely proud and highly trained fighting unit. "We were young and dumb and thought we were going to whip the Germans' behinds and drive them back home as soon as we got there," says Lieutenant Vernon J. Baker, a platoon leader from Cheyenne, Wyoming. Baker arrived in Italy with the first group of Buffalo Soldiers, the crack 370th Combat Team. When they disembarked at Naples on July 30, 1944, African-American soldiers in the service units on the docks cheered them as they marched smartly down the gangways, in full field battle dress, wearing their distinctive circular shoulder patches with a black buffalo on a background of green.

The 370th was put immediately in the line, advancing across the muddy Arno toward the walled city of Lucca and the ultimate Allied objectives in western Italy, the great naval base at La Spezia and the port city of Genoa. After failing to break through the main Gothic Line in the northern Apennines—stymied by torrential autumn rains and relentless enemy shell fire—they moved toward the coast, to the Serchio Valley region, where they were joined in October and November by the remainder of the 92nd. Throughout the winter, they were stationed in these wildly rugged mountains north of Pisa, facing the western anchor of the Gothic Line. "It was," Vernon Baker recalls, "some of the worst country you could fight a war in, but I had grown up in the mountains and knew how to survive in them. From the time I first pulled a trigger at the age of twelve my job was keeping my family going during the Depression by hunting game." [54] By then, the fall offensive against the Gothic Line had failed, and the exhausted, mud-covered Allied troops regrouped for yet a third great push.

The Buffalo Soldiers probably would have remained in the United States for the duration of the war had it not been for pressure from civil rights organizations and an acute manpower shortage in Italy. That summer Eisenhower had stripped the Fifth Army of nearly 100,000 men for the Normandy campaign. At this point in the war, says Captain Hondon Hargrove, a field artillery officer with the 92nd, "Mark Clark's little old 5th Army . . . would have settled for an orangutan." [55] Enlisted men and many of the junior officers of the 92nd were black, while all commanders and staff officers, and most company commanders, were white and predominantly Southern. This was at the insistence of its commander, Major General Edward M. Almond, a Virginian who had graduated from the Virginia Military Institute and who owed his command, some said, to his marriage to the sister of Army Chief of Staff George Marshall. Southern whites, Almond argued, had frequent contacts with black people and knew how to manage them; and he had, accordingly, run the division's rigidly segregated training facility at Fort Huachuca, Arizona, like an antebellum cotton plantation. Not surprisingly, racial distrust and conflict had plagued the unit since it was activated in the spring of 1942.*

In Italy, African-American officers and enlisted men believed they were being used as "cannon fodder" by Almond, who put them in difficult situations under incompetent white officers who believed, as Almond did, that leadership and discipline under fire are "characteristics that are abnormal to [the Negro] race." [56] When an all-black regiment, the 366th, was attached to the 92nd, with its preponderance of white officers, General Almond greeted them with these words: "I did not send for you. Your Negro newspapers, Negro politicians, and white friends have insisted on your seeing

---

*The Army activated a second all-black infantry division, which served in the Pacific.

combat and I shall see that you get combat and your share of the casualties." As another white officer said: "He most certainly kept his word."[37]*

Hatred between whites and blacks ran deep and it affected performance at the front. "The black men I knew wanted to get into combat and smash the enemy," says Vernon Baker. "America wasn't perfect but it was still the best country in the world and it was being threatened by dangerous racist regimes that were a threat to my own people. We wanted to defend our country but at base camp in the South and overseas in Italy we faced the most vicious kind of racism, and that soured a lot of the guys. I tried not to let this get to me; I focused on being a soldier and surviving, but sometimes it was hard to tell who the bigger racists were—the Germans in front of us or the commanders behind us."[38] Staff Sergeant David Cason, of the 92nd, puts it more strongly. "I will say if the 92nd, in the same geographical position, had been told those were southern crackers up in those mountains, 'get 'em,' they would have, myself included, clawed their way up if necessary. We would have waded in our own blood up to our elbows to take them because we would have had a reason: an enemy we knew, despised, and would have enjoyed destroying. The German, what could he mean to us? Nobody bothered to make him our real enemy." Some veterans of the 92nd claim that enlisted men killed their white officers. "There is no doubt," says Sergeant Eugene Lester, a medic, "that a few officers passed through our aid station who had been taken out of the ball game by their own men."[39] Baker never heard of this happening, but admits "sometimes I felt I could put a bullet in the back of one of them. I was there, however, to fight a war not to kill my own people."[40]

General Mark Clark would later call the Buffalo Division the worst in Europe and place the blame directly on its African-American junior officers and enlisted men, the majority of whom were, in the Army's words, "entirely undependable" and "terrified to fight at night."[41] Major General Frederick Davison, who, as a young lieutenant, served in Italy with the 92nd, flatly denies this. Units of the division performed with distinction and the high number of casualties in the division was due, he says, to General Almond and his staff. Their orders "were so flawed, so inept that there was no way that success could have been achieved."[42]

In two operations in the winter of 1944–45, seasoned Nazi mountain units clobbered the Buffalo Soldiers. Their white commanders blamed the defeats on the incom-

---

*A white colonel and four white lieutenant colonels were assigned to the 366th as so-called advisors. But they were, in fact, commanders.

petence and cowardice of the black troops. But Rothacker C. Smith, a medic who witnessed one of these battles and was wounded and left for dead before being captured by the Germans, is amazed that the 92nd fought so bravely when they were treated so badly by their own officers.

AFTER THE WAR, I READ these reports that the Buffalo men "melted away" in combat, but the men I watched—I was a conscientious objector—fought with spirit and guts. That was incredible to me because of the things I saw in training camp in Georgia, things all these guys had seen in the South. Black soldiers on the base had to march German prisoners to the camp theater and wait outside while they watched a movie because it was a "white only" facility. One black soldier had married a white woman up North and brought her down South. They weren't there more than a few days before a gang of white soldiers jumped them at night and beat them to death. How do you fight for your country when you see and hear of things like this? Amazingly, these Buffalo men did.[45]

The Buffalo Soldiers had unusually good relations with the Italian peasants, especially the women, says Vernon Baker, who had a romantic relationship after the war with "a fiery little beauty" from Genoa. This rankled their white officers, even though they looked with disdain on the poverty-stricken mountain people. "Lots of the Buffalo soldiers," Baker says, "married Italian women. That didn't sit well with white southern males."[44]

Both Vernon Baker and Rothacker Smith were near the tiny village of Sommocolonia, in the Serchio Valley, on December 26 to witness one of the great acts of heroism of the war. In what has been called the Battle of the Little Bulge, Nazi troops attacked unexpectedly in the night, many of them dressed as Italian Partisans, and trapped a contingent of Buffalo Soldiers in the village. Lieutenant John Fox, a forward artillery observer, remained in the town with his men, directing defensive fire for retreating troops. When German and Austrian infantry surrounded his position in a house, Fox called down artillery fire dangerously close to himself. "That round was just where I wanted it," he said. "Bring it in 60 more yards." His commander protested, "Fox, that fire will be on you." Fox shouted, "Fire it! There's more of them than there are of us! Give them hell." The bodies of Fox and his party were found in their shattered observation post when the Americans recaptured the town. The fire he had called in killed approximately 100 German soldiers. In 1977, Congress awarded John Fox the Medal of Honor.[45]

Fox had delayed the enemy advance, but only one officer and seventeen men were able to escape the village. And the Germans pushed back the 92nd, which was holding a seventeen-mile front across the Serchio Valley. The Allies moved quickly to send in reinforcements to plug the hole in their lines and take back the valley. By January 1, 1945, the two armies were back at their original positions and the bloody stalemate that extended from the Adriatic to the Ligurian Sea continued through the harsh northern Italian winter.

Relying on Almond's headquarters for its information, the American press roundly criticized the performance of the "luckless 92nd." Its performance was proof, said *Newsweek*, that Negro soldiers couldn't—or wouldn't—fight. But as a white officer of another division pointed out in a letter to *The New Republic*, "The 92nd didn't break nearly so badly as white divisions did under similar conditions at the Kasserine Pass . . . "[46]

"There was disharmony in the 92nd," says Vernon Baker, but "I had no problems with my platoon when the shooting started. None of my platoon 'faded away' or retreated as newspapers alleged of the Buffalo Division. When I went forward under fire, they followed."[47]

Speaking of his Buffalo Soldier comrades, Wade McCree described as well the plight of every Allied unit in the agonizing Italian campaign. "We . . . were put in an area where the war was going to be neither won nor lost. . . . And to witness what happens to spirited men who are forced to accommodate the unacceptable is soul-rending."[48]

Fourteen months after storming ashore on the beaches of Salerno, the Allies still had a lot of fighting to do. They had tied down some of Hitler's best divisions, knocked the Italian Fascists out of the war, and captured air bases in the south to bomb Germany, France, and Eastern Europe. But in the process they had destroyed the greater part of Italy. The narrow, mountainous peninsula had forced the Allies to fight by what Eric Sevareid called "steam-roller advance, crushing towns and villages in their path, laying waste to the countryside. . . .

"The Italian campaign," Sevareid wrote that winter, "is not all debit, by any means. But some day people will want to know whether the returns balanced the enormous investment of Allied lives, ships, transport, and planes. They will ask if we could not have achieved almost as much by stopping in southern Italy at the Volturno line, securing our ports and our bases and using the bulk of our forces in more fruitful encounters elsewhere. They will ask, 'Did not the Italian ground fighting really become a war of attrition and nothing more.' . . .[49]

The answer is in the question.

The men who did the fighting had no knowledge of these big strategic decisions. Their orders were to keep on moving, where next they weren't told. Through his cartoon characters Willie and Joe, Bill Mauldin showed his readers that it was not only the danger of combat that slowly wore men down. "It was perhaps even more," as James Jones put it, "that long haul of day after day of monotony and discomfort and living in perpetual dirt in the field, on and on with no prospect of release and no amenities. Without women, without tablecloths, without a decent bathroom."[50]

Most of Mauldin's readers knew him only from his cartoons in *Stars and Stripes*. But in *Up Front*, the book he wrote in 1944, he gave as fine a portrait as we have of the ordinary "dogface" who slugged his way up the bloody boot to the Gothic Line.

SOME SAY THE AMERICAN SOLDIER is the same clean-cut young man who left his home; others say morale is sky-high at the front because everybody's face is shining for the great Cause.

They are wrong. The combat man isn't the same clean-cut lad because you don't fight a kraut by Marquis of Queensberry rules. You shoot him in the back, you blow him apart with mines, you kill or maim him the quickest and most effective way you can with the least danger to yourself. . . .

But you don't become a killer. No normal man who has smelled and associated with death ever wants to see any more of it. . . . The surest way to become a pacifist is to join the infantry.

I don't make the infantryman look noble, because he couldn't look noble even if he tried. Still there is a certain nobility and dignity in combat soldiers and medical aid men with dirt in their ears. They are rough and their language gets coarse because they live a life stripped of convention and niceties. Their nobility and dignity come from the way they live unselfishly and risk their lives to help each other. They are normal people who have been put where they are, and whose actions and feelings have been molded by their circumstances. There are gentlemen and boors; intelligent ones and stupid ones; talented ones and inefficient ones. But when they are all together and they are fighting, despite their

bitching and griping and gold-bricking and mortal fear, they are facing cold steel and screaming lead and hard enemies, and they are advancing and beating the hell out of the opposition.

They wish to hell they were someplace else, and they wish to hell they would get relief. They wish to hell the mud was dry and they wish to hell their coffee was hot. They want to go home. But they stay in their wet holes and fight, and then they climb out and crawl through minefields and fight some more. . . .

I read someplace that the American boy is not capable of hate. Maybe we don't share the deep, traditional hatred of the French or the Poles or the Yugoslavs toward the krauts, but you can't have friends killed without hating the men who did it. . . .

The very professionalism of the krauts which makes the American infantryman respect the German infantryman also makes him hate the German's guts even more. The dogface is quite human about things, and he hates and doesn't understand a man who can, under orders, put every human emotion aside, as the Germans can and do. . . .

Perhaps the American soldier in combat has an even tougher job than the combat soldiers of his allies. Most of his allies have lost their homes or had friends and relatives killed by the enemy. The threat to their countries and lives has been direct, immediate, and inescapable. The American has lost nothing to the Germans, so his war is being fought for more farfetched reasons.

He didn't learn to hate the Germans until he came over here. He didn't realize the immense threat that faced his nation until he saw how powerful and cruel and ruthless the German nation was. . . . So now he hates Germans and he fights them, but the fact still remains that his brains and not his emotions are driving him. . . .

While men in combat outfits kid each other around, they have a sort of family complex about it. No outsiders may join. . . . That's why, during some of the worst periods in Italy, many guys who had a chance to hang around a town for a few days after being discharged from a hospital . . . didn't take advantage of it. They weren't eager to get back up and get in the war. . . . They went back because they knew their companies were very shorthanded, and they were sure that if somebody else in their own squad or section were in their own shoes, and the situation were reversed, those friends would come back to make the load lighter on *them.*

That kind of friendship and spirit is a lot more genuine and sincere and valuable than all the "war aims" and indoctrination in the world. . . .

ON THE CHOWLINE (SC).

If one man out of a platoon gets a six-hour pass to go back to a town, he will have a good time for himself, of course. . . . It's expected of him. But he will come back with a load of cognac for those who didn't get to go. . . .

If a man in a rifle squad gets a chance to go home on rotation, his friends will congratulate him, tell him they wish to hell they were going themselves, but, as long as they can't, they give him their families' phone numbers. . . . The man who goes home carries a huge list of telephone numbers and addresses, and he makes all the calls and writes all the letters. . . .

Very few of them shoot off their mouths about their own heroism when the inevitable reporter from the home-town paper comes around to see them. They are thinking of their friends who are still having troubles, and how the article will be read by their outfit when the clippings reach them. I've seen few clippings come over here about men who have had a really tough war, and even fewer pictures of them displaying gory souvenirs.

The friends they left behind in Italy "are tired," Mauldin concluded. "[These] guys know what real weariness of body, brain, and soul can be. . . .

"And [these] guys have been getting letters which say, 'I'm so glad you're in Italy while the fighting is in France.' "[51]

After writing this in Rome, Bill Mauldin flew to northern France, where his "doggies" were fighting the climactic battle for Europe.

CHAPTER 8

The Air War

WINGED VICTORY

The decision that made the invasion of Fortress Europe possible was made at the Casablanca meeting between Roosevelt and Churchill in January 1943. The two world leaders had announced a Combined Bombing Offensive to inflict round-the-clock devastation on the Nazi war machine, knocking out the Luftwaffe in the process. The British would bomb at night, the Americans by day.

Roosevelt and Churchill were convinced that the great invasion would fail unless the Allies achieved air superiority from the English Channel to the Rhine. At Casablanca, British and American air commanders assured them that the skies over Northern Europe would be swept clean of German aircraft by the time Eisenhower's armada left England's shores. But unlike George Marshall and other top strategic planners, Air Marshal Arthur Harris, chief of the Royal Air Force Bomber Command, and Carl Spaatz, commander of U.S. Army Air Forces in Europe, were convinced that an all-out bomber offensive would bring Germany to its knees, making a land campaign unnecessary. After years of preparation, trial, and failure, they now had the con-

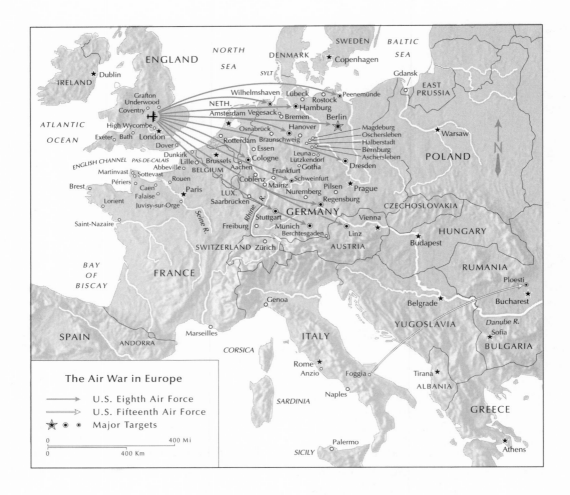

The Air War in Europe

→ U.S. Eighth Air Force
⇒ U.S. Fifteenth Air Force
★ ◉ ○ Major Targets

0   400 Mi
0   400 Km

centrated power, they believed, to crush Germany's will and capacity to wage war. With the invasion tentatively scheduled for May 1944, they had little more than a year to make good their extravagant claim that airpower alone would bring down the Reich.

Harris and Spaatz were under the influence of new ideas about warfare that emerged in the aftermath of World War I. Military strategists were determined not to fight another long war of attrition and close-quarter slaughter. They wanted to shorten the war by returning the advantage to the offense, which since the American Civil War had been battered nearly every time it attacked dug-in defensive positions. The solution the strategists came up was airpower—Winged Victory.

The apostle of airpower was the Italian general Giulio Douhet. He insisted that the next war would be short and total, and would be won from the skies with vast air fleets of long-range bombers. Their chief targets would be industrial cities. Pulverizing entire cities would shatter civilian morale, destroy the enemy's economic infrastructure, and lead to a mercifully quick capitulation. By taking the fight across the battlefield to the enemy's homeland, the bombers would, in the end, save lives.

But the Anglo-American air barons did not completely subscribe to Douhet's ideas. They entered World War II convinced that victory could be had without directly bombing civilian populations. The exigencies of warfare, however, would erode moral caution, first in England, then in the United States.

At first, the only thing the RAF dropped on German civilians was leaflets urging them to rise up against tyrannical Nazism. Then, in retaliation for an accidental Luftwaffe raid on London, England began attacking enemy cities with twin-engine bombers, aiming at strategic economic targets. But when German fighters inflicted heavy losses on their bomber fleets, which had no fighter escorts and poor navigational aids, the RAF began flying only at night. The results were disappointing: losses remained high and bombing accuracy was abysmal. The raids continued, however. After Dunkirk and the German Blitz, Britain, standing alone, had no other way to hit back at Germany. "We have," Churchill declared, "no Continental Army which can defeat the German military power. . . . But there is one thing that will bring him . . . down, and that is an absolutely devastating, exterminating attack by very heavy bombers from this country upon the Nazi homeland."[1]

With precision night bombing impossible, England would do what Churchill swore it would never do: deliberately bomb civilians. The aiming points of the new British air campaign were the built-up areas of cities, the residential centers where most of the workforce lived. Area bombing, as it was called, would slow down German production (a good worker, Harris said, took longer to produce than a good machine) and shatter home front morale, leading perhaps to a workers' upheaval against the war. One British official called the new initiative "de-housing." But the aggressively outspoken Harris never denied that it was terror bombing.

Despite his morale-boosting public pronouncements, Churchill did not share Harris's confidence that bombing alone would bring down Germany. But he had no moral reservations, then or later, about unrestricted air warfare. After the war he wrote to a former officer in Bomber Command: "We should never allow ourselves to apologize for what we did to Germany."[2]

Arthur Harris took over Bomber Command in February 1942, just as British factories were beginning to mass-produce the four-engine Sterlings and Lancasters that

AN 8TH AIR FORCE BOMBER CREW PUTTING ON HIGH-ALTITUDE GEAR (USAAF).

would be the chief instruments of his "city busting" campaign. When the American Eighth Air Force arrived in England later that year it had a different idea about how to win the war from the air. The key to it was the top secret Norden bombsight. Pilots who tested it in the American Southwest claimed they could drop a bomb down a smokestack from 25,000 feet. This technological breakthrough would make high-altitude bombing both more effective and more humane, the Americans argued. Cities could be bombed with surgical precision, targeting only key economic sites like airplane factories and oil refineries.

Pinpoint bombing would be carried out primarily by the B-17 Flying Fortress. It was a fearsome air machine, heavily armored, bristling with machine guns, and capable of carrying enormous bomb loads deep into enemy territory. With planes like this, and the formidable B-24 Liberator, the war could be won, the American bomber barons insisted, without a terrible slaughter on the ground or great loss of life in the air, an idea that appealed to Americans back home. Strategic bombing was warfare suited to the American character. As John Keegan writes: "[It] combined moral scruple, historical optimism, and technological pioneering, all three distinctly American characteristics." [3]

Pinpoint bombing was possible only in daylight. "If the RAF continues night bombing and we bomb by day, we shall bomb them round the clock and the devil shall get not rest," Ira Eaker, commander of the American Eighth Air Force, had assured Churchill at Casablanca.[4] Eaker insisted that daylight bombing would work without fighter escorts. Flying in tight formations—forming, in effect, a self-defending juggernaut—the bombers would have the massed firepower to fight their way to the target. The bombers, it was claimed, would always get through.

The British were understandably skeptical. They had tried daylight bombing without escorts and it had been too costly. They wanted Eighth Air Force to join them in their night raids against city centers. But this dispute was academic in 1942. That summer Eighth Air Force had only enough planes to conduct small raids against targets just across the Channel, while Bomber Command had begun sending air armadas into the beating heart of the Reich.

In May 1942 the RAF conducted the first "Thousand Bomber Raid" of the war against Cologne, destroying 600 acres of the city. Then it hit Lübeck and Rostock, Mainz and Karlsruhe, Düsseldorf and Frankfurt. Improvements in bombers and technique made better results possible. The bomb capacity of the giant Lancasters and Sterlings was increased ten tons; a special "pathfinder" force was developed to go ahead of the bombers to find and illuminate the targets; and a new antiradar device, code-named Window, was introduced. Thousands of bundles of aluminum foil strips, like Christmas tree tinsel, were dropped from planes, jamming German radar screens. By 1943 these improvements began to show results in a succession of paralyzing raids on the cities of the Ruhr. "Bomber" Harris targeted an entire economic region—250 square miles, with a population of over three million—for systematic demolition. Although he did not yet have the bomber fleets to carry through this Douhet-like slaughter, his night raiders brought unprecedented fire and ruin to German towns and factories, including the sprawling Krupp Works.

Hamburg and Berlin

Destruction on this scale came at a deep cost. The RAF lost almost a thousand planes to Germany's fierce night-fighting forces. But Harris believed the damage he was inflicting was worth the pain. In late July 1943 the RAF dealt Germany a staggering blow, devastating the great city of Hamburg with the first man-made firestorm in history.

At least 45,000 people—most of them women, children, and the elderly—were killed and over half of Hamburg was destroyed, leaving 400,000 people homeless. It was suffering and loss never seen before in a bombing raid. In ten days, more civilians were killed in Hamburg than would be killed in Great Britain during the entire war. Harris's crews almost silenced a city.

The English writer Hector Hawton describes the opening days of the Battle of Hamburg:

THE BATTLE OF HAMBURG BEGAN on the night 24–25 July. The main damage then was in the western sections of the city. The ferocity of this first raid—with its obvious implication that Hamburg was threatened with the same fate as the Ruhr—sent a shudder of dismay through Germany. No attempt was made to belittle it. Indeed, on the morning after, a broadcast on the German Home Service took listeners on a conducted tour among the still smoldering ruins.

"It is now 8 A.M.," said the commentator, "five hours after the All Clear, but it is still impossible to comprehend the scale of the damage. Everywhere there are fires burning, the fronts of houses crumble with a great roar and fall across the streets. The smoke lies over the town like an enormous thundercloud, through which one sees the sun like a red disc. Now, at 8 o'clock in the morning, it is nearly dark, as in the middle of the night."

There could be only one reply, according to another propaganda talk: "Terror! Terror! Terror! Pure, naked, bloody terror! Go through the streets of the town which are covered with glass and debris. Set your teeth and do not forget who it was who brought you such misery! Let hatred glow in your hearts! Walk through the streets of Hamburg and from the smoldering ruins of houses see for yourselves at whom bombs and phosphorus were aimed. Forgiveness and conciliation are no longer possible here. The suffering of our heavily tried population has become a sacred vow of hatred."

There was no respite. On that same day the [Americans] delivered a daylight attack, followed by another on the 26th.[5]

July 27 was a beautiful summer night in Hamburg. The city was quiet—no flak, no sirens. Perhaps it was over, people thought. Then at 1:00 A.M. the bombers could be heard approaching. "Suddenly there came a rain of fire from heaven," recalls a Hamburg firefighter. "The air was actually filled with fire. . . . Then a storm started, a shrill howling in the street. It grew into a hurricane so that we had to abandon all hope of fighting the fire."[6] Superheated air raced through the city at hurricane force, sending terrified people scurrying to air raid cellars. "Once inside, they were suffocated by carbon-monoxide poisoning and their bodies reduced to ashes as though they had been placed in a crematorium, which was indeed what each shelter proved to be," said a German secret report. "The fortunate were those who jumped into the canals and waterways and remained swimming or standing up to their necks in water for hours until the heat should die down."[7] But in the canals there was chaos, reported one victim. "People burned to death with horrible suffering; some became insane. Many dead bodies were all around us."[8]

The brains of fire victims fell from their burst temples and tiny children "lay like fried eels on the pavement. Even in death," said a witness, "they showed signs of how they must have suffered—their hands and arms stretched out as if to protect themselves from that pitiless heat." When survivors found dead family members, everything around them was gone—home, photographs, all possessions. "Nothing to remember them by."[9]

The fire, not just the bombing, was a planned act, achieved by a lethal combination of incendiary and blast bombs. Huge bombs were then dropped into the inferno to blow craters in the roads to impede the firefighters. "A wave of terror radiated from the suffering city and spread throughout Germany. Appalling details of the great fires were recounted and their glow could be seen for days from a distance of a hundred and twenty miles," reported a German air commander. "[News of] . . . the Terror of Hamburg spread rapidly to the remotest villages of the Reich."[10]

Photographs of Hamburg in ruins elicited little pity in English households; the sentiment there was that the Germans had brought it upon themselves and deserved what they got. "It was the second biggest city in Germany and I wanted to make a tremendous show," declared Bomber Harris, whose crews approvingly called him "Butcher."[11]

Harris's next big target was Berlin, a city far larger and more heavily defended than Hamburg. Unlike Hamburg, it was situated deep inside the Reich, out of the range of fighter escorts. The Battle of Berlin went on from mid-November 1943 to the following March. Edward R. Murrow went on one of the raids in a four-engine Lancaster named *D for Dog*. "Berlin last night," he told his radio listeners, "wasn't a pretty sight. In about thirty-five minutes it was hit with about three times the

Two elderly women living in the ruins of Berlin (SC).

amount of stuff that ever came down on London in a night-long blitz. This is a calculated, remorseless campaign of destruction." [12]

The people that Harris tried to roast were not voiceless. "The bombs fell indiscriminately on Nazis and anti-Nazis, on women and children, and works of art, on dogs and pet canaries," said a Berliner. Every morning following a raid the people set about repairing their savaged city. This had nothing to do with support of either Hitler or the war, insisted Ruth Andreas-Friedrich, an anti-Nazi activist. "We repair because we must repair. Because we couldn't live another day longer if one forbade us the repairing. If they destroy our living room, we move into the kitchen. If they knock the kitchen apart, we move over into the hallway. If only we can stay 'at home.' The smallest corner of 'at home' is better than any palace in some strange place." [13]

The sprawling German capital was not as easy to destroy as tightly packed Hamburg; and it had hugely superior air defenses. Antiaircraft guns, guided by gigantic searchlights, blew to pieces one bomber after the other; those that survived the flak barrage were attacked by fighters at closing speeds of 600 miles per hour. By early 1944 Harris was taking losses that his critics considered unacceptable.

THE AMERICANS ARRIVE

By this point, Eighth Air Force had finally gotten into the fight. The American effort had come on slowly. In 1942 and early 1943 most American aircraft were sent to the Mediterranean to support the invasion of North Africa. But General Harold "Hap" Arnold, the supreme Army Air Force commander, wanted Eighth Air Force to get into the fight over German-occupied Europe as soon as possible, even if on a limited basis. His impatience wore thin as the British, who had been given some early-model B-17s without Norden sites, publicly ridiculed the plane's combat effectiveness.

On August 17, 1942, a dozen B-17s set out from East Anglia for a railroad yard near Rouen, France, a mere thirty-five miles from the English Channel. The pilot of the lead aircraft was a quietly confident young college dropout from Miami named Paul W. Tibbets, Jr. He was leading the first assault of what would become the biggest American bombing offensive of the war. Three years later, he would drop the most destructive bomb ever built on a place called Hiroshima. Paul Tibbets opened and closed the American bombing campaign in the most destructive war ever waged.

Tibbets describes that first flight of twelve B-17s, escorted by British Spitfires:

GENERAL SPAATZ WAS ON HAND with staff officers from the Eighth and from the RAF to watch the takeoff. Needless to say, the British officers wore an air of skepticism. They had warned against our foolhardy insistence on daylight flights into the unfriendly skies where Goering's Luftwaffe lay in wait. In addition to the brass, the takeoff was witnessed by 30 members of the American and British press. It would have been a hell of a time to blow a mission.

Butcher Shop, which led the first flight into the air, was not my regular airplane and I was not flying with my regular crew. Rounding out a hastily assembled "pickup" crew was Colonel Frank Armstrong, my immediate superior, who occupied the right-hand seat as my copilot. . . .

The plane that is best remembered from the first attack was *Yankee Doodle,* which led the second formation of six B-17s. On board this plane was Brigadier General Ira Eaker, head of the Eighth Bomber Command. The official war his-

A B-17 IS HIT AFTER DROPPING ITS BOMB LOAD (USAAF).

tories will record that General Eaker led the first American daylight raid on occupied Europe. This is a matter of military protocol, for although I led the attacking formation—and all others in which I participated while stationed in England—the highest-ranking officer on the flight is officially credited with being the leader.

It was just past midafternoon when we lifted off into sunny skies. All the planes were in the air at 1539 hours (3:39 P.M.). We started our climb for altitude immediately and had reached 23,000 feet, in attack formation, by the time we left the coast of England and headed south across the Channel. It was comforting to see the British Spitfire V's crossing and crisscrossing protectively about our formation as we set out on our first venture into enemy skies.

Three of our planes carried 1,100-pound bombs for the locomotive workshop at the Sotteville marshaling yards at Rouen, the largest railroad switching facility in northern France. . . .

We caught the Germans by surprise. They hadn't expected a daytime attack, so we had clear sailing to the target. Visibility was unlimited and all 12 planes dropped their bomb loads—36,900 pounds in all. Our aim was reasonably good, but you couldn't describe it as pinpoint bombing. We still had a lot to learn.

At least half the bombs fell in the general target area. One of the aiming points took a direct hit, and there were a number of bomb craters within a radius of 1,500 feet. Bombs intended for the other aiming point fell about 200 feet to the south. While the results did not come up to our expectations, our accuracy was considerably better than that achieved by the RAF in its night attacks, or by German bombers in their raids on England.

By the time we unloaded our bombs, the enemy came to life. Anti-aircraft fire, erratic and spasmodic at first, zeroed in on our formations as we began the return flight. Two B-17s suffered slight damage from flak. Three Me-109s [Messerschmitts] moved in for the attack but were quickly driven off by the Spitfires that accompanied us. . . .

A feeling of elation took hold of us as we winged back across the Channel. All the tension was gone. We were no longer novices at this terrible game of war. We had braved the enemy in his own skies and were alive to tell about it. . . .

The last B-17 from the mission touched down at 1900 hours (7:00 P.M.). The British brass—those generals and war experts who had warned us against venturing across the Channel in daytime—were as elated as were our own commanders. General Eaker received a jubilant note from RAF Air Chief Marshal Sir Arthur Harris: "Yankee Doodle certainly went to town." . . .

The importance of that first raid in establishing a pattern for air warfare over Europe cannot be overstated. British newspapers had been openly critical of American plans to use the B-17 in the daytime, and even our first day's success was not enough to change their opinions. They gave most of the credit to our RAF fighter cover and predicted that our effectiveness would be limited to the range of the escort aircraft.

Future shallow-penetration missions over France and the Netherlands "gave us new respect for our B-17s," Tibbets recalls, "their durability, and their firepower." But the British were right about one thing. The B-17s were highly vulnerable when flying in daylight outside the range of fighter escorts. "Airplanes returned from missions so badly shot up that it was a miracle that they held together," says Tibbets. " 'Coming in on a wing and a prayer' was more than the mere title of a popular wartime song."

In a later attack on a German installation in France, Tibbets had his own brush with death. Messerschmitt 109s jumped on his formation as soon as the fighter escorts left. Just as the worst seemed over, a yellow-nosed Messerschmitt dove from twelve o'clock high straight at Tibbets's plane "on what appeared to be a collision course. . . . A 20 millimeter cannon shell ripped through the right-hand window. There was an explosive sound and a section of the instrument panel disappeared. At that moment, I felt the sting of flying metal, several fragments imbedding themselves in my right side."

Tibbets saw that his co-pilot, Lieutenant Gene Lockhart, was seriously wounded. Part of his right hand had been blown off and blood was spraying all over the shattered cabin. "I struggled with the controls and somehow managed to keep the plane on course even though the whole airframe shuddered from repeated hits."

This was when a crew had to be disciplined. Panic erupted, but it came from an unlikely source, Colonel Newton D. Longfellow, commander of the 2nd Bomber Wing, who was flying with Tibbets on what was called a combat orientation run.

"[Longfellow] had a tough-guy reputation among his subordinates. Half the outfit was scared to death of him," said Tibbets. "In the frenzied moments that followed, all of the . . . bravado that had struck fear into the hearts of Newt's subordinates suddenly left him. Reacting with blind frenzy, he reached over my shoulder and grabbed a handful of throttles and turbo controls, sapping the power of our engines at 25,000 feet.

"There was chaos in the cabin. I was trying to fly the plane with one hand and keep Lockhart from bleeding to death with the other. While he held his shattered hand above his head, I grasped his wrist tightly with my right hand and tried to maintain level flight at the same time."

Tibbets shouted at Longfellow to get his hands off the controls, but with freezing air whipping through a hole in the instrument panel, Longfellow didn't hear him. So Tibbets gave him a "backhand shot" to the chin with his left elbow, knocking him out cold. When Longfellow regained consciousness he grabbed a first aid kit and started bandaging people. Tibbets regained control of the plane, and with Longfellow as his co-pilot, brought it home. "Paul," he turned to Tibbets as they climbed out of the battered plane, "you did the right thing."

Tibbets believed that these early raids over France proved the effectiveness of daylight strategic bombing. But in an interview with an American reporter he confessed to worrying about hitting civilians. "My anxiety is for the women and kids. . . . You see I have a three-year-old boy of my own at home. I hate to think of him playing near a bombed factory. That makes me careful."[14]

Eighth Air Force had begun its first raids into Germany in January 1943, following the Casablanca Conference. But the first sustained American offensive beyond the Rhine did not take place until the last week of July. "Blitz Week," it was called. Flying six missions that week, Eighth Air Force lost almost 1,000 men and more than 100 B-17s. This was ominous. By the end of the year, an American flier would have only one chance in three of surviving a tour of duty, twenty-five missions.

To Hell and Back

"A typical mission started with hearing a jeep stop outside the barracks around 4:00 A.M.," recalls co-pilot Bernard R. Jacobs of Napa, California. "A courtly staff sergeant would come in and go to the officers' bunks who were scheduled to fly. The enlisted men were billeted in another area. We would feign sleep until he stopped at our bunk and gave a tug on the arm. He would say, 'Good morning, sir. You and your [crew] will be flying number 6 in the low squadron, low group today. Breakfast at 4:30, briefing at 5:15, takeoff at 6:15.' "

At the briefing, an officer would pull back a black curtain with a huge map of Europe behind it. Colored ribbons ran from their base in England right to the target; the longer the string the more dangerous the mission. When the crews spotted a long ribbon they would erupt with "whistles, groans, catcalls."

After the briefing, the crews were taken by truck to the flight line to pick up their parachutes and gear, and were then driven to their planes. "The flight surgeon came out to the line before takeoff," says Jacobs, "and gave us some kind of amphetamine if we had flown the day before." With everyone on board, the crew waited for the green flare, the signal that the mission was on.

The runways were usually short and "it was nip and tuck as to whether we would have enough airspeed to get airborne and stay there when we ran out of runway. . . . The engineer called out the speed, '60-70-90-110.' When the end of the runway came in sight we pulled it off the ground and prayed." Every takeoff that eluded disaster was considered routine.

Cloud cover sometimes extended to 23,000 feet, so most planes flew "blind"—on instruments—to that altitude. "Breaking out of the overcast revealed a breathtaking scene. The sun was just coming up and we were now above a carpet of reddish orange cotton as far as the eye could see. Other airplanes were breaking out of the overcast and looked like fish coming up out of their element."

Each bomber fell into its assigned slot in the formation, three groups of eighteen planes each making a wing. Then the formation "headed for the final radio beacon on the coast to fall in train with the other wings that made up the strike force. On the way out to the coast, we turned on the BBC to listen to all the sentimental songs of the day. It somehow didn't compute to be hearing American love songs reminding us of girl-friends [and] family . . . and be heading into combat. It was like a bad dream." [15]

John Keegan, who was a boy in England during the war, writes that "no one—certainly none of the English villagers who watched them depart day after day—could fail to thrill at the sight of the great phalanxes streaming away from their East Anglian airfields. Squadron after squadron, they rose to circle into groups and wings and then set off southeastward for the sea passage to their targets, a shimmering and winking constellation of aerial grace and military power, trailing a cirrus of pure white condensation from 600 wing tips against the deep blue of English summer skies. Three thousand of America's best and brightest airmen were cast aloft by each mission, ten to a 'ship,' every ship with a characteristic nickname, often based on a song title, like *My Prayer*, or a line from a film, like 'I am Tondelayo.' Each Fortress weighed 30 tons and hauled 5,000 pounds of bombs. . . . It was manned by two pilots, bombardier, navigator, top turret gunner, radioman, as well as two waist gunners, a tail gunner and a ball-turret gunner." [16]

The crew's first battle was with the cold. Temperatures dropped to 50 degrees below zero at 20,000 feet, so crew members wore electrically heated flying suits with gloves and boots under thick alpaca coats and pants and sheepskin flying boots. The gunners wore, in addition, lead-lined flak jackets and steel flak helmets with protective earflaps. "I was awesome," said gunner John H. Morris. "But I could hardly move." [17]

Some men tied an extra pair of GI boots to their belts in case they had to parachute out and survive on the ground. Every crew member carried a small escape kit in his pocket: folding money, first aid, a map, and some rations.

Since the planes were not pressurized, the crew wore ill-fitting oxygen masks. Saliva or vomit from airsickness would sometimes get in the mask and freeze, blocking the hose and causing men to pass out or even die from oxygen deprivation. When a gun jammed in the chaos of combat, gunners would sometimes forget and pull off their gloves to try to clear the jam. Their cold hands would stick to the bare metal of the hot guns, and to pull them away they had to tear off the flesh.

The tension heightened when the "little friends"—the fighter escorts—signaled they were heading back when they reached their maximum range. Every eye then began searching the sky for "bandits." In they came, out of the blinding sun. They hit the Forts where they were weakest, in the nose section, attacking head-on, wingtip to wingtip. One plane came in so close that a bombardier, sitting in the plexiglas nose section, said he thought he might recognize the pilot if he ever met him again. [18]

Cannon fire sent glass and metal flying all over the insides of the bombers, and there were shouts of terror, anger, and pain. As other bombers were hit dead-on, the survivors flew through their exploding wreckage. The sky was filled with burning planes and parachutes; and bodies without chutes tumbled out of shattered planes, the men pulling their heads to their knees, spinning and spinning, as they dropped down through the bomber formation.

Flying through this maelstrom, the pilots had no time to think. It took every ounce of concentration and physical strength to hold the shivering planes steady and in rigid formation. If a plane moved too far right or left, up or down, it could crash into another plane in the tightly bunched "combat box." Some formations flew so close together, says Paul Tibbets, that they put dents in each other's fuselages. [19]

Sometimes exertion and fear caused a gunner to breathe heavily and his hot breath would escape his oxygen mask, fog his goggles, and condense into ice. This happened to gunner John H. Morris. "I couldn't unstrap my flak helmet with one hand (the other remained firmly on the gun) to lift the goggles. A blinded gunner! Once or twice I let go of the gun with one hand to reach up and scrape a hole in the goggle ice with my fingertip and peeked out and saw up-close German fighters that had begun to fly through our formation. But the ice would start to form again right away, so I didn't see much. . . . [But] I survived."[20] He survived with German fighters putting cannon holes in his plane big enough, said one airman, to shove sheep through.

After the last of the German fighters left, the bombers entered the dreaded flak field. This was a section of the sky over the target thick with bursting shells hurling shards of razor-sharp steel through the air. The bombers, bumping and shuddering, could not try to evade these deadly fragments of steel, with their puffy traces of black and brown smoke. They had to hold formation right to the target point. As an

THIS B-17 LANDED SAFELY AFTER LOSING ITS NOSE TO GERMAN FLAK GUNS (USAAF).

airman said: "That's when you learned that it's possible to sweat at 30 degrees below zero." [21]

"Sweat covered me," pilot John Muirhead recalled a bombing raid to Regensburg. "It ran down my back and between my buttocks; it streamed down my chest; my eyes burned with it. My crotch and thighs were soaked with urine. I crouched in my small seat, strapped to it so I could barely move. Life-giving air came into my lungs from a slender rubber tube that could be severed with a boy's jackknife. Goggles shielded my eyes from the blasts of ice-cold air pouring through the ragged holes in the windshield. A band of rubber plastic around my throat with two small diaphragms pressed against my vocal cords allowed me to speak; but there were no words." [22]

The big German cities had over 1,200 to 1,500 guns defending them, along with 88mm batteries loaded on railroad cars that could be moved from place to place. "They also had what we called the standard tracking flak, which was very heavy while we were on our ten-to-fifteen-minute run to the target," says Bernard Jacobs. "We used to say it was so thick you could walk on it. . . . The near misses buffeted us around and we could hear the pieces of flak hitting the airplane."

They were now on the bomb run. From here to the target, the bombardier flew the plane. Bombardier Theodore Hallock was not a praying man, but when he got in a tight spot over the target he would whisper to himself, "God, you gotta. You gotta get me back. God, listen, you gotta." Lots of the men promised the Almighty that if they got through they'd swear off liquor and women. Hallock said he never promised that "because I figured that if God was really God he'd be bound to understand how men feel about liquor and women." [23]

Over the target, "there was a sense of the irrevocable," said John Muirhead, "like a door shut and locked behind us. . . . Resolution came to us because we had no choice." When the lead plane dropped a red flare, the bombardiers released their loads. Then the bombers, one at a time, dipped below the flak, turned slowly, and headed out of "hostile land," hoping they had enough gas and guns to slug their way through the fighter formations that would be on them "like wolves" all the way to the English Channel. [24] When Bernard Jacobs's battered plane landed and shut down its engines, with the crash truck and ambulances beside it on the runway, "everyone cheered," said Jacobs. It was not from happiness; it was from relief. Standing on the airstrip, fixed to the ground, pilots and crew exchanged quick glances with the ground crew. Nobody smiled, but it was good to be on firm earth.

After their debriefing, when every crew member had been interrogated about the mission, "four finger shots of Irish or Scotch whisky was poured into water glasses," says Jacobs. "After a couple of those we would be half crocked . . . and we would hit the sack."

Some crews would fly two or three days in a row. Jacobs's crew once flew eight straight days. That got you a pass to go to London.

Every airman fought a never-ending battle with fear. In an Army Air Force survey of combat crews, approximately 40 percent of the men said they were afraid every time or nearly every time they flew. An additional 44 percent said they were afraid up to three quarters of the time. The nature of the men's fear changed over time. At first they feared most being a coward. Later, their greatest fear was physical harm or capture by the enemy. Almost one third of the men asked to be grounded because of fear. Yet only 4 percent quit. No man got through a tour of duty without suffering some symptom of fear: nightmares, bed-wetting, migraine headaches, insomnia, and worse.

There were different views about fear. "We were always afraid when we flew missions, every one of us," says B-17 tail gunner Daniel Behre, "but we grew to love this fear and to welcome it. It was a companion one always had on these missions and without this fear I think every one of us would have been lost." [25]

Small tasks that required attention kept fear under control. "It is routine that saves us," wrote John Muirhead, "the details that must be served to whatever end we go: to a madness five miles above a city in Germany or to a better purpose." [26] Discipline and comradeship also kept men flying. Crews were told never to leave the combat formation to help a crippled bomber. Going to the aid of a bomber in trouble weakened the entire formation. "Don't try any of that heroic buddy stuff," the men were told. "Don't put your buddies ahead of the bigger group." Inside the ship, it was different. "You were a tight-knit team, and you never let anybody down." [27]

The American trait that Hitler most badly underestimated "in his analysis of decadent, undisciplined democracy . . . was not courage, nor patriotism nor mechanical know-how," write Beirne Lay, Jr., and Sy Bartlett, the bomber pilots who wrote *Twelve O'Clock High*, the finest novel of the European air war. "It was the extraordinary, nearly incredible lengths, demonstrated time and again, to which Americans would go rather than fail the other members of their team." [28]

In the Air Force study mentioned above, men were asked to name the three main reasons they continued to fly in combat. The most frequent answers, in this order, were: patriotism, not to let down your crew or unit, and to finish your quota of missions. [29]

The highlight of an airman's career was the day he completed his number of assigned missions, twenty-five—until it was raised to thirty and then thirty-five later in the war. "When I looked down to see the enemy coast sliding under our wings for the last time," says Bernard Jacobs, "I couldn't believe it! I was going home." Jacobs sailed back to New York on the *Queen Elizabeth*, which had been converted into a troopship, and took a train across the country to San Francisco. "When I arrived in Oakland I called home. When I heard my mom's voice I said, 'Hi Mom, I'm home.' She started crying."

OUR FATHER, WHO ART IN HEAVEN

The biggest American air operation of 1943 was the Schweinfurt-Regensburg Raid, a deep-penetration run to a previously inaccessible area of Germany. One fleet of Fortresses hit a major Messerschmitt assembly plant in Regensburg and flew on to North Africa. Another struck the ball bearing factories of Schweinfurt, which a Luftwaffe air commander called the "Achilles' heel" of German industry.[30] No war machine moves without friction-reducing bearings, and Schweinfurt produced almost 50 percent of Germany's ball bearings. The Regensburg Me 109 factory produced 30 percent of the Luftwaffe's single-engine fighter planes.

To get to these cities, Eighth Air Force flew through Germany's most formidable fighter defense zone. As the crews assembled on the runways, "everyone had a case of the nerves," said one flier. "Frequent 'piss calls' were needed behind the planes. . . . Some could not get their cigarettes to their mouths because of nerves."[31]

Lieutenant Colonel Beirne Lay, Jr., was the co-pilot of *Piccadilly Lilly* on the Regensburg raid. This flight would be the inspiration for the culminating chapter of *Twelve O'Clock High*. Lay's wing commander was Colonel Curtis E. LeMay, who would later incinerate the cities of Japan with low-flying B-29s.

Exactly one year earlier, Beirne Lay had watched Paul Tibbets's tiny force of B-17s take off on Eighth Air Force's first raid on Europe. "On that day it was our maximum effort," he wrote on August 17, 1943. "Today, on our first anniversary, we were putting thirty times that number of heavies into the air." As his formation of 147 bombers assembled over the English countryside and crossed into Holland, he experienced "the foreboding that might come to the last man about to run a gantlet lined with spiked clubs."

When the escorting P-47 Thunderbolts left them, enemy fighter squadrons came barreling in. "The main event was on. I fought an impulse to close my eyes, and overcame it." This was the first of "a hailstorm" of fighter assaults that came at them all the way to the target. In front of him a Fortress exploded into an orange ball of fire and no one bailed out. It was the plane to which Lay had been originally assigned.

At that point "I knew that I was going to die, and so were a lot of others. What I didn't know was that the real fight . . . hadn't really begun. The largest and most savage fighter resistance of any war in history was rising to stop us at any cost, and our group was the most vulnerable target." An hour and a half later, their battered bomber column, twenty-four planes short, arrived at the target point. "I knew our bombardiers were grim as death while they synchronized their sights on the great Me-109 shops laying below us in the curve of the winding blue Danube, close to the outskirts of Regensburg." Moments later, a red light flashed on his instrument panel. "Our bombs were away. We turned from the target toward the snow-capped Alps. I looked back and saw a beautiful sight—a rectangular pillar of smoke rising from the Me-109 plant. Only one burst was over and into the town. Even from this great height I could see that we had smeared the objective. The price? Cheap. 200 airmen."

After eleven hours in the air, they landed in the North African desert with their fuel tanks on empty. Beirne Lay slept that night close to the wing of his plane, under a star-filled sky. "My radio headset was back in the ship. And yet I could hear the deep chords of great music." [32]

Schweinfurt was a bigger raid than Regensburg, with almost a hundred more planes deployed, and losses were equally high. "So many guys . . . bailed out from both sides that it looked like a parachute invasion," said radioman George Hoyt. [33] Elmer Bendiner, a navigator, remembers looking down "and counting the fitful yellow-orange flares I saw on the ground. At first I did not understand them. Here were no cities burning. No haystack could make a fire visible in broad daylight 23,000 feet up. Then it came to me as it came to others—for I remember my headset crackling with the news—that those were B-17s blazing on the ground." [34]

On the Regensburg-Schweinfurt raid, the Americans shot down at least ninety-nine German planes but they lost sixty Forts—fifty to fighters—and nearly 600 men. In one day Eighth Air Force lost 10 percent of its aircraft and 17 percent of its crews. "Regensburg-Schweinfurt," said General Eaker, "was the bloodiest and most savagely fought air battle up to that time." [35]

The bombing was accurate but armaments minister Albert Speer relocated fighter assembly plants and actually increased production in the next year. There was a lot of destruction at Schweinfurt but the bombs used by Eighth Air Force were not powerful enough to destroy most of the machine tools on the factory floor. Eaker refused to admit it, but the most critical air battle of the war up to this point was a victory for the German air defense.

Eighth Air Force hit Schweinfurt again on October 14—Black Thursday, the crews would call that day. When they learned at the briefing that they were going back to Schweinfurt, some pilots returned to their rooms to put their possessions in order or to write a final letter. The B-17s did fearsome damage, but they took even heavier losses than on the first raid, 25 percent of the air fleet. "As the crews come in their faces [are] drawn and wan . . . because too many friends have gone down in flames in front of their eyes. Too many," a witness on the ground wrote. "Jerry had thrown so many planes at them, they were bewildered. And for another reason. There was still tomorrow, and tomorrow after that." A surviving airman expressed the feelings of everyone on that terrible mission: "Jesus Christ, give us fighters!" [36]

German air commanders began making the same urgent pleas to Nazi air minister Hermann Goering, for their fighters were taking equally appalling losses. After the second Schweinfurt raid Albert Speer told the Fuehrer that the continuation of these raids could permanently cripple German production. Hitler and Goering replied by pouring more money into revenge weapons like the V-1, and by questioning the courage of their pilots. At one stormy meeting with Goering, General Adolf Galland, chief of German fighters and a renowned fighter ace, became so incensed by these charges that he tore his Knights Cross off his collar and slammed it on the table. "The atmosphere was tense and still," Galland later wrote. "The *Reichsmarschall* had literally lost the power of speech, and I looked him firmly in the eye, ready for anything. Nothing happened, and Goering quietly finished what he had had to say. For six months after that I did not wear my war decorations." [37]

Finally Hitler ordered an emergency increase in fighter production and transferred almost all fighters back to Germany from the Eastern Front. He also built a powerful defensive line of antiaircraft and searchlight batteries in Northern Europe. By November 1943, it was a war of attrition in the sky, the aerial equivalent of the stalemated massacre on the ground that Giulio Douhet had said the big bombers would make unnecessary. A German fighter pilot had a better chance of surviving by joining the infantry and fighting on the Eastern Front against the Russians. An American flier on a deep-penetration bomb run over Germany was in more danger than he would be fighting Kesselring in the mountains of Italy.

With the stupendous American production machine behind them, the Allies could absorb these kinds of losses better than the Germans. But crew morale began to sink. "Somebody I'd be playing ping-pong with one day would be dead the next. It began to look as if I didn't have a chance of getting through." Joseph Hallock summed up the feelings of a lot of the fliers: "I never wanted to go up again," he said after being wounded when a cannon shot exploded in the plexiglass nose of his plane.[38]

A story spread through the ranks of Eighth Air Force that, while not true in its particulars, expressed exactly the new situation. It was about a solitary, shot-up B-17 limping home to England. Someone on the plane radioed the tower:

"Hello Lazy Fox. This is G for George, calling Lazy Fox. Will you give me landing instructions, please? Pilot and co-pilot dead, two engines feathered, fire in the radio room, vertical stabilizer gone, no flaps, no breaks, crew bailed out, bombardier flying the ship. Give me landing instructions."

The reply came a few seconds later:

"I hear you G for George. Here are your landing instructions. Repeat slowly, please, repeat slowly. Our Father, who art in heaven . . . "[39]

Not long after Black Thursday, October 14, 1943, Hap Arnold suspended raids beyond fighter escort range.

As the Germans employed sophisticated radar to combat Windows and put more flak and night fighters into the sky, Bomber Command also began to take far greater losses. But Harris kept his crews flying. He was determined to burn down half of Germany's cities by April 1. Yet even Harris had become convinced that the RAF bomber streams would need long-range fighter escorts to continue their rain of ruin. Britain had lost almost 6,000 bombers in little over a year.

THE DEATH OF THE LUFTWAFFE

A breakthrough in the air war finally occurred with the arrival of the P-51 Mustang. It was a fast, long-range American fighter equipped with drop tanks, auxiliary fuel sources that allowed it to escort bombers all the way to Berlin and back. "That plane," said American fighter ace Don Salvatore Gentile, "put the Huns right up against the wall."[40]

P-51s, along with other fighters equipped with drop tanks, became available in growing numbers in early 1944. With the cross-Channel invasion only months away, the objective became the complete destruction of the Luftwaffe. New commanders were put in charge of what was called Operation Point Blank. Carl Spaatz became

LEFT: P-51 PILOT. THE MARKINGS ON HIS HAND ARE THE TIMES FOR STARTING
ENGINES, TAKING OFF, RENDEZVOUSING WITH BOMBERS, ETC. (USAAF).
RIGHT: P-51 MUSTANG (USAAF).

commander of all U.S. Air Forces in Europe, and he moved Ira Eaker to the
Mediterranean and brought in the more aggressive Jimmy Doolittle from Italy to take
over Eighth Air Force, which had been built up to a prodigious fighting force by
American mass production.

During "Big Week," February 19 to 26, thousands of American bombers, accompanied by swarms of long-range fighters and equipped with new radio direction finders, began focusing almost exclusively on aircraft factories and oil refineries, targets
the Luftwaffe had to come up and defend. The idea was simple: bait them and kill
them.

Goering's fighters were no match for the Mustangs, and he lost an appalling
number of planes and experienced pilots. Captain Don Salvatore Gentile alone
destroyed thirty German planes, the equivalent of two Luftwaffe squadrons. He was
"a one-man air force," said Eisenhower. "If they wouldn't come up into the air,"
Gentile told a reporter, "we would go down against their ground guns and shoot them

up on the ground. Get them, that was the idea; kill them, trample them down." [41] In one month, the American Air Force destroyed more than twice as many enemy planes as it had in the two years of 1942 and 1943.

During Big Week the Allies shot down over 450 German aircraft. "When I pulled my canopy closed I felt like I was closing the lid to my coffin," said a Luftwaffe pilot, recalling his despair. [42] Albert Speer continued to produce enough fighter planes to carry on the air war, but there were soon not enough qualified pilots to fly them, proof that it is men not machines that win wars. "The week of 20–26 February, 1944 may well be classed by future historians as marking a decisive battle of history," Hap Arnold wrote, "one as decisive . . . as Gettysburg." [43]

By April 1944 enormous American bomber fleets—the aerial equivalent of aircraft carrier task forces in the Pacific—were pounding Berlin with terrifying regularity. The "heavies" did big damage, but these were still dangerous missions.

On the morning of April 29, Dale VanBlair, a B-24 gunner from Quincy, Illinois, set out for Berlin on one of the biggest missions of the war. Over the target—the city's central rail station—his Liberator was hit by both flak and fighters and lost an engine. With the plane leaking fuel badly, the pilot had to ditch in the North Sea.

WHEN LIEUTENANT LOCKE attempted to set the plane down, a large wave caught the nose. It was like slamming into a concrete wall. The plane broke behind the rear bomb bay, and the bottom skin of the waist section was ripped off. There was not even time to take a deep breath before we plunged into the frigid sea.

As I fought to get back to the surface, my forehead slammed against a metal object. My lungs were busting, and I thought, "I'm going to drown—what is it going to feel like?"

Then my head hit the surface and I gratefully gulped in the air. It was almost like being brought back from the dead. . . .

I was still inside the waist section, which had not broken completely free of the forward section. . . . Fearing the waist section would break loose any second and sink, I frantically looked for a way out. Spotting a small opening in the side of the fuselage at the water's surface, I paddled over to it. I was relieved to find the fuselage completely ripped away beneath the water with plenty of room for me to swim through. . . .

I pulled myself through, inflated my Mae West [life vest], and began paddling away from the wreckage. . . . Hoping that someone had released a life raft, I looked around. No raft.

VanBlair struggled to stay near other crew members in the water, but high waves washed him away from them.

I HAD NO IDEA of how long I had been in the water, for my watch had stopped when we ditched. It seemed like a long time. I had heard that twenty minutes was about as long as a person could survive during the cold months, and we had not had much warm weather, despite it being the end of April. I felt certain that it had been longer than that since we ditched. . . . My optimism was about used up. . . . I had never felt so completely alone.

Then, off in the distance, I saw the most beautiful object that I had ever laid eyes on in my twenty-two plus years: a boat heading in my direction.

The escort fighters had contacted it and given their position. "After watching the boat pick up two of our crew, I lost consciousness." At Yarmouth, they told him he had been in the water about an hour. They also informed him that his skull was fractured. After a week in the division hospital he returned to base.

WHEN I ENTERED OUR NISSEN HUT, first one man then another came bringing various items of my belongings to me. . . . When a crew was lost, the accepted practice was for the other men in the hut to appropriate any items of equipment other than personal things before Supply came to take everything away. It may sound cold-blooded but . . . we preferred for someone we knew to have an item than for it to go back to Supply. Sometimes two of us would make an agreement. . . . The man who bunked next to me and I had an understanding that if I were lost, he got my sheets; if he were lost, I got his leather jacket. At any rate, every item that belonged to me was returned."[44]

It was this punishing one-two combination, the Americans by day, the British by night, often on the same target, that knocked out the Luftwaffe. "The Americans and the British conduct their large-scale air operations in a way which leaves us no respite," said a German pilot. "Night after night the wail of sirens heralds more raids. How much longer can it all continue?"[45] By May, the Luftwaffe, which was losing an astonishing 20 percent of its planes a month, was no longer an effective fighting force. Germany was virtually defenseless from the air, except for its still formidable flak batteries.

By then the Allies had won air ascendancy over France as well. In the months preceding D-Day, Allied air forces had come under the direct control of Supreme Commander Eisenhower. Overruling Spaatz and Harris, he suspended round-the-clock bombing of Germany in favor of the Transportation Plan of his chief air aide, Sir Arthur Tedder. Under Tedder's directive, Anglo-American air forces destroyed almost the entire transportation network of northern France—railroad yards and rolling stock, bridges and barges, roads and anything hostile that moved on them. The destruction of what a protesting Arthur Harris called "panacea targets" disrupted Hitler's ability to move men and supplies to counter the Normandy invasion and the subsequent movement off the beaches. On the eve of the invasion, Eisenhower could confidently tell his troops. "If you see fighting aircraft over you, they will be ours."[46]

The Great Invasion

PLANNING

In the spring of 1944, the Allies were finally prepared to deliver the greatest blow of the war, the long-delayed invasion of Northern Europe. Winston Churchill explains the genesis of Operation Overlord, as the cross-Channel invasion was code-named:

IN APRIL, 1943, General [Frederick] Morgan, of the British Army, became the head of the British and American Planning Staff, which surveyed the whole project by the decision of the Combined Chiefs in Staff Committee. They made a plan, which I took with me . . . to Quebec [the Quadrant Conference], where it was submitted to the President and the Combined British and American Chiefs of Staff. This plan selected the beaches for the attack and presented the outlines of the scheme, together with a mass of detail to support it. It received, in principle, complete agreement. It is rather remarkable that a secret of this character, which had to be entrusted from the beginning, to scores, very soon to hundreds and ultimately to thousands of people, never leaked out either in these Islands or the wide expanses of the United States.

At Teheran [in November 1944], we promised Marshal Stalin we would put this plan, or something like it, into operation at the end of May or the beginning of June, and he for his part promised that the whole of the Russian Armies would be thrown, as indeed they have been, into general battle in the East. In January of [1944] . . . General Eisenhower assumed the command of the Expeditionary Force gathered in Britain. No man has ever laboured more skillfully or intensely for the unification and goodwill of the great forces under his command than General Eisenhower. He has a genius for bringing all the Allies together. . . .

I do not believe myself that this vast enterprise could have been executed earlier. We had not the experience. We had not the tackle. But, before we launched the attack in 1944 we had made five successful opposed landings in the Mediterranean, and a mass of wonderful craft of all kinds had been devised by our services and by our United States colleagues on the other side of the ocean. The bulk of these had to be constructed in the United States, although our yards were strained and gorged to the utmost. There are more than 60 variants of these landing craft and escort vessels, and they provide for the landing, not only of an Army, but of everything that an Army can need. . . .

An immense system of harbours, breakwaters and landing stages was also prepared which, as soon as the foothold was gained, could be disposed in their appropriate places to give large sheltered water space. In less than a month, harbours had been created compared with which Dover seems small. . . .

Overwhelming air power was . . . indispensable . . . to the carrying out of such an operation. The strategic bombing by the combined British and American Bomber Forces, and the use of the medium bomber and fighter forces, was the essential prelude to our landing in Normandy. Preparations definitely began for the battle in April, and, not only at the point of attack, for that would have revealed much, but necessarily impartially all along the coast and far in the rear. Thus when our ships crossed the Channel, unseen and unmolested, half the guns that were to have blown them out of the water were already dismantled or silent, and when the counter-attack began on the land and under the sea, the Tactical and Coastal air forces held it back while our foothold on shore and our sea-lanes were being firmly established.[1]

After two years of invasion planning, which massed over two million American and Empire troops in the British Isles and supplied them with 16 million tons of material—after giant rehearsal maneuvers in England and false "wet runs" in the Channel, D-Day, June 6, 1944, still was a tactical surprise. The German high command expected the attack to come at the Pas de Calais, north of the River Seine where the Channel is narrowest. It was there, along the coast, that Hitler put the bulk of his panzer divisions. If the Germans had known where and when the Allies were coming they would have hurled them back into the sea with the fifty-five divisions they had in France. The Allies would have been on the offensive with a ten-to-one manpower ratio against them.

Equally surprising was the stupendous size and firepower of the striking force that the Supreme Commander, General Eisenhower, sent over the water in the first hours of D-Day, a fearsome armada of 5,000 vessels and 11,000 planes.

The invasion was a miracle of organization and supply; the only thing the planners could not control was the weather. Just before June 5, the originally scheduled D-Day, the worst June gale in forty years struck along the treacherous Channel. The invasion boats that had started out were called back. Twenty-four hours later the weather showed signs of clearing and Eisenhower ordered the invasion to go ahead, perhaps the riskiest military decision of the entire century. He then issued an order of the day to the men under his command:

SOLDIERS, SAILORS AND AIRMEN of the Allied Expeditionary Force: You are about to embark on a great crusade, toward which we have striven these many months. The hopes and prayers of liberty-loving people everywhere go with you. In company with our brave Allies and brothers in arms on other fronts you will bring about the destruction of the German war machine, elimination of Nazi tyranny over the oppressed peoples of Europe, and security for ourselves in a free world.

Your task will not be an easy one. Your enemy is well trained, well-equipped and battle-hardened. He will fight, fight savagely. But in this year of 1944 much has happened since the Nazi triumphs of 1940 and 1941.

The United Nations have inflicted upon the Germans great defeats in open battle, man to man. Our air offensive has seriously reduced their strength in the air, and their capacity to wage war on the ground.

Our home fronts have given us an overwhelming superiority in weapons and munitions of war, and have placed at our disposal great reserves of trained fighting men.

The tide has turned. The free men of the world are marching together to victory. I have full confidence in your courage, devotion to duty, and skill in battle. We will accept nothing less than full victory.

Good luck and let us all beseech the blessing of Almighty God upon this great and noble undertaking.[2]

This order was distributed to all assault elements. It was read by appropriate commands to other troops in the Allied Expeditionary Force, and it was kept as a memento by the men who went onto the beaches, less than 15 percent of whom had ever seen combat.

"On June 5, in the late afternoon, we formed up in a convoy," recalls Robert E. Adams, a Coast Guard coxswain. "The captain of our ship [USS *Samuel Chase*] read General Eisenhower's message over the public address system and I can tell you it was a great moment. Goose pimples came out on almost everybody that listened."[3]

THE LANDINGS

In preparation for the invasion, Hitler brought in General George Rommel to complete the Atlantic Wall, a network of defenses along the French coast that included six and a half million mines, concrete bunkers and pillboxes containing heavy and fast-firing artillery, tank ditches, and other elaborate beach obstacles. Everett Holles describes the aerial spearhead that sought to soften up the German coastal defenses:

TWENTY HOURS BEFORE H-HOUR, medium and heavy bombers by the hundreds began concentrating on the batteries, the command posts and the control stations of the Target Area. . . . This attack reached its crescendo thirty minutes before H-hour when 2,000 tons of bombs were hurled upon the beaches, to blast open a path ashore. . . .

H-hour was at 6:30 A.M. in the clear early morning. But the invasion of Normandy really began at thirty minutes past midnight when swarms of Allied parachutists and airborne troops began descending on the base of the Cherbourg Peninsula. Theirs was one of the most perilous tasks of the whole undertaking, leaping in darkness into enemy territory, each group with its specific task—a bridge to be blown up, a railroad line to be cut, an enemy defense post to be dynamited, a landing field to be seized and held. Many were killed before they hit

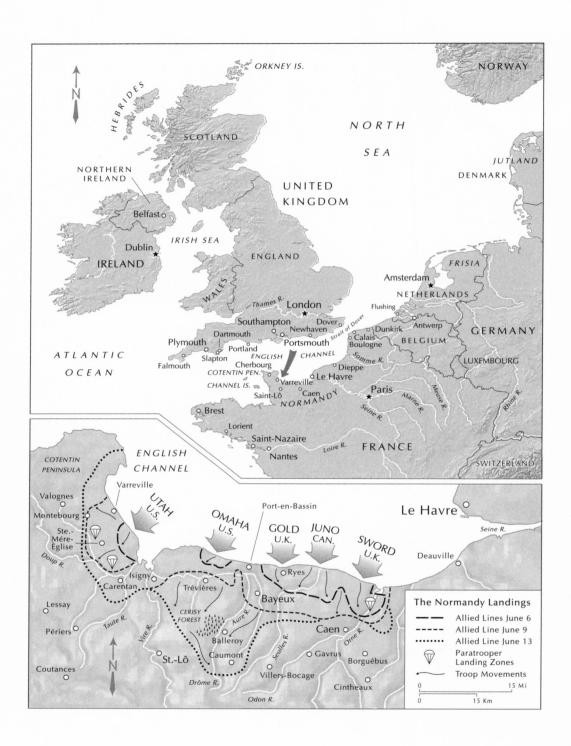

The Normandy Landings

Allied Lines June 6
Allied Line June 9
Allied Line June 13
Paratrooper Landing Zones
Troop Movements

0   15 Mi
0   15 Km

U.S. TROOPS HEADING FOR THE COAST OF NORMANDY (NA).

the ground, riddled with flak or machine-gun fire. Others were encircled the moment they landed and cut down by criss-crossing fire.

Behind the paratroopers came the gliders, towed by [unarmed C-47 transports]. In the glare of bursting flak the tow-lines were cut and the gliders dove steeply down. Now and then one would be caught by the A-A fire and in an instant would be transformed into a plunging ball of flame. The crunch of breaking matchwood could be heard as gliders bounced on rocks and careened into trees. From those that landed safely there poured men, jeeps, guns and small tanks.[4]

While American and British airborne units began securing vital positions behind the beaches to allow the troops to get off the sand and advance inland, the greatest invasion force ever assembled was moving across the storm-tossed waters of the English Channel. Most of the troops traveled in big transports like the USS *Samuel Chase* and were taken ashore in smaller assault barges. These were launched ten miles from the French coast. Robert Adams was the coxswain of a landing craft in the first wave.

The small boats started in toward the beaches in darkness and many of the men had the "invasion shakes." One staff sergeant kept "looking around and wondering for the hundredth time how the hell I got here and what the hell I'm doing here—me, Henry Giles, an old farm boy from Caldwell Ridge, Knifley, Kentucky." [5]

Men talked about dying, about this being a suicide mission. "That was the blessing of seasickness," said John Steber of Reading, Pennsylvania. "We had a big breakfast that morning and everybody got sick and started throwing up and that kept us from thinking about dying."

Vomit filled the bottom of the boats, and as water kept rushing in over the gunwales, taxing the power of the bilge pumps, the green-faced men had to bail this smelly stew of salt water and puke with their helmets. And though it was cold, they were sweating.

"One thing was funny though," Steber recalls. "All the guys had condoms over the muzzles of their rifles to protect them when we jumped in the water. You didn't think that was funny when you put it on your gun, but when you saw a whole shitload of guys with these rubbers on their guns it cut you up, sick as you were." [6]

Some of the men talked about their assignments, what they had to do when they hit the beaches. "It was the only way we could maintain our sanity," recalls Sergeant Alan Anderson, who was in charge of an artillery battery:

IF YOU THOUGHT of the possibilities of what lay ahead, it was more than your mind could take.

I remembered at the time trying to think what this really meant to me, and all I could think about was the fact that I was twenty-five years old, and still single and a college graduate, and whether this was to be all of my life and really what for. I was thinking about the meanings of democracy, and that sort of thing, but it doesn't have any meaning to a man in a situation such as that. I remember that the only thing that meant anything to me was that as long as I was there and some of my relatives, especially my two brothers, were not, that maybe we could

get this mess over with before any more of the family had to be dragged into this situation.

Very few men are very patriotic when they're faced with these suicide missions.[7]

On Robert Adams's landing boat, most of the men were dead quiet, but a few talked in low tones about what "the first kraut will think when he looks out and sees all of us, all of these ships coming his way."[8]

Crouching in a concrete bunker above Omaha Beach, peering through his binoculars, Major Werner Pluskat was one of the first Germans to see the invasion fleet appear on the horizon. "It was dark and foggy. Finally the fog lifted and I saw in front of me part of the armada—it was gigantic. It was the sight of my life.

"There was an armada of at least 10,000 warships moving without the slightest

LANDING CRAFT HEADING IN (NA).

telltale of sound or light. We began searching for signal lights and listening for radio communication—nothing!

"It was a model of discipline among the American and British military—rare among armies. I've never tired of praising the discipline of those troops.

"I called High Command West. . . . They claimed the Allies didn't have such ships. They told me I was imagining things." Pluskat then shouted into the phone: "Those imaginary ships that the Allies don't have are all headed right at me."

When German headquarters finally gave credence to Pluskat's claims he began to get calls. "I got two calls from Hitler's high command in Berchtesgaden. The first was Field Marshal Wilhelm Keitel. He shouted, 'What's happening, Pluskat?' I overheard him say to someone, 'We'll have to wake the Fuhrer.' Then I got another phone call from Berchtesgaden from General [Alfred] Jodl [Keitel's deputy]. . . . I began my report but was cut off when my bunker took a hit from the Allied ships.

"Then I saw a purple flare shot about 300 meters into the air, and then a second one arched into the morning sky. That was the signal for the entire armada to maneuver around and face the coast. They then slowly raised their cannons, and then it began. They unleashed an inferno that made hell seem like child's play."[9]

The firing began just after 5:00 A.M., when the shoreline of France came into view. The giant shells from the battleships went directly over the heads of the troops heading into the beaches and the whole sky turned bright red. The warships laid down a gigantic sheet of flame almost a hundred miles long, and the noise was like nothing anyone had ever heard.

The men thought no one could survive such an attack, but the Germans had built imposing fortifications of concrete and steel. Many of them still stand today.

The enemy, however, was caught off guard, not expecting an invasion at this place and in this kind of weather. One of the first prisoners brought in later that day had been blown out of bed by the opening bombardment. But the Germans quickly regrouped and returned fire from monstrous beachside casemates. It was batteries against battleships, kill or be killed.

Two British and one Canadian division landed near Caen, and after some tough fighting pushed inland to capture the ancient Norman city of Bayeux. The Americans landed at two widely separated beaches, code-named Utah and Omaha. At Utah, geography favored the invaders. There was no easily defended terrain between the beaches and flooded marshes behind them, and the Germans did not have a strong presence in the area. Marauders, twin-engine bombers of Ninth Air Force, flew in as low as 500 feet and pulverized the German fortifications. When General Theodore Roosevelt, Jr., landed, he discovered he was in the wrong place, but he improvised immediately. "We'll start the war from right here," he reportedly declared, and led his men inland, an action typical of the flexibility shown by the Allied command. By the end of the first day, the 4th Infantry Division, led by fast-moving Sherman tanks, had crossed the beaches and was moving into the sniper-covered country beyond the marches.

There it hooked up with the 101st Airborne Division, which had parachuted in the previous night. In putting 23,000 men ashore at Utah, including 1,200 African-Americans, most of them supply personnel, the Americans suffered only 197 casualties, fewer men than they had lost in training exercises for the invasion.

On Omaha Beach everything went bad. The naval bombardment had not been long enough because the Army insisted on going ashore at first light. And B-17s were used to bomb the German positions. These "heavies" were built to destroy cities, not to provide close-in cover for ground troops. Flying at high altitudes, they ran into cloud cover and missed their targets, dropping their loads inland.

Unknown to the Americans, the Germans had recently moved in the 352nd Division, comprised of crack troops from the Russian front. They were dug into the steep, 100-foot-high cliffs that commanded the long, flat beach. When the Americans landed, the men on the hills turned that stretch of sand and gravel into a killing field. "It was terrible," Major Pluskat recalled. "Lambs led to the slaughter. I watched hundreds die in the sea." [10]

As Robert Adams's boat neared the beach, with the high waves crashing in behind it, he saw Army amphibious vehicles all around him in the water. They had been swamped in the choppy sea and then shot to pieces by German 88s and criss-crossing machine gun fire. "I could see bodies of soldiers and their rumps were sticking out of the water. They had belts around their waists and not their chests, and they couldn't keep their heads up when they hit deep water, and so they drowned. All the belt did was to keep their asses up out of the water.

"Then our ramp opened." [11]

The men were to take the four draws, or beach exits, that cut through the bluffs, but the Germans had heavily fortified these draws and they mowed down the Americans as soon as they came within fighting range. The first company to go ashore lost 96 percent of its men without firing a shot.

The Germans had moved their big 88s three miles back from Omaha, but they had artillery spotters on the beach and were able to hit the doors of the landing boats

U.S. TROOPS COMING OFF LANDING CRAFT (SC).

as they opened. On one assault boat, every man was killed when the ramp went down. Some of the men were vaporized.

The troops came in seasick and lugging heavy gear and most had been dropped too far offshore. Under ferocious fire, they couldn't move forward, nor, with the tide coming in, could they retreat. Sergeant Harry Bare took over a broken assault team. "The men were frozen, unable to move. My radioman had his head blown off three yards from me. The beach was covered with bodies, men with no legs, no arms—God it was awful. . . . I could feel the cold fingers of fear grip me."[12]

Bare and his men made it 200 yards to their only available cover, a sloping bank of shingles (smooth round stones), but it was covered with heavy barbed wire and they had no equipment to blow the wire. So they dug in and waited—for what they didn't know. Some of the men in that first wave believed that if the Germans had attacked, they might have pushed the American soldiers back into the sea. But believing they had the invasion stopped, and not willing to risk their outnumbered force, the Germans stubbornly held their positions.

From his landing craft, Alan Anderson watched the first wave go in. He was in charge of an artillery crew with two half-tracks, lightly armored trucks with caterpillar treads in place of wheels in the rear:

AT ABOUT 0600 HOURS I could see the LCIs start approaching the shore, and it seemed that initially they were landing on the shore without too much difficulty. But then the counterfire began in earnest. Some of the larger vessels were unloading men further out in the channel. I could see that machine guns were ripping into the ramps, and that the men were tumbling just like corncobs off of a conveyor belt, and that they were being machine-gunned down and dropping dead into the water. The German machine gunners were firing directly at them from the pillboxes on the beach.

As we approached the slaughter around us, we fired on the gun emplacements that were on the shore. [Then] an 88 shell came through the side of the boat and exploded directly underneath [one of our] half-tracks, and one of the men took the full blast of that exploding shell. We picked him up and put him on a blanket. I heard afterwards that he lived, but he had 206 pieces of shrapnel removed from his body.

As we got in close to shore there was a black man who was part of the crew removing underwater obstacles, and he was badly wounded, and he was in the water, raising his hand for someone to help him.* We were going to go to his rescue. We were trying to find a rope or something we could throw over to him and then the officer received orders for us to put back out to sea, because they were afraid of losing all of the vehicles.

I remember with horror this poor man, as he lay in the water raising his hand and waving to us and then sliding back under the water. The water was tinted red with the blood that was flowing from his wounds.

We then pulled back offshore approximately a quarter of a mile or so, and circled around awaiting further orders. Then, at approximately 1400 hours, we got orders again to land. [When] the ramp opened, the first half-track drove safely through the water and up onto the beach. But when it came time for my half-

*African-American soldiers also set up barrage balloons to prevent the fleet from being hit by low-flying enemy planes, and African-American Coast Guard personnel drove Higgins boats into the beaches. There were some African-American corpsmen on the beaches, as well, and African-American personnel on the ships of the invasion fleet.

track to be unloaded, the landing craft had shifted in the water, and when we started into the water we hit an antitank ditch and the vehicle submerged. I remember looking over at my driver, John Howard, and seeing the water fill the cab and engulf his head so that he was underwater and I was trying to urge him not to take his foot off of the gas pedal because of the danger that we would lose our momentum.

It did no good. We went down deeper and deeper into the hole, and finally the motor stopped as the water went over the top of the breathing pipe that was protruding a foot above the top of the cab.

[We] had to wait inside the cab for the water to fill in completely because we were unable to get the doors open. I stood up on the seat and there was a hole in the tarpaulin that covered the top of the cab. As I stood up my life belt somehow became inflated and I got caught trying to escape and almost drowned. I managed to extricate myself and stand up on top of the cab. John was able to do the same after the water filled the cab. When he got up on top we came under withering machine gun fire and the men were just barely holding on in the back of the half-track, treading water. The vehicle was listing to one side and it was obvious we couldn't stay there, so I gave the word: "Over the side! Let's head for shore!"

So we started to swim for it. The problem was we had helmets on and bandoliers and were carrying rifles, individual weapons and bayonets, and what-not, and this made us top-heavy and flipped us over in the water so that our feet were up and our heads down. We had to abandon our weapons and our helmets and everything else and swim for it.

The undertow was absolutely terrible and I must have floundered in the water for four or five minutes before I managed to make it to shore. Some of the men took ten minutes.

I dug into the sand about thirty feet from an exit from the beach. We were coming under tremendous mortar and machine gun fire. And I noticed that the Germans had zeroed in on this exit route, which was the only route as far as I knew off Omaha Beach, so that anyone in that vicinity who tried to go out through that exit was just committing suicide. Every time somebody tried to make it through that exit they were getting killed.

Then the Germans started blowing up the vehicles on the beach that had been incapacitated and the ammunition in the vehicles started exploding and flying above our heads.

A little later I heard a shell burst not more than five or six feet from me. I heard some fellow ask about his buddy, and one of our fellows, Luther Winkler, said, "He's dead. His whole head is blown away." I went over to see how Winkler was and his face was exactly like raw hamburger. He had been cut and the skin of his face just shredded. I don't know how he survived that shell burst.

Around this time, the Navy started firing against the [German] pillboxes in our area. These big twelve- or sixteen-inch shells that were coming in were landing not more than thirty or forty yards in front of us. Those shells created such a vacuum around them that they practically pulled you right out of your hole in the sand. I remember being lifted up when they went over us and slammed back down in the ground after the shell had gone by and exploded. It was an awful experience and the concussion was beyond belief. We were showered with debris and with sand and smoke and we could hardly hear or see. I was deaf for about three days afterwards.[13]

What goes through men's minds under this kind of duress? "There was so much going on that all you could think about was to keep your ass alive," said Sergeant William H. Lewis.[14]

After dropping off units from the Army's 1st Division—the Big Red One—in the first hours of the invasion, coxswain Robert Adams returned later that day to Red Beach Two to pick up a load of wounded men. Returning with them to the USS *Samuel Chase* he went to one of the upper decks. "Dead soldiers were stacked up like cardboard. Helmets were in a big pile. Most of these dead boys still had their boots on. It was a sight you simply had to turn away from."[15]

Back on the beach it was complete chaos. Units were separated, many of them leaderless, wrecked boats were burning, disabled tanks were floating helplessly in the water, landing craft were hitting mines and exploding, and the men in their shallow holes in the sand were getting raked by enfilading fire from mortars, machine guns, and artillery.

"There were men crying with fear, men defecating themselves," said one Pfc. "I lay there with some others, too petrified to move. No one was doing anything except lay there. It was like a mass paralysis. I couldn't see an officer. At one point something hit [me] on the arm. I thought I'd taken a bullet. It was somebody's hand, taken clear off by something. It was too much."[16]

To Captain Joseph T. Dawson of the U.S. 1st Division, "the beach sounded like a beehive with the bullets flying around. You could hear them hit and you could hear them pass through the air." [17] All the while, bodies kept floating in behind the men huddled on the beach. "It was shocking to see the hundreds of men washing in the surf," says Felix Branham, who was in a unit made up in part with guys from his hometown, "—men I grew up with, double-dated with, puffed off the same cigarette, drank out of the same bottle with—lying there dead. Stark faces with eyes and mouths wide open." [18]

Watching this slaughter from the deck of the cruiser USS *Augusta*, General Omar N. Bradley, commander of the American ground forces in the invasion, considered evacuating Omaha Beach and sending further reinforcements to the British beaches or to Utah. But unknown to him, Brigadier General Norman Cota was onshore helping to save the invasion. Don Whitehead of the Associated Press was with Cota:

> THE ENEMY ON THE RIGHT FLANK was pouring direct fire on the beach. Hundreds of troops, pinned to the cover of the embankment, burrowed shallow trenches in the loose gravel. No one was moving forward. The congestion was growing dangerous as more troops piled in. Snipers and machine gunners were picking off our troops as they came ashore. . . .
>
> Then the brigadier began working to get troops off the beach. It was jammed with men and vehicles. He sent a group to the right flank to help clean out the enemy firing directly on the beach. Quietly he talked to the men, suggesting next moves. He never raised his voice and he showed not the least excitement. Gradually the troops on the beach thinned out and we could see them moving over the ridge.[19]

Cota had seen at once that it would be impossible to take the draws, so he sent the men directly at the cliffs, over the heavily mined beach. That was how the high ground was finally taken that day, by small groups of men, with equally courageous officers in the lead, urging them on, telling them "if you want to live, keep moving" and to "get the hell off this beach and kill some krauts." One lieutenant screamed, "Let's go, goddamn, there ain't no use staying here, we're all going to get killed." He got up, rushed a gun emplacement, and threw a grenade. Minutes later, he returned alone with half a dozen prisoners. "So we thought, hell, if he can do that, why can't we," one of his men recalled. "That's how we got off the beach." [20]

Despite appalling casualties and massive disorganization, the troops advanced to and up the nearly perpendicular bluffs and began taking out the German trench positions. The units that suffered the most crippling losses were the ones that landed in front of the draws and tried to storm them. The first advances were made at the places between the enemy strong points. The draws were opened later in the day, from the rear, with the help of shelling from Navy destroyers fighting at what sailors called "knife-fire range." These destroyers, their captains acting without orders, helped save the invasion.

But even on top of the cliffs the fighting was murderous. "I went back to the medical unit behind the lines, just by a couple of hundred yards," recalls medic Donald M. McKee. "The Germans counterattacked and a squad came back through the aid station which was set up in a barn and just shot everybody, including doctors and wounded. They fired at me and missed, and I fell to the ground and stayed there motionless." [21]

By mid-afternoon, the situation was still critical, but large numbers of men had begun to move off the beach, and Bradley gave up all thought of evacuating. A German officer radioed a final message from his bunker: "Gunfire barrage on the beach. Every shell a certain hit. We are getting out." [22] Germans who hung on were either killed or captured. Soon the engineers and Seabees had blown enormous gaps in the obstacles in front of the draws and a stream of traffic began moving off the beach.

A group of men went into Omaha Beach that day without rifles: Army and Coast Guard photographers sent in to record the battle. One of them was Private Walter Rosenblum, an Army Signal Corps photographer from New York City.

WE WENT ON THE LANDING CRAFT, but we were dispersed. We were two still photographers, two movie photographers, two drivers, and when we got to the beach, we were supposed to get together again and then fan out to make photographs. We were using four-by-five Speed Graphic cameras at the time, which were unwieldy instruments.

When I got to the beach, I looked around me and the water was red with blood. And what you did was you ran up on the beach as far as you could, and then dropped to see what you could photograph. You couldn't lie on the beach. You had to get up and look around to see what was taking place. And you photographed. I'm a very big coward, but somehow if you have a camera in your hand, you're trained to get up and make photographs. And that's what I did, while Germans fired 88s at us from the cliffs.

[The next morning] I noticed that there was a boat in the water that had been

shelled and was taking on water, and there were GIs standing on it, and they couldn't get off. They couldn't swim. A young lieutenant saw what was going on and jumped into the water to swim up there to see what he could do, but since some of them couldn't swim, he came back to shore, found a little rubber raft, and then swam it out and began to take these troops back into shore [with the help of his comrades].

I had a very funny predicament at the time, because I said to myself, "Walter, why don't you jump in and help him swim?" I'm not a bad swimmer. So I said, "Well I could do that or I could take photographs." I felt my role in the Army was to take photographs and so I documented the entire incident.[25]

The swimmer who took the lead in saving the men was Walter Sidlowski. This is an excerpt from Walter Rosenblum's official report on the rescue: "It was almost 1000 hours that morning that an act of heroism was performed that we will always remember . . . How can Hitler win against men such as these! The myth of Aryan supremacy is based on the slogan of everyone for himself and devil take the hindmost. It is cooperation such as this that will win the war." [24]

The photographer Robert Capa of *Life* magazine was with Robert Adams on the *Samuel Chase* and went in to the Easy Red sector with the second assault wave. He was given a gas mask, a life belt, and a shovel, and lowered into a landing boat with his expensive Burberry raincoat over his arm, making him, in his words, "the most elegant invader of them all."

When the coxswain lowered the barge door, Capa stood on the ramp to snap a picture. As he did, the coxswain kicked him in the rear, knocking him into the water. The water was cold and he got behind a steel beach obstacle and began shooting pictures. Then he headed for the cover of a half-submerged tank, passing floating bodies to get to it. "The tide was coming in and now the water reached the farewell letter to my family in my breast pocket. Behind the human cover of the last two guys, I reached the beach. I threw myself flat and my lips touched the earth of France. I had no desire to kiss it."

Beside him on a strip of wet sand was the lieutenant he had been playing poker with on the troopship the night before. The lieutenant asked him if he knew what he saw. "I told him no and that I didn't think he could see much beyond my head. 'I'll tell you what I see,' he whispered. 'I see my ma on the front porch, waving my insurance policy.'"

On his stomach, Capa took out his Contax camera and began shooting again without lifting his head. Just as he ran out of film, his hands, then his whole body, began to shake. "It was a new kind of fear shaking my body from toe to hair, and twisting my face." Just then, he spotted an LCI with medics on it and raced for it. "I stepped into the sea between two bodies and the water reached to my neck. . . . I held my cameras high above my head, and suddenly I knew that I was running away. I tried to turn but couldn't face the beach, and told myself, 'I am just going to dry my hands on that boat.'"

When he climbed aboard he felt a tremendous shock and was suddenly covered with feathers. The ship had been badly hit and the feathers were stuffing from the jackets "of the men that had been blown up. The skipper was crying. His assistant had been blown up all over him and he was a mess."

As the sinking ship limped back to the mother ship, Capa took pictures of the crew giving blood transfusions. Then he helped lift the wounded on stretchers to a rescue ship. When he returned to the *Samuel Chase* the decks were covered with the dead and wounded, the exact scene Robert Adams had to turn away from. "The mess boys

who had served our coffee in white jackets and with white gloves at three in the morn-ing were covered with blood and were sewing the dead in white sacks." As Capa started taking pictures he passed out.

When he woke up, there was a naked man in the bunk above him, staring at the ceiling and muttering, "I am a coward." He was the sole survivor of an amphibious tank group that had gone in on the first wave. He told Capa he should have stayed on the beach. "I told him that I should have stayed on the beach myself." All the way back to England "the man from tank and I both beat our breasts, each insisting that the other was blameless, that the only coward was himself."

When they docked at Weymouth, Capa heard that the only other war correspondent photographer assigned to Omaha Beach had returned earlier and had never left his boat, never been on the beach. Capa was greeted as a hero and was offered a plane to go to London and do a broadcast of his experience. He said no, changed his clothes, and went back to the beachhead on the next available boat.

A week later he learned that many of his photographs were ruined. While drying negatives, 106 of them, the darkroom assistant turned on too much heat, and only ten of them were salvageable. The photographs of the men on Omaha Beach are heat-blurred, yet that gives them an appropriately eerie effect. They are the finest visual documentation we have of that awful morning.[25]

On the evening of D-Day, the reporter Martha Gellhorn was on a hospital ship in the black waters off Omaha Beach. There were six American nurses aboard, all of them young women who had just completed their training back home. All that day they had been working with four doctors to care for the wounded. The wounded men helped by looking after one another: " 'Miss, see that Ranger over there; he's in bad shape. Could you go to him?'

"All through the ship, men were asking after other men by name, anxiously, wondering if they were on board and how they were doing."

As night fell and the ship's crew was unloading more wounded from a water ambulance, someone shouted that there were still hundreds of wounded men scattered along the beach. They had to be picked up before the expected German air raid that night.

Gellhorn went in with a crew from the hospital ship, and had to wade ashore because the water ambulance couldn't get in close enough. "Everyone was violently busy on that crowded, dangerous shore," she wrote later. But soldiers came up to them as they loaded men in stretchers onto an LST and asked them where they were from. "The wounded looked pretty bad and lay very still." But one man called out and Gellhorn noticed that he was speaking German. "We checked up, then, and found that we had an LST full of wounded Germans, and the stretcher-bearer said, 'Well, that's just dandy! . . . If anything hits this ship, dammit, they deserve it.' " With herself and the crew aboard, that seemed to Gellhorn "rather expensive poetic justice."

When their water ambulance found them, the LST floated out to it and the wounded were put on board the launch. That night the hospital ship "began to look very Black Hole of Calcutta, because it was airless and ill-lighted. Piles of bloody clothing had been cut off and dumped out of the way in corners; coffee cups and cigarette stubs littered the decks, plasma bottles hung from cords, and all the fearful surgical apparatus for holding broken bones made shadows on the walls."

CROSSED RIFLES LIE BESIDE AN AMERICAN KILLED ON OMAHA BEACH (NA).

Amid the chaos and clutter, the American doctors and nurses worked through the night on the wounded. There they were, "a ship carrying a load of pain, and everyone waiting for daylight, everyone longing for England." [26]

Almost 900 men were evacuated from France that first day. Most of the dead had to rest where they fell. There was no time that day to bury them. Many could be seen outside aid stations in stacks four and five feet high. Total Allied casualties, killed, wounded, and missing, was approximately 4,900, including over 2,000 on Omaha Beach. Historians consider that light for an invasion of that size, but every death has a meaning beyond statistics.

Nearly 800 of the 2,000 men in the tight-knit 116th Regiment of the 29th Infantry Division were killed or wounded at Omaha Beach. "There were thirty men in my landing craft," recalls Robert Sales, who landed at the Vierville Draw, "and I was the only one who lived long enough to get onto the beach." [27]

Sales lived not far from Bedford, Virginia, a village that lost 19 men under the

AFRICAN-AMERICAN MEDIC ON OMAHA BEACH (NA).

age of thirty at Omaha Beach, all of them in the first fifteen minutes, almost an entire generation of that farming community in the Blue Ridge Mountains.*

That night, Alan Anderson was still trapped on Omaha Beach. "How we survived there, I will never know, but about 9:30 at night the firing quit. I managed to get ahold of an M-1 rifle and clean that up and find some ammunition and then we went up the hill off of Omaha Beach toward the village just above us.

"I passed an aid station. There were a lot of wounded there, and as I went around the corner an American soldier came running, holding his intestines in his hands. He had been hit by shrapnel and he was hollering 'Help me! Help me!' and his intestines were kind of hanging and running out through his fingers, and the next thing I knew he fell, probably dead, I don't know."

*Two more died later of wounds received on June 6, and two more were killed later in the war. With a wartime population of 3,200, Bedford suffered what is believed to be the greatest per-capita loss in the war of any American community.

Anderson spent that night in a ditch that some Rangers were holding. When he stumbled into that ditch, he had not slept for two nights, his clothes were drenched, and he could not close his mouth because it was filled with sand and debris from the beach. Yet all he worried about was "the whereabouts of my crew."

At daylight, he went off to find them. Running as fast as he could, in a zigzag pattern, he came under sweeping machine gun fire. Somehow he made it to the hilltop over the beach where he had told his crew to go with the half-track that had made it off the bench, and there he found them. "The next thing I kind of noticed it was almost noon, and when I looked down on the beach I saw two columns coming ashore without any particular trouble whatsoever. That was the first time I felt that the situation was in hand and that the invasion had succeeded."[28]

"Omaha [is] an epic human tragedy which, in the early hours, came close to total disaster," writes Army historian General S. L. A. Marshall, who interviewed men who took part in the invasion.[29] A medic who landed on Omaha put it more directly: "That invasion could well have been stopped."[30]

Early on the morning of D-Day, on a troopship off shore, twin brothers Roy and Ray Stevens, sons of an impoverished Bedford, Virginia, sharecropper, had shaken hands and made an agreement to meet later that day. Roy never made it to the beach. His boat was hit and sunk, and he was rescued and taken back to England. When he returned four days later, after the beach was secured, he went looking for his brother. "A medic I ran into told me he had been shot and killed, but I refused to believe it. I was so sure I'd meet him," Roy Stevens recalls. "I went to the freshly dug temporary cemetery in the grass just off the beach with Clyde Powers, a friend from Bedford. The first grave I saw was my brother's. There was a small white cross with his dog tags hanging over it." Walking down a line of graves Powers found the grave of his brother. He and Stevens swore revenge. "I wanted to kill Germans, lots of them," Stevens says. "In the next month, I went looking for them, mad as hell."[31]

Because of a mix-up, Ernie Pyle didn't get to the Normandy beaches until the morning after D-Day. By this time, the fighting had moved inland. It was a spectacular June day and Pyle took a walk along the seashore. "The wreckage was vast and startling," he recalled. Scores of tanks, trucks, jeeps, and barges were submerged in the water for more than a mile from the beach. Even more wrecked vehicles were on the beach, which was now "a shoreline museum of carnage." And there were "bodies of soldiers laying in rows covered with blankets, the toes of their shoes sticking up in a

SUPPLIES POUR ASHORE AT OMAHA BEACH. BARRAGE BALLOONS FLOAT OVERHEAD
TO PROTECT SHIPS FROM LOW-FLYING ENEMY AIRCRAFT (USCG).

line as though on drill. And other bodies, uncollected, still sprawling grotesquely in the
sand or half hidden by the high grass beyond the beach. . . .

"On the beach lay, expended, sufficient men and mechanism for a small war.
They were gone forever now. And yet we could afford it."

The Allies could afford it because they had their "toe-hold," and behind them
"there were such enormous replacements for this wreckage on the beach that you
could hardly conceive of their sum total. Men and equipment were flowing from
England in such a gigantic stream that it made the waste on the beachhead seem like
nothing at all."

From the high limestone bluffs behind the beach, near a barbed wire enclosure for German POWs, Ernie Pyle looked out to sea: "Standing out there on the water beyond all this wreckage was the greatest armada man has ever seen. You simply could not believe the gigantic collection of ships that lay out there waiting to unload."

As he stood there, frozen in awe, Pyle noticed a group of recently captured German prisoners standing near him, waiting to be put into the wire enclosure. They, too, were looking out to sea, "almost as if in a trance.

"They didn't say a word to each other. They didn't need to. The expression on their faces was something forever unforgettable. In it was the final horrified acceptance of their doom." [52]

By midnight, June 6, 175,000 fighting men and 50,000 vehicles had landed in Normandy by sea and air. It had been the most successful amphibious assault in history. But at one place, Omaha Beach, it was, in General Bradley's words, a "nightmare." "Even now it brings pain to recall what happened there on June 6, 1944," Bradley wrote long after the war. "I have returned many times to honor the valiant men who died on that beach. They should never be forgotten. Nor should those who lived to carry the day by the slimmest of margins. Every man who set foot on Omaha Beach that day was a hero." [53]

On the afternoon of June 5, 1944, the day he had ordered the invasion to go forward, General Eisenhower hastily scribbled a press release on a piece of paper. "Our landings . . . have failed and I have withdrawn the troops. My decision to attack at this time and place was based upon the best information available. The troops, the air and the Navy did all that bravery and devotion to duty could do. If any blame or fault attaches to the attempt it is mine alone." [54]

He would have taken complete responsibility for the failure. "When one thinks of that . . ." writes James Jones, "it makes the hairs on the back of the neck move." [55]

When Robert Capa returned to the beach on D-Day-plus-two he found his friends from the press corps sitting on the floor of a local barn drinking Calvados, a high-test Norman applejack. They were holding a wake for him, for he had been reported dead by a soldier who had seen his body floating on the water with his cameras around his neck. "The sudden materialization of my thirsty ghost filled my friends with disgust at their wasted sentiment, and they introduced me to the Calvados." [56]

But this was no time to rest and celebrate. The American First Army was moving out from the beaches. Its objective: the port of Cherbourg on the Cotentin Peninsula. Before he left, Roy Stevens went to the cemetery to say goodbye to Ray.

From Normandy to Germany

THE BATTLE OF THE *BOCAGE*

By a miracle of inventive engineering skill the Allies constructed two artificial ports, called "Mulberries," off the Normandy beaches, putting up prefabricated piers and massive artificial breakwaters of scuttled blockships, steel floats anchored to concrete caissons, and vast floating ramps. But the harbor off Omaha Beach was destroyed by a tremendous storm and the port of Cherbourg was needed.

By June 18 the Americans had swept across the Cotentin Peninsula and were prepared to advance on Cherbourg. The Germans withdrew into the town and fought for five days before surrendering, enough time to destroy the port facilities, forcing the Allies to bring in all supplies and reinforcements across the Normandy beachhead until the port was rebuilt about a month later.

Meantime the British Second Army was heavily engaged at Caen, a pivotal city not far from the Normandy beaches, with roads pointing to Paris. Not until five weeks after D-Day were the British able to clear the Germans from Caen, but even then they could not break through the enemy's formidable panzer divisions to link up with the Americans.

With the Cotentin Peninsula cleared of the enemy, the campaign for Normandy and Brittany began. As the fighting moved deeper into Normandy American troops met a new obstacle: the age-old hedgerows of the Normandy farms.

The French called this landscape of small checkerboard-like fields the *bocage*. High-packed earthen walls, thick with deep-rooted vegetation, bordered each pasture and meadow, and narrow, sunken roads traversed the entire area. Chet Hansen, General Bradley's chief aide, admitted after the war that the Allies were totally unprepared for the *bocage*. "No one on our staff had ever been in Normandy. And the British, who should have known, did not. We had all kinds of aerial photographs, but no one imagined that the *bocage* was as difficult as it turned out to be. Every small pasture became a little fortress, where a German squad could easily hold up an American company, and where tanks couldn't break through."[1]

This would be a rifleman's fight, a close-in slugging match, and the Germans excelled at this kind of warfare. "Since obviously we were going to be on the defensive, our infantry had plenty of time to dig in along the sunken roads," a German officer recalled. "Machine-guns and mortars were sited in such a way that all the tracks and gaps in the hedgerows were under observation and zeroed."[2] Rooting out these dug-in defenders in this claustrophobic landscape would be a deadly affair.

An American officer from the Pacific told Ernie Pyle that the man-to-man fighting in the hedges was the nearest thing to the jungle fighting on Guadalcanal that he had seen. Pyle describes the battle of the *bocage:*

> THE FIELDS [OF THE *BOCAGE*] were usually not more than fifty yards across and a couple hundred yards long. They might have grain in them, or apple trees, but mostly they were just pastures of green grass, full of beautiful cows. The fields were surrounded on all sides by the immense hedgerows—ancient earthen banks, waist high, all matted with roots, and out of which grew weeds, bushes, and trees up to twenty feet high. The Germans used these barriers well. They put snipers in the trees. They dug deep trenches behind the hedgerows and covered them with timber, so that it was almost impossible for artillery to get at them. Sometimes they propped up machine guns with strings attached so that they could fire over the hedge without getting out of their holes. They even cut

out a section of the hedgerow and hid a big gun or a tank in it, covering it with brush. Also they tunneled under the hedgerows from the back and made the opening on the forward side just large enough to stick a machine gun through. But mostly the hedgerow pattern was this: a heavy machine gun hidden at each end of the field and infantrymen hidden all along the hedgerow with rifles and machine pistols.

We had to dig them out. It was a slow and cautious business, and there was nothing dashing about it. Our men didn't go across the open fields in dramatic charges such as you see in the movies. They did at first, but they learned better. They went in tiny groups, a squad or less, moving yards apart and sticking close to the hedgerows on either end of the field. They crept a few yards, squatted, waited, then crept again. . . .

FIGHTING IN THE *BOCAGE* (NA).

The attacking squads sneaked up the sides of the hedgerows while the rest of the platoon stayed back in their own hedgerow and kept the forward hedge saturated with bullets. They shot rifle grenades too, and a mortar squad a little farther back kept lobbing mortar shells over onto the Germans. The little advance groups worked their way up to the far ends of the hedgerows at the corners of the field. They first tried to knock out the machine guns at each corner. They did this with hand grenades, rifle grenades and machine guns. . . .

This hedgerow business was a series of little skirmishes like that clear across the front, thousands and thousands of little skirmishes. No single one of them was very big. Added up over the days and weeks, however, they made a man-sized war—with thousands on both sides getting killed. . . .

In a long drive an infantry company often went for a couple of days without letting up. Ammunition was carried up to it by hand, and occasionally by jeep. The soldiers sometimes ate only one K ration a day. They sometimes ran out of water. Their strength was gradually whittled down by wounds, exhaustion cases and straggling. Finally they would get an order to sit where they were and dig in. Then another company would pass through, or around them, and go on with the fighting. The relieved company might get to rest as much as a day or two. But in a big push such as the one that broke us out of the beachhead, a few hours' respite was about all they could expect. . . .

There in Normandy the Germans went in for sniping in a wholesale manner. There were snipers everywhere: in trees, in buildings, in piles of wreckage, in the grass. But mainly they were in the high, bushy hedgerows that form the fences of all the Norman fields and line every roadside and lane.

It was perfect sniping country. A man could hide himself in the thick fence-row shrubbery with several days' rations, and it was like hunting a needle in a haystack to find him. Every mile we advanced there were dozens of snipers left behind us. They picked off our soldiers one by one as they walked down the roads or across the fields.[3]

The terrain was murder on tanks. A tank rolling over the hedge exposed its soft underbelly to the *Panzerfaust*, an antitank gun similar to a bazooka. And the sunken dirt roads were heavily mined. Troops liked to fight behind tanks, but not in the *bocage*. Infantryman J. Robert Slaughter remembers coming across a group of fellow soldiers following a Sherman tank on a road bounded by low hedgerows. "Gathered around the behemoth were riflemen using it for protection, knowing that the 75mm cannon and the 50-caliber machine guns were awesome firepower. Unexpectedly, the monster's tracks rolled over a hidden teller mine. It blew the tracks off the Sherman and killed its occupants. It also blew the men using it for protection to smithereens. I had never seen such grotesque results from an explosion. Legs blown over shoulders and hanging limply as if they were rag dolls. It was sickening. After that I kept my distance from road-bound tanks."[4]

John Gill, a medic from Madison, Wisconsin, recalls how difficult it was to get wounded men to the rear, to the battalion aid station:

OUR JOB WAS TO PICK UP THE WOUNDED where we found them and to stop any bleeding we could. Give them proper morphine, penicillin, and sulfa powder. Other than that there was not a whole lot we could do because we didn't know that much about medicine. We didn't receive a whole lot of training in medicine.

We were the first step in evacuating. Our job was to take them to the battalion aid station and that was always located as close to the front lines as you could get. In Normandy, it was difficult to find it because we would be up with the infantry and both the aid station and the infantry were continually moving. Or we would get plain lost [in the] hedgerows. There was only one opening into these fields . . . and sometimes it was mined or zeroed in. The Germans had artillery and machine guns zeroed on the opening. A lot of the time we had to lift a man over the hedgerow. We had to place the front of the litter on top and then climb over and gradually work him across. It took a lot of effort to get the casualty back, especially if he weighed 200 pounds.

I was in pretty good shape at the time. I played football and I just turned nineteen. So I was in better shape than most of the guys that were over there. I still got tired.

We had a lot of people die on the way. We just left them to find someone else that was still alive.

The battalion aid station usually consisted of a doctor and a couple of medics. They would treat the wounded as best they could, but much of the time they were overwhelmed by the number of casualties. It was like a doctor taking care of ten automobile accidents at the same time. Then we took the wounded by jeep or ambulance to what is called a collection point. Here they received more treatment. From there the casualty went to an evacuation hospital and then finally to a hospital ship.[5]

Some mangled men had to get to help on their own. Crawling through pastures raked by machine gun fire, hiding in shell holes at night, they would stumble into a field hospital with only a slim chance of surviving.

The American photojournalist Lee Miller visited an evacuation hospital in Normandy run by a friend of hers, Major Esther McCafferty, Chief Nurse of the First Army. It was a 400-bed tent city in a Norman pasture staffed by forty doctors and forty nurses. The cows were kept in the pasture as a safety precaution. Wearing tin helmets and surgical whites, the nurses would chase them around the field to disclose mines and booby traps.

Jeeps with battered men on litters, stacked in racks across the hoods, pulled up with sickening regularity. "I am laid across the hood like a slaughtered deer," a wounded man wrote in his diary.[6] In the surgical tent, doctors operated on a hundred patients every twenty-four hours. Surgeons and nurses worked until they were too exhausted to stand. "I have never worked so hard in my life," Lieutenant Aileen

Hogan described her duties in Normandy. "I can't call it nursing. The boys get in, get emergency treatment, penicillin and sulfa, and are out again. It is beyond words."[7]

Soldiers were carried in with legs and arms blown off, faces shot away, and chests ripped open by shrapnel. Belly wounds were given the highest priority, for fully one third of them were fatal. "From the operating rooms . . . [the] men would go to the belly ward, known as 'Wangensteen Alley,' after the inventor of the suction apparatus," Miller wrote. "The ward was like a jungle of banyan trees. A maze of hanging rubber tubes, swaying in the khaki shadow . . . one to the nostril and one to the wound of each man. They are always hungry on their diet of glucose and saline. In a short time they will go by air through England to the hospital nearest their home-town in the U.S.A."

After this batch of patients left, no more would be brought in. The staff would then fold up the brown canvas hospital and move it to a more forward position, nearer the slowly advancing front. The reprieve would give the nurses—the first wave of over 17,000 American nurses who would serve in the European Theater of war—time to get eight hours sleep, "a leisurely shower, a hair-wash, a chance to write a letter or read one, or to lie on the grass."

In World War II, medics, doctors, and nurses, working with the "magic life-savers," penicillin, sulfa, and blood plasma, saved about 95 percent of the men admitted to mobile battlefront hospitals.[8]

"Look at an infantryman's eyes and you can tell how much war he has seen," wrote Bill Mauldin.[9] A GI had not only to watch his buddies die; he sometimes saw or heard of the deaths of local people who tried to help him.

"[One] evening, in a search for eggs, I ran into the nicest French family I have seen so far," Lieutenant Morton Eustis, a New York theater critic, wrote to his mother. "They were refugees from Boulogne and they had many interesting tales of the four years under the German heel. The soldiers, by and large, they said were 'tres correct.' But this good behavior went hand in hand with the most savage atrocities and then they (the Bosch) wondered why everyone didn't love them. In one village, they told me, where a railroad trestle had been dynamited several times by the . . . [French underground], a German officer ordered everyone in the station shot (no matter what they were doing there), and then rounded up the Mayor, the Curé and the village's leading citizens, had them shot in front of all the rest of the inhabitants, and then marched all the remaining men, women and children into the church—locked them up there, saturated the building with gasoline and set fire to it. Something very similar to that happened in another village not too far from where we are. . . .

"If I don't kill at least ten of them personally, I shall be most unhappy!"[10]

FRENCH VILLAGERS GREET GIS (SC).

THE SECOND BATTLE OF BRITAIN

When Lee Miller was at the evacuation hospital in Normandy in July of 1944, she interviewed a group of wounded German prisoners. When they found out she was from London they were astonished that she had survived the attacks of the secret weapon that H.T.W. had assured them would turn the war in their favor.

This was the V-1, a long-range, radio-directed rocket powered by a jet engine. The Germans had begun firing them on London just after D-Day. The Battle of Britain, which the British had thought won, was renewed, and went on all through the summer, exacting casualties almost as heavy as during the dark days of the Blitz.

For a long time British censorship about the new buzz bomb, or cruise missile, was tight, for the War Office was determined to keep from the enemy all information about the results of the bombing. In November, however, after the problem of defense had largely been solved, an official story of the bomb, bomb damage, and counter-measures was released:

> BRITISH SECRET SERVICE AGENTS first reported that the Germans were contriving a new long-range bombardment weapon in April, 1943. . . .
>
> For the first six months it was a battle of wits; the wits of a handful of British agents against those of the German nation; of R.A.F. reconnaissance and aerial photography against German camouflage.
>
> Aerial photographs taken in May, 1943, showed a large experimental station at Peenemünde, on an island in the Baltic. This establishment was seen to possess some mysterious contrivances that the Intelligence Services were at that time quite unable to explain.
>
> Peenemünde was photographed again and again. Eventually a photographic interpretation officer, Flight Officer Constance Babington-Smith, of the Women's Auxiliary Air Force, spotted a tiny blurred speck on one of the prints which, on enlargement, was found to be a miniature aeroplane sitting on a sloping ramp fitted with rails. . . .
>
> From these photographs and other evidence, it was concluded that the speck was a pilotless, jet-propelled, aircraft. . . . This was the secret V-1—the *Vergeltungswaffe*—the "Vengeance Weapon."
>
> In August of 1943 a strong force of . . . the R.A.F. Bomber Command dropped over 1,500 tons of high explosives on Peenemünde. Thus the battle against the flying bomb began at the very source.
>
> Germany's intentions soon became clear. In November it was found that she was building a chain of concrete launching sites like those at Peenemünde all along the French coast, from Calais to Cherbourg. They were pointed in the direction of London.
>
> The Royal Air Force and the U.S. Army Air Forces began their vast bombing operations against the V-1 launching sites in December, 1943. . . .
>
> The bomber offensive dropped some 100,000 tons. It cost nearly 450 aircraft and 2,900 pilots and airmen. . . .
>
> Enough was known about the V-1 by this time to arrange for the defense of London.
>
> Three lines of defense were established. First, a balloon barrage immediately surrounding the city. Next, an anti-aircraft gun belt, placed as near London as

possible to shorten the length of the front and thus obtain the closest concentration of fire with the fewest guns. Then, outside that a fighter zone.

But preparations for the invasion of France were going on simultaneously, and every available gun and balloon was needed for the protection of embarkation ports. Since no one knew when the flying-bomb attack would start, these defenses had to be ready to switch, at a moment's notice, from the defense of the ports to the defense of London.

On D-Day plus six the long postponed attack at last began. The defenses were immediately moved in their prepared positions.

For the eighty days from June 12th until the end of August, an average of 100 flying bombs a day were launched against England—some 8,000 in all.

By day the small pilotless aircraft could be seen skimming the roof tops, or flying over the Kentish villages. At night their tails of flame lit up the blackout. London was a place of demonical noises—the sirens, the guns, the hideous roar as a flying bomb passed overhead, the sudden menacing silence when the bomb's motor cut off, and then the crash that meant more shattered limbs, more crushed bodies.

The bulk of the attack was aimed at London, where ninety-two per cent of the fatal casualties occurred. . . .

It was found that the flying bombs were immensely hard to shoot down; first, because they flew so fast—almost 400 miles an hour; and second, because their flying height of 2,300 feet or less was too low for the heavy guns and too high for the light guns.

They came in droves, often in cloudy weather, when the fighters' visibility was low.

Forty per cent of the number launched was destroyed during the first month, but even so the number of civilian casualties reached front-line proportions. . . .

Scientists went to work on the problem; one of them, Professor Sir Thomas Merton, produced a range-finder, so simple that the whole device costs little more than twenty cents, so ingenious that it answers the purpose completely. . . .

The percentage of bombs shot down by the guns soared up from 17% in the first week to 24% in the second, 27% in the third, 40% in the fourth, 55% in the fifth, and 74% in the sixth week. The total number of flying bombs destroyed by the guns had reached 1,560 by the end of August. Many of these were shot down into the sea.

Fighter pilots of the R.A.F. have shot down over 1,900 flying bombs since the beginning of the bombardment. Some pilots made individual scores of fifty bombs.

Their methods are unorthodox, and sometimes suicidal: but they are effective.

They were evolved out of trial and tragic error. . . . Hurling themselves at the bombs at 400 m.p.h. they shot them down from all angles and at all distances, until they discovered the minimum safety margin before the explosion.

The "nudging" method, discovered by a pilot who had run out of ammunition, calls for split-second timing. The pilot flies alongside the robot, slips the wing tip of the plane beneath it, and, with a flick of the control column, sends it spinning to earth; at high speeds the air cushion formed between the two machines is powerful enough to deflect the bomb, without actually touching it.

"Slipstreaming" was discovered by accident, when a Mustang pilot power-diving down on to a bomb overshot it. Looking back he saw his target spiralling down into the Channel—the slipstream of his aircraft had thrown it out of control.

One R.A.F. pilot destroyed four bombs by three different methods in thirty minutes. He "slipstreamed" two, shot down one and, when his guns jammed, "nudged" a fourth, sending it crashing down onto the Germans in Boulogne.

Out of every 100 flying bombs launched by the enemy in the eighty days of the second Battle of London, forty-six were destroyed by the combined efforts of all three defenses; twenty-five were inaccurate and dived into the sea, or exploded in France, doing considerable damage among the Germans; twenty-nine got through to the London Region—that is, a total of some 2,300. . . .

Secret Service agents reported that tunnels and caves near Paris, formerly used for mushroom growing, had been turned into vast bomb storage depots. During July they were attacked three times by the R.A.F. Great 12,000-pounders crashed through into the caves. Everything inside was lost and many of the caves themselves were utterly destroyed. The enemy's communications were constantly strafed. . . .

Bombing greatly weakened the attacks, but the one completely effective way of stopping them was to capture the firing sites. The first of them were taken by the American troops in the Cherbourg area at the end of July, and the main concentration of them in the Pas de Calais were taken by Canadian troops early in September. . . .

More than 1,104,000 houses have been destroyed or damaged by flying bombs. This number does not include the 149 schools, 111 churches and ninety-eight hospitals. In Croydon, the worst bombed borough of London, three out of every four houses were hit.

Even now the attacks go on. A small number of flying bombs still reach Southern England from a due easterly direction.

These bombs are being launched, not from the ground but from specially adapted German bombers flying over the North Sea . . . and now *Vergeltungswaffe-II* has begun.[11]

"And now *Vergeltungswaffe-II* has begun." The British report on the V-1 had closed with this bravely mild understatement of a new time of terror greater than the eighty days of the V-1.

The V-2 was a short-range ballistic missile, heavier than the V-1, and it traveled faster than sound, achieving a speed on descent of up to 2,200 miles per hour. No public warning was possible. Defensive measures devised against the V-1 were useless against the new weapon, which carried a warhead weighing almost a ton.

When the Allied armies spread out through France and the Low Countries the barrage of the V-1 bombs ceased. But the Germans continued to aim V-2 rockets at London, Antwerp, and Brussels until the last days of the war, when their launch sites and production facilities were captured, with 7,000 V-2s still waiting to be launched.

By then, Wernher von Braun and a team of German scientists were at work on a missile—the A-10—with a range of 2,800 miles. These rockets, called "New York" bombs, were to be aimed across the Atlantic at the United States. Germany also had an atomic weapons program that could have produced lethal warheads for Braun's A-10s. The future of the world could have been horrifyingly altered had the Nazis completed the development of the atomic bomb and the long-range ballistic missile. But Hitler's persecution of the Jews, along with his allocation of resources to other war-winning super weapons, set back both programs, robbing them of scientific talent. In May 1945, an American intelligence team found that German scientists were "about as far as we were in 1940, before we had begun any large-scale work on the bomb at all."[12]

BREAKOUT

In early July 1944, while London was under a rocket assault, the Allied armies were still bottled up in *bocage*. The Americans made the first breakthrough. Two weeks of savage fighting had won St. Lô, on July 18, opening the way to a breach of the German lines. The breakout began with a massive saturation bombardment west of St. Lô. "My front lines looked like the face of the moon," a panzer commander described the impact of this carpet bombardment, "and at least 70 percent of my troops were knocked out—dead, wounded, crazed or numbed." [13] But the bombs fell on American soldiers as well.

Ernie Pyle was with the American Army at St. Lô:

ONE EVENING LIEUTENANT GENERAL OMAR BRADLEY, commanding all American troops in France, came to our camp and briefed us on the coming operation. . . .

The general told us the attack would cover a segment of the German line west of Saint Lô, about five miles wide. In that narrow segment we would have three infantry divisions, side by side. Right behind them would be another infantry and two armored divisions. Once a hole was broken, the armored divisions would slam through several miles beyond, then turn right toward the sea behind the Germans in that sector in the hope of cutting them off and trapping them. . . .

The attack was to open with a gigantic two-hour air bombardment by 1,800 planes—the biggest ever attempted by air in direct support of ground troops. It would start with dive bombers, then great four-motored heavies would come, and then mediums, then dive bombers again, and then the ground troops would kick off, with air fighters continuing to work ahead of them. It was a thrilling plan to listen to. General Bradley didn't tell us that it was the big thing, but other officers gave us the word. They said, "This is no limited objective drive. This is it. This is the big break-through. . . ."

The attack was on. It was July 25. . . .

The first planes of the mass onslaught came over a little before 10 A.M. They were the fighters and dive bombers. The main road, running crosswise in front of us, was their bomb line. They were to bomb only on the far side of that road. . . .

Our front lines were marked by long strips of colored cloth laid on the ground, and with colored smoke to guide our airmen during the mass bombing. Dive bombers hit it just right. We stood and watched them barrel nearly straight down out of the sky. They were bombing about half a mile ahead of where we stood. . . .

The air was full of sharp and distinct sounds of cracking bombs and the heavy rips of the planes' machine guns and the splitting screams of diving wings. It was

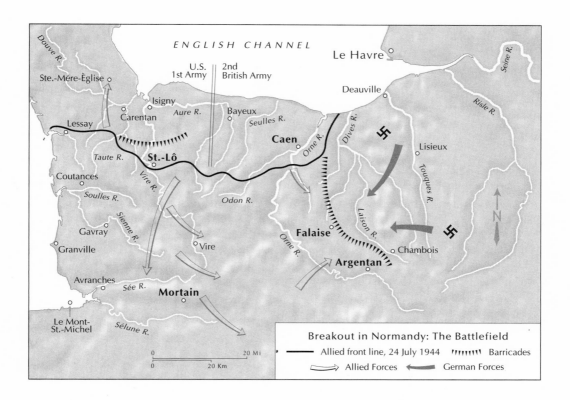

Breakout in Normandy: The Battlefield
— Allied front line, 24 July 1944 ⟨⟨⟨⟨⟨⟨ Barricades
⟨⟨⟩ Allied Forces ⟵ German Forces

all fast and furious, yet distinct. And then a new sound gradually droned into our ears, a sound deep and all-encompassing with no notes in it—just a gigantic far-away surge of doomlike sound. It was the heavies. They came from directly behind us. At first they were the merest dots in the sky. We could see clots of them against the far heavens, too tiny to count individually. They came on with a terrible slowness. They came in flights of twelve, three flights to a group and in groups stretched out across the sky. . . .

The flight across the sky was slow and studied. I've never known a storm, or a machine, or any resolve of man that had about it the aura of such a ghastly relentlessness. . . .

They stalked on, slowing and with a dreadful pall of sound, as though they were seeing only something at a great distance and nothing existed between. God, how we admired those men up there and sickened for the ones who fell.

It is possible to become so enthralled by some of the spectacles of war that a man is momentarily captivated away from his own danger. That's what happened to our little group of soldiers as we stood watching the mighty bombing. But that benign state didn't last long. As we watched, there crept into our consciousness a realization that the windrows of exploding bombs were easing back toward us, flight by flight, instead of gradually forward, as the plan called for. Then we were horrified by the suspicion that those machines, high in the sky and completely detached from us, were aiming their bombs at the smoke line on the ground—and a gentle breeze was drifting the smoke line back over us! . . . And then all of an instant the universe became filled with a gigantic rattling as of huge ripe seeds in a mammoth dry gourd. I doubt that any of us had ever heard that sound before, but instinct told us what it was. It was bombs by the hundred, hurtling down through the air above us. . . .

We dived. Some got into a dugout. Others made foxholes and ditches and some got behind a garden wall—although which side would be "behind" was anybody's guess. I was too late for the dugout. The nearest place was a wagon shed which formed one end of the stone house. . . . I remember hitting the ground flat, all spread out like the cartoons of people flattened by steam rollers, and then squirming like an eel to get under one of the heavy wagons in the shed.

An officer whom I didn't know was wriggling beside me. We stopped at the same time, simultaneously feeling it was hopeless to move farther. The bombs were already crashing around us. . . .

There is no description of the sound and fury of those bombs except to say it was chaos, and a waiting for darkness. The feeling of the blast was sensational. The air struck us in hundreds of continuing flutters. Our ears drummed and rang. We could feel quick little waves of concussion on the chest and in the eyes. . . .

When we came out of our ignominious sprawling and stood up again to watch, we knew that the error had been caught and checked. The bombs again were falling where they were intended, a mile or so ahead. . . .

The leading company of our battalion was to spearhead the attack forty minutes after our heavy bombing ceased. The company had been hit directly by our bombs. Their casualties, including casualties in shock, were heavy. Men went to pieces and had to be sent back. The company was shattered and shaken. And yet Company B attacked—and on time, to the minute! They attacked, and within an hour they sent word back that they had advanced 800 yards through German territory and were still going. Around our farmhouse men with stars on their shoulders almost wept when the word came over the portable radio. The American soldier can be majestic when he needs to be.

I'm sure that back in England that night other men—bomber crews—almost wept, and maybe they did really, in the awful knowledge that they had killed our own American troops. But the chaos and the bitterness there in the orchards and between the hedgerows that afternoon soon passed. After the bitterness came the remembrance that the Air Force was the strong right arm in front of us. Not only at the beginning, but ceaselessly and everlasting, every moment of the faintest daylight, the Air Force was up there banging away ahead of us.[14]

Over 600 American soldiers were killed or wounded by friendly fire. The dead included General Lesley McNair, head of the Army ground forces.

The carpet bombing opened a four-mile gap in the German defenses. Two American armor divisions went racing through it, supported by fast-flying P-47 Thunderbolts. And hundreds of American tanks smashed through the hedgerows by means of a cutting device invented by Sergeant Curtis G. Culin, a cab driver from Chicago.

Culin took scrap iron from a German roadblock, cut it into jagged teeth, and welded these iron teeth to the front of one of his squadron's tanks. The blades made the Sherman tank look like a rhinoceros, so tanks equipped with this device—60 percent of First Army's Shermans—became known as the "rhino tanks." The idea caught on, along with other hedgerow-busting techniques invented by infantrymen in the field.

Armies are reflections of the societies that mobilize them, and these innovations are examples of the mechanical capacity of ordinary Americans. In the rigidly organized Wehrmacht, ideas came from the top down; in the more loosely disciplined American Army, ideas often percolated up from the men on the line.[15]

With six of the eight panzer divisions in Normandy locked up with the British and Canadians around Caen, and the Allies controlling the skies, the Germans were powerless to stop the American onslaught, which one GI called "our second D-Day."[16]

Now it became George Patton's show. The apostle of armored warfare was flown in from England, where he had acted as D-Day decoy, building up a phony force of cardboard tanks and planes that helped convince the Germans the Allies were going to land at Pas de Calais. At St. Lô, Patton took charge of the newly activated Third Army, and began an all-out drive across France, with close coordination among tanks, troops, artillery, and fighter-bombers. Patton's armored columns stormed into the Brittany peninsula to try to capture and open up the Atlantic ports, and then drove south toward the Loire Valley, moving across France, in places at a rate of fifty miles a day. It was the most astonishing achievement in the history of mobile warfare, and it was a kind of warfare that American soldiers—with their love of speed and their mechanical resourcefulness—excelled at.

Correspondents called it a road march. The American reporter Everett Holles describes it:

THE ADVANCE SHOT ACROSS FRENCH SOIL like a thunderbolt. This was the kind of an attack that destroys armies and wins wars, not just battles. From Avranches, [Patton's] tanks raced across the 100-mile base of the Brittany peninsula and down to the Bay of Biscay in less than a week and approached the port of Saint Nazaire. All of Brittany was sealed off, with its great ports of Brest, Lorient, Saint Malo, . . . and their German garrisons. Some thirteen German divisions were either trapped or decimated, and, in the two weeks after Bradley's rocket shot out from Saint Lô, the *Wehrmacht* lost some 250,000 men, including prisoners.

Tank spearheads reached out toward Saint Nazaire and up through the middle of the Brittany peninsula toward Brest. They sent word back asking for instructions to their objectives.

"To hell with objectives, keep going!" was the answer that came from one American commander.

And while Bradley sent [Patton's] tanks racing up into Brittany and down to the Loire River, another column cut eastward in a bold drive pointed directly at Paris. Le Mans was the immediate goal; an important railroad hub, its lines led straight to Paris 110 miles further on. The Germans were fighting to escape annihilation in a triangle that had as its base the line across Brittany, as its sides the Seine and the Loire, and its apex—Paris.

[Patton's] Third Army bumped up against stubborn German resistance around the Breton ports—this was not Nazi fanaticism but part of a shrewd German plan that was to give us plenty of trouble for months to come—and to overcome this resistance might require weeks of valuable time and large forces of men. The Germans defending the ports were hopelessly cut off and so Eisenhower, after talking it over with Bradley and Montgomery, decided to contain the ports with relatively small forces while he turned his main strength eastward to smash the already disorganized German Seventh Army and encircle Paris.[17]

One of the units assigned to the siege of St. Malo was a howitzer battalion of the 333rd Field Artillery. It was made up of African-Americans, commanded by white officers. The correspondent Bill Davidson was with them when they arrived outside the fortress city on the north Brittany coast.

ONE BY ONE THE BATTERIES of the battalion rolled in. . . . By evening they were set up and ready to fire. The big guns pointed short, ugly snouts seaward under camouflage nets. In the battalion fire-direction center men kidded and dug a little deeper while they waited. In the next field a cannoneer sang a song called "Low-down Babe" in a high minor key. At 2035, orders to fire came through.

The gun crew went about firing the round quietly and methodically. There was no time for kidding and singing now. No one even muttered the battalion's now-famous battle-cry which goes, "Rommel—count your men" before firing and then, "Rommel—how many men you got now?" after firing. The projectile slammed into the breech. The crew whirled about rhythmically and the bagged propelling charge flew through the air from man to man. It looked like a well-drilled college backfield handling a tricky lateral-pass play. The breech swung closed. Then No. 1 man, Pfc. Arthur Broadnax of Autaugaville, Ala., pulled the lanyard. There was a blinding flash, a roar and a whistle. Seconds later we heard the 95-pound projectile crash into the crumbling Nazi citadel.

This was the 10,000th round the battalion had fired into the myth of the Aryan superman.

The battalion fired its first round a few hours after debarking on Cherbourg Peninsula June 30. . . . It was the first Negro combat outfit to face the enemy in France. Today it is greatly respected. It is rated by the corps to which it is attached as one of the best artillery units under the corps' control. And I've heard dough-boys of five divisions watch men of the battalion rumble past in four-ton prime movers and say: "Thank God those guys are behind us."

The battalion once fired 1,500 rounds in 24 hours, which didn't leave any time for sleeping. I watched the men set a new unofficial record by firing three rounds in a little over 40 seconds. . . .

The battalion fired steadily for two weeks after it arrived in France and helped pound two vital hills into submission. . . . The battalion poured shells across the Periers–St. Lô road the day of the big July 25 attack and swept on through Normandy and Brittany with the big offensive. It was strafed and bombed and it absorbed occasional counterbattery fire from enemy artillery. It got shelled in foxholes and lost valuable men. . . .

One of the things the battalion is most proud of is the time it scored a direct hit on the turret of a Tiger tank from 16,000 yards. When you consider that 16,000 yards is over nine miles, that the 155 howitzer fires a very heavy projectile at a very high arc, that the target was completely out of sight and that even if it were visible a Tiger tank at that distance would have looked about as big as a Maryland chigger—you realize that was some shooting. . . .

C Battery did the firing. . . . The second round dropped right down through the turret. . . . The tank flew in half like a walnut smashed by a hammer.

They told me at gun No. 2 of C Battery that someone had reverted to the old GI custom and had scribbled some words in chalk on that shell. The words were: "From Harlem to Hitler." [18]

After a two-week siege, the German garrison surrendered.

As Patton's army slashed through France, he was out in front of it in an open jeep so his troops could see him, immaculately attired with his ivory-handled pistols in their holsters, urging the men forward and directing military traffic at blocked country crossroads, using a Michelin road map. This was motorized warfare, the kind of warfare he had spent much of his life preparing for. Robert Capa joined Patton's armored columns as they surged into Brittany along the coastal road. "On both sides of the road, the happy French were shouting *'Bonne Chance!'* And the happy signposts read: '90 kilometers . . . 80 kilometers . . . to Paris.' " [19]

The Germans were threatened everywhere. Military logic called for retreat, but Hitler ordered a counterattack at Mortain in an effort to cut Patton's supply line and destroy his army before the First Army could rescue it. The plan failed disastrously, however, when British intelligence intercepted Hitler's orders and Anglo-American planes and American artillery tore up German armored divisions.

In counterattacking and then failing to withdraw quickly after they were checked, the Germans put their heads into a noose. The British and Canadians had finally broken through at Caen and were coming down from the north to hook up with the Americans, who were driving up from the south, at the town of Falaise. There the two forces hoped to encircle and trap around 100,000 German troops, in what became known as the Falaise Pocket. Here was an opportunity to end the war in 1944 by capturing the entire German Army in Normandy.

As Montgomery moved south, only a small hole in the pocket remained to be closed between Falaise and Argentan. But his Canadian forces moved too slowly to close it. At this point, Patton begged Bradley to let him finish the job, completely enveloping the panicked German forces and destroying them. Bradley refused, fearing that Patton's and Montgomery's armies would come so close to each other at the Falaise Pocket that they would accidentally fire on one another. Instead of pulling the noose shut, Bradley chose to annihilate the Germans with overwhelming air and artillery fire as they tried to escape the pocket.

"It was complete chaos," German Private Herbert Meier recalls of being trapped in the Falaise Pocket. "That's when I thought, This is the end of the world." [20] Men were screaming for their mothers or their wives and children, while artillery fire and bombs rained down on them, and fast-moving Shermans tracked them down like hunted prey. The high ground near the pocket was called the "Balcony of Death." From there American artillery had a perfect observation over a three-mile-long valley. The valley became littered with burned tanks, smashed artillery pieces, overturned carts, dead horses and cattle, and thousands of dead and mangled Germans.

It was a military calamity for the Wehrmacht. The Germans left behind most of their equipment, along with about 50,000 prisoners and 10,000 dead comrades. "The battlefield at Falaise was unquestionably one of the greatest 'killing grounds' of any of the war areas," Eisenhower wrote in his memoirs. "Roads were so choked with destroyed equipment and with dead men and animals that passage through the area was extremely difficult. Forty-eight hours after the closing of the gap I was conducted through it on foot, to encounter scenes that could be described only by Dante. It was literally possible to walk for hundreds of yards at a time, stepping on nothing but dead and decaying flesh." [21]

Yet some 50,000 soldiers, including veteran panzer divisions, managed to escape the fast-closing Falaise Pocket. The Americans would meet them again. They, along with about 150,000 other troops in Normandy who made it back to Germany, would form the foundation of the rebuilt Wehrmacht in the West that launched the Battle of the Bulge, the largest and bloodiest battle American troops ever fought.

The slaughter at Falaise ended the Battle for Normandy, a struggle involving over a million fighting men. The Germans lost almost half a million combatants—killed, wounded, or captured. The Allies suffered almost 210,000 casualties, two thirds of them Americans.

The road to Paris was now open.

The Liberation of Paris

After the almost complete destruction of the German Seventh Army, Patton's forces swept forward on a broad front toward the Seine. By August 19 two columns had reached that river north of Paris; another column swung toward the city from the south through Chartres in time to save its glorious cathedral from irreparable damage; still another headed south through Orléans and the Loire Valley. By the 20th, American soldiers could see the beckoning spire of the Eiffel Tower.

With liberation near, the Parisians rose in revolt. On August 24 Radio France announced: "It is the duty of all Frenchmen to participate in the fight against the Germans." The next day at 2 P.M. General Jacques Philippe Leclerc, head of a Free

PARISIANS CELEBRATING THEIR LIBERATION DUCK FOR COVER AS A GERMAN SNIPER OPENS FIRE (SC).

French army that had fought in Normandy, announced the surrender of the Germans in a scrubby baggage room at Gare Montparnasse. Hitler had demanded the destruction of the city and all its monuments, following up his order with the query, "Is Paris burning?" But General Dietrich von Choltitz refused to carry out that revengeful order.

Robert Capa rode into Paris on a tank with the Spanish Republicans he had fought with against fascism in the 1930s, while his friend Ernest Hemingway, who had landed on Omaha Beach on D-Day, a war correspondent for *Collier's*, had taken a different road to the city. Capa wanted to spend the night at the Ritz, but Hemingway and the private army he had assembled in France had already "liberated" the great hotel and were guarding the doors. When Capa approached the hotel, one of Hemingway's "soldiers" greeted him, "Papa took good hotel. Plenty of stuff in cellar. You go up quick." [22]

As the Germans were struggling to extricate their battered armies from Normandy and pull back from Paris, they were confronted with new difficulties. On August 15 a powerful Allied army landed on the coast of southern France, meeting only light resistance from the overextended Wehrmacht. Leaving the reduction of the ports of Marseilles and Toulon to the First French Army, General Alexander Patch's American Seventh Army swept up the valley of the Rhône to join Allied armies heading for the German border. The Germans were cleared out of Southern France except in some of the ports, among them St. Nazaire, a U-boat base at the mouth of the Loire River.

AT THE SIEGFRIED LINE

In the north, the Allied armies had swept forward almost unopposed from the Seine to the Somme, the Marne and the Belgian border, through territory famous from the First World War. Patton's Third Army reached the Marne on August 28, drove through Château-Thierry, took Soissons, Rheims, and Verdun. The First Army took Sedan at the Belgian border, and still farther north the British and Canadian armies of General Montgomery raced along the coast through Lille, into Belgium and to the Dutch border. Just one hundred days after the Normandy landings, Allied armies were massed—on a 250-mile-long front—near the German border. The Battle for France was over; the Battle for Germany was about to begin.

Guarding the approaches to Germany was the Siegfried Line, or West Wall. At its strongest points, it was a three-mile-deep belt of concrete bunkers, pillboxes, and artillery emplacements protected by minefields, barbed wire, and massive antitank obstacles. The army defending it was perhaps as large as Eisenhower's, although not nearly as well equipped.

With the Allies at the western gates of the Reich, their lightning-like advance came to a halt. "We have advanced so rapidly," Eisenhower wrote George Marshall on September 4, "that further movement in large parts of the front even against very weak opposition is almost impossible." [23] Eisenhower's army was the victim of its own success. It had advanced so fast, so far ahead of schedule, that it outran its supply line, which reached all the way back to the invasion beaches, where 90 percent of its fresh matériel and men still came across from England. The Army was now dangerously short of supplies, especially gasoline.

Getting these necessities to the front was difficult. The French rail system had not recovered from the Allied air assault in preparation for D-Day, and the Germans were still holding tenaciously to a number of major ports, among them Le Havre, Brest, Calais, and Dunkirk. So supplies had to be brought by truck across northern France. In late August, the Army hastily organized the Red Ball Express, a transport system named for the railroaders' term for a fast freight train. Over 6,000 trucks and trailers and 23,000 men were mobilized to rush fuel, ammunition, and rations from the invasion beaches and the only functioning port at Cherbourg to the armies advancing on the Siegfried Line. Three quarters of the drivers on the Red Ball Express were African-Americans. They drove their two-and-a-half-ton trucks around the clock over the approximately 450-mile route from Normandy to the German border.

It was dangerous work. The drivers, two to a truck, were under heavy pressure to deliver their cargoes on the double quick. Some drivers removed the governors on their trucks so they could run at 60 miles an hour, and when one driver was exhausted, he and his relief man would switch seats while the truck was barreling down the road. To avoid detection, the trucks ran at night without headlights, their only identifiable markings two ruby-colored slits, "cat eyes," in the rear and a white slit on the front grille. Many men drove forty-eight hours straight without sleep. "God, it was awful. Sometimes I felt like screaming. You couldn't sleep and they wouldn't let you stop," said Red Ball driver Booker Nance. [24]

Gasoline was often delivered in the heat of combat. "We often refuel and rearm even while fighting," said a GI. "That takes guts. Our Negro outfits delivered gas under constant fire. Damned if I'd want their job. They have what it takes." [25]

This "miracle of supply," said *Time* magazine, "was in the American tradition, a tradition the Germans have never really understood. It was begotten of a people accustomed to great spaces, to transcontinental railways, to nationwide trucking chains, to endless roads and millions of automobiles." [26] But the Red Ball Express could not keep up with the American armies' voracious appetite for supplies, and as the Allied front pressed eastward, the trucks themselves began using unacceptably large quantities of gas.

This logistical nightmare focused attention on Antwerp, Belgium. The British had just captured the city, one of Europe's largest ports, but had failed to take the Schelde River Estuary, the approach to the port. If Antwerp were opened, the Allied fuel problems would end, but instead of applying full force to clear the Germans from the banks of the Scheldt, Eisenhower made a dangerously risky attempt to win the war before the end of the year. Prodded by General Montgomery, he approved a mission to land paratroopers behind the Siegfried Line, in Holland, and have them move through the industrialized Ruhr to Berlin. The invasion was code-named Market-Garden.

On September 17, 4,700 planes flying from England dropped 35,000 American and British airborne troops behind German lines. It was the largest operation of its kind in history. These elite airborne units were to capture the bridges along a sixty-mile-long corridor from the Belgian-Dutch border to Arnhem, a gateway city to the Ruhr. British armored divisions would then storm into the secured corridor and spearhead the invasion of the Ruhr. The American 82nd and 101st Airborne Divisions captured key bridges across the Meuse and the Waal Rivers, but the British 1st Airborne Division, landing at Arnhem, was surrounded and overwhelmed by Waffen SS troops after a deadly battle to take "a bridge too far."

With the failure of Market-Garden, Eisenhower determined to break the Siegfried Line by a series of crushing frontal assaults all along the German border. "People of the strength and warlike tendencies of the Germans do not give in. They must be beaten to the ground," he defiantly declared. [27]

The first attack of that bloody fall and winter was in early October at Aachen, an ancient art center just west of the Rhine. The Germans had turned it into a seemingly impregnable fortress ringed by interlocking concrete bunkers. And the defenders, middle-aged German soldiers thrown into the breach, fought with surprising ferocity. It took three weeks of air and artillery pounding and house-to-house fighting to force the decimated German garrison to surrender. Aachen was the first major German city to fall, but the Americans were unable to break through to the Rhine. At the southern end of the American line, Patton, without sufficient fuel for his tanks, found it equally difficult to reduce the citadel city of Metz, unconquered in 1,000 years.

In his drive across France, Patton had appealed for more tanks—the best-trained tank crews that were available—and the Army sent him the 761st, the first armored unit in the history of the American Army to enter combat with African-Americans

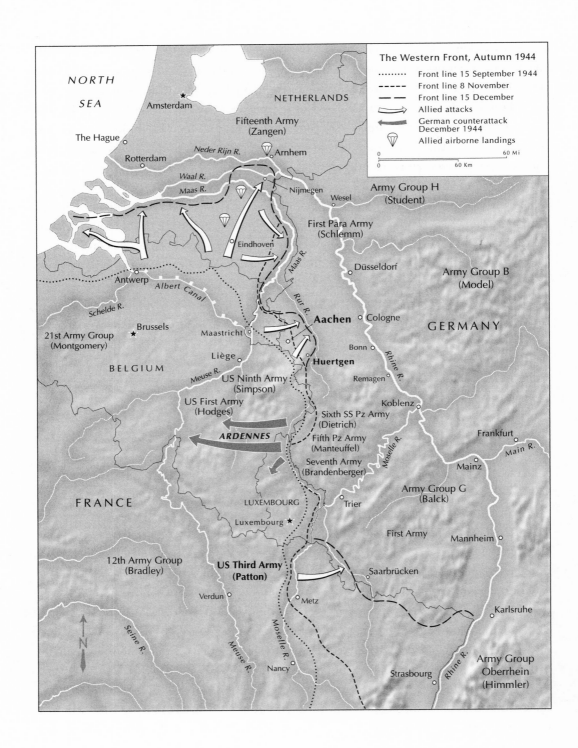

The Western Front, Autumn 1944

Front line 15 September 1944
Front line 8 November
Front line 15 December
Allied attacks
German counterattack December 1944
Allied airborne landings

0   60 Mi
0   60 Km

NORTH SEA

NETHERLANDS

Amsterdam

The Hague

Rotterdam

Neder Rijn R.

Arnhem

Waal R.

Nijmegen

Maas R.

Wesel

Army Group H (Student)

First Para Army (Schlemm)

Düsseldorf

Army Group B (Model)

Eindhoven

Maas R.

Antwerp

Albert Canal

Schelde R.

Rur R.

Aachen

Cologne

GERMANY

21st Army Group (Montgomery)

Brussels

Maastricht

Bonn

Rhine R.

BELGIUM

Liège

Huertgen

Remagen

Meuse R.

US Ninth Army (Simpson)

Koblenz

US First Army (Hodges)

Sixth SS Pz Army (Dietrich)

Frankfurt

ARDENNES

Fifth Pz Army (Manteuffel)

Moselle R.

Main R.

Seventh Army (Brandenberger)

Mainz

Army Group G (Balck)

FRANCE

LUXEMBOURG

Luxembourg

Trier

First Army

Mannheim

12th Army Group (Bradley)

US Third Army (Patton)

Saarbrücken

Verdun

Metz

Karlsruhe

Seine R.

Moselle R.

Meuse R.

Nancy

Strasbourg

Rhine R.

Army Group Oberrhein (Himmler)

N

Fifteenth Army (Zangen)

manning its vehicles. They landed on Omaha Beach on October 10, 1944, and joined the Third Army on the Siegfried Line exactly three weeks later. Their six commanding officers were white, but their thirty company commanders and all 676 enlisted men were black. "I was and am proud of my tankers," Captain John D. Long—called by his men "the Black Patton"—said of the 761st at the front. "They were as good or better than most of the tankers in the whole European theater. . . . We were fighting sons-of-bitches, and our reputation came before us."

On November 2, at St. Nicolas, France, General Patton greeted them. "He was the most dashing thing you ever saw—standing on a half-track with his shining helmet and with those two pearl-handled pistols," says Johnnie Holmes of Chicago, who, like many of the men, came to idolize the Southern general, who did not have positive feelings about black people.[28] In Captain Long's words: "He told us, 'Men, you are the first Negro tankers ever to fight in the American Army. I would never have asked for you if you were not good. I have nothing but the best in my army. I don't care what color you are as long as you go up there and kill those Kraut sons-of-bitches. Everyone has their eyes on you and are expecting great things from you. Most of all, your race is looking forward to your success. Don't let them down, and damn you, don't let me down!'"

The 761st swung immediately into action, covering and leading infantry that seized the town of Morville-les-Vic, and assaulting a series of other strongly held enemy towns on the perimeter of Metz, instantly earning their motto, "Come Out Fighting." "The town of Morville-les-Vic was supposed to be a snap but it was an inferno; my men were tigers, they fought like seasoned veterans," says Captain Long. "We got our lumps but we took that fucking town." [29] The battalion would see uninterrupted action with eight different divisions in France, Belgium, Luxembourg, Germany, and Austria as a "bastard outfit," one that does not belong to any division permanently but fights with any outfit that needs it. "We completed 183 days straight of combat duty," says Charles A. Gates, "and the only reason we didn't see more was because the Germans quit." [30]

The local villagers were surprised to see them. "When we swept into those first towns, blew the Germans out, and crawled out of our tanks, folks were sure surprised to see our black faces," Johnnie Holmes recalls. "And so were the krauts. I captured a house that had a German major in it who spoke perfect English. He told me he was born in Chicago and returned to Germany with his parents when he was fourteen. Then he said, 'Sergeant, what the hell are you doing here?' I said, 'I'm fighting for my country. Why?' He said, 'That's not your country; that's a white man's country. This is not your war; this is a white man's war.' And I said, 'It's my country, too, right or wrong, and I'm here to kill you sons-of-bitches so you don't take it over.'

"Our white troops were glad to see us. But some of them were as racially prejudiced as the Nazis. A lot of guys whose lives we saved made it a point to thank us, but when the shooting stopped, we were niggers again to most of them. They wouldn't say that to our faces. But the local people told us that the white troops told them that there were no black tankers. The black guys just brought the tanks up to the front for the white guys." [31]

Into December the 761st fought in swirling snow and ankle-deep mud along the German border, taking heavy casualties, ending the month with a shortage of 113 men and thirty-four tanks destroyed or disabled. African-American replacement troops did not arrive until the first week of December, but they were not trained as tankers and had to learn on the job. Short of personnel throughout the war, the 761st continued to perform at the highest level because all of its wounded officers and 20 percent of its hospitalized enlisted men returned to duty with the unit.

But even with more tanks, Patton could not break through to the Rhine. When his Third Army finally took Metz, with its twenty-two forts supporting it, in early December, it was still twelve kilometers from the Siegfried Line with no immediate hope of storming it. In the north, meanwhile, Montgomery cleared the Scheldt Estuary and opened the port of Antwerp. Then, all along the Siegfried Line the war settled down to a slugging match, with Allied infantry moving relentlessly and at an awful cost against fixed German positions.

THE HUERTGEN FOREST

The worst fighting—perhaps the worst fighting of the war on the Western Front—was in the Huertgen Forest, near Aachen. "In the [Huertgen] forest proper, our gains came inch by inch and foot by foot, delivered by men with rifles—bayonets on one end and grim, resolute courage on the other. There was no battle on the continent of Europe more devastating, frustrating, or gory," said Major General William G. Weaver, commanding general of the 8th Infantry Division.[32]

The objective of both armies was to kill as many of the enemy as possible, to convince the other side that continuing the war was too costly. Sergeant Mack Morriss was there with the 4th Infantry Division. Morriss wrote this account after the forest was taken in early December, following a punishing two-month struggle:

THE FIRS ARE THICK, and there are 50 square miles of them standing dismal and dripping at the approaches to the Cologne plain. The bodies of the firs begin close to the ground, so that each fir interlocks its body with another. At the height of a man standing, there is a solid mass of dark, impenetrable green. But at the height of a man crawling, there is room, and it is like a green cave, low-roofed and forbidding. And through this cave moved the infantry, to emerge cold and exhausted when the forest of Huertgen came to a sudden end before Grosshau.

The infantry, free from the claustrophobia of the forest, went on, but behind them they left their dead, and the forest will stink with deadness long after the last body is removed. The forest will bear the scars of our advance long after our scars have healed, and the infantry has scars that will never heal.

For Huertgen was agony, and there was no glory in it except the glory of courageous men—the MP whose testicles were hit by shrapnel and who said, "Okay, doc, I can take it"; the man who walked forward, firing tommy guns with both hands until an arm was blown off and then kept on firing the other tommy gun until he disappeared in a mortar burst. . . .

For 21 days, the division beat its slow way forward. . . . There was counterattack, too, but in time the infantry welcomed it, because then and only then the German came out of his hole and was a visible target, and the maddened infantry killed with grim satisfaction. But the infantry advanced with its battle packs, and it dug in and buttoned up, and then the artillery raked the line so that there were many times when the infantry's rolls could not be brought up to them.

Rolls were brought to a certain point, but the infantry could not go back for them because to leave the shelter was insane. So the infantry slept as it fought— if it slept at all—without blankets, and the nights were long and wet and cold. . . .

Huertgen had its roads, and they were blocked. The German did well by his abatis, his roadblocks made from trees. Sometimes he felled 200 trees across the road, cutting them down so they interlocked as they fell. Then he mined and booby-trapped them. Finally he registered his artillery on them, and his mortars, and at the sound of men clearing them, he opened fire. . . .[33]

Nineteen-year-old Robert D. Georgen from Ridgewood, New Jersey, a sophomore in college, fought in the Huertgen meat grinder. He was one of the hundreds of thousands of seventeen- to nineteen-year-old replacements who were being poured into Europe as casualties mounted. When he arrived from a replacement depot in France, he didn't even know what infantry division he had joined. It was, he soon learned, the 28th Infantry, a Pennsylvania National Guard outfit called the Keystone Division. One evening in the Huertgen Forest, his unit received orders to move its position.

IT WAS NECESSARY FOR US to stay close together in single file with our hands on each other's shoulders because of the total darkness. About the sixth man in front of me stepped on a German "S" mine, called a Bouncing Betty. I heard the initial trigger pop and froze in place. The soldier that stepped on the mine did what he had been taught to do. [He] kept his foot on the mine so that it could not jump above the ground and raised his other leg. We moved forward once again and as I passed, the man was lying on the ground with a medic working on him using a flashlight. I noticed his foot was shattered and bloody. He probably had his ticket home, if he ever managed to get out of the forest. . . .

After what seemed like hours on the night march in the Huertgen Forest, the column came to some questionable destination and we were told to try to get some sleep before the light of morning—in the snow! Without my overcoat I was freezing and finally decided to carve out the bank of a small stream nearby and climb into it. . . . By morning my hand (even with gloves) was . . . unable to fit into the trigger guard in order to fire my rifle. On the run, I fixed my bayonet onto the muzzle of the rifle with some difficulty and charged [a] line of foxholes. At one point I saw a German soldier shot down in front of me as he ran from his hole, so I dropped to the ground in a prone position with my elbows and rifle across his chest. Making sure he was dead, I used his remaining body heat to warm up my hands, allowing me to once again fire my rifle.

We captured the position and marched the prisoners down the line.[34]

In the Hürtgen Fwald, the Germans fought with patriotic fury, their backs to the wall, protecting the soil of the Fatherland. The terrain was their ally, for they were on the defensive, in heavily entrenched positions. And they were fighting an enemy without any training in forest warfare and without proper winter gear.

The weather was wretched: drenching rain in October, driving snow and sleet in November. Then there was the green gloom created by the forest canopy of interlocking trees. Men lived in foxholes half filled with water, leading to epidemics of trench foot. When the weather turned cold, thousands of men came down with frostbite and respiratory diseases.

"The forest was a helluva eerie place to fight," said Sergeant George Morgan. "You can't get protection. You can't see. You can't get fields of fire [because of the fog and the morning mist]. Artillery slashes the trees like a scythe. Everything is tangled. You can scarcely walk. Everybody is cold and wet, and the mixture of cold rain and sleet keeps falling."[35] When artillery shells hit the branches of the giant trees they exploded high above the forest floor, splattering troops with lethal shards of steel shell casings and sharp-pointed branches. Units got separated in the dark, dense forest, and men became unnerved by feelings of isolation and helplessness. This and the unending fighting, day after day, led to an alarmingly high rate of combat fatigue.

Soldiers knew when a comrade had had it. The exhausted soldier would sit on the edge of his foxhole, strip off his helmet, and stare into space, his face expressionless, with the Germans firing on him.

Fighting was at close quarters in the Huertgen Forest and inhumanly vicious, particularly when men on both sides reached the limits of their physical endurance. Lieutenant John Forsell of the 110th Infantry was on patrol in a forest village when he came upon a GI hung on the town's crucifixion cross. "We cut him down. We stayed in town and hid in a few houses waiting for the Germans. A German patrol came in, we had a gunfight, they were caught by surprise. A few of the patrol got away but we took three Germans and hung them on three crosses. That ended that little fanfare for both sides."[36]

Most rifle companies had turnover rates of over 100 percent. There were not enough replacements in Europe, so unless a man was wounded or his unit relieved by another, he couldn't get out. Men by the hundreds shot themselves in the foot or the hand to get out of the combat zone; others held on in a state of grim resignation. As the end approached, and the Americans fought for the town of Huertgen at the far end of the forest, the troops went into a killing frenzy, bayoneting and clubbing Germans. In early December, they took the forest, after suffering 31,000 casualties.

When Robert Georgen's 28th Division was pulled out of the Huertgen in the middle of November and replaced with another infantry division, it had suffered horrible losses. His company went in with over 160 men; only twenty walked out. "By the time I left the forest I had the survival instincts of an animal," Georgen recalls.[37]

Early the next year, as American troops were preparing to move into Germany, some units passed through the Huertgen Forest. They descended into the Kall River Valley, where Germans had trapped a regiment of Robert Georgen's 28th Division and destroyed it before the snows fell. "I saw much death and destruction from Normandy onward," recalled Arthur "Dutch" Schultz of the 82nd Airborne, "but never anything even close to what I saw [there]. . . . Much of the snow was beginning to melt and underneath were countless American bodies in all kinds of contorted positions. In some instances only an arm, or a head, or a portion of the lower body, or the entire body could be seen. There were vehicles, tanks, hand weapons, artillery pieces, and other equipment scattered over the valley. What bothered me was that these dead American soldiers were abandoned without any apparent recognition of their sacrifices."[38]

CHAPTER 11

The Battle of the Bulge

NEITHER SIDE GAINED ANYTHING OF VALUE in the terrible fight for the Huertgen Forest. But the battle did help the Germans disguise the tremendous buildup they were making in the Eifel Mountains opposite France's Ardennes Forest. This was in preparation for Hitler's final attempt to turn the tide of the war, a colossal gamble made against the advice of his senior military commanders.

Germany had already suffered four million casualties; its cities and industrial plants were being pulverized from the air; the Luftwaffe had been decimated; and the badly battered Wehrmacht was being pressed from both east and west by huge, highly equipped armies. Rumors flew through the American Army that Hitler was dead, and Eisenhower bet Montgomery £5 that the war would be over by Christmas. In an effort to make that happen, General Bradley postponed orders for winter gear for his troops in order to bring in more military equipment to finish the job.

Hitler knew he couldn't beat the Red Army, but he had contempt for the fighting ability of the Americans. The Americans were winning the war, he was convinced, by the sheer power of their mass production economy. If he cut their precarious supply line he might be able to force them to capitulate.

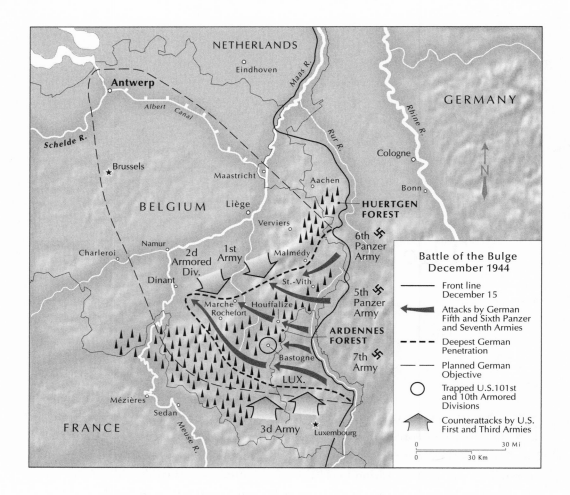

The Fuehrer's plan, announced to his generals in September, was to raise a new army, the Volksgrenadier, a people's infantry of former airmen and sailors, conscripts from Nazi-occupied countries who spoke no German, and grandfathers and young boys, some of them only fifteen years old. It would link up with veteran army units, including the Waffen SS, in a lightning counterattack along an eighty-mile front that ran from southern Belgium to the middle of Luxembourg. The attack would be spear-headed by the hundreds of new tanks that Albert Speer's accelerated armaments pro-gram had produced that summer.

After breaking through the rough terrain of the Ardennes, two armies, with another protecting their southern flank, would swing north, cross the Meuse River, and capture the port of Antwerp, some 125 miles away, cutting the flow of supplies to the

Allies and splitting the British and Canadian forces from the American armies to the south. The Germans would then push the British into the Channel, in a second Dunkirk. At this point, the Western Allies might agree to a separate peace, allowing Hitler to throw everything he had against the oncoming Russians.

Hitler's plan, a masterwork of self-delusion, was based on two things: surprise and bad weather. "Fog, night, and snow," he predicted, would ground the Allied air arm and give him his victory.

After being pulled out of the Huertgen Forest, Robert Georgen's 28th Division and another shattered division from the forest war were moved to a rest area in Luxembourg. There were two other divisions in this thinly defended sector, both of them made up of green replacements. This was considered a "ghost front," an unlikely target of an enemy counterstroke, even though the Germans had attacked through this area in overwhelming force at the start of both this and the last world war. Those assaults had been made in good weather, not in the middle of the worst European winter of the century. So when intelligence units in Robert Georgen's division reported unusual German activity in the area just to the west of them, the reports were disregarded at headquarters.

On the eve of the German attack, Dwayne T. Burns, a radioman with the 82nd Airborne, was in a rest area in France, where the troops were living in comfortable brick barracks and being entertained by Mickey Rooney and other USO stars. Burns had just returned from Operation Market-Garden and the biggest thing on his mind was when his turn would come to get a pass to go to Paris. "Christmas was coming and things were looking up. . . . I was beginning to think that this wasn't too bad of a place to sit out the rest of the war." [1]

That same night, December 15, Field Marshal Gerd von Rundstedt issued the order of the day to the armies he had amassed in the Eifel Mountains: "Soldiers of the West Front, your great hour has struck. Everything is at stake." At 5:30 the next morning a thunderous artillery bombardment announced the only major German counter-offensive of the war in Western Europe.

For Rundstedt, it was to be a repeat performance. Back in May 1940 he had led his panzer divisions through this heavily timbered country that the French thought so unsuitable for armored warfare that they had left it practically defenseless. Now Eisenhower had made the same mistake, posting only 80,000 men along this front.

Almost a quarter of a million German troops and 600 tanks swept through the American lines, causing massive panic and confusion. Defense lines broke down and

A *WAFFEN* SS SOLDIER, ARMED TO THE
TEETH, IN THE ARDENNES (NA).

tens of thousands of soldiers, numb with fear, dropped their weapons and ran. "Germans were all over us, within ten, fifteen yards right in front of us," recalled an American soldier. "If you could see a bunch of wild cattle running wild, that's what it reminds you of. I believe they were doped—they were acting as if, 'I don't care if I get killed or not.' They were like wild men." [2]

German commandos, speaking perfect English and dressed as American soldiers, with dog tags taken from corpses and POWs, created further panic by cutting telephone wires, changing road signs, and misdirecting American tanks and troops.

There were mass surrenders. More than 4,000 men of the green 106th Division gave up, along with 6,000 other American troops. Heavy clouds kept the Allied air force grounded, giving the attackers a huge advantage. A U.S. Army correspondent called Rundstedt's surprise breakthrough "the most frightening, unbelievable experience of the war." [3]

On the night of December 17, Dwayne T. Burns went to a movie with a friend and then stopped at the NCO club:

IT WAS LATE WHEN WE STARTED BACK to the barracks and I was looking forward to a good night's sleep. As we came up the company street, we could see all of the lights burning and everyone was up. As we walked into our room, we could see equipment stacked on the floor and on the bunks. . . . I saw John Hurst standing there in the middle of all the turmoil with a look of uncertainty on his face.

I asked, "Hurst, what in the world is going on?"

"We just got word that the Germans are breaking through the Ardennes in Belgium and we have been ordered to move up to stop them."

"Damn," I exclaimed. "It just isn't fair. I haven't even made it to Paris yet! Why can't they send somebody else?"

At dawn the trucks pulled up. Weary with fatigue and lack of sleep, we reluctantly climbed aboard. I think we were still in shock at having our world turned

CHECKING DOG TAGS TO SPOT GERMAN INFILTRATORS (NA).

around so quickly. Some were complaining that this was no way for an airborne regiment to go into combat. It was a disgrace. Someone joked that after this mission we would get to wear a pair of wheels on our wings along with our stars for our Normandy and Holland jumps. We were riding in open-air trucks and had to stand up, just like a bunch of cows. We drove all day and into the night.

As we went through each town, the French and Belgian people would line the streets to wave and cheer.

We passed through the town of Bastogne and kept going north. Before dawn on the 19th, tired, dirty, and bone weary, we unloaded near Werbomont, Belgium, and established a defensive position. At this time we didn't know where the Germans were. Everything was in a state of confusion.

101ST AIRBORNE MOVES INTO BASTOGNE (SC).

The next day Burns's unit marched all night to a new position near the River Salm, on the north side of the "bulge" in the American line created by the German advance. "Winter weather unleashed the first great snowstorm at about midnight on the 21st. We shivered and watched as the hills around us turned white. . . . Now our biggest enemy was the cold. Lacking winter clothing, we wore what we had. Long Johns and O.D.'s (pants and shirt from our Class A uniform) under our combat suits, two pair of socks and anything else that would help us to stay warm."[4]

Burns and other veterans of the Battle of the Bulge are quick to point out that most American troops did not run when the "Bosch" poured into the Ardennes.

Burns's men hooked up with the troops that had stuck to their positions, and together this first line of defenders made the difference between defeat and victory.

American soldiers in small rifle companies, in engineering groups, and in antitank teams fought in swirling snow and zero degree temperatures, slowing the German penetration and inflicting tremendous casualties on Hitler youth who had no idea how to fight, but kept coming on, machinelike boys, marching straight into enemy fire.

German infantrymen wore white to blend in with the environment; so GIs without winter clothing took sheets wherever they could find them and wrapped them around their bodies. Men grew so tired and listless from moving constantly to stay warm that when they stopped to rest and eat, they would not hesitate to sit on the dead bodies of American soldiers, frozen solid in the snow. Richard F. Proulx, an eighteen-year-old replacement from Maine, described his first encounter with such a corpse: "I said, 'too bad good buddy,' and sat on him and ate my rations."[5]

Proulx was one of the riflemen who helped stop the German juggernaut. His first action was a bayonet fight, one of several hand-to-hand engagements he fought in the Ardennes.

"As we moved into final assembly, we were told to lock and load, keep our M-1s on safety, and to fix bayonets. We were going into our first action with quiet bayonets and knives only. No firing! Our objective was to clear off the top of a small hill . . . without firing on the enemy. We wanted surprise and a show of strength and audacity to shake the morale of the troops facing us."

Moving quietly through the new-fallen snow, with just enough light to see, Proulx's unit achieved complete surprise, but the Germans quickly recovered. "One young German soldier came at me full tilt, head-on, no bayonet on his rifle; aimed straight at me from six feet but could not fire; brought his rifle up to block and screamed. An officer fired at me with a pistol and screamed . . . as my bayonet, sharp as a razor, slashed across his throat. . . .

"All around was screaming, swearing, and the puffing and crunch of body against body. . . . We were all tangled together killing and dying."

After endless minutes of this, the Germans threw up their arms and surrendered. "We had our hill."

Later, Proulx wrote down what happened in an effort to understand what it had done to him.

THERE IS A TREMENDOUS DIFFERENCE between [killing a man with a bayonet] and shooting a man at a distance with a rifle or pistol. In a bayonet attack . . . you see your target close up and feel the shudder when he is cut clear through. . . . You must turn off part of the mind. The real animal instinct must come to the forefront. Even if revenge is the mover, to stand close enough to see the grimace, and hear the scream or shudder and moan as you strike and push the bayonet into the enemy, is one of the things that nightmares are made of. Usually you scream or growl in your throat to take away any sense of being a human being. You become an animal with extended claws and it is to the death. . . . No mercy is asked and none given. . . . No matter that the enemy was a savage, or killer, . . . you too are a killer! It can be rationalized away for a moment, but the fact has to be faced sooner or later. . . . You killed a man with your own hands, up close, and with malice and intent.

When that first bayonet fight ended, Proulx went back to the German officer whose throat he had cut. He was still alive, and he motioned to Proulx to help him. "I stepped over him with my rifle ready. His pistol was out of his reach and as I neared him he reached up quickly with a knife and almost stabbed me in the lower groin. I drove the bayonet clear through his throat pinning him to the ground, and kept it there till his eyes glazed over."

After this, Proulx went over to the other soldier he had hit. He was barely alive. Looking down at him, Proulx became dizzy and sick to his stomach. "Here was a white Christian young man I had just butchered. . . . I began to retch, and only coffee and part of a K ration came up. . . . That was my transition to the unreal world of animal behavior."[6]

Proulx and other GIs who absorbed the shock of the initial German hit were told to "engage, slow, stop, and attack if at all possible."[7] The timetable was critical. They had to delay the Germans until Eisenhower could bring up reinforcements. And unknown to them, the Germans had only enough fuel for a five- or six-day attack. Before their gasoline ran out, the Germans counted on capturing fuel depots behind enemy lines.

The stubborn resistance of American GIs defeated these plans, as small units attacked Tiger tanks with bazookas and rifle grenades and raked infantry outfits with small arms fire, grenades, and mortar. "We filled bottles with gasoline, using cloth wicks, often standing in the open up close, in a rain of bullets and shell fragments, to plaster the tanks with Molotov cocktails. Some GIs even ran through German infantry, got aboard tanks and put grenades and phosphorus in the turrets and hatches," Proulx recalls. "Our orders were to hold or die. Somehow we held." [8] As the English writer Alan Moorehead wrote: "It was this desperate resistance by isolated Americans . . . this and nothing else, which saved Belgium and Holland from being overrun." [9]

The human steamroller these troops tried to slow down was moving in three directions. The major attack, headed by Colonel Joachim Peiper's 1st SS Panzer Division, was to the north through St. Vith, with the objective Antwerp. The other attacks were on the center at the key crossroads town of Bastogne, and south of it. The southern attack was stopped cold, and in the north the Germans were held up by a fanatical American defense around St. Vith. Colonel David Pergrin's combat engineers blew bridges, mined roads, and set up roadblocks to prevent Peiper's armor spearhead from reaching the Meuse River within its forty-eight-hour deadline.

The Germans made the most rapid progress in the center. The American 28th Division was sent reeling back on Bastogne, where several roads led into the thick of the Ardennes. "My 110th Regiment had no place to go except backwards," said Robert Georgen, "defending mile by mile in ever decreasing numbers. . . . At best all we could do was delay the forward movement of the German Army. This we did do, at a great cost, allowing the 101st Airborne Division to occupy and successfully defend Bastogne." [10] Georgen's regiment suffered over 80 percent casualties in the first days of the German counteroffensive.

In areas of the Ardennes where green American troops were facing combat for the first time there was widespread chaos and confusion. Panic-stricken troops threw away their equipment and ran as columns of Tiger tanks came roaring down narrow forest roads, nose to tail. After his unit surrendered, Kurt Vonnegut, Jr., a newly arrived replacement, ran into the forest without a rifle in search of the American lines.[11] On some roads, two lines of troops moved at the same time in opposite directions, one group retreating, the other coming up to meet the enemy. When American reinforcements reached a Belgian village, the priest would ring the church bells in celebration, inadvertently bringing down German fire on the town.

As they were pushed back toward Bastogne, isolated units of the 48th Division disappeared in the chaos of combat. Robert Georgen and two other GIs got separated from their company and began walking, dazed and confused, in a westerly direction. They could hear German guns blowing apart entire villages, and looking up, they watched the horizon turn crimson from enemy 88s.

Clerks, cooks, MPs, musicians, and other noncombat soldiers were thrown into the battle. "A staff sergeant came up to me and asked me to show him how to load and fire his M-1 rifle," Georgen recalls. "At first I thought he was kidding around with me until he told me that the previous week he had been a member of a coastal antiaircraft unit in the United States. They loaded a bunch of these GIs on planes and flew them to Europe to fight in the Ardennes campaign. . . . I gave the staff sergeant a quick course in how to stay alive in combat and wished him well."

GIs were told not to surrender to the enemy's armored groups. If they had to surrender, they should do so only to infantry units. These units had the manpower to take Americans back as prisoners of war; the panzer units did not. These orders hit home when reports of the Malmédy Massacre spread through the front line troops. "The word was out," says Georgen. "Fight to the death or run like hell, but don't surrender." [12]

On the second day of the German attack a small convoy of American trucks was moving along a road near Malmédy, Belgium, when Joachim Peiper's SS panzer unit ambushed and destroyed it, taking 150 prisoners. Peiper, who was pressing to get to the River Meuse, ordered the prisoners, including the medical personnel, to line up in a nearby field. The Germans, in their black SS uniforms, parked Tiger tanks at both ends of the field, giving their machine gunners a clear line of fire on the terrified prisoners. Private James J. Mattera was one of the prisoners:

WE ALL STOOD THERE with our hands up, when a German . . . in a command car shot a medical officer and one enlisted man. They fell to the ground. Then the machine guns on the tanks opened up on [us.] . . . We all lay on our stomachs, and every tank that came by would open up with machine guns on the group of men lying on the ground. This carried on about 30 minutes and then it stopped all at once.

Then about three or four Germans came over to the group of men lying on the ground. Some officers . . . were shot in the head with pistols. After they left, the machine gunners opened up.

Private Homer D. Ford continues the story:

THEY CAME ALONG WITH PISTOLS and rifles and shot some that were [still] breathing and hit others in the head with rifle butts. I was hit in the arm. . . . The men were all laying around moaning and crying. When the Germans came over, they would say, "Is he breathing?" and would either shoot them or hit them with the butt of the gun. . . .

After they fired at us I lay stretched out with my hands out and I could feel that blood oozing out. I was laying in the snow and I got wet and started to shiver, and I was afraid they would see me shivering but they didn't. . . . I heard them shoot their pistols while next to me; I could hear them pull the trigger back and then the click. The men were moaning . . . something terrible. I also heard the butt hit their heads and the squishing noise.

After lying in the field, with their faces in the snow and mud, for about an hour, Homer Ford and James Mattera decided to make a break for it. "My buddies around me were getting hit and crying for help," Mattera told Army officials who questioned him after the massacre. "I figured my best bet would be to make a break and run for my life. I was the first one to raise up and I yelled, 'Let's make a break for it!' About 15 fellows raised up, and we were on our way. About 12 of the men ran into a house, and myself and two other soldiers took out over the open field. They fired at us with machine guns, but by luck we made it into the woods, where we hid until dark. The house into which the 12 men ran was burned down by the Germans. Anyone who tried to escape from the fire was shot by machine guns. After it was dark my buddy and I made our way back to our troops. We landed with an engineering battalion, told them our story and what had happened. They gave us chow and a safe place to sleep." [13]

A German prisoner was asked by his American captors why his fellow soldiers had killed Americans in cold blood. "I have no idea," he replied. "Of course, there are people among us who find great joy in committing such atrocities." [14]

Eighty-six men died in the Malmédy Massacre. Twenty, most of them wounded, escaped the slaughter ground, twelve of them killed by their German pursuers. Before this, Peiper's battle group had shot and killed at least 200 American prisoners and Belgian villagers.

David Pergrin's combat engineers helped dig out the Malmédy dead from under thick piles of snow, an experience that planted in Pergrin a deep desire to kill "the countrymen of the scum who had destroyed my countrymen in the field [at Malmédy]." [15]

Americans had killed prisoners in the heat of battle, but this was mass murder. The Allied high command ordered the atrocity publicized. Word passed through the ranks: Take no SS troops prisoners. Gun them down. Some combat units took no German prisoners at all, SS or otherwise.

Eisenhower and Bradley had been caught by surprise when the Germans burst into the Ardennes, but they did not panic. At a meeting with his senior commanders at Verdun, Eisenhower ordered that the attack be seen as an opportunity. The Germans had come out of their fortifications and were now vulnerable. After listening to this, Patton spoke up: "Hell, let's have the guts to let the sons of bitches go all the way to Paris. Then we'll really cut 'em up."[16]

Eisenhower moved immediately to stop the enemy penetration. Reinforcements were rushed to St. Vith in the north, and the 101st Airborne Division, the Screaming Eagles, then at a rest center behind the lines, traveled to Bastogne by truck to reinforce elements of the 9th and 10th Armored. The Third Army was a hundred miles to the south, facing the Siegfried Line, but Patton agreed to turn three of his divisions north, including the African-American 761st Tank Battalion, to race to Bastogne, in what would be one of the great rescues of the war. "We headed north as fast as tanks can go," says Edward Donald of the 761st.[17] On one day alone, 11,000 trucks, driven mostly by African-American drivers, carried 60,000 men into the Ardennes. By the end of the first week of the German offensive, Eisenhower had moved a quarter of a million men into the fight. No army had ever been reinforced in such numbers at such speed.

Bastogne was the key to the southern Ardennes. By December 20, with Patton still a hundred miles away, the Germans had encircled the town, cutting off the 101st Airborne under the acting command of Brigadier General Anthony McAuliffe. The Screaming Eagles had also commandeered several armored units, including two African-American artillery battalions. One of them, the 969th Field Artillery Battalion, would receive a Distinguished Unit Citation for valor during the siege.

After learning about the trapped paratroopers, Robert Capa requisitioned a jeep and a driver and headed in the direction of Bastogne. Every few miles they were stopped by MPs, who asked them seemingly ridiculous questions: "Who won the last World Series?" "What's the capital of Nebraska?" The guards explained that English-speaking German spies had infiltrated the American lines and were causing problems.

Capa's Hungarian accent was suspicious, and he was arrested several times, and each time he was held for a few hours. When he got to Bastogne on December 23 he heard that the besieged Americans had refused to surrender the day before. That refusal became one of the fabled stories of the war.

Colonel Harry Kinnard, operations chief under McAuliffe, describes the incident:

ON THE 22ND OF DECEMBER, when we were totally surrounded, some German officers, under a white flag of truce, came into our glider regiment with a paper demanding our surrender and telling us all the bad things that would happen if we didn't.

We went into General McAuliffe, who was taking a much-needed nap, and he mistakenly thought that this was some Germans who wanted to surrender to us. We disabused him of that thought very quickly and said, "No, they want us to surrender."

Tony McAuliffe then said, "Us surrender? Aw, nuts."

Then he said, "Well, I wonder if we ought to answer them?" I spoke up and said, "Well, what you first said would be hard to beat," and Tony said, "What do you mean?" And I said, "You said, 'Nuts.' " So he took a pencil and wrote to the German commander: "Nuts!" and signed it, "A. C. McAuliffe, American Commander."

He gave it to Colonel Joseph Harper, who took it back to the Germans. . . . And they said, nice, nice, nuts? What is this? Colonel Harper explained to them that this meant "Go to hell," and gave them a few other choice words.[18]

That story went out to the world and Bastogne became a symbol of resistance. In a fit, Hitler ordered that Bastogne be destroyed to the last man. But the garrison held on through Christmas, paratroopers against tanks.

In Northern Europe, soldiers of the Christian faith—Allied and German—celebrated Christmas as best they could. One of them was Craig S. Fenn of Medina, Ohio. "It was near midnight on Christmas Eve. I was standing guard on the top of a hill overlooking a village. There was snow on the ground, but the sky was clear. There was absolutely no sound. It was possibly the most peaceful setting I've ever been in. Apparently, the Germans were recognizing Christmas, too. It was the perfect Christmas present."[19]

Nineteen-year-old G. F. Fitzgerald of Chicago spent his Christmas in a French village. After singing Christmas carols with members of his platoon, he and some other soldiers walked to the local church on the hill. "The whole village was there. Village officials were in high uniform with colorful silk stockings, britches, and robes for the midnight mass. They were carrying ornate lanterns, illuminated by lighted candles, in a beautiful procession into the church. . . . The rustic priest said a Latin high mass with the choir singing familiar Christmas carols. After he finished his homily to the villagers, he began addressing the soldiers in halting, broken English. He called attention to the fact that we were all men, created by God in His own image, and that even though we were going to live like animals, that we should behave like men and reject the animal instincts that wars bring."

When Christmas Day dawned, Fitzgerald's platoon was given a new assignment. They were to mark and clear enemy minefields, a job, as he described it, "of unimagined, helpless terror, where there is death in every direction."

When Fitzgerald got back that evening he had a big Christmas dinner. A little while later he learned that one of his friends had had the top of his head blown off as he tried to pry a mine loose from the frozen ground of a villager's yard. A mother had told him that her children wanted to play in the yard on Christmas Day and he had offered to remove the mines.[20]

The day after Christmas, Patton's combat teams, Capa riding with them, broke the siege of Bastogne, and in a week of fierce fighting the 761st Tank Battalion helped drive the Germans out of Tillet, a strongly held town near Bastogne that other units had failed to take. "After an hour of fighting we knew we were fighting SS troops we had tangled with before," said Edward Donald. "It might sound odd, but if you have a return engagement with a unit, you know it. You recognize their style of fighting."[21] By then the German advance into the Ardennes had been stopped. Two days before Christmas, the skies had cleared and Allied planes—over 10,000 of them—began chewing up the Wehrmacht. "We'd look up at the sky and say, 'Thank goodness they're flying again,'" said Sergeant Roger Rutland.[22] Running out of fuel and ammunition, harassed by David Pergrin's engineers, and with attack planes blanketing the skies, Colonel Peiper's SS unit abandoned its tanks and began walking back to Germany.

By the first week of January it was the Allies who were on the offensive, pushing the Germans out of the bulge, seventy miles deep, they had driven into the American line. Patton suggested a deep enveloping movement to surround the Germans and bag them. But Bradley and Eisenhower chose another course: to slug it out with the invaders, driving them back to their original position. That would take a month; and that month was a horror for American troops. In January 1945, the U.S. Army suffered more battle casualties—over 39,000—than in any other month in the fight for northwest Europe.

This was the hardest fighting of the battle. The Americans were now on the attack, in waist-deep snow and in the face of sharp winds and relentless artillery fire, which accounted for over half the American casualties in the Battle of the Bulge. "People didn't crumble and fall like they did in the Hollywood movies," said infantryman Bart Hagerman. "They were tossed in the air and their blood splattered everywhere. And a lot of people found themselves covered in blood and flesh of their friends, and that's a pretty tough thing for anybody to handle." [23]

But as Robert Georgen said: "Even when we became emotionally disturbed over the death of a comrade blown to bits, our very next thought was, despite the initial sorrow, 'better him than me.'" Then he added: "You would have to be there under intolerable circumstances to understand our distorted value system." [24]

At night, the men lived in their foxholes, one or two to a hole. These holes were sometimes thirty to fifty yards apart, making some men feel alone and isolated in the dark, brutally cold woods, with German shells falling all around them. "As long as I was with the squad I was always macho," said Morris Metz of Easton, Pennsylvania. "But when I was alone I felt kind of scared, and it was hard to sleep." [25]

If a man got hit at night, and he and his foxhole buddy were under fire, there was nowhere to turn for help. "About midnight I was sleeping—my buddy was on duty—and somehow or other, the Germans got within twenty yards of our position," infantryman Bob Conroy recalls. "Gordon got ripped by a machine gun from roughly the left thigh through the right waist. He then told me that he was hit through the stomach as well. Well, when you're that far from your home base, and it's snowing and the temperature zero, you don't have a chance. We were cut off. The Germans had overrun our position and we were in foxholes by ourselves, so we both knew he was going to die.

"We had no morphine. We couldn't ease [the pain], and so I tried to knock him out. I took off his helmet, held his jaw up, and just whacked it hard as I could, because he wanted to be put out. That didn't work and so I hit him up by the head with a helmet and that didn't work. Nothing worked. He slowly froze to death, bled to death. The next morning, as [I] looked at our gear, it looked as if I'd spent a day in a butcher shop. My clothes were all covered with blood. His clothes were all covered with blood and the territory we were in was all covered—it was a butcher shop." [26]

In January 1945, the American Army was still waiting for its full shipment of winter boots. Without them, some men's toes froze up to the size of softballs and turned black. If gangrene set in, their feet had to be amputated. Men's overcoats became soaked with moisture and caked with mud and freezing rain. The coats became so heavy that troops threw them away. Some men had not received overcoats. "We supplemented our clothing by cutting up burlap sacks found in farmhouses," says John C. Capell. "We wrapped those around our heads, our necks, and legs. Germans

PUSHING THE GERMANS BACK TO THE SIEGFRIED LINE: GROUND TROOPS ON THE ATTACK (SC).

did the same thing, and some of the prisoners we took were so wrapped up they looked like mummies."

Capell carried a supply of TNT and dynamite caps for blasting out foxholes and a handsaw for making shelters from tree trunks. "Sometimes I would be sent on a mission and return after dark. Being unable to take adequate protection against the cold. . . . I would seek a manure pile. There were huge manure piles in front of the peasant houses. They were flattened on top, and by throwing some boards on top of the manure, one could crawl on top and keep warm from the fermenting manure. It was so warm that the snow would melt off and steam rose. There was a strong methane gas being given off and the pungent odor meant that one could survive only a short time without getting away for some fresh air. Then I would have to spend the rest of the night in the cold." But on nights that he had sentry duty, he returned so cold and fatigued he was afraid to fall asleep for fear of freezing.

With the Army constantly on the move, pushing the Germans back, there was no opportunity to set up proper sanitary facilities. "Many of the dead were hidden in snowdrifts and not picked up by the Graves Registration men," says Capell. "Besides many corpses of men and animals, there was much human waste on the frozen ground. Our normal procedure to dispose of waste was to dig a small hole and cover it up. But with frozen ground and snow this was not done, and all waste was simply deposited in the snow. When a thaw came, all the filth from the human waste and corpses of men and animals ran off into the streams. It was from these streams that we obtained our drinking water." [27] The water was supposed to be filtered and chlorinated with tablets, but this was rarely done right. Capell drank this water and came down with dysentery just as a blizzard blew in.

As the exhausted Americans approached the Siegfried Line they started to receive replacements in large numbers. These "greenies" were mostly recent high school graduates. They were assigned as needed to various units in the field and sought whatever acceptance and sympathy they could from indifferent, battle-hardened veterans. "The sad thing about this was that some of them were killed before we ever learned their names," says Dutch Schultz of the 82nd Airborne. "On one occasion, four or five of them were killed by an 88 artillery shell before they were even assigned to any of the platoons." [28] Veterans found men dead on the ground beside them and didn't know who they were until they checked their dog tags. There were no tears shed for them, no sworn oaths to revenge them.

Yet when veterans lost close friends to German fire they sometimes sought an accounting. Prisoners were shot, wounded Germans were left in the snow to die, and GIs went after Germans at night in their foxholes. When you lost a friend, said Richard Proulx, you wanted the enemy "so badly that a chance to close with him [was] actually exhilarating." [29]

Long after the war, Dutch Schultz recounted a time he was ordered to take a prisoner back to battalion headquarters. He didn't want to do it because he was sick and bone-weary. "Reluctantly, I started out with the prisoner and had gone some distance when I spotted two men from another company walking toward me. When our paths crossed, they asked me where I was going with the prisoner, and I told them. They offered to take him back for me, and I said, 'All right,' knowing exactly what they were going to do with him. It seemed that, at the time, I didn't care. We parted ways and I had gone no further than a hundred yards or so when I heard the gunfire. I didn't turn around but kept going until I got back to my foxhole.

"Writing about this moment of weakness is not easy for me, but if it helps someone else who has had a similar combat experience to get it out in the open and deal with it—then it's all worthwhile. In retrospect, what I have learned about my World War II combat experiences is that it has very little to do with battle and victory over the enemy, but rather it's about battle and victory over self." [30]

A few men won that battle right on the field. Caught in a firefight, Robert Georgen was startled to see unarmed German medics run out into the open to take care of their wounded. The Americans stopped firing at once, and their medics joined the German medics. When the medics finished their work both sides resumed the fight as if nothing had changed. "But something had changed. The recognition of a small spark of humanity amidst the ferociousness of battle."

Georgen adds, however: "These feelings of civility were soon banished by the basic primal fear of enemy engagement." [31] Only by killing could you go on living.

Men found it hard to keep mind and body together during this merciless march. "Time, towns, and snow became one big nightmare of a struggle all rolled together," says Dwayne Burns. [32] As extreme fatigue set in, the men began to fight and kill like automatons. Fighting this way—almost in a stupor—they scared themselves, wondering who they were and how they had got that way.

Fatigued men fell into dreamlike trances, and men who fell asleep on the line had strange dreams. After fighting for sixteen straight hours, John Steber dozed off in the foxhole he occupied with two other GIs. He dreamed he was walking straight toward the enemy lines, but at the end of his walk, a voice out of nowhere said, "John, it's not your time. It's not your time." When he awoke his two comrades were dead, both of them shot in the face. [33]

Fortunately, there were moments of relief for some men. One day Dwayne Burns's company set up headquarters in a farmhouse. It was foggy and the snow was coming down hard. After serving on outpost duty all afternoon, Burns returned to the warm farmhouse and found that some of the guys had butchered a cow. "When we opened the door and walked into the kitchen, they were frying hamburgers for the entire company. My mind went back to Fort Worth to my favorite hamburger place, and I could see all of the kids sitting around having a midnight snack after a late movie. The smell was fantastic. I thought that I had died and gone to heaven." [34]

Thoughts of home led to explosions of frustration and anger. "Why can't we have a tour of duty as in the air corps?" rifleman James M. Power complained to his parents. "Certainly we have the most thankless and dirty job in the army. Killing when you see it done just isn't pleasant. . . . Most of the guys are fed on it all, but all of them have seen enough of their buddies die to where they are not only bitter at the Germans, but at the whole world."

All that Power could think of, he said in another letter, was steak and french fries and being behind the wheel of the family car. Yet when Power was wounded and hospitalized he felt guilty that he wasn't with his unit. "How dumb, but it does show true allegiance to a group of dedicated men." This was the ambivalence many soldiers felt—drawn between loyalty to comrades and the desperate desire to go home. On leaving the hospital to rejoin his unit, Power wrote his parents: "I do hate to leave these beds, good food, movies, and lazy life! But it will be grand to see the guys . . . again."[35]

The last ten miles to the Siegfried Line were the toughest. There were fewer replacements, blood plasma was short, and infantrymen who were wounded, physically or mentally, and were "redeemable," were given quick treatment and sent back for the final push. "There was a merciless rule about sending them back in if they were able to go," Captain Ben Kimmelman said in an interview years later. "It's very hard to forget the expressions on their faces. They have a kind of a hollow-eyed, lifeless, slack-jawed expression, and they almost don't see you as you go by. . . . It's almost as though they're going to a hopeless doom. There's a phrase for these men. They are called 'rag men.' "[36]

These were men whose minds had clicked off. A soldier would get out of his foxhole with a blank look on his face and start walking into enemy fire—a war-born zombie. His buddies would tackle him and hold him down, and he would mess his clothes and start screaming. Robert Proulx ran into a lot of this and said it was "the most unnerving thing" he had ever seen.[37]

If he was taken to the rear, a GI suffering from shell shock was put in a special ward and given sodium amytal, a barbiturate that induced a deep, almost trancelike sleep for up to forty-eight hours, depending on the dosage. Ben Kimmelman, who supervised a shell shock center, remembers seeing the drugged men screaming in their sleep. The sodium amytal, which broke down inhibitions, was supposed to have a cathartic effect. When the men came out of this "they'd be walking around completely numb. Sometimes they would be slipping and falling. That took a few more hours. And then they would be given a shower, new clothes, and a pep talk and the attempt was made to send them back. I say attempt," Kimmelman adds, "because it didn't always succeed. They weren't suitable to be returned.

"One time the chief of staff asked me to go out and talk to them. He said, 'You're good at that, you go out and talk.' I said, 'Colonel, I really don't want to do it.' He said, 'I know, Ben, do it anyhow.'

"I went out and tried haphazardly to persuade them to get in the trucks and go back. . . . They just looked at me. And half of them looked as if they couldn't focus.

"And finally one of them said, 'Don't you guys understand? If you can still walk and see, they'll keep shipping you back.' So I didn't do that again, and I told my commanding officer I wouldn't." [38]

Psychiatric disorders were the leading cause of medical evacuation from combat areas and medical discharges from the Army. To gain a better understanding of the problem, the Army sent Captain John W. Appel, Chief of the Mental Hygiene Branch of the Medical Corps, to Europe to conduct a study of men under fire. His conclusions were sobering.

"The key to an understanding of the psychiatric problem," he wrote in his confidential report, "is the simple fact that danger of being killed imposes a strain so great that it causes men to break down. This fact is frequently not appreciated and cannot be fully understood until one has either seen psychiatric cases just out of the lines or himself has actually been exposed to bombing, shell and mortar fire. One look at the shrunken apathetic faces of psychiatric patients as they come stumbling into the medical station, sobbing, trembling, referring shudderingly to 'them shells' and to buddies mutilated or dead, is enough to convince most observers.

"Anyone entering the combat zone undergoes a profound emotional change, which can no more be described than can sexual intercourse. Each man 'up there' knows that any moment he may be killed, a fact kept constantly before his mind by the sight of dead and mutilated buddies around him. To one who has been 'up there' it is obvious that there is no such thing as 'getting used to combat.' Each moment of it imposes a strain so great that men will break down in direct relation to the intensity and duration of their exposure. Thus psychiatric casualties are as inevitable as gun shot wounds in warfare."

Just as a truck wears down after so many miles, so does an infantryman, Appel reported. "He either developed a frankly incapacitating acute neurosis or else became so hypersensitive to shell fire, overly cautious and jittery that he was ineffective and demoralizing to the newer men." This inevitable breakdown usually occurred after about "240 aggregate combat days."

The problem, noted Captain Appel, is that "under the present policy no man is removed from combat duty until he has become completely worthless. The infantryman considers this a bitter injustice. . . . All he can look forward to is being killed, wounded or completely broken down nervously. He feels nobody back home has the slightest conception of the danger his job entails nor of the courage and guts required to do one hour of it."

Appel noted that "the job of a combat infantryman is one of the most difficult a human being is ever called upon to perform. The difficulty, however, lies not in the physical and technical requirements, but in maintaining the tremendous courage and determination needed to stand up under relentless danger of being killed. The job requires 10 percent technical skill and 90 percent guts."

But guts, self-respect, and loyalty to comrades can only carry a man so far, said Appel. "After prolonged, continuous combat all that infantrymen want to do is, not win the war, but get out of combat duty. . . . Thus a wound or injury is regarded not as a misfortune, but a blessing. As one litter bearer put it, 'Something funny about the men you bring back wounded, they're always happy. . . . They're sure glad to be getting out of there.' " [39]

Men in combat for long stretches of time sometimes saw death as inviting. "If you were lucky," says Bob Conroy, "it's going to be a leg wound. If you're not lucky, it'll be worse. And if you're very, very lucky, you'll take it through the head, because after you're in combat a while, dying is a lot easier than living." [40]

J. Glenn Gray, a counterintelligence specialist, who later wrote *The Warriors: Reflections on Men in Battle*, one of the classic accounts of combat, recorded his thoughts of death in his war journal. "The days pass and I become duller of mind and tireder of the war. The way is long and sometimes I question the wisdom of it all, of continuing to live. There may be a real purpose in it all, which is perceived only at the end of the journey. Somehow I feel that is true."

To young men in war, "death appears to be rest; it is quiet, sleep," Gray wrote in *The Warriors*. This is one of the reasons they can face nearly certain death in combat. [41]

The best friend that the GI had in the final weeks of the Battle of the Bulge was the Air Force. Clouds of planes flew in over the treetops, following the tracks of German tanks in the snow, blasting them and their supporting infantry to pieces. Artillery finished them off. "It was our turn to get a bit of rest as we sat and watched as the Germans took it," says Richard Proulx. "A few weeks ago they were the Master Race and Super SS bastards; now they were tasting bitter defeat at the hands of us beardless youths with dirty clothes and faces."

By the end of January, the enemy's slow, fighting retreat turned into a rout, a race back to the Siegfried Line, where the battle had begun six weeks earlier. The

Americans took so many prisoners they didn't know what to do with them. "The Bulge was over." [42]

On January 30, 1945, as his unit finally reached the Siegfried Line, Richard Proulx was cut down by a burst of shell fire. Stretcher-bearers took him to an ambulance and he was rushed to a field hospital. He didn't return to combat, but his war would never be over.

In the field hospital, he began screaming with horror every night and had to be doped until he stopped screaming.

In February, he learned that his unit had cracked the Siegfried Line and was on its way into Germany. It was his nineteenth birthday, and he cried like a baby. A little while later, he was sent home on furlough without therapy or medication.

The Battle of the Bulge was almost entirely an American battle, the biggest and costliest ever fought by the U.S. Army. Over a million German and Allied soldiers were engaged in some capacity, 600,000 of them Americans, and about 50,000 British. Nineteen thousand Americans were killed, 47,000 wounded, and 15,000 captured. The Germans suffered over 100,000 casualties, men that the depleted Wehrmacht could not afford to lose.

The Battle of the Bulge was also almost entirely a soldier's battle, a confusing, close-quarters slugfest won by thousands of small fighting units, without much overall direction from headquarters. While it might have been George Patton's "finest hour," he knew who had won the battle. When asked about his incredible rescue mission, when he turned his Third Army around and fought through ice and enemy fire to reach the "Battered Bastards of Bastogne," he laughed and replied:

"To tell you the truth, I didn't have anything much to do with it. All you need is confidence and good soldiers . . .

"I'll put our goddam, bitching, belching, bellyaching G.I.s up against any troops in the world." [43]

After the war, SS commander Joachim Peiper and seventy-five SS accomplices were tried for the massacre at Malmédy. Peiper was sentenced to death by hanging, but Senator Joseph McCarthy intervened and got his sentence commuted to life imprisonment because Peiper was an ardent anti-Communist.

In 1956, Peiper was released from Landsberg prison for good behavior. After losing two jobs in Germany because of his SS past, he moved to France. On July 14, 1976, Bastille Day, unknown avengers set his house afire. Firefighters at the scene had their hoses cut. The commander's body was found next to an empty rifle with which he had fought his final battle.

When he went home on furlough, Richard Proulx began to develop a fear of being out-of-doors after sunset in the Maine woods. "There was something ominous about the evening in the country. It echoed of faint screams and the crash of shell fire. I just had to get inside and be with someone or I would tremble."

In December 1945, on the first anniversary of the battle, Proulx began to have crying bouts. When his furlough was over, he was assigned to guard duty at a POW camp at Houlton, Maine, just over a hundred miles from his home. He was posted in the guard tower with a machine gun. The Germans in the compound still marched and saluted their officers with the Hitler salute and that infuriated him. He told his commanding officer that if he got into the tower one more time he would open fire and "kill every Nazi bastard." He was disciplined and transferred.

After leaving the Army, he began to withdraw from his family and friends and to be assaulted by terrible dreams. He became so troubled that he had to be put in a mental hospital. It was not until 1978 that he stopped crying at Christmas. But every day that he was healthy he lived in fear that he would slip back into "that nightmare world and be lost there forever."

As he said: "One cannot go to war and come back normal."[44]

The Marianas

THE INVASION OF SAIPAN

In the first week of February 1945, as the American Army was driving the Germans back to the Rhine, great fleets of bombers were pounding Japanese cities from island bases in the Central Pacific captured by American Storm Landings. MacArthur, meanwhile, had landed in the Philippines and his vanguards were fighting in the streets of Manila. The decisive event in this sweeping Pacific offensive was the invasion of Saipan, as important to victory over Japan as the Normandy invasion was to victory over Germany. The invasions took place within nine days of one another, and inaugurated a year of unprecedented carnage for Americans—and in the Pacific, barbaric fighting fueled by racism and revenge.

Two months after Tarawa the Navy was ready to move on the Marshalls, 500 miles to the north of Tarawa and about 1,000 miles east of the formidable Japanese naval base on the island of Truk. Kwajalein Atoll, at the center of the Marshall chain, was the main invasion target. Applying the lessons of Tarawa, the Navy ships and planes pounded the world's largest coral atoll into rubble, and on January 31, Army and Marine infantry landed with a fleet of new armored amphibious tractors, called Alligators or LVTs (Landing Vehicle Tracked). The Japanese fought with predictable fury, suffering a casualty rate of over 98 percent, but by the third day, in an expertly executed operation, Kwajalein was in American hands. Nearby Eniwetok Atoll was then taken in another sharp but decisive battle. In this enormous joint service operation, over 10,000 Japanese were killed, while fewer than 800 Americans died, about half the losses sustained on Betio alone.

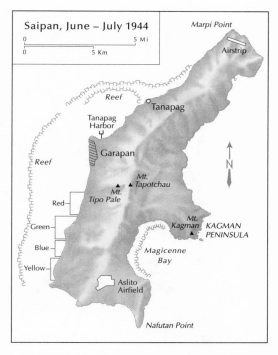

Control of the Gilberts and Marshalls, and shortly after, the Admiralty Islands to the west, which were seized by MacArthur's forces, enabled Task Force 58, the striking arm of Admiral Raymond Spruance's Fifth Fleet, to deliver devastating blows at Japanese air and naval bases in the area. In mid-February, Vice Admiral Marc Mitscher's air fleet destroyed over 200 planes and sank 200,000 tons of merchant shipping in two days of nonstop raids on Truk.

With Truk neutralized, Task Force 58 steamed with impunity into the waters of the Marianas, only 1,300 miles from Tokyo. "The Marianas are the key of the situation," Admiral King declared, "because of their location on the Japanese line of communications."[1] King and Nimitz were convinced that Japan could be brought down by economic strangulation. American naval bases in the Marianas would quicken the inevitable, depriving Japan of the oil, rubber, rice, iron, and other commodities essential to wage war.

Hap Arnold and the Army Air Forces had another idea. They would defeat Japan, as they expected to defeat Germany, with long-range strategic bombing, the executing instrument a fearsome weapon just off the assembly line, the B-29 Superfortress, the world's first intercontinental bomber. The air barons had originally intended to deploy these "Superforts" almost exclusively from bases in China, but Chiang Kai-shek's inability to contain Japanese incursions in the area of the airfields made the Marianas a better location. From long island airstrips, American bombers could, in the words of George Marshall, "set the paper cities of Japan on fire."[2] With the capture of the

U.S. SOLDIER GIVES A WOUNDED JAPANESE A DRINK ON KWAJALEIN (SC).

Marianas, the Navy and Air Force together could apply overwhelming power, making a costly land invasion of the home islands unnecessary, in the opinion of both Nimitz and Arnold. Three awesome weapons of war—the aircraft carrier, the submarine, and the Superfortress—would finish off the enemy by blockade and bombardment. But as journalist Robert Sherrod wrote, "No man who saw Tarawa . . . would agree that all the American steel was in the guns and bombs. There was a lot, also, in the hearts of the men who stormed the beaches." [3]

With the capture of the Marshalls, the war of the coral atolls ended. "We are through with the flat atolls," declared Marine Lieutenant General Holland Smith. "Now we are up against mountains and caves where the Japs can really dig in. A week from now there will be a lot of dead Marines." [4] The principal targets in the Marianas—Guam, Saipan, and Tinian—were large volcanic islands with developed infrastructures of sugar plantations and towns. Tinian was flat, but Saipan and Guam had a varied, luxuriant topography, much like Hawaii's, with flat sugarcane fields, precipitous cliffs, jungle-carpeted mountains, and "big rawboned valleys." [5] Unlike

COFFEE ABOARD SHIP FOR THE MARINE CONQUERORS OF ENIWETOK ATOLL (USMC).

Tarawa, all three islands had sizable native populations—on Saipan, mostly Japanese immigrants. But like Tarawa, all were strongly defended.

There were nearly 40,000 Japanese troops on Saipan, about 6,000 of them Marines under the command of Vice Admiral Chuichi Nagumo, the hero of Pearl Harbor, who had been sent to the Marianas after being disgraced at Midway. The island's army commander, General Yoshitsugu Saito, was under orders to hold Saipan until the Imperial Fleet arrived from the Philippines and drove off the invaders. He had every muzzle trained on the reef the Americans would come over. The island's defense system, however, was not nearly as formidable as it could have been. American submarines had been conducting a devastatingly effective interdiction campaign against supply and troop transports headed for Saipan, sinking ships laden with men and tanks, cement and steel. After Saipan was taken, a Japanese prisoner claimed that if the American assault had come three months later the island "would have been impregnable."[6]

When Marc Mitscher's Task Force 58 sailed from Majuro in the Marshall Islands to launch the Marianas operation, it took nearly five hours to clear the lagoon. The armada of 800 ships, nearly 1,000 planes, 100,000 sailors and aviators, and 127,000 Marine and Army infantry, would be almost as large as the one assembled for the Normandy D-Day landings. "I was at sea on an amphibious assault vehicle, on the 7th of June, when word reached us of the Allied landing at Normandy," recalls Marine General Edwin Simmons. "From the deck, as far as I could see, were the gray shapes of hundreds of Navy ships plodding in convoy toward their targets in the Marianas. I had a realization then of the overwhelming strength of our country—that we could do this at the same time that we were landing in Normandy and reopening a front in Europe. The joint expeditionary force was under the command of the brilliant, sometimes erratic Admiral Richmond Kelly Turner. Kelly Turner, nicknamed Terrible Turner, had a legendary temper. This was his fifth major amphibious operation, going back to Guadalcanal. The expeditionary troops were under General Holland—'Howlin' Mad'—Smith, who while perhaps not as brilliant as Kelly Turner, had a reputation for being equally irascible. The two men struck sparks like flint against steel. But as Smith said in his autobiography, our partnership, though stormy, spelled hell in big Red letters for the Japanese."[7]

There was a heavy preliminary bombing, but naval guns were unable to take out vital targets on the large mountainous island, guaranteeing that Saipan would be terrible to take, with the enemy dug into caves and "spider holes" all over the island. As Admiral Nimitz said later, "The enemy met the assault operations with pointless bravery, inhuman tenacity, cave fighting, and the will to lose hard."[8]

Here, the reef would not be a problem. Underwater demolition teams had scouted the conditions of the reef, the currents, and the beach, and had blown up concrete and steel landing obstacles, taking sixteen casualties in this perilous operation. On the morning of June 15, strong surf pounded over the reef, its sound blocked out by the rumbling of the big battleship guns. Over the loudspeaker of the transport that carried Robert Sherrod to yet another invasion came the chaplain's voice: "With the help of God we will succeed. . . . Most of you will return, but some of you will meet the God who made you. . . . Repent your sins."[9] When they heard this, more than a few men winced.

After the signal went up, over 700 Alligators went tearing ashore, ninety-six abreast in every wave, many of them with turret-mounted cannons. They poured out

SAIPAN. MARINES UNDER ENEMY FIRE ON THE BEACH (U.S. NAVAL INSTITUTE).

of what looked to a Japanese defender "like a large city that had suddenly appeared off shore," and by nightfall they had carried 20,000 men to the beach.[10] The Alligators were to press inland almost a mile in a coordinated blitz, securing a strong defensive position to shield the beach. But their thin skin of armor could not stand up to the heavy Japanese guns, and they were cut to pieces, big plates of steel flying everywhere as they tried to cross the beach.

The Japanese were hidden in shoreline cliffs with a deadly line of fire on the beaches. That first night and the next day Bill Jones's unit, veterans of Tarawa, and others hurled back three enemy counterattacks, one of them a spectacular tank assault, which they broke apart with bazookas, naval fire, and their own "Steel Goliaths." It was the "damned artillery and mortars," veterans would say later, that made Saipan so tough to take; that and the rugged terrain—steep gorges and cliffs and a spine of volcanic mountains culminating in towering Mt. Tapotchau. "Down our throats came this avalanche of artillery fire," recalls rifle platoon leader John C. Chapin, who had just graduated from Yale with honors in history.

THE SHELLS HIT AHEAD, BEHIND, on both sides, and right in our midst. They would come rocketing down with a freight-train roar and then explode with a deafening cataclysm that is beyond description. . . . We had no place to go. We had no foxholes. It was right out of the blue. Later we realized that sitting up on Mt. Tapotchau, 1,554 feet high, Japanese observers had preregistered every

DEAD JAPANESE SOLDIERS ON THE BEACH (USMC).

possible location before we landed. . . . They were zeroed in on us and were hitting us with pinpoint accuracy.

All around us was the chaotic debris of . . . combat: Jap and Marine bodies lying in mangled and grotesque positions; blasted and burnt-out pillboxes; the burning wrecks of LVTs that had been knocked out by Jap high-velocity fire; the acrid smell of high explosives; the shattered trees; and the churned-up sand littered with discarded equipment.[11]

Circling offshore in General "Red Mike" Edson's LVT, listening to the radio reports from the beach, Robert Sherrod penciled in his notebook, "looks like a real crisis."[12]

One of the first of over 1,500 casualties on the beach was Jim Crowe, the Tarawa iron man. He and his aide were hit coming in, and Crowe was in agony with a severe sucking wound near his heart. "I thought I was dying," he recalled of his final hour in combat. "And I thought maybe I'd better take a little interest in things. So I put my carbine in my hand [and] put my fist in this hole, which the doctors said saved me. . . . D'Natilly, my corporal, lying there, pulled his left arm up and looked at his wristwatch. And I said, 'Why are you looking at your wristwatch, Bill?'

"He said, 'Sir, I want to see what time I die.'"

A corpsmen and a surgeon bent over them to try to help. "But then a shell hit down around my knees [and] just laid [the corpsman] wide open . . . and everything in him flew out against me." The doctor also got hit, but survived, and Crowe took some shrapnel in one leg. "Then a shell came up and hit a tree right at my head" and wounded him further in the arm and wrist. "So I got up and left. I wasn't going to stay there any longer."[13] Norman Hatch, the Marine Corps photographer, says that "Crowe had made a $20 bet with the Division surgeon that if he got hit, no matter where, he would get to the aid station. Spotting his big red handlebar mustache, men on the beach offered to help him, but he insisted on walking, holding himself together with one hand while firing his carbine at snipers. When he got to the aid station, he barked at the surgeon, 'Give me my twenty bucks.'"[14]

As Sherrod and Edson passed the battalion aid station, they spotted Crowe sitting in a shell hole, heavily bandaged and "breathing hard," waiting to be evacuated. The surgeon administering morphine looked up and murmured, "not much chance, I'm afraid." But Crowe refused to accept the verdict. "I hate like hell for this to happen, General," he told Edson in a clear voice, "but I'll be all right." Then he turned to Sherrod, "I'll see you stateside. We'll throw a whizdinger."[15] Crowe survived, but he and Sherrod never did meet again. Crowe's battalion was taken over by another hero at Tarawa, the bespectacled, soft-spoken economics professor from Northwestern University, Major William Chamberlin.

Some of the stretcher-bearers at the battalion aid station that day were the first African-American Marines to see combat in the war. The United States Marine Corps had not accepted African-Americans since 1798 and had hoped to fight World War II as an all-white organization. "If it were a question of having a Marine Corps of 5,000 whites or 250,000 Negroes, I would rather have the whites," said the defiant Marine Corps Commandant, Major General Thomas Holcomb.[16] But under mounting pressure from President Roosevelt, the resolutely segregationist Marines had been forced to accept black volunteers and, later, draftees. The Corps formed and trained two Defense Battalions, the 51st and 52nd, and made sure they never saw combat, assigning them to outposts far in the rear of the Central Pacific advance. Ironically, it was the African-American Marines who were not trained for combat who saw heavy action all across the Pacific, beginning, 800 strong, on the beaches of Saipan. These were laborers in military support units.

As infantry swept ashore on D-Day, African-American depot and ammunition companies, standing knee-deep in surf, with mortar shells raining down on them, offloaded shells, food, and water from landing vehicles and hustled them to front line troops. When they were shot at, they returned fire with rifles and machine guns they picked up on the beach. "My company landed about 2 P.M. on D-Day," Captain William C. Adams, commander of the 20th Marine Depot Company, told a combat correspondent. "We were the third wave, and all hell was breaking when we came in. It was still touch and go when we hit shore, and it took some time to establish a foothold.

"My men performed excellently. . . . Among my own company casualties, my orderly was killed." [17]

The orderly was Private Kenneth J. Tibbs of Columbus, Ohio, the first black Marine killed in combat in World War II. Later that afternoon, Private Leroy Seals of Brooklyn, New York, was mowed down. He died the following day. Coming into the beach, four men of an African-American depot company were wounded by mortar fire and had to be evacuated, but the others went in, found guns, and fought as infantry, helping to maintain a precariously held position and to kill enemy infiltrators. The next day, they evacuated hundreds of wounded men to a hospital ship offshore, and under heavy rifle fire they "rode guard on trucks carrying high octane gasoline from the beach." [18]

"The Negro Marines are no longer on trial," said the new Commandant, Alexander Vandegrift. "They are Marines, period."[19] It would have been good if it were true, but throughout the war African-American Marines continued to be treated as separate and unequal.

That first night the Marines and Army reinforcements were pinned to the sand, but there was never any doubt that the landing would succeed. The Americans were here in greater numbers and with more firepower than at Tarawa. Still, in the words of one Marine, "There is something definitely terrifying about the first night on a hostile beach. No matter what superiority you may boast in men and matériel, on that first night you're the underdog, and the enemy is in a position to make you pay through the nose."[20]

THE BATTLE OF THE PHILIPPINE SEA

That night Admiral Spruance got word that the Japanese fleet was steaming toward Saipan. The newly assembled First Mobile Fleet, with almost every warship in the Japanese Navy, had been sighted by American submarines in the Philippine Sea, that part of the Pacific Ocean between the Philippines and the Marianas. Its commander, Vice Admiral Jisaburo Ozawa, had sailed out to slaughter the American landing forces and destroy the United States Pacific Fleet "with one blow."[21] For the still confident Japanese high command, this would be the decisive naval battle that would bring the Americans to the peace table. "Can it be that we'll fail to win with this mighty force?" a Japanese admiral asked in his diary. "No! It cannot be."[22]

The U.S. Fifth Fleet had more firepower, fifteen carriers and over 900 warplanes to Ozawa's nine carriers and 430 combat aircraft. But Ozawa was counting on using Japanese airfields in Guam to refuel and rearm his planes and hit the American carriers, in a devastating shuttle action. Observing radio silence, Ozawa had no idea that Marc Mitscher's carrier planes had knocked out those vital airfields in preparation for the invasion of Saipan.

The fast-approaching Japanese fleet presented Spruance with an agonizing decision: to steam westward after Ozawa or to wait for him near Saipan while protecting the landing force, whose transports and cargo ships were still being unloaded. Remembering Guadalcanal, where the Navy had suffered the greatest defeat in its proud history after Frank Jack Fletcher's carrier fleet pulled out and abandoned the Marines, Spruance stayed in a covering position, against the advice of the aggressive

Marc Mitscher. "I will join up with Mitscher and Task Force 58 and try to keep the Japs off your neck," Spruance told Kelly Turner.

As Spruance sent out scout planes to search for the Japanese, he learned from Nimitz, at Pearl Harbor, that he was under the same imperative as Ozawa. "We count on you to make the victory decisive." [23]

"Those of us on the ground of course knew nothing [of the impending naval battle]," says John Chapin. "The morning when [we] turned and looked out to the sea and saw that this vast fleet was gone—the sea was empty—I want to tell you, that's a sinking feeling." [24]

Ozawa's search planes found Mitscher's fleet on the afternoon of June 18.

Mitscher wanted to push out into combat range, but Spruance doubled back toward Saipan to prevent a Japanese force from passing him in the night and blasting apart the beachhead. The next day, Ozawa launched four massive raids against Task Force 58. With the enemy air fleet closing from 130 miles, the old circus rallying cry of "Hey, Rube!" went up, and fighters scrambled and flew west to meet the threat. This would be the greatest carrier battle of World War II, with almost four times the forces engaged at Midway. But with the inexperienced, poorly trained Japanese pilots outnumbered and fighting superior Hellcats, it was less a battle than an eight-hour aerial massacre. Ozawa lost 373 planes to the Americans' thirty. The pilots called it "The Great Marianas Turkey Shoot." But it was more than a fighter fight. Torpedos from submarines *Albacore* and *Cavallo* sent two Japanese carriers to the bottom of the Philippine Sea.

One of the last of the planes to return to the USS *Lexington* was Lieutenant Stanley Vraciu's F6F Hellcat. As his fighter screeched to a stop on the carrier deck, he pulled back the canopy, looked up at Mitscher standing on the deck with his long-billed lobsterman's cap pulled low over his tanned face, and held up six fingers. Six kills! "The skill, initiative and intrepid courage of the young aviators made this day one of the high points in the history of the American spirit," writes Admiral Samuel Eliot Morison.[25]

"Now the hunter became the hunted."[26] The next day the thin, leather-faced Mitscher sent three carriers after the crippled but still dangerous Japanese fleet. Scout planes failed to locate the enemy's position until 5:40 in the afternoon, but Mitscher, while aware of the extreme risks of a night raid, launched 216 planes from ten carriers in the phenomenal time of ten minutes. "Give 'em hell, boys; wish I were with you," he told them before the cry went out to "Man Aircraft!"[27] At 6:40, after flying almost 300 miles, they spotted the Japanese fleet. With the setting sun barely touching the horizon and the sky filled with brilliant orange and red clouds, the Hellcats struck. They sank the carrier *Hiyo* and blasted from the night sky another sixty-five enemy planes, while losing only twenty of their own, in an engagement that has been called the Battle of the Philippine Sea. This battle left the dispirited and retreating Ozawa with only thirty-five out of the 430 planes he had had on the morning of June 19.

The dusk raiders who smashed Ozawa's fleet now faced a new danger. They had begun this mission knowing they had only a slim chance of returning because the Japanese carriers had been spotted at the maximum range of their planes. And after they had taken off they learned that Ozawa was sixty miles further west than first reported. Now, after a fuel-draining attack, they had to fly back over 250 to 300 miles of ocean on a moonless night to the blackened fleet. The ships' lights had been turned out to avoid detection by Japanese submarines. Many of the pilots were dizzy with fatigue and none of them had been trained to land on a carrier at night.

When the planes came within range, the group commander of four carriers, Rear Admiral Joseph "Jocko" Clark, turned on the deck lights and pointed searchlights into the sky to act as homing beacons. Mitscher ordered all of Task Force 58 to do the same, a decision that Clark considered "one of the war's supreme moments." [28] A pilot who was sent up in a night-fighting Hellcat to help guide the planes home said the scene was like "a Hollywood premiere, Chinese New Year's and Fourth of July rolled into one." [29]

Lieutenant E. J. Lawson, returning to the *Enterprise,* gave an account of the night landings:

WE HAD ALMOST REACHED THE FORCE when we saw the lights come on. It is clear that the task force did all in its power to make it easier for us to get home. Lieutenant Eson led us in over the *Enterprise* but her deck was fouled for some time. We circled for a few minutes, watching the lights of the planes below fan out in the pattern of the landing circle. But there had been too much strain in the last five hours to reduce things to patterns now; and inevitably . . . deck crashes occurred. Many planes—too many—announced that their gas was gone and they were going in the water. . . . Seen from above, it was a weird kaleidoscope of fast moving lights forming intricate trails in the darkness, punctuated now and then by tracers shooting through the night as someone landed with his gun switches on, and again by suddenly brilliant exhaust flames as each plane took a cut, or someone's turtleback light getting lower and lower until blackened out by the waves closing over it. A Mardi Gras setting fantastically out of place here, midway between the Marianas and the Philippines. [30]

Almost half the planes landed on the wrong carriers; one plane tried to land on a red-lit destroyer and had to veer off at the last second and splash into the sea. Pilots and crewmen were scattered all over the waters around the gigantic fleet, blowing the boatswain's whistles they carried for such emergencies and "blinking their little waterproof flashlights. The destroyers, using their 18-inch searchlights to spot rafts and swimmers, did wonderful rescue work. . . . Anti-submarine screening was completely neglected in favor of saving lives. The last laugh of the evening," writes Admiral Morison, "came at the expense of Lieutenant Commander K. F. Musick, torpedo squadron commander of *Bunker Hill*. He had splashed on an earlier operational flight and had been pulled out by destroyer *Hickox*. This time he ditched again for want of gas and was picked up by the same destroyer, on whose stack, next to the painted miniatures of planes shot down, he found a caricature of himself to which a sailor was adding a 'hash mark' to celebrate the second rescue!" [31]

All but forty-nine pilots and crewmen were recovered by the end of the next day, in what was one of the supreme naval victories of the war.

TAKING SAIPAN

Back on Saipan, the ground troops had no idea that this battle had been fought and won, reducing the options of the island defenders to death by one of two ways: at the enemy's hands or by their own. As the Americans gathered up their strength and moved off the beach, the Japanese fell back into a hastily organized defense in depth, using the terrain to maximum advantage. They burrowed into caves all over the islands, and from Mt. Tapotchau they poured down fire on the advancing Marines and Army infantry.

Private Robert F. Graf describes the Marine system for flushing Japanese soldiers out of caves:

QUITE OFTEN THERE WOULD BE multi-cave openings, each protecting another. Laying down heavy cover fire, our specialist would advance to near the mouth of the cave. A satchel charge would then be heaved into the mouth of the cave, followed by a loud blast as the dynamite exploded. Other times it might be grenades thrown inside the cave, both fragment type, which exploded sending bits of metal all throughout the cave, and other times [white] phosphorous grenades that burned the enemy.

Also the flame thrower was used, sending a sheet of flame into the cave, burning anyone that was in its path. Screams could be heard and on occasions the enemy would emerge from the caves, near the entrance. We would call upon the tanks, and these monsters would get in real close and pump shells into the openings.[52]

The cave teams had to be on guard for snipers in nearby trees, or for Japanese who "played possum," as one Marine related, "by smearing blood of other Japs [we had killed] on themselves and lying still as [we] came up. However, within the battalion my instructions were, 'If they didn't stink, stick it.'"[53]

Of the approximately 29,000 civilians on the island, 22,000 were Japanese, the vast majority of them from the prefecture of Okinawa. There were also Korean slave laborers, and Kanaka and Chamorros people, the original inhabitants. The local natives surrendered willingly, but some Japanese and Koreans hid in caves. American soldiers often put their own lives on the line to try to help them. "The thing that really got to me," said one Marine officer, "was watching these boys of mine; they'd take all kinds of risks; they'd go into a cave never knowing whether there would be soldiers in there,

MARINE FINDS WOMAN AND CHILDREN HIDDEN IN A CAVE (USMC).

to bring out these civilians. The minute they got them out, they began to feed them, give them part of their rations, and offer their cigarettes to the men. It made you feel proud of the boys for doing this." [34]

But as the Americans began to lose friends in these cave operations, and as water supplies grew short and polluted, forcing some men to chew on napalmed sugarcane stalks to try to kill their thirst, distinctions were often not made between armed resisters and defenseless civilians. The troops learned a Japanese phrase, which translated loosely meant: throw your rifle away and come out with your hands up. "We tried this," recalls John Chapin, "[and] I never got anybody to come out." [35] If a flamethrower was called for, the people inside the cave, who had learned the English word for it, would usually kill themselves. The cave would then be sealed by a bull-dozer.

When terrified, sick, and starving civilians did come out of their hideouts, there were some heart-tearing scenes. A captured Japanese woman who was crying uncontrollably approached Robert Graf and began hitting him on the arm and pointing to his pack. "I didn't know what she wanted until an interpreter came over and explained that she wanted some food and water for her dead child. She pointed to a wicker basket that contained her dead infant. I gave her what she requested, and she placed the food and water in the basket so that the child could have nourishment on the way to meet [its] ancestors.

"Every illness that we had been briefed on was observed: leprosy, dengue fever, yaws, and many cases of elephantiasis. Most of them were skeleton-thin, as they had no nourishment for many days. Many were suffering from shock caused by the shelling and bombing, and fright because they did not have the vaguest idea as to what we would do to them."

This is a part of the Pacific War few historians deal with, "civilians," in Graf's words, "caught in a war that was not of their making." [36]

On June 23, after capturing the main towns, airfields, and strongholds in the southern half of the island, Marine and Army troops launched a great three-division drive to clear the island of all resistance. Holland Smith spread his forces across the entire middle of Saipan, from east to west, and ordered them to push northward with relentless resolve. The Marines moved on the right and left flanks and the Army's 27th Division, a New York National Guard unit, took the center, fighting slowly and in disorganized fashion through some of the toughest terrain on the island. The plodding movement of the 27th, which had not fought well at either Makin or Kwajalein, incensed Holland Smith, for it dangerously exposed his Marines on the flanks. After a sharp warning to the commander of the 27th, Major General Ralph Smith, and a consultation with Spruance, he relieved Ralph Smith, setting off an interservice feud that continued long after the war. "Ralph Smith is my friend," Holland Smith told Sherrod later that day, "but, good God, I've got a duty to my country." [37] Nimitz, a diplomat as well as a warrior, was not sympathetic. He made sure Holland Smith never again held an active combat command.

On June 25 the Marines took Mt. Tapotchau, a turning point in the battle. There was no celebration; everyone realized that the island would not be taken until nearly every Japanese soldier had been killed. General Saito, wounded and cornered in the

A LONE MARINE WATCHES FROM HIS FOXHOLE AS A MARINE FLAME-
THROWING TANK FIRES ON A JAPANESE PILLBOX (USMC).

cave that served as his command post, sent a final message to his troops, imploring them to follow him in a final charge against the enemy. In another island cave, Admiral Nagumo sent a similar message to his sailors and Marines. But neither the general nor the admiral went forth to lead his troops. Nagumo put a bullet in his brain. Saito fell on his ceremonial sword but failed to strike cleanly. Writhing in agony, he was finished off by a pistol shot from his adjutant.

The final fight, the most fearsome banzai charge of the Pacific war, came at 4:30 in the morning on July 7, 1944. Over 3,000 screaming Japanese soldiers and sailors broke through a gap in the lines of the 27th Division. Some had rifles, grenades, and mortars, but many carried only clubs, rocks, swords, and rusty bayonets wired to bamboo sticks. After this "human storm" overran elements of two Army battalions, a second wave came through and killed the wounded. Those Japanese soldiers who remained hit three artillery battalions of the 10th Marines and were blown to pieces at point-blank range by 105mm howitzers, but not before overrunning twelve guns, engaging in furious hand-to-hand combat with artillery gunners and reinforcements, and blowing up an ambulance that tried to evacuate the wounded.

Later that day, the Marines gathered up their dead. Lying on the field, when Sherrod got there, was Major William L. Crouch, commander of the Marine battalion. His helmet and carbine were close to his body and near his hand were two letters from home, which he was probably trying to read as he bled to death. In a field not far away, the shattered bodies of the enemy were being stacked three high. Sherrod wrote in his notebook, "They are thicker here than at Tarawa." [38]

Mitsuharu Noda, a paymaster for Admiral Nagumo, survived this grisly fight:

ABOUT TWENTY MEMBERS of [Nagumo's] headquarters participated in the final battle. We drank the best Japanese whiskey—Suntory Square Bottle, we'd saved it to the last minute. We smoked our last tobacco—Hikari brand. We were even able to smile. Maybe because we were still together as a group. . . .

On July 7 at 4 A.M., shouting all together, we headed toward the enemy camp. . . . We were not going to attack enemies. We were ordered to go there to be killed. Some probably may have gone drunk, just to overcome fear, but that last taste of Suntory whiskey was wonderful. It was a kind of suicide. We didn't crawl on the ground, though bullets were coming toward us. We advanced standing up.

We had hardly any arms. Some had only shovels, others had sticks. I had a pistol. I think I was shot at the second line of defense. Hit by a machine gun, two bullets in my stomach, one passing through, one lodging in me. I didn't suffer pain. None at all. But I couldn't stand either. I was lying on my back. I could see the tracer bullets passing over. This is it, I thought.

Then I saw a group of four or five men, Japanese, crawling toward each other on their hands and knees. Their heads were now all close together. One of them held a grenade upward in his right hand and called out an invitation to me: "Hey, sailor there! Won't you come with us?" I said, "I have a grenade. Please go ahead."

I heard "Long live the emperor!" and the explosion of a hand grenade at the same instant. Several men were blown away, dismembered at once into bits of flesh. I held my breath at this appalling sight. Their heads were all cracked open and smoke was coming out. It was a horrific way to die. Those were my thoughts as I lost consciousness.[39]

After this, the fight went out of the enemy. They waited in their holes to die or committed hara-kiri with knives or grenades—or by drowning themselves in the sea. (Up to this point in the war, only about 600 Japanese had been captured by all of the Allied powers.)[40] On July 9 the battle was over, although here, as on every other island in the Central Pacific, there was no surrender. It would take over a year to kill or capture the Japanese who remained hidden in caves.

The Battle of Saipan took twenty-four days and the cost was high—16,525 American casualties, including 3,426 killed or missing. Only 921 Japanese of a garrison of nearly 40,000 were taken prisoner. Approximately 14,500 civilians were put into an internment camp, where they would live when they were not working on construction projects.

The Japanese, Koreans, and native peoples were each put in separate, fenced-in sections. Each racial group appointed its own police force to keep order and patrol its perimeter.[41]

While the camp was being set up, and the dead were being buried, American wounded were being taken out to hospital- and troopships anchored offshore. One of the four hospital ships was the *Solace*, which had taken in the wounded in the attack on Pearl Harbor. When Robert Sherrod went on board to gather material for a story, *Solace* had just returned from Guadalcanal for a second shipload of patients. The hospital ships were painted pure white, and the doctors, nurses, and corpsmen wore "spotless white. . . . Everything about the ship was intended to make the wounded man forget about mud and foxholes . . . and the whine of artillery."

Each ship had beds for 480 men, but there were so many wounded at Saipan that patients were put on cots, sofas, and the bunks of ship's personnel. Still, there was not enough space. Only one in five of the wounded could be taken aboard hospital ships. The rest, except for a few evacuated by planes, "sweated it out on the crowded bunks of transports."

The types of wounds the men suffered described the nature of the battle. At Tarawa, 57 percent of the *Solace*'s cases had been bullet wounds. At Saipan, artillery and mortars caused 65 percent of the wounds, and there were five times as many wounds caused by bayonets and knives. Saipan had been an artillery fight, punctuated by savage, close-in fighting and more and larger banzai charges than veterans in the Pacific had ever experienced. And because it was a far longer battle than Tarawa, there

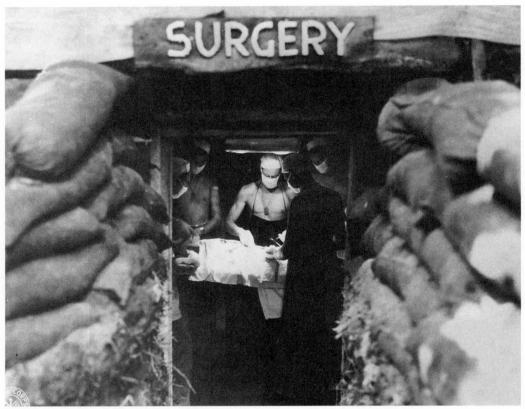

OPERATION AT AN AID STATION (USMC).

were many more cases of combat fatigue. The disorder was treated as callously here as it was in Europe. A third of the men suffering from combat fatigue in the early fighting were returned to shore with only one or two days' rest.

The *Solace* had a crew of seventeen doctors, 175 corpsmen, and seventeen nurses. "Until long after the Saipan battle, the Central Pacific campaign," Sherrod wrote, "was a womanless war except for the nurses aboard the hospital ships. They were a source of curiosity for men who had not seen a woman in months or years." [42]

That was one of the major differences between the war here and in Europe, along with the climate and the incredible distances between the battlefields, often a thousand miles and more, with nothing but water in between. Men felt isolated in the Pacific as they rarely did in Europe, where there were nearby civilizations like their own. "And another adjustment I'll have to make," wrote Ernie Pyle, who was trans-

SITTING ON AN UNEXPLODED 16-INCH NAVAL SHELL, MARINE PRIVATE FIRST
CLASS RAYMOND L. HUBERT SHAKES SAND FROM HIS BOOT (USMC).

ferred to the Marianas from Northern Europe after Saipan was captured, "is the attitude toward the enemy. In Europe we felt our enemies, horrible and deadly as they
were, were still people. But out here I've already gathered the feeling that the Japanese
are looked upon as something inhuman and squirmy—like some people feel about
cockroaches or mice."[43]

Just before Sherrod left the *Solace*, about 9:00 P.M., the ship began to receive
wounded fighting men. As they were loaded from amphtracs, an embarkation officer,

Dr. Richmond Beck, looked at the red-bordered casualty tag that each man had pinned on him and examined the wound, which had been dressed ashore. He made a quick diagnosis and sent the man to the proper ward. There the wounded man received another tag. "When we run out of tags we know we've got a shipload," another doctor told Sherrod.[44] The clothing of each man was cut off and tossed overboard. Then they sailed away from Saipan.

For many of those ashore that evening, sleeping on the bare ground, tired and so far from home, Tinian and Guam were next. Tinian, just across the straits from Saipan, was overrun in nine days. Less important strategically but far more gratifying to the American public was the reconquest of Guam, which was completed by August 10 after weeks of fighting that was as vicious as that on Saipan. It was the first conquered United States territory to be retaken from the enemy. The fall of Guam ended the Marianas campaign. Even as the fighting raged, Seabees had been expanding the runways on Saipan, Tinian, and Guam for the arrival in a few months of the new B-29

Superfortresses. "Saipan was to Japan almost what Pearl Harbor is to the U.S.," Robert Sherrod wrote after the battle, "except that it is a thousand miles closer to Japan's coast than Pearl Harbor is to America's."[45]

MARPI POINT

Before the bombing of the Japanese home islands began, there was a profound perceptual change in both Japan and the United States that would make the last year of the war in the Pacific bloody beyond belief. The triggering incident occurred at Saipan.

During the mopping-up operation on the island, a group of Marines on amphibious tractors saw seven Japanese soldiers on a coral reef and went out to capture them. As they approached the reef, one of the Japanese, undoubtedly an officer, pulled out his sword and began cutting off the heads of the Japanese who were kneeling in front of him. Before the Marines could get to him, there were four heads floating in the lagoon. The officer, swinging his sword wildly, charged the Marines and was gunned down, along with the two remaining men. Marines had seen this kind of behavior before. No one was prepared for what happened next.

On July 11, two days after Saipan was declared "secured," two American reporters, Keith Wheeler of the *Chicago Times* and Frank Kelley of the *New York Herald Tribune*, and a photographer for *Life*, Peter Stackpole, arrived at press headquarters on the island with a story almost too horrifying to believe. During the final days of the fighting, remnants of the Japanese Army and about 4,000 panic-stricken civilians had escaped to Marpi Point, on the northern tip of the island. There they began killing themselves, often in the most gruesome manner. Parents tossed their children off the high cliffs of the point into the sea, or onto jagged piles of rocks. Mothers waded out in the water with their babies and disappeared in the surf. Fathers, mothers, and children stood in circles with grenades pressed to their chests and pulled the pins.

Marine interpreters tried to stop them. They and civilians who had surrendered spoke through amplifiers, pleading with the people on the cliffs to give themselves up, assuring them they would be treated humanely. But their government had told them that the sadistic, hairy-faced Americans would rape, torture, and kill them. Tragically, some who did choose life over death did not survive. The Japanese soldiers assassinated civilians who showed any inclination to surrender.

The next morning, Robert Sherrod drove to Marpi Point. After he returned he wrote one of the most influential pieces of journalism to come out of the Pacific war, "The Nature of the Enemy," which appeared in *Time* magazine:

MARPI POINT . . . IS A LONG PLATEAU on which the Japs had built a secondary airfield. At the edge of the plateau there is a sheer 200-foot drop to jagged coral below; then the billowing sea. The morning I crossed the airfield and got to the edge of the cliff nine marines from a burial detail were working with ropes to pick up the bodies of two of our men, killed the previous day. I asked one of them about the stories I had heard.

"You wouldn't believe it unless you saw it," he said. "Yesterday and the day before there were hundreds of Jap civilians—men, women, and children—up here on this cliff. In the most routine way, they would jump off the cliff, or climb down and wade into the sea. I saw a father throw his three children off, and then jump down himself. Those coral pockets down there under the cliff are full of Jap suicides."

He paused and pointed. "Look," he said, "there's one getting ready to drown himself now." Down below, a young Japanese, no more than 15, paced back and forth across the rocks. He swung his arms, as if getting ready to dive; then he sat down at the edge and let the water play over his feet. Finally he eased himself slowly into the water.

"There he goes," the marine shouted.

A strong wave had washed up to the shore, and the boy floated out with it. At first, he lay on the water, face down, without moving. Then, apparently, a last, desperate instinct to live gripped him and he flailed his arms, thrashing the foam. It was too late. Just as suddenly, it was all over: the air-filled seat of his knee-length black trousers bobbed on the water for ten minutes. Then he disappeared.

Looking down, I counted the bodies of seven others who had killed themselves. One, a child of about five, clad in a ragged white shirt, floated stiffly in the surf.

I turned to go. "This is nothing," the marine said. "Half a mile down, on the west side, you can see hundreds of them."

Later on I checked up with the officer of a minesweeper which had been operating on the west side. He said: "Down there, the sea is so congested with floating bodies we can't avoid running them down. There was one woman in khaki trousers and a white polka-dot blouse, with her black hair streaming in the water. I'm afraid every time I see that kind of a blouse, I'll think of that woman. There was another one, nude, who had drowned herself while giving birth to a baby. A small boy of four or five had drowned with his arm clenched around the neck of a soldier—the two bodies rocked crazily in the waves. Hundreds and hundreds of Jap bodies have floated up to our minesweeper."

Apparently the Jap soldier not only would go to any extreme to avoid surrender, but would also try to see that no civilian surrendered. At Marpi Point, the marines had tried to dislodge a Jap sniper from a cave in the cliff. He was an exceptional marksman; he had killed two marines (one at 700 yards) and wounded a third. The marines used rifles, torpedoes and finally, TNT in a 45-minute effort to force him out. Meantime the Jap had other business.

He had spotted a Japanese group—apparently father, mother, and three children—out on the rocks, preparing to drown themselves, but evidently weakening in their decision. The Jap sniper took aim. He drilled the man from behind, dropping him into the sea. The second bullet hit the woman. She dragged herself about 30 feet along the rocks. Then she floated out in a stain of blood. The sniper would have shot the children, but a Japanese woman ran across and carried them out of range. The sniper walked defiantly out of his cave, and crumpled under a hundred marine bullets.

Some of the Jap civilians went through considerable ceremony before snuffing out their own lives. The marines said that some fathers had cut their children's throats before tossing them over the cliff. Some strangled their children. In one instance marines watched in astonishment as three women sat on the rocks leisurely, deliberately combing their long black hair.* Finally they joined hands and walked slowly out into the sea.

But the most ceremonious, by all odds, were 100 Japs who were on the rocks below the Marpi Point cliff. All together, they suddenly bowed to marines watching from the cliff. Then they stripped off their clothes and bathed in the sea. Thus refreshed, they put on new clothes and spread a huge Jap flag on a smooth rock. Then the leader distributed hand grenades. One by one, as the pins were pulled, the Japs blew their insides out.

Some seemed to make a little game out of their dying—perhaps out of indecision, perhaps out of ignorance, or even some kind of lightheaded disrespect of

*The Marines had obviously never heard that Leonides and his Spartans did the same thing before their last stand at Thermopylae.

A U.S. STOCKADE CAMP ON SAIPAN (USMC).

the high seriousness of Japanese suicide. One day the marines observed a circle of about 50 Japanese, including several small children, gaily tossing hand grenades to each other—like baseball players warming up before a game. Suddenly six Japanese soldiers dashed from a cave, from which they had been sniping at marines. The soldiers posed arrogantly in front of the civilians, then blew themselves to kingdom come; thus shamed, the civilians did likewise.

What did all this self-destruction mean? Did it mean that the Japanese on Saipan believed their own propaganda which told them that Americans are beasts and would murder them all? Many a Jap civilian did beg our people to put him to death immediately rather than to suffer the torture which he expected. But many who chose suicide could see other civilians who had surrendered walking unmolested in the internment camps. They could hear some of the surrendered plead with them by loudspeaker not to throw their lives away.

The marines have come to expect almost anything in the way of self-destruction from Japanese soldiers. . . . But none were prepared for this epic self-slaughter among civilians. More than one U.S. fighting man was killed trying to rescue a Jap from his wanton suicide.

Saipan is the first invaded Jap territory populated with more than a handful of civilians. Do the suicides of Saipan mean that the whole Japanese race will choose death before surrender? Perhaps that is what the Japanese and their strange propagandists would like us to believe.[46]

This is precisely what the Tokyo warlords wanted both their own people as well as the Americans to believe. They wanted the Americans to believe it in order to frighten them into backing off from their insistence on unconditional surrender, which would mean the invasion of Japan and the mobilization of its people into a "Hundred Million Special Attack Force," ready to die like the victims of Marpi Point. And they wanted the Japanese people to believe it in order to prepare them for the sacrifice they would be called on to make if the enemy invaded the home islands.

"I have always considered Saipan the decisive battle of the Pacific offensive," Holland Smith wrote.[47] The capture of Saipan brought down the government of Hideki Tojo. Another military regime, headed by General Kuniaki Koiso, replaced it, but one less convinced that Japan could win the war short of a sacrificial defense of the homeland. With the Americans only 1,300 miles away, Japanese military leaders began making preparations for an expected invasion.

They were not wrong about this. Saipan led to a major change in American policy in the war against Japan. Only a few days after the fall of Saipan, at a meeting of top commanders of the American and British armed forces, General Marshall made the following motion:

"As a result of the recent operations in the Pacific it was now clear to the United States Chiefs of Staff that, in order to finish the war with the Japanese quickly, it would be necessary to invade the industrial heart of Japan."

The Combined Chiefs of Staff then redefined the aims of the war in the Pacific:

"To force the unconditional surrender of Japan by: (1) Lowering Japanese ability and will to resist by establishing sea and air blockades, conducting intensive air bombardment, and destroying Japanese air and naval strength. (2) Invading and seizing objectives in the industrial heart of Japan."[48]

That September, at a meeting in Quebec, Roosevelt and Churchill formally approved this statement of ultimate war aims.

With the likelihood of an American invasion, the Japanese government began a massive propaganda effort to convince the general population to prepare to embrace death, as had the martyrs of Marpi Point. Heavily censored versions of Sherrod's article began to appear on the front pages of Japanese newspapers alongside editorials celebrating the "patriotic essence" of Japanese women and children who chose "death rather than to be captured alive and shamed by the demonlike American forces." [49] Stricken from the Sherrod article were references to Japanese soldiers killing their own countrymen, and to the thousands of Japanese citizens who did surrender. These official versions of Sherrod's article "became fuel for an unprecedented orgy of glorification of death," writes historian Haruko Taya Cook.[50] When the American "beasts" appeared, the government declared, "one-hundred million" must be victorious or die together. Beginning in August, all citizens were to receive military training, with bamboo spears as their chief weapons. And the enemy was to meet not, as at Saipan, "at the water's edge," but "in the interior."[51]

At the same time, Marpi Point convinced many Americans that Japanese civilians were as "fanatical" as Japanese soldiers, and that Japan could be defeated only by a war of mass extermination, a war not only against combatants but against noncombatants as well, as Robert Sherrod had suggested after Tarawa. That kind of war would be fought from the air, from bases in the Marianas, culminating in the flight of the *Enola Gay* from Tinian to Hiroshima. But another kind of total war had already begun at Tarawa and Saipan, a war to the finish with an enemy who would not surrender, no matter how badly he was beaten.

This merciless island fighting was fed by inflamed racism. To the Japanese people, who prided themselves on being genetically "pure," uncontaminated by immigration, Americans were mongrelized brutes—devils and demons. After the fall of Saipan the Japanese government stepped up its organized campaign of racial vilification. Here is an article from a popular Japanese magazine:

> IT HAS GRADUALLY BECOME CLEAR that the American enemy, driven by its ambition to conquer the world, is coming to attack us, and as the breath and body odor of the beast approach, it may be of some use if we draw the demon's features here.
>
> Our ancestors called them Ebisu or savages long ago, and labeled the very first Westerners who came to our country the Southern Barbarians. To the hostile eyes of the Japanese of former times they were "red hairs" and "hairy foreigners," and perceived as being of about as much worth as a foreign ear of corn. We in our times should manifest comparable spirit. Since the barbaric tribe of

MARINES GATHER TO PAY RESPECTS TO THEIR COMRADES WHO FELL ON SAIPAN (USMC).

Americans are devils in human skin who come from the West, we should call them *Saibanki,* or Western Barbarian Demons.[52]

Posters in classrooms and other public places exhorted students to "kill the American animal." American soldiers in the Pacific, however, did not need propaganda slogans to feed their hatred of the enemy. Japanese atrocities against war prisoners and their suicidal banzai charges were seen as signs of their barbarity. The Marine Corps film shot on Tarawa depicted Japanese defenders as "living, snarling rats." As one veteran of the Pacific fighting wrote: "The Japanese made a perfect enemy. They had so many characteristics that an American Marine could hate. Physically, they were small, a strange color, and, by some standards, unattractive. . . . Marines did not consider that they were killing men. They were wiping out dirty animals."[53]

After the fall of Saipan, Japanese military leaders knew the war was lost. Their weakened fleet was powerless to break the American naval blockade, which was able to pull the noose tighter from advanced bases on Saipan. And they had no air arm to protect their vulnerable cities of wood from the long-range B-29s that began to take off from the Marianas four months later. "Our war was lost," said a Japanese admiral, "with the loss of Saipan."[54] Yet Emperor Hirohito and his chief ministers refused to accept defeat; and out in the Pacific, the soldiers of the empire continued to fight with undiminished bravery, confident of victory.

"Do you think Japan will win the war?" an Army interrogator in the Philippines asked a Japanese prisoner not long after the fall of Saipan.

"A. Of course Japan will win the war.

"Q. Why?

"A. Japan can beat anybody.

"Q. What makes you think Japan will win?

"A. Japan has never lost a war. She cannot be beaten. All of Japan is one mind."[55] How does one defeat such an enemy? Justice M. Chambers, a Marine at Marpi Point, answered for countless American troops in the Pacific. "[General William Tecumseh] Sherman was right. To win the war and get it over with, just kill off many of the other side, make it terrible, and the war will stop."[56]

That is what America eventually did. That is how the war against Japan was won. The debate over the morality of it was left to history.

PACIFIC STRATEGY

The conquest of the Marianas and the northern coast of New Guinea, and the smashing of the Japanese fleet in the Battle of the Philippine Sea, opened the way to direct assault of the Philippines. MacArthur's plan was to climb the ladder of the archipelago from Mindanao, at the southernmost tip, to Leyte, and finally to Luzon. Admiral King, however, wanted to bypass the Philippines, which he thought would be too costly to take, and strike directly at Formosa. It was closer to Japan and would allow the Navy to further tighten its economic blockade by completely dominating Japanese sea lanes to the south. For a time both the President and the Joint Chiefs of Staff sided with King.

MacArthur passionately protested to Roosevelt, insisting that he himself, as well as his country, was honor-bound to liberate the Philippines at the earliest possible moment and rescue the soldiers and nurses he had left behind in Luzon. He also

PLANNING THE PACIFIC OFFENSIVE IN HAWAII, JULY 1944. *LEFT TO RIGHT:*
GENERAL DOUGLAS MACARTHUR, PRESIDENT FRANKLIN ROOSEVELT,
ADMIRAL WILLIAM LEAHY, AND ADMIRAL CHESTER NIMITZ (SC).

wanted personal redemption. In 1942 he had presided over the biggest defeat in
American military history, losing over 70,000 American and Filipino troops on the
Bataan Peninsula and in the fortress of Corregidor. Now, after nearly two years of hard
fighting in New Guinea, he wanted to return to free his men and repay the enemy for
the merciless atrocities of the Bataan Death March.

Manila must be liberated on the way to Tokyo, he insisted to Roosevelt. He had
given his word to the Filipino people. And his men, holed up in Japanese prison camps,
were expecting him.

MacArthur also made his case on cold logistical grounds, and this proved more persuasive. Luzon would be a better base from which to attack Japan than Formosa, which could easily be reinforced by Japanese-held China. After a stormy meeting with Roosevelt and Nimitz in Hawaii in July 1944, MacArthur prevailed, and in September the Combined Chiefs of Staff gave him the official go-ahead to invade Mindanao in November and Leyte in December. To protect his right flank, the Navy would take heavily defended Peleliu in the Palau Islands, 550 miles east of Mindanao, knocking out its excellent airbase and building a support facility for initial operations in Mindanao.

Within a week, however, almost everything changed. In conducting softening-up carrier raids on the Philippines and nearby islands, Admiral Halsey downed an incredible 500 planes and met unexpectedly light resistance. Seeing an opportunity here, he immediately sent a top secret message to Nimitz recommending that the Mindanao operation be canceled and that MacArthur strike swiftly at Leyte. This, he argued, would make the invasion of Peleliu, which he feared would be "another Tarawa," unnecessary.[57] Nimitz sent Halsey's recommendation, with his approval only of the acceleration of the Philippines operation, to the Combined Chiefs of Staff, which were meeting in Quebec. After getting MacArthur's consent, they changed the timetable. MacArthur would make an amphibious assault on Leyte on October 20.

Nimitz's decision not to call back the Peleliu invasion force, which was only three days from the island, was a major mistake, for the rationale for the invasion had disappeared. He might been trying to appease MacArthur, who wanted all the air support he could get, but Nimitz had also been informed by American intelligence that Peleliu would be easy to take, a two- or three-day operation.

It was one of the worst intelligence blunders of the war. When finally subdued after months of fighting, Peleliu was virtually worthless. The swiftly advancing Pacific war had passed it by, turning it into a backwater fuel depot. But the cost of taking it was unconscionable—almost 10,000 Marines and Army infantry killed or wounded in perhaps the most savage major battle of the Pacific Theater. "The only difference between Iwo Jima and Peleliu," remarked General Roy Geiger, who commanded the assault troops at Peleliu, "was that at Iwo Jima, there were twice as many Japs on an island twice as large, and they had three Marine divisions to take it, while we had one Marine division to take Peleliu."[58]

The defenders of Peleliu put up a sign. "We will build a barrier across the Pacific with our bodies."[59] That foretold the ferocity of the fight.

A Marine at Peleliu

WITH THE OLD BREED

The 1st Marine Division was given the ugly assignment of taking Peleliu. D-Day was scheduled for September 15, 1944. That summer the division was in rest camp on Pavuvu in the Russell Islands, eighty miles from Guadalcanal. The 1st Marines had done most of the fighting in the epic battle of Guadalcanal and had just completed a tough assignment with General MacArthur, taking Cape Gloucester, on the island of New Britain, in miserable jungle fighting at the peak of the monsoon season. They were a spirited, veteran outfit, nicknamed the Old Breed, even though over three quarters of the men had not yet reached the age of twenty-one. Already legendary among their warriors was Colonel Chesty Puller, whose reckless audacity had won him a Navy Cross and a Purple Heart on Guadalcanal.

One of their newest replacements was a skinny, soft-voiced twenty-year-old from Mobile, Alabama, named Eugene B. Sledge, "Sledgehammer" as he was known to his buddies in K Company, 3rd Battalion, 5th Marine Regiment, 1st Marine Division. Sledge was a doctor's son, a quiet, thoughtful boy who read widely and knew what the

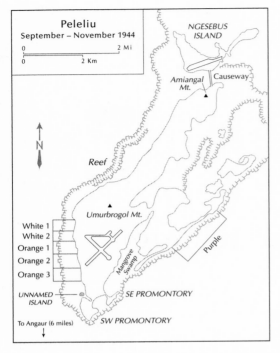

war was about and wanted to get into it. Impatient to see combat, he had quit a Marine officer training program at Georgia Tech to become an enlisted man. By the time he finished officer training the war might be over, he told his protesting parents. He had joined the Marines, he said, to fight not to study. Even so, he wondered if he could face up to combat— and whether he could kill.

Sledge was patriotic and deeply religious. He neither smoked nor drank, and one of his passions was bird watching. After the war he became a professor of biology, specializing in ornithology, at a small Alabama college. There, in his free moments, he completed the war memoir he had begun immediately after returning from Peleliu, *With the Old Breed at Peleliu and Okinawa*. Published in 1981, it has become a small classic, one of the finest personal accounts of combat ever written.

The book is based on a secret diary Sledge kept during the war. "My parents taught me the value of history," he told the writer Stúds Terkel after the war. "Both my grandfathers were in the Confederate Army. They didn't talk about the glory of war. They talked about how terrible it was.

"During my third day overseas, I thought I should write all this down for my family. In all my reading about the Civil War, I never read about how the troops felt and what it was like from day to day. We knew how the generals felt and what they ate.

"We were told diaries were forbidden, because if we were killed or captured, any diary might give the Japanese information. So I kept little notes, which I slipped into the pages of my Gideon's New Testament. . . .

"Some of the supervisors never knew I was keepin' notes: 'We just thought you were awfully pious.'" [1]

When Sledge joined the 1st Marines as a mortarman in a rifle company the men were "bone-tired and decimated from the bloody fighting on the rain-drenched jungle island of New Britain, off the eastern coast of New Guinea," recalls another new replacement, James D. Seidler. "Most of the division was dumped on Pavuvu Island, which had been a British coconut plantation before the war, so there were four years of rotting palm fronds and coconuts, along with thousands of land crabs, huge rats, snakes, and other assorted critters. And mud. It took three months' hard work to make it habitable."[2]

Years later, Sledge described the place: "Huge fruit bats came out all night and flew around and got into fights with rats in the palm trees right above our tents. Land crabs scuttled through the tents all night and each day you had to shake your shoes out to get them out. Morale should have been low, but most of us were in our teens and early twenties and were part of an elite and proud outfit.

"There was no recreation except volleyball, baseball, and B-grade movies we watched on log seats in a coconut grove. But I think this is one of the things that bonded us all so closely together. . . . We didn't have any distractions. We had to lean on each other." In a recently written sequel to *The Old Breed*, Sledge writes that the veterans "treated us replacements like brothers—with the understanding we had to prove ourselves in combat. They were the best teachers in the world in how to kill Japs because, simply said, that is the infantryman's job, to *kill* the enemy. . . .

EUGENE B. "SLEDGEHAMMER" SLEDGE (LRP).

"A passionate hatred for the Japanese burned through all the Marines I knew." When Sledge asked a veteran of Guadalcanal why, he got an unbelieving stare and this emphatic reply, "Because they're the meanest sonabitches that ever lived."[3]

The high point of Sledge's stay on Pavuvu was a visit by Bob Hope. "While we were preparing for Peleliu, which incidentally we weren't told about until the day before we shipped out, Bob Hope was over in [the nearby island of] Banika entertaining the troops in the naval hospital. When he heard the 1st Marine Division was on Pavuvu he flew over with his entertainment group in a Piper Cub and put on a wonderful show with Jerry Colonna, Frances Langford, and [the dancer] Patti Thomas. . . . He said after the war that of all of the shows that he had done for military men, this was the one that stuck in his mind. . . . After we suffered such staggering casualties at Peleliu, Bob saw some of our wounded at a naval hospital in the States. One teenage Marine turned to him and said, 'Hey Bob, remember Pavuvu?' Hope later wrote that he got so choked up he could not go through the ward with its long rows of cots with all the Peleliu casualties. . . . But he sure gave us a spark at Pavuvu. It was a wonderful treat, and that was the last real laugh a lot of my buddies had . . . in their short lives."

The 1st Marines shipped out for Peleliu in the last week of August. Company K boarded a large LST (Landing Ship Tank), a shallow-draft ship as big as a light cruiser, with a load of amtracs in its cavernous belly. It would discharge these Alligators in the waters off Peleliu, twenty men to a vehicle, from its massive bow doors, which opened like the jaws of a clam. The men in the assault companies—the Marines who would hit the beach first—bunked in the rough-riding, flat-bottomed LSTs with the machines that would carry them ashore. The rest of the division rode in more comfortable troopships.

The trip to Peleliu—2,100 miles away—took three weeks in the excruciatingly slow LSTs. It was insufferably hot below deck, but the seas were smooth all the way and the men sat on the deck sunning themselves, reading, playing poker, or writing mother. The enlisted men knew nothing about the island with the "nice sounding name, Pel' e loo" other than that it had a big airfield that Douglas MacArthur wanted knocked out to protect his flank when he returned to the Philippines. Their coldly aloof and unpopular commanding officer, General William Rupertus, told them this would be a "rough but fast" mission, taking only three, maybe four days. Which means "we'll have to kill every little yellow bastard there," a skeptical sergeant mused.[4]

After chow on the evening of the landing, Sledge and a friend leaned on the rail of the slow-rocking ship and talked about what they planned to do after the war, trying their mightiest to appear unconcerned about the next morning. "As the sun disappeared below the horizon and its glare no longer reflected off a glassy sea, I thought of how beautiful the sunsets always were in the Pacific. They were even more beautiful than over Mobile Bay. Suddenly a thought hit me like a thunderbolt. Would I live to see the sunset tomorrow? My knees nearly buckled as panic swept over me. I squeezed the railing and tried to appear interested in our conversation." Sledge excused himself and went below to check his combat pack. Everything was in order. Inside was "a folded poncho, one pair of socks, a couple of boxes of K rations, salt tablets, extra carbine ammo (twenty rounds), two hand grenades, a fountain pen, a small bottle of ink, writing paper in a waterproof wrapper, a toothbrush, a small tube of toothpaste, some photos of my folks along with some letters (in a waterproof wrapper), and a dungaree cap."

His other equipment and clothing included a carbine, an entrenching tool, a steel helmet, a green dungaree jacket and pants, ankle-high "boondockers," light canvas leggings, two canteens, a compass, two clips of ammunition, the regulation Ka-Bar knife in a leather sheath, a larger, meat-cleaver-style knife his father had sent him, and, for good luck, a bronze Marine emblem fastened to one collar.

When his head hit the pillow that night, he thought of home and wondered if he would die tomorrow. "I concluded that it was impossible for me to be killed, because God loved me." His heart racing, he fell asleep whispering the Lord's Prayer.

The Landing

In the blackness of the early morning, he had a breakfast of steak and eggs and headed with his company for the tank deck of the LST. The toilets were so crowded that some men didn't have the chance to empty their bowels. To boost morale, gung-ho Marines were putting on camouflage paint, war paint, they called it. "Puts them in the mood," an officer told K Company's commander, George Hunt, a former newspaperman who would write a riveting account of his part of the upcoming battle, *Coral Comes High.*

Hunt was with Chesty Puller's 1st Regiment, and his company had been given the toughest assignment on D-Day. They were to storm the Point, a Japanese fortification that had been built into the soft coral rock of a small peninsula that jutted out into the sea on the far left of the landing area. If that position was not taken, the enemy would have a free field of fire down the entire length of the beach, and the landing would likely be a massacre.

On the tank deck, the Alligators' engines were rumbling, filling the hold with stomach-turning diesel exhaust, despite the huge fans whirling overhead. When the signal was given, the big bow doors separated and Sledge's amphibious tractor, following others, rumbled down the sloping ramp and settled into the sea "like a big duck." Just ahead, in the rolling, blue-green water, was the Alligator carrying George Hunt. A veteran of Guadalcanal and New Britain, Hunt was scared because he knew what to expect. A greenhorn, Sledge was scared because he didn't know what to expect.

As the Marines passed the patrol boats and rocket ships, the sailors shook their fists and yelled, "Go get 'em, you Marines!" To settle their nerves, the men in one of Hunt's landing boats began singing "Give My Regards to Broadway." "Just before we hit the beach we were all singing it at the top of our lungs," Sergeant Webber said later. "It sure made us feel good." [5]

The men had been ordered to keep their heads down, but Sledge peeked over the high gunwale "and saw several amtracs get hit dead on by screaming shells and watched in horror as the bodies of Marines were blown into the air." Those that were still alive began walking into shore and were slaughtered by machine gun fire. "The noise from the battleships and the Corsairs [Navy fighters] and the dive-bombers was so incredible it was indescribable. You couldn't even yell to the man right next to you and have him hear you. As we moved into position we could see and feel the power of the sixteen-inch salvos fired from the battlewagons right over our heads. Every time they exploded, trees and debris were hurled high into the air. It wasn't hot yet and the sky was blue and the sun was out and I was scared to death, and so was everybody else. The main thing that concerned me was I was afraid I was going to wet my pants.

"I looked at the island and all I could see was a sheet of flame backed by a huge black wall of smoke . . . as though the island was on fire. And I thought, my God, none of us will ever get out of that place."

Back on the troopships, the men lined the rails and shouted, "Burn! Burn!" as tiny Peleliu, only six miles long and two miles wide, vanished in flame and smoke and monstrous clouds of coral dust. "We'll be off here by tomorrow," one Marine yelled.[6]

It was the same reaction as at Tarawa. Hardly a Marine could believe there was an enemy soldier alive after such a shelling. But the Japanese were dug in better than they were at either Tarawa or Saipan. In a cave built deep in one of the island's coral ridges, a Japanese defender wrote in his diary, "We will defend Peleliu! We are imbued with the firm conviction that even though we may die, we will never let the airfield fall into enemy hands. Our morale is sky high."[7] But so was the Marines'. "Over the gunwale of a craft abreast of us I saw a marine, his face painted for the jungle, his eyes set for the beach, his mouth set for murder, his big hands quiet now in the last moments before the tough tendons drew up to kill," wrote Tom Lea, *Life*'s leading war artist in the Pacific.[8]

For more than two months, Lea had lived aboard the carrier *Hornet*, chronicling that ship's role in operations in the South Pacific. This was his first battle experience with the Marines. In their combat packs, he and two other correspondents each had a can of beer. They agreed to have their own little celebration on the beach if they made it there.

There were 10,500 Japanese soldiers and sailors on the island, about 6,000 of them members of the Kwantung Army, veterans of brutal fighting in Manchuria. Their commander, Colonel Kunio Nakagawa, had brought in mining and tunneling engineers to militarize the natural coral caves of Peleliu, which were built into a central spine of hills that ran up the northern half of the island. Sliding steel doors covered the entrances to the caves with the biggest guns, and many of the interlocking caves had electricity, ventilation systems, telephone and radio communications, and hidden exits. The largest of them held a thousand men and a number of the caves were five and six stories deep. The caves were ideally located for defense, in a 300-foot-high mountain of jagged coral, with sheer cliffs, overlooking the flat area at the center of the island, just off the beach, where the airfield was located. It was "a series of crags," Private Russell Davis described it, "ripped bare of all standing vegetation, peeled down to the rotted coral, rolling in smoke, crackling with heat and . . . stained and black, like bad teeth." [9] The natives called this menacing coral mass the Umurbrogol. To Davis and other Marines it became known as Bloody Nose Ridge. Taking it would cost more American lives than were lost in the assault on Omaha Beach.

Aerial intelligence had failed to sight this high ground, for it was covered at the time with dense tropical growth. But the tremendous naval fire had blasted off the vegetation, exposing the coral ridges that began just north of the airport. There in the caves, "with plugs in their ears and hate in their hearts, they waited," Lea wrote. "Through terrifying bombing and shelling they waited for the marines to start across the 675-yard reef to the beach. . . . Then they opened up." [10]

As Sledge's landing craft approached the beach, it hit a coral shelf and the engine stalled. Shells fell all around it, creating huge water geysers, and machine gun bullets pelted the steel sides of the Alligator. "When the first shell came over, I knew my place was back home with mother."

The Alligator began running again, and as the Marines came up on the sand, the lieutenant pulled out a bottle of whiskey and shouted, "This is it boys."

"Just like they do in the movies! It seemed unreal."

Racing ashore a few yards, Sledge sought cover with members of his company. The Marines landed three regiments abreast, the 1st, 5th, and 7th Marines. Most of Puller's 1st Marines, on the left flank, attacked the lower hills of Bloody Nose Ridge and were stopped cold, with heavy casualties. Hunt's K Company, meanwhile, went straight for the Point and took it after a vicious firefight. But holding it would be a lot harder than taking it. Sledge's 1st Marines landed in the center and headed inland through low scrub vegetation toward the airport. The 7th Marines landed on the far right. After knocking out entrenched enemy positions on the southern end of the island, they were to loop north and reinforce Puller.

Tom Lea, with the 7th Marines, found it impossible to do any drawing or sketching on the beach. "My work there consisted of trying to keep from getting killed and trying to memorize what I saw and felt under fire. On the evening of D-plus-one I returned to a naval vessel offshore where I could record in my sketch book the burden of this memory." At his home in El Paso, Texas, Lea transformed his hastily executed pencil sketches into a series of searing color portraits of men at war, which were reproduced in the pages of *Life*.

Lea came across the reef on a Higgins boat. The reef was "barricaded with concrete posts and railroad-track ties, all heavily entwined with barbed wire. There were necklaces of underwater mines around every possible landing point." And the Japanese had "planted inverted 500-lb. aerial bombs and naval torpedoes with special fuses as mines and booby traps. Minefields stretched from the water to 50 yards inland in a pattern which insured explosives every 20 feet."[11] When his boat ground to a stop on the rugged coral, Lea splashed through the shallow surf and fell flat on his face, lying there wet and terrified as he watched a mortar tear a Marine to pieces, his head and one leg sailing into the air.[12]

Lea fell into a shell hole as another mortar came rocketing down on him. "Lying there . . . I saw a wounded man near me, staggering in the direction of LVTs. His face was half bloody pulp and the mangled shreds of what was left of an arm hung down like a stick, as he bent over in his stumbling, shock-crazy walk. The half of his face that was still human had the most terrifying look of abject patience I have ever seen. He fell behind me, in a red puddle on the white sand."[13] That falling, shattered Marine, his "blood-soaked uniform . . . coated with coral grit," became the subject of Lea's shockingly realistic painting *The Price*. It was different from anything Lea had done before. Most of his work up to Peleliu had a sharp documentary quality, with almost no tension or bloodshed. *The Price* is so gory, so brutally grotesque, it makes you want to turn away. Peleliu changed Tom Lea. *The Price* "is a monument," writes James Jones, "to the blood and death that all of us, even those who have been there, prefer not to see or think about when we are away from it."[14]

Lea followed the 7th Marines into the burned and mangled jungle just inland from the beach, where he found cover with other Marines in a long trench. Walking behind an old log, he and his two friends punched holes with their knives in their three beer cans and drank a toast to the Marines on Peleliu. "The beer was hot, foamy and wonderful."

It was just before noon and sun had burned through the overcast of the early morning. Throughout the battle, temperatures would hover around 100 degrees, reaching 115 degrees on some days, and water was in short supply in the early part of the invasion. "Sweat ran in streams from under our helmets which, without cloth covers, were burning to the touch. Our dungarees, wet with sweat, stuck to our legs and backs. The sand under our clothes scratched like sandpaper," Lea wrote.[15]

Just behind the trench, in a large bomb crater, surrounded by splintered trees, an improvised aid station had been set up. No hospital tent had been erected. That would have invited enemy fire. "In the center of the crater at the bottom a doctor was working on the worst of the stretcher cases. Corpsmen, four to a stretcher, came in continuously with their bloody loads." The doctor was performing surgery, while corpsmen administered to the walking wounded. "The padre stood by with two canteens and a Bible, helping. . . . He looked very lonely, very close to God, as he bent over the shattered men so far from home. Corpsmen put a poncho, a shirt, a rag, anything handy, over the grey faces of the dead and carried them to a line on the beach, under a tarpaulin, to await the digging of graves."

Toward evening, the men near the trench started to dig in for the night. Their

AFRICAN-AMERICAN SUPPLY COMPANY PINNED
DOWN ON THE BEACH (USMC).

trenching tools were useless against the bone-hard coral. All they could do was find a hole or a slight depression and pile up stones and debris around it for cover. As they worked, they could be heard muttering. "It's the ferking night time I don't like, when them little ferkers come sneakin' into your lap." [16] When they finished, they cleaned their rifles and sharpened their bayonets.

Up the beach, to the left, Sledge's 5th Marines had moved in close to the airstrip, where they repelled a tank attack with bazookas, mortars, and their own hard-punching Sherman tanks, annihilating thirteen small, thin-skinned tanks and a company of infantry that moved across the airfield behind them. This was a carefully coordinated counterattack, not a banzai charge, the first indication the Marines had that the enemy might fight differently on Peleliu than they had at Tarawa or Saipan.

Still further up the beach, on the extreme left of the line, part of George Hunt's decimated K Company was holding the fortresslike Point in primeval, hand-to-hand fighting, cut off from the rest of the Marines on Peleliu and encircled by the best of Nakagawa's Manchuria veterans. They would be isolated and under incessant attack until they were relieved thirty hours later. Puller and the rest of the 1st Marines could not get to them. They were pinned down by shots of fire from the caves of the Umurbrogol, just to the north of them. (After the war, the Marine Corps built an exact model of the Point at its Quantico training facility to teach new officers how to assault a "doomsday" defense.)

That evening, as he fell into a "restless doze," brushing aside the land crabs that had crawled on his face, George Hunt wondered, "Could I still find my way around New York?—almost unbelievable to see Fifth Avenue again, to buy a newspaper at Whalen's, ride the Eighth Avenue subway and the Staten Island Ferry . . . and feel the stampeding, pulsating, brawling, uproarious spirit of the city—then I must have slept." [17]

Along the beach, as the sun went down, men ate candy bars, drank warm water from canteens, and had their last cigarette before the "smoking lamp" was extinguished. Then the island blackness closed in on them. Most expected it to cool off, but it didn't; and they "sat and steamed in puddles of sweat." Waiting. When the counterattack came in Lea's section of the beachhead, it began with a flurry of small arms fire and the high-pitched screams of enemy soldiers. Then came the mortar shells, smashing down all around them, the Marine howitzers answering every few seconds, "shaking the ground with their blasts." [18] Star shells lit up the sky and the whole beachhead came alive. But again, there was no suicidal assault, just continued and nerve-rattling mortar fire.

"To me, artillery was an invention of hell . . . ," Sledge described that first terrible night on Peleliu. "After each shell I was wrung out, limp and exhausted." As the fight for Peleliu wore on, and the shelling intensified, there were a number of times when Sledge thought he was going to go out of his mind.

BLOODY NOSE RIDGE

Toward first light, after the shelling stopped, Marines climbed out of their primitive shelters with big grins on their smoke-smeared faces, feeling they had beaten the odds, at least for a night. "We wiped the slime off our front teeth and lighted cigarettes," wrote Lea. As they prepared themselves for battle, they saw what the enemy had done that night. The nearest dead Japanese were about thirty yards in front of the trench. They had infiltrated the Marines' lines, wearing the helmets of dead Marines, and sneaked into foxholes and "cut throats. They had been slashed or shot by marines in hand to hand fighting in the darkness and there were bodies now in the morning light." [19]

At 8:00 A.M. Sledge's 5th Marines prepared for an assault on the crushed gravel airfield. The Marines already held two sides of the field, but the Japanese had their heavy guns concentrated on the coral mound overlooking the north side of the field, just west of where Chesty Puller was trying to break through. Planes, tanks, and howitzers would spearhead the advance, followed by the foot soldiers; and the assault would be made under the full force of that other enemy on Peleliu—the blistering sun, heat waves visible to the eye rising up from the furnacelike coral.

Hundreds of Marines had already shriveled and passed out from heat exhaustion and their bodies lay all about, "paralyzed in grotesque shapes." [20] The 5th Marines would need water if they hoped to carry out the attack. Just as the men in Sledge's unit started putting on their gear, a supply detail came up with five-gallon water tanks. "Our hands shook, we were so eager to quench our thirst," Sledge recalls. But the water looked like "thin brown paint" in his canteen cup, and when he first drank it he had to spit it out. It was full of rust and oil and it gave off a vile smell. A supply officer had transported this water to Peleliu in fifty-five-gallon drums that had previously been filled with diesel oil. The drums had supposedly been steam-cleaned but someone had botched the job. There was nothing anyone could do now. The Marines had to drink the oily water or die. Some of the men doubled up and retched.

Four infantry battalions were ordered to cross the airfield at a trot, straight into the enemy's strength. Later, an officer told Sledge the attack had been an appalling mistake. "We moved rapidly in the open, amid craters and coral rubble, through ever increasing enemy fire. . . . The shells screeched and whistled, exploding all around us.

"I clenched my teeth, squeezed my carbine stock, and recited over and over to myself, 'The Lord is my shepherd . . . '

"The ground seemed to sway back and forth under the concussions. . . . Chunks of blasted coral stung my face and hands while steel fragments spattered down on the hard rock like hail on a city street. Everywhere shells flashed like giant firecrackers.

"Through the haze I saw Marines stumble and pitch forward as they got hit. . . . I gritted my teeth and braced myself in anticipation of the shock of being struck down at any moment. It seemed impossible that any of us could make it across."

When Sledge made it to the northeastern side of the field, and found cover in some low bushes, he was "shaking like a leaf. I looked at one of the Guadalcanal veterans and he was shaking as bad as I was." Sledge almost laughed with relief.

Some men bled to death on the fire-swept airfield, for there was no way anybody could get to them in time. The Marines were told to keep moving and not to stop and help the wounded. But an African-American Marine in one of the ammunition companies that was in the thick of the fight picked up a white Marine from Mississippi and carried him all the way to the aid station. Later, Sledge would write that the attack across the Peleliu airfield was his worst combat experience of the war.

That night Sledge's unit moved through the mangrove swamps near the airfield and dug in for the night. It was impossible to get even five consecutive minutes of sleep because of the intensity of the enemy infiltration. "We never used the night," said Marine Benis Frank. "I can only think of two night operations, one on Iwo Jima and one on Okinawa, that were successful. We owned the daytime for the most part. We owned the air, but the Japanese owned the night." [21]

By now it was clear to almost every Marine on the island that the Japanese were not fighting as they had on Saipan and Tarawa, where they had massed their strength on the beachhead and tried to stop the Marines at the waterline. That tactic had failed everywhere. Colonel Nakagawa had contested the landing with one full battalion, inflicting over 1,100 casualties on D-Day, but he had placed most of his troops in caves in the limestone ridges north of the airfield and waited for the Americans to come to him. (The reverse of Rommel's tactics on Omaha Beach.) Beginning with Peleliu, the Japanese would rely on a defense-in-depth strategy, luring the Americans toward their strong points and inflicting horrible casualties from positions that neither naval or air bombardment could reach. Japan could not win the war in this way, but it could hope to make it so hideously costly that the American public would demand an end to the bloodshed short of unconditional surrender.

Peleliu's ungodly landscape was a perfect laboratory to test the new defense-in-depth tactics. Once the airfield was taken, the Marines had to secure it by going north into the Umurbrogol, a wild terrain that resembled a series of reefs that had reared up from the ocean floor, five parallel, razor-sharp ridges extending for two miles up the island. "The ruggedness of the terrain," said Sledge, "was almost indescribable. . . . There were these sheer canyons, the sides at ninety-degree angles, and they would be firing at us from two and three mutually supporting caves. It had a surrealistic appearance because the contours were all at crazy angles, and there was no smooth surface to any ridge."

Japanese terrain and tactics took their heaviest toll on Chesty Puller's 1st Marine Regiment. Puller tried to bull his way through nearly impregnable enemy positions on Bloody Nose Ridge, suffering horrendous casualties. He was a stubborn and fearless fighter, known to take long chances, but there was an almost manic quality to his aggressiveness on Peleliu, perhaps because he had just lost a brother, a fellow Marine, on Guam. He was supported by the equally unbending General Rupertus. When the overall commander of the operation, General Roy Geiger, offered to land an Army regiment being held in reserve to support Puller, Rupertus flatly refused. He distrusted the Army; the Marines would get the job done. To compound the problem, both Rupertus and Puller were hurt. Rupertus had broken an ankle in a training exercise and his injury prevented him from getting to the front to see how badly things were going. Puller aggravated a leg wound he suffered at Guadalcanal, and had to be carried around on a stretcher.[22]

Major Ray Davis's 1st Battalion lost 71 percent of its number, including all the officers in the rifle companies except one; and that man, Captain Everett Pope, had a hair-raising escape from death that won him a Medal of Honor. "We were finished as a fighting force," recalls Davis, "and the survivors were numb." Davis blames Rupertus and Puller, but the entire Peleliu campaign, he says, represented "a total failure of intelligence."[23]

After taking the airport, Sledge's regiment fought for a day or so in the hills next to the 1st Marines and heard their complaints and witnessed their morale sagging. "We had lost too many good men," George Hunt spoke for his entire regiment, "how long could it keep up?"[24]

At this point in the battle, Sledge's regimental commander, Colonel Harold "Bucky" Harris, flew over the Umurbrogol in a scout plane to see what the Marines were up against. He then went to Puller and Rupertus and told them they could never take the coral mountain by frontal assault because "the contours of the ridges were like Swiss cheese, full of caves, situated in mutually supporting positions." He recommended that they pull back and move north, where the cave defense system was weaker. Attacking from north to south, using siege tactics, they could root out the Japanese, one position at a time, with artillery, tanks, and newly developed long-range flamethrowers mounted on armored vehicles. When Rupertus came close to accusing Harris of cowardice, saying he was using too much ammunition and not enough men, Harris replied, "General, I'm lavish with my ammunition and stingy with my men's lives." At that moment, the tent flap opened and in came General Geiger, who looked directly at Harris and said, "That's the most sensible thing I've ever heard. You can't take positions with dead marines." [25]

Geiger overruled Rupertus. On the ninth day of the battle a regiment of the Army's 81st Division, the Wildcats, relieved the shot-up 1st Marines, who had taken more casualties than any Marine regiment in the war up to this point. Trying to force the impossible, Puller and Rupertus nearly destroyed one of the best regiments in the Marine Corps.

"You the 1st Marines?" a correspondent asked as Puller's leathernecks came off the line. "There ain't no more 1st Marines," came the reply from somewhere in the ranks.[26] Many of these men would fight again, but it was the end of Chesty Puller's World War II.

As the exhausted remnants of the 1st Marines walked off to a "safe" area near the sea, George Hunt watched some of his men find beds for themselves on the coral, while others carried their dead comrades to the beach, where "they laid them down respectfully in a straight row. There were no sheets to cover them." [27]

INTO THE UMURBROGOL

Twenty days later Sledge's regiment would be relieved, its ranks almost as decimated as those of the 1st Marines. This was after it went into the Umurbrogol to reinforce the 7th Marines. It was sent there after all the vital positions on the islands had been taken: the airfield, the commanding ridge above it, and all of the island south, east, and north of Umurbrogol Mountain, including the neighboring island of Ngesebus. There would be no more frontal assaults from the south. Instead, the Marines and the Wildcats would follow Harris's plan until they had the enemy sur-

rounded in a "final pocket of resistance."

"We moved much faster, took more positions, and killed just scores of Japs because we could flush them out of the caves with direct fire from artillery, tanks, and flamethrowers," recalls Sledge. Even so, the fighting in the Umurbrogol was "a long nightmare," a struggle between two armies fighting on two surfaces: the Americans above ground and the Japanese below.

The landscape had been blasted free of vegetation and scarred white by thousands of phosphorus shells. "The place had been pulverized by shelling, and we were all covered with coral dust. When it would rain the dust, being lime, would harden, and we would move our arms and the pieces of coral would crack and fall off our dust-hardened dungarees," says Sledge. They became a living part of that terrible terrain. And they stank almost as bad as it did. The heat and the fear made them sweat, and the smell of their bodies was nauseating even to themselves. Worse, it blended with the odor of their dead. "In the tropics, when men were killed in the morning they would begin to bloat and stink pretty badly by night," Sledge recalled in a conversation long after the war.

WE WOULD COVER OUR DEAD with ponchos, from head to toe, and put them on stretchers behind the company area. But the dead Japs were lying all over the place in the ridges. There was no place to bury them in that coral. So they just bloated and rotted. Maggots tumbled out of their mouths and eyes, and big blowflies swarmed around the bodies. The flies would also get after our food and nothing scared them away. . . . You had to pick them off your K rations. Often we had to eat within two or three feet of a dead Jap, and he'd be pretty rotten. And the flies that were on the dead Jap would land on our canteen cups and sometimes fall into the coffee. We didn't have a lot of coffee, so we just pulled the flies out and drank it.

There was another problem. Typically, when a man who was under fire had to defecate he used a grenade canister or ration can and threw it out of his foxhole, covering it up with dirt the next day. If you were not under fire you could go back a little way off the line and dig a small hole. But there was no soil in the limestone hills of Peleliu, so there was this terrible odor from feces. Most of us got severe diarrhea and that added to our sanitary problems. The odor was absolutely vile. You felt you would never get the stench of dead and rot and filth out of your nostrils. And at night the land crabs would come out and swarm over the dead Japs. Then shells would come in and blow big chunks of the rotting corpses all over the place.

Worse than the filth was the fatigue. "The fatigue a combat infantryman is exposed to is absolutely beyond description. . . . [After a couple of weeks], we were literally shuffling around like zombies."

They began to weaken mentally as well. The entire time Sledge was on Peleliu he does not recall a single second when there was not a gun firing. There was no front line; the entire island was the front line. That wore men down and made them feel helpless and vulnerable. "When buddies were killed or wounded, many of us just simply cried."

The men soon realized they had been sent into a death trap. In most Storm Landings, the Marines outnumbered the enemy by about three to one. But on Peleliu there were 9,000 Marines fighting nearly 11,000 Japanese. As casualties mounted, cooks, bakers, drivers, engineers, and supply men, including some African-Americans

1ST MARINES IN THE UMURBROGOL (USMC).

from the ammunition and supply companies, were given rifles and thrown into the fight. And every man in a rifle company, even the company commander, had to serve as a stretcher-bearer at one time or another. "Because of the heat and terrain, it took four people to carry a man on a stretcher," Sledge recalls. "It was dangerous work. The Japs absolutely opened up on stretcher-bearers with everything they had. You cannot imagine the cold hatred we had of people who shot at us as we were taking out our wounded and were unable to fire back. Historians say we hated the Japs because we were racists. Racism had nothing to do with it. It was the way they fought."

Every day, it seemed, Sledge witnessed a new and more ghastly sign of the unyielding ferocity of the enemy. Late in the fight, he saw the bodies of three dead Marines in a small hole. They were badly decomposed, but this was to be expected in the tropics. As he looked closer, however, he was stricken with horror and revulsion— and rage such as he had never felt before. The Marines had been gruesomely mutilated. One man was decapitated. His head and severed hands rested on his chest and his penis had been stuffed into his mouth. The second man had been mutilated in the same way. "The third Marine had been butchered, chopped up like a carcass torn by some predatory animal."

Sledge respected the Japanese soldiers for their loyalty to country and their unbreakable physical courage but believed that they had been brutalized by their training and indoctrination—taught to fight "with savagery beyond necessity." So Sledge killed them without regret or remorse, routinely shooting dead and wounded enemy soldiers after seizing a position "to make sure they were dead. Survival was hard enough in the infantry without taking chances being humane to men who fought so savagely."

George Hunt put this differently. "If it hadn't been for [the Japanese] we would never have been on this goddam island in the middle of no place with all these rocks, the blasted heat and no water or chow. . . . We hated them, and we would kill them and keep killing them or we would be killed." [28]

In the Umurbrogol, there was probably more Japanese infiltration than anywhere else in the Pacific. "They laid up in the caves," says Sledge, "and slept all day. At night we were ready for them. We had a password, a word we knew the Japs couldn't pronounce clearly, and while one man took a catnap, the other was on watch, with a Ka-Bar knife in one hand and a rifle or grenade in the other. The Japs, who knew the terrain down to the last rock and tree stump, would come out in ones and twos and threes and slip up as close as possible and then throw a grenade and come in yelling and swinging a saber or a bayonet. The sounds of the fights in the foxholes were ungodly. Grunts and curses and screams. The fighting was savage, Neanderthal. This was actually more of a raid than infiltration. Its purpose was to inflict casualties and to wear us down, which it did." As Benis Frank remarked: "It was good so many of us were so young. Only a young man could fight all day and all night." [29]

"Sometimes the Japs did truly infiltrate," Sledge says. "They tried to slip through our lines and get to the rear, where often they would set up a machine gun, so that when we woke up they had us covered from the front and rear. Or else they infiltrated to kill our wounded. I lost some buddies that way. They were so good at this, so quiet, you couldn't tell whether it was a Jap out there or a land crab. To try to spot them, we would throw up flares, but you had to be aware of where the dead Jap bodies were around your positions before it became dark, or else you might mistake a live Jap, playing possum, for a dead one. . . . We also put up trip wires with grenades on them, and attached cans and coral pebbles to the wires. If they rattled we opened fire on the position. The remarkable thing about these Jap infiltrators is that they knew that they were going to be killed, but they still came."

Sledge witnessed Japanese "savagery" reduce many of his fellow Marines to an equal savagery. Marines stripped Japanese corpses, looking for souvenirs—sabers, pistols, flags, hara-kiri knives. These were kept or sold for handsome prices to sailors or pilots. "The men gloated over, compared, and often swapped their prizes," which included gold teeth they had extracted with their knives, sometimes before the wounded victim was dead.

"Time had no meaning; life had no meaning. The fierce struggle for survival in the abyss of Peleliu eroded the veneer of civilization and made savages of us all. We lived in an environment totally incomprehensible to the men behind the lines—service troops and civilians. . . .

In a break in the fighting, Sledge saw a dead Japanese soldier squatting on the ground in front of his machine gun. The top of his head had been blown off, cleanly severed as if a saw had cut it. "I noticed this buddy of mine just flippin' chunks of coral into the skull. . . . It rained all that night and the rain collected inside his skull. . . . Each time [my buddy's] pitch was true, I heard a little splash of rainwater in the ghastly receptacle. . . . There was nothing malicious in his action. This was just a mild-mannered kid who was now a twentieth-century savage. . . .

"We all had become hardened. We were out there, human beings, the most highly developed form of life on earth, fighting like wild animals."

The fighting stopped for Sledge on October 30, 1944, when his broken regiment was sent back to Pavuvu after suffering 64 percent casualties. The Wildcats were left to finish the job, and it would take them another six hard weeks. On the night of November 24, Colonel Nakagawa, having carried out his instructions to bleed the Americans—taking 9,615 casualties—burned his colors and killed himself in a cave in the shell-blasted Umurbrogol. Only a handful of his men were still alive. They melted into the coral ridges and did not surface and surrender until a year and a half after the war. To take Peleliu and two nearby islands, Angaur and Ngesebus, cost one American casualty and 1,589 rounds of ammunition for each Japanese defender killed.

The image, more than any other, that captures the agony of Peleliu is Tom Lea's *Two-Thousand-Yard-Stare*. It is the portrait of a young Marine that Lea saw in a sick bay he passed by on his way off the island. "I noticed a tattered marine standing quietly by a corpsman, staring stiffly at nothing. His mind had crumbled in battle, his jaw hung, and his eyes were like two black empty holes in his head." [30] When Lea painted him, he put him against the background of Bloody Nose Ridge, the most frightening feature on earth to 9,000 Marines. Lea's notes tell the man's story: "Last evening he came down out of the hills. Told to get some sleep, he found a shell crater and slumped into it. He's awake now. First light has given his gray face eerie color. He left the States 31 months ago. He was wounded in his first campaign. He has had tropical diseases. There is no food or water in the hills, except what you carry. He half-sleeps at night and gouges Japs out of holes all day. Two thirds of his company has been killed or wounded but he is still standing. So he will return to attack this morning. How much can a human being endure?"[31]

The Japanese defense of Peleliu did nothing to halt the American advance on the home islands, nothing to weaken American resolve to fight to the finish. Neither did taking Peleliu put America closer to winning the war. Peleliu received almost no news coverage while it was being fought and today it is a forgotten battle. All attention was on MacArthur's invasion of the Philippines and Eisenhower's drive to the Siegfried Line. But Peleliu, as Sledge says, must not be forgotten. One of the most murderously fought battles in all of history, it is a frightening reminder of the debasing consequences of unrestrained war, war fought without let up or conscience.

As Eugene Sledge's ship pulled away from Peleliu, with fighting still raging in the smoking canyons of the Umurbrogol, he felt the island pulling him back, like it was some tremendous magnet. He was terrified his regiment would be ordered to return at the very last minute to stop some unexpected counterattack or some threat to the airfield. But perhaps he felt the pull of the place because he had left some part of himself there, never to be retrieved. It wasn't innocence, but it was everything he had known as youth.

That was nothing, however, compared to the unbearable price his 1st Marines paid for a worthless strip of coral in one of the most remote places on earth.

The Return

O N   S E P T E M B E R   1 5 ,   1 9 4 4 ,   T H E   M O R N I N G   the Old Breed went over the reef at Peleliu, General Douglas MacArthur's troops landed on the strategically important island of Morotai, northwest of New Guinea, taking it easily. This gave MacArthur a forward airbase to hit Leyte, the midrib of the Philippines. All the while, Marc Mitscher's Task Force 38 hammered the Philippine island of Luzon, along with Formosa and Okinawa, shattering Japanese airpower in the area. MacArthur was now ready to strike. The invasion plan brought together the two great Pacific offenses—MacArthur's forces advancing from the South Pacific up the coast of New Guinea and Nimitz's forces advancing from Tarawa across the Central Pacific. The U.S. Third Fleet, commanded by Bull Halsey, was the most awesome naval force ever assembled. It would act as a shield, keeping the Japanese Navy away from the assault force—MacArthur's Sixth Army, 200,000 men strong under Lieutenant General Walter Krueger. Providing close support, and putting the troops ashore, would be the job of "MacArthur's Navy," Admiral Thomas Kinkaid's smaller Seventh Fleet of old battleships and small carriers.

The Americans landed on Leyte on October 20, 1944, the culmination, for MacArthur, of a long offensive that had begun 2,500 miles away and sixteen months

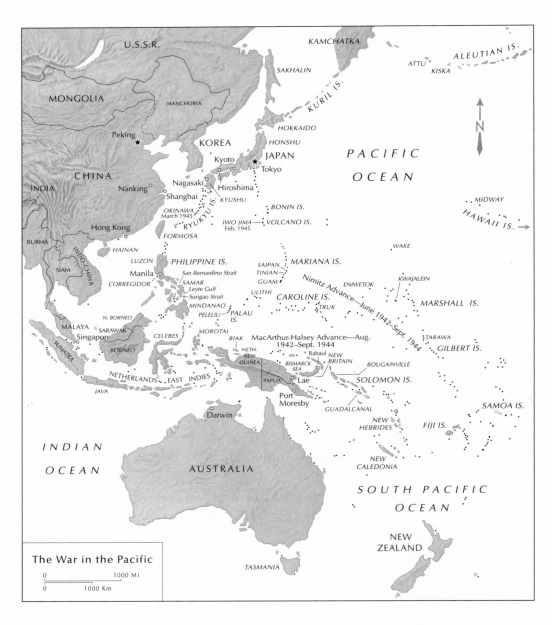

The War in the Pacific

0   1000 Mi

0   1000 Km

ago in New Guinea. Now, finally, he was closing in on the heart of Japan's vast empire. Six hundred vessels brought the Sixth Army to Leyte. Just after the first waves hit Red Beach, General MacArthur, wearing his Philippine field marshal's cap, sunglasses, and freshly pressed khakis, stepped into knee-deep water and walked toward the beach, two and a half years after he had left Bataan. Standing in a rainstorm, holding a

GENERAL DOUGLAS MACARTHUR RETURNS TO THE PHILIPPINES. VICE-
ADMIRAL THOMAS C. KINKAID IS STANDING TO MACARTHUR'S RIGHT (SC).

microphone, he made an announcement: "People of the Philippines, I have returned.
. . . Rally to me. Let the indomitable spirit of Bataan and Corregidor lead. . . . For your
homes and hearths, strike! For future generations of your sons and daughters, strike!
In the name of your sacred dead, strike!"

General Yamashita, the Japanese commander on Leyte, said that had he known
that MacArthur himself was coming ashore he would have formed a suicide squad and
killed him.[1]

THE BATTLE FOR LEYTE GULF

More men went ashore on the first day of the Leyte invasion than landed in
Normandy on D-Day. Meeting unexpectedly light resistance, Krueger's troops swept
inland, captured a vital airfield, and put bulldozers to work preparing two airstrips, one

long enough to land the medium bombers and long-range fighters so sorely needed from Kenney's air force. But before this airstrip could be prepared, the navies of Imperial Japan and the United States met head-on in the greatest sea battle ever fought.

For Japan, the Battle for Leyte Gulf was to be the decisive engagement of a war that had turned disastrously against it. It was Japan's last chance to protect its sea route to its southern empire, through the broad South China Sea, and avoid what Emperor Hirohito called "merciless peace terms."

The Imperial Fleet had lost most of its carrier strength, but its commanders were confident that its battleship and cruiser force was still formidable enough to deliver one perfectly coordinated and devastating blow. When the American invasion force hit Leyte, the Japanese set in motion a huge and highly complex counteroffensive. The key to it was a diversionary move, one that counted on Admiral Halsey's notorious aggressiveness. Admiral Jisaburo Ozawa's carrier force, with the decks of the flattops almost empty, would lure Halsey's fleet away from the Leyte beaches. At that point, two strike forces of battleships and cruisers would steam into Leyte Gulf, one from the north through San Bernardino Strait, the other from the south, through Surigao Strait. This giant pincer movement would converge on the Leyte beachhead and annihilate the smaller American fleet that was covering the beachhead, isolating the troops that had already landed. It was a desperate gamble—an oceanic banzai charge.

Vice Admiral Takeo Kurita's attack force, the strongest to be deployed, was the first to arrive in the Philippines. Two American submarines, *Darter* and *Dace,* sighted it heading for the San Bernardino Strait on the morning of October 23 and closed for the kill, sinking two heavy cruisers, one of them Kurita's flagship. But they could not stop the gigantic fleet, which included five battleships, among them two of the most powerful in the world, *Musashi* and *Yamato.* Switching his flag to *Yamato,* the shaken but implacable Kurita headed for San Bernardino Strait.

When Halsey got word of the fast-approaching Japanese fleet, he launched his Hellcat fighters against it in what turned into a furious, day-long air battle. The Japanese got the worst of it. One of their land-based bombers destroyed the light carrier *Princeton,* but Kurita lost the massive *Musashi,* which was ripped apart by nineteen torpedo and seventeen bomb hits and finally rolled over and sank, taking with her half her crew of 2,300 men. Even more damaging was the loss of 150 planes, nine of them to fighter ace David McCampbell, punishing evidence of massive American air superiority. As night approached, Kurita broke off the engagement, not wanting to risk *Yamato* and his other heavy ships, all of which were pounded in the narrow San Bernardino Strait.

As Kurita steamed west to get beyond range of Halsey's carrier planes, Halsey received a report on the afternoon of October 24 that Ozawa's decoy fleet had been spotted 300 miles to the north. He set out after it at dawn of the next day with his entire Third Fleet, regarding the enemy carriers as his most important prey. In one of the most controversial decisions of the Pacific war, he failed to leave even a picket destroyer to guard San Bernardino Strait. Nor did he tell Kinkaid that he was leaving the pass uncovered. Halsey would say later that he was confident Kurita had no more fight in him.

He was almost right. Kurita had begun to withdraw, but goaded by his fellow commanders, who questioned his resolve, he reversed course and moved to strike the Leyte beachhead. As he passed through San Bernardino Strait on the night of October 24–25 to join the attack force heading up from the south through Surigao Strait, the Japanese believed they were about to win the most momentous naval victory of the war. They might have, had not the American commanders pulled off what Halsey called "one of the prettiest ambushes in naval history."[2]

As darkness fell on the 24th, Admiral Kinkaid's flotilla of PT boats took station just outside Surigao Strait, where Ferdinand Magellan had sailed into the Philippines in 1521. His destroyers lined the thirty-five miles of the strait itself. At the end of the narrow passage Kinkaid placed six old battleships in a line. Five of them had been sunk or damaged at Pearl Harbor, repaired, modernized, and sent to avenge themselves. The cruisers were with them.

About midnight, a PT boat signaled that the Japanese were approaching the strait. In the darkness, the PTs got two hits but the Japanese steamed on, in double column, tearing through the passage at twenty knots. The destroyers held their fire; battleships and cruisers were silent, hidden by the darkness, in the dead calm sea.

About 3:00 A.M. on the 25th, Rear Admiral Jessie B. Oldendorf, commander of Kinkaid's six battleships, ordered "Commence firing!" The destroyers steamed toward the enemy ships and fired their torpedoes. Incandescent flashes lighted Surigao Strait as the torpedoes struck home. The cruisers, ranged on opposite sides of the trap, opened fire on the Japanese caught between them. Colored recognition lights flashed as the confused Japanese, thinking their own ships had attacked them, tried to stop the storm of steel. The lights gave the American cruisers splendid targets—until both the Japanese ships and the U.S. destroyers laid down smoke screens. The one U.S. destroyer crippled by Japanese fire lurched in the smoke, while the others withdrew and opened fire with their five-inch batteries.

Confusion did not alter the enemy's determination: the ships plunged on through

Surigao Strait, firing wildly and inaccurately. This gave Admiral Oldendorf an opportunity granted to few naval commanders. He "crossed the T" of the Japanese battle line—an action where one fleet advancing in column forms a vertical bar and thus can fire only its forward-pointing guns, while the attackers form a horizontal bar (the top of the T) and bring their broadsides to bear, annihilating the opposition.

One after the other the Japanese ships reached a narrow part of the strait and turned, presenting perfect targets. The six American battleships, only twelve miles away, did not even have to shift the range of their radar-controlled guns. Ship after Japanese ship became a torch in the night. The cruisers and destroyers sank the remainder as they fled, leaving only wreckage and long streaks of flaming oil. The southern half of the Japanese pincer was broken. "Silence followed," wrote Admiral Samuel Eliot Morison, "to honor the passing of the tactics which had so long been foremost in naval warfare." All the great naval actions of the past three centuries, including Trafalgar and Jutland, "had been fought by classic line-of-battle tactics. In the unearthly silence that followed the roar of Oldendorf's 14-inch and 16-inch guns in Surigao Strait, one could imagine the ghosts of all great admirals, from Raleigh and De Ruyter to Togo and Jellicoe, standing at attention to salute the passing of the kind of naval warfare that they all understood. For in those opening minutes of the morning watch of 25 October 1944, Battle Line became as obsolete as the row-galley tactics of Salamis and Syracuse."[3]

Early the next morning, Rear Admiral Clifton Sprague, in charge of a flotilla of small escort carriers and destroyers, sighted the tall masts of Kurita's battleships coming over the western horizon, heading for Leyte Gulf, where the beaches were full of ammunition, food, and military hardware. Sprague's escort carriers—lightly armed, converted merchant ships carrying only eighteen to twenty-six planes—were directly in Kurita's path, but were no match for the four battleships and seven cruisers that hove into view.

Kinkaid, and later Nimitz, at Pearl Harbor, sent urgent messages to Halsey asking for help, but Halsey broke off action with Ozawa too late to help Sprague. Realizing he was on his own, Sprague launched every plane he had against the steel Goliaths boring in on him. The Japanese fleet steamed straight on, paying little attention to the four destroyer escorts and three destroyers that laid down smoke screens, darting in and out, matching their small fire against the thunderous volleys of the battleships, in what Kinkaid called the "most daring and most effective action" of the entire war.[4] Heavy Japanese cruisers sank one American escort carrier and hit others with crushing fire, while battleships put down two destroyers and one destroyer escort.

But just as Kurita seemed on the brink of a great victory he turned and headed back toward San Bernardino Strait after losing his third heavy cruiser from air and destroyer attacks. "At 09.25 my mind was occupied with dodging torpedoes," Sprague recalls, "when near the bridge I heard one of the signalmen yell, 'Goddamit, boys, they're getting away!' I could not believe my eyes, but it looked as if the whole Japanese Fleet was indeed retiring. However, it took a whole series of reports from circling planes to convince me. And still I could not get the fact to soak into my battle-numbed brain. At best, I had expected to be swimming by this time." [5]

In the smoke and chaos of battle, Kurita believed he was also facing carriers from Halsey's fleet, for he had been engaging over 400 fighters and torpedo planes, the pilots making dry runs after they ran out of ammunition. Kurita was also convinced, after intercepting and misreading Kinkaid's messages to Halsey, that Halsey was fast approaching with more heavy carriers, and that he would block San Bernardino Strait. Sprague's escort carriers, their destroyer screens, and their brave aviators had stopped what Admiral Morison describes as "the most powerful gunfire force which Japan had sent to sea since the Battle of Midway." [6]

After mauling the Japanese carrier fleet, Halsey steamed back to the waters off Leyte. His vanguard arrived at 1:30 P.M. on the 25th, and his planes joined those of the Seventh Fleet in harrying the fleeing enemy. One more carrier was sent down, and on that evening a submarine made a final kill, a heavy cruiser, completing the destruction of almost the entire Japanese naval force. The official score stood: four carriers, three battleships, ten cruisers, and eleven destroyers sunk—in actual tonnage, more than a quarter of all Japanese losses since Pearl Harbor. A Navy communiqué declared that "this might turn out to be among the decisive battles of modern times." It was. After the three-day Battle of Leyte Gulf, the Japanese Navy was finished.

But just as the battle was concluding, the enemy pulled a wildly unexpected move. After Kurita retreated, several wounded U.S. escort carriers were hit by a new and terrifying weapon, the kamikaze corps. Kamikaze, which means "divine winds," refers to the typhoons that twice destroyed the fleets of Mongol invaders in the thirteenth century. The new suicide planes, armed with heavy bombs, damaged three vessels and sank one.

"Then in succeeding weeks they attacked our ships in Leyte Gulf," Admiral Kinkaid recalls. "Every day I could see the faces from the skippers down to the lowest seamen, getting longer and longer because they just couldn't stop the kamikazes. . . . As they approached, one plane would drop behind, as though there was something wrong with the engine; as the larger group went over the ships, all the antiaircraft would be trained on them, and then the plane that had dropped behind would come in in a dive. The kamikazes had a lot of tricks like that. . . . They did a great deal of . . . damage."[7]

After the Battle for Leyte Gulf both King and Nimitz were convinced that Halsey had made a critical mistake in leaving open San Bernardino Strait. Another commander might have been removed, but Halsey was too important to the cause, and he had MacArthur's complete support. Overhearing a group of Navy men take Halsey to task at an officer's dinner for "abandoning us" while he went after the decoy fleet, MacArthur slammed his fist on the table and roared, "That's enough! Leave the Bull alone! He's still a fighting admiral in my book."[8]

The Fight for Leyte

On Leyte, MacArthur's troops made slow progress against enemy forces using the terrain to maximum advantage in the vast wild interior, despite the fact that Yamashita had planned to meet the Americans in force on Luzon, not here. "Contrary to the views of the Army and Navy General Staffs, I agreed to the showdown battle of Leyte," the Emperor said after the war, "thinking that if we attacked at Leyte and America flinched, then we would probably be able to find room to negotiate."[9] The Japanese pushed in reinforcements from neighboring islands, increasing their garrison from 23,000 to almost 70,000 troops. These troops fought with gritty determination for nearly every inch of ground in the rice paddies and mountains of Leyte. The battle was waged in some of the most horrible natural conditions imaginable. In addition to the difficult terrain, during the fighting, Leyte was hit by three typhoons and an earthquake.

Artillery officer Linwood Crider, twenty-three years old at the time, describes the nearly two-month-long battle for Leyte—like Peleliu, one of the largely forgotten struggles of the Pacific war:

> I WAS A YOUNG ARTILLERY OFFICER and, although I had been in the South Pacific for a while, I had not participated in an operation of this magnitude. The artillery group that I was assigned to was part of the XXIV Corps Artillery. For the Leyte operation we were to provide support to the 96th and 7th Infantry Divisions. . . .
>
> Leyte is a little over 100 miles in length and forty-five miles at its widest point. . . . We entered Leyte Gulf during the night of October 19 and . . . landed on the eastern side of the island just north of the little town of Dulag.

We landed almost unopposed and secured a beachhead. . . . Our landing had been so easy I thought perhaps we were being lured into some kind of trap. . . .

For the next three days we moved south and then I started to earn my money. First of all, the rains came. It rained between thirty and forty inches the first month we were there. Later on the rains increased. It rained over sixteen inches in one day. With the water came lots of mud. It was a special kind of mud. On the surface it was very slick, but once you sank in, it seemed to have an unusual adhesive quality. This mud also did not smell good, probably because it contained a large amount of rotting organic matter.

The worst part came at night. That's when you had to dig a hole to sleep in. Even though you quickly covered the hole with a poncho the water seeped in.

And with the water came the leeches. It wasn't unusual to find a dozen of these little bloodsuckers on you in the morning. . . .

On the night of October 24th . . . we began to hear distant cannonading and could see the flash of big gun fire being reflected off low-lying clouds. . . . The firing increased until it was almost a continuous rumble. It now seemed apparent that a significant naval engagement was taking place off the southeast coast of Leyte. The sound of this gunfire continued until about 0200 the next morning. We had no way of knowing its outcome. . . . The next day we learned [from a downed Navy pilot] that "Kinkaid had kicked their ass. . . ."

During the next few days we continued the push to the west. . . . There is a ridge of mountains running down the center of Leyte that go up to about 4,500 feet. This is extremely rugged terrain. It is covered with dense tropical growth. When you drop an artillery shell into growth like this it seems to get totally lost. . . .

The whole month of November was a miserable time. [Other Army units] had secured the north end of the island but had run into the same problem that we did when trying to push down the west coast to Ormoc. Ormoc was the major town on the west coast and it was through here that the Japanese reinforcements were being brought in from other islands in the Philippines.

The Japanese strategy for the defense of Leyte had also changed during this period. Their initial strategy was to save their best for the defense of Luzon, which was politically more significant than Leyte. They now decided to throw everything available into the defense of Leyte. Air strikes from Luzon were increased and the first kamikaze attacks on the supply ships in Leyte harbor were initiated. The Japanese called this new offensive the "Wa Operation." . . .

It was in our section that [they] launched . . . the Wa Operation. Their objective was to recapture all of the airstrips on eastern Leyte and to bring their planes to these strips to support this offensive. What a stupid thing to do. These airstrips were a sea of mud and therefore worthless.

Some of the things that happened next were almost unbelievable. The Japanese staged their only airborne operation of the war. It began on Luzon, where they loaded about 500 of their best troops onto air transports. They came in to drop these troops in the vicinity of one of the airstrips near Barauen. As the paratroopers floated down they were literally cut to shreds by the antiaircraft and field artillery units. . . .

At about this same time, something even more unbelievable happened. There was a cavalry attack on one of our artillery positions. . . . The horses were of the small, Asiatic variety. There must have been about fifty of them killed. Their riders were dead as well.

The Japanese also launched an offensive which included a heavy mortar attack on our position. An incoming mortar round landed about twenty yards to our front. . . . The people who were standing near me were all hit, including myself. The next round was closer and it got us all. I knew immediately that the company commander and platoon sergeant were dead. My left eye filled with blood so I had a problem assessing any further damage. I lay there for a minute, sort of numbed by what had happened. It was getting dark. I then became aware of someone trying to move me. My left leg hurt and was bleeding. A medic cut

AMERICAN MORTAR SQUAD ON LEYTE (SC).

my pant leg and found a piece of shrapnel sticking in my fibula. He pulled it out and put on a compress to stop the bleeding.

Just when I was thinking that my situation wasn't that bad, I felt a pain in my lower abdomen. The medic took a quick look with a flashlight. I had been gut-shot. . . .

I was quite sure I was going to die. Morning did come though and I was still alive. Three others were not. I somehow got loaded onto the back of a weapons carrier and made the bumpy ride to the battalion aid station. The doctor took a quick look at me and tagged me to go to the field hospital. . . .

My seventh day I was allowed to go back to my unit for "light duty." It was now approaching the middle of December. The 77th Division had assaulted Ormoc and taken it. The Japanese on Leyte were now cut off from receiving outside support from the other islands in the Philippines. . . .

I had about a dozen letters from my parents and my fiancée. . . . We had decided to wait until after the war to get married. I read the last letter from her first. Her opening paragraph began, "When you read this I'm sure you'll understand." . . . Here I lay on some far, distant battlefield and all the while she was with another man. She said since she hadn't heard from me for such a long time she assumed that I had lost interest in her. . . .

On the 15th of December General MacArthur declared that Leyte was secured and the fighting had ended. It's too bad he wasn't there to see what was going on because the fighting wasn't over. There were still thousands of Japanese soldiers on Leyte and they did not plan to surrender. It wasn't until [March] that the Japanese on Leyte were neutralized. [Between Christmas Day and the end of the campaign the Americans killed more than 27,000 Japanese.]

By mid-January . . . we got some good news. We were no longer part of MacArthur's command and therefore would not be going to Luzon. Our destination was Okinawa, another place I had never heard of.

For his service in World War II—and the Korean War—Linwood Crider received twelve military decorations and awards, including a Purple Heart, a Bronze Star, and a Presidential Citation. "All my awards were for merit," he says today. "I got none for valor. I am not a hero." [10]

Sixty-five thousand Japanese soldiers died to hold Leyte, taking with them 15,500 Americans, dead or wounded. Many of the Americans fell in the weeks after

MacArthur, in a publicity stunt typical of him, declared the island secured, to the amazement of Crider and other American troops. The historian of the 11th Airborne describes what MacArthur cavalierly called a mop-up operation. "Through mud and rain, over treacherous, rain-swollen gorges, through thick jungle growth, over slippery, narrow, root-tangled, steep foot trails, the Angels . . . [as 11th Airborne troops called themselves] pushed west to clear the Leyte mountain range of its tenacious defenders. It was bitter, exhausting, rugged fighting—physically, the most terrible we were ever to know." General Robert L. Eichelberger, commander of the U.S. Eighth Army, which relieved the Sixth Army on Leyte on Christmas Day, remarked that "if there is another war, I recommend that the military, and the correspondents . . . drop the phrase 'mopping up' from their vocabularies. It is not a good enough phrase to die for." [11]

LIBERATION

Before the Americans left Leyte their dead and wounded were replaced by new draftees whose average age was nineteen. They went to Luzon.

The first landings were made at Lingayen Gulf on January 9, 1945, on the very spot where General Homma's troops had landed on the fifteenth day of the war. Despite furious attacks by waves of kamikazes, which sank or damaged forty ships of the invasion armada on its way to the beachhead, MacArthur landed a force of 68,000 men by nightfall. It would be the biggest American land engagement of the Pacific war and one the Japanese could not win, having lost so many troops, planes, and ships in trying to stop MacArthur on Leyte. "Now it is their turn to quake!" MacArthur remarked. [12]

In all, MacArthur brought 280,000 men to Luzon. Lying in wait for him but scattered widely on the island were 275,000 Japanese under General Yamashita, the largest enemy army the Americans faced in the Pacific. The stage was set, said *Life* magazine, for "the first large-scale slugging match with the Japanese army." [13]

Yamashita knew that American power made resistance at the beaches futile. His only option was to fight a protracted and bloody delaying action, a battle he was confident of winning. "In Singapore, when I negotiated the surrender there with [General Sir Arthur] Percival, the only words I spoke to him were, 'Yes or no?' I intend to ask MacArthur the same question." [14] The "Tiger of Malaya" withdrew most of his forces to mountain strongholds in the east, opening the way for MacArthur's drive to Manila. Yamashita would sacrifice the capital to win the battle in the badlands.

The first big fight carried the Allies across the Agno River, over low hills, paralleling the gulf, and out onto the great plain leading to Manila, 110 miles southeast of Lingayen. Here American tanks could make use of the open terrain and fine roads.

On January 28, a band of handpicked men from the Army's Sixth Ranger Battalion made a daring raid deep into Japanese-held territory to a prison camp at Cabanatuan. With the aid of Filipino guerrillas, the Rangers freed 513 American and British POWs, including many survivors of the Bataan Death March. MacArthur would soon learn that only a third of the men he had left behind in Luzon had survived. After seeing the wretched condition of the prisoners at Cabanatuan, and learning from his intelligence officers that other POWs and internees were dying of starvation, MacArthur called in the commander of the 1st Cavalry Division, Major General Vernon D. Mudge. "Go to Manila," he ordered. "Go around the Nips, bounce off the Nips, but go to Manila. Free the internees and Santo Tomás."[15] Santo Tomás was the camp where 3,700 American men, women, and children, including the Army nurses of Bataan and Corregidor, had been interned for more than three years.

Mudge assembled two small "flying columns" of infantry and armor, a "modern version of a mounted cavalry unit," and sped for the capital, with Marine Corps dive-bombers covering his advance.[16] Along the way, jubilant Filipinos waved and shouted at them, handing them flowers, eggs, and beer. Forty-eight hours later, on the evening of February 3, they reached the city limits. The *New York Times* reported their entrance into the city:

> THE FIRST TWO FORCES had to fight their way from house to house, in the face of fires and demolitions and through mined streets, to the north bank of the Pasig River, which cuts the city in two. After they crossed the stream in a fleet of amphibious trucks and moved into southern Manila, they were met with steady machine-gun and mortar fire from upper floors and from concrete pill-boxes placed at important intersections by the Japanese, who were still clinging to "Intramuros," the old walled section of the city on the Pasig's lower bank. . . .
>
> Immediately on their entrance into the capital, a flying squadron of cavalrymen sped to the gates of the Santo Tomás internment center where 3,700 persons, mostly women and children, were being detained. The troopers pushed through machine-gun nests and sniper fire up to the camp grounds and then fought from room to room to clean out the Japanese. Other forces, meanwhile, moved against burning Bilibid Prison, where 1,100 war prisoners and civilian internees were saved from flames.[17]

"Tanks were crashing at the gate," one of the Bataan nurses described the liberation of Santo Tomás. "I happened to be in the front building with a room above the front entrance. Tanks rolled to the front door." But in the darkness, no one could tell whose tanks they were. Then a soldier pulled himself out of one of the tanks and said simply, "Hello, folks." This was it. These were Americans. Pandemonium broke loose. The hysterical prisoners mobbed the soldiers of the 1st Cavalry, shouting, screaming, weeping. "The men in the tanks looked like giants to us because we were all so emaciated and thin," said Army nurse Martha Dworsky. "We were all laughing and crying, hanging out the windows, shouting and screaming and waving. It was a wild scene of joy and happiness," another nurse recalled.[18]

With the liberators was a familiar figure to the prisoners. "Carl Mydans. My God! It's Carl Mydans," cried a woman inmate as *Life* photographer Carl Mydans turned a flashlight on his face to identify himself.[19] He had covered the battles of Bataan and Corregidor, and he and his wife, Shelley, a writer for *Life*, had been cap-

ENTERING MANILA (LRP).

AMERICAN NURSES LIBERATED FROM SANTO TOMÁS, MANILA (SC).

tured and interned in Santo Tomás for more than nine months before being sent to Shanghai, where they were freed in 1943 as part of a prisoner exchange. "I was picked up bodily," Mydans dispatched his editors on the morning after the liberation of Santo Tomás, "full camera pack, canteen belt, and all, and carried on the hands of the internees over their heads . . ."[20]

Outside the main building, Mydans found a sight he had dreamed about many times. "In the brilliant light . . . stood three Japanese in officers' uniforms, ringed by soldiers pointing guns at them." The next day, he learned that every one of the prisoners was suffering from malnutrition. Most of them were so emaciated he did not recognize them. And they had been indoctrinated into a state of docility. "Even with husky welcoming Americans on the main gate, the internees would not venture past the swale fence which marked the out-of-bounds area."

On Sunday morning the American flag was raised over Santo Tomás. The whole camp shouted and cheered as the flag went up. Then someone started singing "God Bless America" and everyone joined in. "I have never heard it sung as it was sung that day," said Mydans. "I have never heard people singing 'God Bless America' and weeping openly. And they have never seen soldiers—hard-bitten youngsters such as make up the 1st Cavalry—stand unashamed and weep with them."

Later on, an American sergeant seemed confused when, leading the Japanese prison administrators away from the camp, a group of recently released children shouted to him, "Make them bow. Make them bow."[21]

By early February, MacArthur had more troops on Luzon. Landings had been made at Subic Bay on the west and at Nasugbu on the south. From both points, Allied forces were racing inland. By February 4, two American columns, including the 11th Airborne, led by General Robert Eichelberger, were within fifteen miles of Manila, MacArthur's spiritual home, the city where his mother had died, where he had courted his wife, and where his son, Arthur, had spent the first four years of his life. "We were ready for the dash on Manila," General Eichelberger recalled. "I pressed forward with the infantry, and my headquarters was set up in what had once been the annex of the Manila Hotel. It was a bare and looted building, but the view was just the way I remembered it. And just as beautiful.

"I could see the city of Manila gleaming whitely in the sunshine. I could see Corregidor, and the hook of the Cavite peninsula, which curves into Manila Bay . . . It was strangely like a homecoming. But soon tall plumes of smoke began to rise in Manila, and at evening the tropical sky was crimsoned by many fires. The Japanese were deliberately destroying the magical town which had been traditionally called 'the Pearl of the Orient.' "[22]

The Americans drove in from three sides—the 1st Cavalry Division from the east, the 37th from the north, and Eichelberger's forces from the south. The 1st Cavalry got into the city without much trouble, but the 11th Airborne ran into 12,500 of the 16,000 Japanese Marines that were guarding Manila and had to fight its way into the city, suffering heavy casualties. Up to this point, the Japanese had fought mostly a delaying action: now from the buildings and streets of the capital they put up the same unyielding resistance that Americans had encountered from New Guinea to Peleliu. "Manila was burning. The whole downtown section was smothered in roaring black billows of smoke," *Yank* correspondent H. N. Oliphant described the opening hours of the battle for the city. "The Jap shells were coming in. A sprawling wooden structure across the street got a direct hit. A Filipino girl stood beside us shaking her head. She said her father and baby brother were inside the burning building.

"A pretty, light-skinned woman, dressed in a kimono, was standing across the street. She scolded a little boy, who was pulling at her kimono. She pushed the child and yelled, 'Get away from me, you little Jap bastard!' "[23]

It was probably her own child, his father Japanese, and she did not want to be seen with him for fear of being branded an enemy collaborator. One American soldier, Fred Nixon, was walking along a street with a priest when they passed a procession of men carrying small coffins. "Father Rogers told us that the caskets contained the bodies of Filipino children whose fathers were Japanese. When it looked like we were winning, their families killed them so that they would not appear to be Japanese collaborators. He said the church could not condone the killings, but the children deserved a Christian funeral."[24]

These women feared reprisals for horrible acts of barbarity committed against their people by the Japanese. When Lester Tenney escaped for a short period from Camp O'Donnell after the Bataan Death March, he went into the hills with a small band of Filipino guerrillas. From a hilltop overlooking a village, he witnessed a group of Filipino women being tortured by the Japanese. "The women were tied, with their legs spread, to the stilts that supported their cottages. The Japanese put sticks of dynamite into their vaginas and started asking them questions that we couldn't hear. Then they lit the dynamite and within a matter of three minutes there were loud explosions and I could actually see the parts of bodies flying through the air."[25]

In some of the worst fighting of the war, close-quarter urban warfare akin to that at Stalingrad, Manila, a city of 800,000 people, was utterly destroyed. Nearly 100,000 Filipino civilians were killed in this urban holocaust, many of them in a succession of savage reprisals by a band of Japanese sailors who were determined, against Yamashita's orders, to hold the city or destroy it and die. "Hospitals were set afire after the patients had been strapped to their beds. The corpses of males were mutilated, females of all ages were raped before they were slain, and babies' eyes were gouged out and smeared on walls like jelly," wrote one historian.[26] During the entire war, the only Allied cities to suffer greater human and physical devastation were Warsaw and Stalingrad.

The Japanese fought almost to the last soldier from the sewers of the city, where they were slaughtered by American troops with grenades and flamethrowers. After walking through his ruined city, the Filipino journalist Carlos Romulo wrote: "Wherever I went I felt like a ghost hunting its way in a vanished world."[27] When

MacArthur returned to Manila at the end of February to reestablish the civilian government, he was emotionally overcome by the plunder and slaughter and could not complete his speech, ending with the Lord's Prayer.

THE LOS BAÑOS RAID

Three weeks after the liberation of Santo Tomás, MacArthur ordered an attack on a Japanese internment camp at Los Baños, forty-two miles southeast of Manila, where 2,200 American and European civilians and POWs were slowly starving. "It was a complicated problem," said General Eichelberger, who took part in the planning of the raid:

> LOS BAÑOS WAS ON THE SOUTHERN TIP of shallow Laguna de Bay, and thus some fifty miles behind enemy lines. It was estimated, and accurately, there were between eight and fifteen thousand enemy troops available for counterattack within four hours march of the camp. Past history had given us reason to fear that the Japanese camp guards, if they knew attack was imminent, might execute their prisoners and thus clean the slate. . . .
>
> Trusted guerrilla spies were sent into the area. Five days before the operation they brought back a gentleman named Peter Miles, who had recently escaped from the camp and gone into hiding. Miles had been an engineer in the Philippines before the war, and his careful information was invaluable. Miles drew up an exact map of the camp. . . . He also reported on the physical condition of the internees and accurately estimated the number of sick and helpless who would require evacuation by litter.
>
> All of the planning was highly secret, and few of the troops involved knew anything about their mission until they were plucked from their positions near Fort McKinley under cover of darkness and moved to the positions from which they would make their attacks. Fifty-nine ungainly amphtracs . . . moved noisily into Parañaque from the north. Nine C-47 planes . . . landed on Nichols Field [in Manila] and picked their way hopefully along the pitted runways. A company of paratroopers moved to Nichols Field and slept under the wings of the planes.
>
> [Joseph Swing, commander of the] 11th Airborne, had planned, for the sake of surprise and safety of the internees, one of the oddest expeditions in military history. It was to include a ground force advance, an amphibious expedition, and

GIs with Filipino guerrillas (SC).

a parachute drop. A great deal of faith, too, had to be placed on a reconnaissance platoon [of American soldiers and Filipino guerrillas, led by Lieutenant George Skau]. They departed in bancas [small boats] two days before the operation and, after reaching the southern shore, went into hiding.[28]

Luis M. Burris, commander of Dog Battery, an artillery company with the 11th Airborne, was with the amphibious tractors. He had been told that intelligence reports indicated that the Japanese planned to kill the prisoners thirty minutes before the scheduled attack on the camp. "A mistake of seconds can mean disaster for the prisoners," he told his men. A cousin of one of his men was in the camp.

They started off for Los Baños at midnight and headed into landlocked Laguna de Bay for the seven-and-a-half-mile trip. The skippers of the amtracs were all amateurs, and most of them were confused and scared, unsure they could navigate the lake, on a moonless light, by compass. Burris tells the story from this point:

AT THE ORDER OF "CRANK UP," a noise like a bellowing bull came out of each of those 59 diesel exhaust pipes. The roar could be heard for ten miles. None of us had considered the noise of the amtrac convoy. . . . If this noise alerted the Japanese, would they have time to react? . . . One thing we could assume was that our secrecy was blown right out of those amtrac tail pipes.

We didn't need further proof, but large fires crackled on the shoreline where entire villages cheered us. At a distance of half a mile we saw villagers dancing and waving flaming sticks as if the war was over. They had to know about the raid many hours before in order to have gathered wood for the fires. . . . Were we blundering into a trap? . . . Our adrenaline was pumping so fast we were intoxicated.

As dawn broke, they began to search the skies from the shoreline of the lake for the paratroopers, who were to be dropped right into the camp.

NOTHING WAS THERE. What had gone wrong? Without the jumpers, could we get into camp before the guards shot the prisoners? Had Skau's platoon been able to get to their positions . . . ?

Then some specks were steadier and grew larger. We realized they were our planes. . . . Lt. John Ringler popped the first chute, followed by another. Then the whole sky was full of silk, spilling out of nine transports. We could hear rifle fire of the infiltrators on signal of the first parachute opening.

The amtracs hit the sand, and we headed, as fast as we could go, toward the center of the camp.

As they did, the reconnaissance platoon began killing Japanese sentries, and the paratroopers began mowing down the startled camp guards, who had just started doing their morning calisthenics. The job of the men in the amtracs was to round up the prisoners and get them back across the lake to safety. Burris continues the story:

THE FIRST AMTRAC, WITH . . . MY PARTY, came to a halt in the center of the camp. Prisoners were all out of their barracks milling about in confusion.

It took a short time for them to realize we were Americans. The uniforms had changed so much over the several years they had been locked up. Then came the surge of emotion for prayers answered. Prisoners just stood with arms to the heavens or hands over their faces covering the outpouring of tears. Some were on their knees praying for gratitude. . . . Many of the adults knew of the planned execution, but kept the information from the children and others who would be too upset.

A hardened criminal would have cried.

A group of 2,147 prisoners is a lot of people. They all thought the ordeal was over with no reason to hurry. They already had about as much emotion as they could stand at one time. There was no point in trying to scare them with the idea of 10,000 Japanese troops just over the hill.

We told the prisoners to throw what clothes they needed into two bags and start walking toward the beach.[29]

The amtracs carried the old, the sick, and women with children to the lake, a mile and a half away; everyone else walked. From the lakeshore, all internees were taken by the amtracs to a town across the bay. "When we got to the beach, the Japanese started to fire," recalls Margaret Nash, a Navy nurse who was holding a newborn infant in her arms. "I covered the baby with a great big hat and I lay down on the sand over her. Later I ran across the beach with her and got into another amtrac."[30]

The entire operation lasted only four hours. Among those liberated were 1,589 Americans, including Margaret Nash and eleven other Navy nurses. There were only two American soldiers killed and two wounded in the rescue. The entire Japanese garrison of 250 was killed. "It was said to be the most perfect combat operation of World War II," Burris recalled proudly. "Its success depended on teamwork and not on individual heroism. . . .

Japanese troops closed in on Los Baños the next day and slaughtered every Filipino who did not heed our warning to head for the hills. An estimated 1,500 died."[31]

Following the fall of Manila, MacArthur sent parachute and amphibious troops to capture the tunneled rock fortress of Corregidor, where General Wainwright had made his valiant stand in April 1942. On February 26 the last Japanese defenders blew themselves up inside Corregidor's labyrinthine tunnels. Four days later, and three years after his hasty departure, MacArthur stood on Corregidor and gave the order: "Hoist the colors and let no enemy ever haul them down." As Carl Mydans snapped his photograph, MacArthur turned to General Richard Sutherland and said, "This is home. I am home at last."[32]

The Japanese continued to resist violently on Luzon. More American soldiers fought on Luzon than in either North Africa or Italy, and they died in staggering numbers from enemy gunfire and disease. South of Manila, the strong Shumbu Line was shattered on March 17, trapping the Japanese in caves or forcing them to retire into the remote Sierra Madre Mountains—a malaria-infested region, much of it never thoroughly explored by Westerners. Although hard fighting was to continue in northern Luzon for the rest of the war, the essential parts of the Philippines were now firmly in American hands. It had been a tremendously costly victory in American and Filipino lives for what critics of MacArthur consider a strategically inessential objective. (Sixth Army suffered almost 38,000 casualties in the battle for Luzon, and the American and Australian navies lost 2,000 men, mostly to kamikaze attacks.) The Philippines were to be used as a staging area for attacks on Japan, but with the B-29s about to bomb Japan from the Marianas and the naval blockade of Japan tightening, the Philippine campaign, these critics argue, was unnecessary.

General Eichelberger has another view. "If we were to undertake an armed invasion of Japan—and all planning, necessarily, in 1944 looked forward to that objective—we needed the deep-water harbors, the great bases, and the excellent training areas available in those islands, which, in the main, had a friendly and loyal population. We had no knowledge of the atomic bomb; indeed, it was not until almost a year later that the first atomic bomb was exploded experimentally in New Mexico. Up until then even the scientists weren't sure it would work." [33]

After the war, MacArthur hanged the defender of Luzon, General Tomoyuki Yamashita, who had fought one of the most brilliant defensive battles of the Pacific war. On August 25, 1945, Yamashita, still holding out in northern Luzon, had chosen surrender over suicide in the hope that his execution for war crimes would save the lives of his officers and men. It was a selfless gesture, but in no way counterbalanced the atrocities he and his men had inflicted on innocent Filipinos.

The Japanese lost a staggering 400,000 men in the Philippines. At the end of the fighting on Leyte, American soldiers found a letter from a Japanese soldier to his family:

"I am exhausted. We have no food. The enemy are within 500 meters of us. Mother, my dear wife and son, I am writing this letter to you by dim candlelight. Our end is near. . . . Hundreds of pale soldiers of Japan are awaiting our glorious end and nothing else. This is a repetition of what occurred in the Solomons, New Georgia and other islands. How well are the people of Japan prepared to fight the decisive battle with the will to win?" [34]

The B-29s

THE PLANE

The French journalist Robert Guillain was in Tokyo on March 3, 1945, when he heard the news that MacArthur's forces had liberated Manila. "No Japanese," he wrote later, "would yet let himself say the forbidden words *Nippon maketa*—Japan is beaten—but one could see the thought lurking behind the wooden faces."[1] More than the fall of the Philippines, however, the firebombing raids that began a week later from the Marianas shattered hope on the home front that the war could be won.

On the morning of October 19, 1944, one day before MacArthur landed in the Philippines, Captain I. J. Galantin, skipper of the submarine *Halibut*, approached the clear green waters of Saipan with his pack of underwater raiders. Galantin had last seen Saipan in January of 1944, when his submarine was nearly sunk trying to attack a ship inside the island's anchorage. Nine months later, *Halibut* was greeted in Tanapag Harbor by a Navy band and some old friends. "The harbor had been transformed into a bustling replenishment site for our submarines with the tenders *Holland* and *Fulton* on station."

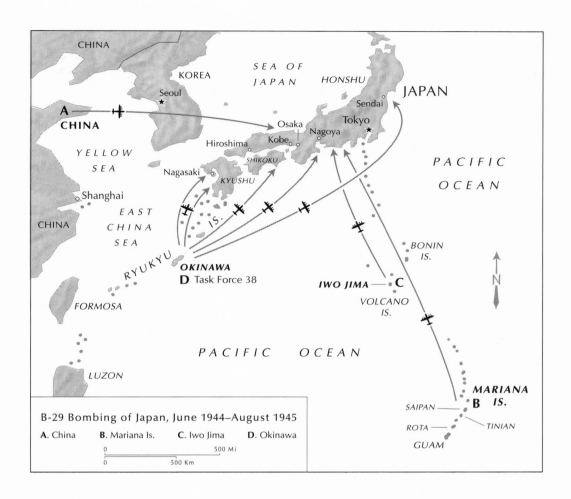

The once beautiful island had been devastated by the awesome firepower of American battleships, bombers, and artillery. There was only one major building on all of Saipan, the Navy port director's headquarters, but Galantin had never seen a busier place. It was a nonstop construction site. "The waterfront was never still. Ships were unloading; hundreds of trucks roared dustily by; new roads were being bulldozed; foundations were being poured; steam shovels and cranes groaned and screeched; huge piles of lumber grew as we watched. Everywhere soldiers and Seabees were at work with what seemed an equal number of indigenous laborers. Nightfall brought little change; powerful lights drowned the shadows until the hot sunlight poured once more over the eastern hills."[2]

The Seabees, with teams of forced Japanese labor, were transforming Saipan and neighboring Tinian and Guam into the main Pacific base for both the United States Navy and the Army Air Forces, building from jungle and shattered coral three major military cities on the Pacific highway to Tokyo. On every inch of usable space, they were hammering and bulldozing by day and night, constructing roads, hospitals, commissaries, Quonset huts, chow halls, pipelines, storage tanks, barracks, warehouses, chapels, wells, palm-thatched officers clubs, and, on Guam's highest peak, spacious homes for the Pacific Theater commander and the island commander. From their wide porches, these Navy luminaries would have splendid views of Apra Harbor, a four-mile-long anchorage that would soon be the second busiest war port in the world, behind Antwerp. One of the two airstrips being built on flat and green Tinian would be the largest in the world.

Wearing blue pants and up-tilted baseball caps, their sweating backs shining red in the blazing sunlight, Seabees were hauling, blasting, and packing down what would eventually be enough coral to fill three dams the size of Boulder Dam. Before the war, the Seabees had been sandhogs, steelworkers, dam-builders, dock-wallopers, and lumberjacks. "[These] are the men who built America's cities, dammed her rivers, strung her wires and dug her sewers," said their chief, Admiral Ben Morcell. Since the Pacific war was an air and sea struggle, fought over "a limitless, unprepared battlefield," it involved more construction than any nation had previously contemplated.[5] And the Marianas was the Seabees' biggest job yet. The islands were to be turned into a vast airdrome for the bombing and burning of Japan.

The Seabees were Navy men, and the capture of the Marianas had been a Navy operation, so the Navy got the best facilities on the islands. When Air Force personnel began arriving around the time the *Halibut* did, they had to camp out in borrowed tents along their uncompleted jungle airstrip, in open places that they hacked out of sugarcane fields with axes and trenching tools. Invited to lavish dinner parties at the hilltop homes of the admirals, Air Force commanders entertained in their tents with canned rations; and every day at dusk, pilots and navigators could be seen lingering outside Navy and Marine officers clubs, hoping to get invited in for a drink.

The Air Force arrived on Saipan in such a hurry and with such high expectations that it had no time to build anything that resembled an amenity. At this point in the war, it was the only branch of the service—with the only weapon—capable of striking the industrial heartland of Japan; and it was under pressure to set up operations and be over target Tokyo by early November.

The Seabees and aviation engineers had begun building an airfield long enough to accommodate the B-29 while the battle for Saipan was still being fought. The first

Air Force service crews would not arrive until later that summer and were assigned a few acres of sugarcane fields by the island commander. Through the miserable rainy season, the Seabees and the engineers built servicing and maintenance installations for the B-29s and their crews, which were still on training exercises back home. Working in the steaming heat, officers and enlisted men fought flies, mosquitoes, dengue fever, and die-hard Japanese soldiers who were still holding out in coral caves. With these "pioneers" was the former managing editor and longtime staff writer for *The New Yorker*, St. Clair McKelway, now serving as staff press censor and public relations officer for the 21st Bomber Command of the Twentieth Air Force, to which the B-29s in the Marianas were assigned.

Later in the war, while he was on leave in the States, McKelway attended a preview of an Army Air Forces film called *Target Tokio*, and watched, with rekindled

A TAIL GUNNER (USAAF).

emotion, the landing on Saipan of the first B-29, Brigadier General Haywood S. "Possum" Hansell's *Joltin' Josie*. Hansell, one of the most valued strategic thinkers in the Army Air Forces, had just been appointed commander of the 21st Bomber Command. "What got me," McKelway wrote after seeing the film of that October landing, "was the movement and noise of the vast mob of people who had been waiting for the airplane for some hours and who, as it landed, moved toward it across the base with the happy, fluttering movement of a crowd going into a baseball park. . . . They had been waiting for this moment, actually, for days and weeks and even months. . . . The sound track for the movie was good and accurate—the noises made by a joyful bunch of men—but it didn't pick up one voice in that crowd which I still remember, the voice of a grease-monkey staff sergeant who shouted over and over, above the racket, as the B-29 people moved across the coral rubble toward the new landing strip and the idling B-29, 'Look at 'er, look at 'er, look at 'er!' "[4]

The B-29 was a gigantic leap forward in aviation technology. It was the longest, widest, heaviest airplane in the world, bigger, faster, and more formidable than its formidable predecessor, the B-17 Flying Fortress. Its 2,200-horsepower engines were the most powerful yet in aviation history. It carried the biggest bomb load of any plane built, ten tons, four tons more than the B-17. Its top speed of 357 miles per hour was fifty-five faster than the B-17. And its range of 3,800 miles with a full bomb load was double that of the B-17. It was a sixty-ton destruction machine capable of flying more than sixteen hours nonstop when fully loaded. Unlike all other aircraft, it had pressurized crew compartments, and a pressurized tube—a crawl space—connecting the front and rear sections of the plane. At altitudes up to 40,000 feet, in minus 50 degree temperatures, its eleven-man crew flew in comfort, without cumbersome heated flying suits and oxygen masks. And this Cadillac of the skies had a revolutionary remote-controlled firing system. "In earlier planes, each gunner manually controlled and aimed just one set of guns," explained pilot Charles W. Sweeney. "With the B-29, a single gunner could control several turrets with one sight and be able to direct all the fire on a single target."[5] It was truly "a super fortress, a super plane," recalls pilot Harry George. "Shirtsleeve atmosphere. Flush rivets. Powerful engines. Big. New type of bombsight. Altitude pressurized. We loved it. It was just a beautiful, beautiful plane."[6]

St. Clair McKelway noticed that the B-29 ground and air crews had an almost reverential affection for their airplanes. "B-24s and B-17s seem to excite an affection, a good-humored familiarity, in fliers and mechanics. I have seen people kick B-24s and B-17s on the tail, or under the belly, and say, 'Well, you were all right today, you old bitch.' . . . Ground crews of B-17s and B-24s like to ignore, and leave unrepaired, minor bits of battle damage that give the airplane a scarred, tough look but do not interfere with flying efficiency. . . . The B-29 crews want their airplanes to look new and shiny all the time. The B-29s are silvery, without camouflage paint of any kind, and the crews laboriously smooth out tiny wrinkles on the exteriors and polish the silver skins far beyond necessity. Any night in the Marianas, you can find B-29 crew members fooling around a perfectly airworthy B-29, fussing with it as an older generation used to fuss with the new car out in the garage after dinner." [7]

The B-29 had been in development since before Pearl Harbor, and the government would spend more money on it than on the Manhattan Project. The plane was initially plagued by mechanical problems, the most persistent being a tendency for the engines to overheat and catch fire. Test pilots were killed flying it; nobody wanted to fly it. So Hap Arnold asked General Doolittle to send him the best bomber pilot in Europe to help make the B-29 operational, and Doolittle sent back Paul Tibbets. Working with aeronautical engineers, Tibbets—who soon became known as "Mr. B-29"—had the plane ready, by Hap Arnold's loose standards, in early 1944.

It still had bugs, but they would have to be worked out in combat. Arnold wanted the Superfortress in the fight as soon as possible. It was mass-produced too late to be deployed in Europe, where all the runways would have had to be lengthened and strengthened. But Arnold was convinced that this tremendous weapon of war could finish off Japan without an invasion of the home islands, making the case, in the process, for the creation of a separate Air Force after the war. To ensure that he had complete control over the use of the bomber, Arnold pressed for the creation of a new Army Air Force, the Twentieth, under his command. He got his wish, and the first B-29s were sent to India in the spring of 1944. From India they flew over the Hump, the Himalaya mountains whose jagged peaks rose to almost 30,000 feet, to bases in the Chengtu Valley in western China, where they conducted raids against coke plants, steel mills, and oil facilities in western Japan, Formosa, and Manchuria. These China airstrips, built by local laborers who smashed stones with primitive hand tools, were, however, out of range of Japan's great industrial cities.

On June 15, the day Saipan was invaded, the China-based B-29s made their first attack on Japan, against a steel mill on Kyushu. Sixty planes reached the target, but only one bomb hit the plant and seven bombers were lost, six of them as a result of mechanical problems and weather. These high-altitude daylight missions were abysmally ineffective. More bombs landed in rice paddies than on steel furnaces and too many planes were lost. Another problem was logistics. Since the Japanese controlled all the ports of China, "we had to fly in all our own gasoline and bombs," recalls Wing Commander James V. Edmundson. "It took roughly fifteen trips over the Hump to get enough gasoline and bombs to fly one sortie to Japan." [8]

In an attempt to turn things around, Hap Arnold sent in one of his top guns from

Europe, General Curtis E. LeMay, who, as a colonel, had led the first Regensburg raid, and at age thirty-eight was the youngest two-star general in the Army Air Forces. A beefy, stern-jawed disciplinarian who bluntly spoke his mind—he was jokingly nicknamed "The Diplomat"—LeMay was one of the most accomplished bomber commanders of the war. He was a large, imposing man whose round face was frozen in a perpetual scowl. But that was the result of a mild form of Bell's palsy, which partially paralyzed the facial muscles at the corners of his mouth; and his exterior toughness hid a ferocious dedication to the men who served under him. He was a fanatic about discipline because he was convinced that discipline

GENERAL CURTIS LeMAY (NA).

under fire saved lives. And he didn't believe in screaming to get results; he spoke so softly he could hardly be heard from a few feet away. LeMay improved crew performance, if not bombing results, but from the time he arrived in August 1944, he realized that the China operation was doomed. "It didn't work," he said later. "No one could have made it work. It was founded on an utterly absurd logistics basis." [9] No air fleet that had to feed its own fuel to itself could hope to be successful.

The only reason bases had been built in China, in LeMay's view, was that "our entire Nation howled like a pack of wolves for an attack on the Japanese homeland." [10] Hap Arnold knew that the future of the B-29 was in the Marianas, and he had pressed the Navy to push up the timetable for its invasion. In the Marianas, Nimitz's ships would be able to meet the bomber's prodigious supply requirements, and from there the plane could reach the concentrated six-city complex around Tokyo that housed more than half of all Japanese industry and 20 percent of the country's population.

As soon as Saipan was taken, China operations began to be phased out. By November, there were over 100 B-29s on Saipan and Hansell had targeted the Japanese aircraft industry, hoping to destroy enemy air defenses in preparation for an American invasion of the home islands. Possum Hansell would first hit the Musashi aircraft engine factory, in a suburb of Tokyo, bombing it with pinpoint precision. General Emmett "Rosy" O'Donnell, commander of the only bomber wing on Saipan at the time, flew the lead plane on this mission. His co-pilot was Major Robert K. Morgan, the first pilot in Eighth Air Force to complete twenty-five missions, flying the *Memphis Belle*. After that, he had volunteered for a Pacific tour. One hundred and eleven of the silvery raiders took off on November 24, to a target thirteen hundred miles away.

It was an unprecedented mission. No aircraft had ever been asked to fly into battle with such loads over so much space, and the entire run up to Japan and back—fifteen to eighteen hours of air time—was over unfriendly waters. Merely getting off the ground could be a hair-raising ordeal. If one engine quit, recalls a B-29 crew member, "you probably wouldn't make it to the end of the runway. One night we didn't fly a mission and we were down at the Quonset hut site and looked up and I could practically read a newspaper five miles from the bases because of the planes burning at the end of the runway. There were four of them down there, burning up gasoline and bombs." On returning to base, pilots had to put down these long-bodied planes, half the size of a football field, on pinpoint spots in the limitless Pacific, often in fast-developing tropical storms and in dangerously overcrowded air traffic patterns.

But Hansell was a pioneer in formulating the doctrine of strategic bombing from what the Air Force called Very Long Range, and he was confident he could train his crews to get good results with their million-dollar machines.[11] His men, who had already begun calling themselves the Saipan Hunting Club, were in high spirits, proud to be part of the first bombing raid on Tokyo since Jimmy Doolittle's in 1942.

One crew member was a twenty-six-year-old published poet named John Ciardi, a gunner who had just arrived on Saipan. "One of my teachers," he wrote in his Saipan diary, "used to say that the best possible job for a writer was in the Fire Department—action in concentrated doses with long spells of musing leisure between. This life fits the requirement. I would like, though, to get over a target—even Tokio."[12] Ciardi would not get his wish until December 3, but more than a thousand other crewmen in 111 planes went up with Rosy O'Donnell. They would meet challenges that November afternoon no one had anticipated.

FEAR

Approaching Tokyo, everyone worried about the flak and the fighters. The flak was heavy but inaccurate, and the Japanese planes that came up after the big silver birds fought cautiously and were easy targets for the bombers' massive firepower. The weather turned out to be the biggest danger: the Siberian jet stream and heavy cloud cover, conditions that would plague almost every future high-altitude mission. "Over

Japan, at 30,000 feet, the winds were from 150 to 200 miles per hour," says pilot John Jennings. "So if you were coming into the wind, you were going probably thirty, forty, fifty miles an hour over the target. You were over the target so long they could shoot the heck out of you.

"All right, so we could turn around and come in downwind. That was the answer. No. Now you're going over 300 miles per hour [sometimes up to 500 miles per hour] and the Norden bombsight couldn't figure out when to drop those things. So . . . we were getting nowhere."

The Norden bombsight couldn't compensate for these furious winds, which played havoc with the bombs, and the clouds were so thick that only twenty-four planes dropped bombs in the vicinity of the aircraft factory. The bomber fleet lost only one plane, but in losing it the surviving crews witnessed the depths of the enemy's desperation. The downed B-29 was rammed by a stripped-down Japanese suicide fighter that managed, without the extra weight of its guns, to reach the altitude of the B-29s. These ramming tactics grew more intense with each raid. Inspired by the kamikaze fliers, the fighter pilots would come boring in on the American bombers at closing speeds of up to 600 miles per hour. Most of the time they would be blown out of the sky, but "we lost considerable planes, wings knocked off, engines knocked out . . . even the noses shattered," says bombardier Ed Keyser. "After the first raid, nothing came at us from behind," recalls John Ciardi. "The Japanese lined up across the sky and came in to ram. They would all swarm on the B-29 and finish it off." [13]

Another of the enemy's weapons was the tiny island of Iwo Jima, squarely astride the B-29 routes, almost exactly midway between the Marianas and Japan. The big bombers had to fly a fuel-consuming dogleg around Iwo Jima, but the Japanese could still pick them up on their radar and radio ahead to the Tokyo air defense system, giving it a two-hour warning. Fighters on the two airstrips on Iwo Jima were also a problem. "They could pick you off coming and going," says Edmundson. "You could be limping back from a bombing raid [with a busted-up plane], trying to squeeze your gas to have enough to get back to Tinian, and these guys would come sailing in on you and jump you out of Iwo."

Precision bombing from the long coral runways of the Marianas never worked the way Hansell hoped it would. Subsequent missions over Tokyo, and over the Mitsubishi Aircraft Engine Works in Nagoya, Japan's third largest city, were only marginally more effective than the first Tokyo raid. The Japanese radio ridiculed Hansell's precision bombing, calling it "Blind Bombing." But for the first month or so, crew morale was surprisingly high. "I was cockeyed proud of the crew . . . ," John Ciardi wrote after his first mission. "This is the pilot's air corps, but it takes eleven men to fly a 29. And eleven men have to lose their fear and be sure of themselves before a crew can function. We functioned." After this mission, Ciardi learned that he had won a prestigious prize back home for his poetry. [14]

The men were not blind to the moral dimensions of their work. "We were in the terrible business of burning out Japanese towns," Ciardi observed in an interview after the war. "That meant women and old people, children. One part of me—a surviving savage voice—says, I'm sorry we left any of them living. I wish we'd finished killing them all. Of course, as soon as rationality overcomes the first impulse, you say, Now, come on, this is the human race, let's try to be civilized.

"I had to condition myself to be a killer. This was remote control. All we did was push buttons. I didn't see anybody we killed." [15]

A few days after flying his first mission, Ciardi went to a movie in the evening. It was called *A Guy Named Joe*, and was about death in the skies over Europe. He found it "too noble," he wrote in his diary. But despite its Hollywood dramatics, the film got him thinking about why America was fighting the war, and why his country had turned him into a killer by remote control. "Wherever one race sets out to take over the rest for private exploitation somebody has to live crazily enough to stop it."

Ciardi thought of himself as a poet, not a soldier. And as he flew more missions, he began to experience doubts that he could do his job. He started to have "sudden chemical anxieties." He was scared, scared in advance of every raid, and he couldn't stop the fear.

He developed little routines to try to settle himself. "Whenever my imagination runs cold and damp I go out and look at a B-29 for five minutes and I'm cured. It's . . . a beautiful thing to look at, and it's pointed the right way." But the fear grew worse with every raid, and he began to try to rationalize it. "I find myself thinking that it's foolish to stick my neck out over Japan when my real usefulness and capability as a person and as a unit of society is in writing what needs to be written well. . . . I'd frankly bow out if I knew how to. I could go to Col. Brannock tomorrow and say I quit and be busted down to private [and be put on permanent garbage detail]. But I can't let myself and won't. All the same I know I'd grab at any reasonable excuse to save face. . . . If I do get killed it will be because I lack the courage to quit. . . ." [16]

FIRE STICKS

In January, Curtis LeMay replaced Hansell and changed bombing tactics, determined that his big bombers would win the war. He experimented with firebombing, with mixed results, and had the planes go in lower, at 25,000 rather than 30,000 feet, to allow the navigators to see the target better and to cut down on mechanical breakdowns by putting less strain on the engines. The men objected. They saw that extra 5,000 feet as their "margin for life." At 30,000 feet, the enemy fighters had difficulty getting to them and the flak was far less accurate. "This 25,000 ft. business is bad stuff. . . . Losses are going to be heavy," Ciardi confided to his diary. "This man I have never seen will very likely be what kills me." That night Ciardi wrote a letter home to be mailed "in case I didn't come back." [17]

LeMay's bombing tactics were as unproductive as Hansell's. "We were still going in too high, still running into those big jet stream winds upstairs. Weather was almost always as bad," LeMay confessed later.[18] In early March, under pressure from Arnold to launch a maximum mission against Japan, he changed tactics radically. Ciardi summed up the new approach: "He said, Go in at night from five thousand feet, without gunners, just a couple of rear-end observers. We'll save weight on the turrets and on ammunition. The Japanese have no fighter resistance at night. They have no radar. We'll drop fire sticks." [19]

These were small cylinders—weighing six pounds—filled with napalm, an insidious new weapon of warfare developed by Standard Oil and DuPont in 1944. Napalm was gelatinized gasoline that created running rivers of fire, ferociously hot fires that were nearly impossible to put out by conventional means. And it stuck to anything it came into contact with: animate or inanimate. Napalm would be shatteringly effective in Tokyo, LeMay reasoned, where 90 percent of the structures were built of wood or heavy paper. Stripping the planes of guns and gunners and going in low would save on gas. Extra gas tanks for the high-altitude missions were stored in the bomb bays. No extra tanks meant extra fire sticks.

The sticks were stored in large cylinders, which were packed together in bundles, "Molotov flower baskets," the Japanese would call them. When these clusters were

B-29 CREW RECEIVING LAST-MINUTE INSTRUCTIONS FROM THE PILOT (USAAF).

dropped, they broke apart above the target, filling the sky with dozens of containers of napalm. Each stick would ignite on contact, setting a small fire, and thousands of these small fires would merge, creating a city-consuming conflagration.

But Curtis LeMay wanted to do more than start a big urban fire. He wanted to start a firestorm—a thermal hurricane that killed by heat and suffocation, as flames sucked oxygen out of the atmosphere. He wanted to create a holocaust.

"We thought he was crazy," Newell Fears, a B-29 flier, describes the reaction of the crews to LeMay's orders to go in at low level. The men protested that they would be suicide missions. As the 334 bombers prepared to take off in the late afternoon of March 9, 1945, the men who were not going to Tokyo that night went down to the flight line to say goodbye to their friends, certain that many of them were not going to come back.

On the morning of March 10, Ciardi recorded in his diary a decisive change in the air war against Japan:

> THE BOYS ARE JUST BACK from a razzle-dazzle play over Tokio. They left a general conflagration behind them. . . .
>
> The planes hit at 3 A.M. All ours got through. Reports are inconclusive, but it must have been terrific. . . . While Tokio burns—there's another one called for tomorrow night [against Nagoya].

Shortly after this, a personnel officer read a recent issue of *Atlantic* with some of Ciardi's poems in it. They needed someone at headquarters to do public relations work, and he was called in and put in charge of awards and decorations. A week or so later, the crew he had been on was killed over Tokyo when their plane was hit and blew up in midair. Years later, Ciardi would say, "it was luck—and poetry—that saved me." [20]

Knox Burger, a correspondent for *Yank* in Saipan, describes that first low-altitude Tokyo fire raid, which he witnessed from one of the B-29s.

> ONE NIGHT IN MARCH 1945 some 300 B-29s, loaded with incendiaries, flew up to Japan from the Marianas to burn out the heart of Tokyo. They set fires which leveled 15.8 square acres of the most densely populated area on earth. By the next morning at least 100,000 people were dead and more than 1,000,000 were homeless. It was probably the worst fire in history.

Subsequent incendiary attacks devastated most of Tokyo, but in this first raid, which was without precedent in air war, more people died than had been accounted for on any other mission thus far in the war. . . .

The target . . . was a mass firetrap of flimsy frame houses and shops which housed a big percentage of the population in Tokyo. . . . Several large factories turned out parachutes and airplane parts, but the real economic strength of the area lay in the thousands of domestic industries that had sprung up with war. Not many of the householders had refrigerators or electric stoves—drill presses were installed instead. And a lathe had come to be a common back-room fixture.

On March 9 a strong wind had been rattling the shaky panes in the doors and windows all day. For the past few nights single B-29s had appeared over the sky, without dropping any bombs but flying very low and setting off a riot of searchlights and antiaircraft fire. A lot of people on the ground had the uneasy feeling that something was due to happen. . . .

The first ships [of the raiding party] were 12 pathfinders whose job it was to light up the outer reaches of the target area for the main force. They were met by searchlights, accurate, intense flak, and strong headwinds.

Then the rest of the B-29s came in.

They were met by terrific flak. . . .

Crewmen looked out at searchlights aimlessly fingering the smoke clouds, picking up a ship, losing it again, picking up another momentarily. There were some fighters up, but most of them refused to close in and shoot. They couldn't see the B-29s blacked out over the target.

The long sky-train droned over the bay for three hours, pouring millions of incendiaries inside roughly patterned circles laid out by the pathfinders. During the first half-hour it was like flying over a forest of brightly lighted Christmas trees. The bombs flickered like faraway candles. Then the fires spread and merged. At the end it was like flying over a super-blast-furnace.

Heat thermals from the fires raging on the ground hurled the bombers thousands of feet upward in a few seconds. Gusts from the inferno were so powerful that crewmen rattled around inside the ships like bones in a dice cup. Floorboards were uprooted. Because of the low altitude, the ships had not been pressurized, and the smoke and soot and smell seeped into the cabins.

The B-29s created large-scale havoc. From 7,000 feet crewmen could see the framework of big buildings in which fires had burned away the roofs and illuminated the window holes. They could see whole blocks like this, and the general impression was of a huge bed of red-hot and burned-out embers.[21]

What was it like to fly over this boiling sea of fire, every bomber feeding it with 20,000 pounds of gasoline and chemicals? Here are the observations of some of the men who were on that mission and the missions that followed it, in lightning succession, against other urban targets, five missions in all—a five-city blitz over a ten-day period.

Captain Charlie Phillips's plane approached the coast of Japan just after midnight, after the pathfinders had marked the target, drawing a huge flaming X with large napalm bombs on ten square miles of one of the most densely populated areas on earth. The first wave of planes set the fire with larger incendiaries; later waves fed

ENEMY FLAK WAS A MENACE ON HIGH-ALTITUDE MISSIONS (USAAF).

it with smaller ones. When Charlie Phillips first sighted Tokyo, it was already in flames. The fire looked to him like the scourgelike forest fires he had seen in California.

Phillips recalls:

NO ONE HAD ANY LIGHTS SHOWING. It was completely dark. If you got picked up by a searchlight, you were so well illuminated that you couldn't see out of the airplane. You'd have to fly on instruments. But most of us went in and came out in the dark.

We had designated targets. We were responsible for our own bombing, unlike daylight missions, where the lead bombardier would make the Norden bombsight run in his aircraft and all of the rest of the bombardiers would drop their bombs as they saw the bombs leave the bay of his plane. On those missions, we would bomb with concentrated destructive power because we were in a very tight formation, our wings overlapping.

The night bombing was completely different and it was horrifying to the crews because of the danger of collisions. When you send 300 airplanes up there with no lights and you didn't know where anybody is, it's serious. You couldn't see other aircraft. You just had to grit your teeth, hold your heading, drive on it, drop the bombs, and make a big, steep turn out of there and head for home.

What surprised us was the terrible turbulence we ran into. Not being the first planes in, we flew into a dirty gray cloud reaching up to 40,000 feet. As we entered that cloud we ran into a huge updraft. [My] plane was tossed about like a leaf in a fall windstorm and it was hard to keep the wings level. You could not see a horizon, so you had to do instrument flying to keep the airplane on a level keel. And there was a monstrous thermal updraft that increased airspeed. I noticed that we were fifty miles an hour over the redline speed. When we talk about the redline airspeed, that's when the guarantee runs out. That's when the wings might come off. The turbulence might tear the plane apart. So I pulled the power back to idle and slowly got the airspeed reduced to below that redline.

We went into the fire cloud at 7,800 feet but came out at 14,000 feet, because of this monstrous updraft.

"Those thermal waves would bounce your plane clear around," observes radio operator George Gladden. "I had my flak suit on and my chair was bolted to me with the seat belt and when the wave hit it jerked the bolts out of the bottom of that thing and I was stuck against the ceiling with a chair tied to me."

"The turbulence was so bad our aircraft was flipped over on its back, and it was a terrific fight to get it back upright," recalls Captain Harry George. "[Then] we looked out and saw Tokyo burning. You could smell it at this low altitude. The smell of it was putrid.

A JAPANESE *BAKA* BOMB (USAAF).

"On the right hand side I [saw] another plane alongside of us about a half a mile out. It was, I learned later, a Jap suicide plane—a Baka Bomb—with a ton of TNT on the warhead. It didn't have any landing gear. It was dropped from a twin-engine bomber in the sky and it drew a bead on one of our planes. Luckily it didn't hit it.

"The incendiary bombs were in 2,000-pound clusters and each of them was small. We had twenty clusters in the bomb bays. When a cluster was dropped it would blow apart about 3,000 feet over the target. And as soon as the [thirty or so] little bombs in the clusters hit the ground they would start things burning. They were filled with napalm. If you threw water on them, they would burn more fiercely. You couldn't stop 'em from burning."

"Our biggest concern was getting caught in a searchlight," says David Farquar, a gunner with the 6th Bomb Wing. "The searchlights would crisscross the sky and as soon as they would focus on a plane you were a target for fighters, because once they had you in one searchlight fifteen or twenty searchlights would be on you. There was no place to hide, and you're blinded by the light. . . . Once you're in the lights your chances of making it through are very slim. . . ."

"Looking down out of the window of the plane was like looking into what I think hell would be like," says Lieutenant Fiske Hanley. "We could smell human flesh burning at 4,000 feet."

"This blaze will haunt me forever," one pilot said to himself as he made the sign of the cross. "It's the most terrifying sight in the world, and, God forgive me, it's the best." [22]

St. Clair McKelway was with Curtis LeMay at his headquarters on Guam during the night of the first Tokyo fire raid. "He had told the rest of his staff to go to bed if they wanted to, that he was going to sit this one out. . . . LeMay was . . . in the operations-control room, whose walls were covered with charts, maps, [and] graphs. . . . He was sitting on a wooden bench smoking a cigar. 'I'm sweating this one out myself,' he said. 'A lot could go wrong.' " [23]

LeMay had not informed Hap Arnold, back in Washington, about the strike until the day before his planes took off, insuring that his commander could not stop the radically risky mission. He had gambled, against the advice of his advisors, that the Japanese did not have the kind of low-level flak that the Germans did, which was deadly accurate at 5,000 to 7,000 feet. If they did, he'd lose a lot of crews. It also bothered him that he could not lead the Tokyo raid, as he had the Regensburg raid. He would have done so had he not been briefed about the atomic bomb. No one who knew about "the big firecracker" was permitted to fly over Japan and risk getting shot down, captured, and questioned.

There was something else on the general's mind. "No matter how you slice it, you're going to kill an awful lot of civilians," he told himself. " . . . But, if you don't destroy the Japanese industry, we're going to have to invade Japan. And how many Americans will be killed in an invasion of Japan? Five hundred thousand seems to be the lowest estimate. Some say a million." [24]

LeMay told McKelway he couldn't sleep.

"I USUALLY CAN, BUT NOT TONIGHT. . . . In a war," he said, "you've got to try to keep at least one punch ahead of the other guy all the time. . . . I think we've figured out a punch he's not expecting this time. I don't think he's got the right flak to combat this kind of raid and I don't think he can keep his cities from being burned down—wiped right off the map. . . . If this one works we will shorten this damned war out here."

He looked at his watch. "We won't get a bombs-away [report] for another half hour," he said. "Would you like a Coca-Cola? I can sneak in my quarters without waking up the other guys and get two Coca-Colas and we can drink them in my car. That'll kill most of the half hour."

We drove the hundred yards to his quarters in his staff car and he sneaked in and got the Coca-Colas. We sat in the dark, facing the jungle that surrounds the headquarters . . . [until] the bombs-away message from the first B-29 formation over Tokio came in. It was decoded and shown to him. "Bombing the primary target visually," it told him. "Large fires observed. Flak moderate. Fighter opposition nil." . . . Then the bombs-away messages from other formations began coming in fast. After the first three, they all reported "Conflagration." . . .

"It looks pretty good," LeMay said. . . . "But we can't really tell a damn thing about results until we get the pictures tomorrow night. Anyway, there doesn't seem to have been much flak. We don't seem to have lost more than a few airplanes." [They lost twelve B-29s.] He shifted his cigar and smiled. . . .

The following night, around twelve, we had the pictures. . . .

The staff officers' five or six jeeps swept up to LeMay's tent like so many cowboys' horses, the officers driving them leaped to the ground, and we all got to the General's bedroom just as the photo-interpretation officer walked in with the pictures under his arm. LeMay [was] in pajamas. . . . The photo-interpretation officer spread the pictures out on a big, well-lighted table and LeMay . . . walked up to it and bent over them.

There was about one full minute of silence. "All this is out," LeMay then said, running a hand over several square miles of Tokio. . . . "This is out—this—this—this. . . ." We crowded in for a better look. "It's all ashes—all that and that and that," said [another officer], bending over the pictures.[25]

In less than three hours, LeMay's B-29s dropped almost a quarter of a million bombs on Tokyo, burning to the bare ground sixteen square miles of the city, an area equivalent to two thirds of Manhattan Island. There was more destruction than any documented fire in history, including the combined earthquake and fire of 1923 in Tokyo. Knox Burger's estimate of the number of people killed—at least 100,000—used to be considered high, but recent studies validate it, and put the number of injured at about one million. Next to Hiroshima, where an estimated 130,000 people were killed by the atomic blast, it was the most destructive air attack of the entire war.[26] Before March 10, only about 1,300 people were killed in all the B-29 raids on Japan. So this raid had as cataclysmic an impact on the Japanese people as did the later, atomic bombing of Hiroshima. For the people in Tokyo that night, nothing in their history or their imaginations could have led them to believe that this was a man-made act. To many, it must have seemed like a furious force of nature. For the first time in the history of humanity, technology approached nature in its destructive capacity.

Knox Burger, who went to Tokyo right after the war and interviewed victims of the fire, describes the panic and devastation inside the city:

SOME PEOPLE, FOLLOWING THE DIRECTIONS given them by police and civilian fire wardens, stayed by their homes and formed bucket brigades, or transferred their families and their valuables into air-raid shelters beside the houses. Whole families were roasted as the flames engulfed these shelters, and wooden doors and supports burst into flames of terrific heat.

Others, several hundred thousand others, with clothes and children piled on their backs, straggled off toward the rivers, the bay, or an open space—whichever happened to be the closest. The wind acted like a lid on the fire, keeping the heat low and forcing the flames to spread out instead of up. Smoke and sparks were everywhere, and white-hot gusts came roaring down narrow streets.

As soon as the big, fluffy coverings on their backs caught fire or a kimono or a jacket started to smolder, the wearers would rip them off. Many people who hadn't had a chance to douse themselves with water were stark naked by the time they reached safety. And safety that night was a sometimes thing. People crowded across firebreaks, hoping the broad lanes had halted the fire's spread, but the fire

ranged on both sides, so people had to fall back into the avenues themselves. They lay down in the center of the streets as far as possible from the flames on each side. The next morning, vehicles couldn't pass because of the litter of corpses. Waves of heat had swirled across the firebreaks, and people burned to death without being touched by flame. Other blasts of pure heat killed people as they ran.

The wind seemed to blow the fire in all directions. A wave of flame would follow the people out of a block of houses like a breaker on the beach. Then, in front of the people, it would catch a load of incendiaries, and they would be walled in.

Many times the flames, lashed by cross-drafts, reversed their field. All that night the general direction of the flight across the lowlands surged one way and then another as new fires started and the ground wind shifted. . . . The fire commissioner of the Fugawa district, perhaps the worst hit of all, said, "Everything burned so quickly it was like a bad dream. We couldn't stand up against the wind."

By dawn the wind had died and most of the fires had burned themselves out. . . . The next day was clear and cold. What had been the marrow of one of the world's most congested cities was a bed of ashes. Here and there a building burned, orange against a pall of smoke and dust that overhung the city. Blackened bodies lay strewn among the embers. Charred telephone poles stood along the streets, their tips glowing like cigars. For acres the only structures that rose above the horizon were an occasional double-decked storage vault, some schools, and a few gutted factories. A forest of chimneys stood like sentinels, marking the sites where other factories had stood.

The survivors sat or stood looking stupidly at the monstrous flatness. They were too exhausted for anger or bitterness, too stunned to comprehend what had happened. Their throats and eyes ached from smoke and wind; almost all of them had painful burns. People got in line in front of aid stations and rice-distribution centers almost automatically. There was very little noise. Occasionally a brick wall would tumble.

The police took charge of the dead, collecting corpses in piles and burning them. The piles gave off a blue-white smoke, heavy with the stink of death.[27]

Even those who had managed to get out of their tinderbox neighborhoods to the fetid canals that coursed through the Tokyo flats died. Those in the deeper water were boiled alive. Those in the shallow places, buried in muck up to their mouths, were later found dead; not drowned, but suffocated by the burning air and smoke.

LeMay called it a strategic raid, an attack on Japanese war industries. As he wrote after the war:

IT WAS THEIR SYSTEM of dispersal of industry. All you had to do was visit one of those targets after we'd roasted it, and see the ruins of a multitude of tiny houses, with a drill press sticking up through the wreckage of every home. The entire population got into the act and worked to make those airplanes or munitions of war . . . men, women, children. We knew we were going to kill a lot of women and kids when we burned that town. Had to be done.[28]

Morality aside, this was not "strategic bombing." The Japanese had the right word for it: slaughter bombing. Did "moral considerations" affect his decisions to firebomb cities? LeMay was asked by an Air Force cadet after the war. "Killing Japanese didn't bother me very much at that time. It was getting the war over that bothered me. . . .

"I guess the direct answer to your question is, yes, every soldier thinks something of the moral aspects of what he is doing. But all war is immoral and if you let that bother you, you're not a good soldier."

Then he added, tellingly: "I suppose if I had lost the war, I would have been tried as a war criminal. Fortunately, we were on the winning side." [29]

As soon as LeMay got the damage assessments for Tokyo, he ordered more raids. "It would be possible, I thought, to knock out all of Japan's major industrial cities during the next ten days." [30]

Charlie Phillips flew all five of these missions and afterward wrote to his wife that he had never been more exhausted in his life. "It was wam bam. We flew to Nagoya, to Osaka [Japan's second largest city], to Kobe [Japan's major port and ship-building center], back to Nagoya again, all in ten days' time." In ten days, LeMay burned out half of the built-up area of four of Japan's biggest cities, and killed at least 150,000 men, women, and children.

"Then," says LeMay, "we ran out of bombs. Literally." Later, he gave an accurate assessment of the murderous efficiency of his raids. "The ten-day blitz of March was a turning point. The morale of the Japanese people began a steady decline, never to rise again. Industries ceased to exist, or operated at greatly reduced rates. The panic-stricken people began an exodus from the major cities. The rate of absenteeism in the war industries recorded an alarming rise. . . . Fire, not high explosives, did this. And we possessed no more fire with which to speed the capitulation." [31]

When the Navy brought more bombs to the Marianas, thousands of tons of scalding chemicals, the city-burning campaign resumed and intensified. Now LeMay bombed by day and night, at low and high altitudes, because there was soon nothing to fear. Japan's air defense system had been obliterated. "We had nothing in Japan that we could use against such a weapon. . . . We felt that the War was lost," said Prince Higashikuni, commander of Japan's home defense headquarters.[32] Historian Michael S. Sherry argues that "for many Japanese, the March 10 raid and the ones to follow it triggered the plunge into a mood of desperation even more than did the apocalyptic events of August." [33]

On June 15, LeMay ended his campaign against six of Japan's seven largest cities. (The fourth largest city, Kyoto, the ancient imperial capital, was spared by order of

Secretary of War Stimson.) In the six cities of Tokyo, Osaka, Nagoya, Yokohama, Kobe, and Kawasaki over 126,762 people were killed—according to conservative estimates—and a million and a half dwellings and over 105 square miles of urban space were destroyed. In Tokyo, Osaka, and Nagoya alone the areas leveled (almost 100 square miles) exceeded the areas destroyed in all German cities by both the American and English air forces (approximately seventy-nine square miles).[34] The cost to the United States was 136 bombers and their crews—light, by the cold calculations of modern war.

The men most opposed to LeMay's initial decision to go in low became his strongest supporters, both during the war and afterward. "It turned out to be the greatest decision that LeMay ever made. It's what really turned the tide and put us in control of the Japanese," says John Jennings. "In my opinion, the fire raids were what won the war. . . ." The leading Japanese historian of the fire raids, Katsumoto Saotome, agrees. He argues that the government should have surrendered after the first Tokyo raid, with its terrible promise of more to come.

Harold Tucker, a B-29 gunner, believes, as LeMay did, that if the fire raids had continued, "we may not have had to drop the atomic bomb. We could have just burned them out."

These men were motivated, in part, by revenge. Those that were not shot down and made prisoners—those that never met the Japanese face-to-face in combat—did not have Eugene Sledge's visceral hatred of the enemy. But they remembered Pearl Harbor and were keenly aware of atrocities committed by the Japanese in the Philippines and elsewhere. What really motivated them, however, was loyalty, not the lust for revenge, loyalty to their fellow crew members—and an overwhelming desire to end the war as quickly as possible, and by any means possible, so that they could get back to their "real lives."

We weren't motivated by "patriotism," John Ciardi said forty years after the war. "I think it was a certain amount of pride. The unit was the crew. You belonged to eleven men. You're trained together, you're bound together. I was once ordered to fly in the place of a gunner [on another crew] who had received a shrapnel wound. I dreaded that mission. I wanted to fly with my own crew. . . . I did not want to run the risk of dying with strangers."

But Ciardi is quick to add that he knew why he was in the war. "As an American, I felt very strongly I did not want to be alive to see the Japanese impose surrender terms." [35]

While they killed, they did not think of themselves as killers. "We had to kill to

end the war," says pilot Harry George. By starting a war of aggression and then refus-ing to surrender when there was no hope of victory the Japanese militarists were responsible for the incineration of babies and grandmothers, Harry George and other B-29 crewmen insist. "We knew. We heard about the thousands of people [we killed], the Japanese wives, children, and elderly. That was war. But I know every B-29 air crewman for the next two or three years would wake up at night and start shaking. . . . Yes, [the raids] were successful, but horribly so."

These men saw the war as the journalist Russell Brines did. Brines had lived in Tokyo; he knew the people, spoke the language. And he had been a prisoner of the Japanese. In a best-selling book, *Until They Eat Stones,* published in 1944, he explained what the Americans were up against in the final year of this war:

"WE WILL FIGHT," THE JAPANESE SAY, "until we eat stone!" The phrase is odd; now revived and ground deeply into Japanese consciousness by propagandists skilled in marshaling their sheeplike people. . . . [It] means they will continue the war until every man—perhaps every woman and child—lies face downward on the battlefield. . . .

American fighting men back from the front have been trying to tell America this is a war of extermination. They have seen it from foxholes and barren strips of bullet-strafed sand. I have seen it from behind enemy lines. Our picture coincides. This *is* a war of extermination. The Japanese militarists have made it that way.[56]

Only one Medal of Honor was conferred on a B-29 crew member during the war. The recipient was Staff Sergeant Henry Eugene "Red" Erwin of Bessemer, Alabama, a hard-muscled former steelworker who was in the habit of calling his wife, whom he wrote to every day, "Cupcake." His act of heroism will have to stand for other brave men who, unfairly, were not decorated. St. Clair McKelway tells his story:

ERWIN'S B-29 WAS LEADING a formation to Japan on one of the first incendiary raids. He had been given the additional duty of shoving phosphorus bombs down a chute near the rear end of the forward crew compartment. These bombs were being used on that mission to spread smoke over a certain area of Japan and thereby aid the other airplanes to make an effective rendezvous. One of Erwin's phosphorus bombs was faulty. It began to sputter and smoke as he put it into the chute. The sputtering phosphorus flew into his face, ate part of his nose away, and blinded him. The stuff splattered on his clothes, on his hands, inside his shirt. . . . The airplane quickly filled with smoke and fumes, and the pilot lost control of it. It went into a spin. Erwin knew what to do and he did it. A phosphorus bomb weighs about twenty pounds. Erwin pulled the sputtering bomb out of the chute, picked it up in his bare hands, and started carrying it to the nearest opening—the pilot's windows. From where he was, this was a distance of about twenty feet. He couldn't see, so he felt his way along the passage with his shoulders, holding the bomb in his hands.

In a B-29 certain crew members have tables to work on during a flight, tables which, when raised, cut off this passage. The navigator's table was raised when Erwin got to it. The navigator didn't know what was going on, for he was blinded by the smoke and fumes, as was everybody else in the airplane, and was sitting with his back to the table, having swung around in his swivel chair. Erwin felt the table against his thighs. He held the bomb then for a few seconds in one hand, resting it against his chest, and with the other unlatched the table and lowered it so he could get by. All the time the bomb was sputtering and burning, throwing white-hot phosphorus all around. Erwin carried it to the front of the compartment. The pilot and co-pilot had opened their windows, trying to get rid of the fumes and smoke. Erwin threw the bomb out the co-pilot's window. Then he walked a few steps back toward his post, near the other end of the compartment, and fell.

The pilot managed to bring the airplane out of its spin three hundred feet above land a few seconds after that [and headed back to safety.] . . . The rest of the crew did what they could for Erwin. His face was burned all over and his nose was half gone. The flesh around his eyes was raw, his skin was blistering, and it seemed certain to his comrades that he would never see again. His hands were burned to the bones. His shirt and pants were afire when the crew got to him and the skin under his clothes was burned away.[37]

Five weeks later, in a Navy hospital on Guam, a general pinned the Medal of Honor on the bandages that covered Red Erwin's entire body. The crew, whose lives he saved, gathered around his cot during the brief ceremony. Erwin breathed and was fed through a tube, but his eyes were all right. The rest of him was patched together by plastic surgeons back home.

THE BLOCKADE

"The strikes are still going," wrote McKelway in June of 1945, after returning from Saipan on leave. "I see by the New York papers that LeMay is throwing his B-29s at the Japs in different ways, with different tactics. . . . Flying low and only at night, specially trained B-29 squadrons have mined the harbors of Japan's main islands, strengthening the naval blockade, and preventing the Japs from moving their war industries to Manchuria before they are entirely wiped out on Honshu."[38]

These missions had begun in March 1945, and came at the culmination of an overwhelmingly successful campaign against enemy shipping by American submarines. The campaign was intended to bottle up Japanese harbors and major waterways, chiefly Shimonoseki Strait, between the southern island of Kyushu and the island of Honshu, the main channel from Japan's Inland Sea to the Sea of Japan and the Asian mainland. Most of the Japanese shipping that had survived naval air and submarine attacks had to pass through this strait to reach the great ports of the Inland Sea. Mining operations, first suggested by the Navy and grudgingly supported by LeMay, were designed to cut off imports—including food and vital raw materials—from Japanese-occupied Asia; prevent the flow of supplies to Japanese armies in the Pacific; and disrupt coastal shipping. It was called Operation Starvation.

The men who carried out this dangerous operation, the crews of the 313th Bomb Wing, describe it:

"The Inland Sea's outlet was the Shimonoseki Strait, which was comparable to our Panama Canal. All traffic that flowed from the four major Japanese islands to the Asian mainland went through it. We had to cripple it," observes Robert Rodenhaus. "General John C. Davis was the commanding general of the 313th Wing. He chose my plane, *The Lucky Strike,* to lead the planes that went in. We were number one."

"Japan was perfect for mining," explains John Jennings. "It had very shallow waters. The Navy provided the mines. Some were 1,000 pounds, some 2,000 pounds, and they would be dropped from 5,500 to 7,500 feet at night with parachutes." There were three types of mines: magnetic, pressure, and acoustic, and they were almost impossible "to sweep," adds Fiske Hanley. "They lay on the bottom of these shallow waterways and would listen for noises, or feel for pressure, or for the magnetic influence from a ship. They were set so they might go off on the first ship to go over them or the tenth. They were devilish things."

Many B-29 crewmen considered the mining missions the most dangerous ones they flew. "We were conned immediately from both sides with searchlights," Rodenhaus continues his story. "Powerful [radar-directed] searchlights. They were demoralizing. They are psychologically wrenching, because they illuminate completely the interior of the airplane. You gotta wear dark glasses, and as you travel they are passing you from one searchlight battery to the next. You're never out of their sight." As John Jennings says, "the mining missions are where we lost most of our planes and people."

Over 12,000 mines were laid, 2,100 of them in the Shimonoseki Strait. By the end of the war, these mines had sunk or disabled 650,000 tons of Japanese shipping. As early as May 1945, however, mining operations had blockaded every Japanese shipping lane, virtually cutting off communications between Japan and the Asian mainland. Submarines, meanwhile, had severed communication between Japan and its southern resource colonies, and LeMay's B-29s had destroyed a good part of Japan's industrial war machine. By the end of May, the lethal combination of burning and blockade had closed the huge ports of Nagoya, Yokohama, and Tokyo.

The Japanese also used mines, to defend their shores against the expected American invasion. Finding these minefields and plotting them was one of the most harrowing and least known operations of the war. Marty Schaffer, a Navy enlisted man from Allentown, Pennsylvania, served on the submarine *Polaris* in the waters off Japan in the last year of the war.

THE JAPANESE MINES were anchored to the ocean floor, just jiggling there, swinging on a chain. Our job was to plot them, using sonar. When we went in to plot them, "silent running" was announced over the PA system. That meant four knots on the propeller screws, real quiet. Everyone who wasn't on duty went to their bunks, sometimes for ten hours—and waited in absolute silence, in the dark, listening to the eerie "ping, ping" of the sonar. When we picked up a mine you would hear an echo. Then everybody would tense up. Sometimes I'd try to read to steady the nerves, but that didn't work. I'd sometimes fall asleep but that was bad, because I'd have these terrifying dreams of the boat getting blown apart by a mine.

The most awful thing was the sound of the chains. You could hear the chains, or cables, that held those mines scraping the side of our boat, and that was hair-raising. Any second, you thought—kabang! you're blown to bits. I'll never forget that sound, that nerve-rattling scraping. I can still hear it. I don't call myself a veteran. I call myself a survivor.

Sometimes we weren't down very far, and the sea was so rough it would toss our boat around. And there were loose mines floating around, mines that had been torn loose by monsoons or storms. We always worried about running into those. We'd go after them when we came topside to recharge our batteries. We had a yeoman who was a sharpshooter, a good old boy. The other kids would try to get the mines with machine guns, but he'd say, "step aside, lads," and with one shot would hit the detonator and explode the mine.

When I think about it now, we were in a hell of a mess when we went into those fields. Minefield plotting became so tight that you actually had to back out of the minefield. There wasn't enough room to turn around. But nobody on the boat ever broke down or panicked. It was the training, the tough training we went through, and the screening. We were an elite service, all volunteers, and everyone did his job.[39]

Submarines participated in nearly every type of Navy operation in the war, including setting up, with Navy destroyers and long-range patrol planes, a search-and-rescue lifeline for B-29 crews, like Charlie Phillips's, that had to ditch in the Pacific or parachute into its dangerous waters. Submarines alone rescued 247 downed airmen in the last three months of the war.

But the main job of the silent service was to cut off enemy shipping. From the day Pearl Harbor was attacked, it was a campaign of unrestricted submarine warfare against Japan, with no warning given to enemy ships, armed or not. Navy code breakers spearheaded the effort. They deciphered the Japanese shipping codes, which gave the location of every convoy in the Pacific, and guided submarines to these easy targets. By the end of the war, it was, as Marty Schaffer said, "like shooting fish in a barrel," for there was no Japanese Navy or Air Force to contend with.[40] It had not always been this easy. In World War II, one out of every seven men in the submarine service was lost at sea.

With only 2 percent of the Navy ships and personnel, the U.S. submarine service accounted for more Japanese shipping sunk than all other arms of the services put together. By 1945 Japan's five great Pacific ports handled less than one eighth of their 1941 trade; and three quarters of the Japanese fishing fleet was destroyed. In the summer of 1945, Japanese planners doubted that the country could feed itself into the next year.

According to Vice Admiral Charles A. Lockwood, Jr., commander of the Pacific Fleet submarine force, American submarines sank a total of 1,256 Japanese ships, 167 combatant ships, including four carriers, and over 1,000 tankers, transports, and cargo ships. Eight million tons of Japanese merchant marine shipping was sunk in the war, over half of it by American submarines. Most critically, the submarine service cut off oil supplies from Southeast Asia to oil-dependent Japan and created desperate shortages of food and essential raw materials, including rubber, coal, lumber, iron ore, and nitrates for explosives. In the end, blockade would be far more damaging to the Japanese war economy than bombing. But before the war against shipping strangled its economy, Japan, "a maimed but still vicious tiger," amassed the strength for one final, furious struggle on the islands of Iwo Jima and Okinawa.[41]

FOR THE B-29S

On a night in May 1945, B-29 co-pilot Harry George was on a fire raid over Tokyo:

THE SEARCHLIGHTS LOCKED IN ON US. . . . Then the flak hit and the plane started to rock. The engineer behind me said, "I'm losing number one." Then he said, "Now I'm losing number three." Then the interphone went dead. No conversation at all. I used the emergency interphone and asked for a crew report. We had four men in the rear waist compartment. I waited probably ten seconds. Not a sound. Then all of a sudden the tail gunner reported he was okay. But no word from the waist compartment. So I took off my flak suit and went back there to see what happened.

We had dropped our bombs but were still on the edge of Tokyo with the flames, the burning. The navigator was beating out fires in the forward gun turret.

I got to the tunnel—there was thirty-five feet of narrow tunnel—and I went in with my parachute on. That made it tough for me to get through, and I started to think, "If we go down and I'm caught in this tunnel. . . ."

When I got through and stuck my head out at the other end it was an awful sight. Our left gunner was badly wounded. His jaw had been shot away by flak. He had lost the whole calf of one leg. The other gunner had a flak wound in his leg. The radar man, God bless him, was giving first aid. We had a top gunner there who also had a couple of small flak wounds. Meanwhile, we were being followed by a Baka Bomb, but he dropped off. . . .

As I started to help these guys we started back to Iwo Jima, which we had captured from the Japanese a couple of months before. That was three good hours away. We went through weather. We only had two engines. The bomb bay doors were hanging open. Couldn't get 'em closed. Finally got back to Iwo. The place was covered with fog. We couldn't get back to Tinian, another three and a half hours, so we just said we'd circle and wait. The control command at Iwo Jima said our best bet was to ditch the airplane near the beach and we said, "No, we will not ditch because our gunner will not survive a ditching." We had given him three pints of plasma and morphine. He thought he was going to die.

Then the engineer said, "We're about to run out of gas." So we had to try to land. It was light by this time, about nine o'clock in the morning. They directed us around the top of Mount Suribachi and down through the clouds. We got down to about fifty feet and didn't see the runway. All we saw was a cemetery and we didn't want to go there, so we pulled up around again trying to line up again over the island, which was only seven miles long. . . .

On the third pass around, the engines started cutting out. We were about out of gas. We just had enough to pull to 1,200 feet and we rang a bell for the crew to bail out. The bombardier had gone back and they were going to dump the badly wounded gunner, Dick Neil, out the back with his ripcord tied to a rope that was tied to the plane. But even though his jaw was gone, he was able to say he would get tangled up. He said, "I'll pull it." And so he bailed out and pulled his own ripcord. He landed about 500 yards from a MASH [Mobile Army Surgical Hospital] unit and they saved him.

The rest of us—all ten of us—bailed out and landed on the island, except the commander, Gus, who went into the water. A Navy boat went out to find him in the heavy fog, and they only found him because he was blowing that police whistle that's attached to the Mae West.

I landed in a big foxhole, a bomb shell hole. Then this big Marine comes sliding down in that volcanic dust, dust that's sand only it's black and a little more gravelly, and he says, "Are you all right?" And I said, "Boy, am I glad to see you Marines!"

That is why the Marines had been ordered to Iwo Jima—to save the bomber boys. After Iwo Jima was taken in late March, about 2,400 shot-up, fuel-starved B-29s would make emergency landings on or near the island. Iwo Jima saved almost 27,000 American airmen. But the cemetery that Harry George's crippled plane flew over, the largest American cemetery in the Pacific, contained almost 6,800 graves. In the sulfuric ash of barren Iwo Jima, the Marines fought their bloodiest battle ever, suffering more than 26,000 casualties. "The Marines did it," said a grateful Harry George, "for the B-29s."

Make Them Remember

TARGET: PLOESTI

The American air command in Europe was as determined as Curtis LeMay in the Pacific to end the war with bombing raids of ever greater ferocity. Airpower had been decisive in the Battle of the Bulge. German panzer divisions had run out of fuel before they could capture oil, gasoline, and diesel stocks in the Ardennes Forest. When the clouds lifted, the tanks, along with the entire German Army, had been savaged from the skies. Nazi armaments minister Albert Speer actually increased production of fighter planes and tanks in 1944, but Germany lacked the fuel to make them combat effective because American bombers had been hammering Nazi oil facilities since before D-Day.

Oil—the blood of modern warfare—was the fatal flaw in Hitler's war machine. Germany had been experiencing oil shortages since the beginning of the war, but except for a spectacular American raid in 1943 on the oil fields at Ploesti, Romania, the source of 35 percent of Hitler's oil, the Allies had failed to strike hard at the Reich's petroleum resources until April 1944.

That was when Spaatz and Doolittle went after Germany's entire oil infrastructure. Eighth Air Force targeted Germany's synthetic oil industry in an area north of Munich, while Fifteenth Air Force, operating from bases in Foggia, Italy, bombed Ploesti, as well as synthetic plants in Prussia and Germany's conquered satellites. By the conclusion of the Battle of the Bulge, the Americans had disabled Hitler's oil industry.

As the Wehrmacht was pushed back onto home soil on both the Eastern and Western Fronts, the Americans began hitting Germany's transportation system to prevent Hitler from mounting a final fight inside the Reich. This transportation offensive was massively effective, destroying the mobility of the German Army and crippling the entire national economy. Without a transportation network to move its products, and with oil reserves heavily depleted, German industry ground to a halt in early 1945.

Eighth Air Force was the darling of the American news media; and, in fairness, it did carry the burden of the air war. But Fifteenth Air Force—captured forever in Joseph Heller's *Catch-22*—contributed greatly to Germany's demise, knocking out vital economic targets beyond the reach of British-based bombers.

The Foggia plain, with its bombed-out German fighter bases, had been captured by the British Eighth Army in September 1943. But a year later, when ball turret gunner Clayton Ogle of Helena, Montana, arrived, conditions at the rebuilt Foggia airfields were still primitive. "Personnel were housed in pyramidal tents scattered among the trees in an almond and olive grove. . . . Beds were canvas cots with three GI blankets. Electrical wires from a generating plant were strung about the grove, but having no service we initially used candles. Lighting the tent was left to our own resourcefulness. . . . [A] GI helmet mounted on the center tent pole served as our wash basin."

The men used empty fuel drums to make gas stoves, which blew up with alarming frequency; and even when the snake- and bug-infested tents were wired with electricity, each tent had only one light. The fliers supplied the bulbs. The airfield was a converted grain field on the Foggia plain, whose runway "was 'paved' by interlocking steel matting which rattled unmercifully as we took off and landed. The rest of the Fifteenth Air Force's Bomb Groups were scattered in every direction in this Italian breadbasket."

Living quarters did improve at Foggia, but they were never as good of those of Eighth Air Force. Toward the end of the war, plumbing was installed and an officers

club was built by cheap Italian labor. For its opening, a band was hired and three B-17s were sent to Rome for women, arriving back at Foggia "loaded with ladies of easy virtue. . . . An enlisted man, I was not privy to the activities within their club," says Ogle. "I could only imagine the decadence behind those walls. For the next week great care was needed when opening the doors of tents about the squadron. One might interrupt more than one expected." [1]

The enlisted men consorted with Italian women from nearby villages. Sex was cheap: a few cigarettes, some rations, a handful of lira. When the enlisted men had dances, local prostitutes showed up and every room in the building was filled with copulating couples. The incidence of venereal disease shot up.

Some guys just stayed in their tents, loyal to loved ones at home. One bombardment outfit in Italy formed a Lonely Hearts Club, whose motto was "They break it and we can take it." War shattered engagements and marriages. The club's constitution put this melancholy fact in rhyme:

> *If you're bothered with an affair of the heart,*
> *If you feel you are drifting apart,*
> *If she says she met an interesting fellow,*
> *If instead of "Dear," she says "Hello,"*
> *Then, brother, you can sign*
> *On the dotted line.[2]*

In the spring and summer of 1944, Fifteenth Air Force's primary target was Ploesti. It was, said the Fifteenth's commander, General Nathan Twining, "Number One on the Hit Parade." The morning the crews first learned they were going to Ploesti there was silence in the briefing room, broken only, says pilot John Muirhead, "by half-stifled groans, by men shifting in their seats as if to try to move out of harm's way. I felt the edge of panic, the saving, urging impulse to run, to get away from it, the word, the terrifying word—Ploesti. The man beside me leaned forward and muttered, 'Oh, Christ, here we go.'"

Then the group commander lifted the black cloth that covered the big map. "He was barely able to restrain a proud smile at the stunned reaction to the long, eastward journey of the tape that stretched deep into Romania to a point just north of Bucharest. The colonel tapped his pointer on the map. 'There, gentlemen; there it is—Ploesti, a complex of eleven refineries with all the support installations: rail yards, tank farms, pumping stations, cracking plants—plenty for everybody. Every plane that can fly will be in the air today. . . . This is the beginning, gentlemen. This is the beginning."

The commander was smiling as he said this, and every man in the room hated him for that. Then came the words that dissolved the contempt. "I'll be leading the group today. There's no way you're going to leave the old man home on this one." The room broke into cheers and laughter. "We were all mad, as mad as men must be to cheer the words that would send them against this terrible fortress halfway round the world from home, to cheer as though it were a splendid game that only they could play."[3]

Flying escort on these hazardous missions were the Air Force's Black Eagles, the Tuskegee Airmen. Their job was to clear out the German fighters that would rise to intercept the big bombers.

THE RED TAILS

Since the summer of 1941 the Air Force had been training African-American cadets for flight duty at a segregated base in Tuskegee, Alabama. Black leaders had joined Eleanor Roosevelt to pressure her husband to integrate the all-white Army Air Corps, but few Air Force officials expected the all-black 99th Pursuit Squadron to see combat.

The Tuskegee Airmen lived in segregated and embarrassingly inferior facilities, even though a high percentage of the recruits had college degrees. There were separate drinking fountains and rest rooms, and a separate and unequal officers club. A black flier described a nearly identical club at Selfridge Field, near Detroit, where other African-American aviators were trained a year later. "Our officers' club was a small wooden building with a bar that literally shouted, 'Okay, niggers, this is good enough for you.' "[4]

There was not a base on which African-American soldiers and airmen were trained that was not rocked by racial incidents. In May 1943 the white commander at Selfridge Field, Colonel William T. Coleman, got staggering drunk at a base picnic and called for his staff car. When it arrived, he shouted, "I made it perfectly clear I didn't want a colored chauffeur!"[5] At which point he pulled out a pistol and shot the driver, Private Willie McRae, nearly killing him. Coleman was court-martialed and convicted—not of attempted murder but of assault.

When American forces landed in North Africa in early 1943 and started to run short of fliers, the call went out for the 99th Fighter Squad. The Tuskegee Airmen arrived too late to get into the fight against Rommel, but they saw action in Sicily and Italy with a succession of fighter groups. The black fliers were not prepared for combat. They were given obsolete planes and had received no training from battle-tested pilots. The pilots they served with in Italy were no help. Forty percent of the first fighter groups they joined were Southern whites, who called them "boys" and failed to take them seriously. They were in Italy only ninety days when the Air Force recommended that they be pulled from combat for failing to fight aggressively. One general wrote Hap Arnold that "the Negro type has not the proper reflexes to make a first-class fighter pilot."[6]

By the time these charges were filed, the commander of the squadron, Captain Benjamin O. Davis, Jr., a West Point graduate and the son of the Army's only African-American general, had been sent back to the States to assume command of another contingent of black aviators. This was the 332nd Fighter Group, in training at Selfridge Field. Davis's impressive testimony before a War Department committee on Negro Troop Policies, along with pressure from General George Marshall, kept the 99th in combat. When the 332nd Fighter Group arrived in Italy that summer, the 99th Pursuit Squadron was attached to it. It was the only black Air Force unit to serve in combat in World War II.

Iron-disciplined Benjamin Davis, who had bulled his way through West Point without a single cadet ever speaking to him, turned the 332nd into one of the finest

TUSKEGEE AIRMEN (M25).

fighter outfits in Europe. And morale soared when the group was transferred to silver P-51 Mustangs with bright red tails. "There, lady, was a plane!" Lieutenant Alexander Jefferson told a woman interviewer after the war. "The Mustang was the most beautiful thing to fly in the world."[7] From their base at Ramitelli, on the Adriatic, the "Red Tails" escorted heavy bombers to targets both across the Adriatic and over the Alps, most frequently to "Number One on the Hit Parade."

Ploesti was one of the most heavily defended targets in the Reich. Enemy fighter bases surrounded the vast field of refineries, and antiaircraft guns threw up a protective canopy of flak "so thick," said one Tuskegee flier, "it looked like a huge black doughnut suspended in air."[8] The Germans also placed 2,000 smoke generators around the oil fields, which created a Dantesque ring of swirling smoke: "When [the bombers] . . . came out of that holocaust of black smoke they were in tough shape," says Lieutenant Colonel Henry Peoples of the 332nd.[9]

The fighters covered the bombers when they were most vulnerable: after they had dropped their loads and were breaking off from the target. "It was then," writes John Muirhead, "when we came out of the barrage of flak, when damaged planes staggered and began to lag, when the empty spaces left by our fallen had to be filled, it was always then that the German fighters hit us hard."[10]

"From watching the bottom of the grotesque doughnut we had a good idea of what to expect," recalls Alexander Jefferson. "Planes fell in flames, planes fell not in flames, an occasional one pulled out and crash-landed. . . . Men fell in flames, men fell safely in their parachutes, some candle-sticked. Pieces of men dropped through that hole, pieces of planes. The sights we saw at Ploesti would make an addict's hallucinations look good. Have you any idea what it is like to vomit in an oxygen mask?" Jefferson asked an interviewer. "Some of the most battle-hardened of us did at the grisly sights we saw."

Those bomb boys "had seen the inside of hell, and if they could stay airborne we damned sure were going to take them back. . . . A large number of the bombers were totally unable to protect themselves on the return trip." To stay in the air, they had thrown almost everything overboard, even their guns. The holes in the bombers were so big that the fighter pilots would see inside the planes and tell how badly the crews had been mauled. If some "cripples" fell back, the Tuskegee airmen would fly in close, rock their wings in greeting, and nurse them back home. "I have often wondered," says Jefferson, "if any members of those bomber crews we flew escort for ever remembered after they came home that black men who did their jobs, sometimes going beyond orders, are the reason they came back to enjoy the privileges of this country."[11]

But the Red Tails *were* appreciated, at least during the war. On leave in Bari, Italy, Henry Peoples and a group of other fliers from the 332nd sat across from some bomber pilots in a local taverna. "One of them noticed us and said, 'Pardon me, but are you guys with the Red Tails?' We answered yes and before we knew what was happening we were surrounded and being kissed. If it was possible I was beet red, a man kissing me!" This happened a number of times and it always seemed to be a group of white Southerners who showed their appreciation with kisses, hugs, and free drinks. "I just could not help thinking to myself," said Peoples, a tough street kid from Chicago, "when I get back to the States I'll have to kill 'em but here we are kissing kin. Why couldn't we have saved some nice Northern liberals?" [12]

Fifteenth Air Force made its final raid on Ploesti on August 19, 1944. Several days later, the Soviets occupied the city and Romania surrendered. After this, the Red Tails concentrated on escorting bombers across the Alps and into Austria, Poland, and Germany. At first, the bomber pilots were reluctant to be escorted by the Black Eagles, but the word got out quickly. The Red Tails never went chasing after enemy fighters in combat looking for kills; they stuck with the bombers. Soon the Black Eagles, whose number would increase to 450, were in demand by all the bomber groups. Flying 200 missions, the 332nd never lost a bomber to an enemy fighter, a unique record.

But occasionally there was opportunity for glory. The Germans introduced jet fighters in the closing months of the war and the 332nd shot down three of them. "The jets . . . had to slow down to hit the bomber[s]," Captain Roscoe C. Brown said, describing a fight over Berlin. "That's when we'd get them. I pulled down and came up underneath this one jet as he was slowing down. I climbed right up his behind and got him." [13]

After the war, some of the men of the 332nd remarked that it was strange to work in close cooperation with white fliers in combat and not be able to socialize with them afterward. On one occasion, bad weather forced a white bomber squadron to land at their field at Ramitelli. "They remained with us either two or three days," says Captain Samuel Fuller. "Of necessity they had to eat with us, sleep with us, and a lot of guys gave up their beds and slept on pallets on the floor; they were our guests. We talked together, played cards together, had bull sessions together, did all of those things normally done by pilots and crews when they are socked in. . . . This was, to my knowledge, the only time a white squadron had a chance to live with Negroes and find out what we were all about. They found we lived the same, spoke the same language, didn't smell up the place, and were doing the same job they were doing and doing it well."

When it came time to leave, some of the white fliers "actually had tears in their eyes," says Fuller. "It stands out in my mind even today because it took an act of God, bad weather, to integrate the black and white air force for a few days."[14]

One of the most dangerous missions the Red Tails flew was to southern France to strafe radar installations guarded by German 88s. On one raid, seventy-two Red Tails were put over the target. They were to fly low, under the radar, but the Germans were ready for them. "When we got over the target they . . . shot up a wall of fire," recalls pilot Richard Macon. "We ran through [it] and my buddy was hit and his plane exploded. The parts flew everyplace. That does something to you. First of all it makes you feel happy. Happy because it wasn't you. And then you get angry. Angry because you've got to do something to avenge the death of your buddy. So I went in with this anger at those guys who were shooting the guns.

"But I ran through the same wall of fire and [one] wing was half ripped off. The plane was completely disabled, flipped over upside down." Macon prepared to parachute out, but flying at only 200 feet, upside down, with no control of the plane, he didn't think he had a chance of surviving. "Suddenly I was unconscious." At that point, the plane started to ascend and as it did, Macon, who had already loosened his safety belt and opened the canopy, was blown out. "About an hour later I regained consciousness on the ground. . . . My parachute was open, but I don't remember having pulled the [ripcord]."

When he regained consciousness, he noticed that his shoulder bone was sticking out through the skin, and although he didn't know it at the time, he had broken two vertebrae in his neck. Looking up, he saw three German soldiers standing over him with machine guns.

That night they put him in a stable. He heard some noises. He thought it was an animal, but when he went to check he discovered it was two other pilots from the 332nd. One of them was Alexander Jefferson.

The next day they were on their way to a prison camp fifty miles east of Berlin. At Stalag 3 they joined 5,000 or so other American fliers, including, a little later, more pilots from the Black Eagles. They remained there until near the closing weeks of the war.[15]*

---

*Sixty-six Tuskegee Airmen, out of a total of 450, were killed in combat and another thirty-three were either forced or shot down and became prisoners of war. They downed 108 enemy planes and earned a Presidential Unit Citation for courage in combat.

Dresden and the End

In late February 1945, Fifteenth Air Force participated with Eighth Air Force in one of the most controversial operations of the entire war, code-named CLARION. The Battle of the Bulge had just concluded, and American war leaders were alarmed by the continuing strength of German resistance. At this point, Generals Spaatz and Arnold proposed a radical measure to break the enemy's will to fight. The Americans would join the RAF in a series of systematic terror raids on small and medium-sized German towns. Light bombers, escorted by fighters, would be sent out against undefended targets all over Germany, chiefly railroad stations, bridges, and marshaling yards. After the dive-bombers had dropped their loads, the fighters would sweep in and finish these small-scale massacres. The air barons knew that these were the raids the German people dreaded most of all. The fighter-bombers came in suddenly, without warning, strafing houses and fields with machine guns, even killing the animals in the fields.

Doolittle and General Ira Eaker opposed Operation CLARION for strategic as well as moral reasons. The raids, they told Spaatz, would divert attention from the highly successful oil war and kill thousands of innocent civilians. "We should never allow the history of this war to convict us of throwing the strategic bomber at the man in the street," Eaker wrote Spaatz. CLARION, he said, would "absolutely convince the Germans that we are the barbarians they say we are, for it would be perfectly obvious to them that this is primarily a large scale attack on civilians, as, in fact, it of course will be." One protesting Air Force general called CLARION "a baby killing plan." [16]

CLARION went forward because Marshall and Roosevelt wanted Germans everywhere, not just in big cities, to feel the full weight of the war. Although this abbreviated operation had only limited success, it was an alarming indication of a loosening of moral restraints against terror bombing on the part of the Americans.

These restraints burst completely with Operation Thunderclap. Under pressure from Churchill, Allied air commanders issued new bombing directives in the early winter of 1945. When bad weather prevented pinpoint bombing of oil targets, bombers were to hit big population centers in eastern Germany, chief among them Berlin, Leipzig, and Dresden. These attacks would crowd roads and rail stations with panicked refugees, preventing the Germans from conducting a fighting retreat against the

Russians. The targets in Berlin and Leipzig were rail yards, but since the weather was bad, "blind bombing"—bombing by new and still inaccurate radar—was, in reality, terror bombing. This was not new policy. For over a year, Eighth Air Force had been sacrificing accuracy in order to fly more bombing missions, regardless of the weather. As the official Air Force historians put it: "Radar bombing was better than no bombing." [17]

On February 3, 1944, the Americans struck Berlin with over 900 bombers, the first of a succession of city-killing raids. B-17 waist gunner John Morris was on the biggest of these missions.

In *The Warriors,* J. Glenn Gray calls attention to the "enduring appeals of battle," the "powerful fascination" and emotional attraction of warfare. John Morris felt the pull of what Gray calls "war as spectacle" in the skies over Berlin, just after his air fleet had dropped its bombs.[18] "We must have been quite a sight: [over a] thousand heavy bombers, with their fighter cover high above them, strung out in a disciplined stream. . . . As we [led] the bomber stream curving away to the west, I could see for the first time off our portside the whole fantastic spectacle of the mighty machine of which I was a tiny, insignificant cog."

Even the devastation was strangely beautiful from 30,000 feet. There was a hole in the cloud bank and "slowly the glow of the fires of Berlin lit up the hole and smoke began pouring through. I watched for ten or twenty minutes—totally mesmerized. And the greatest spectacle I ever saw till then got more so. I could see another bomber stream coming up from the south. It was all the heavy bombers of the Fifteenth AAF . . . coming over the Alps from Italy. Their lead squadron arrived over Berlin just as our last one emptied its bomb bays, amazing coordination when you consider that our bases were separated by almost 1,000 miles.

"The memory of it all is still vivid for me today: the crystal clear skies, the extended suspense, and then the shock over the target, the magnificent display of the entire heavy bomber force of the United States in Europe passing with a stately cadence through the north German skies."

In the sky over shattered Berlin, Morris had another thought: these great bombers and their courageous crews were coordinated killing machines. "I do regret the human suffering we caused in Berlin," he writes in retrospect.[19]

On February 3, an estimated 35,000 civilians died in Berlin under the American bombs. At least that number died in Dresden on the night of February 13–14.

*   *   *

The Americans were scheduled to strike Dresden first, but were stalled by bad weather. Two waves of RAF Lancaster bombers flew ahead and obliterated the city, which was known for its splendid parks and fanciful architecture. As at Hamburg, the catastrophic combination of explosive and incendiary bombs ignited a firestorm that incinerated or suffocated a minimum of 35,000 people, many of them refugees fleeing the Red Army. Eighth Air Force followed the British that day and the next, hitting the marshaling yard, strafing the flaming buildings, and bombing the wide green spaces outside the city where the homeless sought shelter.

"The inner city was 100 percent destroyed," reported Joe Kleven and Art Kuespert, two American POWs who were sent to Dresden the next day to help with the cleanup. "Some areas, including the marshaling yard, escaped total destruction, thanks to the stupidity of the bomber command. Residents killed in this massive cremation will never be accounted for. Of the fifteen city hearses, fourteen were destroyed. Farmers and peasants from surrounding villages were ordered to drive their teams into Dresden for the task of hauling the dead to mass graves. Some of the victims were wrapped in brown paper. POWs were used to remove charred bodies from buildings. . . . A term that can be applied to what we saw—the people were 'broasted.'"

Kleven and Kuespert couldn't get the putrid smell of burning flesh off their clothing and they couldn't wash their clothing because they had nothing else to wear.[20]

Kurt Vonnegut, Jr., a POW working in a baby food factory in the area, had been moved to Dresden several days before the bombing. "The boxcar doors were opened, and the doorways framed the loveliest city that most of the Americans had ever seen." It looked to Vonnegut like Oz.

The prisoners were marched to a slaughterhouse and put into one of the buildings, a concrete shelter for pigs that were being readied for the butcher. The number over the building was five. Vonnegut was down in the meat locker when the bombs fell. It was a safe place.

They were not able to come out of the shelter until noon the next day. "Dresden was like the moon now, nothing but minerals. The stones were hot. Everybody else in the neighborhood was dead," Vonnegut would later write in his novel *Slaughterhouse-Five, or the Children's Crusade*. The prisoners noticed "little logs" lying on the pavements. "They were people who had been caught in the fire storm."

That afternoon American fighter planes strafed the city, killing survivors. "The idea was to hasten the end of the war."[21] Vonnegut would say later: "Only one person ever got any benefit from the bombing of Dresden, and he is me. I wrote an antiwar novel that made lots of money."[22]

Former POW Art Kuespert agrees with Vonnegut that "the bombing of Dresden didn't make that much difference in the outcome of the war."[23] John Morris, who flew on one of the strikes against Dresden, disagrees. "I don't rejoice in the 35,000 Germans killed there. Incidentally, I doubt that there were many Jews in that number; the good burghers of Dresden had shipped the last of them off to Auschwitz." Morris believes that the attacks on the transportation hubs on the eastern border of Germany—Berlin, Stettin, Frankfurt, Leipzig, and Dresden—shortened the war by disrupting the rearward movement of the Wehrmacht and preventing it from conducting a "last-ditch fight" on German soil. When people ask him why Dresden was bombed so late in the war, Morris replies that he and other airmen had no idea when the war would end. "The Ardennes [Battle of the Bulge] had taught us how dangerous it was to count the Germans out. We thought we had a lot of fighting left to do."[24]

With the bombing of Dresden, Eighth Air Force crossed a moral threshold. Both Eisenhower and Roosevelt went along with this. Eisenhower preferred precision bombing, but he wanted to end the war as quickly as possible. And Roosevelt believed that it was "of the utmost importance," as he wrote Secretary of War Stimson, "that every person in Germany should realize that this time Germany is a defeated nation. . . . The fact that they are a defeated nation, collectively and individually, must be so impressed upon them that they will hesitate to start any new war."[25]

What kind of behavior is morally justifiable to win a war against a ruthless enemy? That question would soon surface again, with even greater urgency, in the final weeks of the war against Japan. But in Europe the bombing was over, ended by the air barons on April 16, 1945, when they finally ran out of targets. The human cost of the air campaign in Europe is staggering. Some 650,000 German civilians died under the bombs, 20 percent of them children. Another 800,000 civilians were injured. The Americans lost 9,949 bombers, 8,420 fighter planes, and suffered 79,265 casualties. British losses were even greater. They were bombing much earlier than the Americans, their bombers were not so heavily armored as the Americans', and German night defense systems were awesomely effective, giving the lie to Bomber Harris's claim, early in the war, that night bombing would be safer than daylight raids. In total, the two forces lost 158,000 flying personnel. By comparison, the U.S. Marine Corps suffered 75,000 casualties (20,000 deaths) in the entire war.

The air campaign was bloody but undeniably effective. As the American reporter Allan A. Michie wrote at the end of the war, "The combined damaged areas of London, Bristol, Coventry and all the blitzed cities of Britain could be dumped in the ruins of just one medium-sized German city and hardly be noticed. The raid on Coventry in 1940 marked the peak of the Luftwaffe destructiveness; and there the Germans dropped 200 tons of bombs. By that standard Berlin suffered 363 Coventrys, Cologne 269, Hamburg 200 and Bremen 137." [26]

AMERICAN TANKS MOVE THROUGH THE BOMBED RUINS OF NUREMBERG (SC).

Every major German industry suffered serious setbacks. Oil production was stopped and not even two million foreign slave laborers, including American POWs, could repair the rail damage. By early 1945 the entire transportation system collapsed. Only the Allied postwar occupation, with its infusion of food, technology, loans, and medical supplies, prevented widespread starvation.[27]

The German economy did show amazing resilience, but it gives pause to consider how much more it would have produced had it not been bombed ruthlessly and relentlessly. The Allied air offensive also crushed the Luftwaffe, giving an enormous impetus to the Allied ground offensive in the last year of the war; and two million German workers had to be diverted to air defense operations, more than the entire workforce in the aircraft industry. Bomber Harris's city-shattering campaign also provoked Hitler to pour an enormous proportion of his resources into vengeance weapons in order to sustain home front morale. This prevented Germany from developing a more effective antiaircraft system, making more vulnerable her cities, factories, and workers. And it was a wounding financial drain. By some recent estimates, the V-2 program alone cost Germany, proportionally, as much as the Manhattan Project cost the United States.[28] The air campaign did not completely crush German civilian morale. But it dealt it a punishing blow; and it often took police state methods to meet production quotas and discourage discontent and passivity.

Nazi Germany could not have been brought to the brink of defeat without the Allied Air Forces. Except in official propaganda, and a few scholarly studies, the Air Forces' contribution to victory has been greatly undervalued to this day, perhaps because bombing is such an odious and randomly destructive way of conducting war, killing as it does both combatants and noncombatants. And to give strategic bombing its just due in bringing down Hitler's Reich is almost to sanction total war, the most awful invention of all time.

It has become fashionable to see World War II as preeminently a war of machines, with the side with the best and the most machines winning. Some historians even argue that the war was won in the factories and foundries of America, in places like Henry Ford's Willow Run Plant, near Detroit, where an assembly line a mile long poured out B-24 bombers at a rate of a plane every sixty-three minutes. But there were human beings operating these great killing engines, in the sky and on the ground. In every aspect of the war, and in every theater of the conflict, the human factor was paramount. We have to believe this, if only to distribute the blame for the massive destruction these machines delivered.

One of the most powerful of the war engines was the bomber, a terrifying instrument, especially when tightly massed in combinations of over a thousand. Yet in the end, the war in Europe would be won on the ground. In 1945, millions of tired and grubby foot soldiers, advancing like converging avalanches from east, west, and south, prepared to deliver Nazi Germany the lethal blow the air barons never could.

From the Volga
to the Oder

After the Russian victory at Stalingrad on February 2, 1943, it was ebb tide for the Germans. Russia had inflicted upon the German Army irreparable losses of manpower, tanks, planes, and military equipment, and Germany was now fighting a man-draining two-front war, with incessant bombing seriously cutting into its production. And Russia, despite its huge losses of troops and territory in the first eighteen months of the war, was growing steadily stronger. New armies were being raised, new generals were forging to the front, new arms and equipment were coming off the nation's production lines and pouring in from Britain and the United States.

As soon as Germany had attacked Russia, Britain initially sent over token aid, and thereafter it gave generously of its own limited production. U.S. lend-lease had been extended to Russia early in the war, as well, and eventually its contribution was tremendous. Altogether, to January 1944, the United States sent Russia under lend-lease 7,800 planes, 4,700 tanks and tank destroyers, 170,000 trucks, millions of boots and shoes, over a million tons of steel, and two and a quarter million tons of food.

With new armies and equipment the Russians could seize and hold the offensive. The westward movement of the Red Army that started before Stalingrad and in the

Caucasus at the end of 1942 never stopped until the Red banner was planted in the ruins of Berlin. All through 1943 and 1944 the Russians drove relentlessly forward in the greatest counteroffensive in the history of land warfare. One after another, vast areas that the Germans had occupied and gutted were rewon: the Caucasus, the Donbas, Ukraine, White Russia, the Crimea.

THE LIBERATION OF RUSSIA

As the Russians were annihilating the German Sixth Army before Stalingrad, 1,000 miles to the north the long siege of Leningrad was drawing to a close. The first blow in the counteroffensive that was to liberate Russia's former capital was struck from Oranienbaum—"the Tobruk of the Leningrad front." The main attack came on the morning of January 12, 1943, and within a few hours the Russians had crossed the ice, stormed the formidable defenses, and established themselves on the left bank of the Neva River.

But the Germans were not driven away from the Leningrad region for fully a year, as the Red Army had to root them out of each pillbox and fortification, at a cost of more than 250,000 casualties. During that year there was continuous fighting, usually on a small scale. Now that access to Leningrad was easier, the striking power of the Russian Army there could be reinforced.

Some of the most ferocious fighting of the entire war took place in July 1943 in the Kursk-Oreal region, the spacious grasslands north and east of Stalingrad. There the Germans and Russians fought the greatest tank battle of the war and the largest land battle in all of history. The Germans struck first with almost half a million men and over 3,000 massive tanks and self-propelled 70-ton tank destroyers against the million and more Soviet defenders of Kursk, 3,200 tanks, and 13,000 artillery pieces and mortars, this vast assemblage of men and arms lined up behind massive field fortifications with heavily mined approaches.

When the German tank attack failed, the Russians, under cover of a cloud-splitting artillery barrage, launched a furious counteroffensive, and, just one month after the Nazis had begun their last major offensive of the war, pushed them back to where they had begun. From this point in the war, the German armies in Russia were in retreat.

As the Wehrmacht pulled back from Stalingrad and the region of the Caucasus it ran into the Cossacks, among the most feared horse soldiers in the world. Pyotr

Pavlenkio, covering the conflict for a Soviet publication, reported how the older men came out of retirement to teach the trade of war as the Cossacks had been practicing it for centuries:

I WAS THEIR GUEST for a few days. They were holding a sort of training course in saber fighting. Nikifor Natluck, a Cossack from the *stanitsa* [village] of Labinskoy, a patriarchal old man, whose sons are prominent Cossack Red Army commanders, proposed that young Cossacks should be taught the immortal saber blow of the Zaporozhye Cossacks.

"The German must be slashed from the shoulder to the groin," he said. "Anyone can cut off a head or slice off an arm, but a Cossack must wield his saber as his great-grandfathers did."

Another of the instructors was Trofim Njegoduyko, whose forefathers came with the first settlers from the mouth of the Dnieper in the time of Empress Catherine II. . . .

Now, at 54 years of age, he is a senior sergeant, a volunteer in the Red Army. He fought near Moscow . . . and later back home in the Kuban. . . .

"I've known 16 generals in my time," he told me, "and honestly they all treated me like a brother."

"Why was that?"

He smoothed the flowing gray-black beard which spreads over his Circassian coat, and kept silent for some time, loving to keep our curiosity suspended in mid-air. Finally he said, "I do a Cossack's job well. What do they want from a Cossack? Fierceness. They expect him to deal heavy strokes. Well, I deal such strokes. A good stroke, boys, is never forgotten. It lives forever." . . .

In 1914, near Gumbinen, Trofim's father cut a German in six parts with two blows of his sword. It was the famous "criss-cross" blow, and the fame of it drew young officers to study with Alexander Njegoduyko. He showed them how to cut a calf in two, or a piece of cloth thrown up into the air.

Trofim Alexandrovich has upheld the honors of his family. . . . The silver hilt [of his sword] is . . . covered with 131 copper dots like freckles. That is Trofim's score of killed Germans. Trofim Alexandrovich says that eight dots are missing; they dropped off by accident.

Not all the 139 Germans were cut up: many of them tasted lead bullets, others were destroyed with the rifle butt or crushed under Trofim's horse. With his sword he killed 43 Germans. . . .

With one blow he cut a German officer near Rostov in three parts: head and shoulders, half the body and an arm, and the rest of the body.

Now he has been invited to show young Cossacks the art of sword play. Upright on his horse, he gallops spiritedly up to the clay figure of a German with out-spread arms. The young folks have been hacking away unsuccessfully at this "German" since the early morning. But their swords have got stuck in the moist clay at the level of the heart, or they have struck off only the head, which of course cannot be considered a decent stroke. Even a child can strike off a head.

So 54-year-old Trofim Njegoduyko, with set teeth, dashes up on his russet horse. The sword glitters brightly in his hand. He rises in his stirrups, raises the blade, and the clay German falls in two pieces.

The young folk shout "Hurrah!" Trofim, reining in his horse, explains: "The hardest thing, my lads, is to cut clay. I can feel no hatred for a clay figure, and therefore there is no heat in doing it. Why do I cut it? Only for the sake of your education.

"But my heart's not in it. I feel no anger. The conclusion to be drawn from this is that it is easier to strike at a German. In the first place, he usually turns tail. So if you stick a sword into him he'll run up it himself. He'll cut himself up. In the second place, you've got to apply pressure along the length of the blade, not downwards. It's not the same as chopping wood.

"Use your imagination. Pretend that the German is very broad and you're cutting him open like a cake. Don't hurry. Take it easy, and everything will turn out well.

"Of course, psychology plays a part too," adds Trofim mockingly. "But it's none of our business if a German yells. If the Germans don't like it they should have stayed at home in Germany. But once they've come on to our territory, friend, crying won't help. Run, damn you, run up the blade!" [1]

The fighting in the Kuban, the Kerch Peninsula, and the Crimea was as tough as any in the great 1943–44 counteroffensives. Not until October 1943 did the Germans finally retire from the Caucasus to the Crimea, and not until December were the Russians able to establish a beachhead on the Kerch Peninsula.

Meantime the Russians were fighting their way, village by village and town by town, from Rostov to Melitopol and the Perekop Peninsula. In October Melitopol was cleared, street by street. With control of the entire Sea of Azov, the Russians moved in

April 1944 to reconquer the Crimea and its naval base at Sevastopol. It had taken the Germans seven months to take Sevastopol. The Russians retook it in as many days.

By early summer of 1944 Russian armies were fighting in Poland, Finland, and Romania. During June, Finland's Mannerheim Line was breached and by September Finland had asked for an armistice. This was granted, but German divisions there kept on fighting—as they did in Italy—and in the frozen north the war went on for months.

That summer the Russians pushed steadily into pre-1939 Poland and by July they were storming at Pinsk, Lvov, and Lublin. The Nazis fought furiously to defend Lublin, for near here was the notorious Majdanek death camp—one of many which they had set up in Poland.

In August, Romania quit and joined the Allies, while the Russians drove on Bulgaria and Hungary. Meantime the British had landed in the Peloponnesus and liberated Athens, as the Germans hastily tried to pull out what divisions they had in the Balkans.

By the end of 1944 the situation in the East had undergone a convulsive change. All Russia was free. The Nazis were extricating themselves from the Balkans, and of the Eastern European countries only Hungary remained a reluctant Axis ally. Finland was out of the war against Russia and in the war against Germany. Half of Poland had been liberated and the assault on Warsaw was about to begin. The Red Army was already in East Prussia, and Germany had lost over a million men in the slashing Soviet counteroffensive.[2]

INTO GERMANY

During 1945 the attention of Americans was fastened on the swift campaign across the Rhine and into Germany. The Russian campaigns in the East seemed distant and confused. Yet these gigantic campaigns were on a far larger scale than those in the West. Far more soldiers were engaged and far more territory was involved than in the fighting in any other theater of the war.

While the Red Army was storming ahead in the Balkans and in the far north, the enormous armies along the center of the line were regrouping and reorganizing for the final lunge. Then, at the beginning of the new year, the grand strategy of this last series of campaigns unfolded. From the south, Russian armies advanced into Hungary

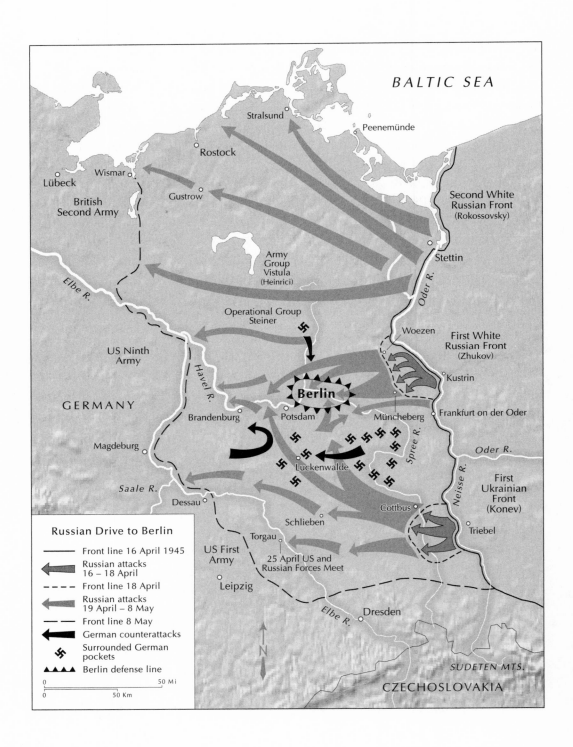

BALTIC SEA

Stralsund

Peenemünde

Rostock

Wismar

Lübeck

British
Second Army

Gustrow

Second White
Russian Front
(Rokossovsky)

Stettin

Army
Group
Vistula
(Heinrici)

Elbe R.

Oder R.

Operational Group
Steiner

Woezen

First White
Russian Front
(Zhukov)

US Ninth
Army

Havel R.

Kustrin

Berlin

GERMANY

Brandenburg

Potsdam

Müncheberg

Frankfurt on der Oder

Spree R.

Oder R.

Magdeburg

Luckenwalde

Saale R.

First
Ukrainian
Front
(Konev)

Dessau

Neisse R.

Cottbus

Triebel

Schlieben

US First
Army

Torgau

25 April US and
Russian Forces Meet

Leipzig

Elbe R.

Dresden

Russian Drive to Berlin

—— Front line 16 April 1945

◄ Russian attacks
16 – 18 April

----- Front line 18 April

◄ Russian attacks
19 April – 8 May

– – – Front line 8 May

◄ German counterattacks

卐 Surrounded German
pockets

▲▲▲ Berlin defense line

0   50 Mi

0   50 Km

N

SUDETEN MTS.

CZECHOSLOVAKIA

and Austria, seeking to flank Germany in one of the greatest encircling operations in military history. To the north, Soviet forces leaped forward from their line along the Vistula in a race for the Oder, which forms the border between eastern Germany and Poland. Still farther to the north other armies drove on Danzig, and Koenigsberg in East Prussia.

The speed of the new offensive caught the world by surprise. The drive from Warsaw to the west started on January 12; in three weeks the Red Army was attacking Frankfurt an der Oder—275 miles away, on the German border.

The capture of Warsaw was the climax to one of the cruelest tragedies of the war. At the beginning of the previous August the patriot forces of that decimated city, believing that the current Russian offensive would

SOVIET INFANTRY AND ARMOR TAKING A GERMAN TOWN (M25).

carry across the Vistula, rose against their German conquerors urged on by Soviet radio. But the Russians stopped in the suburbs of Warsaw on the east bank of the Vistula, and for sixty-three days the Poles waged an unequal conflict, fighting from street to street and house to house, enduring bombing, starvation, and death against ruthless SS troops. There was little left of Warsaw when the Russians entered in January 1945. In a two-month reign of revenge, the Nazis had slaughtered over 200,000 Poles and demolished their ancient city block by block. Stalin was complicit in the crime. He had refused to send aid and prevented the British and the Americans from using his air bases to ship matériel to the anti-Communist rebels. He allowed the Nazis to do his dirty work for him, eliminating a likely source of resistance to future Soviet tyranny in Warsaw.[5]

After the first advance to the Oder there was another pause while the main Red armies of Generals Georgi Zhukov and Ivan Konev regrouped and brought up supplies for the last offensive—the assault on Berlin. The two great drives to the Brandenburg Gate, one that had started from the banks of the Volga, the other from the beaches of Normandy, were about to join.

Across the Rhine

"CLEAN 'EM OUT"

With victory in Europe close at hand, Roosevelt, Churchill, and Stalin met in February 1945 at Yalta in the Crimea to draw up plans for the final offensive. The Big Three also reiterated their demand for unconditional surrender and formulated terms for the dismemberment of Germany, with the United States, England, France, and the Soviet Union given separate zones of occupation.

That month the Allies began the drive to the Rhine, one of the great campaigns of the war. Hitler again gambled and decided to make his stand west of the Rhine, with the river at his Army's back. From his new headquarters and residence, an eighteen-room underground bunker in Berlin, he appealed to the patriotism of his troops, warning them that the enemy's insistence on unconditional surrender meant that the Fatherland would be turned into powder and dust by the invading hordes. You are fighting, he told his troops, for Fatherland and family. And he promised new "miracle weapons" that would turn the tide.

These were empty appeals, vacant threats. The Ardennes campaign had depleted

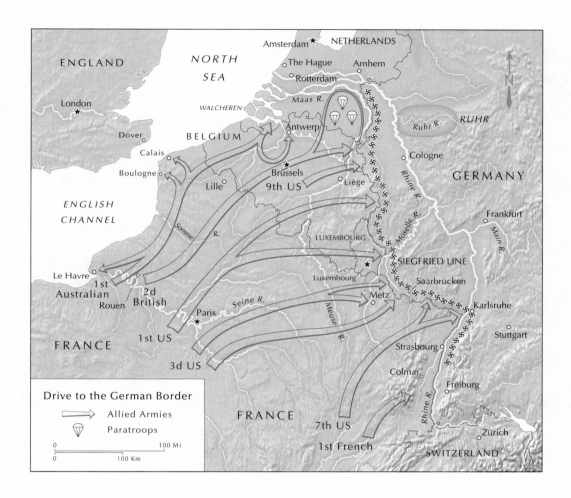

Drive to the German Border

→ Allied Armies

⛉ Paratroops

0 _____ 100 Mi
0 _____ 100 Km

the German Army in the West. It had the equivalent of twenty-six divisions, all of them under-equipped, against Eisenhower's fully armed eighty-five divisions. From mid-February to late March, Nazi power west of the Rhine was shattered. In a little over a month, the Germans were pushed back across the Rhine, with Montgomery's armies doing the hardest fighting, in assaults launched from Holland across flooded fields and through the dense Reichswald Forest. "It was in March of 1945," Chet Hansen, General Bradley's chief of staff, wrote in his diary, "that we broke the back of the German Army."[1]

U.S. tanks and infantry pass dead German troops near Hanover (SC).

In places along the Rhine where the fighting was toughest, some men managed, in rare moments, to acknowledge the humanity of the enemy. On guard duty one evening, Albert W. Scribner, an American GI, stood his watch with a dead German lieutenant at his feet, his "still helmeted body profiled against the white snow. One sees many dead in combat areas," he said later, "however such occasions are usually brief encounters occurring when moving along the way." It was entirely different to stand next to a man for hours and "to wonder about who he was, what his aspirations were," who his loved ones were, and what they were doing at this moment, not knowing he was lying dead on frozen mud on the German frontier.

At one point during the night, Scribner lightly pressed his boot against the side of the German's "now freezing body in an earnest but futile attempt to convey to him some sort of final farewell." [2]

* * *

At Cologne, Coblenz, Bonn, and every other point that the Allied troops reached the Rhine, the Germans blew the bridges as they retreated eastward. But on March 7, when a task force of the 9th Armored Division moved up the left bank of the Rhine to the little town of Remagen, south of Bonn, it found an enormous railroad bridge miraculously intact. *Yank* correspondent Ed Cunningham describes the fight for the Bridge at Remagen:

FOR TWENTY-SEVEN YEARS the Ludendorf Bridge connecting the pictur-esque riverside villages of Remagen and Erpel was known to very few people outside the wine-growing Ahr Valley. But for ten days during World War II this obscure span across the Rhine was probably the most important military property on the whole of the Western Front. . . .

On March 7, 1945, the U.S. Army's 9th Armored Division rumbled into the

THE BRIDGE AT REMAGEN (NA).

Rhine village of Remagen for what it thought would be the climax of its seven-day drive across 40 miles of German territory. The tankmen and armored infantrymen expected to reach the banks of the Rhine and stop there for a rest while the Allied high command completed plans for the crossing of that last barrier to the heart of Germany.

The bridges spanning the Rhine at Cologne, Bonn, and Coblenz had been blown up by the retreating Germans. When the 9th Armored reached Remagen it naturally looked for the blasted remains of the Ludendorf Bridge. Instead, the three-span structure was still standing. The German engineers assigned to destroy it had apparently delayed their work too long.

Realizing the value of their find, the armored infantrymen rushed past the pair of fortress-like towers guarding the bridge's main spans and headed for the east bank of the Rhine. The Germans on the far bank, now equally conscious of the Ludendorf's importance, set off two demolitions. One of the explosions damaged the eastern span, but it failed to stop the armored infantrymen from continuing across the bridge and establishing the first Allied bridgehead on the east bank of the Rhine.

The Ludendorf Bridge, overshadowed for twenty-seven years by its more important sister spans across the Rhine, had won its place in history.

For ten days the Ludendorf basked in its glory as the world's most important bridge. It was a high-priority military objective now. American troops and tanks rolled across it to enlarge the bridgehead. German air artillery, realizing its importance, attacked it daily. Maybe such belated attention was too much for the Ludendorf. Anyway, on the afternoon of March 17, the bridge suddenly crumbled and its three spans dropped into the Rhine. But the Ludendorf, while meeting the same fate as the other bridges of the Rhine, had won a space in history that the more important bridges could never attain.

The Ludendorf's ten days of fame began at 1550 hours on March 7. First Lt. Karl Timmermann of West Point, Neb., was telling his men of Able Company of the 27th Armored Infantry Regiment that he had just received orders to cross the bridge. The Germans were scheduled to blow it at 1600. . . .

The lieutenant had barely finished his announcement when an explosion shook the east span of the structure. Timmermann hollered, "As you were!" Then, seeing the three spans still standing, he repeated the order of attack and shouted, "Let's go!"

The 1st Platoon . . . started across, followed by the 3d and 2d Platoons, in that order. With them went three armored engineers, a lieutenant, and two sergeants, to cut the demolition wires so the Germans would not set off further charges.

Running and ducking like halfbacks on a broken-field gallop to avoid the machine gun and sniper fire, A Company reached the towers on the far side of the bridge.

"The bullets didn't worry us half as much as the bridge," . . . Gaccarino Mercandante, a mortarman from Brooklyn, explained later. "We expected the Heinies to blow the bridge right out from under us at any minute, so we didn't waste any time getting to the other side. It didn't mater how many Germans might be there; we just wanted to get off that bridge fast . . ."

Rushing up the winding stairs of the right tower, . . . Sgt. Joseph Delisio of New York City, the 3d Platoon leader, broke in on a Jerry machine gun nest on the second floor, expecting a fight with the two-man crew who had been spraying the advancing Americans. Instead, he found the two Jerries meekly waiting to be captured. . . . [Three other men from the 3rd Platoon] got the same result in the left tower. The lone German manning the machine gun there surrendered immediately. . . .

Meanwhile the three armored engineers had cut all the wires on the west and center spans of the bridge, which prevented electricity getting through to set off the caps on the 40-pound charges the Jerries had planted under the decking on the bridge's crossbars. Then they made a dash for the far side to cut the main cable which controlled the entire demolition set-up. When they found it, it was too heavy to cut with their small pliers. But Sgt. Eugene Dorland of Manhattan, Kans., solved that problem by riddling the cable with three well-aimed shots from his carbine. Then he went back to hunting other demolitions along with his platoon leader, 1st Lt. Hugh Mott of Nashville, Tenn., and Sgt. John Reynolds of Lincolnton, N.C., the other two engineers.

They found one 500-pound TNT charge set up with time fuses near the north railing, about two-thirds of the way across the bridge. It had not exploded, even though the cap went off. Across the board-covered railroad tracks was another charge, which had been set off just before Able Company started across the bridge. That blast knocked out one of the main diagonal supports on the upstream side of the main arch, destroyed a section of the bridge flooring, and left a six-inch sag at the damaged pier point.

"Both piers had 350-pound TNT demolitions in them which hadn't been set off," Lt. Mott said. "The Germans had enough stuff in that bridge to drop it right to the bottom of the Rhine but we were lucky. The one heavy charge that didn't explode had either a faulty cap or something was wrong with the explosive itself. Besides that, before we started across, one of the cables to the main charge had been cut in two, evidently by a million-to-one direct hit by our artillery."

Under the cover given the Able Company men in the two towers, Sgt. Alexander Drabik of Holland, Oh., and Pfc. Marvin Jensen of Slayton, Minn., ran down the bridge approach and on to the east bank of the Rhine. They were followed almost immediately by [seven other men] . . .

For the first thirty minutes of the crossing, Able Company fought alone on the east bank of the Rhine. The men cleared the nearby village of Erpel and the roads leading to the bridge. . . .

At 1630, with the bridge safe for heavy traffic and a company bridgehead firmly established on the pay-off side of the Rhine, Brig. Gen. William H. Hoge of Lexington, Mo., commander of Combat Command B, which swept through Remagen to grab the war's most unexpected prize, gave the orders for reinforcements to cross. Armored infantryman, engineers, tanks, . . . and antiaircraft crews started rolling.[5]

Furious at the loss of this critical bridgehead, Hitler changed theater commanders, replacing Rundstedt with Kesselring, the cagey defensive fighter who had given the Allies so much trouble in Italy. But there was no stopping the Allied advance from the Rhine on the west and the Vistula on the east.

After crossing the Rhine at Remagen, the American First Army fanned out and poured across the Rhineland plain. As the Germans hurried up reinforcements, they weakened their defenses elsewhere along the river. In the last week of March, four armies crossed the Rhine on barges and on pontoon bridges constructed with spectacular speed by their engineers. And in the last airborne operation in Europe, British and American paratroopers were dropped on the east bank of the Rhine at Wesel, right on the German defense line. Robert Capa was with them.

Before they took off the American paratroopers shaved their heads in Mohawk style. Capa wouldn't let them touch his hair, but he did fly in the lead plane and was the second to jump, right behind the regimental commander. Capa was scared, but he tried not to let on, conspicuously reading a mystery novel as his plane flew over France. When it came time to jump he was only on page sixty-seven. "For a moment, I had the foolish idea of saying, 'Sorry, I cannot jump. I have to finish my story.'"

As he stood in front of the open door behind the colonel, 600 feet above the

U.S. TANKS LADEN WITH TROOPS ROLL INTO INNSBRUCK, AUSTRIA. THE SURRENDERING
GERMAN TROOPS ON THE STREET HAVE NOT YET BEEN COLLECTED (SC).

Rhine, bullets began smashing into the plane. The airborne boys screamed
"Umbriago!" and Capa leaped out the door with his cameras wrapped around him. As
he descended he took out a camera and shot some pictures. When he landed he kept
clicking, catching the men running toward gliders that carried the big guns. "We lost
many of our men, but this was easier than Salerno or Anzio or Normandy. The
Germans of those campaigns could have murdered us here, but these Germans were
beaten."[4]

With seven armies across the river, the German resistance was broken. Only 250
miles separated the Allied armies in the West from the Red Army in the East. That
tremendous Army was massed in front of the Oder River preparing for the final,
revengeful drive on Berlin.

The culminating battle of the Rhineland campaign was the fight for the Ruhr,
Germany's industrial heart. In an audaciously conceived strategy, Eisenhower and
Bradley had their armies encircle the Ruhr, then split it in two. In the cleanup opera-

GERMAN PRISONERS ON THE AUTOBAHN, AS THIRD ARMY
ROLLS PAST THEM TO THE FRONT (SC).

tion, the Allies captured 325,000 prisoners of the dying Reich. It was the largest mass
surrender of the war. Walter Model, the German commander, blew his brains out
rather than surrender. "A Field Marshal," he declared, "does not become a prisoner." [5]

Thereafter, the drive became a pursuit. Montgomery's armies liberated most of
the Netherlands and drove into Bremen and Hamburg. The American First and Ninth
Armies went straight for the Elbe River. Patton's tank men, led by the 761st Tank
Battalion, sped into southern German toward the Austrian Alps, where Eisenhower
believed, erroneously, that Hitler was building a National Redoubt, a mountain stronghold from which he would mastermind a last-ditch guerrilla war. "At last we had Jerry
on the run everywhere, and it was just a matter of running him to earth and destroying him, and getting this damned war over," a member of the 761st told Trezzvant W.
Anderson, an African-American correspondent for the Army who wrote *Come Out*

Fighting, a history of the tank battalion.[6] The Americans had no trouble with the regular German soldiers they met up with, who surrendered willingly. "[But] we had to kill the SS men because they wouldn't surrender," says Christopher Sturkey of the African-American 614th Tank Destroyer Battalion. "They wanted to fight to the death; they wanted it the hard way and that's just the way they got it."[7]

Toward the end of the war, some of the men of the 761st began to wonder "what the history writers would say about us. Not much we thought, for we had not seen a war correspondent since Anderson . . . had left us late in November 1944." As Anderson wrote in 1945, when he reunited with the 761st in Austria: "There were 32 different combat units in service on the Western Front and in Italy. Very few . . . of these were visited by correspondents." Only three correspondents, including Anderson, visited the 761st, whose soldiers earned eight Silver Stars, sixty-two Bronze Stars, and 296 Purple Hearts in 183 days of combat without a break.[8]

Moving across Germany on the autobahns with their powerful Sherman tanks, "firing on enemy troops hidden in the woods along the great highway," it was thrilling for the men of the 761st to be conquering mile after mile of the sacred soil of the world's most infamous racists. "It was during this period," writes Trezzvant Anderson, "that Sergeant Jonathan B. Hall had to stand and watch a German SS trooper pull a razor and slash his own throat from ear to ear, in front of Hall's tank, rather than surrender to these colored tankers. He slowly bled to death writhing on the ground, as Hall and his crewmen watched the life ebb from his body."[9]

As the Allies penetrated deep into Germany, opposition melted. Nazi Party leaders ordered old men and boys into battle without uniforms or training. Some obeyed and were either bypassed by the advancing Allied troops or mowed down. Other *Volkssturm* units assembled but broke up and returned to their homes when long lines of Shermans came rumbling into their towns.

About this time a lot of GIs started to become extra cautious. No one wanted to be one of the last men killed in a war that was already won. In the waning moments of a fight near the Elbe River, Dutch Schultz heard a German machine gun open up on his unit from a wooded area nearby. "For the sake of glory, I decided to go after it with hand grenades. After running into the woods and crawling about fifty feet in the general direction of the machine gun, I suddenly thought, 'Why in hell am I doing this?'

"Without so much as a second thought, I retraced my steps and rejoined my platoon."[10]

* * *

A DYING REICH RECRUITS GRANDFATHERS AND GRANDCHILDREN (NA).

Everywhere, American soldiers witnessed symptoms of the German collapse. *Yank* correspondent Allan B. Ecker was on an Elbe River ferryboat when he met a German woman with four children, all of them crying uncontrollably. Ecker asked her where she was going. She replied in words that epitomized the plight of a people caught in a gigantic, fast-closing vise: "We left Bradenburg two days ago because the Russian bombs and shells leveled our home there. Where are we going? To a big city where we have relatives.

"Perhaps you've been there? It's called Aachen."[11] No one had told her that Aachen was no more.

"From the Rhine to the Oder the shooting war quickly changed into a looting war," wrote Robert Capa. "The GIs fought their way ahead, meeting less and less resistance and finding more and more cameras, Lüger pistols, and frauleins."[12] Ordered, under penalty of court-martial, from associating with white women in the

Texas town where they trained, members of the 761st found themselves, in the land of the master race, besieged by its women.

As American troops cut through Germany they heard one refrain from the defeated citizenry: "We are not Nazis!" Nazis were in the next neighborhood, the next village. And Jews? "There weren't any Jews in this town." And no one, wrote Martha Gellhorn, had any relatives who were in the Army. "I worked on the land. I worked in a factory. That boy wasn't in the army, either; he was sick. Ach! How we have suffered! The bombs. We lived in the cellars for weeks. We have done nothing wrong. We were never Nazis!"

Some Germans tried to befriend the American conquerors, claiming they had been waiting to be liberated from Nazi tyranny. The GIs didn't go for it. "They can talk their heads off; sing the *Star-Spangled Banner*. They are still Germans," wrote Gellhorn, "and they are not liked. No one has forgotten yet that our dead stretch back all the way to Africa." [13]

It is often assumed that the citizen soldiers who knocked out the Fascists did not fight for flag and country—for high purpose—but only for their buddies. As John Steber, a veteran of Omaha Beach and the Bulge, put it: "When guys are dying around you, you don't think of your country. You fight to save your ass; and you keep on fighting because you don't want to let your buddies down or look like a coward in front of them." But then, Steber added: "When things quiet down sometimes you'd think: it's those fucking Nazis who started this thing and we've got to take 'em out before they take over the world. By the time we got to Germany we'd seen a lot of the evil things the krauts had done. We wanted to make 'em pay, clean 'em out and head home." [14]

A few GIs even thought they were liberating the Germans. "Why are you making war against us?" a German soldier asked an American prisoner who spoke perfect German. His unforgettable reply was: "We are fighting to free you from the fantastic idea that you are a master race." [15]

The armies of the master race were now confronting, to their disgust, African-American infantrymen, in addition to African-American armored and artillery units. "Negroes are now being used in volunteer platoons with our divisions and according to Bradley they are doing well," Chet Hansen wrote in his diary on April 8.[16] The decision to allow African-Americans to serve in formerly all-white infantry platoons was made during the Battle of Bulge when the Army's pool of manpower ran dangerously low, with no reservoir of available troops back in the United States. African-American members of service units like the old Red Ball Express were asked to volunteer for combat duty and serve as replacements in white platoons. This was the initiative of General John C. H. Lee, a logistics officer who had advanced views on racial relations, suggesting that white and black troops should fight "shoulder to shoulder to bring about victory." [17] It was a radical change in Army policy. Before this, some commanders in the field had brought together white and African-American artillery battalions and attached black armored units, like the 761st, to white organizations. The only African-American infantry unit fighting in Europe, the 92nd Division in northern Italy, fought as a separate black unit, commanded by white officers. Nowhere in Europe—or anywhere else—were black and white American infantrymen fighting "shoulder to shoulder" in the same platoons.

George Patton adamantly opposed the new policy, claiming that Southern-born white troops would find it reprehensible to serve alongside African-Americans, eating, sleeping, and fighting together. And Eisenhower's chief of staff, General Walter Bedell Smith, argued that it would encourage civil rights organizations in their fight to integrate the entire Army. But, for strictly military reasons, Eisenhower went ahead with the experiment. He simply didn't have enough white soldiers to finish the job.*

There was no great rush to volunteer. "The way I felt about it was what's the use of going out and fighting when you're a second class citizen," recalls James Rookard.[18] But by February 1945, over 4,500 African-Americans had signed on for combat duty. Hundreds of them were sergeants or noncommissioned officers who took a cut in pay and a drop in rank to serve on the line. "Oh, I was generous," says James Strawder. "I gave 'em my stripes. I went from buck sergeant to buck private for a chance to get shot at." [19]

After taking an accelerated training program, roughly half of the volunteers were organized into thirty-seven African-American rifle platoons under white officers or sergeants. The platoons were incorporated into white rifle companies, and Eisenhower made sure that none of the black units joined Patton's Third Army. It was hardly complete integration, but it was a promising start.

African-American soldiers marched proudly with Eisenhower's Army to and across the Rhine. "I was just boiling for a fight," says James Strawder. "When we got up there the white guys were glad to see us. They were catchin' hell. We got there right in the thick of things and they taught us a whole lot real quick." [20] James Staton, another black combat volunteer, claims that "the relationship between the black and

* In late 1944, the U.S. Army (including the Army Air Forces) had 2,700,000 men in The European Theater of Operations. But only about 300,000 were front-line infantry troops, with another 300,000 or so serving in armor, artillery, or other combat-support units.

white soldiers was very good. They were more like family. Anytime anyone goes in combat you are a family man."[21]

Black volunteers found that the closer they got to combat the less prejudice they encountered. Horace Evans, of the 761st, was wounded and spent time in a hospital as a walking patient with another wounded man who was an amputee. "They didn't have enough help. I stuck with that soldier for a solid week and tried to do what I could for him. Near the end of the ordeal he called me a 'nigger,' and that is the one time I cried. After I left the hospital . . . I was real glad to get back to the front line because there was much more freedom up there!"[22] Nearly all the black platoons performed well in combat, and gained the respect of whites in the outfits they joined. "In courage, coolness, dependability and pride, they are on a par with any white troops I have ever had occasion to work with," reported one infantry battalion commander. "In addition, they were, during combat, possessed with a fierce desire to meet with and kill the enemy, the equal of which I have never witnessed in white troops."[23]

"We proved to the world we could fight," says Frank Barbee.[24]

By early April, with the Allied armies across the Rhine and the Oder, the only strategic question that remained was who would get to Berlin first—the Red Army or Eisenhower's Army. Churchill pleaded with Eisenhower to release Montgomery to take Berlin before the Soviets did. Eisenhower refused. He doubted that Montgomery could beat the Russians to Berlin and was unwilling to sacrifice a hundred thousand men, by Bradley's estimate, in the attempt. In any event, Churchill himself had agreed at Yalta to a Russian zone of occupation extending sixty miles west of Berlin. Why take territory at great cost, Eisenhower reasoned, that would have to be turned back to Stalin after the war? Instead he concentrated on crushing what remained of the German Army with his massive force, nearly two million strong.

After receiving support from George Marshall, Eisenhower ordered Montgomery to move toward Lübeck, sealing off the Danish peninsula, and preventing the Russians from occupying Denmark. Refusing to let the British, or his own Army, move on Berlin may have been the correct military decision, but it was one Eisenhower himself would question, in private, when the Russians blockaded Berlin in 1948.

The End in Italy

With the Allies closing in on Berlin, Italy became a sideshow, virtually ignored by the American press and public. Hitler's irrational dream that he could make a separate peace with the Western Allies if he held out in Italy prolonged the savagely contested campaign until the very end of the war.

In March 1945, when the weather cleared, General Mark Clark began preparing for another assault in force on the Gothic Line. The main attack would come in the center, near Bologna, but the first big breakthrough occurred at the western part of the line, where the African-American 92nd Division was positioned. After losing confidence in the offensive capabilities of the Buffalo Division, General Clark, in consultation with George Marshall, put together a new assault force comprised of the Japanese-American 442nd Infantry Battalion, the all-white 473rd, and the African-

JAPANESE-AMERICAN TROOPS (SC).

American 370th, reorganized to include only "the most reliable elements," in Marshall's words, of the 92nd.[25] The rest of the 92nd was turned, in effect, into a service outfit, relegated to hauling ammunition, gathering up prisoners, and carrying out the wounded. An injustice had been done to the Buffalo Soldiers, but Clark had unintentionally created the most racially diverse American fighting force of the war—and one of the toughest. The 442nd, made up entirely of second-generation Americans of Japanese ancestry (Nisei) from Hawaii and the mainland United States, was the most decorated infantry unit in the American Army, and arguably the most aggressive. The motto of the "little men of iron," taken from a Hawaiian dice game, was "Go For Broke!" They were part of 33,000 Nisei who served in the armed forces in World War II, fighting for a government that had incarcerated their people in American-style concentration camps.

Following the attack on Pearl Harbor, over 100,000 Japanese-Americans from the Pacific Coast had been pulled from their homes and jobs, without charges or due process of law, and placed in ten government-run internment camps on barren lands in the interior of the continent. Over 70,000 of them were native-born American citizens; the others were resident aliens, many of whom were, by law, ineligible for citizenship. Allegedly, they posed a grave threat to national security, yet no other Americans with Axis country affiliations were interned, and not a single Japanese-American was arrested during the war for espionage, subversion, or sabotage. No Japanese-Americans from Hawaii were relocated, but only because they made up nearly half the islands' population. "If you had evacuated all of the Japanese-Americans, the economy would have collapsed," said Daniel Inouye.[26] Yet Hawaiian-born Nisei like Inouye had their civil rights stripped from them when the Selective Service discontinued Nisei inductions and classified all Nisei 4-C, "enemy alien." When Roosevelt lifted this restriction in January 1943, thousands of young Hawaiian Nisei flooded the enlistment centers. The 100th Infantry Battalion was formed in Honolulu and sent to Italy the following September, where it fought at Salerno, Anzio, and Monte Cassino, taking so many casualties that it became known as the Purple Heart Battalion.

This performance encouraged the Army to form another Nisei unit, the 442nd Combat Team, made up of Hawaiians and mainland Nisei, many of whom had families in barbed-wire-enclosed relocation camps. The average Nisei soldier was only five feet, three inches tall and weighed 125 pounds, and some volunteers were under five feet and weighed barely a hundred pounds. Most of the officers were Caucasians, but, unlike the Buffalo Division, there was strong rapport between them and their men.

"I joined the army because I always felt very strongly about patriotism; I felt that this was my country . . . and I wanted to defend it," says Tom Kawaguchi, who was living in an internment camp with his family when Army recruiters sought him out. "I was a little confused. I thought, wait a minute, here I want to defend my country and they lock me up. . . . Then I said . . . I've got to get out of here. And I've got to demonstrate in one form or another that I am what I am." He wanted to prove his loyalty and erase what he saw as his family's disgrace.

In Italy, the 442nd was attached to the Purple Heart Battalion, which had arrived in Italy with 1,300 men and suffered more than 900 casualties. Transferred to France in the summer of 1944, the unit participated in one of the most daring combat operations in modern military history, rescuing a "Lost Battalion" of Texans in the Vosges Mountains, where the delirious and starving men were surrounded for eight days by SS tankers and infantry. "I never saw men get cut down so fast, so furiously, caught in machine-gun crossfire. . . . It was just a tree-to-tree fight, and a tank couldn't go there," says Shig Doi. "I was getting shot at from the enemy, [while] . . . at home in my own country, [vigilantes] were [firing] a shotgun through our house." [27]

In this suicidal mission, the 442nd suffered 1,400 casualties to save 217 fellow soldiers. In 1978 the Department of Defense named the rescue of the Lost Battalion—the Battle of Bruyeres—one of the U.S. Army's "ten most heroic battles." [28]

What sustained them and drove them to perform with such self-sacrificing courage? "I think the Japanese culture really came into play," says Tom Kawaguchi, "all the things we were taught as kids—honesty, integrity, honor. And *haji*, not bringing shame on the family. . . . All of us were scared, no question about it. None of us felt like heroes, but we didn't want to bring shame upon our families" [29] A veteran of the 442nd who enlisted from a concentration camp remembers his mother telling him before he left for basic training: "This country has done a great wrong to you, but it does not lessen your obligation and duty to your country." [30] In a year of fighting, not one member of the 442nd deserted.

When they had first started training at Camp Shelby, Mississippi, there was friction between the "Kotonks" (mainlanders) and "Buddhaheads" (Hawaiians). "We—in Hawaii—were of darker shade than the mainland guys. And we spoke in pidgin, [while] they spoke a better brand of English," says Senator Inouye. "We thought they were looking down at us. . . . There was constant violence between the two groups, and we were the ones who were beating up the mainlanders. That's how the name 'Kotonk' came up. We used to laugh every time you hit a guy and he hits the floor, it goes 'kotonk.'

"At one point, the senior officers of the regiment were seriously considering disbanding the regiment. . . . They tried everything—social programs, discussion groups. Nothing worked until somebody had the bright idea to [send] ten noncoms from Hawaii—opinion molders—to visit the Rohwer internment camp in Arkansas. We were prepared for a fine weekend of 'Kotonk' girls, good food. When we saw the camps with barbed wire all around, with machine gun towers, men with rifles and bayonets, this was the first time we realized what our mainland brothers had to go through and, instantaneously, we looked upon them differently—with great respect and pride. In fact, till this day many of us from Hawaii have asked ourselves the question: 'would we have volunteered if we were in those camps?' Almost immediately after we returned to Camp Shelby, the 442nd became a fighting unit."[31]

Mark Clark's transfer of the 442nd Infantry Regiment from France to Italy in the spring of 1945 was done in deep secrecy. When the men arrived, they were hidden at an assembly point near Lucca to avoid detection by German sentries. Their mission, along with the 370th and the 473rd, was to head a diversionary assault on the western sector of the Gothic Line, drawing German troops away from the Bologna area, to clear the way for an Allied breakthrough in that sector.

Lieutenant Vernon Baker of the all-black 370th, the first African-American unit to arrive in Italy, describes the opening of this operation:

"My platoon's objective was Castle Aghinolfi, a heavily fortified German observation point on the extreme western end of the Gothic Line. It commanded the mountain passes in the area and Highway One, the main coastal road to Genoa. It was the anchor of what the local partisans called the Triangle of Death. The triangle consisted of Castle Aghinolfi and two of the loftier peaks in the mountains behind it—Mount Folgorito and Mount Carchio. We had to take that castle if we wanted to break the Gothic Line. We had already tried to take it four times. It was an imposing place.

"The attack on the castle was to begin before dawn on April 5th. Our company led it. That night, around midnight, before we headed out, the 442nd—a Japanese-American unit—started climbing the other two legs of the Triangle of Death, Mount Folgorito and Mount Carchio, to try to get in the rear of the Germans and surprise them. They started at midnight and scaled steep cliffs and crossed dangerous gorges in the dark, maintaining absolute silence. It was to be a pincer movement. Additional units of the 442nd were to climb other German-held hills and come up from the south. The objective of the Japanese-Americans was to capture the high ground overlooking the castle. My attention was focused solely on the castle. They had a job to do. I had a job to do."

That morning, Baker wore his dress uniform. "The day spelled death. I wanted to go sharp. . . . I topped off my outfit with my customary cap, a wool helmet liner, and left my helmet near my bed roll." Baker thought the "old steel bucket" was useless against shrapnel, and it impeded his hearing, which had been damaged by mortar fire.

"My platoon had twenty-six men. I should have had ten more but there were no replacements for black troops. Our company was also undermanned . . . twenty-seven short of the more than two hundred that should have been on hand. . . . My commander—the commander of Company C—was Captain John F. Runyon, a white guy. He didn't have a lot of combat experience.

"I told my guys, no talking when we go up that hill. Hand signals only. . . . I felt a rush of hope, 'Today we're going to do it,' I added. My men nodded.

"The hill was heavily mined, we went up it so fast we outran our artillery. We had to keep running so we didn't get annihilated by our own fire. We got to the top in two hours.

"We were in front of a ravine, about 250 yards from the castle. I went down in the draw to see if I could find any Germans."

The Medal of Honor citation that Baker received describes, in spare, military prose, what he did on that hill in northern Italy: "Lieutenant Baker observed two cylindrical objects pointing out of a slit in a mount at the edge of a hill. Crawling up and under the opening, he stuck his M-1 into the slit and emptied the clip, killing the observation post's two occupants. Moving to another position in the same area, Lieutenant Baker stumbled upon a well-camouflaged machine-gun nest, the crew of which was eating breakfast. He shot and killed both enemy soldiers. After Captain John F. Runyon . . . joined the group, a German soldier appeared from the draw and hurled a grenade, which failed to explode. Lieutenant Baker shot the enemy soldier twice as he tried to flee. Lieutenant Baker then went down into the draw alone. There he blasted open the concealed entrance of another dugout with a hand grenade, shot one German soldier who emerged after the explosion, tossed another grenade into the dugout and entered firing his sub-machine gun, killing two more."

When asked what he did next, Baker replied, "I looked for more Germans to kill."

After he returned to his men, the Germans spotted their position in front of the castle and began hitting it hard with mortars. They also started taking heavy antiaircraft fire from their own batteries down below. Runyon radioed their position but "no one believed we had gotten this far behind enemy lines this fast," says Baker. Mortars chewed up six men. Three lay dead, three wounded, screaming in agony. Just then, machine gun fire from the castle swept their position. "I swore at the Germans and swore at the American intelligence officers who doubted our location." Finally, their radioman succeeding in getting the artillery fire zeroed in on the castle, but they were under a hail of mortars that were ripping up the trees they had been using for cover. As the Germans added artillery fire to the murderous mix, Baker screamed at his men, "Move. Move or die."

"Men dropped. A few pitched forward, others went bulleting backward, as if struck by a freight train. I ran to them, saying, 'Please, God, let him be alive.' When I got to each man, I saw an arm or a leg or half of their face blown off."

They had been promised reinforcements. None were in sight. Baker screamed, "Where the hell's Runyon?" A man pointed. Baker crept through the scrub and found Runyon in a small stone building, sitting on the dirt floor, his knees pulled up to his chest, his head lowered. When Runyon said he was going to order a withdrawal Baker broke into tears and said, "We can't withdraw. We must stay here and fight it out."

Then Runyon told Baker he was going for reinforcements. "I knew he was lying," says Baker. "He was going to abandon us." When Runyon informed the men he was leaving, one of them called out, "Motherfucker." Runyon left with his radioman and some of the wounded.

Baker had the men strip their dead comrades of rifles and ammunition and build a low defense perimeter with logs and rocks. Minutes later, German soldiers came straight at them, some of them disguised as medics, with machine guns hidden under blankets on stretchers. Only eight of Baker's men were still alive and, in his words, "they radiated hopelessness and exhaustion." They were nearly out of ammunition.

Baker ordered a retreat, but his men ran into German machine gun nests. Baker covered them, taking out two of the enemy positions.

When Baker and six other surviving members of his platoon got to the bottom of the hill, Baker sent the walking wounded to an aid station, sat down, put his head between his legs, and emptied his insides. Later that day, a senior officer he reported to chewed him out for not wearing a helmet into battle. Then he ordered Baker to lead a battalion of white soldiers back up to the castle the next day. It was eventually taken.[32]

Vernon Baker's shooting war was over.

Meanwhile, the 442nd had accomplished its objective. After an all-night climb up a nearly vertical mountainside, they had completely surprised the Germans. "Most of them were lining up for chow when we hit them," recalls Daniel Inouye. "All the high points were taken and the ridgeline secured. Barely forty-eight hours had elapsed

COMPANY I OF THE 370TH INFANTRY REGIMENT ON THE GOTHIC LINE (SC).

since the commanding general had asked if we could do the job in a week—and this over terrain that had stymied the best effort of Allied troops for fully five months."[33]

With the help of 14,000 partisans and elements of the 92nd, the Go For Broke Battalion drove the Germans up and down 3,000-foot-high mountains toward La Spezia and Genoa, while the main elements of the Fifth Army smashed through the center of the Gothic Line near Bologna. "Our biggest single advance," recalls Inouye, "came on the day word reached us that President Roosevelt had died. Men just got up out of their holes and began fighting their way up. 'Where the hell are they going?' the brass hollered at regimental headquarters, and of course no one in the [headquarters] section knew. But down on the line, we knew. Every Nisei who had been invested with first-class citizenship by virtue of the uniform he wore knew. We were moving up for FDR. He had given us our chance and we had a lot of aloha for that man."[34]

The Buffalo Division's tank battalion was attached to the 442nd for the drive through the mountains and up the coast. "Our biggest problem with the little Japanese-Americans was keeping up with them; they moved like greased lightning," says Lieutenant Harry Duplessis. "Instead of following the paths, which tanks have to do, they went up and across those mountains like crazy. We worked out a system. As they took out across the mountains we'd wind our way along until we received a signal from them. Then we would lay down a barrage as a diversionary. Jerry would be concerned about us and the Nisei would move in swiftly from the rear and mop up. I do mean mop; they turned those Germans every way but loose. We soon ended up in Genoa sitting out the rest of the war." [35]

After capturing Genoa on April 27 the Japanese-Americans drove on to Turin, in the northern Po Valley, while the American Fifth and British Eighth Armies pursued the Germans across the Lombard Plain and into the Alpine passes, where their lines of retreat were severed. What had begun as a diversionary attack turned into a full-scale offensive that cracked the Gothic Line in the Apennines. [36] By now, most of the fighting had ended. The Japanese-American unit had won every battle it had been in and had been awarded over 9,400 Purple Hearts and a Presidential Unit Citation. But many of the men felt that their hardest fight lay ahead of them, when they returned home to face, yet again, racial prejudice based on the color of their skin and the slant of their eyes.

On April 28, while Kesselring's replacement, General Heinrich von Vietinghoff, moved to end hostilities in Italy by a local surrender, Mussolini and his mistress, Clara Petacci, tried to escape to Switzerland. They were captured by Italian Partisans and executed in a village near Lake Como. Their bodies were taken to Milan. Vernon Baker was there. He had gone to Milan by himself to see its cathedral, and afterward went exploring in the city. Huge, noisy crowds filled the streets, jamming the intersections. He got out of his jeep and pushed his way into a mob in a small square, and there in front of him was a pile of bodies on the street, with a group of Partisans, rifles in hand, standing over them like hunters over their killed prey. "As the cheering intensified, the partisans gathered each body and hoisted it feet first to a long concrete beam exposed along the front of a bombed-out building. Mussolini, his mistress . . . and a half dozen other fascist officials soon dangled from the beam by their feet. . . . An enterprising young partisan climbed to the beam and painted the name of each dead fascist above their feet. A Who's Who of Hatred, a piece of history." As Baker walked away, he noticed that someone had tied Clara Petacci's dress to her legs so it would not fall down and expose her body. [37]

Before the surrender could be signed on May 2, Sergeant Daniel Inouye had a brush with death.

Leading his platoon against a ridge being held by die-hard Italian Fascists, he came under withering machine gun fire. Inouye got up to throw a grenade and felt a blow in his side, as if someone had punched him hard. He fell back for a few seconds and then charged the machine gun emplacement. "I threw the grenade and it cleared the log bunker and exploded in a shower of dust and dirt and metal, and when the gun crew staggered erect I cut them down with my tommy gun."

His men raced up the hill after him and he waved them toward two other gun positions on the rocky slope. Holding his side where a bullet had gone through his stomach and just missed his spine, he struggled ahead to attack the machine gun that now had his men pinned down. "I lobbed two grenades into the second emplacement before the riflemen guarding it ever saw me." He fell again, but managed to crawl to within ten yards of the third machine gun position. As he cocked his arm to throw his last grenade an enemy soldier fired a rifle grenade and shattered his arm, nearly tearing it off. "It dangled there by a few bloody shreds of tissue, my grenade still clenched in a fist that suddenly didn't belong to me any more."

The grenade was live and about to go off. " 'Get back!' I screamed, and swung around to pry the grenade out of that dead fist with my left hand." This time he beat the Italian, and the grenade blew up in the soldier's face as he was loading his rifle. "I stumbled to my feet, closing on the bunker, firing my tommy gun left-handed, the useless right arm slapping red and wet against my side."

Just when Inouye thought the fight was over, a wounded enemy soldier "squeezed off a final burst from the machine gun and a bullet caught me in the right leg and threw me to the ground and I rolled over and over down the hill." As his men gathered around him and tried to pick him up, he kicked free and yelled, "Get back up that hill! Nobody called off the war!" He refused to be evacuated until his platoon had carried the hill.

Axis resistance in this sector ended two days later. Nine days after that the war in Italy was over.

After surgeons finished operating on Inouye's arm, someone showed him a bottle of blood. "It had a name on it—Thomas Jefferson Smith, 92nd Division—and while they were rigging it for transfusion into my left arm, I thought how funny that was, showing me the blood, like a waiter displaying the label on a bottle of wine for your approval." He had seventeen transfusions that week, and a lot of that blood had been donated by the Buffalo Division. "The bottles of blood were shown to recipients without comment," Inouye wrote later, "as silent evidence that fighting men did more than fight, that they cared enough about each other . . . to donate their blood against that time when somebody, maybe the guy in the next foxhole, would need it to sustain life." [38]

If Daniel Inouye had been white, he would not have received the blood of those black soldiers, for in the great war against genocidal racists, the American Red Cross segregated blood. And if Vernon Baker had not been black, he would have received the Medal of Honor fifty-two years before President William Jefferson Clinton pinned it on his chest.

No Wonder the Flowers Were So Beautiful

After receiving a Presidential Citation for his photograph of a rescue mission on Omaha Beach, Signal Corps photographer Walter Rosenblum had accompanied the American Army through France and into Germany. Near Munich, he went off by himself for a ride in the magnificent Bavarian countryside. It was the last week of April 1945.

"I'm going down the road [in a jeep] and I see a series of boxcars lined up along the side of the road. So I stopped and climbed up to the top of the boxcars to look inside and they were full of dead people. . . . I was so upset by what I saw I never thought of taking photographs. Can you imagine coming on forty boxcars full of dead people in the middle of nowhere?" [39]

Rosenblum returned to Dachau on April 30 with units of the U.S. Seventh Army, including Japanese-American soldiers from the 442nd combat unit. On a desolate railroad siding outside town, the troops came upon the forty or so cattle cars he had discovered. Opening their doors was like opening "the gates of hell," said an American officer.[40] The cars were filled with more than 1,500 corpses piled four and five deep, with excrement all around them. The bodies were "skin and bones," and some of them had bullet holes in the back of their shaven heads. They had been transported from another camp and were murdered by SS guards the day before Dachau was liberated. One man was still alive and crawled out from under a ghastly pile of corpses.[41]

Overcome with horror and rage, the troops "banged down the gate of the camp," Rosenblum recalls, "And I began to photograph with my movie camera." They found corpses strewn all over the camp, and near the crematorium, a stack of naked bodies "about as high as a man could reach." Deep inside the stack, the soldiers could see a few of the victims' eyes still blinking.

"Some of the American troops were so upset by what the Nazis had done that they shot some of the German guards," said Rosenblum. A U.S. squad guarding about 122 SS prisoners, who continued swearing threats at their former prisoners, opened fire with machine guns and killed all of them. "I photographed the whole thing," says Rosenblum.[42]

At that point, the soldiers turned over the remaining guards to the inmates. One GI gave an inmate a bayonet and watched him behead a guard. Many of the guards were shot in the legs and could not move. A number of these disabled guards were ripped apart limb by limb.

Some hysterically happy prisoners lifted up their liberators and carried them on their shoulders around the camp, kissing and hugging them, waving a makeshift American flag, and shouting, "Long Live America!" Other prisoners were too weak even to smile. In the excitement of the moment, several inmates were killed when they tried to break through the electrically charged wire fence that ringed the enclosure.[43]

When the Americans came into the camp one woman, Janina Cywinska, was standing in line with a blindfold on waiting to be shot, "but the shot didn't come. So I asked the woman next to me, 'Do you think they're trying to make us crazy, so we'll run and they won't have to feel guilty about shooting us?' She said, 'Well, we're not going to run.' . . . So we stood and stood and suddenly someone was tugging at my blindfold and . . . pulled it off. I saw him and I thought, 'Oh, now the *Japanese* are going to kill us.' And I didn't care anymore. I said, 'Just kill us, get it over with.' He tried to convince me that he was an American and wouldn't kill me. I said, 'Oh, no, you're a Japanese and you're going to kill us.' We went back and forth, and finally he landed on his knees, crying, with his hands over his face, and he said, 'You are free now. We are *American* Japanese. You are free.' "[44]

Walter Rosenblum stayed around for only a few hours. He wanted to get back to his Signal Corps unit with his film. "So nearby, and I don't remember how it happened, I found a little Piper Cub. The pilot had been doing reconnaissance. And I persuaded him to take me back so I could drop this film off. I had a great moral predicament. I said to myself, 'What do I do with this film now? Do I send it into the Army and get these people into trouble [for killing the guards]?' But again, I said to myself, 'You are a photographer, you have to send in all this film.' "

Rosenblum never learned what happened to his film. "It just disappeared from public view."[45] He suspects the censors confiscated it. With the war tribunal trials coming up, the Americans did not want to let the enemy know that GIs had shot German troops in cold blood.

As horrible as conditions were in Dachau, it was not a murder mill on the order of Treblinka or Sobibor, where Jews were gassed on arrival in accordance with the directives for the "Final Solution"—Hitler's plan to exterminate all Jews in Nazi-occupied territory. Dachau had been built in 1933 as a camp for political opponents of the Nazi regime. Early in the war it was primarily a labor camp, but the Nazis used it for hangings, torture, and fiendish medical experiments. A gas chamber was also constructed. When Walter Rosenblum arrived there, it was actually two camps: a work camp for political prisoners and a place where sick and dying Jews were either detained before being sent to large death camps, or executed on the spot.

After an inspection of the camp, Lieutenant Colonel Walter J. Fellenz described the crematorium:

FIRST, I WAS LED to the execution grounds, a small plot of ground entirely enclosed by a hedge. There, I saw a mound of earth about thirty feet long and four feet high. Here, prisoners, six at a time, were lined up; required to kneel down facing the mound, while the SS nonchalantly murdered them by shooting them in the back of the head from a range of two or three feet. The mound of earth was still wet with blood. . . .

Next, I was led to the storage warehouse. This large building contained the naked dead bodies of over 4,000 men, women and children, thrown one on top of the other like sacks of potatoes. The odor was terrific. I vomited three times in less than five minutes. It was the most revolting smell I had ever experienced.

Next to the warehouse of dead bodies, was the crematorium itself: a large, double furnace, each capable of being stuffed with five or six corpses at once. The dead bodies were dragged from the warehouse [and] jammed into the red-hot furnace. But even then, the Nazis were not through! The ashes of the victims were used as fertilizer for the flower gardens and the vegetable gardens—no wonder the flowers were so beautiful.[46]

In his official report of camp conditions at Dachau, Brigadier General Henning Linden recommended that all German citizens living in the area of the camp be forced to walk through it so they could see the kind of government they had been supporting. This was done. At captured camps, local citizens were also put on burial details.

After helping to liberate Dachau, Lieutenant William J. Cowling of Leavenworth, Kansas, wrote to his parents. "When I tell you [this story] you probably won't believe all the details. I knew when I heard such stories back in the States I never believed them and now even after seeing with my own eyes, it is hard for me to believe it." After describing what he had seen, he vowed he would "never take another German prisoner armed or unarmed. How can they expect to do what they have done and simply say, 'I quit,' and go scot-free. They are not fit to live."

Then he added:

"Incidentally, your griping about my going to the South Pacific. I have only been in the Army a couple of years. Some of these people were in the hell hole of Dachau for years. If I spend ten years in the Army during war I will never go through what those people [went] through. Even if I were killed, I would be lucky compared to those people. So if you still feel the jitters, remember the people of Dachau and think how lucky I am no matter what happens." [47]

Several freed American POWs witnessed the liberation of Dachau. Two of them were Richard Macon and Alexander Jefferson, the Tuskegee Airmen who had been shot down over southern France. After spending nine months in Stalag 3 outside Berlin, in January 1945, "they got us out on the road and told us to march or be shot," Jefferson described their late-war ordeal as the Germans moved POWs out of the way of the advancing Russians. "It was cold as all get-out and we walked about thirty kilometers. We were put in boxcars on a train and ended up . . . about twenty miles north of Munich. We were freed by black tankers, what group I do not know. . . .

"We had heard about this place at the stalag but we believed the stories to be exaggerated. We rushed right to it when freed to see for ourselves. . . . The stories we had heard had been understated. The imagination could not conjure up this sickening reality. Some of the fellows went on to see some of the other camps in the area, but I had seen all I wanted to see. For the first time the doughnut of smoke over Ploesti didn't seem so bad. At least those guys died fighting back and their deaths were quick. But this, Dachau, men, women, and children, unarmed, terrorized; herded together like sheep and exterminated like cockroaches. No, I didn't want to see the rest of man's ingenuity in mass murder and bestiality." [48]

When questioned, the residents of the town of Dachau said they had no idea what went on inside the camp. Yet it was known that when they rode their bicycles past it, they had to put handkerchiefs over their mouths and noses to keep out the ghastly smell.

Although the 761st Tank Battalion did not liberate Dachau, as some writers and filmmakers have recently claimed, it did help to liberate a satellite camp of the Mauthausen concentration camp network in Austria, near the Danube. "At the camp you could not tell the young from the old," says the "Black Patton," Captain John Long. "When we busted the gate the inmates just staggered out with no purpose or direction until they saw a dead horse recently struck by a shell. Have you ever seen ants on a few grains of sugar? They tottered over to that dead carcass and threw themselves upon it, eating raw flesh. We cut ourselves back to one-third rations and left all of the food we could at the camp. There was just one thing wrong. We later learned our food killed many of them. . . .

U.S. GENERALS INSPECT OHRDRUF
CONCENTRATION CAMP (SC).

"From this incident on Jerry was no longer an impersonal foe. The Germans were monsters! . . . We had just mopped them up before but we stomped the shit out of them after the camps."[49]

Other atrocities fired the soldiers' hatred. "The worst enemy was not the German soldier," says Johnnie Holmes of the 761st. "It was the Nazi SS. They would kill their own mother and father to satisfy Hitler's wishes. This was the guy I had to eliminate. Here's why.

"Just before we hit Wels, Austria, the SS captured the 14th Reconnaissance Division. They tied the hands and feet of all the prisoners behind their backs and laid them out in the road, and put a bullet right between their eyes.

"We killed every damn one of those SS every time we caught them. I killed seven point blank with my machine gun. I counted those sonofabitches."[50]

Long before Mauthausen and Dachau were liberated, American officials had known that Hitler had set in motion a barbaric campaign of ethnic cleansing. As early as the spring of 1942 word had come into Washington from a number of sources of extermination camps in Poland. "One is almost stunned into silence by some of the information reaching London," Edward R. Murrow announced in a broadcast in December 1942. "Some of it is months old, but it's eyewitness stuff, supported by a wealth of detail and vouched for by responsible governments. What is happening is this: Millions of human beings, most of them Jews, are being gathered up with ruthless efficiency and murdered." It was, Murrow said, "mass murder and moral depravity unequaled in the history of the world."[51]

The massacre had begun in 1941 when Nazi murder squads shot and killed over a million Russian Jews at mass murder sites near cities like Kiev and Riga. One year later Hitler put Adolf Eichmann in charge of the Final Solution and he set up gas chambers to replace mass shootings. The most barbarically efficient of Eichmann's assembly line killing plants was Auschwitz, where 10,000 skeletonlike inmates were herded into the gas chambers every day in 1943. By the end of that year most of the extermination camps had finished their work and were closed down. But Auschwitz as well as Majdanek ran their gas chambers and cremation ovens until the Red Army arrived. When the Russians pushed into Poland, many of the remaining Jews in Polish concentration camps were taken on hunger marches to Dachau, Buchenwald, and other camps inside Germany.

The Nazis murdered six million Jews between 1939 and 1945. They also murdered three million non-Jewish Poles; one million Serbs; over four million Soviet prisoners of war; and hundreds of thousands of Gypsies, slave laborers from Southern Europe, and mentally ill and homosexual Polish and German citizens. Political dissidents were also killed in harrowing numbers. At least 12 million people died in the Nazi concentration camp and slave labor system. As historian Victor Davis Hanson writes, "While other countries—the Soviet Union and Mao's China—would eventually murder more than Hitler's Germany, no country killed so efficiently, so scientifically, so rapidly, and so completely on the basis of race, ethnic background, physical and mental impairment, and sexuality."[52]

America's complete focus on the war, and its acceptance of anti-Semitism, which infiltrated the highest levels of government, stopped it from doing what it should have done: publicize Hitler's genocidal policies and turn America into a refuge for persecuted Jews. The War Refugee Board, which Roosevelt had established at the insistence of his Secretary of the Treasury, Henry Morgenthau, urged that the crematoria and gas chambers at Auschwitz be bombed, even at the risk of killing some of the prisoners. These innocents, it was reasoned, were doomed anyway in a place where so many millions were slaughtered or starved to death by the end of the war.

Churchill called the systematic murder of European Jews "the greatest and most horrible crime ever committed in the whole history of the world."[53] But he and Roosevelt believed that the only thing they could do for the Jews caught in the Nazi net was to end the war as quickly as possible. That meant bombing German cities, factories, and rail lines, not its death camps. But Jewish leaders pointed out that Allied bombers were already conducting raids on oil refineries near the camp at Auschwitz, and that bombing it would not detract from their major mission.

On April 12, 1945, Generals Eisenhower, Bradley, and Patton toured the Ohrdruf camp, near Gotha. It was the first concentration camp that the Americans liberated. "The smell of death overwhelmed us even before we passed through the stockade," Bradley recalled after the war. "More than 3,200 naked, emaciated bodies had been flung into shallow graves. Others lay in the streets where they had fallen. Lice crawled over the yellowed skin of their sharp, bony, frames."[54] Patton vomited behind a barracks building; Eisenhower turned pale and grew quiet, but insisted on seeing the entire camp.

Leaving the camp, Eisenhower spotted an American soldier accidentally bump into a Nazi guard and laugh nervously. "Still having trouble hating them?" he asked the soldier coldly.[55] Later that day, Eisenhower learned that President Roosevelt had died of a stroke at Warm Springs, Georgia.

The day after Roosevelt's death, Eisenhower ordered every Allied unit in the vicinity of Ohrdruf that was not engaging the enemy to tour the camp. "We are told that the American soldier does not know what he is fighting for. Now, at least, he will know what he is fighting *against.*" The Supreme Commander then cabled President Truman, asking him to send over a congressional delegation to personally witness the "full horrors" of the camps.[56]

When they arrived, they toured the camp at Buchenwald, in beautiful Weimar, the home of Goethe. The camp was built near the Goethe oak, the tree stump that marked the poet's favorite spot in this fragrant beech forest north of the city. Like Dachau, Buchenwald began as a camp for political prisoners, but during the war it had also become a relocation center to supply slave labor to war industries. By the spring of 1945, 60,000 prisoners were packed into an enclosure designed for 8,000. When the Americans liberated Buchenwald, soldiers and inmates killed at least eighty camp officials.

"I had studied German literature while an undergraduate at Harvard College," said Dr. Philip Lief, an Army surgeon, "and I could not really believe that . . . a cultured people like the Germans would undertake something like this. . . . I saw the pocketbook made out of human skin that supposedly Ilse Koch, the wife of the commandant of Buchenwald concentration camp carried about, and also saw the lampshade made out of human skin that had been stretched over a frame and used as a lampshade in her apartment."[57] Combat correspondents noticed that the only American soldiers that did not fraternize with German women were the ones who liberated the camps.

American soldiers liberated prison camps as well as concentration camps. Some of the prisoners were in decent shape, but a lot of them had been brutalized. Ed Cunningham talked to a group of Yanks who had just been freed by the 104th Division.

THE DEAN OF THE PRISONERS had spent two years and eight months in a PW camp. He had been captured in August 1942 and had been shot in the ankle and thigh by a German sniper just before he was taken prisoner. Despite his wounds, the Germans made him walk twelve miles to a prison camp without medical attention.

After a week in a French prison, he and 1,500 other Allied prisoners were herded into French 40-and-8 cars and taken to Stalag VIII-B at Lamsdorf in Ober Silesia. . . .

"When we got to Lamsdorf," the dean of the prisoners said, "they . . . tied our hands with binder twine from eight in the morning until eight at night. Later they used handcuffs instead of twine. That went on for a whole year. . . ."

Despite temperatures that dropped to ten and twenty below zero, the Germans made no effort to heat the prisoners' barracks. Men had to sleep in their clothes with their overcoats for blankets. Many of them suffered frozen feet and fingers. Later some of these frozen feet and fingers had to be amputated by Allied military doctors in the prison.

"The food at Lamsdorf was terrible," the soldier said. "They gave us a loaf of bread for seven men, and it was usually green with mold. Sometimes we'd get about a quart of watery soup made from the water the Germans boiled their own potatoes in, with a few cabbage leaves thrown in to make it look like soup. I lost about fifty pounds in two years and five months."

Along with 8,000 other Allied prisoners at Lamsdorf, he was evacuated from the Silesian prison camp on Jan. 23, 1945, because the Russian Army had advanced to within five miles. All the men who were able to walk were forced to do so. A few invalid prisoners went by freight.

"They put me on a train, but some of the other boys who had frozen feet and hands never made it. Their guards clubbed them with rifles and left them lying there along the roadside in the snow and zero weather when they dropped out because of bad feet. God knows what happened to them. . . ."

Another GI, an infantryman from the 14th Armored Division, was captured at Bitchie on Jan. 2, during the German breakthrough in Belgium and Luxembourg.

Along with 200 other Americans he was loaded on a freight train and sent to eastern Germany. They had neither food nor water on the trip, which took four days and five nights. Their overcoats, blankets, field jackets, and shoes were taken away from them, together with their watches and other personal belongings.

"We licked the ice on the hinges of the box car for water," he said. "There were sixty or seventy of us in each car with no blankets or warm clothes or even straw to sleep on. And just to make sure we didn't get any sleep, German guards stopped outside our car several times a night and fired a couple of rounds in on us. They weren't trying to hit us; because they always fired high, but they kept us awake, so we wouldn't have energy to try to escape." [58]

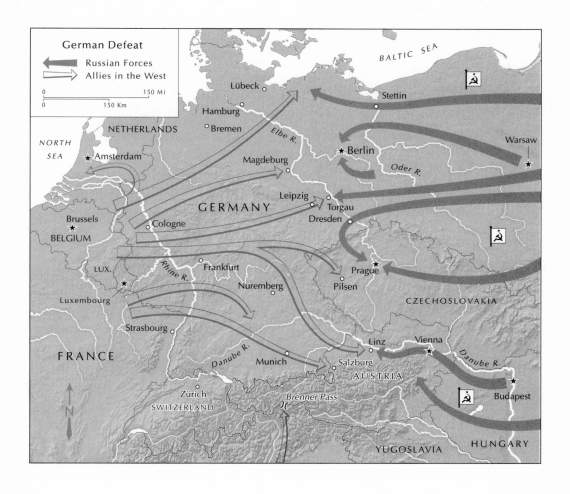

RUSSIAN AND AMERICAN TROOPS MEET AT THE ELBE RIVER (NA).

A WHIRLPOOL OF DESTRUCTION

Throughout the first weeks of April the people of Berlin waited in terror for the end, beseeching God that the Americans would get to the city before the Russians. When the Russians reached the doomed city from the Oder on April 22, their artillery commanders gave the orders: "Open fire at the capital of Fascist Germany." [59] In minutes, the center of the city was in flames.

At this time the Allied armies were at the banks of the Elbe River, almost within earshot of the death rattle of Berlin. On April 27, the American and Russian Armies met at the Elbe, northwest of Dresden. For Nazi Germany, it was the end.

Germany's only chance against the Russians was to get the Americans and the English to sign a separate peace. A captured German officer told Chet Hansen that the German officer corps could be used by the Allies to build a Germany strong enough to

destroy the Communism that will surely "engulf Germany."[60] Perhaps they thought that Eisenhower, a German-American, would agree to this. They didn't understand the man. "Every victory is sweet," Eisenhower wrote his wife, Mamie, "—but the end of the war will come only with complete destruction of the Hun forces. . . . God, I hate the Germans!"[61]

On May 1, 1945, Radio Hamburg made a "grave and important announcement": "It is reported from the Fuehrer's headquarters that our Fuehrer, Adolph Hitler, fighting to the last breath against Bolshevism, fell for Germany this afternoon in his operational headquarters in the Reich Chancellery." After the announcement came the sound of muffled drums and then a Lutheran hymn was played.

The end for the former "beerhall demagogue" came this way. After eating a light lunch with his two secretaries and his dietician, the fifty-six-year-old Fuehrer and his new bride, Eva Braun, for years his mistress, retired to their private quarters in the *Fuehrerbunker*, where Braun took cyanide and Hitler shot himself in the head with a pistol.[62] The bodies were placed in a Russian shell crater, covered with gasoline,

RUSSIAN SOLDIERS CELEBRATING THE FALL OF BERLIN (M25).

and ignited. As the flames shot up, Hitler's staff stood at attention and gave their leader a final Nazi salute. The Russians found the remains a few days later.

Joseph Goebbels, Hitler's fanatically loyal propaganda minister, was next. He had himself and his wife Magda shot by an SS official after they had poisoned their six children. Admiral Karl Doenitz succeeded Hitler and pledged to carry on the fight against Bolshevism.

Asked by a reporter what he thought about Hitler's death, a hospitalized GI replied: "I wish I was the guy who killed him. I'd have killed him a little slower, awful slow." [63]

On the night he learned of Hitler's death, Chet Hansen made an entry in his diary:

THIS WAS THE WORD the world had been waiting for. And tonight it seemed so anticlimactical . . . so slight in the magnificence of our victories.

Unannounced, unheralded . . . the German armies have been destroyed. The German generals have lost control. And the nation is speeding headlong into total collapse. Only the voice of a government can halt the disorder. And tonight there is no government. Only the night, and the Allied armies, the specter of their torture camps, the smell of their dying, the mounds of mass graves and the threat they hold for those who perpetrated them.

Vengeance is coming quickly. [64]

The next day Berlin fell to the Red Army. The correspondent Virginia Irwin was one of the first three Americans to enter the city just before the Russians took it. She went, without permission, with another journalist, Andrew Tully, in a jeep driven by a GI named John Wilson. Military authorities delayed the publication of her story and stripped her of her credentials as a war correspondent.

Heading north toward Berlin, the trio encountered Russian troops riding toward the city in trucks and huge hay wagons. "It was the most fantastic sight I have ever seen. The fierce fighting men of the Red Army in their tunics and great boots, shabby and ragged after their long war, riding toward Berlin in their strange assortment of vehicles, singing their fighting songs, drinking vodka, were like so many holiday-makers going on a great picnic."

They followed this motley convoy into the capital. In the suburbs, dead Germans lay on the sidewalks and in their front yards, and the horses of the Red Army were running loose in the streets. As they got near the center of the city the Russians went wild with joy.

There were few live Germans to be seen. "They fear the Russians as no nation has ever feared a conquering army," Irwin wrote. The Russians showed no mercy, destroying Berlin with "barbaric abandon." It was, said Irwin, "a giant whirlpool of destruction." [65]

Over 350,000 Russian and Polish soldiers died in the Battle of Berlin, an appalling indication of the cost the Allied armies would have incurred had they tried to take the city. The Red Army had its revenge for Leningrad and Stalingrad, going on a rampage of rape, pillage, and murder.

On the outskirts of Berlin a unit of motorized Russian infantry came storming into a small village looking for women. One young woman named Ellen had not believed the atrocity stories about the Russians and greeted them on the street with a smile. "She was immediately seized, thrown on the ground and raped," reported another villager. "She then ran into the woods and returned at night, hiding in a barn. Her original assailant and several of his comrades found her and raped her repeatedly after beating her with their belts.

"Near daybreak they had reached such a state of drunkenness and enfeeblement that she was able to slip out and shelter with a neighbor, who hid her in the stable. At noon they could hear drunken voices and knocks at the door. When there was no answer the Russians smashed it open with their rifle butts.

"One of the children, a thirteen-year-old girl, was lying in bed with scarlet fever. A drunken Russian threw himself upon her and when she struggled he shot her through the throat. She bled to death. The oldest child was a girl suffering from almost complete paralysis who had been unable to move for years. Several drunken liberators threw her on the table, forced her paralyzed legs apart, and raped her in turn. As she lay unconscious on the table they fired their revolvers into her from three paces' distance."

The village was occupied by several groups of troops in the next several weeks. Ellen, who now had gonorrhea, was forced to work for them. Finally her father, a German soldier, deserted and returned to the village and took her back to Berlin. On the train, Ellen was raped by a group of Russian soldiers while her father was forced to guard their luggage and rifles. Just before they got to Berlin they allowed her to dress.[66]

The capital of what was to have been the Thousand Year Reich was obliterated. Once a city of four million people, it was now dead and deserted, the air filled with the stench of decomposing bodies. The wreckage was like that of other German cities, but here there was the feeling that not just a city but a nation, and with it, a "titanic force" had "come to catastrophe," wrote *Yank* correspondent Mack Morriss.[67]

On May 7, 1945, at Eisenhower's headquarters in Rheims, France, the enemy signed an instrument of unconditional surrender. May 8 was officially proclaimed V-E Day, for Victory in Europe. "We've heard the news for which the world and we have been awaiting for so long," GI James Power wrote his parents from a small Austrian village, ". . . but it came rather as an anticlimax. There were no celebrations or parties where we were. Instead we are wondering what the next move will be. We're taking it easy, but it's too good to last." Most of the guys, he said, were worried they would be transferred to the Pacific.[68]

Paris was one big party—crowds and song, wine and cognac. Infantryman Albert Scribner celebrated V-E Day there and then took a train for London, coming into the city just in time to join in the week-long V-E celebrations. He noticed a difference. "The general tone was of total thanksgiving. I stood . . . and watched hundreds and hundreds of rather shabbily dressed civilians marching along the street in a triumphant manner loudly singing hymns, particularly 'Onward Christian Soldiers,' all the refrains . . . bursting from their innermost feelings of deliverance."[69] England had won her fight for survival.

On V-E Day, ex-POW Craig Fenn was on a troopship setting out for home. "A week or so later we reached New York City and its magnificent Statue of Liberty. Men cheered and cried. When we disembarked, some of us kissed the ground. We had been so used to seeing ruin and desolation all around us that we couldn't believe the sight of all these buildings intact."[70]

News of the German surrender came over the B-29 squadrons' loudspeakers on Saipan. It hardly got a reaction.

Iwo Jima

THE FINAL BATTLES

In the early fall of 1944, Captain William Sanders Clark of Cleveland, Ohio, was stationed with the Marines on Saipan. He had fought to take the island from the Japanese, knowing it would become a base for the B-29s, and now he eagerly awaited their arrival. "None of us had ever seen a B-29," he wrote in his war diary, "so all hands were on the lookout for the first one." Sanders was there when *Joltin' Josie* touched down, and he was there when Possum Hansell's crews took off on their first bombing raid against Tokyo.

"In our officers club we talked with B-29 crews who had been over Tokyo. We envied these fellows and also greatly admired them. During these early raids there were a lot of Marines who would have paid money to go along on a bombing mission. However, the losses of bomber personnel rose steadily and this early enthusiasm waned. The 3,000-mile bombing run from Saipan to Tokyo and back was [one of] the most dangerous in the world. For several months there was nothing but the enemy on Iwo Jima. The only place that planes could set down in case of trouble was in the sea!

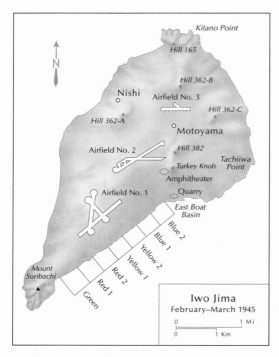

Iwo Jima
February–March 1945

0   1 Mi

0   1 Km

Destroyers, search planes, and submarines did a magnificent job of rescue work but the toll of casualties continued to mount. It was this condition more than anything else that made the conquest of Iwo a military necessity."[1]

The decision to invade Iwo Jima had been made before the first B-29 took off from Saipan. On October 3, 1944, the Joint Chiefs of Staff approved Chester Nimitz's plan to avoid taking Formosa and go straight for the kill, seizing the islands of Iwo Jima, about 700 miles south of Tokyo, and Okinawa, only 350 miles from Kyushu, the southernmost main island of Japan. The Iwo Jima landing was scheduled for February 19, 1945; D-Day at Okinawa would be only six weeks later, on April 1. Without knowing it, the high command had chosen the sites for the last great battles of World War II.

Okinawa, a large island with excellent harbors and airfields, would be an ideal staging base for an assault on the home islands. Iwo Jima was seen as more than a refuge station for distressed B-29s. Although only a tiny speck in the limitless Pacific, Iwo would provide air bases for P-51 Mustangs to escort the B-29s to Japan and to harass enemy airfields. It was a base from which to hit the enemy; taking it would also prevent the enemy from hitting the B-29s on their landing strips in the Marianas.

That October, Japanese fighter-bombers from Iwo Jima had begun a series of "vengeance raids" on Saipan. "Their first raid came as a real surprise," William Clark recalls. "Toward dusk, several Japanese planes suddenly swooped low over Isley Field and proceeded to bomb and strafe the parked Superforts. The enemy pilots were audacious and were only fifty feet above the runways. They [took us by] surprise and left the field littered with burned and blasted B-29s."

On later night raids, the enemy bombers were picked up by batteries of crisscrossing searchlights as they flew in tent-high over Isley Field. Clark and his fellow Marines, who were camped near the airfield, had "ringside seats" for these aerial duels. "We would cheer wildly and shout, 'Get the yellow bastard, don't let that goddamned son-of-a-bitch get away.' Every man on the ground felt that he could help the gunners' aim with a little profanity."

The raids stopped after December, when the Japanese began to lose too many aircraft to American fighter planes. But the enemy bombers destroyed more B-29s on the ground than were lost in the air over Japan, helping to persuade Admiral Nimitz—who was having second thoughts about invading heavily fortified Iwo Jima—that the operation had to go forward.

The battles of Iwo Jima and Okinawa "sound like oft-repeated tunes," James Jones writes in his history of the war. "So familiar by now that the reader can just about chant them in unison with me. . . . The sequence of landings, moves inland, fierce resistance, head-on attacks, final splitting of the defenders into isolated pockets—they were like the choreographed movements of some classic military ballet." But each of the two battles had its own "diabolical hardship" that set it off from all previous Pacific struggles.[2]

At Iwo Jima, it was an end-of-time environment of volcanic rubble and ash and the way the enemy used it to create a killing field like none other in history. It was the Marines' costliest battle ever. In one month, they suffered one third of the total number of deaths they would incur in World War II. The eight-square-mile island cost the Americans—Marines, Navy, and Army—28,686 casualties, including 6,821 killed. It was the first time in the Central Pacific campaign that the enemy inflicted more casualties on an American invasion force than it sustained itself.

Okinawa's extra hardships were its size (sixty miles long by two to eighteen miles wide), its large Japanese population, and the unprecedented waves of kamikaze attacks—by air and sea—that would kill or wound almost 10,000 sailors. For three months, Okinawa was the scene of the greatest air-naval-and-land battle in history. The Americans suffered over 49,000 casualties, more than 110,000 Japanese soldiers were killed, and 150,000 to 170,000 non-combatants died. Okinawa was a horrifying foretaste of what an invasion of the Japanese mainland would cost—for both sides.

The assaults on Iwo Jima and Okinawa took place with the war in Europe winding down; and the fighting on Okinawa went on for seven weeks after Germany surrendered on May 7, 1945. Americans at home watched these two epic struggles closer than they had ever watched events in the Pacific, for these battles would determine how much longer this death-dealing war would last. We today, of course, know it ended in August of 1945, but they feared at the time that it could go on for another two to three years. For combat-battered veterans stationed in Europe, nervously reading about developments in the far-off Pacific, this was almost too cruel to contemplate.

IWO JIMA

On a cold, rainy morning in late January 1945, William Sanders Clark left Saipan's Tanapag Harbor with an invasion convoy headed for Iwo Jima. Like almost every man on board he knew little about the mission ahead. Back on Saipan, he and other Marines had talked to bomber crews who had been "softening up" the target. Their photo interpreters had found no signs of life on the island. "All you'll need is about one regiment to walk ashore and bury the dead," a B-29 pilot assured them.[3]

But the men who would head the invasion were not convinced. The bombing, the Marine and naval commanders believed, had merely driven the dug-in defenders deeper underground. On February 16, three days before D-Day, Admiral Richmond Kelly Turner, commander of what was the largest Navy-Marine operation up to that time, held an emotional press conference on his flagship, USS *Eldorado*. Granite-featured Harry Schmidt, commander of the three Marine divisions that would make the assault, predicted the island would be taken in ten days. It would be a small campaign between two large ones—Luzon and Okinawa. "But everyone [knew] we would lose a lot of men," recalled Robert Sherrod, who was there that day. "We knew the underground defenses of this little island were as nearly impregnable as man could devise, and that seventy-four straight days of bombing had not knocked them out."

"Iwo Jima is as well defended as any fixed position that exists in the world today," Admiral Turner informed the reporters assembled in his palpably tense briefing room. Then Colonel Thomas Yancey, the chief intelligence officer, spoke. "Iwo is 625 miles north of Saipan and 660 miles south of the Japanese empire. It is of the greatest importance to the enemy. It is small: five miles long and two and one-half miles wide at its widest point. Mount Suribachi on the southern tip is a volcano, 554 feet high. About one third of the island is airfields and revetments, one-third cane fields and scrub growth, one third is barren. The beaches we will land on are volcanic ash, the northern two thirds of the island is a plateau whose height goes up to about 350 feet." The invasion beaches were between the plateau and the volcano, at the southern tip of the island's eastern side.[4]

When Yancey finished his briefing, a member of General Schmidt's staff outlined the plan of attack. This had already been given to all officers in the amphibious force, and William Clark described it accurately in the memory book he wrote during the battle and immediately afterward. "The 5th Division was to land near the base of Mount Suribachi. Its mission was to secure the volcano, thus denying the Japs perfect positions from which to subject our landing beaches to severe enfilade fire. When this was accomplished, it was to turn north and drive up the west side of the island. The 4th Division [to which Clark was attached as a radio operator] was to land near the center of the island. [Our] mission was to cut directly across the island, capturing Motoyama Airfield No. 1. This was the primary enemy airstrip. This accomplished, the division was to make a right pivot and drive up the east side of the island. The 3rd Division was to be a floating reserve to be used only in case of emergency."

With the Japanese dug in, it would be a "frontal assault," the reporters were told, a slugging match, yard by yard, with no place for maneuver or strategy on such a confined space. "We have got to dig them out." At least one of the generals was "misty-eyed," and the reporters filed out of the briefing room with what Sherrod describes as "the sort of the pit-of-the-stomach emotion one feels when he knows that many men who love life are about to die." [5]

First to hit the beaches were the frogmen. Navy underwater demolition teams swam into the invasion beaches two days before D-Day, covered by a storm of fire from a dozen gunships, backed up by destroyers and cruisers. In an interview given long after the war, frogman Andy Anderson describes the work of the men who were known as "half-fish and half-nuts":

I'LL NEVER FORGET when we first arrived in the waters off Iwo on D-minus-three and stood on the deck and looked at that island. It was the most god-forsaken place I'd ever seen, with the rising smoke and haze and that frightening-looking volcano. It flashed through my mind that this would be a great place to film a Dracula movie. We all thought, "Why do we want that miserable piece of real estate?"

Our job was to swim in to the invasion beaches, locate mines and detonate them, identify other beach obstacles, and bring back samples of the sand to see if our landing vehicles could operate on that brown volcanic ash. The operation had to be done in daylight to be sure we got all the mines. At a thousand yards, the gunboats—converted LCI (Landing Craft Infantry) ships—fired their rockets and we raced by them in speedboats and were dropped into the water seven hundred yards off the beach. Five pairs of swimmers went in at one hundred yards apart.

Our first shock was the temperature of the water. When you hit that water at fifty-eight degrees it was a real character builder. We had no rubber suits or scuba tanks. They weren't used until the Korean War. We were the naked warriors; that's what they called us. We went in with swim trunks, a pair of fins, a mask,

NAVY FROGMEN (USN).

a knife, a slate and pencil, and blasting caps for detonating mines, which we kept in condoms to keep the powder dry. We strapped the condoms to our belts. In fact, we used so many condoms in training back in Florida that the Navy sent down a morals officer to look into the situation.

We painted our bodies with grease that was mixed with silver paint, to give us camouflage. When we got close to the beach, an awful lot of enemy fire was coming at us. I rolled over in the water and looked back and all those gunboats that were supposed to be giving us cover had been either sunk or disabled. When the Japanese mortar shells came down they actually popped us up, almost out of the water. And we could look down in the water and see the shells that missed us, spiraling to the bottom. But bobbing out there, with silver paint on, we were hard targets to hit.

When we almost reached the beach we saw an abandoned boat with a sniper in it. He kept popping up and shooting at us. My swim partner was a young Irish kid with a hot temper and he stood up, shook his fist, and shouted, "Why don't you come down here and fight like a man." I screamed at him, "Matt, get your tail down or it's going to get blown off." On the beach, all I remember is looking up and seeing this sixteen-inch stuff exploding out of these cliffs and the tremendous return fire of our ships. It was terrifying, and the noise was deafening.

After we got our sand samples and other information we swam back to the rendezvous point with the speedboat. Going back you didn't know whether to zig or zag as the shells came in on the left and then the right, one after the other, till they pulled us out of the sea.

Part of our mission that day was to get the Japanese to fire on us, so we could locate their big beach guns, which were hidden in cliffs and hills. We fooled them. They thought we were the first wave of the invasion force. That night Tokyo Rose went on the radio and congratulated the valiant defenders of Iwo Jima for repulsing the American invasion. But all we did was force them to make a mistake by firing on us. The next day the Navy pulverized those beach guns, saving lives on D-Day.

Our operation was successful in other ways. We didn't find any mines or obstacles and there were no sandbars. It was well graded for bringing up LSTs. We didn't have to do any demolition and only two swimmers were killed in the whole operation, one after he got back on the boat. [Two hundred sailors, however, were killed or wounded on the disabled gunboats.]

As soon as we were pulled out of the water, we were debriefed. Then a chart of the beach was made and sent to the Marines.[6]

That night, after singing religious hymns on the deck to settle himself, William Clark "slept better than I had slept before many a college exam." The next morning was bright and clear; high clouds, calm seas—a perfect invasion day. After watching the third and final day of the greatest naval bombardment of the Pacific war, Clark boarded a boat to guide in the first waves of assault vehicles. After this he became a kind of water cop, keeping boats moving to and from the thickly congested beach. "This gave me an opportunity to view the whole attack."

The first assault waves came ashore at nine o'clock, right on schedule. It was a surprisingly easy landing, even though the Marines had to scale steep terraces of soft volcanic ash when they walked out of the surf, each man carrying sixty and more pounds

MARINES IN LSVP (LANDING SHIP, VEHICLE, PERSONNEL) ON A THIRTY-MINUTE RUN TO THE BEACHES AT THE FOOT OF MOUNT SURIBACHI (USMC).

of equipment. The island looked abandoned. "Where's the reception committee?" asked Private Louie Adrian.[7] Around 11 A.M., when the beach became jammed with men and equipment, Adrian got his answer.

The Japanese used monstrously large mortar shells, "flying ashcans" the Marines called them, which blew parts of men and machines as high as a hundred feet in the air. Landing that afternoon, Pfc. Thomas H. Begay, a full-blooded Navajo, said the beach was the "scariest damn thing" he had ever seen. "I got numb . . . all over my body. No feeling, I was scared as hell, I mean scared. Even though I'm walking, I feel like I'm standing in one place. And that place was like wrecking yard. They had things blown to pieces, it's like traffic jam. . . . There was piles of bodies, and wounded ones. . . . I grow up that day. I age about two years right on that beach, got my Ph.D. about war."[8] The enemy zeroed in from Mount Suribachi and from the cliffs and hills north of the beachhead, and anywhere they put a shell it hit a man or a machine. "No man who survived that beach knew how he did it," said Joe Rosenthal, the Associated Press photographer who would take the most famous picture of the war on Iwo Jima. "It was like walking through rain and not getting wet."[9]

That evening, Captain Clark, working close to the beach, watched the Marine tractors, the only vehicles capable of negotiating the soft ash with little trouble, scurrying "back and forth like a bunch of ants. Some of our fellows carried badly needed

supplies right to where the fighting was in progress. These cumbersome vehicles were choice targets for Jap gunners and mortarmen." It was a job, in the pitch black of night, requiring "daring and cool courage," the tractors' only guide being a blinking flash-light on the beach held by a Marine officer who directed the unloading of ammunition and other supplies. A lot of this work was being done by African-American Marines with the ammunition and depot companies, eleven of whom were wounded, two fatally.

When Robert Sherrod was preparing to go ashore around five o'clock that after-noon, he ran into his friend Keith Wheeler of the *Chicago Times*. Wheeler was just getting back from the beach to write his D-Day story. "There's more hell in there than I've seen in the rest of this war put together," he told Sherrod. "I wouldn't go in there if I were you, it's plain foolishness. The Nips are going to open up with everything they've got tonight." Sherrod shook his head and headed in. When his Higgins boat

A Marine hands a cigarette to a wounded Japanese soldier half-buried in a shell hole, after knocking away a grenade that was near his hand. The embittered local conscript gave the Marines information about Japanese defenses on Mount Suribachi (Lou Lowery/USMC).

crunched ashore, he found it almost impossible to dig a foxhole in the loose volcanic ash. "It's like diggin' a hole in a barrel of wheat," a Marine next to him shouted.

By this time, the 5th Division had cut across the tail of the pork-chop-shaped island, isolating Suribachi from the rest of Iwo Jima, and General Schmidt had 30,000 Marines ashore, against about 21,000 Japanese defenders. Aside from the beach and a small portion of Motoyama Airfield No. 1, the Japanese owned the rest of the real estate, and no place on it was beyond the range of their heavy guns. When the remainder of the assault force, over 40,000 men, landed over the course of the next week, Iwo Jima would be one of the most heavily populated seven and a half square miles on earth.

When Sherrod arrived on the beach, the mortar fire had quieted down, and he was even able to get a little sleep. But just after 4:00 A.M. the Japanese opened up with everything they had. "The first big mortar shell hit only a few yards from my foxhole, and it sounded like the break of doom. . . . All night the Japs rained heavy mortars and rockets and artillery on the entire area between the beach and the airfield. Twice they hit casualty stations on the beach. . . . The corpsmen were taking it as usual."[10]

"Our medical team had landed with two doctors and forty corpsmen," recalls squad leader Albert J. Ouellette. "Before the day was out, one doctor was killed when he lost both legs, and only two corpsmen were left. All the rest were dead or wounded."[11]

Navy corpsman Stanley E. Dabrowski landed under heavy fire near Mount Suribachi. "I had a carbine and a .45. Unlike the Army in Europe, we were armed. That was because of our experience on Guadalcanal. At that time corpsmen still wore Red Cross brassards on their arms and a red cross on their helmets. They were the first ones to be knocked off." Even after that, the Japanese, spotting the medical kits that corpsmen carried on both shoulders, focused their fire on them.

On landing, Dabrowski and his team of corpsmen picked the deepest shell hole they could find and set up an emergency aid station. "Evacuation of wounded was extremely hazardous. The stretcher-bearers were under constant fire. . . . When we started experiencing heavy casualties, it was almost impossible to comprehend. Because of the heavy artillery and mortar fire there were a lot of traumatic injuries, traumatic amputations. . . . No arms, or both legs. And then there were abdominal injuries, torn-out intestinal tracts. Often I was beside myself trying to decide what to do with these people. . . .

"Sometimes these young men would be covered by a poncho and lying on a stretcher. And I'd say, Hey, Mac, how are you doing? Pretty good, doc. What's the problem? Oh, my left arm got it. So you'd lift the poncho and you'd see a stump."[12]

When the firing let up at daylight, Sherrod walked back to the beach. He saw only a dozen or so dead Japanese. "The Jap plan of defense was plain," he wrote in his first story from Iwo Jima. "Only a few men would defend the beaches. The mortars and machine guns from the hillside caves . . . would stop the landing."

By the second morning, there were 2,400 casualties among the landing force, and most of them had "died with the greatest possible violence. Nowhere in the Pacific war have I seen such badly mangled bodies," wrote Sherrod. "Many were cut squarely in half. Legs and arms lay fifty feet away from any body."[13] The velocity and intensity of the mortar and artillery fire on the compacted battleground was the reason nearly

IWO JIMA'S MOONSCAPE (USMC).

8 percent of the Americans wounded on Iwo Jima would die of injuries, as against the World War II number of 3 percent.

On that rainy second day, with the wind off the ocean blowing the volcanic dust in their faces, the Marines got a close look at the piece of bleak Pacific cinder they had been sent to take. The pre-invasion bombardment had annihilated the island's vegetation. Between Suribachi on their left and the sloping wasteland of black crevices and cliffs on their right, there was nothing but a flat field of volcanic ash. Flies and mosquitoes were so thick in places men dared not open their mouths, and orders went out not to drink the sulfur-contaminated water. Big "slit-faced" bats soared out of smoking caves on shell-scarred Suribachi and clouds of black sulfur gas flared up through piles of steaming rocks, giving off the smell of rotten eggs. Iwo Jima means "sulfur island" in Japanese, and it was the sulfur deposits that had originally drawn prospectors to the island. On at least one occasion, Marines could feel the whole island shaking. "It was as if the very earth itself was alive," recalls William Clark. "At first we were deathly afraid that the entire beach was mined and it would soon erupt. However, successive tremors made us realize that volcanic action was still taking place."

But it was the barren and blasted landscape that provoked the greatest concern. "There was no cover and concealment as we had practiced in our training exercises," says Captain Lawrence Snowden. "There wasn't anything to hide you."[14] When men walked in soft ash up to their knees, and pulled one leg out, it left no imprint. The only marks in the tundra of sand and ash were huge craters created by the naval shelling. Hundreds of them gave the place a lunar appearance. And like walking on the moon, it was as if no one had been there before. There were Marines who fought on Iwo Jima for the entire six-week campaign who never saw a living enemy soldier. "It was an eerie landscape," says Marine Fred Hayner. "While you couldn't see them, you had a feeling that the Japanese had you always in their sights."[15]

Like Peleliu, the battle was fought in two dimensions: the Marines were *on* Iwo Jima, the Japanese were *in* it. Robert Sherrod had not been to Peleliu, so he had no idea what the Marines were in for. After the third day, he filed a cautiously optimistic report. "It seems certain that we will take Iwo Jima at a smaller cost in casualties than Saipan's 16,000. Probably no large percentage of the Jap defenders have yet been killed, but henceforth the Japs will kill fewer Marines and the Marines will kill more Japs."[16] As Sherrod admitted later, "I did not then know the real underground strength of Iwo, nor the capabilities of its defenders."[17]

Iwo Jima had been turned into the world's greatest underground citadel. "[When the invasion comes] every man will resist to the end, making his position his tomb," announced the man who masterminded its defenses, General Tadamichi Kuribayashi.[18] Iwo Jima was of more than strategic value to Japan. It was home territory, administered as part of the Tokyo Prefecture; the mayor of Tokyo was the mayor of Iwo Jima. Anticipating an American invasion before one was planned, the Japanese had begun bolstering the island's defenses after the Americans landed on Saipan. The invasion of Peleliu gave them an additional six months to turn Sulfur Island into a subterranean death trap, defended by blooded veterans of the Kwantung Army. Emperor Hirohito, the Son of Heaven, had taken a personal interest in preparing the island's defenses, sending Kuribayashi, the commander of his Palace Guards, to defend it. Kuribayashi was iron-spirited and aggressive, the most formidable adversary the Marines would face in the Pacific War. He was from a distinguished samurai family and he fought like a true professional warrior.

The general brought hard discipline to Iwo Jima, abolishing the consumption of alcohol and evacuating all civilians, including his officers' "comfort girls." He then brought in Korean laborers, military engineers, and demolition experts, and supervised the construction of a phantasmagoric warren of interwoven caves and gun galleries inside Suribachi and under the rock-strewn badlands at the northern end of the island. His cave defenses were stocked with weapons, fuel, and rations, and all had myriad secret entrances and exits. They were mutually supporting, and if one position was threatened, his men could easily sneak through tunnels to the next, above, below, or behind the original position, surprising the Marines with exterminating counterfire. Over the entrances to these tunnels and caves Kuribayashi built double-layered concrete blockhouses and pillboxes, which were concealed by volcanic ash. Only the gun muzzles were exposed. Suribachi itself had seven levels of tunnels, connecting almost 1,000 gun galleries.

Kuribayashi respected his enemy. Serving in the Japanese embassy in Washington before the war, he had traveled around the United States and was impressed by its prodigious industrial strength. "The United States is the last country in the world that Japan should fight," he had written his wife.[19] Preparing for the American assault he told his men what to expect and how to die. A list of "courageous battle vows" was posted in every underground position: "Each man will make it his duty to kill ten of the enemy before dying; until we are destroyed to the last man we shall harass the enemy with guerrilla tactics."[20]

He would fight as Colonel Kunio Nakagawa's forces had at Peleliu. American intelligence had a name for it, "the cornered rat defense." The Japanese would hole up and wait for the Americans to come to them, bleeding them in a battle of attrition. A dying officer who was found on the ground at Iwo Jima said over and over, "wait for them, wait for them, make them come to you."[21] But while Kuribayashi learned the lesson of Peleliu, American commanders ignored it, paying scant attention to their own intelligence reports. That is why they had been surprised on the beaches, first by no resistance, and then by the nature of the resistance— flaming metal rather than fighting men.

A MARINE SNIPER ON THE SLOPES OF SURIBACHI (USMC).

On D-plus-two, the 28th Marines of the 5th Division began the assault on Mount Suribachi. From this combination fortress and watchtower the enemy was pouring down fire on the beaches, and artillery spotters were siting targets for guns all over the island. It had to be taken out, and quickly.

Sergeant Bill Reed, a correspondent for *Yank,* recounts the opening of the battle for "Hot Rocks," as the Marines called Suribachi:

FOR TWO DAYS THE MEN who landed [at the foot of the mountain] were pinned to the ground. Murderous machinegun, sniper, and mortar fire came from a line of pillboxes 300 yards away in the scrubby shrubbery at the foot of the volcano. . . . Men lay on their sides to drink from canteens or to urinate. An errand between foxholes became a life-or-death mission. . . .

Towering over them was Mount Suribachi, a gray unlovely hulk with enemy pillbox[es] . . . in its sides. Marines . . . grew to hate the mountain almost as much as they hated the Japs who were on it. Reaching the summit was almost as much of a challenge as destroying the men who defended it.

The supporting air and naval fire did much. . . . But when it came to the specific four-foot-square machinegun emplacements and the still smaller snipers' pillboxes there was little the offshore and air bombardment could do except silence them for a few minutes. Everyone knew that in the end the troops would have to dig them out.

The foot troops made their drive on the third day. They were aided by a naval and air bombardment so terrific that the Tokyo radio announced that the mountain itself was erupting. They were also aided by their own artillery and rocket guns, landed with superhuman effort the previous day in spite of a choppy ocean and the enemy's guns.

But the foot troops were aided most by the tanks that advanced with them and lobbed shells into the stone-and-concrete revetments that blocked the way of the foot troops. The Japs were afraid of our tanks—so afraid that they ducked low in their shelters and silenced their guns when they saw them. . . .

As soon as the tanks had passed or had been blown up by mines, the Japs came out of their holes and attacked our men from behind with machineguns and mortars. . . . The enemy had hundreds of pillboxes and emplacements connected by a network of tunnels. When the Japs were driven from one pillbox, they would disappear until the Marines advanced to another, and moments later they would appear at their old emplacements, lobbing grenades at our men who had just passed.

By early afternoon of D-plus-two the Japs at the foot of Suribachi had been silenced. However, everyone knew there were Japs still around . . . [in] their shelters. . . .

There were also many Japs who were dead. They were dead in every conceivable contortion of men who met death violently. Their arms and legs were wrenched about their bodies and their fists were clenched and frozen. Those who had been killed by flamethrowers were burned to a black darker than the ashes of Suribachi or scorched to a brilliant yellow. Their clothes had been burned off, and the heat vulcanized their buttocks together with ugly black strips. It was good to see these sights after having been pinned down to [the beach] for two terrible days.

There were dead Marines too. Some platoons had been entirely stripped of their officers and noncoms. Some had lost more than three-fourths of their men since morning. . . . But the worst of the battle for Suribachi was over. Our men had fought their way in under the guns higher up on the mountain.[22]

That night, half of the small enemy force of 300 that was still inside the mountain made a breakout, trying to reach their comrades on the northern side of the airfield. Not more than twenty made it. The following morning, February 23, a patrol led by Lieutenant Harold G. Schrier began the ascent of still dangerous mountain. Their job was to secure the summit. "Just before we set out, Colonel Chandler Johnson, our battalion commander, handed Harold Schrier a small American flag," says Charles W. Lindberg, one of the two flamethrower men in the platoon, a Marine respected for his almost inhuman poise under fire. "He said, 'If you get to the top, raise it.' I remember he used that word, if.

"Staff Sergeant Lou Lowery, a photographer for *Leatherneck Magazine,* went with us."[23]

That morning the fleet had been notified of their mission and told to withhold all fire on Suribachi. Sailors stood by their silenced guns, watching the ascent with binoculars. The volcanic ash and broken rock on the steep path made it tough going, and the men slipped and slid. "We all expected trouble, but not a shot was fired at us," says Lindberg. When they reached the crater's rim, two of the Marines claimed the mountain for their country in their own way: by urinating on it. Then some of the men found a fragment of old pipe, shot a hole through it, and tied the flag to it. "Towards ten thirty, we found the highest point we could and we raised it." As the men gathered around the flag, Lou Lowery recorded the event with his camera. "Then things broke loose down below," says Lindberg. "Our troops started to cheer and our ships whistled and blew their horns. I was so proud. It's a feeling I'll never forget."

The cheering grew louder when the beachmaster turned up the volume of his public address system and announced that the flag was flying on Suribachi. That entire area of the island erupted with noise, the cheers and whistles of the Marines accompanied by the sirens and bells of the fleet. "Talk about patriotism!" says Coast Guardsman Chet Hack. "The uproar almost shook the sky." [24]

The men on the summit didn't have time to celebrate. "Just after we had the flag up, all of a sudden from our right side some shots were fired," Lindberg recalls. "Some Japs were running out of caves, one of them swinging a broken saber, and we drove them back into their hiding places. . . . Then we went around the crater and burnt out some other holes and threw some explosives into whatever caves we could. By about one thirty, we had the mountain secured. . . .

"I found out later that they had changed the flag. I didn't pay any attention to it."

After the first flag went up, Colonel Chandler Johnson had sent a runner to the beach to get another and larger flag. He was concerned that Secretary of the Navy James Forrestal, who was with the invasion fleet, would want the flag on Suribachi for himself. "It was the first American flag to fly over Japanese home territory in World War II. He wanted to preserve that flag [for the battalion]," says Lindberg. Johnson's man got a larger flag, eight feet by four feet eight inches, from the communications officer of an LST, who had picked it up in a salvage depot at Pearl Harbor. Johnson handed the flag to nineteen-year-old Rene Gagnon and told him to get it to the top of the mountain as fast as he could. When Gagnon reached the summit, Sergeant Mike Strank, who had climbed Suribachi with him, took the flag from him, handed it to Schrier, and announced, "Colonel Johnson wants this big flag run up high, so every son a bitch on this whole cruddy island can see it." [25]

When Tarawa veteran Norman Hatch, the 5th Marine Division photo officer, had learned that a larger flag was going up he sent two of his men, Sergeant Bill Genaust, a movie cameraman, and Private Bob Campbell, a still photographer, to the top of Suribachi to cover it. The diminutive Associated Press photographer Joe Rosenthal joined them. As the three photographers ascended Suribachi they ran into

MOUNT SURIBACHI. THE FIRST FLAG GOES DOWN AS THE
SECOND FLAG GOES UP (LOU LOWERY/USMC).

Lou Lowery, who was on his way down, and apparently was not aware there was going
to be a second flag raising. "You guys are a little late," he said, "the flag is up, but it's
a helluva view up there."

When they reached the rim of the crater about noon, a couple of Marines were
attaching a flag to a twenty-foot iron pipe they had found in a pile of rubble. Schrier

ordered the replacement flag raised at precisely the moment the original flag was low-
ered. Six men raised the flag: Mike Strank, Rene Gagnon, Ira Hayes, Harlon Block,
Franklin Sousley, and Navy corpsman John Bradley. When the flag started to go up,
Rosenthal was talking to Genaust, and then shouted, " 'There it goes!'

"Out of the corner of my eye, as I had turned toward Genaust, I had seen the
men start the flag up. I swung my camera, and shot the scene," Rosenthal later
remembered. Campbell got a different still shot, one of the first flag going down while
the second one went up. And Genaust caught the replacement flag going up with his
color movie camera.

Rosenthal feared there might have been too much movement for him to have
gotten a good picture. A few minutes later, he took a second shot, a posed picture with
a group of Marines crowded around the replacement flag cheering and raising their
rifles and helmets high.

Colonel Johnson got the original flag and put it in the battalion safe. The replacement flag flew on Suribachi for three weeks, before it was torn to shreds by the wind.
And the country got one of the most famous photographs ever made, and one of the
finest. It became the most widely reproduced photograph of all time. An engraving of
it appeared on a three-cent postage stamp, a painting of it was used in the most successful bond drive of the war, and after the war, the sculptor Felix de Weldon spent
nine years on a 100-ton bronze statue based on it that stands on the grounds of
Arlington Cemetery.

The story of Joe Rosenthal's photograph has been mired in myth and misrepre-
sentation. To this day, some people still believe, despite several excellent books on the
flag raising, that Rosenthal staged his photograph. Rosenthal himself added to the
confusion. Nine days after taking the picture, he walked into press headquarters on
Guam and a correspondent walked up to him.

"CONGRATULATIONS, JOE," he said, "on that flag raising shot on Iwo."
"Thanks," I said.
"It's a great picture," he said. "Did you pose it?"
"Sure," I said. I thought he meant the group shot I had arranged with the
Marines waving and cheering, but then someone else came up with the [flag rais-
ing] picture and I saw it for the first time.
"Gee," I said. "That's good, all right, but I didn't pose it. I wish I could take
credit for posing it, but I can't."

One of the correspondents had overheard only the first part of the conversation and he wrote that Rosenthal had posed it, that it was a "phony."

"As I left for home," says Rosenthal, "I had the fear that, through no fault of my own, I was in the doghouse. When I arrived in San Francisco, however, I found that I was now a celebrity." [26]

When Rosenthal's packet of pictures had been sent by mail plane to Guam to be developed the Associated Press photo editor picked up a glossy print of the flag raising, whistled, and said, "Here's one for all time!" [27] He at once radioed the image to AP headquarters in New York, and it made every front page in America.

The picture arrived at exactly the right time and with exactly the right message. The war in Europe was almost over, but news from the Pacific was discouraging. "The Pacific names are all news to me," wrote Ernie Pyle that February—Kwajalein, Saipan, Peleliu, Tarawa—and now Iwo Jima. Americans had died in places that people back home had difficulty finding on a map. And at Iwo Jima they were dying in horrifying numbers, and for what? Was this awful little island worth it? (In 1944, the Navy had come up with a secret plan to shoot shells filled with poison gas onto the island, taking it without losing a single American life, but Roosevelt had scotched that plan, insisting that poison gas only be used as a last-ditch retaliatory measure.) [28]

At the same time, the conservative press was excoriating Nimitz for his costly island-hopping battles, demanding that the President turn over the Pacific war to MacArthur. Americans were impatient, and they were exhausted, and they could not see the end to this war with a people who seemed to have a collective death wish. "The Pacific war is gradually getting condensed, and consequently tougher and tougher," wrote Ernie Pyle. "The closer we go to Japan itself, the harder it will be. . . . To me it looks like soul-trying days for us in the years ahead." [29] As Americans read this on February 24 their spirits must have dropped; he actually said "in the *years* ahead."

The next day, Sunday, February 25, they opened their papers to Rosenthal's majestic photograph of six heroic Marines putting up that wonderfully big victory flag. Maybe Ernie Pyle was wrong. Suddenly, the end of the war seemed in sight. The message of the photograph also matched the wartime mood. Here were "six Americans," as the writer Hal Buell has observed, "all for one, working together in victory and valor, and above them, Old Glory. Finally, for the first time, a clear, simple statement from the Pacific gripped the United States." [30]

No major paper carried Lowery's photograph or mentioned the first flag raising. There was only one flag raising, the one captured for all time by Joe Rosenthal. Second only to the one that flew over Fort McHenry on the night Francis Scott Key wrote "The Star-Spangled Banner," this became the most famous American flag that ever flew. To the men on Iwo Jima it was the flag that didn't count. But to Americans back home that replacement flag was the only flag they wanted to hear about. They weren't looking for truth, after all, they were praying for encouragement.

The morning that the first flag went up there were still thirty days of combat ahead. The 28th Marines had paid a stiff price for Suribachi, and now the regiment moved north, with almost every assault unit on the island, into the teeth of Kuribayashi's defenses. One of the first Marines to be wounded in the drive north was Charles Lindberg. After he was evacuated from the island and read the reports in the papers about the flag raising he found it difficult to suppress his anger. "It just didn't make sense to me that something like that could happen. We went up the mountain and we raised the flag. We took the enemy off the top of the mountain. Somebody comes up four hours later and puts up another flag and they're national heroes."

By the morning of the fifth day, over 5,000 Marines had fallen—three for every two minutes of action on Iwo Jima. And now the Americans faced an obstacle greater than Suribachi—the barren stone plateau to the north of the airfields, where Kuribayashi had constructed his most imposing defenses, including his own underground headquarters. On D-plus-six the Marines moved northward, three divisions strong (the "emergency" 3rd Division had been put ashore right after D-Day). They now had the enemy outnumbered by at least three to one, but by going underground the Japanese nullified the Americans' prodigious firepower. "For all our technical skill, we had on Iwo no method and no weapon to counteract the enemy's underground defense," wrote Sherrod. "The Japs made us fight on their own terms." [31] A team of Marine Corps correspondents described the attempt to smash through these defenses at a place called "The Wilderness":

WHEN THE 24TH REGIMENT'S 2ND BATTALION reached . . . "The Wilderness" . . . they spent four days on the line, with no respite from the song of death sung by mortars among those desolate and gouged shell holes. The Wilderness covered about a square mile inland from Blue Beach 2, on the approaches to Airfield No. 2, and there was no cover. Here stood a blasted dwarf tree; there a stubby rock ledge in a maze of volcanic crevices.

The 2d Battalion attacked with flamethrowers, demolition charges, 37-millimeter guns, riflemen. A tank advancing in support was knocked out by a mortar shell. After every Japanese volley, Corsair fighter planes streamed down on the mortar positions, ripping their charges of bombs into the Wilderness. But after every dive was ended, the mortars started their ghastly song again.

Cracks in the earth run along the open field to the left of the Wilderness, and hot smoke seeped up through the cracks. Gains were counted in terms of 100 or 200 yards for a day, in terms of three or four bunkers knocked out. Losses were counted in terms of three or four men suddenly turned to bloody rags after the howl of a mortar shell, in terms of a flame-thrower man hit by a grenade as he poured his flame into a bunker. The assault platoon of flame throwers and demolitionists, spearheading the regiment's push through the Wilderness, lost two assistant squad leaders killed.

The Japs were hard to kill. Cube-shaped concrete blockhouses had to be blasted again and again before the men inside were silenced. Often the stunned and wounded Japs continued to struggle among the ruins, still trying to fire back. A sergeant fired twenty-one shots at a semiconcealed Jap before the latter was killed. Another Marine assaulting a pillbox found a seriously wounded Jap trying to get a heavy machine gun into action. He emptied his clip at him but the Jap kept reaching. Finally, out of ammunition, the Marine used his knife to kill him.

Forty-eight hours after the attack began, one element of the Third Division moved into the line under orders to advance at all costs.

Behind a rolling artillery barrage and with fixed bayonets, the unit leaped forward in an old-fashioned hell-bent-for-leather charge and advanced to the very mouths of the fixed Jap defenses. Before scores of pillboxes the men flung themselves at the tiny flaming holes, throwing grenades and jabbing with bayonets. Comrades went past, hurdled the defenses and rushed across Airfield No. 2. In three minutes one unit lost four officers. Men died at every step. That was how we broke their line.

Across the field we attacked a ridge. The enemy rose up out of holes to hurl our assault back. The squads reformed and went up again. At the crest they plunged on the Japs with bayonets. One of our men, slashing his way from side to side, fell dead from a pistol shot. His comrades drove his bayonet into the Jap who had killed him. The Japs on the ridge were annihilated.

And now behind those proud and weary men, our whole previously stalled attack poured through. Tanks, bazookas, and demolition men smashed and burned the by-passed fortifications. In an area 1,000 yards long and 200 deep, more than 800 enemy pillboxes were counted.

The survivors of this bold charge covered 800 yards in an hour and a half. Brave men had done what naval shelling, aerial bombardment, artillery and tanks had not been able to do in two days of constant pounding. What was perhaps the most intensively fortified small area ever encountered in battle had been broken.[32]

Iwo Jima would have been tougher to take without the help of the Navajo "code-talkers," who had been serving in the Pacific since Guadalcanal. The Navajo language has no alphabet, and in 1941 was known to no more than forty non-Navaho in the world, none of them Japanese. The Marine Signal Corps recruited 420 of the 3,600 Navajo that served in all services in the war. It trained them as radiomen and had them develop a highly secret metaphoric code, which included hundreds of words of their own invention for military terminology like "machine gun" and "bazooka." The code was never written down—it had to be memorized—and it remains one of the few unbroken codes in military history. (The Army recruited Comanches for the European theater and used them on the Normandy beaches and in the drive to the Rhine.) "We named the airplanes 'dive bombers' for *ginitsoh* (sparrow hawk)," says Cozy Stanley Brown of Chinle, Arizona, "because the sparrow hawk is like the airplane—it charges downward at a very fast pace. . . . We usually used the harmful animal's names that were living in our country for the alphabet. . . . We were well taken care of. The generals would not allow other soldiers to come near us. . . . We were not supposed to take order[s] except from high [officers] we were assigned to."[33]

The code-talkers were generally split up into two-man teams, "one on either end of a field telephone or walkie-talkie so they could transmit coordinates for artillery or air strikes, relay information on enemy positions, and provide other valuable intelligence without the Japanese being able to decipher the information," explains one of their historians.[34] On Iwo Jima's impossible terrain, where secure communication between ground troops and supporting tanks, artillery, planes, and ships meant life or death, the code-talkers relayed almost a thousand messages without an error, including the one announcing the flag raising on Suribachi. "They told us that being a code-talker, we can't make mistakes," says Thomas Begay. "Has to be perfect. Because if we make a mistake, say the wrong word, could kill a lot of our men."[35] The code-talkers gave the Marines on Iwo Jima something the enemy did not have, a rapid, reliable, and absolutely secure system of communication. Most of the messages were sent in the fury of combat, and three code-talkers were killed.

"Why do you have to go?" a Navajo mother asked her son who volunteered for the Marines. "It's not your war. It's the white man's war." [36]

"My main reason for going to war was to protect my land and my people because the elderly people said that the earth was our mother," and it was being dominated by foreign countries, explains Cozy Stanley Brown. "There are Anglos and different Indian tribes living on the earth who have pride in it. . . . I believe what we did was right, and it was worth it. We protected many American people, also the unborn children, which would be the generation to come. . . .

"I brought one of the enemy's scalps home," he declares with a warrior's pride. "The Squaw Dance was performed on me for the enemy scalp that I brought home with me." [37]

When Motoyama Airfield No. 1 was secured and cleared of mines, transports flew in from Guam to evacuate the badly wounded and to bring in cases of whole blood. Twenty-three-year-old Norma Crotty from Cleveland, Ohio, was on one of the first R4D cargo planes to land on Iwo Jima.

TWELVE OF US NURSES had been flown from Honolulu to Guam, where we lived in hospital tents. We were there only a few days when our chief nurse said we were going to fly to Iwo Jima to bring back patients to the hospital on Guam. We didn't know much about the place, and we were astonished to hear that we would be flying into a combat area.

We left Guam about four o'clock in the morning and tried to sleep a little bit on the plane. When we approached Iwo, the pilot woke us up, and we looked out and saw the whole fleet in the water around this tiny island, ships of all kinds firing away and you could see the smoke coming up from the island. It was impressive. I felt like I was living in a newsreel.

When we landed we ran to the aid station, which was nothing but a big tent, a sandbag tent. Iwo was almost indescribable. There was tremendous noise and dirt and it was all gray sand, which I found out later was volcanic ash, nothing green, no vegetation whatsoever. It was cool and the island smelled, and there were smashed planes and equipment all over the place, and big bulldozers at work. It was so far removed from any experience I ever had.

The patients were on the ground. With the help of the doctors we picked out the worst cases and took them to the plane. The worst thing you would see were burns, and men who were torn up by shrapnel. We had some men who were flamethrowers and their tanks had blown up, and it was horrible—the pain, the terrible pain. On the four- to five-hour trip back, we worked with corpsmen—there were no doctors—to stabilize the men and monitor their condition, checking for bleeding, giving them plasma, and feeding them sliced peaches in little paper cups, which we would sit on their chests. It was like they were swallowing little goldfish.

We gave them morphine occasionally, but we didn't have oxygen, or water to wash our hands. We worried about that, going from patient to patient without being able to wash our hands. The men, about thirty of them, were on stretchers and they were stacked up three and four high on the plane, and it was cold and drafty. Generally there was only one nurse and one corpsman on every plane. We were on our own.

The fellows were so much younger than us, seventeen or eighteen years old, and some of them looked younger than that. Like little boys. And they wanted their mothers, and we sort of became their mothers and comforted them. They were all very courteous and appreciative of anything we did. As much as we did for them medically, I think it was the comforting that was most important to them, and to us. Mostly, they wanted to talk to us, and they enjoyed watching us comb our hair and put on lipstick. They'd ask us to do that. The feeling of closeness to these boys I didn't have again until I had children.

What was touching to me was that so many of them were replacements, right out of high school. And now a lot of them were ruined for life.

The thing that matters most to me now, fifty years later, are the friendships I made with the eleven other nurses I worked with on those trips between Guam and Iwo. We stayed very close through the years. You must remember that women and girls back in the 1940s hardly left their mothers. It was quite a thing to be away, without any family support, on your own. That meant a lot, because then you knew through the rest of your life you could do just about anything that you put your mind to, that nothing could stop you. You knew you were in control. That was the good thing we got out of our war experience.[38]

Almost 2,500 wounded men were airlifted out of Iwo Jima. Not one patient was lost in the flight to Guam.

* * *

On March 4, a Sunday, the Marines around the airfield got an unexpected visitor. A "monster" landed on Iwo Jima. This was Air Force slang for a B-29. The plane, named *Dinah Might*, developed fuel problems on its way back from Japan. After it skirted past Suribachi, it slammed down and skidded to a stop at the end of a runway less than half the size of the one it had taken off from in the Marianas. "As the silver craft came to a stop at the northern end, shellfire began hitting near it. The Japanese wanted that B-29 badly," says Iwo veteran Richard Wheeler. "But *Dinah Might* swung around and taxied out of range toward Suribachi. Hundreds of Seabees and Marines cheered their throats dry as the sixty-five-ton plane stopped and cut its engines." The hatch opened and four or five crew members "jumped down and fell to their hands and knees and kissed the runway," another Marine recalls. "What a contrast! Here were men so glad to be on the island they were kissing it. A mile or two to the north were three Marine divisions who thought the ground . . . [was] not even good enough to spit on." [39]

The plane had a faulty fuel valve, and thirty minutes later it was airborne again, soaring out to sea. "If anything was needed to tell the Marines why they were dying on this unholy island," wrote correspondent Keith Wheeler, "the successful landing of *Dinah Might* furnished the demonstration." [40]

Then there were the dead. At this point in the battle, William Clark was still back at the beach, living in a foxhole, working with the supply companies. The fighting had ended in his sector but all around him was the smell and physical presence of death. "Directly offshore from our bivouac area lay a pontoon barge which held several rows of white-clad figures laid in stretchers. These were the mortal remains of men who had died aboard hospital ships and had been towed in shore awaiting burial. There was no time to tender them this decency. For days the barge rocked back and forth on the waves and one by one the bodies would slip overboard. . . . Some were washed ashore; others went to sea."

On the beach, burial detachments were at work. "Anyone who thinks that death on the field of battle is a hero's end should be made to watch a burial party picking up the remains of some poor devil whose luck had run out," says Clark. "We kid ourselves into calling this man a hero. Calling him a hero does not bring life into this limp mass of flesh. Such a man as this was sacrificed by the stupidity of mankind which made such an end possible."

By D-plus-fourteen, many of the Japanese cross-island defenses had been broken and Kuribayashi had only about 3,500 battle-ready troops left. On the high ground in the center of the island, Marines of the 3rd Division had driven a wedge into the northern third of the island still held by the Japanese. This wedge was exploited in fighting through a "jungle of stone"—wild lava ledges, smoking sulfur pits, chasms, cliffs, caves, boulders. Four days later the breakthrough to the sea was accomplished and the Japanese force was split. Turning southward, Marines cleaned out the eastern pocket in vicious cave warfare, and it was on the northernmost tip of the island, at Kitano Point, that Kuribayashi reputedly was killed leading his men in a final attack, although his body was never found. "Let's hope the Japs don't have any more like him," said one Marine.

On March 14, General Schmidt declared the island officially occupied by the forces of the United States, and the Army was brought in to finish the job. But the battle really ended on March 25, D-plus-thirty-four, when the last enemy stronghold was taken in a place called Death Valley. A week before this, General Nimitz had issued a statement that summed up the fight. "On Iwo island, uncommon valor was a common virtue." That was good to hear, but it was thin consolation for the battered and bleeding Marines, among them the company that had raised the flag on Iwo Jima. Easy Company had landed with about 235 men and received seventy replacements, and had suffered 240 casualties, more than 100 percent of its original number. Among the dead were three of the Marines who had raised the second flag on Suribachi: Mike Strank, Harlon Block, and Franklin Sousley, and one of the photographers who immortalized the act, Bill Genaust.

On March 17, Primer Minister Kuniaki Koiso, speaking by radio, called the fall of Iwo Jima "the most unfortunate thing in the whole war situation." He was quick to add, however, that the nation would fight to the last man "to shatter the enemy's ambitions." [41]

As if to bear out that threatening prophecy, a remnant of Kuribayashi's men mounted one final attack in the early morning hours of March 26, the day after the Americans had declared the battle over. "About three hundred of them took off straight down the center of the island," recalls Fred Hayner. "They went right down the airfields and they caught a group of young pilots who had come in with P-51's to escort the B-29's over Tokyo and Yokohama. These fellows, along with some Seabees and Marine construction units, were sleeping in tents or on the ground and the Japanese killed about fifty of them." [42] Some of the sleeping airmen had their throats cut before they had a chance to hear the alarm. "The ensuing battle, which lasted into the daylight hours, was confused and wild," writes Richard Wheeler, "with hand grenades exploding, rifles and machine guns crashing, and men on both sides shouting and cursing and lamenting in pain and terror. The Seabees employed their training as infantrymen, the Army brought up flame tanks, and the Marines first formed a defense line and then counterattacked. With the Marines was a shore-party unit made up of blacks who had seen no previous action, and they performed splendidly." [43]

One of the dead Marines was Lieutenant Harry L. Martin. He earned the Medal of Honor that morning, the last of twenty-seven to be won on Iwo Jima.

The "clean-up" operation went on into the summer, conducted by the 147th Regiment of the U.S. Army, which killed another 1,600 Japanese. "On moonlit nights," a Japanese cave survivor wrote after the war, "I was particularly sad. Watching the moon, I counted the age of my son or thought of my wife's face." [44] Only about 1,000 Japanese were captured. The remains of thousands of their comrades are still in the rocks and caves and shifting ash of desolate Iwo Jima.

On April 7, 108 P-51 Mustangs took off from Iwo Jima to escort a fleet of Curtis LeMay's silver "monsters" on a daylight raid on Tokyo. That extra margin of safety for the bombers came at an immeasurable cost.

Before leaving Iwo Jima, William Clark attended the dedication ceremonies of the 4th Division cemetery. The Marines had begun setting up this cemetery on the third day of the battle and the first burials took place three days later. "From that point on, the number of bodies collected was much more than we could handle in any one day," observes Lieutenant Gage Hotaling, a Navy chaplain assigned to the Graves Registration Section. "At one time, we had four hundred or five hundred bodies stacked up, waiting for burial. . . . I am not a smoker, but I found that the only way that I could go around and count bodies was to smoke one cigarette after another. . . . I was addicted to smoking for twenty-six days. . . .

"Once we had bodies lined up, I would give a committal to each one, with Marines holding a flag over the body. And I said the same committal words to every Marine, because they were not buried as Protestants or Catholics or Jews. They were buried as Marines." [45]

The cemetery was dedicated on March 15. As the band played the Marine Corps Hymn, William Clark sang along with the other survivors of the battle gathered around the fresh graves. "Never in my life had I beheld such a sobering experience. Before me stretched row upon row of new white crosses and headboards. I stood there looking at the somber scene and in my mind formed a question, Why? Why must men be such fools? No war can possibly be won when so much human suffering must be endured."

Okinawa

IN FEBRUARY 1945, EUGENE SLEDGE and the 1st Marines were at their rest camp on Pavuvu preparing for another island "blitz." In the evenings, after training exercises, they gathered around radios and listened to news reports of the desperate fighting on Iwo Jima. To many of them, it sounded "like a larger version of Peleliu." It was also a foretaste of what they would confront on their next landing, where the Japanese would employ the defense-in-depth tactics of Peleliu and Iwo Jima with even more appalling effectiveness.

Sledge and the other enlisted men had no idea where they were headed next. Their first hint was a map they were shown, without names on it, of a long, narrow island about 300 miles south of the Japanese mainland. A few days later, a friend "came excitedly to my tent," Sledge recalls, "and showed me a *National Geographic* map of the Northern Pacific. On it we saw the same oddly shaped island. . . . It was called Okinawa."

The Old Breed sailed from Pavuvu on March 15, while fighting still raged on Iwo Jima, and on the other side of the world Eisenhower's columns poured into Germany. They were bound for Ulithi Atoll, about 260 miles northeast of Peleliu, where their

IE SHIMA

MOTOBU
PENINSULA

OKINAWA

EAST
CHINA
SEA

Mt. Yaetake ○ Nago

PACIFIC
OCEAN

USMC III
TENTH
XXIV

Yontan Airfield
Kadena Airfield

EASTERN
ISLANDS

Naha

Shuri Line

Naha
Airfield

Shuri
OROKU PENINSULA

Okinawa
April–June 1945

0   5 Mi

0   5 Km

convoy would join the assembling invasion fleet. They arrived there six days later, anchoring in the spacious, necklace-shaped lagoon, with its crystal clear water.

Ulithi was the biggest dividend of the Peleliu campaign. While the 1st Marines were suffering and dying in the smoking coral of the Umurbrogol, the Army's Wildcats had captured this long atoll, with its 110 square miles of anchorage, without firing a shot or losing a man. Ulithi, not worthless Peleliu, was turned into the marshaling yard for the vast armadas that would be hurled against Iwo Jima and Okinawa. "We lined the rails of our transport and looked out over the vast fleet in amazement," Sledge remembers. "It was the biggest invasion fleet ever assembled in the Pacific, and we were awed by the sight of it." [1]

This was only part of an amphibious force that would equal the size of the one that had landed at Normandy the previous spring. From San Francisco to the Philippines, from Hawaii to Guadalcanal—from eleven ports in all—almost 1,500 vessels, carrying over half a million men and covering thirty square miles of ocean, would converge at Okinawa at approximately the same time, in what would be one of the logistical miracles of modern warfare. Their mission was to take the island and turn it into the England of the Pacific, the assembling point for the even greater invasion fleet that would strike the Japanese homeland later that year.

While Sledge and his friends were admiring the ships at anchor, they saw what turned out to be an awful omen, had they known it. Anchored near them was "a terribly scorched and battered aircraft carrier. . . . A Navy officer told us she was the *Franklin*. We could see charred and twisted aircraft on her flight deck, where they had been waiting loaded with bombs and rockets to take off when the ship was hit. It must have been a flaming inferno of bursting bombs and rockets and burning aviation gasoline. We looked silently at the battered, listing hulk until one man said, 'Ain't she a mess! Boy, them poor swabbies musta caught hell.' " [2] They had; 724 of *Franklin*'s crew were dead and 265 more were wounded, many of them badly burned. No ship in the entire war suffered more damage and managed to stay afloat. "It seemed to us beyond human belief that the shattered *Franklin* could have made port," wrote Robert Sherrod, who had flown to Ulithi from Guam for what everyone thought would be the last and largest battle of the Pacific island campaign. Unknown to Sledge and his pals, *Franklin,* along with three other carriers, *Enterprise, Wasp,* and *Yorktown,* had been hit by Japanese kamikazes while conducting raids against airfields on Kyushu. "Any mention of suicide planes was taboo for six months," Sherrod recalls. "In our news stories we simply had to ignore one of the most lurid stories of the war, or of any war."[3] Nimitz would not remove these restrictions on the press until April 13. He did so less than an hour before

SAILORS ON LEAVE ON ULITHI ATOLL (USN).

Franklin Roosevelt died, so the kamikaze threat went to the back pages of the American papers—but only for a few days.

During the week they were anchored at Ulithi, the Old Breed went ashore on the tiny islet of Mogmog for what Sledge called some "recreation and physical conditioning," but which another Marine described as a raucous beer-blast. Mogmog was a sixty-acre "recreational island" capable of accommodating over 15,000 sailors who had been at sea for weeks or months. On Mogmog they could swim, play baseball and basketball, and drink—beer for enlisted men and blended whiskey for officers at their segregated "lounges," where they had exclusive access to the company of visiting Navy nurses, and where they were entertained by African-American Navy bands.

After calisthenics, the officers of the 1st Marines broke out warm beer and Cokes, and Sledge and some of the guys played a game of pickup baseball. "Everybody was laughing and running like a bunch of little boys," Sledge recalls. William Manchester of the 6th Marines describes a different scene. "Each of the . . . U.S. fighting men heading into the battle was to be allowed . . . all the beer he could drink while PA systems belted out songs popular at home. It was a thoughtful gesture. Unfortunately, the picnic wasn't left at that. Some recreational officers thought red-blooded American

boys deserved another outlet. It was his idea to issue us sports equipment so we could burn up all that energy accumulated during the long voyage here. It didn't work quite as expected. He had no notion of what it meant to be psyched up for combat. We quickly got loaded and called . . . for madder music and stronger wine. When none was forthcoming, we destroyed most of the sports gear, and the hardchargers among us began hitting people over the head with Louisville Sluggers. The officer was furious, but his threats were as futile as a clock in an empty house. What could he do? Deprive us of the privilege of getting shot at?"[4]

At island closing time, 6:00 P.M., the men jammed Mogmog's single jetty for the short ride back to their ships. Onboard, the fights continued, with sailors and Marines throwing each other overboard and having to be fished out by the neutral Coast Guard.

Back on the troopships, company commanders met with their men to give them their final briefings for Operation Iceberg. This time there was no promise of a short battle. "This is expected to be the costliest amphibious campaign of the war," an officer told Sledge's company. "We can expect 80 to 85 percent casualties on the beach." Standing on the fantail of the assault transport *George C. Clymer,* with his men gathered around him in a tight semicircle, Lieutenant William Manchester unrolled a map of Okinawa, a place almost none of the men had heard of until the last week or so. Americans with a sense of history remembered it as the island Commodore Matthew Perry had landed on in 1853 on the journey that ended Japan's 200-year-long isolation from the rest of the world. The Commodore had planted the American flag on a hill adjacent to ancient Shuri Castle, a center of pre-Japanese culture where both Sledge and Manchester would experience some of the severest fighting of the war. Perry signed a treaty with the regent of Okinawa that declared that "whenever citizens of the U.S. come to Luchu [Okinawa] they shall be treated with great courtesy and friendship [and] shall be at liberty to ramble where they please without hindrance." [5]

Okinawa is a big island, sixty miles long and two to eighteen miles wide, Manchester told his assault unit. "In the north it is rugged and thickly forested; in the south it is rolling and farmed," but there were a series of steep ridges and cliffs near Shuri, where General Mitsuru Ushijima's forces had built fortifications of great scope and strength. The Okinawans buried their dead in elaborate concrete tombs that dotted the landscape, and the 110,000 defenders, about 24,000 of them Okinawan conscripts, were also expected to use these as shelters and fire points. On April 1, Easter Sunday, Army General Simon Bolivar Buckner, Jr., the overall commander, would land four divisions—two Army, the 96th and the 7th, and two Marine, the 1st and the 6th— on beaches just south of the island's "midriff." The immediate objective was the seizure of Yontan and Kadena airfields, not far from the beachhead. Once the airstrips were in American hands, Manchester explained, the GIs would swing south, into the most densely populated area of the island, while the Marines wheeled northward against isolated, heavily fortified Motobu Peninsula. Easter Sunday would be William Manchester's twenty-third birthday. "My chances of becoming twenty-four were, I reflected, very slight." [6]

Admiral Nimitz was more worried about this invasion than any previous one. The fleet expected to be hit hard from the air—both by kamikazes and conventional aircraft—from the hundred or so airfields within range of Okinawa. "This is the biggest thing yet attempted in the Pacific," declared the naval intelligence officer at the briefing Robert Sherrod attended on the command ship *Panamint,* "all the forces available in the Western Pacific are involved except those in the Philippines and the Aleutians." This included the B-29 force of Curtis LeMay, which had been pressured by Nimitz to suspend its fire raids against Japanese cities in order to hit the homeland bases of the suicide planes. At the time, Manchester thought the Marines had been given the toughest assignment. But the intelligence people on *Panamint* expected the fiercest resistance in the south, where "we know there are caves by the thousands, and pillboxes, bunkers, and trenches. . . . Okinawa will be the first heavily inhabited enemy island we have invaded. The population is about 450,000, and we have no reason to believe they are any different people from the mainland Japanese. We expect resistance to be most fanatical."[7]

The Japanese garrison *would* fight with suicidal defiance, but most of the civilian population of Okinawa would try to stay out of harm's way. Japan had not claimed the island until 1879, and the Okinawans, who were not ethnically Japanese, were treated as second-class citizens of the empire. It was difficult for them to see this war as theirs. Still, fed by Japanese propaganda, they lived in mortal terror of the American devils, who, they feared, would torture, rape, and kill them in great numbers. "We spent the last week of March like criminals on death row," recalled a recently conscripted Okinawan. "The instrument of execution was there . . . all ready for us. . . . It was the American fleet instead of an ax or noose."[8]

As Sherrod and forty or so other correspondents boarded their ships the next day, Coast Guard Commander Jack Dempsey, the former heavyweight champion of the world, was there to see them off. "Keep your head down," someone shouted at Ernie Pyle, who would land with the Old Breed. "Listen, you bastards," Pyle shot back at the reporters standing near him. "I'll take a drink over every one of your graves." Then he swung around, put up his fists, and asked the champ if he wanted to go a few rounds.[9]

The landing was one of the pleasantest surprises of the war. "We were in a Higgins boat," Sledge recalls, "and when an amtrac came to pick us up and take us into the beach the driver told us he had just taken some troops ashore and there was no opposition, nobody was fired at. We couldn't believe it. It was the first good news we had heard during the war and everybody started singing 'Little Brown Jug,' and we sang it all the way into the beach. When the tailgate went down we just walked out, formed up, and moved inland to cut the island in half."

Another surprise was Okinawa itself. "We had been warned about terrible terrain, jungle rot, and an infestation of the world's deadliest snakes," says Sledge. "But the island was pastoral and handsomely terraced, like a postcard picture of an Oriental landscape, and hardly anyone ran into the *hubu* snakes whose bites were supposed to be fatal. The island looked like a patchwork quilt, with little farms and fields and rice paddies, all surrounded by low stone walls. The weather was cool, about sixty-five degrees, and there was the wonderful smell of pines, which reminded me of home. It was such a beautiful island; you really could not believe that there was going to be a battle there." [10]

As they moved inland over the next few days, Sledge found the Okinawans friendly and easy to like, but Pyle, a notorious cultural chauvinist, described them as "filthy," "rather stupid," and "pitiful" in their poverty. [11]

From a mountaintop, a Japanese officer watched 60,000 American troops (of the 183,000 assault troops available to General Buckner) walk ashore and seize two important airfields. "As I observed the landing operations, I was convinced this was a complete defeat. The soldiers felt the same way. But we thought it was our destiny to share the fate of the island, and so held on to our pride." [12]

Where was the enemy? every American wondered those first days on Okinawa. Had the Japanese played some kind of strange April Fool's joke on them? "I may be crazy but it looks like the Japanese have quit the war, at least in this sector," Admiral Richmond Kelley Turner radioed to Nimitz. Nimitz replied: "Delete all after 'crazy.' " [13]

While the Old Breed cleaned out pockets of resistance at the center of the island and two Army divisions moved south against the first line of Japanese defenses, Manchester and the 6th Marines drove north into the steep, densely wooded hills and ravines of Motobu Peninsula. "There was no role here for mechanized tactics; tanks were useful only for warming your hands in their exhaust fumes," Manchester described the six-day-long battle for Motobu Peninsula. "This was more like French and Indian warfare." [14] In hand-to-hand fighting with bayonets and knives, the 6th Marines captured Motobu Peninsula and then subdued the rest of the thinly populated northern part of Okinawa.

While fighting in the north, the Marines learned of the death of Franklin Roosevelt. He was the only President the younger Marines had ever known, but most of the talk was about his successor. "Who the hell is Harry Truman?" Marine Raymond Sawyer spoke for thousands of other concerned warriors who felt their fates were suddenly in his hands. [15]

Six days later, on April 18, Ernie Pyle was killed on the small island of Ie Shima, four miles off Motobu Peninsula. He was accompanying the 77th Army Division on an amphibious operation to take the island's airfield when a jeep he was riding in was hit by a burst of machine gun fire. Pyle fell into a roadside ditch unhurt. There was

ERNIE PYLE ON OKINAWA (NA).

another burst and he died instantly when a bullet pierced his helmet and entered his left temple. When his body was recovered, his hands still clutched the battered knit cap he carried at all times.

When Pyle had been assigned to the 6th Marines, many of the men did not recognize the small, frail, balding man with the stubby white whiskers and the frayed woolen cap. But when they learned who he was, they invariably asked him what he thought of the Pacific war. Pyle would smile wearily and say, "Oh, it's the same old stuff all over again. I am awful tired of it." [16]

The last time Sherrod saw him was April 9, when they were in a room aboard the *Panamint*, writing stories. Sherrod told him he was heading home in a few days, and Pyle said he was going back too in a month or so. "I'm getting too old to stay in combat with these kids. I think I'll stay back around the airfields with the Seabees and the engineers in the meantime and write some stories about them." He had made his last landing, he said. Nine days later, Sherrod was in Hawaii when he heard that Pyle had been killed. "I never learned which doughboy of the Seventy-seventh Division persuaded Ernie to change his mind and go on the Ie Shima invasion. . . . But Ernie rarely refused a request from a doughboy." [17]

After northern Okinawa was secured on April 20, the victorious 6th Marines "expected a respite, hot chow, and a few days in the sack. We didn't get any of them," says Manchester. They had been hearing "ominous rumors of stiffening resistance in the south. GIs were encountering unprecedented concentrations of Japanese artillery fire. Progress was being measured in yards, then feet. . . . It was Peleliu and Iwo all over again, but to the nth degree." The Japanese strategy was now revealed. "Looking back, I can't imagine how we could have been so ignorant," says Lieutenant General Victor "Brute" Krulak, operations officer for the 6th Marines. General Ushijima *had* played a cruel April Fool's joke on the Americans. Abandoning the beaches and most of the north, he concentrated his forces along three formidable defensive lines in the south, the strongest of them the Shuri Line, what Manchester called "the war's great Gethsemane." He used every hill and ravine as his ally, hiding his troops and artillery—the most powerful artillery the Japanese had available in the Pacific war— in a sixty-mile network of caves and tunnels, subterranean defenses far deeper and more extensive than those on Iwo Jima. He had already lured Army units into his trap and was butchering them. Now the Marines were rushed south to reinforce them. Wedged together on a terrain-constricted battlefield, Marines and Army infantry and a determined enemy would wage one of the most terrible struggles in the history of warfare.

With American ground forces bogged down in a close-quarter slaughter, the Japanese unleashed a new weapon on the enemy fleet—not individual kamikaze attacks, but massed suicide raids of up to 300 planes. These were called *Kikusui*, or "floating chrysanthemums." "Ultimately they failed," Manchester writes, "but any-one who saw a bluejacket who had been burned by them, writhing in agony under his bandages, never again slandered the sailors who stayed on ships while the infantrymen hit the beach." [18]

FLOATING CHRYSANTHEMUMS

By the late spring of 1945, Japan's situation was so grave, with Iwo lost and the Americans on Okinawa, that its military rulers turned to a desperate scheme, code-named Ten-Go, to protect the most vulnerable points of its rapidly deteriorating defense perimeter. Almost 5,000 aircraft based on Formosa and the home islands were assigned to suicide missions against the American fleet. As Japan-based reporter Robert Guillain noted, the military leaders committed "the nation's total air power to an all-out battle. It was not even a question of winning or dying, but of dying in any case and winning if possible." [19]

Most of the planes were reliable but outmoded Zeroes, but the Japanese did unveil the Baka Bomb that the B-29 crews, as we have seen, would later confront in the skies over Japanese cities. At Okinawa it was used against ships. Piloted by one man and launched like a glider from the underside of a two-engine bomber, it contained in its nose a ton of TNT. It was powered by three rockets and could dive on a vessel at a speed of up to 550 miles per hour, making it almost impossible to hit once it was launched. "The small size and tremendous speed of Baka made it the worst threat to our ships that had yet appeared, almost equivalent to the guided missiles that the Germans were shooting at London," wrote Admiral Samuel Eliot Morison.[20] But before it was launched, the Baka Bomb's weight slowed down the mother ship and impeded its maneuverability, making it an easy target for American interceptors.

Most of the kamikaze raids at Okinawa were made in daylight by waves of planes that attacked continuously, inflicting more casualties in ships and personnel than in any previous battle fought by the American Navy. "It is absolutely out of the question for you to return alive," the suicide pilots were told. "Your mission involves certain death. . . . Choose a death which brings about the maximum result." [21]

The suicide pilots, called "treasures of the nation," were abysmally trained, but they were a cross section of the country's educated elite. Most of them were college students in the humanities who had recently been called into service. These "hero-gods of the air" were not the mindless fanatics, hopped up on saki, that many American sailors believed them to be. With few exceptions, they flew to certain death for what they considered unselfish causes—patriotism, family honor, and unflagging loyalty to the Emperor. They were willing to die to protect loved ones back home from an unimaginably destructive American invasion. If Iwo Jima gave Americans pause about the costs of an invasion of Japan, Curtis LeMay's fire raids on the cities of the empire revealed to the Japanese people the terrible power of an avenging enemy that could only be stopped, they believed, by the most desperate measures.

Here are parts of two typical letters from young suicide pilots:

MY DEAR PARENTS,

The Japanese way of life is indeed beautiful and I am proud of it, as I am of Japanese history and mythology, which reflect the purity of our ancestors and their belief in the past. . . . And the living embodiment of all wonderful things from our past is the Imperial Family, which is also the crystallization of the splendor and beauty of Japan and its people. It is an honor to be able to give my life in defense of these beautiful and lofty things.[22]

Please do not grieve for me, mother. It will be glorious to die in action. I am grateful to be able to die in a battle to determine the destiny of our country.[23]

On April 6 and 7, 355 kamikazes, along with 345 conventional dive-bombers and torpedo planes, hit the great fleet assembled in the waters off Okinawa, in what was the first and largest of ten massive attacks. On that same day, American submarines spotted an enemy naval force coming out of the protection of the Inland Sea and heading for Okinawa. It was *Yamoto*, the biggest battleship afloat, escorted by a cruiser and eight of Japan's latest and largest destroyers. The sleekly proportioned dreadnought, a masterwork of naval design, was on a suicide mission. After inflicting maximum damage on the enemy's amphibious force, she was to beach herself and use her enormous guns, whose projectiles had a range of well over twenty miles, as artillery support for the armies on Okinawa.

Yamoto was also an expensive decoy. Sailing without aircraft cover, she could be expected to draw to herself great numbers of Hellcats, Avengers, Corsairs, and Dauntlesses that might be used against the suicide bombers. Admiral Mitscher summoned over 386 planes for the slaughter, and wave after wave of them tore into *Yamoto* until she exploded tremendously and capsized, taking down with her almost the entire crew of 3,300 officers and men. The Navy interceptors also sank a cruiser and four destroyers, while losing only twelve fliers.

It was the Imperial Navy's last sortie of the war but it helped half of the kamikazes to get through to the American fleet, which had been joined by the Royal Navy's Pacific Fleet. In one of the most fantastic air duels in naval history, the Japanese lost almost 400 planes to American fighters and withering antiaircraft fire, but they inflicted grievous damage, sinking eleven ships, including three destroyers. Altogether, Japan would mount 900 attacks on the fleet, mass raids as well as individual sacrificial sorties, from early April until the middle of June, when it began to run out of both pilots and planes that were not being husbanded for the "final battle" in the home islands.

To protect the fleet, a ring of early-warning radar picket stations was established. Small destroyers and other light vessels, including minelayers, gunboats, and landing craft, were stationed on the outer perimeter of the invasion armada. They picked up incoming enemy planes with their radar and vectored circling carrier aircraft to them. It was these smaller ships on lonely picket duty, heavily armed but thinly plated, that took the brunt of the Japanese air attacks. Rarely was a destroyer on picket duty for more than five hours without being hit by enemy bombers. "Get the destroyers," said Admiral Matome Ugaki, commander of Japan's 5th Air Fleet. "Without their radar warning of our approach, we will enjoy great success."[24]

Inside the radar picket screen were the larger destroyers of the gunfire support

A KAMIKAZE HEADED FOR THE BATTLESHIP *MISSOURI*. THE PLANE BOUNCED
OFF A GUN MOUNT AND CAUSED ONLY MINOR DAMAGE TO THE SHIP (NA).

screen. They had long-range, rapid-firing antiaircraft guns with nasty five-inch shells. Kamikazes flew directly into "as formidable an assembly of gun power as could be found perhaps anywhere in the war," in the opinion of Vice Admiral M. L. Deyo, commander of the naval force protecting the beachhead. Still, they made a "high percentage of hits," says Deyo. "Two hits out of seven [attempts.]"[25] The blows they delivered, while serious, were rarely mortal—not a single aircraft carrier or battleship was sunk in the waters off Okinawa. But a number of destroyers took a fatal beating.

In the first and largest *Kikusui* attack, the destroyer *Newcomb*, part of the gunfire support screen, was assaulted in lightning succession by three kamikazes, two of them scoring direct hits. Then a fourth one smashed into the forward stack, "spraying the entire amidships section . . . which was a raging conflagration, with a fresh supply of gasoline," wrote her skipper, Commander I. E. McMillian.[26] Lieutenant Leon Grabowsky of the destroyer *Leutze* risked his ship to try to save *Newcomb*. Correspondent Evan Wylie describes the heroic efforts of both crews, beginning his story just before a fifth kamikaze missed *Newcomb* and slammed into *Leutze*.

AT ALMOST COLLISION SPEED, [*Leutze*] swept up alongside the *Newcomb.* There was a grinding crash . . . as the two ships came together. The men jumped across and made the ships fast. Fire hoses were snaked across the rails. Powerful streams of water leaped from their nozzles and drove the flames back from the prostrate men. Rescue parties rushed in and dragged them to safety.

The suicide boys were not through. Another plane was roaring in, headed straight for the *Newcomb*'s bridge. Looking up, Joseph Piolata of Youngstown, Oh., saw the other destroyer firing right across the *Newcomb*'s deck. The gunners did their best, but the *Newcomb*'s superstructure hid the plane from their sights. On both ships the men watched helplessly. This was the kill. The *Newcomb* could never survive another hit.

But the battered, burning can still had fight in her. Incredulously the men of the *Newcomb,* crouched on her stern, struggling in the water, lying wounded on the deck, heard their ship's forward batteries firing. There was no power, but the gunners were firing anyway—by hand.

The gunnery officer stood at his station shouting the range data to the men in the forward five-inch turrets. In the No. 2 turret Arthur McGuire of St. Louis, Mo., rammed shells with broken, bleeding fingers. His hand had been caught by a hot shell while he fired at the third plane, but he was still on the job. The Jap had the *Newcomb*'s bridge in his sights. It looked as if he couldn't miss. But the burst from McGuire's gun caught him and blew him sideways. The hurtling plane missed the bridge by a scant eight feet, skidded across the *Newcomb*'s deck and plowed into the other destroyer.

With a gaping hole in the afterdeck and the portside a tangled web of broken lines and wildly sprouting fire hoses, the *Leutze* drifted slowly away.

Without water to fight the fire still raging amidships, the *Newcomb* was doomed. But the destroyer's crew contained some obstinate people. Donald Keeler of Danbury, Conn., was one of them. Keeler had been at his station in the after steering compartment. He was knocked down by the explosions but got up and put the ship in manual control. When it became evident that all the power was gone he joined the crowd on the stern just in time to hear that the after ammo-handling rooms were burning and the magazines were expected to go any minute.

Keeler elected to fight the fire. His only hope lay in a "handy-billy," a small, portable pump powered by a gasoline engine. The engine was started like an outboard motor—by winding a rope around the flywheel and giving it a quick tug.

Like all outboard engines, sometimes it started and then again sometimes it didn't.

Groping around in the blistering heat, Keeler found the handy-billy. Carefully he wound the rope around the flywheel, held his breath and yanked. The engine kicked over and kept going. Now Keeler had water. He and [three other sailors] . . . got the fire under control. Then they dragged the pump forward.

The No. 3 handling room was a roaring furnace. Steel dripped like solder from overhead. . . . Flames shot from the ammo hoists like the blast of a huge blow torch. It looked hopeless, but Newcomer shoved the hose in the doorway. No sooner had he done so than a wave came over the side and doused the pump. The chattering handy-billy spluttered and died. Keeler rushed back to the pump. Again he wound the rope around the flywheel, gritted his teeth and yanked. "I think I even prayed that second time," he said. "But the damn thing popped right off, something it wouldn't do again in a million years."

The men went back into the handling room. They kept the hose in there, taking turns. The magazines didn't blow up.

Up forward sailors were trying to fight the fire with hand extinguishers. A withering blast of heat drove them back. Their life jackets were smoking; their clothing was afire. The *Newcomb*'s doctor, Lt. John McNeil of Boston, Mass., . . . found one of the crew battling the flames with hair ablaze, half blind from the blood dripping from the shrapnel wounds in his face and forehead. With difficulty [he and another man] . . . dragged him off to the emergency dressing station in the wardroom. Many of the pharmacist's mates were out of action. Men with only first-aid training helped McNeil mix blood plasma for the burn cases.

Early Sayre of Roseville, Oh., was trapped on the stern unable to get his casualties forward. He was working on a fracture when someone tugged on his sleeve. "Blue Eyes has been hit bad. Looks like he's bleeding to death."

Blue Eyes was the youngest member of the crew. He had come aboard claiming eighteen years, but the men had taken one look at him and decided he must have lied to get in. Now he lay on the deck, blood spurting from a vein in his neck. Sayre had no instruments. He knelt down beside Blue Eyes and stopped the flow of blood with his fingers. He stayed there while the second plane came in and hit the other destroyer twenty feet away. He stayed there for almost an hour longer until they could come and take Blue Eyes away and operate on him and save his life. But Early Sayre had saved it already.

The rest of the Japs had been driven off. It was beginning to get dark when a ray of hope came to the exhausted men of the *Newcomb*. Keeler's volunteer fire department seemed to be holding the fires. Perhaps now they could save their ship. But the wave that had stopped the handy-billy was followed by another and another.

The *Newcomb* was sinking. The weight of the water that the hoses had poured into her after compartments was dragging her down. The rising water moved steadily forward. It reached the after bulkhead of the forward engine room. If it broke through, the *Newcomb* was done for. And the bulkhead already was leaking. . . .

In the forward engine room the damage-control party shored up the bulging bulkhead. Water oozed from it, but it held. With less than one foot of freeboard between the sea and her decks, the *Newcomb* stopped sinking.

Now the blinkers flashed in the darkness. Other destroyers were coming alongside. Over their rails came men with fire hoses and pump lines, doctors and pharmacist's mates with plasma and bandages. Tugs were on the way. The fight was over.

The *Newcomb*'s men had answered the question: Just how much punishment can a destroyer take?[27]

After this action, both destroyers were scrapped. Although they lost only forty-seven men killed or missing, many of the wounded in this and other kamikaze attacks were horribly burned. "They suffered excruciating agony until given first aid; for a man blown overboard, hours might elapse until a pharmacist's mate could relieve him," Morison has written. "The medical officers did wonders if the wounded survived long enough to receive attention. And many men in rear hospitals, who looked like mummies under their bandages, breathing through a tube and being fed intravenously while their bodies healed, were cured by virtue of new methods of treating burns."[28]

An American aircraft carrier was the dream target of every suicide pilot. On May 11, Admiral Mitscher's flagship, *Bunker Hill*, her deck crowded with thirty-four planes waiting to take off, their tanks filled with highly volatile aviation gas, their guns loaded with ammunition, was hit by two suicide planes almost simultaneously. The ship lost 396 men and was put out of commission after fifty-nine consecutive days at sea. Reporter Phelps Adams was nearby, on the bridge of the carrier *Enterprise*, when the kamikazes came tearing out of the low-hanging clouds.

TWO JAPANESE SUICIDE PLANES carrying 1,100 pounds of bombs plunged into the flight deck of Admiral Marc A. Mitscher's own flagship early today, killing several hundred officers and men, and transforming one of our biggest and finest flattops into a floating torch, with flames soaring nearly a thousand feet into the sky.

For eight seemingly interminable hours that followed, the ship and her crew fought as tense and terrifying a battle for survival as has ever been witnessed in the Pacific, but when dusk closed in the U.S.S. *Bunker Hill*—horribly crippled and still filmed by thin wisps of smoke and steam from her smoldering embers, was valiantly plowing along under her own power on the distant horizon—safe! Tomorrow she will spend nearly eight equally interminable hours burying at sea the men who died to save her.

Only once before during the entire war against Japan has any American carrier suffered such wounds, fought such fires, and lived—and that was when the battered, gutted hulk of the *Franklin* managed miraculously to steam away from these waters under her own power.

From the deck of the neighboring carrier a few hundred yards distant I watched the *Bunker Hill* burn, and I do not yet see how she lived through it. It is hard to believe that men could survive those flames, or that metal could withstand such heat.

I still find it incredible, too, that death could strike so swiftly and so wholly unexpectedly into the very heart of our great Pacific fleet. At one minute our task force was cruising in lazy circles about sixty miles off Okinawa without a care in the world and apparently without a suggestion of the presence of an enemy plane in any direction. In the next minute the *Bunker Hill* was a pillar of flame. It was as quick as that—like summer lightning without any warning rumble of thunder. . . .

Before General Quarters could be sounded on this ship, and before half a dozen shots could be fired by the *Bunker Hill,* the first kamikaze had dropped his 550-pound bomb and plunged squarely into the midst of the thirty-four waiting planes in a shower of burning gasoline.

The bomb, fitted with a delayed action fuse, pierced the flight deck at a sharp angle, passed out through the side of the hull and exploded in mid-air before striking the water. The plane—a single-engine Jap fighter—knocked the parked aircraft about like ten-pins, sent a huge column of flame and smoke belching upwards and then skidded crazily over the side.

Some of the pilots were blown overboard, and many managed to scramble to safety; but before a move could be made to fight the flames another kamikaze came whining out of the clouds, straight into the deadly anti-aircraft guns of the ship. This plane was a Jap dive bomber. . . . A five-inch shell that should have blown him out of the sky, set him afire and riddled his plane with metal, but still he came. Passing over the stern of the ship, he dropped his bomb with excellent aim right in the middle of the blazing planes. Then he flipped over and torched through the flight deck at the base of the island. The superstructure, which contains many of the delicate nerve centers from which the vessel is controlled, was instantly enveloped in flames and smoke which were caught in turn by the maws of the ventilating system and sucked down into the inner compartments of the ship, where the watertight doors and hatches had just been swung shut and battened down. Scores of men were suffocated in these below deck chambers.

Minutes later a third Jap suicider zoomed down to finish the job. Ignoring the flames and the smoke that swept around them, the men in the *Bunker Hill*'s gun galleries stuck courageously to their posts, pumping ammunition into their weapons and filling the sky with a curtain of protective lead. It was a neighboring destroyer, however, which finally scored a direct hit on the Jap and sent him splashing harmlessly into the sea.

That was the end of the attack and beginning of an heroic and brilliant fight for survival. The entire rear end of the ship was burning with uncontrollable fury. It looked very much like the newsreel shots of a blazing oil well, only worse—for this fire was feeding on highly refined gasoline and live ammunition. . . .

The carrier itself had begun to develop a pronounced list, and as each new stream of water was poured into her the angle increased more dangerously. Crippled as she was, however, she ploughed ahead at top speed and the wind that swept her decks blew the flame and smoke astern over the fantail and prevented the blaze from spreading forward on the flight deck and through the island structure. Trapped on the fantail, men faced the flames and fought grimly on, with only the ocean behind them, and with no way of knowing how much of the ship remained on the other side of that fiery wall.

Then, somehow, other men managed to break out the huge openings in the side of the hangar dock, and I got my first glimpse of the interior of the ship. That, I think, was the most horrible sight of all. The entire hangar deck was a raging blast furnace, white-hot throughout its length. Even from where I stood the glow of molten metal was unmistakable.

By this time the explosions had ceased and a cruiser and three destroyers were able to venture alongside with hoses fixed in their rigging. Like fireboats in New York Harbor, they pumped great streams of water into the ship and the smoke at last began to take on that greyish tinge which showed that somehow a flame was dying.

Up on the bridge, Capt. George A. Seitz, the skipper, was growing increasingly concerned about the dangerous list his ship had developed, and resolved to take a gambling chance. Throwing the *Bunker Hill* into a 70-degree turn, he heeled her cautiously over onto the opposite beam so that tons of water which had accumulated on one side were suddenly swept across the decks and overboard on the other. By great good fortune this wall of water carried the heart of the hangar deck fire with it.

That was the turning point in this modern battle of the *Bunker Hill*. After nearly three hours of almost hopeless fighting, she had brought her fires under control, and, though it was many more hours before they were completely extinguished, the battle was won and the ship was saved. . . .

Late today Admiral Mitscher and sixty or more members of his staff came aboard us to make this carrier his new flagship. He was unhurt—not even singed by the flames that swept the *Bunker Hill*, but he had lost three officers and six men of his own staff and a number of close friends in the ship's company. . . .

As he hauled aboard in a breeches buoy across the churning water that separated us from the speedy destroyer that had brought him alongside, he looked tired and old and just plain mad. His deeply lined face was more than weather beaten—it looked like an example of erosion in the dust-bowl country—but his eyes flashed fire and vengeance. He was a man who had a score to settle with the Japs and who would waste no time going about it.[29]

After the fire was put out, the flight deck of *Bunker Hill* looked like "the crater of a volcano," and below deck that night corpsmen prepared 396 bodies for burial at sea, starting the next day.

Three days after Mitscher transferred his flag to *Enterprise* that carrier was hit

THE MINESWEEPER *LINDSEY* TOOK TWO KAMIKAZE HITS OFF OKINAWA (USN).

by a kamikaze and lost for the remainder of the war. The admiral had to transfer his flag to *Randolph*. Having had two flagships shot from under him in four days, Mitscher said, "Any more of this and there will be hair growing on this old bald head." Three British carriers were also hit, but suffered little damage because they had steel decks. The American carriers were fitted out with light wooden decks to give them added speed and maneuverability. "When a kamikaze hits a U.S. carrier, it's six months' repair in Pearl," said an American officer. "In a Limey carrier, it's 'Sweepers, man your brooms.' " [30]

Admiral Mitscher, even with his Jonah-like luck, told reporters that the kamikazes "don't worry us very much." But Robert Sherrod "knew the sailors were worried, and so was I." [31]

In the Okinawa campaign, the Japanese made over 3,000 kamikaze sorties against the American fleet, in addition to the 5,000 to 6,000 sorties by conventional aircraft. In these raids, both massive and intermittent, they lost an astounding 7,830 planes. But they sank thirty-six American ships and damaged 368 others, including thirteen carriers, ten battleships, and five cruisers. The 9,731 officers and men killed or wounded at Okinawa represented one seventh of the Navy's total casualties in World War II. The Navy suppressed these horrifying casualty figures until a month after the conclusion of the battle.

"When the kamikazes started to come in the rule was never fire until one of them came directly at you. Don't provoke the guy," says Mort Zimmerman, a signalman on an LCI that laid smoke screens to camouflage the fleet.

THEY WOULD COME IN AT YOU in such numbers and so low that you could see the expressions on the faces of the pilots from the deck of the ship. Some destroyer crews would lower their guns into the water and throw up these huge walls of water, and when some of the older planes hit them they would just disintegrate.

It was awful to see the guys who got burnt in the fires these planes set off. They looked like mummies with the wraps off. They looked like charcoal logs.

DEAD SAILORS WRAPPED IN CANVAS BUNK BOTTOMS (NA).

One day I saw a destroyer escort that was on picket duty come into harbor and it was so beat up that the highest-rated man on the ship was a chief. Water was pouring out of the hull, everything above deck was charred and shattered, and from bow to stern I counted ninety bunk bottoms, dead guys wrapped in bunk bottoms. And I wondered how many other guys had gone over the sides. You could not believe what this ship looked like. Later they beached it and put up a sign that said, essentially, "Look at this thing. This is what you are fighting against."

Close to shore, we also encountered Japanese suicide swimmers. They would swim out in the morning, under the fog, dive beneath a ship and blow it and themselves up. So every morning, beginning at daybreak, we would put out watches and fire on anything that moved in the water. I was a bad shot, so I used a Thompson submachine gun. Anything I saw I sprayed.

You know, waiting for a kamikaze raid was sometimes worse on your nerves than the actual raid. Because once those sons-of-bitches started coming in there was no time to worry or think. Then it was a game of survival, and almost all your instincts were on high alert. And one of them wasn't fear. You were too damn worried about protecting your ship to be afraid.[32]

Radar and radio communications allowed the Navy time to prepare for the larger kamikaze attacks and to alert the crews. "But this practice had to be stopped," said one reporter. "The strain of waiting, the anticipated terror, made vivid from past experience, sends some men into hysteria, insanity, breakdown."[33] Admiral Halsey would later write that the kamikaze was "the only weapon I feared in the war."[34] Yet even on the biggest kamikaze raid of the war, on April 6–7, the Americans had more ships in the water than the Japanese had planes in the air. A picture released by the Navy after the Battle of Okinawa tells the larger story. It is called "The Fleet That Came to Stay."

SLAUGHTER ON THE SHURI LINE

As the kamikazes swarmed on the American fleet, the Tenth Army, reinforced by the 1st and 6th Marines, made excruciatingly slow progress against the Shuri Line, which extended across the island, with Naha, Okinawa's capital, on the west, the heights of Shuri Castle in the center, and the hills around Yonabaru on the east coast. As the battle of brute attrition wore on into May, Admiral Nimitz grew increasingly irritated with General Buckner, the son of the Confederate general who had surrendered to Ulysses Grant at Fort Donelson. Nimitz complained to the general that his methodical method of fighting was causing the Navy to lose "a ship and a half a day." But even when assault-trained Marines were brought in, the enemy line held, and Buckner, backed by Nimitz, jettisoned a proposal for a daring amphibious landing behind the Shuri Line, reminiscent of the Anzio operation, when the Allies had made an end run around Italy's formidable Monte Cassino. "We poured a tremendous amount of metal in on those positions," recalls a Marine commander. "Not only from artillery but from ships at sea. It seemed nothing could possibly be living in that churning mass where the shells were falling and roaring but when we next advanced, Japs would still be there, even madder than they had been before." [35]

Before the Americans landed on Okinawa, the Japanese had dug for over three months, with hand tools, to build an interlocking network of deep, heavily fortified caves on the faces of hills, cliffs, and sharply pitched ravines. From these hidden positions they resorted to "sleeping tactics," putting heavy artillery and mortar fire on the enemy trapped below them on flat fields and farms, and coming out only at night in small infiltration parties, as they had at Peleliu and Iwo Jima. "Counting both sides, the [Shuri Line] represented an extraordinary concentration of 300,000 fighting men and countless terrified civilians, on a battleground that was about as wide as the distance between Capitol Hill in Washington and Arlington National Cemetery," writes William Manchester. "In the densest combat of World War I, battalion frontage had been approximately eight hundred yards. Here it was less than six hundred yards. The

ATTACKING THE SHURI LINE (SC).

sewage, of course, was appalling. You could smell the front long before you saw it; it was one vast cesspool." As Manchester caught his first glimpse of the front, from a high hill overlooking it, his mind went back to the photographs his father, a World War I veteran, had shown him as a boy. "This, I thought, is what Verdun and Passchendaele must have looked like. The two great armies, squatting opposite one another in mud and smoke, were locked together in unimaginable agony. . . . [And] there was nothing green left; artillery had denuded and scarred every inch of ground."[36]

Throughout the month of May, the 1st and 6th Marines launched attack after bludgeoning attack against the western end of the ten-mile-long Shuri Line, while the Army did the same against the eastern side. Much of the battle was fought in driving rain and knee-deep mud. "Our division [the 6th Marines] entered the southern battle lines on May 1," wrote Raymond Sawyer, who in 1941 had left home to join the

Marines at the age of fifteen, lying about his age to an over-eager enlistment sergeant. "We joined our 1st Marine Division near the bluffs above the Asa Kawa River [on the right flank of the Shuri Line, above Naha]. The next forty days would witness the most intense fighting encountered in the South Pacific." [37]

In an unpublished memoir written after the war, Sawyer describes the opening rounds of the fight for Sugar Loaf Hill, a 100-foot-high mound of coral and volcanic rock that was the anchor of the Shuri Line. It stood about one mile from General Ushijima's command center in a tunnel under Shuri Castle and at the time was the bloodiest battlefield in the world:

BY MAY 12, WE HAD PUSHED to within one mile of the Shuri Ridge and Sugar Loaf Hill. Sugar Loaf Hill was an unpretentious elevation that formed one leg of a triangular system which protected the left of the Shuri Line. The capture of Sugar Loaf Hill spelled doom to the Shuri defense position. . . . Behind Sugar Loaf and its attendant hills lay a broad corridor, which led into the Shuri Fortress. General Ushijima had organized [his] positions to make the most of the Japanese soldier's feral instinct to live, fight, and die underground. They set the highest of prices on access to this corridor. The prospective customer was the striking 6th Marine Division.

With Sherman tanks at our side our attack commenced. Our unit pushed within 1,000 yards of Sugar Loaf and there heavy fire from 47mm guns, well concealed in caves, battered our advance. The battle for Sugar Loaf Hill took place from May 13 to May 17. During those four days we reached the top of Sugar Loaf thirteen times only to be driven back by Japanese counterattacks twelve times.

On May 15, our eighth assault on this hill took place. Our battalion led it. Machine gun fire, mortar shells, and rifle fire hit us hard. Our own heavy guns were pounding the gun positions on the hill. It was apparent within a couple of hours that our assault would not permit us to hold the summit. Orders were given to withdraw to the perimeter line from which we had earlier commenced the assault. My machine gun squad and a supporting rifle team failed to receive the withdrawal orders.

Suddenly we found ourselves about 150 feet below the summit of Sugar Loaf Hill and then realized we were alone except for the Japanese garrison above us. There were seventeen of us. . . . Corporal Mike Sabo, our squad leader, myself as [machine] gunner, my assistant gunner, and [fourteen] riflemen. We dug in on the slope and this would be our real estate for the next ten to twelve hours. . . .

We managed to hold out throughout the very long day, with my machine gun and our rifle fire . . . keeping the Japanese from our position. [We] killed a large number of Japs. I did not know how many.

That night we attempted to get off the hill. I provided machine gun fire for my fellow Marines [a number of them were wounded]. Within a minute of leaving our hole on the hill about five or six Japs appeared and were about to fire upon the Marines who were now below. I took them out using about thirty rounds from my machine gun. I started down when I saw the Marines before me drop into the ravine. I carried my machine gun supported by a shoulder strap. . . . How, I do not know, but I did reach . . . our position.

After our ordeal on Sugar Loaf Hill I was convinced that I would never be hit during a campaign.

It would require five more assaults on Sugar Loaf Hill before we captured the site.[38]

On Okinawa, the Japanese had more and better artillery than in any previous island campaign. So did the Americans. The consequent shock and carnage was almost unendurable for the men on both sides. "The ground swayed and shook from concussion as shells erupted all around and steel fragments tore through the air and through men's bodies," Eugene Sledge recalled. Some artillery barrages went on for four or five days. "When the shells finally stopped we were all shaking. You could not hold your rifle steady."[39] Because of the intensity of artillery fire, neuropsychiatric casualties were higher on Okinawa than any previous Pacific battle.

In was no better for the GIs on the other end of the Shuri Line. *Life* photographer W. Eugene Smith, a veteran of thirteen Pacific actions and twenty-three bombing missions, was nearly killed in this sector by mortar fire while putting together a photo essay on "the working day" of Terry Moore, a foot-slogging Pfc. of the 7th Division. They were on a muddy ridge together when the artillery and mortar fire started coming in on them. "They had us zeroed in and we just lay and took it," wrote Smith.

TERRY LAY A FEW YARDS AWAY. I adjusted my camera, judged the footage and waited. I wanted to show Terry under close mortar hits, it was part of his day.

The trouble with taking photographs when the air is full of lead is that you have to stand up when anyone with any sense is lying down and trying to disappear right into the earth. I got to my feet. . . .

The next thing I remember was a spiral ringing in my ears and I knew I was regaining consciousness. I knew I had been hit but I did not hurt. I felt warm and cozy. I heard the cry, "Medic, medic over here, the photographer." I had a surge of happiness: I could hear. My ears were all right. I rolled over on my left elbow and warm blood came gushing from my mouth and face, but I could see. Another surge of happiness, my eyes were okay. But then I saw. My left hand was what I focused on first. It was messed up badly. The index finger was hanging by a cord. . . .

I could not swallow and I choked as I breathed. The blood gurgled in my throat at each breath. I had a moment of fright, overwhelming fright. I could not breathe. . . .

Then consciousness again: the face was Terry's and the voice was Terry's. . . .

"Take it easy, Smitty." He was holding my smashed hand. . . . Then I realized I couldn't talk. I just gurgled. But Terry understood.

With Terry's help, Smith made it to the road, where he was placed into a supply jeep. He was losing a lot of blood. " 'Move fast through the villages,' I heard some one say. 'Artillery.' I prayed, 'Oh please God, no more artillery.' "[40]

Smith was evacuated to a hospital on Guam and underwent a number of surgeries before he was able again to use a camera. He wrote the text for his story of Terry Moore from a hospital bed, and it appeared with his photographs in *Life*. Not shown in the picture story was the badly blurred photograph of the explosion that nearly killed him. Smith took it less than a second before he was hit. He left it out because it had nothing to do with Terry.

W. Eugene Smith took some of the finest combat photographs of the war. One is a classic, a shot of a grubby, hard-as-nails-looking Marine on Saipan. It failed to get through the military censors, however, because they didn't want the home front to know what combat was doing to the attitude and appearance of our fighting boys.*

While Raymond Sawyer and the 6th Marines were still assaulting Sugar Loaf Hill, Eugene Sledge's Company K moved onto a barren, muddy ridge called Half

*It is the photograph that appears on the cover of this book.

Moon Hill, a key supporting position for Sugar Loaf Hill, just to the right (west) of them. They had relieved a company of 6th Marines that had taken horrendous casualties. "They could not remove their dead because of the thousands of Jap shells unleashed on the area," Sledge recalls. "The day we moved onto Half Moon, torrential rains began and did not slacken for ten days. Tanks bogged down and all our attacks had to stop, so we occupied the Hill amid death and heavy shellfire. Almost every shell hole in the area had a dead Marine in it, and they were all infested with maggots. The rain washed the maggots off the dead and into our foxholes. . . .

"The Japs were attacking every night, and we were killing them in our lines every night. In the Pacific, decay is rapid. We threw mud on the dead bodies with our entrenching tools to hold down the swarms of big flies and maggots. The next day . . . a few shells came in and blew the corpses apart. There were body parts lying all over the place; we called it 'Maggot Ridge.' If we went down the ridge and slipped and fell, we slid all the way to the bottom. When we came to our feet, the maggots were falling out of our dungaree pockets, our cartridge belts and everything else." And "many of us who fell," Sledge says, "were covered with our own vomit."

With rain pouring down on them, with mud up to their knees, with decaying bodies all around them, with flies swarming in their food, with the landscape butchered beyond recognition, and with amoebic dysentery breaking out among the company, "[we] believed we had been flung into hell's own cesspool." Beginning on Okinawa, and continuing for the next twenty years or so, Sledge was afflicted by terrifying nightmares.

On Okinawa, the dream was always the same. "The dead got up slowly out of their waterlogged craters . . . and with stooped shoulders and dragging feet, wandered around aimlessly, their lips moving as though trying to tell me something. I struggled to hear what they were saying. They seemed agonized by pain and despair. I felt they were asking me for help. The most horrible thing was that I felt unable to aid them." [41]

Adding to the men's torment was their complete ignorance of how the battle was going elsewhere, not just in this gully or on that ridge—and their feeling, as more and more of their friends died, that death had become "a kind of epidemic." As the divisions were bled down, veteran Marines like William Manchester started to see, to their despair, dozens of seventeen-year-old boys, fresh out of boot camp. If he were to die, Manchester wanted to die among raggedy-ass Marines like himself, not these pallid, innocent-looking kids. [42]

"What kept you going," Sledge says, "was the fact that you felt like you had to live up to the demands of your unit and the buddies that were depending on you." [43]

Manchester believes it was that and more. "To fight World War II you had to have been tempered and strengthened in the 1930s Depression by a struggle for survival—in 1940 two out of every five draftees had been rejected, most of them victims of malnutrition. And you had to know that your whole generation, unlike the Vietnam generation, was in this together, that no strings were being pulled for anybody; the four Roosevelt brothers were in uniform, and the sons of both Harry Hopkins, FDR's closest advisor, and Leverett Saltonstall, one of the most powerful Republicans in the Senate, served in the Marine Corps as enlisted men and were killed in action. . . .

"You also needed nationalism, the absolute conviction that the United States was the envy of all other nations." And you needed to believe in certain core values. "Debt was ignoble. Courage was a virtue. Mothers were beloved, fathers obeyed. Marriage was a sacrament. Divorce was disgraceful. . . . [And] you assumed that if you came through this ordeal you would age with dignity, respected as well as adored by your children. . . .

"All this led you into battle, and sustained you as you fought, and comforted you if you fell, and, if it came to that, justified your death to all who loved you as you had loved them.

"Later the rules would change. But we didn't know that then. We didn't *know*." [44]

As the 6th Marines continued to hurl themselves against Sugar Loaf Hill, a reporter from *Time* described one of their assaults: "There were fifty Marines on top of Sugar Loaf Hill. They had been ordered to hold the position all night, at any cost. By dawn, forty-six of them had been killed or wounded. Then, into the foxhole where the remaining four huddled, the Japs dropped a white phosphorus shell, burning three men to death. The last survivor crawled to an aid station." [45]

The Marines tried every tactic, every weapon they had, but the courageous enemy seemed to get even stronger. The Americans could tell by their morning examinations of the Japanese dead that the enemy wasn't ready to give up. The corpses looked healthy and well fed, the uniforms almost brand new.

On May 8, the troops on the Shuri Line learned that Nazi Germany had surrendered. "No one cared much. . . ." admits Sledge. "We were resigned only to the fact that the Japanese would fight to total extinction on Okinawa . . . Nazi Germany might as well have been on the moon." [46]

By sundown on May 17, the 6th Marines had almost given up hope of taking Sugar Loaf Hill. They were worn down and nearly out of ammunition. But they stayed and prevailed. Elements of the Tenth Army, including Sledge's unit, had taken the hills

THE STEEPLE OF A CATHOLIC CHURCH BELOW SHURI CASTLE
PROVIDED A SNIPER'S NEST FOR THE JAPANESE (USMC).

that flanked Sugar Loaf, threatening to envelop Ushijima, and the next morning Manchester's 29th Marines, with new tanks, captured the summit and held it. After smashing through the Shuri Line, the Americans pursued the Japanese Army as it retreated to a strong line of ridges on the southern end of the island. In fifteen days of fighting on the Shuri Line the Japanese had lost nearly 50,000 soldiers. The Marines lost almost 3,000 men, killed or seriously wounded, roughly the same as at Tarawa. The Army took even greater casualties during the same period. As George Feifer writes in *Tennozan,* his searing account of the Battle of Okinawa, "Gaining control of the 'pimple of a hill,' . . . [was] by some measures the hardest single battle in the Pacific War and hardest for Americans anywhere in World War II."[47]

While Sledge's 1st Marines fought the rear guard that had been left on Shuri

Heights, Raymond Sawyer's regiment marched south on May 22 to join other units of the 6th Marines in the capture of Naha. On the morning of June 5, while engaged in a firefight near the city, Sawyer was knocked out by the blast of a 60mm mortar shell. He woke up in a cave that had been set up for emergency surgery and learned he had shrapnel wounds all over his body. A surgeon from his hometown of Woburn, Massachusetts, sewed up his abdomen and sent him to a hospital plane to be flown to Guam for additional surgery. On June 25, 1945, in a brief ceremony at the fleet hospital on Guam, Admiral Nimitz presented him with the Navy Cross for heroism on Sugar Loaf Hill.

Back on Okinawa, on June 2, William Manchester suffered a superficial gunshot wound, the million-dollar wound that was "the dream of every infantryman." He was out of the war, temporarily, in a well-run field hospital, eating hot food on clean plates and listening to Jack Benny on the radio. But when he learned that his 6th Marines were going to bypass Naha and make an amphibious landing behind Japanese lines he went AWOL and made the successful landing with them. Early the next morning, he was standing around with some friends when he heard a familiar shriek. Seconds later, an eight-inch shell landed yards away from them. One of his buddies disintegrated, flesh and bones and blood flying everywhere. When Manchester woke up on the ground he was blind (temporarily) and deaf (with both eardrums ruptured) and his body was punctured by shards of shrapnel and pieces of his dead friend's bones. He was left for dead, but a corpsman found him, gave him two shots of morphine, and arranged for his evacuation to Saipan.

Pursuing the enemy south of the Shuri Line, the Tenth Army was forced to do a lot of "cave flushing." Working in small teams, sometimes with tanks equipped with long-range flamethowers, infantrymen would call into a cave, often with bullhorns, demanding that the occupants come out with their hands high. If the Japanese refused, the cave blowers dropped fifty-five-gallon drums of napalm into the mouth of the cave, ignited them with phosphorus grenades, and mowed down every enemy soldier who tried to escape. To avoid death by fire and suffocation, some soldiers crawled into the deepest reaches of caves and took their lives. Civilians hid with soldiers in these caves and uncounted thousands of them were buried alive.

If the Japanese soldiers agreed to come out with their hands up, they were sometimes shot anyway. Americans did not trust their intentions. A surviving Japanese officer recalls that "when Americans called Japanese soldiers to come out of their caves, they would put hand grenades under their armpits. Outside, they'd get as close as pos-

A DEMOLITION SQUAD PREPARES TO BLOW UP A JAPANESE CAVE (SC).

sible to the Americans, throw the grenades and try to fly back into the caves. Not very noble, but there was simply nothing else they could do to resist. Anyway, such tactics only work once. The Americans learned to order us to raise our hands higher."

Another enemy trick was to put on an Okinawan kimono and hide a grenade or a demolition charge under it. This caused many innocent citizens to be killed by nervous American soldiers who shot anyone who moved suspiciously. One Marine who was religious found it "pretty hard at first" to accept that "our people were shooting human beings who weren't necessarily military. But after I saw what their people—including civilians—did with their hands up, I worried about us, not them. I wanted to leave Okinawa alive!"

To the Japanese and Okinawans, the flamethrower was the most terrifying weapon in the American arsenal. But the men carrying them were as frightened of the enemy as the enemy was of them. A flamethrowerman had ninety-five-pounds of lethal firepower strapped to his back. One bullet in the tank meant instant incineration. And because of the weight of the tank, he could not crawl or lie flat if fired upon;

A FLAMETHROWER ATTACKS A HIDDEN ENEMY POSITION (SC).

nor did he carry a rifle. "You couldn't see them in there, but they could see you—a perfect bull's eye without a rifle," recalls Evan Regal, a farm boy from upstate New York. "Every time I had to walk up to a hole, I was scared out of my mind because I was a sitting duck." Casualties among flamethrowers were far higher than for riflemen. "I stepped over hit flamethrowers like logs," said one infantryman.

Regal describes a typical cave-flushing operation: "You pulled the triggers—there were two—just as soon as you thought your flame could reach them. In it went and all hell'd break loose. You heard the shuffling and the screaming and almost always some would come running, their hair and clothes on fire, for the riflemen to pick them off. . . . Gasoline could glance off sometimes, just searing them, but napalm stuck to their skin like jelly glue even when they ran out, and we used napalm most of the time on Okinawa. . . .

"You have utterly no compassion for their screams because you've seen so many of your own cut down and you know it can be *you* the next second; if you give them the slightest chance, they'll put a bullet between your eyes. . . . All you care about the Japs is that they fry fast." [48]

For civilians, the battle south of the Shuri Line was a massive slaughter. Up to 100,000 noncombatants died in the month of June. As the Japanese troops retreated, the terrified civilian population went with them, filling the roads and villages with an almost indistinguishable mixture of combatants and noncombatants. So they were killed in nearly equal numbers, "grandfathers, grandmothers, mothers with children on their backs, scurrying along, covered in mud," in the words of one refugee. [49] Those not killed by random American fire died of disease, starvation, and a score of other war-related causes, including suicide. As at Marpi Point, many jumped from high cliffs into the shallow surf. The Navy tried to stop them, and tried to rescue those who were pinned to the bottom of the cliffs, terror-stricken at the sight of the American naval guns glaring at them. "Those who can swim, swim out!" Navy translators in a rescue boat shouted to a group of Okinawans standing in the breakers. "Those who can't swim, walk toward Minatogawa! Walk by day. Don't travel by night. We have food! We will rescue you!"

"They actually did!" recalls Miyagi Kikuko, a sixteen-year-old member of an Okinawan student defense group who was trapped with her friends in the churning surf. "They took care of Okinawans really well, according to international law, but we only learned that later. We thought we were hearing the voices of demons. From the time we'd been children we'd only been educated to hate them. They would strip the girls naked and do with them whatever they wanted, then run over them with tanks. We really believed that. . . . So what we had been taught [by the Japanese] robbed us of life. . . . Had we known the truth, all of us would have survived. . . . Anyway, we didn't answer that voice."

The next day three of Miyagi Kikuko's friends were killed by random American fire and ten classmates gathered in a cliffside cave and pulled the pin of a hand grenade they had been carrying. "When the firing stopped I . . . stepped out over the corpses. . . ." she recalls. "The automatic rifles of four or five American soldiers were aimed right at me. My grenade was taken away. I had held it to the last minute."

Miyagi Kikuko was fed and taken to a camp in the north, where she was reunited with her mother and father. "Mother, barefoot, ran out of a tent in the camp and hugged me to her. 'You lived, you lived!' "[50]

In the Battle of Okinawa at least a third of the island's population of almost 490,000 died, and nearly every town and burial tomb was turned into smoking rubble. Few people suffered as greatly in modern warfare as the Okinawans. Their losses indicate how horrible an invasion of Japan would have been for the Japanese people.

In early June, Sledge's 1st Marines were sent south to assault the western anchor of the enemy's final defensive line at Kunishi Ridge, a sheer coral cliff laced with caves and gun emplacements. As Sledge approached Kunishi "its crest looked so like Bloody Nose [Ridge] that my knees nearly buckled. I felt as though I were on Peleliu and had it all to go through again." The vicious week-long battle for Kunishi finished off the Japanese on Okinawa, and on June 20 Sledge's battalion was one of the first American units to reach the southern tip of the island. They stood on a high hill overlooking the sea and felt a surge of accomplishment. "This was different from Peleliu. We could see its meaning."[51]

The next morning, Sledge went with his company's corpsmen to assist some Marines who had been attacked by two Japanese officers wielding samurai sabers. One of the officers lay dead on the ground when Sledge arrived at the scene. "Nothing remained of his head from the nose up—just a mass of crushed skull, brains, and bloody pulp. A grimy Marine with a dazed expression stood over the Japanese. With a foot planted firmly on the ground on each side of the enemy officer's body, the Marine held his rifle by the forestock with both hands and slowly and mechanically moved it up and down like a plunger. I winced each time it came down with a sickening sound into the gory mass. Brains and blood were splattered all over the Marine's rifle, boon-dockers, and canvas leggings. . . .

"The Marine was obviously in a complete state of shock. We gently took him by the arms. . . .

"The poor guy responded like a sleepwalker as he was led off with the wounded. . . .

"We dragged the battered enemy officer to the edge of the gun emplacement and rolled him down the hill. Replete with violence, shock, blood, gore and suffering, this was the type of incident that should be witnessed by anyone who has any delusions about the glory of war."

On June 21, 1945, the Tenth Army declared the island secured, after eighty-two days of fighting. But it went on for Sledge and Company K. They were ordered to clean out die-hard Japanese defenders and to bury the enemy dead in their area. "It was the ultimate indignity," Sledge says, burying the men who had been trying to kill them for the last seven weeks.[52]

When they were sent back up north Sledge looked for old friends, but could not find many. Only twenty-six Peleliu veterans who had landed with the company had survived Okinawa.

It was the bloodiest campaign of the Pacific war. Total American combat casualties were 12,510 killed and missing in action (4,675 Army, 2,928 Marines, and 4,907 Navy), 36,613 wounded, and a slightly lower number of noncombat casualties, principally victims of battle fatigue and accidents. The American Army counted 107,539 enemy dead, but thousands of others were sealed in caves and never became statistics.

Okinawa was the only major battle in the Pacific in which the commanding officers of both sides died. Ushijima committed suicide, and Buckner was killed near the end of the fight by enemy artillery fire. A sizable number of prisoners were captured,

7,401. Although about half of them were conscripted Okinawans, this was more than had surrendered in the entire Pacific campaign, evidence, perhaps, of growing disillusionment among recent conscripts in the Japanese Army. Even so, far greater numbers committed suicide or fought on when death was a certainty. No American soldier who participated in the death struggle on Okinawa believed that the Japanese Army could be beaten short of utter annihilation.

In early July rumors started to run through the ranks that the troops on Okinawa would hit Japan next. As Sledge said, "No one wanted to talk about that."[55]

CHAPTER 21

The Setting Sun

BURMA

The invasion of Okinawa in April 1945 was the climactic moment of the war against Japan. In China, a huge Japanese Army was bogged down in the greatest guerrilla war of the century, carrying out well-organized "annihilation campaigns" against guerrillas and their village supporters, extermination operations that killed over two and a half million noncombatants. In every other Asian theater the Imperial Army had either been defeated or backed up on its heels. "The Japs in this area are on the run," Marvin Kastenbaum, an American GI, wrote his family from Namhpakka, Burma, "and where I was sitting yesterday, I could see the famous Burma Road."[1]

The turning point in Burma had come in August 1943. At the Quebec Conference, Roosevelt and Churchill decided that the time was propitious for a counteroffensive against Chinese-held Burma. Lord Louis Mountbatten was named Supreme Commander in Southeast Asia and Vinegar Joe Stilwell, who had led a heroic retreat from Burma in the spring of 1942, was given command of Chinese and American ground forces. With the Japanese controlling the Burma Road, Stilwell's most urgent task was to reopen a supply line to China. He had already established an air transport system over the Hump, the high and dangerous Himalayas, to supply Chiang Kai-shek's Chinese Nationalist Army from India. By the end of 1943, the American "Humpsters," flying woefully under-powered cargo planes through some of the most wretched weather in the world, were delivering more supplies to China than had ever gone over the hairpin turns and gorges of the Burma Road.

This allowed the Chinese to tie down over a million Japanese troops that could have been deployed in the Pacific against MacArthur and Nimitz. "Strong winds, with speeds sometimes exceeding one hundred miles per hour, created mountain waves and vertical sheers that could overturn an aircraft, send it rocketing upward for thousands of feet or plunge it downward into the mountains. According to the season, thunderstorms, torrential rains, hail, sleet, snow, and severe icing held sway," recalls an American flier. "Bring me men to match my weather," was the Humpster's motto. If pilots survived a hit by Japanese Zeros they parachuted into unfathomable jungle, a fifteen-minute fall from 17,000 feet. Those not picked up by rescue teams, among them the reporter Eric Sevareid, walked out of "tiger country" with the help of upcountry headhunters. Sevareid writes of his experience. "Tonight one of the [native] guards said to Private Schrandt: 'India *there*'—and pointed west. 'China *there*'—and pointed east. 'American *there*'—and pointed *up*." [2]

Late in 1943, American engineers and 15,000 American troops, 60 percent of them African-Americans, began building a new road to connect Ledo, Assam, in eastern India, with that part of the Burma Road still in enemy hands. But first the Japanese had to be cleared from northern Burma. Major General Orde Wingate and his raiders, called Chindits, after the statues of dragons that guard Burmese temples, had already begun this operation, crossing from India through Japanese lines and wrecking airfields, blowing up bridges, and dynamiting railways. Wingate's British Chindits were second-line troops—nearly all of them married men from the north of England, aged twenty-eight to thirty-five. Wingate told them they had to imitate Tarzan. "For six sweltering months in the Indian jungles he trained them in river crossing, infiltration tactics and long forced marches with heavy packs, until they were the toughest of shock troops," wrote Charles Rolo, war correspondent for the *Atlantic Monthly*. On returning from the raid one private remarked: "The whole job was a piece of cake compared to the training."

The Chindits lived on rice, vultures, jungle roots, and grass soup, and kept in touch with one another by carrier pigeons, birdcalls, and messenger dogs. Elephants carried their mortars and folding boats; carts drawn by oxen were stacked high with machine guns and boxes of grenades. Supplies were dropped in by air. Looking like some minor prophet with his long beard and a blanket draped over his shoulders, Wingate drove his raiders mercilessly, reminding them that their security lay in speed.[5]

Wingate's Raiders and their American prototype, Merrill's Marauders, organized by General Frank D. Merrill, harried the enemy in northern Burma while Stilwell fought down from China to protect the construction of the Ledo—later named the Stilwell—Road. Meanwhile the Japanese went on the offensive in March 1944, attacking across the Indian border at Imphal, the main base of General William Slim's Fourteenth Imperial Army. They ran into unexpectedly strong resistance, and the British were soon counterattacking, aided by revengeful Burmese hill men. The miserably supplied Japanese invasion Army was slaughtered and a starving remnant limped back into Burma. Fifty thousand of the 80,000 elite troops that had begun the confident push into India died. British losses were equally appalling. But in 1944 the Japanese were in full retreat down the road they had come up in 1942, the road to Mandalay, to Rangoon, and to Tokyo.

In the closing months of 1944, Stilwell's army, now commanded by General Albert C. Wedemeyer, who replaced Stilwell as Chiang Kai-shek's chief-of-staff, cleared the way for the opening of the Stilwell Road. This prodigious engineering achievement rose as high as 4,500 feet through the Patkai Mountains and passed through untouched wilderness. "The work was done principally by black combat engineers," recalls one of the African-American truck drivers on the Ledo Road. "I take my hat off to those guys, talk about cliff-hangers, and in bulldozers, no less. They took the turns out of the road and made curves."[4] On January 28, 1945, the first convoy, consisting of fifty African-American and fifty Chinese drivers, drove over the Hump and crossed into China.

Over the next four months the Allies launched a coordinated offensive. Three armies converged on the Japanese in Burma: the American-trained Chinese from the north, General Slim's Fourteenth Imperial Army from the center, and three divisions of Indian and African troops from the south. Before these overwhelming forces Mandalay fell on March 20, Rangoon on May 3. After liberating Burma and inflicting over 300,000 casualties on the Japanese Army, General Slim began planning the liberation of Malaya and Singapore, an enormous operation that the end of the war would thankfully make unnecessary.

HELL SHIPS AND DOG CAGES

As Japanese power crumbled in Southeast Asia and the Central Pacific, and as military conscription drained Japan's industrial workforce, the government began shipping great numbers of prisoners of war to the home islands. There they worked as laborers in shipyards, steel mills, coal mines, and other vital sectors of the economy. These industrial slaves were transported by sea in the steaming overcrowded holds of merchant vessels, where thousands died of starvation, disease, and suffocation. The death toll rose alarmingly in late 1944 when Allied warships and planes gained domination of Japan's shipping lanes in preparation for the invasion of the Philippines. The Japanese refused to mark the ships that carried its prisoners of war, and these slow-moving, lightly armed vessels were easy prey for Allied submarines and fighter planes. Over the course of the war, approximately 21,000 Allied POWs died at sea, about 19,000 of them killed by friendly fire. By comparison, about 20,000 Marines died in the entire Pacific War.[5] The *Arisan Maru*, torpedoed by an American submarine, took down with it over twice as many American POWs, almost 1,800, as died on the Bataan Death March. No combatants in the war suffered and died more horribly than did the prisoners on these hell ships. And driven insane by their conditions, prisoners sometimes killed one another.

Sergeant Forrest Knox was one of ninety-nine men from the small town of Janesville, Wisconsin, to be captured by the Japanese after the surrender of Bataan. In September 1944, as MacArthur's armies prepared to land in the Philippines, he was working with an 800-man crew on airfield construction at a camp near Manila. He worked barefoot, in a G-string and straw hat, digging ditches and draining mosquito-infested rice paddies with shovels made out of thin sheet iron. He was losing his sight and the sensation in his legs, he had malaria and hookworm, and he weighed barely ninety pounds. He had managed to keep only two things from the Bataan Death March, a toothbrush and a filthy neck towel, which had kept him from dying from heat stroke. As Admiral Halsey's planes pounded the airfields around Manila, he was moved with prisoners from other camps to Bilibid, a compound in Manila where he ran into some old buddies from his Janesville National Guard tank unit. They and a thousand or so other prisoners were to be shipped to Japan in the stinking hold of a rusty freighter called the *Haro Maru*, a place that soon became, in Forrest Knox's words, "a madhouse."

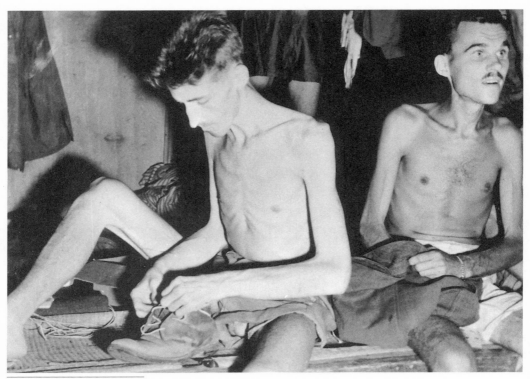

DEATH SHIP POWs (SC).

THEY PUT 500 OF US in one hold and 500 in the other. . . . After the ship was loaded, tugs pulled us away from the dock and moored us to a buoy in the harbor. Tropical sun on a steel deck. Body heat from 500 men packed together. All around men began passing out. They just slid down out of sight, where men stepped or stood on them. . . .

As a guy goes crazy he starts to scream—not like a woman, more like the howl of a dog. . . . It must have been 120 or 125 degrees in that hold. The Japs' favorite trick was to cut off our water. It was bad enough in other places when they did this, but there, in this oven, when they cut it off, guys started going crazy. People running, people screaming. An American colonel was on deck. There was always some Americans topside who were used to raise and lower the honey buckets and food tubs. The Japs told the colonel to tell us to be quiet. He shouted down, "Be quiet or the Japs will completely cover over the hatch with canvas." . . .

With the temperature we were in, if they'd closed off that little air we got, I don't know how many of us would have been alive by morning. I had picked up the habit of wearing a small sweat towel around my forehead. . . . The next guy that went by screaming they caught and killed. . . . He was strangled with my little towel. A guy that had worked in a mental institution in Pennsylvania knew how to do it. Several others were also killed [strangled or beaten to death with canteens]. The crazy ones . . . howled because they were afraid to die— but now the ground rules changed. If they howled, they died. The screaming stopped. . . . The Japs didn't cover the hatch.

"No one was ever punished for these deaths," says Private William R. Evans, who was in the hold with Knox, "and the Japs didn't give a shit."[6]

The last of the death ships to leave the Philippines was the passenger-cargo vessel *Oryoku Maru*. It pulled away from the Manila docks on December 13, carrying 1,619 POWs in her holds, along with over two thousand Japanese merchant seamen and civilians, who were quartered above deck. All but thirty of the prisoners were Americans.

"We were jammed in the holds," recalls Lieutenant Melvin Rosen, a young American artillery officer. "There was no place to lie down; some people couldn't even sit down, and everybody had diarrhea. The floorboards were full of human waste and vomit, and the stench was unbearable. The temperature was over one hundred degrees, and people started going mad that first night, screaming for water and air. Some guys drank their own urine, and it drove them crazy." Others scraped the sweat off the steel sides of the ship and tried to drink it. "One person near me," says Pfc. Lee Davis, "cut another person's throat and was holding the canteen so he could catch the blood."

About fifty men died that first night, an unknown number of them strangled or beaten by other prisoners. Others were killed to stop them, in their frenzy, from murdering fellow Americans.

The next morning the ship was bombed and strafed by Navy planes as it headed north, hugging the shore. The slaughter was above deck. More than 300 Japanese were killed and hundreds more were injured seriously. Waiting for the cover of night, the ship's crew offloaded the passengers to the site of a former U.S. naval base, leaving only the guards, the gun crews, and the prisoners on the battered *Oryoku Maru*. That night, thirst-crazed men turned into "human vampires," says Major John M. Wright, "biting men and sucking blood in their mad lust for liquid in any form."[7] Toward morning it got quiet, as most of the exhausted prisoners passed out, sleeping fitfully in their own vomit and urine. Then the dive-bombers returned.

"They put a 500 pound bomb in the hold with us," recalls Colonel Maynard Booth, "and there was a terrible bloody mess. Arms and legs and blood and guts were flying all over the place, and one guy who got blasted to pieces landed right on top of me. About 200 guys were killed, and the whole ship was on fire. Then it got real quiet. And as you heard people groaning, the Japs ordered us to swim to shore, which was only a couple of hundreds of yards away. I stayed on the ship and went up into the cabins and got life preservers and put them on our wounded, and heaved these men over the side of the ship. Then I bailed out with my life preserver and started swimming. Japanese on shore were machine-gunning us, but most of us managed to make it."

"When we got to shore," says Melvin Rosen, "they herded us into an old tennis court surrounded by a chicken-wire fence and gave each of us a tablespoon and a half of raw rice and a little water. That was our diet for the next five days. After that we were taken on trucks to a town we had passed through on the Bataan Death March, San Fernanado, Pampanga."

"They said they were going to take our wounded to the hospital," recalls Booth. "They were beat up real bad and the Japs didn't have any medicine. They loaded fifteen of them on the back of a truck like they were sides of beef and went down the road two or three miles, kicked them out into a ditch, and [beheaded] them, as we found out later."

The 1,333 prisoners that survived were jammed into boxcars and taken to a small port on northern Luzon. "We were lined up and packed into two Jap freighters," says Captain Marion "Manny" Lawton. "The *Enoura Maru* housed almost 1,000 of us. The rest were loaded on the *Brazil Maru*."

"The *Enoura Maru* was a freighter that had just unloaded horses for the Japanese horse artillery," says Booth. "There was horse manure on the floors and we were so hungry we picked the bugs out of it and ate them and crawled on the floor looking for barley that the horses hadn't eaten." As the two hell ships headed for Formosa, rice was lowered to the men in tubs. "The flies were like hornets coming out of their hive. When the tub got to the bottom you couldn't see the rice for the flies," says Lawton. "We were so hungry it didn't make any difference." Twenty-one POWs died along the way and their bodies were tossed overboard to the sharks. The ships arrived in Formosa on New Year's Eve. Just after the prisoners on the *Brazil Maru* were transferred by barge to the *Enoura Maru*, an American dive-bomber hit that ship and it sunk at anchor in shallow water. Almost 300 men were killed instantly in the forward hold and at least another 250 were wounded. "The Japanese kept us down in the hold with our dead and wounded for three days, and then sent down a cargo net to load the dead," says Rosen. "After a few days, sitting in the smashed hull, we were put on the *Brazil Maru* and headed in a convoy for Japan." They left without four doctors who had died of exhaustion assisting the wounded, using old razor blades and rusty scissors for surgical instruments.

There were only about 900 POWs remaining and they kept dying on the two-week passage to Japan, as many as thirty a day. Officers and men traded their wedding bands and service academy rings to their Japanese guards for cupfuls of water and dry rice, and the stealing and fighting continued. "Let me tell you what it felt like to be hungry all the time," says Major William G. Adair. "It was a stomach pain. Not a great pain, but an annoying one. And it never went away while I was a prisoner. Never." As they headed further north, they ran into snow and ice storms and men started coming down with pneumonia. A tarpaulin had been put over the hatch, but the freezing wind whipped through the hold. "When it rained, the dirty water from the deck would pour down on us. Men drank it—filthy, dirty water. The diarrhea and pneumonia just started wiping us out. We buried an average of twenty-five a day," says Lawton.

At least half of the prisoners had malaria; and the genitalia of men with beriberi swelled, causing excruciating pain. Men with dry beriberi experienced stabbing pains, like electric shocks, in their legs and feet, and almost everyone had dysentery. When they landed in northern Kyushu after a forty-eight-day journey, only 450 of the original 1,619 were still alive, and about 150 more died from maltreatment the first week in Japan. "The Japanese weighed some of us when we came ashore," says Rosen, "and I weighed exactly eighty-eight pounds."

The prisoners were divided into groups and sent to three different camps. When Manny Lawton arrived at Camp No. 3 there was snow on the ground and the men were moved into an unheated barracks. Lawton learned from a corpsman that his closest friend, Captain Henry Leitner, had pneumonia and was in danger of dying. "The next morning I looked up and there was Henry in his undershorts, nothing else on, strolling toward the door. I called to him and asked him where he thought he was going. He said, 'I'm going to get some of that snow. I'm thirsty.' I said, 'Henry, please come back. There's plenty of hot tea here.' 'No,' he said, 'I'm hot. I've got to have something cool.' His fever was burning. He strolled on out. That night he died."[8]

"Unlike a lot of the guys, I don't have nightmares today," says Melvin Rosen. "But every morning when I come down and pick up the kettle on the stove and empty the old

LIBERATED POWs IN THE PHILIPPINES (USN).

water in it, I think of how many lives that little bit of water might have saved when we were in those hell ships." [9]

Before being transferred to Korea, Rosen was taken to a slave labor camp on Kyushu, where one of the prisoners was Lester Tenney, a fellow survivor of the Bataan Death March. This was Fukuoka Camp No. 17 in Omuta, just east of Nagasaki. It was a compound built by the Mitsui Coal Mining Company and run by the Army. And it had a reputation. "This camp was as tough as they came," says Staff Sergeant Harold Feiner. "It was mean. If there was nothing else that had gone wrong, the work itself would have made it bad. We mined coal twelve hours a day, had a thirty-minute lunch break, and were given one day off every ten days." [10]

Lester Tenney had been with the initial group of prisoners to open the camp. When he was first taken underground he was ordered to build ceiling supports. "When I asked why this was needed, one of the civilian workers told me that the mine had been shut down years before because all the coal that was safe to extract had already been removed. . . . We paid a price for doing this. . . . Even with the ceiling sagging, and only three feet high, we went in and got the coal on our hands and knees; and men got hurt doing it—from cave-ins especially. A lot of guys died in that mine."

Men mutilated themselves to get out of work. Tenney describes how it was done:

I TOOK A BIG STEEL LOCKING PIN from one of the coal cars, put my hand over a piece of timber and took that bar and smashed it into my hand as hard as I could. The pain was excruciating. But my hand started to swell up, and it looked like it was broken. I had to make it look like an accident. So I got a pick ax and tore some coal down on myself and let out a yell. I showed my bleeding and swollen hand to the Japanese supervisor, but the hand wasn't broken and I had to go to work the next day. The next time, I said to myself, I'll go to an experienced bone breaker and have it done right.

We had bone crushers, guys who would break a bone with a shovel or a jack-hammer for a price, usually cigarettes or rations of rice. A hand cost one ration of rice, a foot five to eight rations. You didn't get out of work for long, even with a broken leg, but it was worth it to some guys who reached the point where they felt that if they went in that mine the next day they'd die there.

Another way to get out of work was to manufacture ulcers on your feet, so you couldn't put on a shoe. Making an ulcer was simple. I took a pin and pricked twenty or so holes in my foot in a pattern about the size of a dime. Then I got some lye from the bathroom and mixed it with lye soap to make a paste. I put that paste on the bleeding area and put a bandage over it. The next morning I took off the bandage and I had a nice burn scab. I picked away at the crust with a knife and saw that I had a beautiful, fresh looking ulcer. Every day I made it bigger, until it was the size of a half-dollar. The medics, who were Americans, let me off work for a week.[11]

There were other ways to make ulcers. Some men put battery acid from their miner's lamps on their festering sores.

"The diet of the prisoner of war was based solely on rice," reported Thomas Hewlett, an American Army doctor at Omuta, "and all the men lived in a state of chronic starvation." This led desperate men to steal food from the prison gallery. Those caught were denied rice and water for days and were beaten with bamboo poles, baseball bats, and pick handles. When the guards were finished with them they would urinate in their faces. At Omuta, several prisoners were executed for stealing canned food and Red Cross parcels that were supposed to be given to them. Thirty-eight percent of the 36,260 American military personnel captured and interned by the Japanese died in captivity, a total of 13,851. By contrast, 99 percent of the 93,941 Americans captured by the Germans survived the war.[12]

For some prisoners, tobacco was as essential as food. "They would desperately trade off some of their rice for a little bit of tobacco, either cigarettes or shaved tobacco, which they made into cigarettes with the thin rice paper of the little Bibles that GIs were issued," says one prisoner.[13] Traders would go around the camp calling out, "nicotine for protein," and there were always takers, as some men smoked themselves to the point of death.[14]

Conditions grew worse in the winter and spring of 1945 when LeMay's B-29s began their fire raids. "Instead of merely hitting us with their hands or fists, the Japanese used shovels, picks, and sections of steel chain," says Tenney. "They swung the chains around overhead until they reached a high speed. Then, using the chain's momentum, they inflicted brutal blows upon our bodies. . . . In one attack, my cheekbones were gashed; the skin above my eyebrow was broken, my nose . . . was smashed, and my entire chin was gushing with blood." Dr. Hewlett told him his left scapula was broken, but he was sent back into the mine because he could still shovel coal with one hand. "The beatings were bad," says Tenney, "but the more of them we got the better we felt about the war effort." [15]

The Japanese saved their cruelest treatment for downed B-29 crews. In February, at Chichi Jima in the Bonins, eight downed fliers were executed and the men of the garrison ate the flesh of four of them. In Japan, captured "B-29ers" were segregated from other POWs, usually in small torture camps run by the *kempeitai*, the Gestapo-like secret military police. They were interrogated and tortured brutally. Some were put on public trial as war criminals and executed; others were beheaded or bayoneted on the spot. One group of fliers was shot with bows and arrows and then decapitated. At another camp, three airmen were tortured and burned alive. In one of the most ghastly atrocities, eight B-29 crewmen were offered as specimens to the medical professors at Kyushu Imperial University. "The professors," writes historian Gavan Daws, "cut them up alive, in a dirty room with a tin table where students dissected corpses. They drained blood and replaced it with sea water. They cut out the lungs, livers, and stomachs. They stopped blood flow in an artery near the heart, to see how long death took. They dug holes in a skull and stuck a knife into the living brain to see what would happen." [16]

Records are incomplete, but it is likely that over 200 fliers were killed after being captured by the Japanese military.

Flying out of Saipan, a B-29 named *Rover Boys Express* was shot down by Japanese fighters over Tokyo on January 27, 1945. Five crew members survived a terrifying explosion, and with their ordinary escape hatch damaged, parachuted out of the bomb bay. One of them was Ray "Hap" Halloran, a twenty-two-year-old navigator from Cincinnati, Ohio. Japanese civilians followed the flight of his chute and captured him and beat him into a state of unconsciousness with wooden and metal poles. Then they stoned him with large rocks. As he slipped in and out of consciousness, he looked up and saw six military police standing over him. They cut his parachute, stuffed part of it into his mouth, tied his hands and feet, beat him with the butts of their rifles, and tossed him into the bed of a truck. After a brutal interrogation at a nearby airbase, he was again beaten in the chest and back with rifle butts.

THEY TOOK ME TO A SHOPPING AREA and made me stand and bow to jeering crowds of people. I think the purpose was to build morale among the civilians who had taken quite a beating from the B-29s. After people finished throwing stones at me, I was blindfolded again and taken to the *kempeitai* torture prison in downtown Tokyo. That's where I spent the next sixty-seven days in a cage.

The cage was elevated about four feet off the floor. I was covered with blood. I was cold. And I was crying with pain. The other prisoners, Japanese conscientious objectors, complained to the guards that they couldn't sleep with all the noise I was making. So they pulled me out of my cage and took me to a doctor. He had a big tube in his hand, with a needle at the end of it. There was green liquid in the tube. The doctor said this would make me sleep. Somehow I convinced him not to inject me. Later I learned the greenish liquid was poison. Six other prisoners were injected and died.

After a few days, they carried me—I couldn't walk—across a courtyard to what we called the stables, and I was locked in another cage. It was small and you entered through a door on the floor. They pushed you in like you were a dog, and it really was a dog cage. I was ordered to lie in my cell with my head to the door, and the guards played a game of punching my head with their rifle butts.

It was cold and I had only one blanket and there was a hole in the floor for a toilet. The biggest thing in my life was a rice ball the size of a golf ball that they'd roll in through a small feeding slot at the base of the door. I was a big guy and I lost over 100 pounds in prison.

Firm rule. No speaking. No noise. There was one young guy in another cage, an eighteen-year-old gunner who kept saying, "Okay, Mom, I'll be right down for breakfast." He violated the rule. He was taken out and he never made it home.

Each day, you try to hang in there. At first I tried to cope by thinking of my family but that was no good. It broke me down internally. I prayed a lot. I said, "Please God, I'm really in trouble. I need your help." No one came to help me.

I was always in darkness. The only light I ever saw was a low-wattage bulb on the ceiling of my cage. The darkness makes you go nuts. The only time I saw the light of day was from under a blindfold when they carried me out to interrogate me and beat me. But, crazily, I looked forward to the interrogations. They broke the everlasting boredom and were a chance to get out of the cavelike darkness. I missed them when they stopped.

The next thing I remember is the big Tokyo fire raid of March 10. I heard multiengine planes at low altitude and I thought that was strange. We always flew at 30,000 feet. Then the bombs started to fall and my cage jumped; and for the next two or three hours fire was all around us. At the back of my cage was a small window. There was a black cloth covering it, but on that night I could see the red sky and the flames through the covered window. And though it had been a calm night before the bombers came, I heard the wind blowing like a tornado. I was frightened out of my mind, 'cause fire really scares me. I was convinced I was going to burn to death.

HAP HALLORAN IN CAGE AT THE TOKYO ZOO
(ILLUSTRATION BY NORMAN ROCKWELL).

I could hear mothers and children screaming and running. The prison was right across from the Emperor's Palace and they were jumping into the moat to escape the flames and heat. But I didn't know that at the time.

The next morning an interpreter came in, a polite guy, and told me what had happened the night before, like he was trying to be informative. He spoke of bodies stacked three and four feet high in the streets and of thousands of bodies floating down the river to Tokyo Bay. Then he looked at me and said, "Hap, I regret to advise you that at our meeting this morning the decision was made to execute you B-29ers."

A few days later I was taken out and told to take off my shoes. I thought—death sentence. They blindfolded me, tied my hands and feet, and loaded me on a truck. They dropped me off at the Tokyo Zoo, just tossed me off the truck. Then they pulled off my blindfold, put me in a tiger cage, stripped off my clothes, and tied my hands

RAY "HAP" HALLORAN
(COURTESY OF RAY HALLORAN).

to the bars. The purpose was to let civilians see me. "Do not fear these B-29 fliers. They are not super beings. Look at this one." I was a pathetic sight, standing there, skinny as a rail, with a long, filthy beard, shivering from the cold, with my body covered with running sores from lice and fleas. I was trying desperately to act like an air corps guy, you know, with dignity. It was pretty tough, but you've got to do it, maintain your dignity as best you can.

They left me at the Ueno Zoo overnight and the next day they took me to a place with some other B-29ers and a bunch of other prisoners, the Omori Prisoner of War Camp, about twelve miles from downtown Tokyo. It was on a little island in Tokyo Bay, only a couple of hundred yards out in the bay. Thank God for that little separation because the subsequent fire raids burned down everything right across from us.

At Camp Omori, Hap Halloran met Air Commander Robert Goldsworthy, who had also been tortured in a *kempeitai* prison. "Sometimes I'd get so low that I wanted to quit," Goldsworthy recalls, "and Hap would buck me up. And days when Hap would get like that I'd take him off to the side and buck him up. . . . We used to say 'home alive in '45.' We knew it couldn't go on much longer because our guys were devastating Japan from the air." [17]

DECISIONS

On June 15, when General Curtis LeMay ended his incendiary campaign against Japan's six largest cities, having turned them into charred wastelands, he began attacking smaller cities, destroying an additional sixty of them by the end of the war, killing one million Japanese and leaving ten million homeless. His crews also targeted shipping and harbors, oil facilities, and railroads. By now, the enemy's air defenses had been destroyed. "At this time," LeMay recalled, "it was actually safer to fly a combat mission over Japan in a B-29 than it was to fly a B-29 training mission back in the United States." [18] While LeMay's "burn jobs," as he called them, obliterated Japan's urban culture, Admiral Halsey's Task Force 38 cruised at will up and down the coast of Japan, shelling port cities and military installations, even Tokyo Harbor. Navy planes ripped up airfields and burned planes on the ground; and they attacked railroad trains and passenger ferries filled with women and children, attacks the Japanese considered more reprehensible than "Devil LeMay's" napalm raids. Every Japanese citizen became a military target. "I did want every Japanese dead," John Ciardi admitted. "Part of it was our propaganda machine, but part of it was what we heard accurately. This was the enemy. We were there to eliminate them. That's the soldier's short-term bloody view." [19]

LeMay dropped leaflets as well as bombs, his own foray into psychological warfare. In bold red and black script, the leaflets warned the citizens of cities targeted for incineration to "evacuate at once!" On the other side of the leaflet were these words:

THESE LEAFLETS ARE BEING DROPPED to notify you that your city has been listed for destruction by our powerful air force. The bombing will begin within seventy-two hours.

This advance notice will give your military authorities ample time to take necessary defensive measures to protect you from our inevitable attack. Watch and see how powerless they are to protect you.[20]

LeMay writes: "At first they thought we were bluffing. . . . There wasn't any mass exodus until we knocked the hell out of the first three towns on the list. Then the rest were practically depopulated in nothing flat." The leaflets had a crushing impact on civilian morale, producing defeatism and terror. Their government, the Japanese people realized, *was* powerless to protect them.

With thousands of American and British heavy bombers on the way from Europe and with 5,000 more B-29s on order, LeMay was convinced he "could bomb and burn them until they quit," avoiding a humanly costly invasion of the home islands.[21] He informed General Arnold, however, that by October he would run out of cities to burn, except for four he had been ordered not to touch—Kyoto, Niigata, Kokura, and Hiroshima. LeMay soon learned why they were off-limits to him.

On June 18, 1945, President Harry Truman was scheduled to meet with his top military advisors. "I have to decide Japanese strategy—shall we invade Japan proper or shall we bomb and blockade?" the President wrote in his diary the day before the meeting. "That is my hardest decision to date."[22] Truman was concerned about casualties, hoping to prevent "an Okinawa from one end of Japan to the other."[23]

At the meeting, General George Marshall presented an invasion plan, supported by the Navy and the Air Forces, code-named Downfall. It was to be a two-phase operation. The Americans would land on the Japanese island Kyushu on November 1 with 760,000 assault troops, seize the southernmost part of the island, and build naval bases and air fields for the larger invasion of Honshu and the Tokyo Plain in March 1946, should that be necessary. The first landing was called Olympic, the second, Coronet. MacArthur would be in charge of the ground troops, Nimitz would command the naval forces. It would be a combined operation larger than the Normandy invasion, requiring over 1.7 million troops, the entire Pacific fleet, and 5,000 combat aircraft. Marshall told Truman that there would probably be 350,000 defenders on Kyushu. A precise estimate of American casualties might not have been mentioned at this meeting but Truman had been led to believe that the number of dead Americans would probably be higher than 25,000 in the first thirty days.

Airpower alone could not bring down Japan, Marshall was convinced, even combined with a tightened naval blockade. The ground troops would have to finish the job.

Truman commented that the effect of Olympic would be to create "another Okinawa closer to Japan," and approved the Kyushu operation, adding that they could decide "later" whether to proceed with Coronet.[24]

There was no mention of the atomic bomb, which had not yet been tested. But as the meeting was breaking up, Truman asked Assistant Secretary of War John J. McCloy, who had sat silently through the proceedings, for his views. Speaking with some reluctance, McCloy suggested that the threat of the bomb might provide a "political solution," making an invasion unnecessary. "I said I would tell them [the Japanese government] we have the bomb and I would tell them what kind of a weapon it is. And then I would tell them the surrender terms."[25] The Japanese, he said, should also be told that they could keep the Emperor.

Truman said he would take this under consideration and hurried off.

Momentum for using the bomb—when it was ready—was already building. Reports about Japanese atrocities against American POWs were being headlined in newspapers and magazines, fueling demands for retribution. The American public—and many of Truman's advisors—were also convinced that the Japanese would slaughter all prisoners of war in the event of an invasion. They were apparently not wrong. In August 1944, the Japanese government had sent a directive to commandants of POW camps. What later became known as the "Kill-All Order" outlined "extreme measures" to be taken against prisoners when the military situation became "urgent . . . Whether they are destroyed individually or in groups, or however it is done, with mass bombing, poisonous smoke, poisons, drowning, decapitation, or what, dispose of the prisoners as the situation dictates. . . . It is the aim not to allow the escape of a single one, to annihilate them all, and not to leave any traces."[26]

The American public was also weary of war and deeply alarmed by the rising numbers of American casualties. Over 64 percent of American battle fatalities in World War II took place in the one-year period between June 1944—the month of the Normandy and Saipan invasions—and May 1945. An invasion of the home islands would mean a large-scale redeployment of troops from Europe to the Pacific and yet one more battle—the bloodiest of them all—for weary Pacific assault troops like Eugene Sledge. "After [Okinawa] . . . we all knew that General MacArthur was already planning our role in the next damned landing, the biggest one in history . . . right down the gut to Tokyo. None of us veterans," said Sledge, "expected to survive that epic carnage."[27]

The families of these men were as concerned as they were. That June, Marvin Kastenbaum's father had four of his sons serving in the military, and another son had just been killed in April. One son was likely to be discharged early, but Jimmie Kastenbaum was with the infantry in the Philippines, Jack Kastenbaum was in Europe, waiting to be transferred to the Pacific, and Marvin had been moved from Burma to China. "The prospect that Jack and Jimmie and I would converge on Japan from three different directions had to be a cause of some concern to my father," Marvin wrote later.[28]

The invasion that never occurred was a real and awful thing to American fighting men in August 1945. The assault troops had been chosen and were already in training. And that summer almost half a million Purple Hearts were being made and stockpiled for the operation.[29]

That July and August, Army intelligence intercepts, code-named ULTRA, reported an enemy buildup on Kyushu greatly in excess of what the Joint Chiefs had originally anticipated. Decoded messages indicated that the Japanese would have 900,000 troops on Kyushu by November and that they would be prepared to meet the Americans on the first high ground behind the beaches. Suicide squads were being trained to throw themselves on American tanks with handheld bombs capable of penetrating heavy armor; and Japanese military planners expected the 5,000 kamikazes they had held back for the invasion to destroy over 40 percent of the American fleet. The Emperor himself took a personal interest in developing plans for repulsing the American invasion. He attended ceremonies at court for the regiments being raised for the defense of the divine homeland and encouraged the formation of citizen suicide units.[30] Intelligence sources predicted a "titanic confrontation," with possibly "unbearable" American losses—losses sufficient, perhaps, to force the Americans to back off from their demand for unconditional surrender.[31] That, not victory, had become the only realizable aim of even most die-hard Japanese militarists. This is why the defeat at Okinawa was actually encouraging to the Japanese military. On Okinawa, a badly outnumbered force, cut off from supplies and vigorous civilian support, had held off the invaders for almost a hundred days, inflicting frightful casualties. In a statement made after the war, General Masakazu Amano, an architect of defensive preparations on Kyushu, declared: "We were absolutely sure of victory. It was the first and only battle in which the main strength of the air, land and sea forces were to be joined. The geographical advantages of the homeland were to be utilized to the highest degree, the enemy was to be crushed, and we were confident that the battle would prove to be the turning point in political maneuvering."[32] When American political leaders "said that the Japanese were likely to fight to the death rather than surrender unconditionally, they were not exaggerating what the Japanese government itself was saying," writes historian Herbert Bix.[33] The paradoxical effect of the decisive American victory at Okinawa was to discourage the Americans "while inspiring the Japanese."[34]

Japan had already been defeated. Now, the American objective was to force a defiant government to surrender, a government that still had the support of its people. Residents of Tokyo hurled ridicule on their conquered ally for surrendering unconditionally, verbally accosting Germans on the streets and in the trains. "The Tokyo papers," Robert Guillain reports, "blamed Germany's defeat on its lack of *bushido*. With *bushido* . . . one never dies, never surrenders unconditionally."[35]

While the President and his advisors plotted the final stroke against Japan and a team of nuclear scientists at a secret facility at Los Alamos, New Mexico, hurried their world-altering work to conclusion, a new Air Force unit was conducting highly secret training operations in the Marianas. Flying stripped-down B-29s designed to achieve maximum speed and altitude, pilots and crews of the 509th Composite Group were dropping enormous pumpkin-shaped bombs, one to a plane, on a desolate island near Tinian and practicing dangerously sharp diving turns away from their targets. Their commander was pipe-smoking, thirty-year-old Colonel Paul Tibbets, who had been chosen to head this operation because he knew the B-29 better than anyone else in the service. A year before arriving in Tinian, he had suggested to Curtis LeMay, while the General was in the States, en route to the Marianas, that he finish off Japan with low-level fire raids. Now Tibbets was awaiting the arrival in the Marianas of a new kind of fire that he was sure would end the war.

Vice Admiral Frederick L. Ashworth, who would fly on the Nagasaki mission, had picked Tinian as the base for Tibbets's operation. At the time, Ashworth was a thirty-five-year-old Navy commander working at Los Alamos for General Leslie Groves, administrator of the Manhattan Project, the vast scientific and industrial enterprise—unprecedented in size—created in 1942 to build the world's first atomic bombs. "I was what was known as a 'weaponeer,'" Ashworth said in a recent interview.

THERE WERE TWO OF US, both Navy men. The other was Captain William "Deak" Parsons [the Manhattan Project's chief of weapons development], who flew on the Hiroshima mission. We were in change of the bombs, since the crews knew nothing about them.

In February 1945 General Groves sent me to Guam to deliver a letter from Admiral King to Admiral Nimitz, saying that a highly secret . . . "new weapon will be ready in August of this year for use against Japan by the 20th Air Force." . . .

The letter asked Nimitz to provide the necessary support for this operation, and it also said that the bearer would search for a proper base for this operation in the Marianas.

I went back to Washington to pick up the letter. I had a money belt with a zipper on it and I put it in there, under my khaki uniform shirt. When I got to Guam, the admiral's aide escorted me to Nimitz's office and I told Nimitz that I had to deliver the letter to him with no one else in the room. After his aide left, I pulled up my shirt, unzipped this sweaty old money belt, and handed him the letter. He read it and said grimly, "Don't they know we've got a war going out here? This is February now. You're talking about August. Why can't we have it out here sooner?" Nimitz wanted it to be available for Iwo Jima and Okinawa.

I told him that this was the schedule and it was a very tight schedule. He wasn't happy with this. He thanked me and I left his office.

I went from there to Tinian, after scratching Guam and Saipan as sites for the operation. Tinian was a natural because it had the longest runway in the world. The island commander took me to a spot on the north end of the island and I thought this is the place to put it. It was isolated from the other bomber groups on Tinian and would be ideal for top secret operations.[36]

After training at desolate Wendover, Utah, the 509th began arriving in Tinian in late May. Tibbets was confident his group of 1,800 men "would do the work of two million soldiers."[37] "The 509th was totally isolated within its own compound, connected by taxiways to North Field," recalled Major Charles W. Sweeney, the crack B-29 test pilot from North Quincy, Massachusetts, who was in charge of training exercises. "The compound was enclosed by a high fence with a main gate that was guarded around the clock by armed sentries. . . . This area contained the only windowless, air-conditioned buildings in the Pacific. . . . Here the various components of the bombs would be assembled. . . . Anyone trying to gain access without proper clearance could be shot."[38]

Tibbets and Sweeney were the only members of the 509th who had been officially informed that the unit was preparing to drop an atomic bomb. "The men were only told what they needed to know to do their jobs," Tibbets says, although it is likely that the bombardiers, at least, soon figured out what they would be asked to do.

Tibbets had little contact with the Los Alamos scientists and no interest whatsoever in the deep physics behind the bomb. "They told me it would explode with the equivalent of 20,000 tons of TNT. . . . All's I could say was that's going to be a damn big explosion." [39]

J. Robert Oppenheimer, director of the Los Alamos laboratory, explained to Tibbets that once the atomic bomb was released the delivery plane would have to make a dizzying 155 degree diving turn to get as far away from the point of explosion as possible. Otherwise the delivery plane was likely to be blown out of the sky. "This was difficult to do," Tibbets found out, "[without] snapping the tail off the airplane." In dry runs over the island of Rota, and later over Japan itself, Tibbets had his pilots practice these radical turns after releasing a single 10,000-pound bomb. These bombs were the shape and color of a pumpkin, the same size and configuration of the plutonium bomb that would be used against Nagasaki.* "I wanted them to get shot at," says Tibbets. "I wanted them to experience every possible emergency before they had an atom bomb and were really playing for keeps. I wanted the Japanese to see planes, flying alone, and to think they were on reconnaissance operations." Tibbets planned to fly these "pumpkin runs" himself but LeMay insisted the Army could not risk having him fall into enemy hands, with knowledge of the bomb. [40]

Other airmen on Tinian resented Tibbets's "glory boys." They had the best living quarters on the island and flew the safest missions—and some of them bragged to friends in the other bomber groups that they were personally going to win the war. "The other guys had lost a lot of crews and they had to come in low, while we went in

*The Manhattan Project produced two types of atomic weapons, one using uranium (U-235), the other plutonium, which was created from uranium. The explosive power of the bombs resulted from the instantaneous release of energy upon the splitting, or fission, of the atomic nuclei in uranium-235 or plutonium.

These weapons had different detonation systems. The uranium bomb was set off by using a gun-like device which fired a subcritical slug of uranium (one not compact, or dense, enough to explode) into a subcritical core of uranium. The slug, or bullet, was placed at one end of a long hollow tube similar to a gun barrel, with an explosive packed behind the bullet, and the core was placed at the other end of the sealed tube. When the bullet was fired and hit the core it produced a critical mass, setting in motion a self-sustaining chain reaction and a nuclear explosion.

The plutonium bomb was detonated by an implosion process. Plutonium was arranged inside the bomb in the form of a hollow sphere and surrounded by a sphere of conventional chemical explosives. When the fuse was ignited, the explosion of the outer sphere compressed the inner spere of plutonium into a ball-like critical mass, the size of a baseball. A chain reaction and an explosion followed instantaneously.

high where they couldn't get any antiaircraft or fighters up to us, so we were relatively safe," says airman Raymond Biel. "And we had brand-new planes and were getting the best of treatment from the government. To the other men, it didn't seem we were doing anything to end the war."[41]

On July 29, General Carl "Tooey" Spaatz arrived from Europe, via Washington, D.C., to take command of the Strategic Air Forces, which was created expressly for the atomic bomb missions. LeMay was made his chief-of-staff. Spaatz carried with him top secret orders drafted by Groves and approved by Truman:

> THE 509 COMPOSITE GROUP, 20th Air Force, will deliver its first special bomb as soon as weather will permit visual bombing after about 3 August 1945 on one of the targets: Hiroshima, Kokura, Niigata and Nagasaki. To carry military and civilian scientific personnel from the War Department to observe and record the effects of the explosion of the bomb, additional aircraft will accompany the airplane carrying the bomb. . . .
>
> Additional bombs will be delivered on the above targets as soon as made ready by the project staff.[42]

Stricken from the target list, at the instigation of Secretary of War Stimson, was Kyoto, the ancient religious and cultural capital of Japan. Nagasaki replaced it. It was a major military port in western Kyushu that was the home of the enormous Mitsubishi Steel and Armament Works and of a plant that had made the torpedoes that were used against the American fleet at Pearl Harbor. Hiroshima, the primary target, was the southern headquarters and supply depot for the homeland army that would mount the defense of Kyushu. Located on the main island, just across the Inland Sea from Kyushu, it had a population of about 350,000 and contained a number of war industries.

The United States was about to commit the most destructive single act in the history of civilization. How had it come to this decision?

The world's first nuclear explosion occurred in the New Mexico desert, at a remote area of Alamogordo Air Force Base, in the early morning hours of July 16, 1945. Truman was notified immediately and received a detailed description of the plutonium explosion five days later at Potsdam, an undamaged suburb of Berlin where he was meeting with Stalin and Churchill. Groves's report was euphoric. The "awesome roar" of the bomb had been heard at a distance of 100 miles and the "searing light" from the explosion had been seen 180 miles away. "All seemed to feel," wrote Groves's deputy, General Thomas F. Farrell, "that they had been present at the birth of a new age." But Groves concluded soberly, "We are all fully conscious that our real goal is still before us. The battle test is what counts." [43]

On July 26 the Allied leaders at Potsdam issued an ominous ultimatum calling for "the unconditional surrender of all the Japanese armed forces. . . . The alternative for Japan is prompt and utter destruction." [44]

None of the President's advisors opposed using the atomic bomb. But Stimson, Assistant Secretary of State Joseph Grew, and a number of others had tried to persuade Truman to eliminate the unconditional surrender clause of the Potsdam Declaration or at least modify it to assure the Japanese that the Emperor would be retained. They did so not to avoid dropping the A-bomb (Grew didn't know about the bomb), but to make unnecessary an invasion. To Secretary of State Jimmy Byrnes, this was rank appeasement. The Germans had to accept unconditional surrender. Why should not the Japanese? Byrnes was also concerned about Truman's standing with the American people. A Gallup poll taken on May 29 showed the American public overwhelmingly opposed to retaining the Emperor, whom they saw as a Hitler-like figure who had encouraged Japanese aggression. A third of those polled wanted him executed as a war criminal. Only 7 percent favored retaining him as a figurehead.

That spring, Americans had learned of the Palawan Massacre. To prevent American POWs from falling into enemy hands, Japanese soldiers on the Philippine island of Palawan had put 150 of them into an air raid shelter, doused them with gasoline, and set them on fire with long torches. Some of the men—their bodies in flames—managed to escape the shelter but most were cut down by gunfire and finished off with bayonets. Miraculously, a few escaped to tell their grisly story, which inflamed anti-Japanese sentiment in the United States. Giving in to Stimson, Byrnes warned, "would mean the crucifixion of the President." [45]

Some scholars criticize the "uncompromising" nature of the Potsdam Declaration. But Truman wanted to overthrow the imperial system, or *kokutai*, that was behind Japan's racist war of conquest in Asia, in the same way that Franklin Roosevelt wanted to eradicate Nazism root and branch. Truman intuited correctly that the Emperor was not a mere ceremonial figure, but an active advocate, until the dying days of the war, of a fight to the finish with the Americans. Historian Herbert Bix points out, in addition, what Truman could not have known—that the peace faction in the Japanese cabinet wanted to retain this authoritarian system. They were fighting not for a constitutional monarchy, Bix argues, but "for a monarchy based on the principle of oracular sovereignty," a system that could allow them to continue to control the people.[46]

It is unlikely, moreover, that an American guarantee of the imperial system would have caused Japan to surrender on terms acceptable to the Americans before the November invasion.[47]

On July 24, after agreeing to the wording of the Potsdam Declaration, Truman had learned from Stimson that one bomb would probably be ready by August 1. Stimson wrote in his diary that the President "was highly delighted."[48] Did he make his final decision to drop the bomb that day? We will never know. Probably, there was no one moment when he made up his mind. The only real decision he had to make was whether or not to stop the almost unstoppable momentum of events. Leslie Groves would later observe that Truman's "decision was one of noninterference—basically, a decision not to upset the existing plans."[49]

Truman knew the bomb would kill tens of thousands of innocent people, and that did not sit well with him. But he weighed this against the horrendous cost in American lives if the invasion were to go forward. He has been accused of crossing a moral threshold, but America had crossed that ethical boundary the previous March with the indiscriminate terror bombing of Dresden and Tokyo. "Every step in the bomber's progress since 1937," the editors of *Life* observed just after the atomic bombs were dropped, "has been more cruel than the last. From the concept of strategic bombing, all the developments—night, pattern, saturation, area, indiscriminate—have led straight to Hiroshima."[50] By this point in the war the mass killing of innocents had come to be seen as a narrowly military decision, independent of ethical considerations. There was no debate in Truman's circle over the ethics of the bomb.

Philip Morrison, a scientist who helped build the plutonium bomb and was at Tinian to assemble it, argues that the bomb "was not a discontinuity. We were carrying on more of the same, only it was much cheaper." One bomb, one city. "For that war, it was just one more city destroyed."

The scientists who made the bomb, he argues, bear as much responsibility for its use as President Truman. The Army did not approach the physicists. "*We* went to the Army. I mean the scientific profession. Einstein, the pacifist, at its head. We beat on the doors and said, We must be allowed to make this weaponry or we're going to lose the war. Once we did that, we didn't stop. I didn't stop. I didn't work a forty-hour week. I worked a seventy-hour week . . . [making] weapons. . . .

"I was wildly enthusiastic, 'cause I was a long-time anti-Nazi and this was the war I expected and feared. I was caught up spontaneously and naively in this terrible war. It was a great crusade." The scientists he worked with realized, Morrison adds, "that the idea of dropping it was implicit in making it."[51]

On July 26, the day Truman released the Potsdam Declaration, the cruiser *Indianapolis* arrived at Tinian with the firing mechanism and a uranium bullet (U-235) for the first bomb, nicknamed "Little Boy." The uranium core arrived by air shortly thereafter, along with the plutonium core for the second bomb, "Fat Man," named, for its shape, after Winston Churchill. This bomb was bigger and more powerful than "Little Boy." A third bomb was scheduled to be sent from Los Alamos in late August, according to Groves's original timetable.

After delivering her top-secret cargo, the *Indianapolis* headed for the Philippines. On July 30 she was sunk by a Japanese submarine. Only 317 of the sailors survived, most of them dying horribly in shark-infested waters because of a botched rescue mission. "The *Indianapolis*," Leslie Groves wrote later, "was a very poor choice to carry the bomb. She had no underwater sound equipment, and was so designed that a single torpedo was able to sink her quickly."[52] (She was hit by two torpedoes.)

While the Japanese had already attempted feeble peace overtures through Russia, Prime Minister Kantaro Suzuki, a seventy-seven-year-old admiral, publicly announced that they would "ignore" the Potsdam Declaration—"kill it with silence"—and continue to fight. The Japanese cabinet was almost evenly split between die-hards who wanted to continue the war and those who wanted peace, albeit on terms exceedingly favorable to Japan. No one in the cabinet was willing to accept the Allied demand for unconditional surrender.

Truman gave the order to the air command at Tinian: "release when ready but not sooner than August 2."[53]

Bad weather canceled the first flight, scheduled for August 3, but on August 5 the meteorologists called for several consecutive days of clear visibility. "Now we were ready," Tibbets recalls. Two planes would fly to the target with the *Enola Gay*, the lead plane that Tibbets named after his mother. *The Great Artiste*, piloted by Chuck Sweeney, would drop instruments to record heat, blast, and radiation, and an unnamed plane with George Marquardt at the controls would photograph the blast. At a tense preflight briefing, Captain Parsons told the crews they would be delivering the most powerful weapon in the history of the world, but the words "atomic" and "nuclear" were apparently not used. Nor, of course, were the crews told that the uranium bomb had not, and could not be, tested because of the slow production of U-235. (The uranium bomb was used because Los Alamos had exhausted its entire "immediate sup-

THE FLIGHT AND GROUND CREW OF THE *ENOLA GAY* AFTER THE HIROSHIMA MISSION. PAUL TIBBETS IS STANDING WITH HIS HAT ON IN THE CENTER UNDER THE PROP (NA).

ply" of plutonium in the test bomb.) Afterward, the men went to the mess hall for a preflight meal. It was 12:30 A.M., August 6, 1945. When Tibbets got up to leave, flight surgeon Don Young handed him a pillbox containing twelve cyanide capsules, one for each member of his crew. They were to be passed out if an emergency occurred. The crewmen could use them or not. There were no suicide orders.

As Chuck Sweeney's crew stowed their gear and prepared their airplane, Sweeney jumped into a jeep and drove over to Tibbets's plane. "The scene I encountered was surrealistic. There had to be two hundred people . . . standing in an island of intense light. Mobile generators were powering all forms of illumination: stands of high-intensity shop lights, floods, popping flashlights, and klieg lights like those you'd see at a grand opening of a movie. . . . Army photographers and film crews, MPs, technicians, senior officers, and civilians—who, I presumed, were the scientists—milled about."[54] As Tibbets climbed into the cabin of *Enola Gay* he felt he was about to be a part of "the greatest single event in the history of warfare."[55]

With his plane overweight because of the four and a half ton bomb, Tibbets burned practically every inch of the runway before he eased back on the yoke and *Enola Gay* rose majestically into the air. It was 2:45 A.M. Tinian time. Eight minutes into the flight, Captain William Parsons, the weaponeer, and his assistant, Morris Jeppson, crawled into the cramped bomb bay and inserted the explosive propellant powder into the bomb's gun-like firing mechanism and hooked up the detonator.

The arming was done in the air because Parsons had feared the plane stood a good chance of crashing on takeoff.

It was a perfect tropical night, with clear skies and a light breeze. As *Enola Gay* approached the target six and a half hours later, after rendezvousing with the two other planes over Iwo Jima, the sun was shining brilliantly and visibility could not have been better. Bombardier Thomas Ferebee released the bomb just seventeen seconds behind schedule. The plane jumped violently, 9,000 pounds lighter, and Tibbets made the dangerous diving turn he had been practicing for almost a year. "When we completed the turn, we had lost 1,700 feet and were heading away from our target with engines at full power. . . . Then everyone was quiet as a church mouse because we had nothing else to do," Tibbets recalls. They were about eleven miles from the drop point when a bright light filled the plane and a tremendous shock wave smashed into them. "The plane shook, and I yelled 'Flak!' thinking a heavy gun battery had found us." At a press conference the next day, co-pilot Robert Lewis told reporters he "felt as if some giant had struck the plane with a telephone pole." No one, not even Oppenheimer, was sure the plane would be able to withstand the shock of the blast. But after the second, and lighter, shock wave hit them Tibbets knew they'd survive. "And for the record, I announced over the intercom, 'Fellows, you have just dropped the first atomic bomb in history.'"[56]

George "Bob" Caron, the tail gunner, had the best view; and he had been on the intercom describing the mushroom-shaped cloud that rose high above the city and seemed to be coming right at them. "But we were not prepared for the awesome sight that met our eyes as we turned for a heading that would take us alongside the burning, devastated city," Tibbets wrote later. "The giant purple mushroom . . . had already risen to a height of 45,000 feet, three miles above our altitude, and was still boiling upward like something terribly alive. It was a frightening sight, and even though we were several miles away, it gave the appearance of something that was about to engulf us.

"Even more fearsome was the sight on the ground below. At the base of the cloud, fires were springing up everywhere amid a turbulent mass of smoke that had the appearance of bubbling hot tar. . . . The city we had seen so clearly in the sunlight a few minutes before was now an ugly smudge. It had completely disappeared under this awful blanket of smoke and fire.

"A feeling of shock and horror swept over all of us."

"My God!" Lewis wrote in his log.

The bomb detonated at 1,900 feet above the ground at 8:16 Hiroshima time, forty-three seconds after it was dropped. Almost in that instant, there was no city.

"I think this is the end of the war," Tibbets said to Lewis as they headed back to Tinian.[57]

President Truman thought the same. When he got the news, four hours later aboard the cruiser *Augusta* on his return from Potsdam, he grabbed the messenger by the hand and said, "This is the greatest thing in history."[58]

Caron could see the mushroom cloud for an hour and half as the *Enola Gay* sped southward from the horror of Hiroshima. The cloud did not disappear until they were almost 400 miles away. On their smooth return to Tinian, Tibbets quietly smoked his pipe and then dozed off, the first time he had ever been able to sleep in an airplane.

"When we landed, someone yelled, 'Attention!' and General Tooey Spaatz came forward. He pinned the D.S.C. [Distinguished Service Cross] on me while I stood at attention, palming the bowl of my pipe and trying to work the stem up my sleeve."[59] A crowd of exuberant airmen milled around the plane, cheering and shouting, and all the military brass in the Marianas was on hand.

At a press conference, none of the correspondents questioned the use of the atomic bomb. "These reporters had seen the war at first hand," Tibbets said later, "and, like every soldier I met, welcomed anything that would shorten the conflict."[60]

When news of the bomb was announced on Armed Forces Radio, American soldiers in the Pacific at last saw the end in sight. "We whooped and yelled like mad, we downed all the beer we'd been stashing away," recalled a Marine veteran of Okinawa. "We shot bullets into the air and danced between the tent rows, because this meant maybe we were going to live."[61]

That afternoon there was a raucous beer party at the Tinian officers club. "All

work on the island had stopped, and . . . the order of the day was to get drunk," Chuck Sweeney recalls. But Sweeney was exhausted and ready to leave after an hour. As he started for the door of the big Quonset hut, Tibbets spotted him and waved him over. "Chuck, if it becomes necessary, the second one will be dropped on the ninth. Primary target will be Kokura. The secondary target will be Nagasaki." Then he paused and said, "You're going to command the mission."[62] It would be Chuck Sweeney's first combat mission command.

"Everything into Nothing"

None of the physicists on Tinian went to the party that night. "We obviously killed a hundred thousand people and that was nothing to have a party about," recalls Philip Morrison. "We knew a terrible thing had been unleashed."[63]

The bomb had been terrifyingly successful. Pedestrians who were alive one second were vaporized the next, leaving behind nothing but shadows etched eerily into the concrete sidewalks. A Japanese journalist described the bomb's effects:

EVERYTHING STANDING UPRIGHT in the way of the blast—walls, houses, factories, and other buildings were annihilated and the debris spun round in a whirlwind and was carried up in the air. . . . Horses, dogs and cattle suffered the same fate as human beings. Every living thing was petrified in an attitude of indescribable suffering. . . .

Beyond the zone of utter death in which nothing remained alive houses collapsed in a whirl of beams, bricks and girders. Up to about three miles from the center of the explosion lightly built houses were flattened as though they had been built of cardboard. Those who were inside were either killed or wounded. Those who managed to extricate themselves by some miracle found themselves surrounded by a ring of fire. . . .

About half an hour after the explosion, whilst the sky all around Hiroshima was still cloudless, a fine rain began to fall on the town and went on for about five minutes. It was caused by the sudden rise of over-heated air to a great height, where it condensed and fell back as rain. Then a violent wind rose and the fires extended with terrible rapidity, because most Japanese houses are built only of timber and straw.

By the evening the fire began to die down and then it went out. There was nothing left to burn. Hiroshima had ceased to exist.[64]

Victims walked around in shock, with burnt skin hanging from their arms and faces. When one infirmary ran out of medication, volunteers sterilized the wounds with salt water. People were so damaged, one volunteer soldier recalls, "We took a broom, dipped it into . . . salt water, and painted over the bodies."[65]

Dr. Michihiko Hachiya was the director of the Hiroshima Communications

Hospital, which was 1,500 yards from the hypocenter, the point directly under the blast. He began keeping a diary the evening the bomb hit.

THE HOUR WAS EARLY; the morning still, warm and beautiful. . . . Clad in drawers and undershirt, I was sprawled on the living room floor exhausted because I had just spent a sleepless night on duty as an air warden in my hospital.

Suddenly, a strong flash of light startled me—and then another. . . . Through swirling dust I could barely discern a wooden column that had supported one corner of my house. It was leaning crazily and the roof sagged dangerously.

Moving instinctively, I tried to escape, but the rubble and fallen timbers barred the way. . . . A profound weakness overcame me, so I stopped to regain my strength. To my surprise I discovered that I was completely naked. . . .

All over the right side of my body I was cut and bleeding. A large splinter was protruding from a mangled wound in my thigh, and something warm trickled into my mouth. . . . Embedded in my neck was a sizable fragment of glass.

Dr. Hachiya and his wife, Yaeko, who was also hurt, managed to escape the house. Just as they came to the street, a house across from theirs collapsed almost at their feet.

OUR HOUSE BEGAN TO SWAY, and in a minute it, too, collapsed in a cloud of dust. Other buildings caved in or toppled. Fires sprang up and whipped by a vicious wind began to spread.

It finally dawned on us that we could not stay there in the street, so we turned our steps toward the hospital [only a few hundred yards away]. Our home was gone; we were wounded and needed treatment; and after all, it was my duty to be with the staff. . . .

I was still naked, although I did not feel the least bit of shame.

Dr. Hachiya collapsed in the street and sent his wife ahead of him to get help. After a while, he struggled to his feet and walked on, blood spurting from his leg wound.

I PAUSED TO REST. Gradually things came into focus. There were shadowy forms of people, some of whom looked like walking ghosts. Others moved as though in pain, like scarecrows, their arms held out from their bodies with forearms and hands dangling. These people puzzled me until I realized that they had been burned and were holding their arms out to prevent the painful friction of raw surfaces rubbing together. A naked woman carrying a naked baby came into view. I averted my gaze. . . . An old woman lay near me with an expression of suffering on her face; but she made no sound. Indeed, one thing was common to everyone I saw—complete silence.

Dr. Hachiya made it as far as the Communications Bureau, located in the building adjacent to the hospital. It was being used as an emergency hospital. His friends saw him outside the building and carried him in on a stretcher. As he was being treated, he looked up and saw that the hospital was on fire. He and the other patients were evacuated to a rear garden.

THE SKY WAS FILLED WITH BLACK SMOKE and glowing sparks. Flames rose and the heat set currents of air in motion. Updrafts became so violent that sheets of zinc roofing were hurled aloft and released, humming and twirling, in erratic flight. Pieces of flaming wood soared and fell like fiery swallows. . . .

The Bureau started to burn . . . until the whole structure was converted into a crackling, hissing inferno.

Scorching winds howled around us, whipping dust and ashes into our eyes and up our noses.

The Communications Bureau was evacuated, and after being carried out and finding his wife by the main gate, Dr. Hachiya passed out.

MY NEXT MEMORY is of an open area. The fires must have receded. I was alive. . . .

A head popped out of an air-raid dugout, and I heard the unmistakable voice of old Mrs. Saeki: "Cheer up doctor! Everything will be all right. The north side is burnt out. We have nothing further to fear from the fire. . . .

She was right. The entire northern part of the city was completely burned. The sky was still dark, but whether it was evening or midday I could not tell. . . .

The streets were deserted except for the dead. Some looked as if they had frozen to death while in the full action of flight; others lay sprawled as though some giant had flung them to their death from a great height.

Hiroshima was no longer a city, but a burnt-over prairie. To the east and to the west everything was flattened. . . . How small Hiroshima was with the houses gone." [66]

Of Hiroshima's 76,000 buildings, an astounding 70,000 were destroyed or damaged, for in this pancake-flat city there were no hills or ridges to blunt the sensational power of the blast. "Such a weapon," said one victim, "had the power to make everything into nothing." [67]

Helping the burn victims, doctors took some time to realize that they were dealing with a new and horrifically deadly phenomenon, radiation sickness—what they called atomic bomb disease. "People who appeared to be recovering developed other symptoms that caused them to die. So many patients died without our understanding the cause of death that we were all in despair," Hachiya observed in his diary.[68] Those who suffered only minor burns lost their hair; their gums bled; they vomited blood; they developed raging fevers; and they died. For weeks they died at a rate of a hundred a day.

No one will ever know how many people died at either Hiroshima or Nagasaki. Robert Oppenheimer had predicted a death toll of 20,000. At Hiroshima, an estimated 100,000 to 140,000 died almost immediately. Five years later, perhaps another 100,000 had died. Curtis LeMay would later boast that "we scorched and boiled and baked to death more people in Tokyo on that night of March 9–10 than went up in vapor at Hiroshima and Nagasaki combined." [69] He is wrong. More people died in the atomic blasts.

LeMay has argued that it is no more "wicked" to kill people with atomic weapons than with conventional bombs. But that fails to account for radiation disease, one of the worst ways to die imaginable. Nuclear bombs continue killing long after they detonate; and they kill insidiously and across generations. Nuclear power is the fire that mankind has not yet learned to put out. "If a person picks up one rem it can linger in your cells all your life," says Marine veteran Victor Tolley, who was stationed in Nagasaki shortly after the bomb was dropped. "It may lie dormant and nothing may happen to me. But when I die and I'm cremated and my ashes are scattered out over some forest, that radiation is still alive. Twenty-seven thousand years from now, somebody might pick up that rem of radiation from those ashes of mine and come down sick." [70]

But LeMay was correct when he said "the crew who freighted the ordnance up to Hiroshima and Nagaski and dumped it, didn't know just what they really had. Nobody was sure about the destructive capacity, not even the scientists." [71]

After Hiroshima, Truman warned the Japanese leaders that "if they do not now accept our terms they may expect a rain of ruin from the air, the like of which has never been seen on this earth."[72] There was no response; the cabinet was still deadlocked. To their everlasting discredit, the Japanese ruling elite, including the Emperor, was more concerned about the destruction of its power than the destruction of its country. At any point, now or before this, the rulers could have stopped the insane violence. In delaying, they risked not only more nuclear destruction, but an invasion that would have had catastrophic consequences for the Japanese people.

Orders had already been cut to drop the second bomb, and Truman made no effort to intervene. This was the most frightening aspect of early atomic diplomacy—there *was* no diplomacy. Once in place, the technology dictated the decision-making. Even Truman sensed this. "I fear that machines are ahead of morals," he had written in his diary after learning of the first atomic test.[73]

Although a third bomb was not yet ready, Groves wanted the Japanese to believe that the Americans had an unlimited supply of super bombs and were prepared to use them. If two were dropped in quick succession, the enemy would not know what to expect. Or as one of Tibbets's fliers put it, "Hit 'em twice and make them think we've got a barrel full of these things at home. That was the psychology."[74]

Early plans called for an August 11 drop day for the second bomb, but forecasters predicted bad weather for that day and the following five days. So Sweeney's mission was moved up to August 9. The target was still Kokura, with its enormous arsenal, a great source of strength for the Army that was being mobilized to repel the American invasion. Since the intricate measuring instruments for the Hiroshima flight had been installed in Sweeney's plane, *The Great Artiste*, Sweeney and his crew would fly Fred Bock's airplane, *Bockscar*, and Bock's crew would fly *The Great Artiste*. This would lead to considerable confusion in reportage of the event. William L. Laurence of the *New York Times*, who would win a Pulitzer Prize for his coverage of the Manhattan Project, flew in *The Great Artiste* with Bock's crew yet erroneously reported in the *Times*, and in his later book, that Sweeney dropped the bomb from *The Great Artiste*. For years afterward, other authors repeated his error.

LeMay had assumed that Tibbets would fly this mission. But Tibbets told him, "I'm getting enough publicity. The other guys have worked long and hard and can do the job as well as I can."[75] He would regret that decision.

Victory

THE FORGOTTEN BOMB

This was "the forgotten bomb," says Navy Commander Frederick Ashworth, the weaponeer in charge of Fat Man, the plutonium bomb dropped on Nagasaki. "The Nagasaki strike was a kind of sideshow to the first one. There was no fanfare when we left and no fanfare when we got back. Yet few people realize that our mission was almost a national disaster." [1]

Chuck Sweeney wanted to fly a flawless mission, as Tibbets had done. [2] But from start to finish, the second most important bombing strike of the war was a succession of near-disastrous accidents, bad command decisions, and broken orders. The bomb was dropped a mile and a half from the designated target. *Bockscar* came perilously close to running out of fuel and ditching at sea. And the bomber nearly crashed on an airfield where it was not scheduled to land. One man saved the mission and the careers of the pilot and the weaponeer, who, together, broke strict orders about how the bomb was to be dropped, orders that had come down from the highest authority.

It all began with a typhoon off Iwo Jima.

BOCKSCAR AFTER THE NAGASAKI MISSION (USAAF).

"The night we were getting ready to go to Hiroshima, there were thunderstorms in the area, lightning all over the place, and you get a little skittish about lightning," recalls Ashworth, a coolly composed aviator who had commanded a torpedo squadron in the South Pacific earlier in the war. "That's bad news in the airplane business. Then we got word about a storm at Iwo Jima."

The three planes flying to the target, *Bockscar*, *The Great Artiste*, and an observation plane piloted by Colonel James Hopkins, were to take off from Tinian and rendezvous over Iwo Jima. The weather, however, forced them to take a different route and reassemble at Yakushima, a small island off the coast of Kyushu. "Because of the bad weather at low altitudes and our proximity to the Japanese mainland, the rendezvous would be at 30,000 feet instead of at 8,000, as on the Hiroshima mission," Sweeney wrote in his memoir, *War's End*. "This meant we would be flying through some turbulent weather for about five hours in complete radio silence. Then all three of us had to arrive at a tiny spot in the ocean within one minute of each other."[3]

At the preflight briefing, Sweeney's crew was told that they were to drop the bomb visually. These were the "only stringent orders that we had," Ashworth recalls. "General Groves wanted to be sure that we knew exactly where we were putting it and radar bombing equipment at that time was notoriously inaccurate. There was a provision that if it couldn't be dropped by visual bombing with a Norden bombsight then we should bring it home."

Out on the flight deck, Philip Morrison and his team of scientists had just finished loading the "man-made meteor" into *Bockscar*.[4] The bomb bay doors were open, so Sweeney bent down and took a look. "There it was. . . . Ten feet eight inches long, five feet across, painted with high-gloss yellow enamel and black tail fins. It weighed 10,300 pounds, at least 1,000 pounds heavier than Little Boy. It resembled a grossly oversized decorative squash. I could see that many people had signed the bomb or left poems and messages with varying degrees of vitriol."[5]

The takeoff would be "dangerous because there was no way of rendering [the bomb] safe," Morrison notes.[6] Unlike the uranium bomb used at Hiroshima, the complicated implosion system was sealed inside the bomb. Ashworth would not be able to wait until after takeoff to load Fat Man, as Parsons had "late-armed" Little Boy, with its gun-like firing mechanism. If the plane crashed and burned on takeoff, as so many B-29s did on Tinian, the bomb might detonate. "You probably would not have had a full-scale detonation," says Ashworth, "but you'd have had a smaller one. With all that fuel aboard, you would have had a raging fire and the heat would have set off the explosives in the bomb, causing a cook-off, a low-level detonation, that would have torn the bomb apart, spreading chunks of radioactive plutonium all over that part of the island. This was a very serious consideration. The only thing that could be done was to reinforce all the fire-fighting and ambulance equipment on the field and hope that if it happened, we could put the fire out before anything went radically wrong." Chief scientist Norman Ramsey was so concerned about a nuclear accident that he stood at the end of the runway with the emergency equipment so that in the event of an explosion he'd be blown up and wouldn't have to do any explaining.

The only people there to see the plane off were a few Army photographers and "the boss," Paul Tibbets. Just as Sweeney was ready to take off, his flight engineer, John Kuharek, leaned in and said, "Major, we have a problem. The fuel in our reserve

THE CREW OF BOCKSCAR ON ARRIVAL AT TINIAN AFTER THE NAGASAKI MISSION. MISSING ARE ASHWORTH AND HIS ASSISTANT, LT. PHILIP M. BARNES. SWEENEY IS ON THE FAR LEFT (USAAF).

tank in the rear bomb bay bladder isn't pumping. We've got six hundred gallons of fuel trapped back there."[7] Kuharek thought the problem was a solenoid and that it would take several hours to fix.

Sweeney pulled off his harness and climbed out of the plane to consult with Tibbets. "Sweeney and Kuharek walk up to the jeep I'm sitting in," Tibbets recalls, "and Sweeney says, 'We can't transfer fuel from our bomb bay.'

"I said, 'What do you give a damn about it. The fuel is only carried as ballast' [to balance the bomb in the forward bomb bay]. . . . With my airplane I had 1,000 gallons of fuel more than I needed."

Sweeney still looked concerned.

"'Chuck,' I told him, 'you've lost a lot of time now. If you're waiting for me to tell you . . . to cancel the mission, I'm not going to. You're the airplane commander. You can say cancel or don't cancel.'

"He said, 'Well, we're gonna go.'

"When Sweeney got ready to walk away, I said, 'Chuck, you've already lost about forty-five minutes. Get back in that airplane, go to your rendezvous point and tell the other planes the same thing I told you at Iwo Jima [where Tibbets and Sweeney rendezvoused on the Hiroshima mission]: "Make one 360 degree turn, be on my wing, or I'm going to the target anyway." ' " [8]

Tibbets also advised Sweeney that if he ran into any problems on the bomb run to consult with Kermit Beahan, the bombardier, who had plenty of combat experience in Europe. As they prepared for takeoff, with lightning flashes streaking across the black sky, everyone was on edge. "Young man, do you know how much that bomb cost?" Admiral W. R. E. Purnell, a high official in the Manhattan Project, asked Sweeney. "About 25 million," said Sweeney. "See that we get our money's worth," Purnell cautioned.

Tibbets had used the entire runway with a lighter load; with orders for complete radio silence, Sweeney had no communication with the tower. As they raced down the runway at 150 miles per hour a horrible thought went through his mind: Had the Japanese figured out the point of origin of the first flight? Were they out there, over the ocean, waiting for him? But the takeoff went smoothly and they cruised to the assembly point off the coast of Japan at 17,000 feet to try to get above the rough weather. At 5:30 A.M. sunlight started to fill the flight deck and the storm was behind them. "All seemed right," Sweeney recalls, "in our pressurized, air-conditioned, encapsulated universe." [9]

Sitting in the cabin of *The Great Artiste,* reporter William Laurence took out his notebook and began to write. "Somewhere beyond these vast mountains of white clouds ahead of me there lies Japan, the land of the enemy. In about four hours from now one of its cities, making weapons of war for use against us, will be wiped off the map by the greatest weapon ever made by man. In one-tenth of a millionth of a second, a fraction of time immeasurable by any clock, a whirlwind from the skies will pulverize thousands of its buildings and tens of thousands of its inhabitants. . . .

"Does one feel any pity or compassion for the poor devils about to die? Not when one thinks of Pearl Harbor and of the Death March on Bataan." [10]

When *The Great Artiste* reached Yakushima, *Bockscar* was waiting for it. The two planes began circling, waiting for the third ship, piloted by Colonel Hopkins. Sweeney's orders were to wait fifteen minutes and then leave for the target. But he considered the observation plane vital to the mission, perhaps because the photographic equipment had malfunctioned on the Hiroshima flight. The minutes ticked away. They were flying under radio silence; there was no way to contact Hopkins. Sweeney circled for forty minutes, wasting precious fuel.

"I couldn't see what was going on," says Ashworth. "I was down below, in the navigator's compartment, just behind the flight deck. We started to circle and circle. . . . I remember Sweeney coming on the intercom and saying, 'Look, gang, we gotta do this right for Paul.' He wanted a perfect operation, like Tibbets had flown. That meant that three planes proceeded to the target. That's probably why he overrode his instructions to spend no longer than fifteen minutes at the rendezvous." In wasting gasoline, he "very nearly lost the mission right there.

"Finally, after forty-five minutes, I went up to Sweeney and said, 'Look, we've gotta get going. I don't care about the observers [in Hopkins's plane]. I want to be sure that the airplane carrying the instruments is the one that's with us. . . . Is it?' That's when he told me it *was* the instrument plane. . . .

"The other plane never showed up. We found out later that he was up at 39,000 feet while we were at 30,000 feet, where we were all supposed to be."

One error led to another. In frustration, unable to find the two other planes, Hopkins broke radio silence and asked Tinian, "Has Sweeney aborted?" The message caused consternation at Tinian. "Here was this plane," says Ashworth, "that was supposed to be with *Bockscar* and it had no idea where *Bockscar* was, with a ten-thousand-pound nuclear weapon on board. When General Thomas Farrell, Groves's deputy on Tinian, got word of this he was having breakfast. He immediately became sick and raced outside the officers' mess and vomited." [11]

Sweeney blames Hopkins for the delay at the rendezvous point, but Tibbets blames both Ashworth and Sweeney. Tibbets is convinced that Ashworth told Sweeney to wait for the observation plane. "Sweeney didn't have sense enough to know that that Navy Commander couldn't tell him a damn thing. Sweeney was browbeaten by Ashworth. I told Sweeney to his face, 'Sweeney, you forget who was in command of that airplane. . . . You wasted your envelope.' " [12]

But Sweeney insists that he, not Ashworth, made the decision to "give Hopkins a little more time." [13] Tibbets was correct about one thing, however. This was the critical mistake of the mission. From here on, nothing went right.

* * *

At 9:45 *Bockscar* and *The Great Artiste* arrived over the Kokura arsenal. It was hazy and there were broken clouds, but Sweeney thought he had a chance to spot the target. He began the bomb run, turning the plane over to bombardier Kermit Beahan, the most highly qualified member of the crew. By acclamation, his fellow crew members had named their plane—the plane Captain Fred Bock was flying that day—*The Great Artiste* after this brawny, handsome twenty-six-year-old Texan, an artist with the bombsight as well as with the ladies, in the crew's estimation. A graduate of Rice University and a former football player, Beahan had flown in North Africa and Europe and been shot down four times. Although he developed a slight stutter after surviving a crash that killed his pilot and co-pilot, he was rock-steady under pressure. He may have been unlucky in combat, but he was good.

"[Beahan] hit those bomb bay doors and they opened up and the ship started to wobble a little because of the drag of the doors," recalls assistant flight engineer Ray Gallagher. "So now you're waiting. You've got your welder's goggles on to protect your eyes from the blast. You're waiting, bracing yourself for the ship to go up, because you're dropping 10,000 pounds of weight." Only seconds into the bomb run, Beahan said he couldn't see the aiming point. Smoke and clouds obscured it.

Two nights earlier, Curtis LeMay's B-29s had firebombed a steel mill in Yawata, just to the north, and shifting winds had begun carrying the heavy black smoke of the still burning factory over Kokura. Sweeney yelled, "No drop," and "at that," says Gallagher, "we were told 'no talking on the ship!' We didn't want the Japanese to be able to pick up anything. Complete silence." Flak was exploding all around the plane, making it buck and shiver. The enemy gunners had the right altitude and were zeroing in. Kokura, the Pittsburgh of Japan, was one of the most heavily defended cities in the empire.

Then Sweeney did something almost no combat pilot ever did: he made a second bomb run, giving the flak gunners another chance. "Oh boy!" said Ray Gallagher to himself. Ashworth admits he pressured Sweeney to make the second run. "I suggested to Sweeney, 'Why don't we go around 120 degrees and come in from a different direction, and maybe the wind will be such that Beahan can see what he's looking for. But we still couldn't see the target.

"I did this, even though we had a potential fuel problem, because I knew General Groves wanted the second bomb dropped as soon as possible after the first one, to try to convince the Japanese we had more of these things and would use them. There was great pressure to get that second bomb dropped quickly."

"We're not playing here too long," Sergeant John Kuharek announced on the intercom, "because we've got a problem with gas." But Sweeney made a third run! The flak got closer and Gallagher looked out and saw fighters climbing to intercept them. Beahan said, "I can't drop," and Sweeney closed the bomb doors. As he did, Gallagher muttered into his mike, "Let's get the hell out of here."[14]

"In hindsight, I recognize that this was a stupid way of doing it," Ashworth admits. "Sweeney was told at this briefing to make only one pass at the target. If he couldn't drop it he was supposed to take it to the secondary target, or bring it home. So here again, Sweeney was violating his instructions.

"We spent fifty minutes over the target and I finally said to Sweeney, 'We gotta get to Nagasaki, our secondary target.' That was a suggestion. It was Sweeney's decision. He was the commander of the aircraft, and he agreed." Sweeney was determined not to fly back to Tinian—humiliated—with the bomb.

Tibbets is convinced that neither Ashworth nor Sweeney wanted to return to Tinian because "they wanted to beat Tibbets. Well the elements wouldn't let 'em do it. They didn't have enough sense to see that. . . . I said to Sweeney later: 'You should have turned around and come back home. Nobody had the gun to your head.'

"I don't know why even Ashworth didn't make that decision to turn around and bring it back." In going to Nagasaki dangerously low on fuel, Sweeney jeopardized his own life and the lives of his crew. "We haven't talked about it in great length, but I told Chuck, 'You're the only bad mistake the 509th ever made.'"

Ashworth agrees. "We had the wrong guy flying the plane." Yet he blames Tibbets for picking Sweeney. "He had a bunch of experienced, combat-tested guys like Fred Bock. Yet for some reason, God only knows why, he chose Sweeney, who was green. It was a disastrous mistake and a shoddy operation. We were lucky we didn't get into more trouble than we did." Yet it was Ashworth, under pressure from Groves, who had suggested they go on to Nagasaki, knowing the plane had a fuel problem. In this way, atomic diplomacy figured strongly in what was nearly a catastrophic atomic mission.

On the way to Nagasaki, Kuharek informed Sweeney that he had only enough fuel for one bomb run if they were to make it to Okinawa, their alternative landing field. As they approached the target, the heart of the port city's downtown, there was dense cloud cover. A visual drop looked impossible. What would they do with the bomb? Drop it in the ocean? "We couldn't take the bomb [back] with us," says Gallagher. "We were running out of gas and there was too much weight." As Gallagher put it, things couldn't have been any worse.

Back at Tinian, the generals and scientists worried that Sweeney, hours behind schedule, had crashed or been shot down.

"I was responsible to see that the bomb got off and got on the target," says Ashworth. "So I said to Sweeney: 'We'll make this approach by radar and hopefully the visual bombardier may be able to see the target when we get closer to it.'" Sweeney claims that he made that decision. That is unlikely, for Ashworth was in complete charge of the bomb. According to Gallagher, Ashworth made the decision and told Sweeney, "I'll back you." Sweeney didn't balk; this is what he wanted to do. Having come this far—having gotten this deeply into trouble—neither man felt he had any other choice. They didn't want to jettison the bomb in the ocean or disconnect the firing circuit and crash-land at sea with the bomb in the bomb bay, losing it in the ocean. "We were violating orders," says Ashworth, "but in tight situations like this the man in charge has to make a decision on the spot. You simply have to step up and do it. I thought making a radar drop was the right thing to do. You can't just wring your hands. Our mission was drop the bomb on one of two targets and the second target was right below us. I wouldn't have jettisoned the bomb under any circumstances. We needed to get two off, back to back, to force a capitulation."

Now it was up to Kermit Beahan. "On his shoulders," Ashworth said later, "rested one half of the Manhattan Project's finances, namely a billion dollars that had been put into making this plutonium bomb that had to be dropped someplace."

The crew was told to prepare for a radar run. It was still overcast; no one could see the city. Thirty seconds before the bomb's release, the bomb bay doors snapped open. Twenty seconds later Beahan spotted a thin break in the clouds and hollered, "I can see it, I can see it, I've got it!" Sweeney answered, "You own it." [15] Immediately, the radar run was stopped and Beahan "took over, set up the bombsight and dropped the bomb," says assistant co-pilot Fred Olivi. "So actually, we did in the end follow orders." But they had come within seconds of violating them.

Beahan said later that he had studied the target thoroughly before the mission and knew he was somewhere over the industrial area of Nagasaki. "It was not," says Ashworth, "a blind drop, as Olivi claimed later."

"There she goes!" someone said on *The Great Artiste*, which was about a mile and a half in back of *Bockscar*.

"Captain Bock [piloting *The Great Artiste*] swung around to get out of range; but even though we were turning in the opposite direction, and despite the fact that it was broad daylight in our cabin, all of us became aware of a giant flash that broke through the dark barrier of our arc-welder's lenses and flooded our cabin with intense light," William Laurence wrote.

"We removed our glasses after the first flash, but the light still lingered on, a bluish-green light that illuminated the entire sky all around. A tremendous blast wave struck our ship and made it tremble from nose to tail. This was followed by four more blasts in rapid succession, each resounding like the boom of cannon fire hitting our plane from all directions.

"Observers in the tail of our ship saw a giant ball of fire rise as though from the bowels of the earth, belching forth enormous white smoke rings. Next they saw a giant pillar of purple fire, 10,000 feet high, shooting skyward with enormous speed."

Less than a minute later the purple fire reached the altitude of both planes. "It was no longer smoke, or dust, or even a cloud of fire. It was a living thing, a new species of being, born right before our incredulous eyes." [16]

Back in *Bockscar*, Ray Gallagher shouted to Sweeney over the intercom, "the mushroom is coming toward us! It's right under us!" That got everybody's attention because the scientists had emphatically told them to steer clear of the radioactive cloud. "When Sweeney became aware of it," says Fred Olivi, "he dove the aircraft down and to the right with full throttles, to pull away from the oncoming mushroom cloud. For a while I couldn't tell whether we were gaining on it, or it was gaining on us. . . . But then we began to see that we were pulling away and we escaped the radiation."

The cloud kept rising "in an elemental fury" to a height of almost 60,000 feet. [17]

The mood in *Bockscar* was relief, not elation. Beahan had gotten rid of the bomb. "If Beahan doesn't accomplish the release," Ashworth said later, "we're in a disaster situation. There would have been a Board of Investigation if we had bombed by radar, and we might even have missed Nagasaki, because radar bombing was notoriously inaccurate. That would have caused a national embarrassment and might even have prolonged the war. If Beahan hadn't done his job, Sweeney would never have become a general and Ashworth would never have become an admiral."

But now the pilot and the weaponeer had another problem: they had no idea exactly where the bomb had landed. Beahan had had one quick look at Nagasaki before releasing Fat Man, which turned the city into a boiling inferno of fire and smoke, reducing ground visibility to zero. "To be able to tell headquarters back in Tinian precisely where it had gone was impossible," Ashworth admits. "I sent Tinian a coded strike report saying just that we had hit Nagasaki, but added, 'Conference recommended before any news release.' This shook them up at Tinian, I learned later. But this was the first time they had heard from us. We were running over two hours late and, before this, they had no idea where we were or what we were doing."

When they left Nagasaki, Sweeney asked Kuharek, "What are your readings for gas?"

"You've got two hours."

"What's your time from here to Okinawa?" Sweeney asked navigator Jim Van Pelt.

"You've got two hours."

Sweeney instructed radio operator Abe Spitzer to start putting out calls to the air-sea rescue teams. Spitzer got no response. With the mission running hours behind schedule, Navy rescue teams had probably left their prearranged positions, assuming that *Bockscar* was on its way safely back to Tinian. No one would be waiting for them if they had to ditch at sea.

By the time they sighted Okinawa they were flying on fortune and fumes. Sweeney repeatedly called the tower at Yontan airfield, but couldn't get a response. Losing patience, the volatile Irishman ordered the crew to fire the emergency warning flares. "Red and green flares were fired out in an arc, bursting away from the airplane." There was no answer from the field. "Mayday, Mayday," Sweeney shouted into the mike. "I yelled back toward Olivi and Van Pelt, 'Fire every goddamn flare we have on board.'" The color-coded flares went out, nearly every color in the rainbow, each color signifying a different type of problem: "aircraft out of fuel"; "prepare for crash"; "heavy damage"; "dead and wounded on board." That got their attention on the ground and the crew could see planes peeling away from runways and emergency equipment racing toward the edge of the airstrip.

Sweeney told the crew to "brace themselves for a rough one." He was going in without clearance—into the busiest airfield in the world. And it was hard to see because the plane was filled with gray smoke from the flare guns. A B-24 was taking off just where *Bockscar* was heading and the two planes almost collided in midair. "We were hot," says Olivi. "We were going in about 160 miles an hour and when we hit the ground it must have been at least 150." When *Bockscar* touched down halfway up the runway it bounced into the air almost twenty-five feet, and "veered violently to the left toward a line of B-24s parked wingtip to wingtip along the edge of the runway." But Sweeney muscled the plane under control with the help of its specially installed reversible propellers. Just barely missing the row of B-24s, the big bomber came to a screaming stop at the end of the island. As it rolled onto a taxi strip, one of the engines quit. Sweeney killed the other engines and slumped back in his seat. "Total silence fell over the compartment. No one made a sound."

Emergency vehicles came racing toward them, sirens blaring. Sweeney opened the nosewheel door. A rescue worker stuck his head in. "Where's the dead and wounded?"

"Back there," said Sweeney, pointing to the north, toward Nagasaki.[18]

Kuharek later measured the fuel. They had seven gallons left, about one minute of flight time.

As soon as they landed at Okinawa, Ashworth had to quickly figure out where the bomb had hit so he could make a report to Tinian. "The instrument-carrying airplane landed on Okinawa shortly after we did," he recalls, "and strangely who should arrive shortly thereafter but the third plane that had never joined us. It had gone on to Nagasaki and done some observing after the bomb was dropped. So I got the three pilots together, and Beahan, and I spread out a target map on the hood of a jeep, right on the runway. After we talked it over, it became obvious that the point of detonation was the industrial Urakami River Valley, which was a mile and a half from the center of the city, our aiming point, and directly over the huge Mitsubishi Steel and Armament Works. That was good enough for me." This long industrial valley was separated from the downtown by a ridge of hills, which contained the blast and saved tens of thousands of lives. And Beahan, by missing the intended target by almost two miles, had turned to cinder and ash one of Japan's stupendous industrial complexes, employing some 40,000 workers.

Ashworth and Sweeney commandeered a jeep and had the driver take them to a communications center, but "the guy manning it said, 'I'm too busy, get out of here,'" Ashworth recalls. So they went over to General Jimmy Doolittle's tent and Ashworth told a staff officer, "We have just dropped an atomic bomb on Nagasaki and need to inform Tinian." Doolittle's aide told them they had better see the general first. Doolittle had just transferred the headquarters of Eighth Air Force from England to the Pacific, in preparation for the invasion of Japan. He was all business. There would be no messages sent until they told him what they had hit. Ashworth pulled the target map out of his leather pouch. "Doolittle looked at it for a while and said, 'You know, General Spaatz will be far happier that it went off over there than if it had over the city, because there will be far fewer casualties.' Then he let me send my detailed letter message.

"After this, we returned to the plane. It was refueled and we flew back to Tinian. On the way we heard on Armed Forces Radio that the Russians had entered the war against Japan." There was no word of the surrender of Japan, however, which got some of the men thinking that they might be flying another of these missions very soon. They flew the rest of the way in a somber mood, smoking cigars, drinking pineapple juice, and listening to the tunes of Glenn Miller and Tommy Dorsey.

At 10:30 P.M., *Bockscar* landed on Tinian, twenty hours after taking off. No one was there to greet them except their ground crew and one photographer—and Paul Tibbets, standing at a distance with a high-ranking Navy officer. (In a recent revision of his memoirs, Tibbets claims he had gone to bed, but that seems unlikely. Sweeney says he was there, and he would have wanted to attend the post-flight briefing.)

The next morning, Tibbets thought he would have to make a difficult decision: "what, if any action should be taken against the airplane commander, Charles Sweeney, for failure to command." But LeMay made the decision for him. After a press conference on Guam, in which nothing came out about the problems the crew experienced, LeMay called together Sweeney and Tibbets. "You fucked up, didn't you, Chuck?" LeMay confronted him. Sweeney did not respond. LeMay turned to Tibbets and told him that an investigation into the conduct of the Nagasaki mission "would serve no useful purpose."[19] So a cloak of official secrecy was thrown over the operation.

That evening, in a meeting in the Imperial Library, the militants in the Japanese cabinet were still arguing for a continuation of the war, for a decisive battle on home soil. But the double blow of the second bomb and the Russian invasion of Manchuria gave Emperor Hirohito the leverage he had been recently seeking. He feared, as did the moderates in the cabinet, growing popular criticism of the throne and the possibility that the people might eventually revolt against their authoritarian leaders for allowing the war to continue for much longer. We must "bear the unbearable," he told the cabinet in the early hours of August 10.[20] Later that morning, President Truman received Japan's "conditional" acceptance of the Potsdam Declaration. Japan would surrender, but only if the Emperor retained his sovereignty. To this Truman consented, over Secretary of State Byrnes's objections, with the stipulation that the Emperor would submit to the authority of the Supreme Allied Commander in Japan. The Emperor would stay, but the institution was now under the control of the United States, which was quite different from recognizing the Emperor's power as a condition of surrender. As Truman wrote in his diary, if the Japanese people want to keep the Emperor "we'd tell 'em how to keep him."[21]

While the Japanese considered this counterproposal, Truman suspended B-29 raids and further use of the atomic bomb. "Our production facilities were operating at such an accelerating rate," Groves wrote later, "that the materials for the next bomb would be ready for delivery to the field momentarily." During this period, seven "pumpkin" raids were made on Japan "in preparation for further atomic attacks, if they should become necessary." And General Groves says his organizations at Los Alamos and Tinian were in a state of readiness to prepare additional bombs immediately should peace talks break down.[22]

After receiving no word from the Japanese for three days, Truman had Marshall order an all-out air attack on August 14, although Groves continued to hold up shipments of fissionable materials to Tinian, convinced that Japan would soon surrender. It was the most awesome air display of the war; more than 2,000 planes participated. "On the third day, we got orders for a maximum effort," Fred Olivi describes that raid. "Everything that could fly was supposed to fly against the Japanese empire. Our crew participated in that raid in a plane called *Straight Flush*. Other aircraft from islands closer to Japan got to the empire first so I think the bombs we dropped were the last bombs that were dropped on Japan." When Chuck Sweeney and his crew returned to Tinian, after dropping a "pumpkin" on the Toyoda Auto Works at Koromo, the booze was flowing and bedlam had broken out on the island. Japan had surrendered. World War II was over. It was August 15 in the Marianas. Back in the United States, across the International Dateline, it was still Tuesday, August 14, 1945.

"I had occasion to meet some of Doolittle's fliers at an air show after the war, and one of them signed their book for me," recalls Fred Olivi. "It says 'from the first to the last.' They were the first to bomb Japan and we were the last."

In New York a crowd estimated at two million jammed Times Square and the surrounding area in the biggest celebration in the nation's history. The "din," said the *New York Times*, was "overwhelming." [25] It was victory, but at what a cost! An estimated 60 million people died worldwide, almost 40 million of them civilians. New research indicates that as many as 25 million Russians died. China lost at least 15 million people, Poland six million, Germany over four million, Japan over two million, Yugoslavia between one and a half and two million. Millions of innocents died in calculated acts of violence and annihilation. In the bombing of England, Germany, and Japan, 1,300,000 people perished, more than half of them women. The Germans, the Russians in Germany, and the Japanese in China murdered political and racial enemies in staggering numbers. And to defeat fascist and fascist-style regimes, the Allies lost twice as many fighting men as the Axis, among them 409,399 Americans. [24] It was too much death to contemplate, too much savagery and suffering; and in August 1945 no one was counting. For those who had seen the face of battle and been in the camps and under the bombs—and had lived—there was a sense of immense relief. They had survived the greatest explosion of violence in human history, a war so terrible that even the atomic bomb was seen by some as an instrument of deliverance.*

"When the atom bomb ended the war, I was in the Forty-fifth Infantry Division, which had been through the European war so thoroughly that it needed to be reconstituted two or three times," writes Paul Fussell. "We were in a staging area near Rheims, ready to be shipped back across the United States . . . [to] the Philippines. My

---

*Had the atomic bombs not been dropped, and had Japan prolonged the war, Curtis LeMay would have continued, and greatly accelerated, his bombing campaign, turning Japan into a scorched wasteland and killing many more people than died at Hiroshima and Nagasaki.

A NAVAL CONSTRUCTION BATTALION CELEBRATES THE END OF THE WAR (NA).

division . . . was to take part in the invasion of Honshu. . . . I was a twenty-one-year-old second lieutenant of infantry leading a rifle platoon. Although still officially fit for combat, in the German war I had already been wounded in the back and the leg badly enough to be adjudged, after the war, 40 percent disabled. But even if my leg buckled and I fell to the ground whenever I jumped out of the back of a truck, and even if the very idea of more combat made me breathe in gasps and shake all over, my condition was felt to be adequate for the next act. When the atom bombs were dropped and news began to circulate that 'Operation Olympic' would not, after all, be necessary, when we learned to our astonishment that we would not be obliged in a few months to rush up the beaches near Tokyo assault-firing while being machine-gunned, mortared, and shelled, for all the practiced phlegm of our tough facades we broke down and cried with relief and joy. We were going to live. We were going to grow to adulthood after all." [25]

In Okinawa, Eugene Sledge and his 1st Marines received the news of the bombs and the surrender "with quiet disbelief coupled with an indescribable sense of relief. . . . Except for a few widely scattered shouts of joy, the survivors of the abyss sat hollow-eyed and silent, trying to comprehend a world without war." [26]

In the tiny village of Leedsville, New York, a parade of cars moved slowly down the main road, the drivers honking their horns in celebration, while women and children hung out the windows shouting "the Japs have surrendered." Lewis Mumford, who had kept a tight lid on his emotions since the death of his son, Geddes, in Italy, looked out the window of his farmhouse and turned on the radio to hear the news. Before the broadcast was over, he turned around and walked out the back door to the sandpit where he and Geddes used to shoot targets with their hunting rifles, a place that had become a symbol for him of Geddes's life and of their best days together. There, alone, he broke down and wept uncontrollably.

My father, Donald L. Miller, was serving in the Army Air Corps when Japan surrendered.

"Think of the survivors of the German death camps cheering our troops," he wrote my mother, "and then think of Nagasaki. The war was insane but we had to fight it—and to the finish. No regrets."

LIBERATION

On August 15, when the Emperor spoke for the first time to his people, telling them the war was over, the American airmen in the Omori prisoner-of-war camp were going to work. "I didn't hear it and wouldn't have understood it anyway," recalls Hap Halloran. "The day the war ended for us was August 29, when the [Navy] came into Tokyo Bay."

Evacuation of prisoners held in Japan was to begin after the representatives of the Japanese government formally signed the articles of surrender on September 2. But when Bull Halsey was presented with evidence that prisoners were still being brutally treated he ordered a rescue mission of sailors and Marines into Tokyo Bay on August 29. It was commanded by Harold Stassen, the future governor of Minnesota and a presidential candidate. "We saw about six landing craft with American flags flying," says B-29 flier and POW Fiske Hanley. "It was the most beautiful sight I've ever seen in my life." Frank "Foo" Fujita, one of the only two Japanese-Americans to be captured in the Pacific war, became so excited he jumped into the bay and swam out to meet them, along with about a dozen other prisoners.

"After I had made about forty yards, my strength left me and I started to sink. I was completely underwater but somehow managed to get my head up for one more breath. . . . The next thing I knew . . . the two largest hands ever created on earth . . . were pulling my frail 110 pounds out of the water. As the other landing craft picked up the rest of the swimmers, I lay on the deck too exhausted to move.

"As the boats pulled in the Omori docks, the whole camp was crowded at the little island's edge, and from somewhere American, British, and Dutch flags appeared and were being wildly waved. . . . We [were] about to be the first POWs liberated from Japan.

"All the POWs in camp were whooping and yelling as the landing party came ashore. . . . [Then] the Japanese camp commander . . . came storming to the dock and walked up to the commodore [Stassen] and . . . shouted: 'What are you doing here? The war is not over, officially. You must not do this!' . . .' "

Stassen was ready for him. "We are taking these prisoners of war out of here, starting right now! What's more, you are to have every Allied prisoner in the Tokyo area right here by tomorrow morning so that we can take them too!"

Then, said Fiske Hanley, "the meanest-looking Marines I've seen in my life climbed off those boats and surrounded the camp. They loaded us onto those landing craft and took us out to a beautiful hospital ship, the SS *Benevolence*, and we were in heaven. We ate till it came out of our ears." Hap Halloran shoved down eighteen Milky Way bars in a matter of two hours.[27]

"When I stepped on that hospital ship, all my senses were suddenly bombarded with new experiences," recalls Halloran's prison comrade, Robert Goldsworthy. "We lived like pigs for so long. All of a sudden there were nurses with starched uniforms, clean, smelling good. But my greatest thrill took place a few hours earlier, when I first boarded the ship. I had beriberi, my ankles were swollen. I had amoebic dysentery and I had yellow jaundice, and I weighed about eighty-five pounds. I was lifted onto the deck by two sailors and I stumbled over to the railing and looked at Omori prison camp and shook my fist and yelled, 'You bastards, I beat you.' Then I took a big deep breath of free air." [28]

That evening, all the ships of the liberation task force were lit, breaking the wartime procedure of blacking out ships at night. "It was a wonderful picture," says one Marine, "with all the ships flying large battle flags both at the foretruck and the stern. In the background was snowcapped Mount Fuji." [29]

During the next two weeks, more than 19,000 Allied prisoners were liberated. Freedom came for some prisoners a little earlier, when their Japanese guards capitulated. On the morning of August 15, Lester Tenney and other prisoners on the brink of death at Fukuoka Camp No. 17 were about to enter the coal mine when the guards told them to turn around and walk back to camp. The Japanese ordered everyone into the mess hall and passed out full Red Cross boxes. Everyone knew they were about to be freed. But when? Would it be that night? They were looking for a sign. Tenney, who spoke Japanese better than most of the other prisoners, was prodded to go out into the

GENERAL DOUGLAS MACARTHUR'S REUNION IN JAPAN
WITH GENERAL JONATHAN WAINWRIGHT (NA/SC).

prison yard "and just say hello to one of the guards, without saluting or bowing. I took the challenge. Out of the barracks I went, and I walked on the parade ground until I saw a guard. With one mighty heave of my hand, I waved at him and said, 'Hello.' He smiled at me, bowed, and said in English, 'Hello.' . . .

"The war was over!"[30]

On August 31, the most famous POW of the war, General Jonathan Wainwright, the commander Douglas MacArthur had left in charge of Corregidor, arrived in Tokyo and was taken to the Grand Hotel, where he had an emotional reunion with MacArthur. Wainwright had just been released by the Russians from a Manchurian POW camp four days earlier. "I rose and started for the lobby," MacArthur described that meeting, "but before I could reach it, the door swung open and there was Wainwright. He was haggard and aged. . . . He walked with difficulty and with the help of a cane. His eyes were sunken and there were pits in his cheeks. His hair was snow white and his skin looked like old shoe leather. He made a brave effort to smile as I took him in my arms, but when he tried to talk his voice wouldn't come. For three years he had imagined himself in disgrace for having surrendered Corregidor. He believed he would never again be given an active command. This shocked me." MacArthur embraced him and said, "Your old corps is yours when you want it."[31]

Two days later, a destroyer took Wainwright to the battleship *Missouri*, anchored in Tokyo Bay. Standing at a place of honor in the center of the deck with General A. E. Percival, who had surrendered the British forces in Singapore and spent the balance of the war in a prison camp, Wainwright watched MacArthur sign the instrument of capitulation. MacArthur presented the first fountain pen he used to Wainwright, the second to Percival. After all the delegates signed the surrender document, the general,

ADMIRAL NIMITZ AND GENERAL MacARTHUR ON THE USS *MISSOURI* (NA).

dressed in plain suntans, like the other American officers, spoke: "Let us pray that peace be now restored to the world and that God will preserve it always."[32] At that moment 462 silver B-29s filled the sky, flying low over the massive slate-gray battleship. They made a long majestic turn and disappeared in the mists hiding Mount Fuji. Standing on the deck of the *Benevolence*, Hap Halloran looked up and cried tears of happiness.

As the big leather folders containing the surrender documents were gathered, a GI was heard to say: "Brother, I hope those are my discharge papers."[33]

So the greatest of all wars came to an end. It ended, fittingly enough, in such a holocaust as made clear to every man and woman that humanity could not survive another total war.

"How would you like to go up to Japan tomorrow?" Paul Tibbets asked Chuck Sweeney at almost the very hour MacArthur was signing the formal surrender on the *Missouri*.[34] The next morning, with Tibbets at the controls, twenty members of the 509th, along with a few scientists, flew to Tokyo in a C-54 transport. They wanted to see Hiroshima but the runways there were in no condition to handle their plane, so, after a brief stay in Tokyo, they flew to a field sixteen miles from Nagasaki. They were the first group of Americans to visit the area after the bomb blast—and they were not supposed to be there.

Tibbets was "amazed" by the terrible destruction in the Urakami Valley. "Block by block had been flattened, as if by a tornado. . . . Strangely, however . . . there were no bodies anywhere. . . . There were not many people in the streets in the heart of the city. But outside the areas where the damage was heaviest, in the major residential and business districts of the city, life was proceeding in an almost normal manner. The people were polite and didn't even seem to think it unusual that American airmen were there so soon after the long war."[35]

Sweeney walked alone to where ground zero would have been, 2,000 feet from the obliterated Mitsubishi Steel and Armament Works, in what had been a poverty-stricken community of small homes and industrial plants. Although there had been no firestorm as there was at Hiroshima, the bomb had obliterated this entire industrial valley. Of the approximately 70,000 people who eventually died in Nagasaki as a result of the bomb (about 40,000 immediately), almost all were from this area. Standing in this tremendous field of rubble and ruin Sweeney "thanked God that it was we who had this weapon and not the Japanese or the Germans. . . . But I felt no remorse or guilt that I had bombed the city where I stood. . . . My crew and I had flown to Nagasaki to end the war, not to inflict suffering." [36]

Tibbets's reaction mirrored Sweeney's. He had no animosity toward the Japanese people. He saw himself fighting against an evil system imposed on the people by a powerful military regime. That's why, he says, "I have no personal feeling of guilt about the terror that we had visited upon their land." Tibbets has never deviated from that position. [37] "Please try to understand this," he told reporter Bob Greene forty-five years after the war. "It's not an easy thing to hear, but please listen. There is no morality in warfare. You kill children. You kill women. You kill old men. You don't seek them out, but they die. That's what happens in war." [38]

He also has no patience with revisionist historians who claim the bomb would not have been used on Caucasians. "If the Germans had not surrendered, I would have flown the bomb over there. I would have taken some satisfaction in that—because they shot me up. . . . My instructions were to create an elite bombing force . . . with the understanding that, when trained, they would be divided into two groups: one to be sent to Europe and the other to the Pacific . . .

"There was no Japanese target priority," he argues in his own book on the flight of the *Enola Gay*. "All our early planning assumed that we would make almost simultaneous bomb drops on Germany and Japan." [39]

Where were the dead victims of the Nagasaki blast that Tibbets failed to see on his visit to the city? Where were the wounded? The dead were vaporized or already in their final resting place. The wounded were packed into emergency centers, like the one run by Dr. Takashi Nagai, a professor of radiology at the medical school of the University of Nagasaki. Dr. Nagai had been swept into the air and wounded by the atomic blast. His house was buried and his wife killed. A few days later, he carried her blackened bones to a relief center in the countryside, where he gathered together a small band of doctors, nurses, and students who were working night and day to help the sick and dying while Sweeney and Tibbets were touring the city. Nagai and his colleagues were in the country because the bomb had destroyed the Nagasaki Hospital and Medical College and had killed half of the city's medical personnel.

Nagai was a devout Catholic and most of the victims he treated were from his parish church, the Urakami Cathedral, only 500 yards from the hypocenter. The area around the cathedral, the largest in East Asia, contained over half of the city's 14,000 Roman Catholics, who traced their religious roots back to the conversion efforts of St.

Francis Xavier in the sixteenth century. Almost all of them were killed by the blast, which also destroyed the cathedral.[40]

After closing down his relief center in the mountains, Nagai moved to a small hut built on the site of his former house. He began a life of meditation and prayer, surrendered almost all his earthly belongings, and dedicated his life to the desperately poor people of the neighborhood. He died in 1951 and today his home is a shrine, visited by people from all over the world. Some of them remember Nagai's dying words. "Grant that Nagasaki may be the last atomic wilderness in the history of the world."[41]

"I REMEMBER THE WAR"

For those who lived through the worst of it, it was a war that was never over. "Instead of talking about it, most [American fighting men] didn't talk about it," says James Jones. "It was not that they didn't want to talk about it, it was that when they did, nobody understood it. It was such a different way of living, and of looking at life even, that there was no common ground of communication in it."

Long after the war, an infantryman who had fought in the Battle of the Bulge got talking to Jones at a bar. He said his platoon had taken some prisoners near St. Vith. "There were eight of them, and they were tough old timers, buddy. Been through the mill from the beginning. It was about the fourth or fifth day, and we needed some information. But they weren't talking, not those tough old birds. You had to admire them. So we took the first one off to the side, where they could see him, and shot him through the head. Then they all talked. They were eager to talk. Once they knew we were serious. Horrible? Evil? We knew all about Malmédy, man. . . . We needed that information. Our lives depended on it. We didn't think it was evil. Neither did they. But how am I going to tell my wife about something like that? Or my mother?"[42]

Nor could folks back home understand the esprit, the comradeship, and love that kept Marines like Sledge together under the most awful assaults on their humanity— or the horrifying mental torture that some men experienced, pain that didn't go away soon.

Ray Halloran walked through a hell storm after the war.

WHEN I GOT HOME I was not that boy my parents saw go away. I met them, for a few hours, at the train station on my way to a hospital in West Virginia. They looked real worried. I was limping badly and they were convinced I'd lost a leg. I told them I hadn't, but I didn't want to prove it by pulling up my pants. If I had they would have seen the nasty scars from the lice and flies that had bit me in my cage. I think they could also see that, mentally, I wasn't in good shape. I was a little strange.

At the Army hospital at White Sulphur Springs, I got excellent care, but I couldn't talk to the doctors and nurses about my feelings. They didn't know what was inside me. Only the other patients did, those who had suffered in the war. We hardly ever talked about our experiences; but you looked at another patient and you knew he understood. They were the only people I could communicate with, so I was afraid to leave the hospital.

After a while, I made a try of it, took a shot at normal life. I got a job and in 1953 I got married and we adopted three children. I was O.K. most of the time but the nights were bad. I broke windows, and did a lot of other dumb things, like running out in the streets screaming. That terrified my wife and children.

I had horrible nightmares. I dreamed I was falling through space and was trying to reach out for something. I saw fires all around me, and people beating me. I'd crawl in closets and under the bed to get away from what was happening to me. I didn't talk much about it. I thought it was my problem to solve.

I never wanted to go back to Japan—never! They had done this to me, especially the guards that beat me, like this guy we called "Horseface." I could have killed him. But then I decided to go back. I did it because I thought it would help me get rid of the nightmares. I had to get better. I couldn't go on the way I was. If I could see things that were still real inside my head—the torture prison, the city burning down around it, almost killing me, the people who beat me—see them as they are now, not as they were back then, maybe that would help me get better. My wife thought I was goofy but nothing else was working.

I had a contact. I had been in touch with one of my former prison guards, the only one in the prison who treated me like a human being. Before this, I arranged for him to come to study at the University of Illinois. There should be a reward for good people, I think. He would be the anchor I needed over there.

He and his wife met me at the airport and we had dinner at the Palace Hotel overlooking the Palace grounds, right near where I was a prisoner of the kempeitai. This worked out well. I started feeling blood and air coming back into me. I even got up in the middle of the night and walked around the perimeter of the Palace grounds. Was I looking for the torture prison? Maybe I was.

Later I found out where it had been. At first, no one would tell me. Everyone claimed they knew nothing about it. But some people arranged to have me taken there. It was done in secret. The people in the building said I was at the wrong place. I knew they were wrong. I looked around, and then left. No one there could hurt me anymore. I started to feel better.

I traveled all over Japan on the trains. I went to a town called Shizuoka, where I met a doctor who spoke perfect English. He took me to a small mountain in the middle of the town that had been turned into a memorial. Two B-29s had slammed into one another and crashed in the town. A Buddhist monk found the mangled bodies and buried them on the mound. They were human beings, he told the angry townspeople. They deserved a proper burial. He also built a memorial for them, a simple but handsome obelisk. On the other side of the mound he had built an identical memorial for the 2,000 people of the town who had been killed during that raid.

The doctor brought along two bouquets of flowers. He handed me one. He said, "You put yours by the monument for our people and I'll put mine by the monument for your people." It was a beautiful setting, on the crest of a hill over-looking the town. We both prayed and then quietly walked down the hill, each lost in our own thoughts. We went to his home and he made me feel at ease.

After this trip, I saw Japan in a different way. I wasn't ready to change my final judgment. Nor had I conquered all my demons. But I was getting better. And now after five trips over there I have lots of Japanese friends and I can say that I have no animosity toward the Japanese people. And gradually, I've become a more settled person. I'm not normal yet. But I don't have anger in me.

I guess it's kind of selfish. I've used the people who made me sick to help me get better.[43]

The writer Robert Crichton struggled all his life to write a book about his experiences as an infantryman in Europe. He never completed it. "He was torn," says his wife, Judy, "between revealing the truth as he knew it, and a sense that he was violating the veteran's code of silence."

Here is a passage from the book.

THIRTY YEARS GONE NOW since The War ended.

I lie to myself, it is longer ago than that. I lie about time these days, along with a lot of my generation, and this is one of the reasons for this book. The years are beginning to skid away like logs down a flume, each one indistinguishable from the one that went before it, each one equally forgotten. This distresses me because I have come to believe in something Céline found out:

The greatest defeat, in anything, is to forget . . .

Forgetfulness dismantles time, the ultimate gift of life. Death might be seen as the condition of running out of time. If something is forgotten it never happened and it is correct to say that loss of memory murders life.

Knowing this, I keep on forgetting. . . . Failing to find any acceptable reason for this willful even suicidal forgetfulness, I have come to blame it on The War.

Because I remember The War.

I can't remember what I had for breakfast two mornings ago or where I might have been on this day two years ago but I can remember the meal I had on the morning of the day I am writing this, November 28—admittedly a special day for me—in 1944. I can, with no effort at all, summon up the nostril-stinging mix of hot water and dark Barbados rum being poured into my metal canteen cup, meant to lend me courage and help wash down the half-stale loaf of British bread someone slapped into my hand in the dawn darkness.

I could go to the stone barn where I had been sleeping and find the garden where I squatted later in the day, eating a can of American cheese and sucking lemon sourballs, staring across the black stalks and rain-swollen rutabagas, unharvested, at the bodies of two German soldiers lying in the leaves, harvested. One of them held a tin of Spanish sardines in his hand and I wanted them but I wouldn't pry them from his grip . . . not from delicacy, I had gone beyond that by then but because I was afraid of the transference of his death into me through the eating of the bodies of his fish. Death is catching.

I could, this minute, go to the drainage ditch where I was hiding at five o'clock that afternoon, alone in a sweep of beet fields that ran to the horizon like dark green swells of the sea, waiting for darkness to come and free me. I could, if pressed to do it, name every man in my outfit who died on this day.

Memory, then, is out of balance, the past is out of proportion. Sometimes, especially in winter when snow is in the fields, old images come back with such authority, the past luminous and magnified by time, whirring in my memory like . . . an old newsreel, that it becomes hard for me to accept the present as the real and these lantern slides as the past, and gone.

For a long time this didn't bother me because I couldn't see then how this dominance in me by the past led to the paring down of the present. Nothing in the present ever seemed quite as compelling and real, nothing on such a grand scale, as to what had gone before. This I can see now resulted in a considerable loss of life, a muffling and muting of life, the present always diminished and disappointing by the excess of the past.

In this sense, I have come to see myself, along with many others of my time, as a casualty of war.[44]

ABBREVIATIONS
DLM: Donald L. Miller
EC: Eisenhower Center

PREFACE

1. Allan Nevins, "Henry S. Commager as Historian: An Appreciation," in Harold M. Hyman and Leonard W. Levy, eds., *Freedom and Reform: Essays in Honor of Henry Steele Commager* (New York: Harper & Row, 1967), 7.

2. Henry Steele Commager, *The Story of the Second World War* (Boston: Little, Brown, 1945), v.

3. John Steinbeck, *Once There Was a War* (New York: The Viking Press, 1958), xvii.

4. Quoted in James Tobin, *Ernie Pyle's War: America's Eyewitness to World War II* (New York: The Free Press, 1997), 122.

5. Steinbeck, *War*, xvii, xviii.

6. Irwin Shaw, *The Young Lions* (New York: Random House, 1948), 463–65.

7. Quoted in Richard Holmes, *Acts of War: The Behavior of Men in Battle* (New York: The Free Press, 1989, originally published, 1985), 7. I have learned much from Holmes's powerful book.

8. Steinbeck, *War*, xvi.

9. Quoted in Neil Jumonville, *Henry Steele Commager: Midcentury Liberalism and the History of the Present* (Chapel Hill: University of North Carolina Press, 1999), 93.

10. "The GI," in *"Yank," the GI Story of the War*, by the staff of *Yank, the Army Weekly*, edited by Debs Myers, Jonathan Kilbourn, and Richard Harrity (New York: Duell, Sloan & Pearce, 1947), 11.

11. Eugene B. Sledge, *With the Old Breed at Peleliu and Okinawa* (New York: Oxford University Press, 101–2.

12. Eugene B. Sledge interview by Donald L. Miller (hereinafter DLM).

13. Frank Clark, "The 36th Mission," *American Heritage* (May-June 1995), 46, 48.

14. Steinbeck, *War*, xxi.

1: NAZI JUGGERNAUT

1. Herbert P. Bix, *Hirohito and the Making of Modern Japan* (New York: HarperCollins, 2000), 195–203.

2. Iris Chang, *The Rape of Nanking: The Forgotten Holocaust of World War II* (New York: Basic Books, 1999); estimates of the number of Chinese killed in Nanking and its vicinity range up to 340,000. See Daqing Yang, "Convergence or Divergence? Historical Writing on the Rape of Nanking," *American Historical Review*, 104, no. 3 (June 1999): 850.

3. G. E. R. Gedye, *Fallen Bastions: The Central European Tragedy* (London: V. Gollancz, 1939), 295.

4. Ian Kershaw, *Hitler, 1936–45: Nemesis* (New York: W. W. Norton, 2000), xi. This is one of the most impressive studies of Hitler and his hold on the German people.

5. Quoted in Keith Feiling, *The Life of Neville Chamberlain* (London: Macmillan, 1946), 381.

6. Quoted in Kershaw, *Hitler*, 112.

7. Quoted in ibid., 123.

8. William L. Shirer, *Berlin Diary* (New York: Alfred A. Knopf, 1941), 21; for an insightful survey of the European side of the war, see Gordon Wright, *The Ordeal of Total War, 1939–1945* (New York: Harper & Row, 1968).

9. Otto D. Tolischus, *They Wanted War* (New York: Reynal & Hitchcock, 1940), 289–92.

10. Virginia Cowles, *Looking for Trouble* (New York: Harper & Brothers, 1941), 292–94, 297.

11. Shirer, *Berlin Diary*, 291, 307.

12. Arthur D. Divine, "Miracle at Dunkirk," *Reader's Digest* (December 1940), 108–15.

13. Quoted in Desmond Flower and James Reeves, eds., *The War, 1939–1945: A Documentary History* (New York: Da Capo, 1997), 91; for Hitler's "halt order" see, Kershaw, *Hitler*, 296–97. Kershaw claims that Rundstedt first suggested to Hitler to hold back the motorized forces and repair the worn-down tanks for coming operations in the south against the French Army; see also, Gerhard L. Weinberg, *A World at Arms: A Global History of World War II* (Cambridge: Cambridge University Press, 1994), 130–31; at this time there were powerful groups in England, led by Lord Halifax, Chamberlain's former Foreign Secretary, that wanted to sue for peace terms. See John Lukacs, *The Duel, The Eighty-Day Struggle between Churchill and Hitler* (New Haven: Yale University Press, 2001 edition).

14. Cowles, *Looking for Trouble*, 376.

15. Shirer, *Berlin Diary*, 419.

2: BRITAIN STANDS ALONE

1. Winston S. Churchill, *Blood, Sweat, and Tears* (New York: G. P. Putnam's Sons, 1941), 296–97.

2. Quoted in David M. Kennedy, *Freedom From Fear: The American People in Depression and War, 1929–1945* (New York: Oxford University Press, 1999), 440.

3. Quoted in Allan A. Michie and Walter Graeber, *Their Finest Hour* (New York: Harcourt, Brace, 1941), 164–73; for a recent account of the Battle of Britain, see Richard Overy, *The Battle of Britain: The Myth and The Reality* (New York: W. W. Norton, 2001).

4. Ernie Pyle, *Ernie Pyle in England* (New York: Robert McBride, 1941), 30–33.

5. Mollie Panter-Downes, *Letters from England* (Boston: Little, Brown-Atlantic Monthly Press, 1940), 254–59.

6. Edward R. Murrow, *This Is London* (1941); quoted in Samuel Hynes, et al., eds., *Reporting World War II: Part One: American Journalism 1938–1944* (New York: Library of America, 1995), 80.

7. Quoted in *Reporting the War, Part One,* 174.

8. Interview with Erich Topp, Lou Reda Productions.

9. Commander Griffith B. Coale, *North Atlantic Patrol: The Log of a Seagoing Artist* (New York: Farrar & Rinehart, 1942), 21–27.

10. Churchill, *Blood, Sweat, and Tears,* 462.

11. Quoted in Flower and Reeves, *The War,* 267.

12. John Gunther, *D Day* (New York: Harper & Bros., 1944), 95–96.

13. Quoted in Alan Moorehead, *The End in Africa* (New York: Harper & Bros., 1944), 479–82.

14. Quoted in Flower and Reeves, *The War,* 474.

3: FROM THE VISTULA TO THE VOLGA

1. Quoted in Kershaw, *Hitler,* 385.

2. Quoted in Flower and Reeves, *The War,* 204.

3. Frederick C. Oechsner, *This Is the Enemy* (Boston: Little, Brown, 1942), 181–82.

4. Frederick C. Oechsner, "The Bloodiest Front in History," *Saturday Evening Post* (September 19, 1942), 22, 105.

5. Weinberg, *World At Arms,* 267.

6. C. L. Sulzberger, "The Russian Battlefront," *Life* (July 20, 1942), 78–79.

7. Henry C. Cassidy, *Moscow Dateline* (Boston: Houghton Mifflin, 1943), 162–75.

8. Walter Kerr, *The Russian Army: Its Men, Its Leaders, and Its Battles* (New York: Alfred A. Knopf, 1944), 76–78.

9. Quoted in Oechsner, *This Is the Enemy,* 184.

10. "Batya," *Soviet War News Weekly* (August 20, 1942), 1.

11. William Mandel, "Leningrad Under Siege," *Soviet Russia Today* (February 1943), 1–2.

12. Alexander Werth, *Leningrad* (London: Hamish Hamilton, 1944), 50, 165–66.

13. Major Velichko, "The 62nd Army," *Soviet War News Weekly* (February 11, 1943), 1.

14. Quoted in John Keegan, *The Second World War* (New York: Viking, 1989), 230–31.

15. Quoted in Antony Beevor, "Stalingrad," in Robert Cowley, ed., *No End Save Victory: Perspectives on World War II* (New York: G. P. Putnam's Sons, 2001), 258; for a powerful account of the Battle of Stalingrad, see Antony Beevor, *Stalingrad, The Fateful Siege: 1942–1943* (New York: Viking Penguin, 1998).

16. Edgar Snow, *People on Our Side* (New York: Random House, 1944), 128–29.

17. Albert Parry, *Russian Cavalcade* (New York: Ives Washburn, 1944), 311–18.

18. Quoted in Flower and Reeves, *The War,* 491.

19. Quoted in ibid., 493.

4: THE RISING SUN

1. Hull and Nomura quotations are from Gordon W. Prange, with David M. Goldstein and Katherine V. Dillon, *At Dawn We Slept: The Untold Story of Pearl Harbor* (New York: Penguin, 1991; originally published, 1981), 554.

2. David Kahn, "Why Weren't We Warned?" *World War II*, Pearl Harbor Commemorative Issue, (2001), 97.

3. Captain Mitsuo Fuchida, "I Led the Air Attack on Pearl Harbor," *U. S. Naval Institute Proceedings* (September 1952), 939–52.

4. Daniel K. Inouye, with Lawrence Elliot, *Journey to Washington* (Englewood Cliffs, N.J.: Prentice-Hall, 1967), 54–56.

5. Interview with James F. Anderson by John T. Matson, U.S. Naval Institute, 1981.

6. Young's account is pieced together from the following sources: interview with Young by DLM; interview with Young, Lou Reda Productions; and Young's riveting personal account, *Trapped at Pearl Harbor: Escape from Battleship Oklahoma* (Croton-on-Hudson, N.Y., North River, and Annapolis, Md.: Naval Institute Press, 1991).

7. Samuel Eliot Morison, *Two-Ocean War: A Short History of the United States Navy in the Second World War* (Boston: Little, Brown, 1963), 59.

8. Quoted in Bix, *Hirohito*, 437.

9. Quoted in Keegan, *Second World War*, 240.

10. Robert Guillain, *I Saw Tokyo Burning: An Eyewitness Narrative from Pearl Harbor to Hiroshima* (Garden City, N.Y.: Doubleday, 1981), 1–3.

11. James Jones, *WW II* (New York: Ballantine, 1975), 25.

12. Edwin Ramsey, oral history, WGBH, American Experience, Boston.

13. Lester I. Tenney, *My Hitch in Hell: The Bataan Death March* (Washington and London: Brassey's, 1995), 20–21.

14. William Manchester, *American Caesar: Douglas MacArthur, 1880–1964* (New York: Dell, 1978), 230, 233.

15. Quoted in ibid., 233.

16. Quoted in ibid., 269; see also 274.

17. MacArthur and Romulo quotes in ibid., 311–12.

18. Quoted in D. Clayton James, *The Years of MacArthur, 1942–1945*, vol. 2 (Boston: Houghton Mifflin, 1975), 127–28.

19. Tenney, *Hitch*, 32–33.

20. Ibid., 34.

21. Quoted in Elizabeth M. Norman, *We Band of Angels: The Untold Story of American Nurses Trapped on Bataan by the Japanese* (New York: Random House, 1999), 13.

22. Tenney, *Hitch*, 42.

23. Interview with Hattie Brantley, Lou Reda Productions.

24. Frank Gibney, ed., *Senso: The Japanese Remember the Pacific War* (New York: M. E. Sharpe, 1995), 53–54; on Japan's armed forces, see Hayashi Saburo, *KOGUN: The Japanese Army in the Pacific War* (Quantico, Va.: Marine Corps Association, 1989).

25. Interview with Kermit Lay, Lou Reda Productions; Gavin Daws, *Prisoners of the Japanese: POWs of World War II in the Pacific* (New York: William Morrow, 1994), 75.

26. Lester Tenney's account is pieced together from three sources, his interview with *DLM*, his interview with Lou Reda Productions and his book *My Hitch in Hell*.

27. Quoted in Arthur Zich, *The Rising Sun* (New York: Time-Life Books, 1977), 100.

28. Lay interview.

.29. Tenney interview, Lou Reda Productions.

30. Ibid.

31. Lay interview.

32. Quoted in Nathan Miller, *War at Sea: A Naval History of World War II* (New York, Oxford University Press, 1995), 235–36.

33. Ted W. Lawson, *Thirty Seconds over Tokyo* (New York: Random House, 1943), 64–66.

34. Guillain, *I Saw Tokyo Burning*, 59; on the Japanese home front, see Thomas R. H. Havens, *Valley of Darkness: The Japanese People and World War II* (New York: W. W. Norton, 1978).

35. Walter J. Boyne, *Clash of Titans: World War II at Sea* (New York: Simon & Schuster, 1995), 167.

36. Mitsuo Fuchida and Masatake Okumiya, *Midway: The Battle That Doomed Japan: The Japanese Navy's Story* (Annapolis: Naval Institute Press, 1955), 3.

37. Gilbert Cant, *America's Navy in World War II* (New York: John Day, 1943), 233–34.

38. Quoted in Walter Lord, *Incredible Victory* (New York: Harper & Row, 1967), 86.

39. Quoted in Morison, *Two-Ocean War*, 156.

40. Fuchida and Okumiya, *Midway*, 177.

41. Keegan, *Second World War*, 275, 278.

42. Clarence E. Dickinson and Boyden Sparks, "The Target Was Utterly Satisfying," in S. E. Smith, *The United States Navy in World War II* (New York: William Morrow, 1966), 279–80.

43. Fuchida and Okumiya, *Midway*, 177.

44. Fletcher Pratt, *The Navy's War* (New York: Harper & Bros., 1944), 128–31.

45. Quoted in Boyne, *Clash of Titans*, 193.

46. Fuchida and Okumiya, *Midway*, 11.

47. Quoted in Morison, *Two-Ocean War*, 162.

48. Jones, *WW II*, 39.

49. Jack Belden, *Retreat with Stilwell* (New York: Alfred A. Knopf, 1943), 305–58.

5: THE HARD WAY BACK

1. Jones, *WW II*, 48.

2. "The Right Way. The Wrong Way. The Navy Way," William J. Murphy, unpublished MS, Eisenhower Center (hereinafter EC), New Orleans.

3. Quoted in Ronald H. Spector, *Eagle Against the Sun: The American War with Japan* (New York: Random House, 1985), 195.

4. Thayer Soule, *Shooting the Pacific War: Marine Corps Combat Photography in WWII* (Lexington: University of Kentucky Press, 2000), 4.

5. William Manchester, *Goodbye, Darkness: A Memoir of the Pacific War* (Boston: Little, Brown, 1987), 209.

6. Quoted in Miller, *War at Sea*, 286.

7. Ira Wolfert, *Battle for the Solomons* (Boston: Houghton Mifflin, 1943), 341.

8. Quoted in Richard B. Frank, *Guadalcanal: The Definitive Account of the Landmark Battle* (New York: Random House, 1990), 441.

9. Robert L. Schwartz, "The Big Bastard" in *The Best from "Yank, the Army Weekly"* (New York: E. P. Dutton, 1945), 43–47.

10. Quoted in Morison, *Two-Ocean War*, 208.

11. Interview with Paul Moore, Jr., Columbia University Oral History Collection.

12. Quoted in Flower and Reeves, *The War*, 715.

13. Moore interview.

14. Major General Carl W. Hoffman, U.S. Marine Corps (ret.), oral history transcript, Marine Corps Oral History Collection, Marine Corps Historical Center, Washington, D.C.

15. John Hersey, *Into the Valley: A Skirmish of the Marines* (New York: Alfred A. Knopf, 1943), 56.

16. Quoted in Kenneth S. Davis, *Experience of War* (Garden City, N.Y.: Doubleday, 1965), 308.

17. Quoted in Hersey, *Into the Valley*, 56.

18. James Jones, *The Thin Red Line* (New York: Charles Scribner's Sons, 1962), 156–57.

19. Quoted in Eric M. Bergerud, *Touched with Fire: The Land War in the South Pacific* (New York: Viking, 1996), 411–12.

20. Quoted in ibid., 412.

21. Jones, *WW II*, 28.

22. Quoted in Richard Tregaskis, *Guadalcanal Diary*, (New York: Random House, 1943), 401.

23. John Hersey, "The Battle of the River," *Life* (November 23, 1942), 116.

24. Jones, *WW II*, 54.

25. Samuel E. Stavisky, *Marine Combat Correspondent: World War II in the Pacific* (New York: Ballantine, 1999), 80–81.

26. Quoted in Manchester, *Goodbye, Darkness*, 231.

27. Jones, *WW II*, 122–24.

28. George H. Johnston, *The Toughest Fighting in the World* (New York: Duell, Sloan & Pearce, 1943), 167–68.

29. Robert L. Eichelberger, *Our Jungle Road to Tokyo* (Nashville: Battery Classics, 1989), 21–23.

30. Ibid., 33–34.

31. Dave Richardson, "No Front Line in New Guinea," in *"Yank," the GI Story of the War*, 43.

32. Patrick J. Robinson, *The Fight for New Guinea* (New York: Random House, 1943), 165.

33. Eichelberger, *Our Jungle Road*, 48–49.

34. Diaries collected by Eichelberger's staff, in ibid., 53–55.

35. Quoted in ibid., 51.

36. Jay Luvass, ed., *Dear Miss Em: General Eichelberger's War in the Pacific, 1942–1945* (Westport, Conn: Greenwood Press, 1972), 64–65.

37. Quoted in Geoffrey Perret, *Old Soldiers Never Die: The Life of Douglas MacArthur* (New York: Random House, 1996), 329.

38. Dwight D. Eisenhower, *Crusade in Europe* (New York: Doubleday, 1948), 155.

39. Ernie Pyle, Scripps Howard wire copy, May 6, 1943.

40. Ernie Pyle, *Here Is Your War* (New York: Pocket Books, 1945), 555–57.

41. Eisenhower, *Crusade in Europe*, 157; for a brilliant account of how the Allies recovered from the

low point of 1942 and turned the tide of the war, see Richard Overy, *Why the Allies Won* (New York: W. W. Norton, 1997).

42. Quoted in Miller, *War at Sea*, 349. Ronald H. Spector gives a riveting history of naval operations in World War II in his sweeping study, *At War at Sea: Sailors and Naval Combat in The Twentieth Century* (New York: Viking, 2001).

43. Quoted in Keegan, *Second World War*, 104.

44. Quoted in Michael Gannon, *Operation Drumbeat: The Dramatic True Story of Germany's First U-Boat Attacks Along the American Coast in World War II* (New York: Harper & Row, 1990), 141; for a different view on Operation Roll of Drums see Clay Blair, *Hitler's U-Boat War*, vol. 1, *The Hunters, 1939–42* (New York: Modern Library), 689–96; the best one-volume account of submarine warfare in World War II is Peter Padfield, *War Beneath the Sea: Submarine Conflict, 1939–1945* (New York: John Wiley, 1998); see also Dan Van Der Vat, *The Atlantic Campaign: World War II's Great Struggle at Sea* (New York: Harper & Row, 1988) and John Terraine, *The U-Boat Wars* (New York: Putnam, 1989).

45. Quoted in Samuel Eliot Morison, *The Battle of the Atlantic: September 1939–May 1943* (Boston: Little, Brown, 1957), 157.

46. Quoted in Ernest J. King and Walter Muir Whitehall, *Fleet Admiral King: A Naval Record* (New York: W. W. Norton, 1952), 455–56.

47. Gannon, *Operation Drumbeat*, 399.

48. Quoted in Felix Riesenberg, Jr., "Atlantic Slaughter," in Smith, *United States Navy in World War II*, 119–20.

49. Helen Lawrenson, "Damn the Torpedoes!" *Harper's*, (July 1942), 208–11.

50. Quoted in Miller, *War at Sea*, 343.

51. Rear Admiral Daniel Gallery, Jr., "U-Boat War from Iceland to Murmansk and the Coasts of Africa," oral testimony reprinted in John T. Mason, *Pacific War Remembered: An Oral History Collection* (Annapolis: Naval Institute Press, 1986), 117.

52. Karl Doenitz, R. H. Stevens, with David Woodward, *Memoirs: Ten Years and Twenty Days* (Cleveland: World, 1959), 341.

53. Morison, *Two-Ocean War*, 122.

54. Winston Churchill, *The Hinge of Fate* (Boston: Houghton Mifflin, 1950), 125.

55. Jones, *WW II*, 85.

56. Hugh Sebag-Montefiore, *Enigma: The Battle for the Code* (New York: John Wiley, 2001), 299.

57. Gallery's account is taken from two sources, Gallery, "U-Boat War," in Mason, *Pacific War*, 120–36; and Gallery, *Twenty Million Tons Under the Sea* (Annapolis: Naval Institute Press, 2001; originally published, 1957), 291–311.

6: THE DEAD OF TARAWA

1. Robert Sherrod, *Tarawa: The Story of a Battle* (New York: Bantam, 1983; originally published, 1944), 30–31.

2. Quoted in Miller, *War at Sea*, 375.

3. Samuel Eliot Morison, *The History of U.S. Naval Operations During the Second World War*, vol. 4, *Coral Sea, Midway and Submarine Actions, May 1942–August 1943* (Boston: Little, Brown,

1953), 409; interview with Major General John P. Condon, Lou Reda Productions. As Operations Officer of the Solomon's Fighter Command, Marine officer Condon helped plan the interdiction strike against Yamamoto.

4. Quoted in Manchester, *American Caesar*, 391–92.

5. Joseph Alexander, *Storm Landings: Epic Amphibious Battles in the Central Pacific* (Annapolis: Naval Institute Press, 1997), 6.

6. Paul W. Kearney and Blake Clark, " 'Pete' Mitscher, Boss of Task Force 58," *The American Legion Magazine*, (July 1945); for the great carrier fleets, see James H. Belote and William M. Belote, *Titans of the Seas: The Development and Operations of Japanese and American Carrier Task Forces During World War II* (New York: Harper & Row, 1975).

7. Jones, *WW II*, 104.

8. Hanson W. Baldwin, "The Bloody Epic That Was Tarawa," *New York Times Magazine* (November 14, 1958), 19.

9. U.S. Marine Corps Correspondents, *Betio Beachhead* (New York: G. P. Putnam's Sons, 1945), passim.

10. Quoted in Baldwin, "The Bloody Epic," 19.

11. Interview with Robert Sherrod, Lou Reda Productions.

12. Interview with Michael Ryan, Lou Reda Productions.

13. Baldwin, "The Bloody Epic," 68.

14. Karl Albrecht, "Tarawa Remembered," *Follow Me* (November–December, 1993), 28–31.

15. Quoted in Baldwin, "The Bloody Epic," 69.

16. Sherrod, *Tarawa*, xiii, 64.

17. Interview with Harry Jackson, Lou Reda Productions.

18. Quoted in Manchester, *Goodbye, Darkness*, 267.

19. Sherrod, *Tarawa*, 66.

20. Interview with Norman Hatch by DLM; interview with Norman Hatch, Marine Corps Oral History Collection, Marine Corps Historical Center, Washington, D.C.

21. Lieutenant Bonnie Little to wife, quoted in Joseph Alexander, *Utmost Savagery: The Three Days of Tarawa* (New York: Ivy Books, 1977), 106.

22. Sherrod interview.

23. Quoted in Manchester, *Goodbye, Darkness*, 267.

24. Hatch interview with DLM.

25. Sherrod interview.

26. Hatch interview, Marine Corps Oral History Collection; Hatch interview with DLM.

27. Interview with Eddie Albert, Lou Reda Productions.

28. Quoted in Alexander, *Utmost Savagery*, 192.

29. Hatch interview with DLM; interview with Norman Hatch, Lou Reda Productions; Hatch interview, Marine Corps Oral History Collection.

30. Sherrod, *Tarawa*, 90–92.

31. Quoted in Alexander, *Utmost Savagery*, 187.

32. Sherrod, *Tarawa*, 96.

33. Ibid., 96–97, 110.

34. Interview with Colonel William Jones, Lou Reda Productions; Joseph H. Alexander, *Across the Reef: The Marine Assault of Tarawa* (Washington, D.C.: Marine Corps Historical Center, 1993), 42.

35. Quoted in Sherrod, *Tarawa*, 113.

36. Manchester, *Goodbye, Darkness*, 282.

37. William Jones interview.

38. Quoted in Alexander, *Across the Reef*, 46.

39. Quoted in Sherrod, *Tarawa*, 100; Sherrod interview.

40. Hoffman, Marine Corps Oral History Collection.

41. Sherrod, *Tarawa*, 113–14.

42. Albert interview.

43. Quoted in Baldwin, "The Bloody Epic," 72.

44. Sherrod, *Tarawa*, 100–101.

45. Ibid., 132.

46. Quoted in ibid., 129.

47. Sherrod interview.

48. William Jones interview.

49. Quoted in Sherrod, *Tarawa*, 139.

50. Sherrod, *Tarawa*, 140; Sherrod interview.

51. *Life*, October 11, 1943; Davis quoted in Frederick S. Voss, *Reporting the War: The Journalistic Coverage of World War II* (Washington, D.C.: Smithsonian Institution Press, 1994), 34.

52. George S. Horne, "Tarawa's Captor Reviews Victory," *New York Times*, November 30, 1943.

53. Sherrod interview.

54. "Mid-Pacific Stronghold," *New York Times*, (December 27, 1943).

55. Quoted in Alexander, *Utmost Savagery*, 71.

7: UP THE BLOODY BOOT

1. Robert Capa, *Slightly Out of Focus* (New York: Modern Library, 1999), 111; on the decision to invade Italy, see Michael E. Howard, *The Mediterranean Strategy in the Second World War* (London: Weidenfeld & Nicolson, 1968); on the invasion of Sicily, see Carlo D'Este, *Bitter Victory: The Battle for Sicily, July–August 1943* (London: Collins, 1988); for the Italian campaign, see Dominick Graham and Shelford Bidwell, *Tug of War: The Battle for Italy, 1943–1945* (New York: St. Martins, 1986); Albert N. Garland and Howard McGaw Smyth, *United States Army in World War II: The Mediterranean Theater of Operations: Sicily and the Surrender of Italy* (Washington, D.C.: Center of Military History, U.S. Army, 1965); and Richard Lamb, *War in Italy, 1943–1945: A Brutal Story* (New York: Da Capo, 1996).

2. Quoted in Kennedy, *Freedom From Fear*, 594.

3. Quoted in *"Yank," the GI Story of the War*, 52.

4. *New York Herald Tribune*, October 3, 1943, 43.

5. *New York Herald Tribune*, October 4, 1943, 13.

6. "Germans Burned Library in Naples," *New York Times*, October 12, 1943.

7. Interview with Carter Roland, Lou Reda Productions.

8. Ibid.

9. Capa, *Slightly Out of Focus*, 111.

10. "Road to Mud, Fatigue—and Glory," *New York Times*, December 26, 1943.

11. Bill Mauldin, *Up Front* (New York: Henry Holt, 1944), 144–47.

12. Quoted in John Ellis, *On the Front Lines: The Experience of War Through the Eyes of the Allied Soldiers of World War II* (New York: John Wiley, 1991), 206–7. This is a first-rate study of men under fire.

13. Quoted in Gerald Astor, *A Blood-Dimmed Tide: The Battle of the Bulge by the Men Who Fought It* (New York: Dell, 1992), 11.

14. Ernie Pyle, *Brave Men* (New York: Henry Holt, 1944), 97–100.

15. Mauldin, *Up Front*, 143–44.

16. Capa, *Slightly Out of Focus*, 116.

17. Pyle, *Brave Men*, 159–62.

18. Quoted in *"Yank," the GI Story of the War*, 22.

19. Quoted in Ellis, *On the Front Lines*, 42–43.

20. Interview with Bill Mauldin, Lou Reda Productions.

21. Bill Mauldin, *Up Front*, 35–38.

22. Quoted in Ellis, *On the Front Lines*, 210.

23. Paul S. Green, "GI Journalist: A *Stars and Stripes* Reporter in World War II Europe," unpublished MS, EC, 73–75.

24. Quoted in Don Congdon, *Combat WW II: European Theater of Operations* (New York: Arbor House, 1983), 404.

25. Quoted in "Capture of Rome Preceded D-Day," *Stars and Stripes* (June 6, 1944), 26.

26. Green, "GI Journalist," 75–76.

27. "The Italian Ordeal Surprises Members of Congress," *New York Times*, (December 23, 1944).

28. "The Price We Pay in Italy," *The Nation* (December 9, 1944), 713–14.

29. Sergeant Harry Sions, "The Partisan from Brooklyn," in *Best from "Yank,"* 25–28.

30. Martha Gellhorn, "Cracking the Gothic Line," *Collier's* (October 28, 1944), 24, 57–58.

31. These letters are reprinted in Lewis Mumford, *Green Memories: The Story of Geddes Mumford* (New York: Harcourt, Brace, 1947), 304–41; interview with Lewis Mumford by DLM; Donald L. Miller, *Lewis Mumford, A Life* (New York: Wiedenfeld and Nicholson, 1989), 424–27.

32. Mauldin, *Up Front*, 57.

33. Quoted in Mumford, *Green Memories*, 339.

34. Interview with Vernon J. Baker by DLM.

35. Quoted in Mary Penick Motley, ed., *The Invisible Soldier: The Experience of the Black Soldier, World War II* (Detroit: Wayne State University Press, 1975), 322.

36. "Recollections and Reflections: Transcripts of the Debriefing of Gen. Edward M. Almond by Capt. Thomas G. Fergusson," March 25, 1975, Edward M. Almond Papers, U.S. Army Military History Institute, Carlisle Barracks, Carlisle, Pa., 39–40.

37. Quoted in Motley, *Invisible Soldier*, 339.

38. Baker interview.

39. Cason and Lester quoted in Motley, *Invisible Soldier*, 304, 269, 307.

40. Baker interview.

41. Official reports quoted in Vernon J. Baker, with Ken Olsen, *Lasting Valor* (New York: Bantam, 1999; originally published by Genesis Press, 1977), 276.

42. Interview with Major General Frederick Davison, United States Army.

43. Interview with Rothacker C. Smith by DLM.

44. Baker, *Lasting Valor*, 220; Baker interview.

45. Major Paul Goodman, *A Fragment of Victory* (Carlisle Barracks, Carlisle, Pa.: Army War College, 1952), passim; Major E. A. Raymond, "Black Buffalo," *Field Artillery Journal* 36 (January 1946), 14–16; James Bennet, "I See 'Em! We'll Fight 'Em: Profiles in Courage Beyond the Call," *New York Times* (January 19, 1997), 4, 7; Ulysses Lee, *Employment of the Negro Troops* (Washington, D.C.: Office of the Chief of Military History, Department of the Army, 1966), 564–65.

46. "The Luckless 92nd," *Newsweek* (February 26, 1945), 34; Lieutenant Colonel John H. Sherman, Letter to the Editor, *New Republic* (November 19, 1945), 677–78.

47. Baker, *Lasting Valor*, 76.

48. Quoted in Motley, *Invisible Soldier*, 303–5.

49. "The Price We Pay in Italy," *The Nation* (December 9, 1944), 713–14.

50. Jones, *WW II*, 130.

51. Mauldin, *Up Front*, 11–57.

8: THE AIR WAR

1. Quoted in Max Hastings, *Bomber Command* (New York: Simon & Schuster, 1989; originally published, 1979), 116.

2. Quoted in ibid., 107; interview with General Bernard A. Schriever, Lou Reda Productions; interview with General Ron Fogleman, Lou Reda Productions; for a brilliant account of the history of American strategic bombing, see Michael S. Sherry, *The Rise of American Air Power: The Creation of Armageddon* (New Haven: Yale University Press, 1987); Gerald Astor has assembled a wonderful collection of first-hand accounts in *The Mighty Eighth: The Air War in Europe as Told by the Men Who Fought It* (New York: Dell, 1997); for a biography of the man who was most responsible for creating the largest air armada ever assembled, see Dik A. Daso, *Hap Arnold and the Evolution of American Airpower* (Washington, D.C.: Smithsonian Institution Press, 2000).

3. John Keegan, "'We Wanted Beady-Eyed Guys Just Absolutely Holding the Course,'" *Smithsonian Magazine* 14, no. 5 (1993): 34–35.

4. Ira Eaker, "Senior Officers Debriefing Program," U.S. Army Military History Institute, Carlisle Barracks, Carlisle, Pa.

5. Hector Hawton, *Night Bombing* (London: Thomas Nelson, 1944).

6. Quoted in Martin Middlebrook, *The Battle of Hamburg: Allied Bomber Forces Against a German City in 1943* (London: Allan Lane, 1980), 258.

7. Quoted in Flower and Reeves, *The War*, 564–65.

8. Quoted in Middlebrook, *Battle of Hamburg*, 268.

9. Quoted in ibid., 276.

10. Quoted in Flower and Reeves, *The War*, 564–65.

11. Quoted in Earl R. Beck, *Under the Bombs: The German Home Front, 1942–1945* (Lexington: University Press of Kentucky, 1986), 64.

12. CBS radio broadcast, December 3, 1943.

13. Both quotations in Beck, *Under the Bombs*, 87–88.

14. All Tibbets quotations in Paul W. Tibbets, *The Flight of the Enola Gay* (Reynoldsburg, Ohio: Buckeye Aviation, 1969), 81–100.

15. Bernard Jacobs, unpublished memoir, EC. All Jacobs quotations are from this source.

16. Keegan, "'We Wanted,'" 37–38.

17. John H. Morris, testimony, EC.

18. Dale VanBlair, "Three Years in the Army Air Forces," unpublished MS, EC.

19. Interview with Paul Tibbets, Lou Reda Productions, October 14, 2000.

20. Morris, EC.

21. Interview with Donald L. Miller (father) by DLM; interview with Paul Slawter by DLM.

22. John Muirhead, *Those Who Fall* (New York: Random House, 1986), 55.

23. Quoted in Brendan Gill, "Young Man Behind Plexiglass," *New Yorker* (August 12, 1944), 484.

24. Muirhead, *Those Who Fall*, 49–50.

25. Daniel Behre, testimony, EC.

26. Muirhead, *Those Who Fall*, 47.

27. Miller interview.

28. Beirne Lay, Jr., and Sy Bartlett, *Twelve O'Clock High* (New York: Dodd, Mead, 1975; originally published, 1948), 122.

29. Quoted in Kenneth P. Werrell, *"Who Fears?": The 301st in War and Peace, 1942–1979* (Dallas: Taylor Publishing, 1991), 100.

30. Adolf Galland, *The First and the Last: The Rise and Fall of the German Fighter Force, 1938–1945* (New York: Henry Holt, 1954), 179.

31. Brian D. O'Neill, *Half a Wing, Three Engines and a Prayer: B-17s over Germany* (New York: McGraw Hill, 1999), 40.

32. Beirne Lay, Jr. "I Saw Regensburg Destroyed," *Saturday Evening Post* (November 6, 1943), 9–11, 85–88.

33. Quoted in O'Neill, *Half a Wing*, 43.

34. Quoted in Keegan, "'We Wanted,'" 41.

35. Quoted in Edward Jablonski, *Flying Fortress* (Garden City, N.Y.: Doubleday, 1965), 130.

36. Quoted in Mark Caidin, *Black Thursday* (New York: E. P. Dutton, 1960), 209–11.

37. Quoted in Flower and Reeves, *The War*, 571.

38. Quoted in Gill, "Young Man Behind Plexiglass," 485.

39. *"Yank," The GI Story of the War*, 71.

40. Quoted in Don Salvatore Gentile and Ira Wolfert, *One-Man Air Force* (New York: L. B. Fischer, 1944), 16.

41. Gentle and Eisenhower quoted in ibid., 17.

42. Interview with Paul Bauer by DLM.

43. Quoted in Werrel, *"Who Fears?"* 77.

44. VanBlair, EC.

45. Heinz Knoke, *I Flew for the Führer* (London: Greenhill, 1953), 161.

46. Quoted in Wesley Frank Craven and James Lea Cate, eds., *The Army Air Forces in World War II*, vol. 3 (Chicago: University of Chicago Press, 1948), 58, 163.

9: THE GREAT INVASION

1. Winston Churchill, *The Dawn of Liberation* (Boston: Little, Brown, 1945), 190–94.

2. Eisenhower's order of the day, in the possession of Donald L. Miller.

3. Robert E. Adams, oral testimony, EC.

4. Everett Holles, *Unconditional Surrender* (New York: Howell-Soskin, 1945), 206–7.

5. Jon E. Lewis, *Eyewitness to D-Day: The Story of the Battle by Those Who Where There* (New York: Carroll & Graf, 1994), 36.

6. Interview with John Steber by DLM.

7. Alan Anderson, testimony, EC.

8. Adams, EC.

9. Quoted in Ed Reavis, "A German Officer Remembers," *Stars and Stripes* (June 6, 1994). Pluskat claims that the rumors that he was in Paris and not at his post in Normandy, and that he lied to Cornelius Ryan, author of *The Longest Day*, to cover up his absence, are "totally untrue."

10. Quoted in ibid., 9.

11. Adams, EC.

12. Harry Bare, testimony, EC.

13. Anderson, EC.

14. "Eyewitness Accounts of Omaha Beach," EC. Interview with Lt. John Spaulding, U.S. Army Military History Institute, Carlisle Barracks, Carlisle, Pa.; in his revisionist history *Omaha Beach: A Flawed Victory* (Chapel Hill, N.C.: University of North Carolina Press, 2001), Adrian R. Lewis blames the strategic planners, among them General Omar Bradley, for the needless loss of American lives because they ignored the past lessons of Allied amphibious landings.

15. Adams, EC.

16. Anonymous Pfc, quoted in Lewis, *Eyewitness to D-Day*, 103–4.

17. Joseph T. Dawson, testimony, EC; Gerald W. Heaney testimony, EC.

18. Quoted in Cindy Killion, "Within Minutes Private Sales Was the Only One Left," *Stars and Stripes* (June 6, 1994), 8.

19. Quoted in Charles Wertenbaker, *Invasion* (New York: Appleton-Century, 1944), 40–41.

20. William Lewis oral history, in an unpublished manuscript by John Robert Slaughter, EC.

21. Interview with Donald M. McKee, Lou Reda Productions.

22. Untitled order, EC.

23. Interview with Walter Rosenblum, EC.

24. Walter Rosenblum report, June 21, 1944, D-Day Museum, New Orleans, Louisiana.

25. Capa, *Slightly Out of Focus*, 136–52.

26. Martha Gellhorn, "Wounded Come Through," *Collier's* (August 5, 1944), passim.

27. Quoted in Killion, "Within Minutes," 3.

28. Anderson, EC.

29. S. L. A. Marshall, "First Wave at Omaha Beach," *Battle at Best* (New York: William Morrow, 1963), 43–66.

30. McKee interview.

31. Interview with Roy Stevens by DLM.

32. Ernie Pyle, Scripps-Howard wire copy, June 16, 1944.

33. Omar Bradley and Clay Blair, *A General's Life: An Autobiography* (New York: Simon & Schuster, 1983), 249.

34. Quoted in Stephen E. Ambrose, *D-Day, June 6, 1944: The Climactic Battle of World War II* (New York: Simon & Schuster, 1994), 190.

35. Jones, *WW II*, 159.

36. Capa, *Slightly Out of Focus*, 153.

10: FROM NORMANDY TO GERMANY

1. Interview with Chet Hansen, Lou Reda Productions.

2. Quoted in Flower and Reeves, *The War*, 885.

3. Pyle, *Brave Men*, 302–12.

4. J. Robert Slaughter, unpublished testimony, EC.

5. John Gill, oral testimony, EC.

6. Quoted in Stephen E. Ambrose, *Citizen Soldiers: The U.S. Army from the Normandy Beaches to the Bulge to the Surrender of Germany, June 7, 1944–May 7, 1945* (New York: Simon & Schuster, 1997), 320. This is an outstanding account of the Battle for Normandy, as is the comprehensive work by Carlo D'Este, *Decision in Normandy* (New York: Harper Perennial, 1994); the on-the-line experience of the American combat soldier is covered revealingly in Gerald F. Linderman, *The World Within War: America's Combat Experience in World War II* (Cambridge: Harvard University Press, 1999 edition), and John C. MacManus, *The Deadly Brotherhood: The American Combat Soldier in World War II* (Novato, Calif.: Presidio Press, 2000); for the battle for North-West Europe from the perspective of the American high command, see Russell F. Weigley, *Eisenhower's Lieutenants: The Campaign of France and Germany, 1944–1945* (Bloomington: Indiana University Press, 1981); Chester Wilmont's *The Struggle for Europe* (London: Collins, 1952) is a modern military classic from the pen of a crack war correspondent.

7. Judy Litoff and David Smith, "Today We Have Lived History: The D-Day Letters of U.S. Women," p. 20, paper given at EC, May 16, 1994; Jeanette A. Wasco, "Memoirs of an Army Nurse," EC.

8. Lee Miller, "U.S.A. Tent Hospital," *Vogue* (September 15, 1944), 138–39, 204–12.

9. Quoted in Flower and Reeves, *The War*, 885.

10. *War Letters of Morton Eustis to His Mother: February 6, 1941, to August 10, 1944* (New York: Spiral Press, 1945), 226–27.

11. "The Flying Bomb," British Information Services, November 1944; more than one-half of the V-1 were fired at targets in Belgium, primarily Antwerp; for a fascinating account of the development of the V-2 rocket, the first ballistic missile, see Michael J. Neufeld, *The Rocket and the*

Reich: Peenemünde and the Coming of the Ballistic Missile Era (Cambridge: Harvard University Press, 1996).

12. Quoted in Keegan, *Second World War,* 582.

13. Quoted in ibid., 394.

14. Pyle, *Brave Men,* 295–301.

15. Michael D. Doubler, *Closing with the Enemy: How GIs Fought the War in Europe, 1944–1945* (Lawrence: University Press of Kansas, 1994), 5.

16. Quoted in Ralph G. Martin, "Breakout from St. Lô," in *"Yank," the GI Story of the War,* 115.

17. Holles, *Unconditional Surrender,* 232–33.

18. Bill Davidson, "Rommel—Count Your Men," *Yank* (September 29, 1944), in *Reporting World War II: Part Two: American Journalism, 1944–1946,* 221–26.

19. Capa, *Slightly Out of Focus,* 166.

20. Quoted in Ambrose, *Citizen Soldiers,* 102.

21. Eisenhower, *Crusade in Europe,* 279–80; Hansen interview; for a fresh appraisal of this controversial engagement, see Martin Blumenson, *The Battle of the Generals: The Untold Story of the Falaise Pocket* (New York: Morrow, 1993).

22. Capa, *Slightly Out of Focus,* 188.

23. Quoted in Kennedy, *Freedom From Fear,* 732.

24. Quoted in David P. Colley, *The Road to Victory: The Untold Story of World War II's Red Ball Express* (Washington, D.C.: Brassey's, 2000), 112.

25. Quoted in *Stars and Stripes* (August 31, 1944).

26. "The Miracle of Supply," *Time* (September 25, 1944), 20–22.

27. Quoted in Ambrose, *Citizen Soldiers,* 142; for Operation Market-Garden, see Cornelius Ryan, *A Bridge Too Far* (New York: Fawcett Popular Library, 1975).

28. Interview with Johnnie Holmes by DLM; Tom Brokaw has an interview with Holmes in *The Greatest Generation* (New York: Random House, 1998), 193–202.

29. All Long quotations are in Motley, *Invisible Soldier,* 151–52.

30. Charles A. Gates, oral testimony, Department of Defense.

31. Holmes interview.

32. Quoted in Doubler, *Closing with the Enemy,* 172.

33. Mack Morriss, "Yank" (January 5, 1945), in *"Yank," the GI Story of the War,* 162–66.

34. Robert D. Georgen, "The Fortunes of War: A Teenage Soldier's Story of WWII Combat Infantry Experience," EC.

35. Quoted in Edward G. Miller, *A Dark and Bloody Ground: The Hürtgen Forest and the Roer River Dams, 1944–1945* (College Station: Texas A&M University Press, 1995), 1; for another outstanding history of the battle, see Charles B. MacDonald, *The Battle of the Huertgen Forest* (Philadelphia: Lippincott, 1963).

36. Quoted in Dorothy Chernitsky, *Voices from the Foxholes, by the Men of the 110th Infantry* (Uniontown, Pa.: privately published, 1991), 62–63.

37. Georgen, "Fortunes of War," EC.

38. Arthur "Dutch" Schultz, oral testimony, EC.

11: THE BATTLE OF THE BULGE

1. Dwayne T. Burns, unpublished account, EC.

2. Roger Rutland, oral testimony, WGBH, American Experience, Boston.

3. Ed Cunningham, *"Yank," the GI Story of the War*, 167.

4. Burns, EC.

5. Richard F. Proulx, "Twilight of the Gods—Remember Us," unpublished essay, EC.

6. Ibid.

7. Ibid.

8. Ibid.

9. Alan Moorehead, *Eclipse* (New York: Harper & Row, 1968; originally published, 1948), 224.

10. Georgen, "Fortunes of War," EC.

11. Interview with Kurt Vonnegut, Jr., by DLM.

12. Georgen, "Fortunes of War," EC.

13. Quoted in Ed Cunningham, *"Yank," the GI Story of the War*, 171–73.

14. Quoted in ibid., 173.

15. David Pergrin, *First Across the Rhine* (New York: Atheneum, 1989), 193–94; interview with Pergrin, Lou Reda Productions.

16. Quoted in Charles B. MacDonald, *A Time for Trumpets: The Untold Story of the Battle of the Bulge* (New York: William Morrow, 1985), p. 68; for this climactic battle, see also John S. D. Eisenhower, *The Bitter Woods* (New York: Da Capo, 1996); for an excellent biography of Patton, see Carlo D'Este, *Patton: A Genius For War* (New York: Harper Perennial, 1996).

17. Quoted in Motley, *Invisible Soldier*, 156.

18. H. W. O. Kinnard, oral testimony, WGBH, American Experience, Boston.

19. Craig S. Fenn, oral testimony, EC.

20. G. F. Fitzgerald, "My Most Memorable Christmas," unpublished essay, EC.

21. Quoted in Motley, *Invisible Soldier*, 156.

22. Rutland, WGBH.

23. Bart Hagerman, oral testimony, WGBH, American Experience, Boston.

24. Georgen, "Fortunes of War," EC.

25. Interview with Morris Metz by DLM.

26. Bob Conroy, oral testimony, WGBH, American Experience, Boston.

27. John C. Capell, oral testimony, EC.

28. Schultz, EC.

29. Proulx, "Twilight of the Gods."

30. Schultz, EC.

31. Georgen, "Fortunes of War," EC.

32. Burns, EC.

33. Steber interview.

34. Burns, EC.

35. James M. Power, letters home, EC.

36. Ben Kimmelman, oral testimony, WGBH, American Experience, Boston; Proulx, "Twilight of the Gods."

37. Proulx, "Twilight of the Gods."

38. Kimmelman, WGBH.

39. John W. Appel, "Prevention of Manpower Losses from Psychiatric Disorder," Unclassified Document, Mental Hygiene Branch, Medical Corps; John E. Sloan Papers, U.S. Army Military History Institute, Carlisle Barracks, Carlisle, Pa.

40. Conroy, WGBH.

41. J. Glenn Gray, *The Warriors: Reflections on Men in Battle* (Lincoln: University of Nebraska Press, 1970; originally published, 1959), 104.

42. Proulx, "Twilight of the Gods.'

43. Quoted in Carlo D'Este, "Patton's Finest Hour," *Military History Quarterly* (Spring 2001), 23.

44. Proulx, "Twilight of the Gods."

12: THE MARIANAS

1. Quoted in Samuel Eliot Morison, *History of United States Naval Operations in World War II*, vol. 8, *New Guinea and the Marianas, March 1944 to August 1944* (Boston: Little, Brown, 1964), 5.

2. Quoted in Richard B. Frank, *Downfall: The End of the Imperial Japanese Empire* (New York: Random House, 1999), 48.

3. Robert Sherrod, *On to Westward: War in the Central Pacific* (New York: Duell, Sloan & Pearce, 1945), 14.

4. Quoted in Alexander, *Storm Landings*, 70.

5. Manchester, *Goodbye, Darkness*, 309.

6. Quoted in John C. Chapin, *Breaching the Marianas: The Battle for Saipan* (Washington, D.C.: Marine Corps Historical Center, 1994), 17, 36.

7. General Edwin Simmons, oral testimony, Lou Reda Productions; interview with Simmons by DLM.

8. Quoted in Alexander, *Storm Landings*, 62.

9. Sherrod, *On to Westward*, 50.

10. Quoted in Haruko Taya Cook, "The Myth of the Saipan Suicides," *Military History Quarterly* 7 (Spring 1995): 13.

11. Interview with John C. Chapin, Lou Reda Productions; Chapin, *Breaching the Marianas*, 2.

12. Sherrod, *On to Westward*, 55.

13. Henry Crowe, Oral History Collection, Marine Corps Historical Center, Washington, D.C.

14. Hatch interview by DLM.

15. Sherrod, *On to Westward*, 58.

16. Quoted in Bernard Nalty, *The Right to Fight: African-American Marines in World War II* (Washington, D.C.: Marine Corps Historical Center, 1995), 1.

17. Quoted in Henry Shaw and Ralph W. Donnelly, *Blacks in the Marine Corps* (Washington, D.C.: History and Museums Division, U.S. Marine Corps, 1975), 34.

18. Quoted in Nalty, *Right to Fight*, 20–21.

19. Quoted in Shaw, *Blacks in the Marine Corps*, 35.

20. Quoted in Morison, *New Guinea and the Marianas*, 200.

21. Quoted in ibid., 213.

22. Quoted in Boyne, *Clash of Titans*, 298.

23. Spruance and Nimitz quoted in Spector, *Eagle Against the Sun*, 305.

24. Chapin oral testimony.

25. Morison, *New Guinea and the Marianas*, 278.

26. Morison, *Two-Ocean War*, 343.

27. Quoted in Morison, *New Guinea and the Marianas*, 291.

28. Quoted in Boyne, *Clash of Titans*, 302.

29. Quoted in Morison, *New Guinea and the Marianas*, 302.

30. Quoted in ibid., 302–3.

31. Morison, *New Guinea and the Marianas*, 304.

32. Quoted in Chapin, *Breaching the Marianas*, 17–18.

33. Quoted in ibid., 29.

34. Quoted in ibid.

35. Chapin interview.

36. Quoted in Chapin, *Breaching the Marianas*, 19.

37. Quoted in Sherrod, *On to Westward*, 89; for this controversy, see Harry A. Gailey, *Howlin' Mad versus the Army: Conflict in Command, Saipan 1944* (Novato, Calif.: Presidio Press, 1986).

38. Sherrod, *On to Westward*, 23–24, 140.

39. Quoted in Cook, "Myth of the Saipan Suicides," 15.

40. Arnold Krammer, "Japanese Prisoners of War in America," *Pacific Historical Review* 52 (1983): 71–72, 82–83.

41. Philip A. Crowl, *The Campaign in the Marianas* (Washington, D.C.: Office of the Chief of Military History, 1959), 265–67.

42. Sherrod, *On to Westward*, 119–23.

43. David Nichols, ed., *Ernie's War: The Best of Ernie Pyle's World War II Dispatches* (New York: Simon & Schuster, 1987), 367.

44. Sherrod, *On to Westward*, 119–23.

45. Robert Sherrod, "Saipan," *Life* (August 28, 1944), 75.

46. Sherrod, "The Nature of the Enemy," *Time* (August 7, 1944), 27; Sherrod, *On to Westward*, 144–47; interview with John McCullough by DLM.

47. Quoted in Cook, "Myth of the Saipan Suicides," 12.

48. Quoted in Frank, *Downfall*, 30.

49. Quoted in Cook, "Myth of the Saipan Suicides," 17.

50. Cook, "Myth of the Saipan Suicides," 17.

51. Quoted in Bix, *Hirohito*, 480.

52. Quoted in John W. Dower, *War Without Mercy: Race and Power in the Pacific War* (New York: Pantheon, 1986), 247.

53. Quoted in Andrew A. Rooney, *The Fortunes of War: Four Great Battles of World War II* (Boston: Little, Brown, 1962), 37.

54. Quoted in Chapin, *Breaching the Marianas*, 36.

55. Quoted in H. N. Oliphant, "How the Jap Soldier Thought," in *"Yank," the GI Story of the War*, 148–54.

56. Justice M. Chambers, Oral History Collection, Marine Corps Historical Center.

57. Quoted in James H. Hallas, *The Devil's Anvil: The Assault on Peleliu* (Westport, Conn.: Praeger, 1994), 281.

58. Quoted in ibid., 280.

59. Sherrod, *On to Westward*, 148.

13: A MARINE AT PELELIU

1. Studs Terkel, *"The Good War": An Oral History of World War II* (New York: The New Press, 1984), 65–66.

2. James D. Seidler, testimony, EC.

3. Unless otherwise indicated, all quotations from Sledge are from the following sources: E. B. Sledge, *With the Old Breed at Peleliu and Okinawa* (New York: Oxford University Press, 1990; originally published, 1981, Presidio Press); Sledge, oral testimony, Lou Reda Productions; Sledge interview with DLM. "The Old Breed and the Costs of War," in John V. Denson, ed., *The Costs of War: America's Pyrrhic Victories* (New Brunswick, N.J.: Transaction Publishers, 1997); Sledge, "Peleliu 1944: Why Did We Go There?," *Naval Institute Proceedings*, 120 (September 1994); Sledge, with Colonel Joseph H. Alexander, "Sledgehammer's War and Peace: Reflections on Combat, North China Duty, and Homecoming," 1999, manuscript. I am grateful to the late Dr. Sledge for allowing me to quote from this forthcoming book.

4. Quoted in George P. Hunt, *Coral Comes High* (New York: Harper & Brothers, 1946), 13.

5. "Officer" and Webber quoted in ibid., 40, 43.

6. Quoted in Hallas, *Devil's Anvil*, 41.

7. Quoted in ibid., 36.

8. Tom Lea, *Peleliu Landing* (El Paso, Tex.: Carl Hertzog, 1945), 4.

9. Russell Davis, *Marine at War* (New York: Scholastic, 1961), 95.

10. "Peleliu: Tom Lea Paints Island Invasion," *Life* (June 11, 1945), 61.

11. Lea, *Peleliu Landing*, I, 1–8; Lea, "Peleliu," 61–66.

12. Lea, *Peleliu Landing*, 6–7.

13. Ibid., 7; Lea, "Peleliu," 61.

14. Jones, *WW II*, 118.

15. Lea, *Peleliu Landing*, 12–13.

16. Ibid., 12–15.

17. Hunt, *Coral Comes High*, 98.

18. Lea, *Peleliu Landing*, 17–18.

19. Ibid., 20–21.

20. Lea, "Peleliu," 66.

21. Interview with Benis Frank by DLM.

22. Interview with General Paul Henderson, Lou Reda Productions; for Puller, see Lt. Col. Jon T. Hoffman, *Chesty: Lieutenant General Lewis B. Puller, USMC* (New York: Random House, 2001); for a fine account of the battle, see Harry A. Gailey, *Peleliu, 1944* (Annapolis: Nautical and Aviation Publishing Co. of America, 1983).

23. Interview with General Ray Davis, Lou Reda Productions.

24. Hunt, *Coral Comes High*, 112.

25. This encounter is based on Sledge's later conversations with Harris.

26. Quoted in Hallas, *Devil's Anvil*, 176.

27. Hunt, *Coral Comes High*, 144.

28. Ibid., 112.

29. Frank interview.

30. Lea, *Peleliu Landing*, 34.

31. Lea, "Peleliu," 65.

14: THE RETURN

1. Quoted in Manchester, *American Caesar*, 388–89; the campaign to recover the Philippines is covered exhaustively in Louis Morton, *The United States Army in World War II: The War in the Pacific: The Fall of the Philippines* (Washington, D.C.: Office of the Chief of Military History, Department of the Army, 1953).

2. Quoted in Flower and Reeves, *The War*, 750.

3. Morison, *Two-Ocean War*, 449.

4. Interview with Admiral Thomas C. Kinkaid, Columbia University Oral History Project.

5. Quoted in Samuel Eliot Morison, *Leyte* (Boston: Little, Brown, 1958), 288.

6. Morison, *Two-Ocean War*, 463.

7. Kinkaid interview.

8. Quoted in Manchester, *American Caesar*, 459.

9. Quoted in Bix, *Hirohito*, 481.

10. Linwood B. Crider, personal testimony, EC; interview with Linwood Crider by DLM.

11. Eichelberger, *Our Jungle Road*, 182; 11th Airborne historian quoted in ibid.

12. Quoted in Manchester, *American Caesar*, 475.

13. "The Battle Begins for Luzon," *Life* (January 22, 1945), 19.

14. Quoted in Guillain, *I Saw Tokyo Burning*, 189.

15. Quoted in Rafael Steinberg, *Return to the Philippines* (New York: Time-Life Books, 1979), 114; for the Cabanatuan Raid, see Forrest B. Johnson, *Hour of Redemption: The Ranger Raid on Cabanatuan* (New York: Manor Books, 1979); and Hampton Sides, *Ghost Soldiers: The Forgotten Epic Story of World War II's Most Dramatic Mission* (New York: Doubleday, 2001).

16. Carl Mydans, "My God! It's Carl Mydans," *Life* (February 19, 1945), 20.

17. *New York Times*, Week in Review, February 11, 1945.

18. Nurses quoted in Norman, *We Band of Angels*, 203–4.

19. Mydans, "My God!" 98.

20. Quoted in Norman, *We Band of Angels*, 204.

21. Mydans, "My God!" 98–101.

22. Eichelberger, *Our Jungle Road*, 194–95.

23. H. N. Oliphant, "How the Jap Soldier Thought," 22.

24. Fred Nixon, written testimony, EC.

25. Tenney interview with Lou Reda Productions.

26. Manchester, *American Caesar*, 413.

27. Carlos Romulo, *I See the Philippines Rise* (Garden City, N.Y.: Doubleday, 1946), 229.

28. Eichelberger, *Our Jungle Road*, 198–89.

29. Lieutenant Colonel Luis M. Burris, edited by Carol Heckman-Owen, "Blazing Trails with 'D' Battery in the War Against Japan," manuscript at EC.

30. Quoted in Norman, *We Band of Angels*, 213.

31. Burris, "Blazing Trails."

32. "MacArthur Is Home," *Life* (April 9, 1945), 31.

33. Eichelberger, *Our Jungle Road*, 166.

34. Quoted in Stephen E. Ambrose, *American Heritage New History of World War II*, original text by C. L. Sulzberger (New York: Viking), 530.

15: THE B-29S

1. Guillain, *I Saw Tokyo Burning*, 191.

2. I. J. Galantin, *Take Her Deep!: A Submarine Against Japan in World War II* (Chapel Hill, N.C.: Algonquin Books, 1987), 208–9.

3. Quoted in William Bradford Huie, "The Navy's Seabees," *Life* (October 9, 1944), 52; interview with Lou Reda by DLM. Reda served in the Seabees in the Pacific in World War II.

4. St. Clair McKelway, "A Reporter with the B-29s, IV—The People," *New Yorker* (June 30, 1945), 35, 37–38, 40–43.

5. Charles W. Sweeney, *War's End: An Eyewitness Account of America's Last Atomic Mission* (New York: Avon, 1997), 43–44.

6. Interview with Harry George, Lou Reda Productions. Unless otherwise indicated, all quotations by B-29 crew members are from interviews conducted by Mark Natola, some of them for Lou Reda Productions, and by DLM.

7. McKelway, "B-29s, IV," 40–41.

8. Interview with General James V. Edmundson, Lou Reda Productions.

9. General Curtis E. LeMay, with MacKinlay Kantor, *Mission with LeMay* (Garden City, New York: Doubleday, 1965), 332.

10. Ibid., 322.

11. McKelway, "A Reporter With the B-29s, I—Possum, Rosy, and the Thousand Kids," *New Yorker* (June 9, 1945), 28.

12. John Ciardi, *Saipan: The War Diary of John Ciardi* (Fayetteville: University of Arkansas Press, 1988), 35.

13. Terkel, *"The Good War,"* 201.

14. Ciardi, *Saipan*, 40.

15. Terkel, *"The Good War,"* 200.

16. Ciardi, *Saipan*, 44, 58, 83, 90–94, 99–101.

17. Ibid., 93, 99–100.

18. LeMay, *Mission*, 345.

19. Terkel, *"The Good War,"* 200.

20. Ciardi, *Saipan*, xi, 97, 103.

21. Knox Burger, "Tokyo Fire Raid," in *"Yank," the GI Story of the War*, 274–76.

22. Quoted in Keith Wheeler, *Bombers Over Japan* (Alexandria, Va.: Time-Life Books, 1982), 168.

23. McKelway, "A Reporter with the B-29s, III—The Cigar, the Three Wings, and the Low-Level Attacks," *New Yorker* (June 23, 1945), 36.

24. LeMay, *Mission*, 352.

25. McKelway, "B-29s, III," 36–38.

26. Sherry, *American Air Power*, 406, 278–79.

27. Burger, "Tokyo Fire Raid," 276–77; Interview with Knox Burger by DLM.

28. LeMay, *Mission*, 384.

29. Quoted in Richard Rhodes, *Dark Sun: The Making of the Hydrogen Bomb* (New York: Simon & Schuster, 1995), 21–22.

30. LeMay, *Mission*, 353.

31. Ibid., 354–355, 368.

32. Quoted in Wheeler, *Bombers Over Japan*, 98.

33. Sherry, *American Air Power*, 280.

34. Williamson Murray and Allan R. Millett, *A War To Be Won: Fighting the Second World War* (Cambridge, Mass.: Harvard University Press, 2000), 508; this is the best single-volume military history of the war.

35. Terkel, *"The Good War,"* 199–200.

36. Russell Brines, *Until They Eat Stones* (New York: J. B. Lippincott, 1944), 9, 11.

37. McKelway, "B-29s, IV," 42–45.

38. McKelway, "B-29s, III," 39.

39. Interview with Marty Schaffer by DLM.

40. Ibid.

41. Manchester, *Goodbye, Darkness,* 338; for the devastating impact of the blockage on Japan's economy, see United States Strategic Bombing Survey, Report no. 42, *The Japanese Wartime Standard of Living and Utilization of Manpower* (Washington, D.C.: Manpower, Food and Civilian Supplies Division, 1947); Mark P. Parillo, *The Japanese Merchant Marine in World War II* (Annapolis: Naval Institute Press, 1993); and Jerome B. Cohen, *Japan's Economy in War and Reconstruction* (Minneapolis: University of Minnesota Press, 1949).

16: MAKE THEM REMEMBER

1. Clayton Ogle, "Clancy's Crew," EC.

2. Paul Green, EC.

3. Muirhead, *Those Who Fall*, 132–33.

4. Quoted in Motley, *Invisible Soldier*, 218.

5. Quoted in Geoffrey Perret, *Winged Victory: The Army Air Forces in World War II* (New York: Random House, 1993), 383.

6. Quoted in Benjamin O. Davis, Jr., *American: An Autobiography* (Washington, D.C.: Smithsonian Institution Press, 1991), 103.

7. Quoted in Motley, *Invisible Soldier*, 219; Lewis C. Huff to Donald L. Miller, June 6, 2001.

8. Quoted in Motley, *Invisible Soldier*, 220.

9. Quoted in ibid., 233.

10. Muirhead, *Those Who Fall*, 135.

11. Quoted in Motley, *Invisible Soldier*, 220–21.

12. Quoted in Motley, *Invisible Soldier*, 234.

13. Quoted in Stewart Leuthner and Oliver O. Jensen, eds., *High Honor: Recollections by Men and Women of World War II Aviation* (Washington, D.C.: Smithsonian Institution Press, 1990), 244–45; Daniel Behre, personal testimony, EC; Stephen Ambrose tells the story of the 15th Airforce's B-24 bombing raids on Germany in *The Wild Blue: The Men and Boys Who Flew the B-24s Over Germany* (New York: Simon & Schuster, 2001).

14. Quoted in Motley, *Invisible Soldier*, 215.

15. Interview with Richard Macon, Lou Reda Productions and United States Army.

16. All quotes in Ronald Schaffer, *Wings of Judgment: American Bombing in World War II* (New York: Oxford University Press, 1985), 92.

17. Quoted in Sherry, *American Air Power*, 261.

18. Gray, *Warriors*, 25–58.

19. John H. Morris, testimony, EC.

20. Joe Kleven and Art Kuespert, "Rainwater and Potato Peelings," EC.

21. Kurt Vonnegut, Jr., *Slaughterhouse-Five or the Children's Crusade* (New York: Dell, 1969), 128–31, 153–54.

22. Vonnegut, Jr., interview.

23. Kleven and Kuespert, "Rainwater and Potato Peelings," EC.

24. Morris testimony.

25. Quoted in Schaffer, *Wings of Judgement*, 88.

26. Allan A. Michie, "Germany was Bombed to Defeat," *Readers Digest* 47 (August, 1945): 77–81; for a splendid account of the final days of the air war in Europe, see Thomas Childers, *Wings of Morning: The Story of the Last American Bomber Shot Down Over Germany in World War II* (Reading, Mass.: Addison-Wesley, 1995).

27. Weinberg, *World at Arms*, 835–36; the best study of the breakdown of the German economy is Alfred C. Mierzejewski, *The Collapse of the German War Economy, 1944–45: Allied Air Power and the German National Railway* (Chapel Hill, N.C.: University of North Carolina Press, 1988).

28. For two fresh and arresting appraisals of the impact of the air campaign, see Murray and Millet, *A War To Be Won;* and Williamson Murray, *War in the Air, 1914–45* (London: Cassell, 1999). I have relied on these studies, and have profited from conversations with Allan Millet; see also several other excellent studies, Conrad C. Crane, *Bombs, Cities, and Civilians: American Airpower Strategy in World War II* (Lawrence: University Press of Kansas, 1993); Sir Charles Webster and Noble Frankland, *The Strategic Air Offensive Against Germany, 1939–1945*, 4 vols. (London: Battery Press, 1994); Richard J. Overy, *The Air War, 1939–1945* (New York: Stein and Day, 1985); Richard G. Davis, *Carl A. Spaatz and the Air War in Europe* (Washington, D.C.: Center for Air Force History, 1993); and the indispensable *The Army Air Forces in World War II*, 7 vols. edited by Craven and Cate.

17: FROM THE VOLGA TO THE ODER

1. Pyotr Pavlenko, "Cossacks of the Kuban, *Soviet War News Weekly* (September 23, 1943); David M. Glantz and Jonathan M. House have written a splendid account of *The Battle of Kursk* (Lawrence: University Press of Kansas, 1999).
2. Weinberg, *World at Arms*, 752; see also David M. Glantz and Jonathan M. House, *When Titans Clashed: How the Red Army Stopped Hitler* (Lawrence: University Press of Kansas, 1995).
3. For the Warsaw uprising, see Joanna K. M. Hanson, *The Civilian Population and the Warsaw Uprising of 1944* (Cambridge: Cambridge University Press, 1982).

18: ACROSS THE RHINE

1. Chet Hansen diary, U.S. Army Military History Institute, Carlisle Barracks, Carlisle, Pa.
2. Albert Willis Scribner, "A Debtor's Life," unpublished testimony, EC.
3. Ed Cunningham, "The Bridge at Remagen," in *"Yank," the GI Story of the War*, 205–7.
4. Capa, *Slightly Out of Focus*, 219.
5. Quoted in John Keegan, *World War II: A Visual Encyclopedia* (London: PRC Publishing, 1999), 355.
6. Trezzvant W. Anderson, *Come Out Fighting: The Epic Tale of the 761st Tank Battalion, 1942–1945* (Salzburg: Salzburger Druckerei und Verlag, 1945), 125.
7. Quoted in Motley, *Invisible Soldier*, 171.
8. Anderson, *Come Out Fighting*, 125.
9. Ibid., 83, 93.
10. Shultz, EC.
11. Allan B. Ecker, "Fall of Germany," in *"Yank," the GI Story of the War*, 239–40.
12. Capa, *Slightly Out of Focus*, 226.
13. Martha Gellhorn, "Das Deutches Volk," *Collier's* (May 26, 1945), in *Reporting the War, Part Two*, 671–78.
14. Steber interview; Sergeant Tom Warner of Easton, Pa., echoed my Uncle John Steber's remarks. "We knew why we were in this war. Hitler and his people were evil. They were doing wrong things, and we were there to get it over with. We wanted to get the job done and go home." Personal testimony, EC.
15. Quoted in Ambrose, *Citizen Soldiers*, 472–73.
16. Hansen diary.
17. Lee, *Employment of Negro Troops*, 689.
18. Quoted in Colley, *The Road to Victory*, 178.
19. Interview with James Strawder, U.S. Department of Defense.
20. Ibid.
21. Interview with James Staton, U.S. Department of Defense.
22. Quoted in Motley, *Invisible Soldier*, 159–60.
23. Quoted in Lee, *Employment of Negro Troops*, 702.
24. Interview with Frank Barbee, U.S. Department of Defense.
25. Goodman, *Fragment of Victory*, 115.

26. Interview with Daniel K. Inouye, in Col. Hiroaki Morita, "The Nation's Most Decorated Military Unit: The 100th/442nd Regimental Combat Team," Study Project, U.S. Army War College, Carlisle Barracks, Carlisle, Pa.

27. Tom Kawaguchi and Shig Doi interviews in John Tateishi, *And Justice for All: An Oral History of the Japanese American Detention Camps* (New York: Random House, 1984), 165, 181.

28. Morita, "The Nation's Most Decorated."

29. Quoted in Tateishi, *And Justice for All*, 182–83.

30. Survey Data, "United States Army Military History Institute's World War II Army Service Experience Questionnaire," Carlisle Barracks, Carlisle, Pa.

31. Inouye interview in Morita, "The Nation's Most Decorated."

32. This account of the assault on the castle was assembled from Baker's book, *Lasting Valor*, Chapters 19 and 20, an interview with Baker by DLM, Baker's Medal of Honor citation, and Captain Runyon's report. Runyon's report, naturally, differs radically from Baker's account on the matter of his own conduct. But he does credit Baker with displaying "magnificent courage." Runyon's report is reproduced in part in Goodman, *Fragment of Victory*, 130–33.

33. Inouye, *Journey to Washington*, 143.

34. Ibid., 147.

35. Quoted in Motley, *Invisible Soldier*, 334.

36. General Orders, War Department, VII Battle Honors, April 10, 1946, National Archives.

37. Baker, *Lasting Valor*, 206; Baker interview with DLM.

38. Inouye, *Journey to Washington*, 150–58.

39. Interview with Walter Rosenblum, EC.

40. Walter J. Fellenz, in *The Liberators: Eye Witness Accounts of the Liberation of the Concentration Camps*, vol. 1, *Liberation Day*, edited by Yaffa Eliach and Brana Gurewitsch (Brooklyn, N.Y.: Center for Holocaust Studies Documentation and Research, 1981), 1.

41. William Cowling to his parents, April 28, 1945, in Sam Dann, ed., *Dachau 29 April, 1945: The Rainbow Liberation Memoirs* (Lubbock: Texas Tech University Press, 1998), 22; Marguerite Higgins, *New York Herald Tribune*, (May 1, 1945).

42. Rosenblum interview.

43. Robert H. Abzug, *Inside the Vicious Heart: America and the Liberation of the Nazi Concentration Camps* (New York: Oxford University Press, 1985), 87–103.

44. Quoted in "Reunion," *The New Yorker* (November 11, 1991), 33.

45. Rosenblum interview.

46. Quoted in Dann, *Dachau*, 33–4.

47. Quoted in ibid., 21–24.

48. Quoted in Motley, *Invisible Soldier*, 224–25.

49. Quoted in ibid., 155.

50. Interview with Johnnie Holmes by DLM.

51. Edward R. Murrow, CBS Radio Broadcast, December 13, 1942.

52. Victor Davis Hanson, *The Soul of Battle: From Ancient Times to the Present Day, How Three Great Liberators Vanquished Tyranny* (New York: The Free Press, 1999), 380–81. Despite

painstaking efforts by demographers, we will never know for certain how many people died at the hands of the Nazis. For estimated numbers killed, see R. J. Rummel, *Democide: Nazi Genocide and Mass Murder* (New Brunswick: Transaction, 1992) and Weinberg, *World at Arms,* 894–900. For German war losses, see Martin K. Sorge, *The Other Price of Hitler's War: German Military and Civilian Losses from World War II* (Westport, Conn.: Greenwood Press, 1986).

53. Quoted in Ambrose, *World War II,* 441; for the American government's insensitivity to the plight of the European Jews, see two exhaustive studies by David S. Wyman, *Paper Walls: America and the Refugee Crisis, 1938–41* (Amherst, Mass.: University of Massachusetts Press, 1968) and *The Abandonment of the Jews: America and the Holocaust, 1941–1945* (New York: Pantheon, 1984).

54. Omar N. Bradley, *A Soldier's Story* (New York: Henry Holt, 1951), 539.

55. Quoted in Abzug, *Inside the Vicious Heart,* 30.

56. Abzug, *Inside the Vicious Heart,* 30.

57. In Eliach and Gurewitsch, *Liberation Day,* 17.

58. Ed Cunningham, "How the Germans Killed," in *"Yank," the GI Story of the War,* 212–13; Prison diary of Major Francis Gerald, in the possession of Pat Caruso.

59. Roman Karmen, *Soviet War News* (April 26, 1945), 1; for the Red Army's drive on Berlin, see John Erickson, *The Road to Berlin* (London: Grafton, 1983).

60. Hansen diary.

61. Quoted in Ambrose, *Citizen Soldiers,* 101.

62. Kershaw, *Hitler,* 841.

63. Quoted in *"Yank," the GI Story of the War,* 244.

64. Hansen diary.

65. Virginia Irwin, "A Giant Whirlpool of Destruction," *St. Louis Post-Dispatch* (May 9–11, 1945).

66. Claus Fuhrmann, quoted in Flower and Reeves, *The War,* 1006–8.

67. Mack Morriss, "Fall of Berlin," in *"Yank," the GI Story of the War,* 238; in a vividly written account, *Band of Brothers: E. Company, 506th Regiment, 101st Airborne from Normandy to Hitler's Eagle's Nest* (New York: A Touchstone Book, 2001), Stephen E. Ambrose tells the story, mostly in the men's own words, of one rifle company's combat experience in Europe.

68. Power, EC.

69. Scribner, EC.

70. Fenn, EC.

19: IWO JIMA

1. William Sanders Clark, unpublished account of personal experiences, 1945, EC. All subsequent quotations by Clark are from this source.

2. Jones, *WW II,* 235–36.

3. Typed copy at EC of article on the Battle of Iwo Jima by Brigadier General Wendell Duplantis, (originally published in *Battle Creek Enquirer and News,* February 21, 1965), 1.

4. Sherrod, *On to Westward,* 153–56; Sherrod, "The First Three Days," *Life* (March 5, 1945), 41.

5. Sherrod, *On to Westward,* 154, 159.

6. Interview with Andy Anderson, Lou Reda Productions.

7. Quoted in Keith Wheeler, *The Road to Tokyo* (New York: Time-Life Books, 1979), 60.

8. Quoted in Lynn Kessler, ed., with Edmond B. Bart, *Never in Doubt: Remembering Iwo Jima* (Annapolis: Naval Institute Press, 1999), 168–69.

9. Joe Rosenthal, with W. C. Heinz, "The Picture That Will Live Forever," *Collier's* (February 18, 1955), 62; interview with Frank Crossland Caldwell, Lou Reda Productions.

10. Sherrod, *On to Westward*, 178; Sherrod, "The First Three Days," 44.

11. Quoted in Kessler, *Never in Doubt*, 12.

12. Quoted in ibid., 206–8.

13. Sherrod, "The First Three Days," 44.

14. Quoted in Kessler, *Never in Doubt*, 55.

15. Interview with General Fred E. Hayner, Lou Reda Productions.

16. Sherrod, "The First Three Days," 44.

17. Sherrod, *On to Westward*, 190.

18. Quoted in Keith Wheeler, *Road to Tokyo*, 41.

19. Quoted in Richard Wheeler, *Iwo* (New York: Lippincott & Crowell, 1980), 10.

20. Ibid., 33.

21. Quoted in Duplantis, 3.

22. Bill Reed, "Battle for Iwo," in *"Yank," the GI Story of the War*, 219–21.

23. Interview with Charles Lindberg, Lou Reda Productions; all subsequent quotations by Lindberg are from this source.

24. Quoted in Richard Wheeler, *Iwo*, 159.

25. Quoted in ibid., 161.

26. Rosenthal, "The Picture That Will Live Forever," 62–62; Hal Buell, *Moments: The Pulitzer Prize-Winning Photographs* (New York: Black Dog & Leventhal, 1999), 22; Richard Wheeler, *Iwo*, 157–64; Hatch interview with DLM.

27. Quoted in James Bradley, with Ron Powers, *Flags of Our Fathers* (New York: Bantam, 2000), 220; for another fine account of the battle, see Bill D. Ross, *Iwo Jima—Legacy of Valor* (New York: Vintage Books, 1986); for the battle from the perspective of a medical officer, see James S. Vedder, *Combat Surgeon: Up Front With the 27th Marines* (Novato, Calif.: Presidio Press, 1984).

28. Jeremy Paxman and Robert Harris, *A Higher Form of Killing: The Secret Story of Gas and Germ Warfare* (New York: Hill & Wang, 1983), 138; John Ellis van Courtland Moon, "Chemical Warfare: A Forgotten Lesson," *Bulletin of the Atomic Scientists* 45, no. 6 (July–August 1989): 40–43; Brooks E. Kleber and Dale Birdsell, *The Chemical Warfare Service: Chemicals in Combat, United States Army in World War II* (Washington, D.C.: Government Printing Office, 1966), 648–52.

29. Nichols, *Ernie's War*, 368, 374–77.

30. Buell, *Moments*, 23; Interview with Hal Buell, Lou Reda Productions.

31. Sherrod, *On to Westward*, 202.

32. C. P. Zurlinden, Jr., and others, "Iwo: The Red-Hot Rock," *Collier's* (April 4, 1945), 16–17.

33. Cozy Stanley Brown in Broderick H. Johnson, ed., *Navajos and World War II* (Tsaile, Navajo Nation, Ariz.: Navajo Community Press, 1977), 54–56.

34. John P. Langellier, *American Indians in the U.S. Armed Forces, 1866–1945* (Mechanicsburg, Pa.: Stackpole Books, 2000), 8.

35. Quoted in Kessler, *Never in Doubt*, 166.

36. Quoted in Bruce Watson, "Jaysho, moasi, . . ." *Smithsonian Magazine* 24, no. 5 (August 1993): 36; see also Ron McCoy, "Navajo Code-Talkers of World War II," *American West* 18 (1981): 67–73; and Alison R. Bernstein, *American Indians and World War II* (Norman, Oklahoma: University of Oklahoma Press, 1991).

37. Quoted in Broderick, *Navajos and World War II*, 59–61.

38. Interview with Norma Crotty, Lou Reda Productions.

39. Richard Wheeler, *Iwo*, 201; George Green testimony, EC.

40. Keith Wheeler, *Road to Tokyo*, 55.

41. Quoted in Richard Wheeler, *Iwo*, 223.

42. Hayner interview.

43. Richard Wheeler, *Iwo*, 231.

44. Quoted in ibid., 234.

45. Quoted in Kessler, *Never in Doubt*, 112–13.

20: OKINAWA

1. Sledge, *Old Breed*, 171–73, 178.

2. Ibid., 179.

3. Sherrod, *On to Westward*, 265, 293–94.

4. Sledge, *Old Breed*, 179; Manchester, *Goodbye, Darkness*, 399–400.

5. Sledge, *Old Breed*, 179; "Okinawa," *Life* (May 28, 1945), 90.

6. Manchester, *Goodbye, Darkness*, 400–4.

7. Quoted in Sherrod, *On to Westward*, 268–69.

8. Quoted in George Feifer, *Tennozan: The Battle of Okinawa and the Atomic Bomb* (New York: Ticknor & Fields, 1992), 136; this book and three others are excellent histories of the battle: Roy E. Appleman, James M. Burns, Russell A. Guegeler and John Stevens, *Okinawa: The Last Battle* (Washington, D.C.: Historical Division, Department of the Army, 1948); William M. Belote and James H. Belote, *Typhoon of Steel: The Battle for Okinawa* (New York: Harper and Row, 1970); and Benis M. Frank and Henry I. Shaw, Jr., *Victory and Occupation* (Washington, D.C.: U.S. Marine Corps, 1968); Col. Hiromichi Yahara and Frank Gibney gave an eyewitness account of the battle from the Japanese perspective in *The Battle for Okinawa* (New York: John Wiley, 1995).

9. Sherrod, *On to Westward*, 270.

10. Interview with Sledge, Lou Reda Productions; interview with Sledge by DLM.

11. Nichols, *Ernie's War*, 408–9.

12. Quoted in Gerald Astor, *Operation Iceberg: The Invasion and Conquest of Okinawa in World War II* (New York: Dell, 1995), 158; this is one of Astor's several absorbing oral histories of World War II combat.

13. Quoted in E. B. Potter, *Nimitz* (Annapolis: Naval Institute Press, 1976), 372.

14. Manchester, *Goodbye, Darkness*, 409.

15. Raymond Sawyer, oral testimony, EC.

16. Evan Wylie, "Death of Ernie Pyle," in *"Yank," the GI Story of the War*, 230.

17. Sherrod, *On to Westward*, 296–97.

18. Manchester, *Goodbye, Darkness*, 406–7; interview with Lieutenant General Victor Krulak, Lou Reda Productions.

19. Guillain, *I Saw Tokyo Burning*, 204.

20. Morison, *Two-Ocean War*, 550.

21. Quoted in Flower and Reeves, *The War*, 743.

22. Quoted in Feifer, *Tennozan*, 206.

23. Quoted in Astor, *Operation Iceberg*, 174.

24. Quoted in Feifer, *Tennozan*, 224.

25. Vice Admiral M. L. Deyo, "Kamikaze," unpublished MS, U.S. Naval Historical Center, Washington, D.C.

26. Quoted in Morison, *Two-Ocean War*, 545.

27. Evan Wylie, "Kamikaze: Jap Suicide," in *"Yank," the GI Story of the War*, 269–70.

28. Morison, *Two-Ocean War*, 548–49.

29. Phelps Adams, "Attack on Carrier Bunker Hill," *New York Sun* (June 28, 1945).

30. Both quotations in Miller, *War at Sea*, 526.

31. Sherrod, *On to Westward*, 294; Mitscher quoted in Miller, *War at Sea*.

32. Interview with Mort Zimmerman by DLM.

33. Hanson Baldwin, *Battles Lost and Won: Great Campaigns of World War II* (New York: Harper & Row, 1966), 377.

34. Quoted in Ambrose, *World War II*, 572.

35. Major General Wilburt S. Brown, oral history interview, Marine Corps Historical Center.

36. Manchester, *Goodbye, Darkness*, 411–12.

37. Sawyer, EC.

38. Ibid.

39. Sledge, "Sledgehammer's War and Peace," 21.

40. W. Eugene Smith, "24 Hours with Infantryman Terry Moore," *Life* (June 18, 1945), 20–25.

41. Sledge, "Sledgehammer's War and Peace," passim; Sledge interview, Lou Reda Productions; Sledge, *Old Breed*, 252–53, 269; Sledge interview with DLM.

42. Manchester, *Goodbye, Darkness*, 420, 429–30.

43. Sledge interview, Lou Reda Productions.

44. Manchester, *Goodbye, Darkness*, 451–53.

45. Quoted in ibid., 435.

46. Sledge, *Old Breed*, 223.

47. Feifer, *Tennozan*, 276.

48. Evan Regal and others quoted in Feifer, *Tennozan*, 415–19; Manchester, *Goodbye, Darkness*, 441–43.

49. Miyagi Kikuko, in Haruko Taya Cook and Theodore F. Cook, *Japan at War: An Oral History* (New York: The New Press, 1992), 357.

50. Ibid., 360–62.

51. Sledge interview, Lou Reda Productions.

52. Sledge, *Old Breed* 306–8; Sledge interview, Lou Reda Productions.

53. Sledge, *Old Breed*, 312.

21: THE SETTING SUN

1. Marvin A. Kastenbaum, "A Teenage Warrior," unpublished MS, EC; for the Japanese annihilation campaigns in China, see Bix, *Hirohito*, 365–68.

2. Quotations in Richard Rhodes, "The Toughest Flying in the World," *World War II Chronicles* (New York: American Heritage, 1995), 40–47; interview with Ruven Greenberg, EC.

3. Charles J. Rolo, "Wingate's Circus," *Atlantic Monthly* (October 1943), 91–94.

4. Quoted in Motley, *Invisible Soldier*, 119.

5. Gregory F. Michno, *Death on the Hellships: Prisoners at Sea in the Pacific War* (Annapolis: Naval Institute Press, 2001), 282–83; for different—and lower—figures, see Gavan Daws, *Prisoners of the Japanese: POWs of World War II in the Pacific* (New York: William Morrow, 1994), 297.

6. Forrest Knox, in Donald Knox, *Death March: The Survivors of Bataan* (New York: Harcourt Brace Jovanovich, 1981), 338–40; William R. Evans, *Kora!* (Rogue River, Ore.: Atwood, 1986), 107, 112.

7. Melvin Rosen interview by DLM; Davis quoted in Knox, *Death March*, 350; John M. Wright, Jr., *Captured on Corregidor: Diary of an American P.O.W.* (Jefferson, N.C.: McFarland & Co., 1988), 92; Daws, *Prisoners of the Japanese*, 294.

8. Maynard Booth interview, Lou Reda Productions; Melvin Rosen interviews, by DLM and Lou Reda Productions; William Adair interview, Lou Reda Productions; all Lawton quotations in Knox, *Death March*, 356.

9. Rosen interview, Lou Reda Productions; for a powerful account of the journey of the last hell ship, see E. Bartlett Kerr, *Surrender and Survival: The Experience of American POWs in the Pacific, 1941–1945* (New York: William Morrow, 1985), Chapter 12. For graphic eyewitness accounts, see, in addition to the books previously mentioned, Manny Lawton, *Some Survived* (Chapel Hill, N.C.: Algonquin Books, 1984) and Sidney Smith, *Give Us This Day* (New York: W. W. Norton, 1957).

10. Quoted in Knox, *Death March*, 364–65.

11. Tenney interviews with DLM and Lou Reda Productions; Tenney, *Hitch*, 122–37.

12. Hewlett quoted in Knox, *Death March*, 368; these figures are from The Center for Internee Rights, Inc. and include Merchant Marines. In *Surrender and Survival*, p. 339, Kerr states that 25,600 American military personnel were captured by the Japanese and that 10,650 were killed or died in captivity, a mortality rate of 41.6 percent. Kerr does not include Merchant Marines; to put the German figures in perspective, 60 percent of the Russian military personnel captured by the Nazis did not survive the war.

13. Interview with Frank "Foo" Fujita by DLM; Fujita interview, Lou Reda Productions.

14. Tenney interview by DLM; Daws, *Prisoners of the Japanese*, 308.

15. Tenney, *Hitch*, 164; Tenney interview, Lou Reda Productions.

16. Daws, *Prisoners of the Japanese*, 322; for the terrifying ordeal of one captured American flyer, see Fiske Hanley II, *Accused American War Criminal* (Austin, Tex.: Eakin Press, 1997).

17. Interview with Ray Halloran by DLM; interviews with Ray Halloran and Robert Goldsworthy by Mark Natola.

18. LeMay, *Mission*, 376.

19. Terkel, *"The Good War,"* 201.

20. LeMay, *Mission*, 375.

21. Ibid., 375, 381.

22. Truman diary, June 17, 1945, in Robert H. Ferrell, ed., *Off the Record: The Private Papers of Harry S. Truman* (New York: Harper & Row, 1980), 47.

23. "Minutes of Meeting Held at White House on Monday, 18 June at 1580," in Frank, *Downfall*, 143.

24. "Minutes," in Frank, *Downfall*, 139–43.

25. Interview with McCloy, in David McCullough, *Truman* (New York: Simon & Schuster, 1992), 401.

26. Daws, *Prisoners of the Japanese*, 325.

27. Sledge, "Sledgehammer's War and Peace," 1; Sledge interview by DLM.

28. Kastenbaum, EC.

29. D. M. Giangreco and Kathryn Moore, "Half a Million Purple Hearts," *American Heritage* (December 2000), 81–83; see also, Giangreco, "Casualty Projections for the Invasion of Japan, 1945–46: Planning and Policy Implications," *Journal of Military History* 61, no. 3 (July 1997): 535; and Giangreco, "The Truth About Kamikazes," *Naval History* (May–June 1997), 25–30.

30. Herbert Bix, "Japan's Delayed Surrender: A Reinterpretation," *Diplomatic History*, 19 (Spring 1995), 210; *Army Battle Casualties and Non-Battle Deaths in World War II, Final Report, 7 December 1941–31 December 1946* (Washington, D.C.: Statistical and Accounting Branch, Office of the Adjutant General), 10; for ULTRA intercepts, see Edward J. Drea, *In the Service of the Emperor: Essays on the Imperial Japanese Army* (Lincoln: University of Nebraska Press, 1998) and Drea, *MacArthur's ULTRA: Codebreaking and the War Against Japan, 1942–1945* (Lawrence: University Press of Kansas, 1992).

31. Frank, *Downfall*, 194, 202.

32. Quoted in ibid., 196.

33. Bix, "Japan's Delayed Surrender," 214.

34. Spector, *Eagle Against the Sun*, 543.

35. Guillian, *I Saw Tokyo Burning*, 209.

36. Interview with Frederick L. Ashworth by DLM.

37. Tibbets, *Enola Gay*, 183.

38. Sweeney, *War's End*, 137–38; Sweeney retired from the service as a Major General.

39. Tibbets interview.

40. Ibid.; Tibbets, *Enola Gay*, 192; it was LeMay's idea to have the bomb dropped by a single, unescorted plane. See Leslie R. Groves, *Now It Can Be Told: The Story of the Manhattan Project* (New York: Harper & Row, 1962), 284.

41. Interview with Raymond Biel by Mark Natola.

42. Groves, *Now It Can Be Told*, 308.

43. General Groves, Memorandum to the Secretary of War, 18 July 45, in ibid., 433–40; for a bril-

liant analysis of the story of the bomb, see Martin Sherwin, *A World Destroyed: Hiroshima and the Origins of the Arms Race* (New York: Vintage, 1987).

44. Quoted in Kennedy, *Freedom From Fear*, 845.

45. Quoted in Barton J. Bernstein, "The Perils and Politics of Surrender: Ending the War with Japan and Avoiding the Third Atomic Bomb," *Pacific Historical Review* 46 (February 1977): 5.

46. Bix, "Japan's Delayed Surrender," 222–23; for a suggestive essay on this issue, see Ian Buruma, "The War Over the Bomb," *New York Review of Books* (September 21, 1995), 26–34.

47. Barton J. Bernstein, "Understanding the Atomic Bomb and the Japanese Surrender: Missed Opportunities, Little-Known Near Disasters, and Modern Memory," *Diplomatic History*, 19 (Spring 1995), 240.

48. Stimson quoted in McCullough, *Truman*, 437.

49. Groves, *Now It Can Be Told*, 265.

50. "The Atomic Age," *Life* (August 20, 1945), 32.

51. Terkel, *"The Good War,"* 506–13.

52. Groves, *Now It Can Be Told*, 306. Groves initially expected a second plutonium bomb "to be ready about August 24," with "additional ones arriving in increasing numbers from there on." Ibid., 309; for the sinking of USS *Indianapolis*, see Doug Stanton, *In Harm's Way: The Sinking of the USS* Indianapolis *and the Extraordinary Story of Its Survivors* (New York: Henry Holt and Company, 2001).

53. Quoted in McCullough, *Truman*, 448.

54. "Immediate supply" in Groves, *Now It Can Be Told*, 309. Sweeney, *War's End*, 163–64.

55. Tibbets, *Enola Gay*, 186.

56. Colonel Paul Tibbets, Jr., as told to Wesley Price, "How to Drop an Atom Bomb," *Saturday Evening Post* (June 8, 1946), 136; Tibbets, *Enola Gay*, 226–27; Tibbets interview.

57. Tibbets, *Enola Gay*, 228; Tibbets interview.

58. Quoted in McCullough, *Truman*, 454.

59. Tibbets, "How to Drop an Atom Bomb," 136; Tibbets interview.

60. Tibbets, *Enola Gay*, 237.

61. Quoted in Feifer, *Tennozan*, 567.

62. Sweeney, *War's End*, 176.

63. Terkel, *"The Good War,"* 513.

64. Quoted in Flower and Reeves, *The War*, 1032.

65. Hajimi Kito in Terkel, *"The Good War,"* 539.

66. Michihiko Hachiya, *Hiroshima Diary: The Journal of a Japanese Physician, August 6–September 30, 1945* (Chapel Hill: University of North Carolina Press, 1955), 1–9.

67. Quoted in Robert Jay Lifton, *Death in Life: Survivors of Hiroshima* (New York: Random House, 1967), 79.

68. Hachiya, *Hiroshima Diary*, 97.

69. LeMay, *Mission*, 387.

70. Terkel, *"The Good War,"* 544.

71. LeMay, *Mission*, 382.

72. Quoted in McCullough, *Truman*, 455.

73. Farrell, *Off the Record*, 52.

74. Interview with Ray Gallagher by DLM; interview with Ray Gallagher by Mark Natola.

75. Quoted in Gordon Thomas and Max Morgan Witts, *Enola Gay* (New York: Stein & Day, 1977).

2 2 : V I C T O R Y

1. Ashworth interview. Unless otherwise indicated all quoted passages are from interviews by DLM and Mark Natola with the men on *Bockscar*. Frederick Ashworth was especially helpful in recreating the ill-fated flight of *Bockscar*. General Sweeney was interviewed by my associate Mark Natola but would not release the interview for publication. Subsequently, I made several unsuccessful attempts to get in touch with him to have him talk further about the Nagasaki mission. The interview he did with Natola stays close to the substance of his autobiography, *War's End*, which I have used in this chapter to give his account of the mission.

2. Sweeney, *War's End*, 4.

3. Ibid., 198.

4. William L. Laurence, "A Giant Pillar of Purple Fire," *New York Times* (September 9, 1945).

5. Sweeney, *War's End*, 200.

6. Terkel, *"The Good War,"* 513.

7. Sweeney, *War's End*, 203.

8. Tibbets interview; Paul Tibbets, *Return of the Enola Gay* (Columbus, Ohio: Mid Coast Marketing, 1998), 248. (This is a revised edition of Tibbets's earlier book.)

9. Sweeney, *War's End*, 209; Purnell quoted in Groves, *Now It Can Be Told*, 344.

10. Laurence, "A Giant Pillar of Purple Fire."

11. Sweeney claims that Hopkins's message was garbled in transmission and came out as "Sweeney aborted." Sweeney, *War's End*, 212.

12. Tibbets interview.

13. Sweeney, *War's End*, 211.

14. Ibid., 213–15.

15. Ibid., 217.

16. Laurence, "A Giant Pillar of Purple Fire."

17. Ibid.

18. Sweeney, *War's End*, 223–26.

19. Tibbets, *Return of the Enola Gay*, 250; Tibbets interview.

20. Quoted in McCullough, *Truman*, 459.

21. Farrell, *Off the Record*, 61; Robert J. C. Butow's *Japan's Decision to Surrender* (Stanford, Calif.: Stanford University Press, 1954) remains the standard volume on the end of the war in the Pacific.

22. Groves, *Now It Can Be Told*, 352–53.

23. *New York Times*, August 15, 1945.

24. For recent data on the human cost of the war, see Murray and Millett, *A War to Be Won*, chapter 20; and Weinberg, *A World at Arms*, 894–920.

25. Paul Fussell, "Thank God for the Atomic Bomb," reprinted in *Hiroshima's Shadow*, Kai Bird and Lawrence Lischultz, eds. (Stony Creek, Conn.: Pamphleteer's Press, 1998), 217–18.

26. Sledge, *Old Breed*, 312–15.

27. Interview with Fiske Hanly by DLM; interview with Fiske Hanly, Lou Reda Productions; Frank Fujita, oral testimony, Lou Reda Productions; Frank Fujita, *Foo: A Japanese-American Prisoner of the Rising Sun* (Denton: University of North Texas Press, 1993), 1–5, 312–16; Halloran interview by DLM.

28. Goldsworthy interview.

29. Quoted in Charles Smith, S*ecuring the Surrender: Marines and the Occupation of Japan* (Washington, D.C.; Marine Corps Historical Center, 1997), 10.

30. Tenney, *Hitch*, 172.

31. Quoted in Manchester, *American Caesar*, 448.

32. Quoted in Morison, *Two-Ocean War*, 576.

33. Dale Kramer, "Fall of Japan," in *"Yank," the GI Story of the War*, 291.

34. Sweeney, *War's End*, 247.

35. Tibbets, *Enola Gay*, 240–43.

36. Sweeney, *War's End*, 257.

37. Tibbets, *Enola Gay*, 243; Tibbets interview.

38. Bob Greene, *Duty: A Father, His Son, and the Man Who Won the War* (New York: William Morrow, 2000), 19–20.

39. Tibbets, *Enola Gay*, 8.

40. The Committee for the Compilation of Materials on Damage Caused by the Atomic Bombs in Hiroshima and Nagasaki, trans., Eisei Ishikawa and David L. Swain, *Hiroshima and Nagasaki: The Physical, Medical, and Social Effects of the Atomic Bombings* (New York: Basic Books, 1981), 6.

41. Takashi Nagai, *The Bells of Nagasaki* (Tokyo: Kodansha International, 1984), 6, 114–18.

42. Jones, *WW II*, 255–56.

43. Halloran interview; Chester Marshall, with Ray "Hap" Halloran, *Hap's War: The Incredible Survival Story of a P.O.W. Slated for Execution* (Collierville, Tenn.: Global Press, 1998).

44. Private papers of Robert Crichton, New York.

Page numbers in italics refer to illustrations.

Broz, Josip (Tito), 51, 66
Bruckner, Anton, 76
Buchenwald, 521
Buck, John P., 139–41
Buckner, Gen. Simon Bolivar, Jr., 561, 563, 577, 590
Buell, Hal, 548
Bulgaria, 51, 58, 489
Bulkeley, Lt. John D., 104
Buna, New Guinea, 156–58, 159, 210
Bunker Hill, 373, 571–74
Burger, Knox, 449–51, 456–58
Burma, 114, 126–28, 592–94
Burma Road, 126, 128, 592–93
Burns, Dwayne T., 339, 340–43, 354
Burris, Luis M., 432–34
Byrnes, Jimmy, 614, 639

Caen, 289, 306–7, 321, 324
California, 99
Callaghan, Adm. Daniel J., 134, 135, 142
Campbell, Pvt. Bob, 545, 547
Canadian forces:
    in France, 317, 321, 324–25, 327
    in Italy, 242
    in Pacific War, 186
Cant, Gilbert, 121
Canton, 113
Capa, Robert, 224, 228, 298–300, 305, 324, 327, 348, 350, 498–99, 502
Cape Gloucester, 187, 393
Capell, John C., 351–52, 353
Cape Matapan, 50
Carlson, Evans, 207
Caroline Islands, 188
Caron, George "Bob," 618–19
Casablanca, 161, 162, 255
Cason, S/Sgt. David, 248
Cassidy, Henry C., 63–65
Catch-22 (Heller), 472
Catton, Bruce, 12
Cavallo, 371
Celebes, 114

Chamberlain, Neville, 23, 30
Chamberlin, Maj. William, 202–3, 204, 368
Chambers, Justice M., 390
Chapin, John C., 366–67, 370, 375
Chartres cathedral, 326
Chatelain, 180
Cheek, Chief Yeoman, 141
Chennault, Gen. Claire, 126
Cherbourg Peninsula, 283–84, 305, 306, 323
Chiang Kai-shek, 126, 361, 593, 594
Chikuma, 80, 81
China:
    Burma Road to, 126, 128, 592–93
    guerrilla war in, 592–93
    isolation of, 128
    Japanese invasions of, 21–22, 100, 392
    Japanese reprisals in, 118
    Long March, 127
    over the Hump to, 442, 593, 594
    rape of Nanking, 21–22, 105, 118
    supply roads to, 128
    U.S. airstrips in, 442–43
    war losses of, 640
Chindits, 593–94
Choiseul, 141
Choltitz, Gen. Dietrich von, 327
Chuikov, Gen. Vasily, 71–73
Churchill, Winston, 34, 53, 613, 616
    on Battle of Atlantic, 167, 175, 178
    on the Holocaust, 520
    inspiration from, 30–31, 37, 53, 153, 257
    and Pacific war, 103
    and second front, 162, 214, 215
    strategies of, 52, 103, 160, 162, 229, 255, 280, 387, 479, 492, 505, 592
    and U.S. aid, 49

Ciardi, John, 444, 446–47, 448, 449, 460, 606
Cigoi, Walter, 108
Clark, Frank, 17
Clark, Adm. Joseph "Jocko," 372
Clark, Gen. Mark W.:
    and Buffalo Division, 248
    in Italy, 215, 218, 221, 224, 226, 228, 229, 231, 232, 234, 235, 241, 506, 509
Clark, Capt. William Sanders, 529, 530, 532–33, 535–37, 540, 554
Clinton, William Jefferson, 515
Coale, Griffith B., 47–48
Coleman, Col. William T., 475
Cologne, 259, 495
Colonna, Jerry, 395
Commager, Henry Steele, 12–16
Conroy, Bob, 351, 357
Cook, Haruko Taya, 388
Coral Sea, 118–19
Corregidor, 102, 103, 104, 105, 119, 391, 426, 434, 644
Cossacks, 486–88
Cota, Brig. Gen. Norman, 295
Courageous, 44
Coventry, England, 43, 483
Cowles, Virginia, 27, 35
Cowling, Lt. William J., 517–18
Crichton, Robert, 650–52
Crider, Linwood, 420–24, 425
Crimea, 70, 486, 488–89
Cronin, Whitey, 195
Crotty, Norma, 552–53
Crouch, Maj. William L., 378
Crowe, Henry "Jim," 196–98, *197*, 200, 201, 367–68
Culin, Sgt. Curtis G., 321
Cunningham, Ed, 522–23
Cyclops, 168
Cywinska, Janina, 516
Czechoslovakia, 23, 24, 38

Dabrowski, Stanley E., 539
Dace, 416
Dachau, 515–18, 519
Darlan, Adm. Jean, 162